First civilizations

Second edition

First civilizations

Ancient Mesopotamia and Ancient Egypt

Second edition

Robert Chadwick

equinox

LONDON   OAKVILLE

Published by
Equinox Publishing Ltd.
UK: Unit 6, The Village, 101 Amies St., London SW11 2JW
USA: DBBC, 28 Main Street, Oakville, CT 06779
www.equinoxpub.com

First edition published by Les Éditions Champ Fleury, Montréal, in 1996.
This second edition first published 2005.

British Library Cataloguing-in-Publication Data

A catalogue record for this book is available from the British Library.

ISBN   1 904768 77 6   (hardback)
          1 904768 78 4   (paperback)

Library of Congress Cataloging-in-Publication Data

Chadwick, Robert, 1941-
   First civilizations : ancient Mesopotamia and ancient Egypt / Robert
Chadwick.— 2nd ed.
      p. cm.
   Previous ed.: Montreal : Les Editions Champ Fleury, 1996.
   Includes bibliographical references and index.
   ISBN 1-904768-77-6 (hb) — ISBN 1-904768-78-4 (pb)
      1. Iraq—Civilization—To 634. 2. Egypt—Civilization—332 B.C.-638
A.D. I. Title.

DS69.5.C43 2004
935—dc22

Typeset by Kate Williams, Swansea.
Printed and bound in Great Britain by Antony Rowe Ltd., Chippenham.

To Karina

Contents

Preface

Robert Chadwick
Bishop's University and Université
de Sherbrooke, Estrie, Québec, Canada
October 2004

This is an expanded and revised edition of *First Civilizations: Ancient Mesopotamia and Ancient Egypt*, which originally appeared in 1996 (Les Éditions Champ Fleury, Montréal, Canada). *First Civilizations* is a one-volume, introductory overview of two of the world's oldest civilizations: ancient Mesopotamia and ancient Egypt. It grew out of three decades of teaching the history and culture of the ancient Near East at college and university level using a variety of books and articles that were, in many instances, unsuited to the needs and scholarly capabilities of undergraduates. *First Civilizations* was conceived primarily for students who have little or no knowledge of ancient history or archaeology, and will take only one general interest course about the ancient Near East as part of their broader educational experience. Even though most people who use this text will pursue studies in other areas it is hoped that a few will be stimulated to continue their studies in the field of Near Eastern or pre-classical antiquities.

Although *First Civilizations* contains much historical information, it is not, strictly speaking, a history book; it also offers glimpses of religion, mythology, art, architecture, technology and an overview of historical and archaeological methodology. To assist students in the preparation of class reports and research papers, endnotes and complete bibliographies are included at the end of the book. Although there are a number of highly valuable sources in French, German, Italian, and other European languages, this book was designed for English language readers, and almost all bibliographical sources included are in English. Instead of emphasizing specialized journals and monographs, many of which are beyond the knowledge of introductory students, *First Civilizations* takes advantage of a number of recently published encyclopedias and dictionaries specializing in Near Eastern civilizations, including *Civilizations of the Ancient Near East*, *The Anchor Bible Dictionary*, *The Oxford History of Ancient Egypt*, *The Oxford Encyclopedia of Archaeology in the Near East* and *The Oxford Encyclopedia of Ancient Egypt*, among others, as its principal sources of information. These publications were favoured over specialist journals and monographs for several reasons. First, and perhaps most importantly, they are widely available even in most small- and medium-sized educational institutions. Secondly, the articles in these compendia are short, up to date, and written by recognized experts in the field in a style and on a level that is comprehensible to entry-level students. Thirdly, they contain excellent bibliographies for those who wish to expand their research. It should be noted that most of the very old titles that appear in the bibliography have been included mainly as sources for illustrations and not necessarily for their sometimes outdated content.

Finally, a word to teaching professionals using this book: I know full well that there is so much more that could have been included in a one-volume treatment such as this, but the most difficult task I encountered in writing this book was not deciding what to include, but what to leave out.

Acknowledgements

I would like to thank everyone who helped and encouraged me in preparing the updated and expanded edition of *First Civilizations: Ancient Mesopotamia and Ancient Egypt*, in particular, Dr John Baines of Oxford University, who read the entire manuscript and made many valuable comments and corrections. During various stages of development of the 1996 edition and the 2005 edition the following people read various parts of the manuscript and made many valuable suggestions and corrections: Professors Michel Fortin, of Université Laval and Joe Seger of the Cobb Institute of Archaeology, Mississippi State University; as well as Professors Grant Frame, Douglas Frayne and Ronald J. Leprohon of the Department of Near and Middle Eastern Studies at the University of Toronto; Donald Redford (now at Pennsylvania State University); Professors Robyn Gillam, York University, Toronto; Eugene Cruz-Uribe, Northern Arizona University, Flagstaff; Professors Marcel Leibovici, Philip Smith and Jean Revez of Université de Montréal; Professor Paul-Alain Beaulieu, Yale University; as well as Edwin C. Brock and Lyla Pinch-Brock of Cairo.

I would also like to thank Deborah Cunningham for her numerous drawings and maps, which appear throughout the text, along with John Mahoney of Tomifobia, Québec, who edited the 1996 manuscript, Tim Doherty of *visimage.ca*, who designed the front cover and helped facilitate many improvements in the 2005 edition and Kim Prangley of the Haskell Free Library, Stanstead, Québec, who proofread the entire manuscript. Finally, to my wife Karina who read the manuscript numerous times and yet persevered with charm, patience and understanding through the longer than expected gestation period of this book. My heartfelt thanks to all. Any errors herein are, of course, my own and not those of my friends and colleagues mentioned above.

In addition I would like to thank Drs Horst Klengel of the Vorderasiatisches Museen, Berlin, Beatrice André-Salvini of the Musée du Louvre, Paris, W.V. Davies, Keeper of Egyptian Antiquities, British Museum, London, Dr Elisabetta Valtz of Museo Delle Antichità Egizie and Dr Mohamed Saleh, Egyptian Museum, Cairo, for allowing me to make or use drawings of objects in their respective institutions.

My thanks to the following people who provided photographs used in this book. Professor John Holladay Jr. of the University of Toronto as well as Nicola Woods of Royal Ontario Museum and Barbara Lawson of the Redpath Museum of McGill University for the use of photographs of objects in their collections. Special thanks to Professor Michel Fortin of Université Laval for allowing me to use a number of excavation photographs and drawings from his excavations at Tell 'Atij and Tell 'Acharneh, Syria that appear in Chapter 1. Other photographs were kindly provided by my wife Karina Gerlach, and by Professors Michael Weigl of the Catholic University of America, Washington D.C., Professor Grant Frame of the University of Toronto and Mr Wallace Eldredge of Nesconset, New York.

List of illustrations

Colour plates

Part I: Introduction

1 History and archaeology as tools for understanding the past

Ancient Mesopotamia and ancient Egypt were located in that part of the world now referred to as the Near East or the Middle East. In this book this region will be referred to as the ancient Near East; it is a geographical area that includes the lands of Egypt, located in northeastern Africa, extending north through modern-day Israel, Palestine, Jordan, Lebanon, Syria, and the southeastern portion of Turkey. In addition, it encompasses the regions to the east towards the valleys formed by the Tigris and Euphrates Rivers, which flow from eastern Turkey through Syria, Iraq, and western Iran, ending in the south where the two rivers empty into the Persian Gulf. The ancient Near East refers to the peoples and civilizations that developed in that part of the world many thousands of years ago. The word "Egypt" refers to a geographical area situated in North Africa adjacent to the Nile River. However, it also refers to the Egyptians, the people who lived in this area and to Egyptian culture, language, and religion.

In modern scholarship the word Mesopotamia[1] refers to the geographical area located in the region of the Tigris and Euphrates Rivers, roughly equivalent to present-day Iraq. "Mesopotamia" referred to the northern portion of the Tigris and Euphrates regions in third-century BC Greek translations of the Old Testament,[2] and in the works of the first-century BC Greek historian Strabo.[3] Unlike Egypt, there was never a country called "Mesopotamia", nor did any ancient group of people ever refer to themselves as "Mesopotamians". Mesopotamia was the home of numerous peoples who either invaded or migrated to the Tigris and Euphrates region and made it their home. The peoples of Mesopotamia who will be discussed in this book are usually identified according to their chronological appearances, the languages they spoke, and the geographical regions they occupied. These include the Sumerians, the Akkadians, the Babylonians, the Assyrians, and others.

During the early centuries of its history Egypt was the home of a somewhat more homogeneous people, most of whom spoke the same language, worshipped many of the same gods, and, like the peoples of Mesopotamia, shared a number of similar cultural traditions. Egypt was bounded on the east and west by deserts, and to the north lay the Mediterranean Sea. These geographical barriers protected Egypt from attack by invading armies; in contrast, the open plains of Mesopotamia were easily accessible to friendly, as well as hostile, outsiders.

Why study ancient Mesopotamia and ancient Egypt?

There can be no doubt that the ancient civilizations of Greece and Rome formed the basis of modern Western societies. However, a number of important elements of Western civilization predate the Greeks and Romans, and come directly from the earlier civilizations of ancient Mesopotamia and ancient Egypt. Our 365-day calendar and 24-hour day

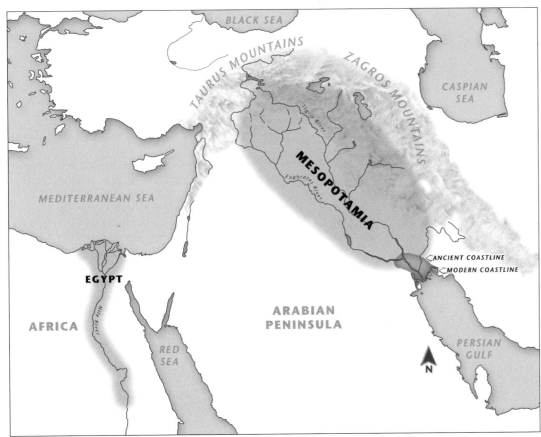

The ancient Near East.

Date palm tree, central Iraq.

Foothills of northern Iraq near Marmatra.

originated in Egypt. Scientific astronomy originated in Mesopotamia and spread west to the Greeks and Romans, who made their own important contributions to this science. Astrology, one of the world's oldest and most enduring superstitions, also originated in Mesopotamia, and had a profound influence on art and religion in the Greco-Roman, and ultimately Christian and Islamic, world. Key elements of architecture such as the vault and the arch were in use in Egypt and Mesopotamia at least two thousand years before the Romans used them. Before the Greeks and Romans, the first rational theory of the causes of disease, which influenced later developments in scientific medicine, came from the Egyptians. Monotheism, the belief in one god, originated in Egypt centuries before it became a key spiritual element in Judaism, Christianity, and Islam. Monotheism was further developed in neighbouring Israel and Arabia, both situated between Mesopotamia and Egypt and strongly influenced by both of these older civilizations. If we add to these accomplishments the invention of the alphabet, which also originated in the ancient Near East, it is clear that some of the most important and valuable elements of our own Western tradition came from the world's first civilizations: ancient Mesopotamia and ancient Egypt

Sand dunes near the banks of the Nile River, Aswan, Upper Egypt.

Egyptian mud-brick arches at the Temple of Ramesses II (13th century BC).

METHODOLOGY I: WHAT IS HISTORY?

How are ancient Mesopotamia and ancient Egypt studied? How do scholars and researchers get information about them? There are basically two methods that can be used to study an ancient civilization: history and archaeology. (Archaeology will be covered in Part II of this chapter.) History relies on the written word and its principal method of gathering knowledge is the decipherment and translation of ancient texts. For historians the key to understanding the past is learning to read ancient languages.

Reading the past

To obtain written information about ancient people it is not necessary to study texts of a strictly historical nature. Non-historical material, such as myths, stories, and religious texts, can reveal a great deal about the lives of ancient peoples. The earliest examples of writing in ancient Egypt and Mesopotamia were not history books but records of business transactions. Texts that record the exchange or sale of goods can provide valuable information about the economic structure of a society. If an economic text lists farm animals and agricultural produce that were traded in the marketplace, the historian learns something about the diet and eating habits of a particular people. In some instances the goods produced and sold go beyond economics and may reveal clues about the social structure or values of a society. For example, if a text mentions the sale of slaves, the historian obtains a clearer idea about the values and the treatment of certain segments of a society. There is a wealth of knowledge to be gained from ancient texts. Everything from military campaigns to peace treaties, from eclipses to sensitive poetry or moving prose, can be found in the writings of ancient Mesopotamia and ancient Egypt. Even the simplest written document may contain valuable information that will help the historian to reconstruct the past.

The origins of history

Many ancient historians maintain that the first history book was written about 440 BC by a Greek named Herodotus. The title of his book was *Historia* (or *History*), the word we still use today when speaking about the recording of the past. Even though the first book to be called a history book appeared 2500 years ago, it must be emphasized that humans had been recording their own story, and thus writing history, for many centuries prior to the time of Herodotus. In ancient Egypt most writing was done on a substance called *papyrus*. Papyrus, the Greek word meaning paper, was made from reeds growing along the riverbanks and marshes in the Nile river valley. Reeds were gathered, split open, and soaked in water for a month or so, releasing natural sugars that acted as glue. Then the reeds were stacked at right angles and pressed together. After they dried they made a very suitable writing surface. In Egypt's dry climate, papyrus can last for thousands of years. Nevertheless, papyrus is fragile, often crumbling into tiny fragments after a few centuries, so much of the Egyptian historical record has been lost. As a result, Egyptologists must turn to other sources, such as inscriptions on stone monuments, to obtain their information. Inscriptions in stone reflect the views and aspirations of the rich and powerful and tell us much about the rulers of Egypt, but nothing about the majority of the population, who were illiterate and too poor to record their stories. The largest number of written documents from the ancient Near East come from Mesopotamia. Texts from Mesopotamia were written on clay tablets, which is why so much written material from this part of the world still survives today. Compared to papyrus, clay tablets are practically

History may be defined as the enquiry into the past of people in society through the medium of written sources.

indestructible. An estimated half a million clay tablets from Mesopotamia have been recovered and are now stored in museums and private collections around the world.

Calendars and astronomical dates

One of the principal goals of historical research is to determine when things happened, and calendar dates are a reliable source for determining when a person lived or an event took place.[4] The Egyptians had several calendars. One of them was based on the flood cycle of the Nile River and was developed to meet the needs of farmers, who depended on the flooding of the great river for their survival. Of more value to the historical researcher is the Sothic cycle,[5] which concerns the flooding of the Nile River combined with the rising of Sothis, the brightest star in the heavens. The Sothic cycle may be explained as follows. After a 70-day absence from the night sky, Sothis (known in modern astronomy as the star Sirius) appeared low on the eastern horizon just before sunrise at about the time in summer that the Nile River began its annual inundation. However, the 365-day Egyptian calendar did not precisely match the length of the regular or solar year, which is close to, *but not precisely*, 365¼ days in length. As a result the calendar finished too early and lost about one day every four years. After 120 years the calendar and the solar year would be off by one month; after 730 years they would be off by six months. As a result Sothis only rose at dawn with the sun on the first day of the New Year once about every 1460 years. By a fortunate chance, the Roman writer Censorius tells us that in AD 139 the sun and Sothis rose together on New Year's Day. Subtracting 1460 years from this date (and adding a zero between 1 BC and 1 AD) it is possible to calculate that the star Sothis rose at sunrise on New Year's Day in the years 1320 BC and 2780 BC.

Many centuries ago, an Egyptian scribe recorded the rising of Sothis during the 16th year of the reign of King Sesostris III. Such information allows historians to calculate this date to be 1872 BC, a date that is considered to be the oldest fixed calendrical date in history.[6] In addition, Sothic dates have also been established for two other kings of the second millennium BC: Amenhotep I and Thutmosis III. When these dates are used in conjunction with other historical data, such as lists of kings, letters, inscriptions on buildings, and economic texts, it is possible to establish when certain kings ruled and when important events took place. Even though the Sothic cycle gives scholars a few reliable dates on which they can build a chronology, it is controversial, and still leaves many dates in doubt.

Astronomical dates from Mesopotamia are more numerous than those from Egypt, but none are older than the Sothic cycle date for King Sesostris III (1878–1841 BC). The earliest astronomical date from Mesopotamia comes from the reign of King Ammisaduqa, who ruled during the First Babylonian Dynasty. During a 21-year period of his reign some unknown person observed and recorded the movements of the planet Venus, which have been preserved in a later copy from the first millennium BC. These movements are dateable through astronomical calculations and thus it is possible to date the first year of the reign of the Babylonian King Ammisaduqa to 1702 BC.[7] Since the length of the reigns of other kings from the same period are recorded on lists of kings, a reliable chronology for this period has been established. However, not all of these dates can be accurately tied to events of the time and there are still many chronological gaps and undateable events from the second millennium BC.

In contrast, the first millennium BC has provided researchers with many calendar dates that have been determined by astronomical and other methods. In Mesopotamia, the Babylonians and Assyrians used a lunar calendar and in their letters to the king, scribes

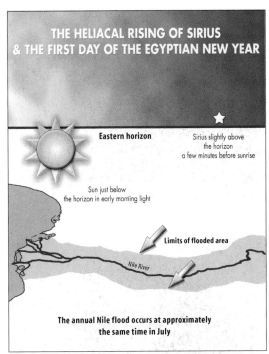

The Sothic cycle. This figure shows the star Sothis in relation to the sun at the time of the flooding of the Nile River.

often noted the position of the moon in relation to the constellations and planets. Assyrian and Babylonian kings wrote lengthy accounts of their military campaigns that contain valuable information about their reigns, while their court scribes wrote letters, administrative documents, and religious texts that have important astronomical data. Again, because it is sometimes possible to calculate when such phenomena occurred, the dates of a number of events have been established with a high degree of certainty, which has enabled historians to give accurate dates to many events that took place during the first millennium BC.[8]

Annals and king lists

In the third century BC, a priest named Manetho wrote a history containing a list of all the kings and ruling families of ancient Egypt. Despite a number of problems, Manetho's list has been useful in helping scholars to reconstruct Egyptian chronology.[9] Manetho divided Egyptian history into 31 periods spanning nearly 3000 years from the first king, Narmer, to the conquest of Egypt by Alexander the Great in 332 BC.

The Sumerian king list[10] gives a chronology of the reigns of the early kings of Mesopotamia from a mythical past down to about 2000 BC. Like Manetho's list of Egyptian kings, the Sumerian list is only of limited use to historians. In some instances it accords impossibly long reigns of hundreds or even thousands of years to the early rulers of Mesopotamia. The deeds of these early kings, and the periods they were on the throne, are mixed with myth and legend and it is difficult to separate fact from fiction. The most important chronological texts from Mesopotamia are the Assyrian king lists. These lists begin around 1800 BC and continue until about 700 BC. The Assyrian king lists,[11] written on clay tablets, are neatly divided into little boxes containing a paragraph concerning the reign of a particular king. Each entry tells us the name of the king, the length of his reign, and his ancestor. This record covers a thousand years of history and is a very valuable chronological tool that has helped reconstruct the chronology of Mesopotamia, as well as much of the rest of the Near East. Similar to the king lists were *limmu* lists, which contained the years named after officials who were appointed annually to important positions. Lists of these *limmu* officials were used to identify the years during which the king held office and helped keep track of the years. Over the past 150 years scholars have combined archaeological and historical information from a variety of sources to create a realistic and, all things considered, reasonably accurate chronology of past events in the ancient Near East. Dates from the third millennium BC are generally accurate to within plus or minus 50 years, while the margin of error in the second millennium BC is usually less than that. In the first millennium BC accuracy is even better, and in many cases precise dates are known.

Interpreting the past: early ideas about history

To the people of ancient Mesopotamia and Egypt the distinction between the realm of the gods and the realm of humans was not always clearly defined.[12] Because of this, history had only one causal agent: the gods. The worlds of the mythical and spiritual were often mixed together to explain how things happened. Despite this, the scribes of these two ancient civilizations left numerous documents that record actual historical events. Everything from military campaigns, the reigns of kings, and peace treaties were recounted, often in a reliable and believable fashion. Centuries later, the ancient Greeks had a different view of history and the causes of historical events. Although they too believed that the gods were important forces in history, they were among the first to consider the possibility of non-divine forces. They believed that history was cyclical, and things and events repeated themselves on a regular and predictable basis. The historian Thucydides (fifth century BC) believed there was a pattern in history and that events repeated again and again. Civilizations rose, became strong then eventually declined because of their increasing pride and greed. Political power led to increased prosperity and wealth; wealth led to excess and indulgence, which in turn caused people to believe they were exempt from the rules of proper human behaviour.

Centuries later, in the early fifth century AD, the Christian theologian Augustine of Hippo (St Augustine) enlarged on the biblical view that history was linear and not cyclical. Events began, happened in a straight line, and then came to an end. History had a definite beginning in the Garden of Eden and the passing of events would ultimately lead to the establishment of a better, divine kingdom at some future point. To St Augustine history was progress; history was going somewhere and things got better along the way. The ideas of the classical Greeks and St Augustine dominated historical thought for centuries, until the Enlightenment. Starting in the 17th century, with the increasing importance of science and discovery, historians argued that, as in physics and astronomy, there were laws that determined the course of historical development. The Italian Giambattista Vico believed that history was a combination of both linear and cyclical development, events repeating cyclically yet moving upwards in a spiral. At about the same time historians argued that civilizations went through stages, beginning with a "savage" stage then advancing to what was referred to as the "barbaric" stage and finally to true "civilization", always improving as things moved along. It was Vico who introduced the modern idea of "progress" into historical theory. The idea of progress, combined with Charles Darwin's evolutionary theory, led historians and philosophers of the 19th century to believe that certain groups of people (usually Europeans and their relatives scattered around the world in colonies) were destined to reach higher and better ways of life than other peoples.

At one time it was thought that the task of the historian was simply to record how things really were.[13] It was believed that historians would seek out facts and that the past would be known once and for all. It was naively believed that there was only one way to interpret past events and that everyone would agree how and why things happened. However, interpretations of history are continually changing because new facts, and new ways of interpreting the facts, are constantly being discovered. Ideas and concepts about the world change. Each new generation re-examines past events and interprets them from its own unique point of view. The philosopher Karl Marx expressed this more than a century ago when he said, "History is contemporary thought about the past". Fifty years ago historians lived in an era dominated by empires, world wars, and the superpowers, and they wrote histories that reflected these factors. The current generation of historians lives in a somewhat different world, one concerned with ethnic strife, the roles of women and minorities, and ecological issues. As a result, these matters are often emphasized in the contemporary historian's interpretation of the past.

Historians (and archaeologists), like all other people, are products of their own societies and share the cultural values and prejudices of their particular group. The historian's view of the world, and therefore its history, is shaped and influenced by his or her ethnic background, economic conditions, and religious beliefs. Because of this, history, like many other forms of enquiry, is to a certain extent subjective in nature. This does not mean that the work of the historian is wrong or inaccurate. Modern historians spend years studying and preparing themselves to practise their craft, and are constantly striving to maintain the highest levels of excellence and objectivity. Despite these limitations, the past is about people and it can only be studied and interpreted by people; if people are not capable of writing their own story, then who is?

Historians carry out one additional task vital to our understanding of the past: they decide which events they will include in their interpretation of history, and which ones they will leave out. History has traditionally been written by the winners of wars and the educated, and by men. Only in recent years have members of minority groups and women started to write history from their own perspective. If the history of North America had been written by slaves, native peoples, or women, how much different would our interpretation of it be? Of course, the important dates and personalities would remain the same: Napoleon would still have fought the Battle of Waterloo in 1815, the American Civil War would still have ended in 1865, and Columbus would still have voyaged to the New World in 1492. But seen from the point of view of the groups just mentioned, these events would be interpreted from a different perspective.

Continuing historical research

Historical research is being carried out in many parts of the world. At the University of Chicago work is nearing completion on a research project called *The Chicago Assyrian Dictionary*. This project has produced a 20-volume dictionary that serves as the basic research tool for those interested in reading the languages of ancient Assyria and Babylonia. Currently, at the University of Toronto, a team of scholars is busy translating and publishing all royal inscriptions from Mesopotamia. Periodically, the Royal Inscriptions of Mesopotamia Project publishes another volume of texts in the original language, along with an English translation, so that both specialists and non-specialists can read the words of the people of ancient Mesopotamia. Other historical research projects are underway in Finland (*The State Letters of Assyria*), France (*Les Archives Royales de Mari*) and Germany (*Lexikon der Ägyptologie* and *Reallexikon der Assyriologie und Vorderasiatischen Archäologie*). Projects such as these take years of commitment and research to complete, and add a great deal to our knowledge of ancient peoples. In addition, individual historians doing their own research are producing new or updated translations of magical and religious texts, ancient literature and poetry, military campaigns, astronomical texts, and divination (fortune-telling) texts, as well as groups of texts that deal with chemistry, metallurgy, and other subjects. Even though historical research projects seldom make the daily newspapers and thus are not well known to the public, they nevertheless produce results that are just as important and spectacular as those in archaeology.

The free exchange of ideas

Both historical and archaeological research must be published in specialized and learned journals so that their findings can be shared with other scholars and analysed and criticized by qualified people in the field. In this manner research is constantly being checked and rechecked for errors by the scholarly community. In addition, historians meet on a regular basis at conferences to present their ideas in the form of learned papers to their colleagues. Such presentations are often followed by lively debate and discussion, which serve to clarify and enhance new ideas and discoveries. In an atmosphere where ideas are continually checked and rechecked, faulty or erroneous opinions do not survive for long and the overall quality of our knowledge about the past is constantly improving. As a result, historians have accumulated more data than ever before concerning ancient humans, and modern researchers know more about the past than any other group of people who have ever lived before us.

The limits of history

Even though written documents are about as close as we can ever come to actually hearing the voices and understanding the thoughts of our ancestors, history has one major shortcoming: it has existed only for a relatively short time. Human ancestors who were physically and mentally similar to modern people (*Homo sapiens sapiens*) have existed for more than 50 000 years, and our more ancient human ancestors go back in time more than four million years. However, writing only appeared about 5000 years ago, leaving most of the human story unrecorded. When written documents are not available to give information about the past, scholars must turn elsewhere for their sources of information. The other method used to obtain information about past civilizations is called archaeology.

What time is it? How to understand the dating system used in this book

Strictly speaking this is not a history book, even though it contains much historical data. Since it deals with the ancient world, some dates must be included to give the reader an idea of the time periods being discussed. This book uses the standard BC–AD system of dating that has been used for well over a century by historians and archaeologists when referring to events in the distant past. About 1700 years ago, when Christianity became the dominant religion of the Roman Empire, Christian calendar-makers decided their calendar would begin with the date of the birth of Jesus Christ. Before the Christians, the Romans had used a 365-day calendar they had borrowed from the Egyptians. This calendar was quite accurate and, like the Romans, the Christians adopted it and modified it to fit their own needs. Like calendar-makers before them, they decided to begin their calendar with the date of the birth of an important person such as a king or a religious leader; in this case they began it with the birth of Jesus.

For historians and archaeologists, all events that took place before the birth of Jesus happened "before Christ", abbreviated BC. When it is stated

that King Hammurabi ruled from 1792 to 1750 BC, this means that he ruled that many years before the birth of Jesus. Dates after the birth of Jesus are followed by the letters AD, from the Latin *anno Domini* meaning "in the year of Our Lord" (not "after death" as some people mistakenly believe). Thus the end of the Roman Empire is generally given as AD 476, the death of Charlemagne as AD 814, the creation of the Magna Carta as AD 1215, and so on. In the modern world few people actually bother to add the letters AD after dates. More recently scholars have begun to use the letters BCE, which stand for "Before the Common Era"; BCE dates are chronologically equivalent to BC dates but without a religious reference. Similarly CE, standing for "Common Era", dates are chronologically equivalent to *anno Domini* dates.

The Christian calendar is used in many parts of the Western world today, but it is not the only calendar in use. China, India, and a number of other civilizations developed their own calendrical systems thousands of years ago. The Islamic calendar is somewhat younger, beginning in AD 622. It dates from the time when Mohammed, the prophet of the religion of Islam, was forced to flee to the city of Mecca to avoid religious persecution. Dates in the Islamic calendar are hundreds of years younger than those in the Christian calendar, and it is based on a lunar cycle, so years in the Islamic calendar don't correspond to years in the Christian calendar. For example, the year AD 2000 corresponds to the year 1420/1421 AH, where AH stands for *anno Hegirae*, meaning after the time of Mohammed's flight to Mecca.

In order to calculate the age of BC dates, that is, how many years ago an event took place, simply add 2000 years to the BC date and you will have a very good approximation of how long ago someone lived or how long ago an event took place. Thus, for King Hammurabi we add 2000 to 1750 BC, the year of his death, and we know that he died about 3750 years ago or 3750 BP, where BP stands for "before present". For AD dates simply calculate the difference between the current year and the date given to determine the number of years before the present that an event took place.

Centuries and millennia

If this is the year 2005, or any year after that, why do we refer to the present century as the twenty-first century? If we are living in the century from 2000 to 2099 shouldn't this be the twentieth century? No. The first century contained years 1–99. It should really have contained years 0–99, but calendar-makers early in the Christian era decided that the year of Jesus's birth would be year 1. The first century (both AD and BC) really only contains 99 years; all other centuries contain 100 years, as indicated by the diagram below. Historical time is measured in years, centuries, and a period of time called a "millennium". A millennium (plural millennia) contains 1000 years. Thus, the second millennium AD, which only recently ended, contained the years 1000 to 1999. When the calendar reached the year 2000 both the century and the millennium changed. We are currently living at the beginning of the third millennium AD, that is the period from AD 2000 to AD 2999. Returning again to King Hammurabi (recall that he ruled 1792–1750 BC), we see that he ruled in the 18th century BC, which was in the second millennium BC.

Years BC			Years AD			
Third century	Second century	First century	First century	Second century	Third century	Fourth century
299–200	199–100	99–1	1–99	100–199	200–299	300–399

Counting years and centuries.

METHODOLOGY II: WHAT IS ARCHAEOLOGY?

The word archaeology comes from the Greek *archaios*, meaning "old", and *logos*, meaning "the study of"; thus, archaeology means "the study of old things". However, history is also concerned with the study of "old things", so how do we differentiate between them? Archaeology relies on the retrieval and interpretation of artifacts to understand ancient people. An artifact is anything made by people, regardless of its beauty, value, or function. An artifact can be a simple stone tool, a piece of pottery, or a farming implement. Retrieval of artifacts generally takes place at a *habitation site*, or some other location where people have lived and carried out activities. A habitation site can be a simple campsite used by nomadic hunters, or it can be a larger area such as a village or a city.

Instead of dealing with languages and manuscripts, archaeology is concerned with objects, what is referred to as "material culture". While historians often spend long hours studying ancient papyrus scrolls or clay tablets in museums or libraries, archaeologists spend extended periods of time in distant lands, sometimes living in harsh and inhospitable conditions, in order to carry out their fieldwork. Together, archaeology and history give much reliable information about ancient societies, and they are both of equal value in helping to understand the past.

The archaeologist as treasure hunter

The image of the two-fisted, rough-and-tumble archaeologist–adventurer made so popular through Hollywood films in no way represents what professional archaeologists do in real life. Archaeologists must spend many years at university to gain the

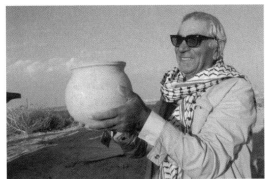

The thrill of discovery. Architect and archaeologist Elias Marcou displays a freshly excavated jar that was part of a burial cache from an Early Dynastic period grave at Tell 'Atij, Syria.

specialized training necessary to undertake serious research. Even though it is true that in the early days of archaeological exploration adventure was easy to find in distant lands often inhabited by exotic, sometimes hostile, peoples, today archaeology has become a more mundane social science.

The explorers of the 18th and 19th centuries who first began the search for ancient civilizations had little in common with today's highly trained archaeologists. In fact, early explorers were not really archaeologists at all (no universities offered degrees in the subject), since they had little or no training to guide them in their quests for ancient artifacts. Instead, they were treasure hunters more interested in plundering ancient civilizations to fill their personal collections than in understanding the lives of ancient people. Throughout the 18th and 19th centuries, explorers, or *antiquarians*, took the wealth of ancient civilizations and sold it to private collectors, while countries such as the United Kingdom, France, Prussia (later Germany), and the United States competed with each other to fill their museums with

statues, mummies, and art objects.[14] In the mid-19th century, Cairo was the centre for the open traffic of stolen and illegally excavated antiquities. Many other Near Eastern cities, like Damascus and Baghdad, fulfilled a similar function, draining away the precious cultural heritage of the surrounding areas for a few dollars, francs, or pounds. Ironically, it was Europeans who eventually insisted that government agencies for the protection of antiquities be established. In 1858 Frenchman Auguste Mariette established an antiquities organization (*La Direction des Services d'Antiquités*) that was designed to bring some order to the chaotic state of exploration in Egypt, and to stop the trafficking of stolen artifacts. Soon after, similar agencies were established in other Near Eastern countries. Twenty years later, Englishman and pioneer archaeologist William Matthew Flinders Petrie took some of the first steps towards the development of scientific methods of retrieval and recording of artifacts in Egypt. Slowly, the trafficking in antiquities began to diminish, and scientific methods of excavation began to be adopted by excavators as the treasure hunters began to disappear. However, despite local and international laws, theft and trafficking of stolen artifacts still persists to this day, and continues to grow at an alarming rate.

Of course, not everyone who searched for artifacts did so only for profit and personal gain. Many of the early explorers were genuinely interested in learning about the past and eventually were able to take control of archaeological exploration. In the early days of exploration in the Near East ancient civilizations that had been lost and forgotten for centuries were rediscovered. In the 18th and 19th centuries ancient languages were deciphered, and the literary richness of the past was once again brought to light. Museums were established that, over the years, have proved to be safe depositories for artifacts as well as

Archaeology is the study of people in past societies through the retrieval and analysis of artifacts

places where the public can view artifacts and appreciate them, and scholars can study them. By the turn of the twentieth century improved methods of excavation and preservation were being used by more and more excavators, and what had started as the exploitation of artifacts had become the scientific study and analysis of the past in many parts of the world.

Proving the Bible and Homer

Along with the treasure hunters and explorers there were others who wanted to prove the validity of stories found in the Bible and classical works written by the ancient Greeks. One of the important early archaeological discoveries concerned the lost city of Troy, known from an ancient story called the *Iliad*. This story was particularly famous for its episode about a giant wooden horse that enabled the Greek invaders to conquer the besieged city of Troy after a ten-year struggle. In the 19th century a rich merchant and amateur archaeologist called Heinrich Schliemann discovered the location of the city of Troy and brought to light many of its treasures and other interesting elements. Schliemann's discovery of Troy was set in an era of mystery and romance that makes for great reading. In his biography,[15] Schliemann recounts how, with a copy of Homer's *Iliad* in one hand to guide him, he searched the coast of western Anatolia (Turkey), examining numerous abandoned mounds until he found one that matched the description of Troy in Homer's story. After he had excavated the site for many seasons, Schliemann's adventure came to an exciting climax. During the last days of his final campaign he uncovered a cache of golden treasures that he believed belonged to Priam, one of the main characters in the story. As it turned out, these artifacts were much older than Schliemann claimed they were. He smuggled these treasures out of the country illegally and gave them to his wife for her personal adornment. Back in Europe she made quite an impression,

boasting that her jewellery came from Homer's fabled city and were undoubtedly worn by the legendary Helen of Troy herself.

Romantic stories abound about amazing discoveries from the nineteenth and twentieth centuries, and indeed it was an exciting era for archaeological discovery. Recent research has forced scholars to reinterpret some of the earlier spectacular discoveries, but many of them remain valid and important. One discovery in particular that shocked the world in the 1870s was the reported discovery of the original Biblical flood story.[16] George Smith, a young, self-taught specialist of the ancient Akkadian language, was working at the then newly established British Museum in London, which had been built to house and display the wealth of archaeological treasures pouring into the United Kingdom at the time. Smith had been given the task of joining together the numerous fragments of broken tablets in order to read and catalogue them. While reading through the tablets he discovered a story about a man named Utnapishtim (see Ch. 8), who, having been warned about a coming flood, built a huge boat into which he gathered his farm animals and his family. Together they rode out a terrible storm that lasted seven days and seven nights. Eventually, the boat landed on a high mountain. After a few days this Babylonian Noah released a dove, a swallow, and a raven before determining that it was safe to exit the boat.

Smith was convinced that he had found the original story that had inspired the version of the flood story found in the Bible. However, he could not be sure because his broken tablet was missing an important section containing about 17 lines of the story. Despite this, Smith's discovery was extremely important, and in 1872 he presented it to an assembly of scholars in London at the annual meeting of the Society of Biblical Archaeology. The United Kingdom in the 1870s was a very religious nation, but new ideas such as Charles Darwin's theory of evolution and the discoveries by geologists of impressions

of extinct creatures preserved in rock formations that were millions of years old, had shaken the foundations of biblical truth. Many people were very anxious to see some archaeological proof of the validity of the stories in the Bible. When Smith read a paper concerning his discoveries before the members of the Society of Biblical Archaeology, the audience was spellbound. Afterwards, members of the society passed a unanimous resolution calling on the British Museum to undertake further investigations to search for the missing fragments of the story. The process was accelerated when a London newspaper, the *Daily Telegraph*, gave a donation of £1000 to help finance an immediate expedition to the ancient city of Nineveh, in Iraq, where it was thought more tablets might lie buried. Everything was arranged quickly and a month after his discovery was announced, Smith travelled from London to the Near East in search of more tablets.

After months of delay in Turkey he was able to begin excavating. Amazingly, after only five days he not only unearthed tablets, but also discovered a fragment that contained most of the lines that were missing from the story he had found in the British Museum. Smith triumphantly telegraphed the details of his archaeological scoop to the *Daily Telegraph* in London. The world was amazed by Smith's discovery and reaction in the United Kingdom and elsewhere was remarkable. Although it was a moment of triumph for Smith, it would be his last, for upon hearing from him the owners of the newspaper cut their financial aid to his excavation and he was forced to return home. George Smith's discoveries caused an uproar among religious scholars and historians, and the debate concerning the ancient Sumerians and Babylonians and their influence on stories in the Bible raged for years afterwards. This debate continues today, albeit in a more subdued manner. Although through archaeological research new light has been shed upon the stories and myths from the past, the main purpose of archaeology is not to prove or

Syria and the eastern Mediterranean showing the location of Tell 'Atij.

View of Tell 'Atij from the Khabur River in eastern Syria.

Mud-brick house at night. The area on the left served as a kitchen and dining area, and that on the right as a laboratory for examining and preserving artifacts.

disprove the Bible or ancient Greek stories any more than it is to fill up museums with treasures from ancient lands.

What, then, is the purpose of archaeology? Archaeology has two main tasks:

- to establish a chronology, that is, to determine the age of the artifacts found at a particular site;
- to reconstruct the past lifeways of ancient people, which involves determining such things as the technology, economy, political system, religion, and art.

To clarify these objectives, this chapter will draw examples from an archaeological excavation in the Near East. Even though this excavation cannot explain all aspects of archaeological research, it will nevertheless serve as a good example of how archaeologists get their information.

EXCAVATING IN SYRIA

In 1983 the government of the Syrian Arab Republic announced plans for a giant project to build a number of dams to exploit the Khabur river valley for irrigation purposes.[17] With the damming of this tributary of the Euphrates River, more than 60 important archaeological sites from all periods of history would be lost under the waters of a vast shallow lake. To explore these sites the Syrian government called on the international community of archaeologists to come to its aid. Teams of archaeologists from Belgium, the Netherlands, Poland, Germany, Japan, the United States, France, Denmark, Lebanon, and Canada answered the call to save the precious cultural heritage buried along the banks of

A worker dumps a load of dirt at the edge of the tell with a view of the Tell 'Atij encampment in the background.

Local workers at Tell 'Atij.

Accurate measurements and detailed plans are an essential element of any excavation. Here one archaeologist takes measurements and calls them out to the architect seated nearby, who records them on a top plan.

Local workers at Tell 'Atij.

A Bedouin worker hands a *guffa* or basket of dirt to another worker.

The project photographer records the excavation data on film or with a digital camera.

Burial of a small child found on the summit of the tell. The site architect and his assistant will measure and record the orientation of the skeleton and the accompanying grave goods before they are removed and sent to a laboratory for further study.

Archaeologist Hillary Gopnik supervises the removal of a wall from an area of the site that was used for administrative purposes.

Workers remove earth from the main excavation area by passing *guffas* filled with dirt up a ladder.

the Khabur River. The Canadian team was led by Professor Michel Fortin and a group of archaeological researchers and graduate students from the University of Toronto and Laval University (Université Laval) in Québec City. In exchange for Canadian help and expertise, the Syrian government agreed to give the fragmentary material and a percentage of the artifacts recovered to Laval University. These artifacts are a welcome addition to Laval's museological centre and constitute one of the finest collections of its kind. Researchers, students, and the public will be able to view and study these objects for generations to come.

Professor Fortin chose a small site called Tell 'Atij (Arabic for "the old mound"), located about 20 km south of the nearest town, and 500 km to the east of the Syrian capital of Damascus. Before archaeologists could begin their work they had to build a mud-brick house, which served as a kitchen and dining area. In the second season the house was enlarged, toilets and showers were added (no longer was it necessary to bathe in the river), and a small laboratory and drafting area were set up. Finally, a wall of mud bricks was built around the compound to keep stray animals, especially vicious dogs, from wandering into camp. The excavators slept in army tents that were purchased locally. The Syrians provided the Canadian group with a representative from the Directorate of Antiquities and Museums to help coordinate the excavation and to ensure that no Syrian laws were contravened. However, the government representative was present not only to look out for Syrian interests. He helped to find and hire local workers, supervised their hours, and made sure that they were paid every two weeks. The representative also helped the team to get settled and meet local merchants and people in the service trades. If someone was sick the representative knew the location of the nearest hospital; often in a Near Eastern country what seems bewildering to foreigners can be done quickly and easily by the government representative.

The principal mound at Tell 'Atij (its ancient name is not known) measured a modest 200 m long by 40 m wide and was about 8 m above the plain at its highest point. Right from the start this mound was very promising because its surface was littered with hundreds of pieces of broken pottery, or "potsherds", most of which were dateable from the Early Dynastic period (called the Ninevite V period in northern Mesopotamia), roughly 3000–2500 BC. From the surface pottery evidence it was clear that the site was a centre of intense activity and that there was an excellent chance it would be of significant archaeological value.

Getting started

Before work could begin the site had to be surveyed using a theodolite, measuring tapes, and a ranging rod. Site contours were then mapped on a plan and divided into a grid of 6 m by 6 m squares. All archaeological sites must be surveyed so that when objects are found their exact location can be determined. Before the survey could begin, a single location called the "datum point" was established, and it is in relation to this point that walls, rooms, burials, pottery, and occupation areas are drawn on a series of detailed plans for the entire site. Each artifact or architectural feature is clearly indicated and drawn to scale and photographed, so that the whole site can be understood and studied long after the excavation is terminated. It is important to remember that a site can only be excavated once. After the artifacts have been unearthed the whole excavation process cannot be repeated because as the site is excavated much of it is also destroyed. As the excavation proceeds artifacts are retrieved, recorded, and safely stored. When the excavation is completed the walls and floor surfaces of the last level will remain, but the material above will have been removed. One of the most important tasks of archaeology is to establish the "chronology" of the site. There are numerous dating methods available to do this, but not all of them are equally useful in all parts of the world or on all types of sites. Some provide greater accuracy than others; some are useful in one context but not in another.

Types of dating techniques: relative dating methods

Stratification means the deposition or arrangement of the different layers of human occupation at an archaeological site. The most widely used dating method is called "stratigraphy",[18] meaning the study of the different layers or levels of occupation. Stratigraphy is based on the "law of superposition". Simply stated, the law of superposition means that artifacts found at the deepest levels of an excavation are the oldest, and those found nearest to the surface are the youngest. The date of each layer or *stratum* may be determined by the latest or most recent artifacts found in the soil that constitutes a given layer. Stratigraphy is an excellent dating method since it can be used in the field on any kind of site, anywhere in the world, and can usually be learned quickly by students. In addition, stratigraphy requires no specialized or costly laboratory equipment to obtain results. Despite its simplicity, stratigraphy does have its limitations since it can never give an exact numerical date to an artifact. Because of this, all stratigraphic dates are *relative dates* and indicate only which layers (and the artifacts found in those layers) are older or younger *relative* to other layers above or below them. The term "relative" should not be understood as meaning inaccurate. In fact, relative dates can be quite accurate and form the backbone of archaeological chronology.

In most parts of the ancient Near East buildings were made of mud bricks. Unburnt mud-brick structures will not last more than a few decades before they must be rebuilt with new bricks. When the walls of a building were intentionally thrown down, the old walls were not removed, but simply toppled over and levelled out to make room for the new structure, which was built on top of the remains of the old one. Each time a structure was rebuilt a new layer or stratum was created. After repeating this process a number of times a mound containing many strata was

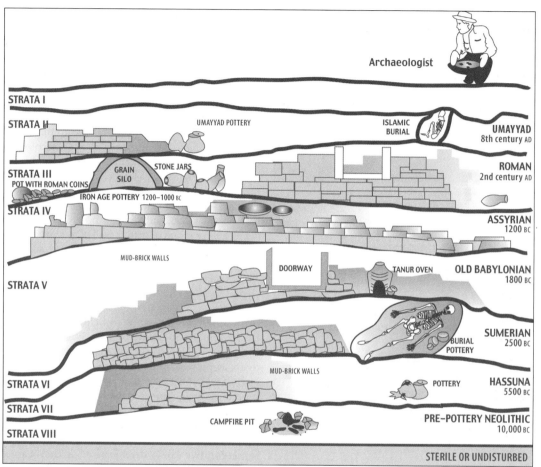

The principles of stratigraphy.

formed. Some of these mounds are only a few metres high, while others such as the ancient site of 'Acharneh are 30 m or more above the original ground level.

Strata could be formed in other ways as well. If the site was abandoned because of enemy attack, drought, or disease, it may have remained unoccupied for years or even centuries, then resettled later. In addition to buildings, after many centuries of occupation a habitation site will build up debris from normal human activities. Such things as garbage, broken pottery, and discarded or lost tools and valuables accumulate in and around areas where people have lived. Mixed in with this debris are the remains of

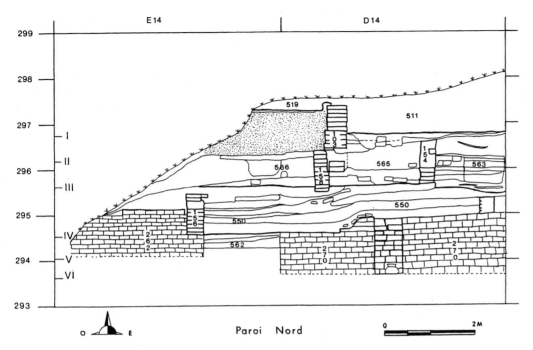

Stratigraphy from Tell 'Atij showing different levels of occupation and the remains of brick walls.

The massive Bronze Age mound at Tell 'Acharneh, Syria, 40 m high × 300 m long.

Pottery in the local market, Amman, Jordan.

houses and other buildings in which the former occupants lived and worked, and all of this material helps to form the different strata of a habitation site.

At Tell 'Atij the first artifacts recovered close to the surface were recent burials of local villagers, some of which were only a few decades old. Being close to the surface these artifacts were the youngest objects found on the site. Below these most recent burials were earlier ones from the Islamic period (seventh to fourteenth centuries AD), while below them (in one part of the site), Roman burials from the second century AD were found. Deeper still were the remains of the original inhabitants of the tell.

Pottery

Pots were used to cook and store cereal grains and were essential to prepare foods such as porridge, gruel, and beer. Pots are vermin proof and prevent mice and other rodents from eating stored grain. In addition, pots keep grain dry and free from rot and mildew.[19] Pots, jars, and even potsherds provide valuable clues that help to determine the economy, technology, and age of a site. But if pots and potsherds have no dates stamped on them how can archaeologists use them for dating? The type of pottery found at Tell 'Atij is called Ninevite V pottery, and has been known since the 1930s when the British archaeologist Max Mallowan first encountered this type of pottery in the number five stratum while he was excavating at Nineveh, hence its name. Over the years pots like those retrieved at Tell 'Atij have been found in strata that also contained dateable artifacts such as written documents or plant remains that could be dated using the radiocarbon method (see below). Based on this, Ninevite V pottery had been previously dated to 3000–2500 BC. When the same type of pottery was found at Tell 'Atij it was reasonable to conclude that it dated from the same period. Because there are slight variations even within

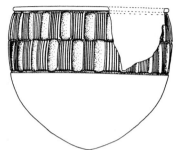

Drawing of an example of Ninevite V pottery. Important items such as pottery that has distinguishing or "diagnostic" characteristics are both drawn and photographed.

Ninevite V pottery (about 2500 BC), Tell 'Atij, Syria.

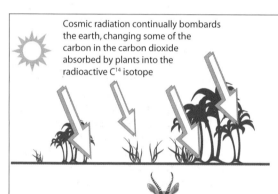

Cosmic radiation continually bombards the earth, changing some of the carbon in the carbon dioxide absorbed by plants into the radioactive C^{14} isotope

People and animals eat the plants, thus ingesting the C^{14} isotope

When the person or animal dies, no more C^{14} is ingested

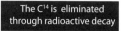

The C^{14} is eliminated through radioactive decay

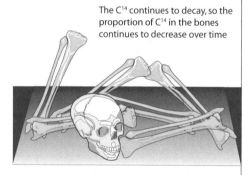

The C^{14} continues to decay, so the proportion of C^{14} in the bones continues to decrease over time

A bone can be tested in the laboratory and its remaining amount of C^{14} compared with that of a modern sample. The difference in the proportion of C^{14} in the two samples gives us the amount of C^{14} decay. From this, the time elapsed since the sample stopped ingesting C^{14} can be determined.

a given type of pottery, it was possible to date the site even more precisely to the middle of the third millennium BC.

Nuclear physics and absolute dating: the principles of radiocarbon dating

Up until the late 1940s, stratigraphy, pottery, numismatics, and calendars were the only tools available to scholars for determining ancient chronologies. However, in 1949 a new dating system was introduced that radically changed archaeology. An American, William F. Libby, developed a technique that was a spin-off of nuclear physics. In 1960 Libby received the Nobel Prize in Chemistry for his revolutionary discovery: radiocarbon dating. Radiocarbon or carbon-14 (C^{14}) dating may be explained as follows.

The earth is constantly being bombarded by cosmic radiation, or rays, consisting of small subatomic particles. When these particles reach the earth's atmosphere they cause changes in one of the very common elements present in our atmosphere, the gas carbon dioxide. The carbon atoms in carbon dioxide are a carbon isotope called carbon-12 (C^{12}), which is one of the fundamental elements found in all living organisms. When cosmic radiation comes in contact with carbon-12 atoms, a small number of them are altered and changed into carbon-14 atoms, another carbon isotope. Carbon-14 isotopes are simply carbon-12 atoms whose nuclei have been modified so that their atomic mass is increased from 12 to 14. There is only about one carbon-14 isotope in the atmosphere for every million carbon-12 atoms.

Both carbon-12 and carbon-14 combine with oxygen to form carbon dioxide. Carbon dioxide is

The principles of radiocarbon dating. Besides bone, radiocarbon dating can be used on wood, seeds, shells, cloth and other organic materials.

taken into plants during their growth cycle and eventually animals eat the plants, so that ultimately all living organisms ingest carbon-12 and carbon-14. The proportion of carbon-12 to carbon-14 is the same in plants and animals as it is in the atmosphere: about a million to one. Carbon-14 differs from carbon-12 because it is radioactive, meaning that it decays or deteriorates at a constant rate over a given period of time. This radioactive decay is going on all around us all the time in the air, the oceans, and the soil. It is important not to confuse the normal organic decay that takes place after the death of any living organism with the radioactive decay of carbon-14. Even though dead creatures may chemically decay in a few days or weeks, this in no way affects the amount of carbon-14 they contain because whatever remains of the organism – bones, shells, sticks, seeds or whatever – still has the same ratio of carbon-12 to carbon-14. When a plant or animal dies it no longer takes in carbon-12 or carbon-14 and the carbon-14 that it has ingested while it was alive begins to decay.

It will take approximately 5600 years for half of the carbon-14 in any given sample to decay, so the "half-life" of carbon-14 is 5600 years. In another 5600 years half of what remains will decay, and this process will continue until the amount left is so small that it can no longer be measured. Thus, if a sample of human bone contains only half the amount of carbon-14 found in living human bone, then the sample died 5600 years ago, and anything found in the same stratigraphic layer dates from the same period.

Radiocarbon or carbon-14 dates are typically given within a range of a certain number of years, which can vary. The symbol ± is used after the date to indicate the range. Thus, for example, a date may be expressed as 750 BC ± 25 years. This means that the date falls somewhere within a 50-year range between 775 BC and 725 BC. Even though carbon-14 dates do not produce exact calendar dates, they are still considered absolute dates because, unlike relative dates, they are not relative to the date of another artifact.

One of the tasks of the modern archaeologist is to find suitable samples of organic material that can be dated by the carbon-14 method. Wood charcoal is a good material since it is almost pure carbon. One or two grams of charcoal provides plenty of material for a dating sample. Finding some old wooden beams or the remains of a cooking fire may not seem very important to an outsider, but to an archaeologist it can provide as much valuable information about the age of an ancient society as a burial containing many fine artifacts. At Tell 'Atij, samples of wood suitable for carbon-14 dating have been retrieved and analysed by the geophysical sciences laboratory at Laval University. To ensure accuracy, other samples of the same material were also sent to two laboratories in the United States. The radiocarbon dates confirm the pottery and stratigraphic dates, and the combined results of the three methods place Tell 'Atij firmly in the middle of the third millennium BC.

Exact dates: numismatics

Numismatics is the study of coins. Coins are made of metals such as gold, silver, or, more commonly, copper, and last for thousands of years. Pieces of money offer one of the most reliable dating sources known because they either have a date stamped on them (most ancient coins did not), or they have a representation of a person or symbol that is dateable. If a coin is found with the likeness of a particular king on it and the exact dates of that king's reign are known, then artifacts found with that coin in the same strata can be dated from the same period. Coins can give very precise, even exact dates for their own manufacture, and are one of the few artifacts that can do so. However, coins are rare or absent from most sites and since they only appeared in the seventh century BC,[20] they have limited use as chronological indicators. As explained above, along with coins, written material such as letters, economic texts, and annals may also yield exact calendar dates.

Interpreting the data

The excavators at Tell 'Atij were struck by the lack of any evidence of living quarters on the main tell. Instead of houses, they found a number of mud-brick silos that were used for storing grain. Most of the silos were about 1.5 m square at the base and 2 m high, although a few were larger. Most of them were plastered on the inside to keep their interiors clean and dry. There were a dozen such silos at Tell 'Atij and each could hold 2–4 tonnes of grain: enough to feed a family of five for one year. On top of one of the clusters of silos were the remains of a building that was probably used for administrative purposes. But where were the remains of the inhabitants of Tell 'Atij? The main tell produced no evidence that would indicate that anyone actually lived there. About 30 m from the tell a smaller habitation site was found. Here, the remains of a number of brick houses were uncovered where the merchants who ran the grain storage operation on the main tell once lived. Apart from the fact that the principal tell only revealed structures used for grain storage, additional evidence was accumulated that corroborated the hypothesis that the site served as a grain storage and distribution centre. One interesting piece of information was the retrieval of a number of tokens or counters similar to the ones that will be discussed in the section on writing in Chapter 2.

It has been established that such clay tokens were used to record business transactions before writing was developed, and were in use from the Neolithic period down to the second millennium BC (8000–1800 BC).[21] Several of the tokens were shaped like the heads of cattle (see Ch. 2) and several of the round

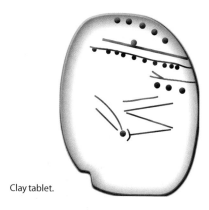

Clay tablet.

tokens indicate sheep. These types of tokens have led researchers to believe that, in addition to cereal grains, animals and animal by-products were also being raised and processed at Tell 'Atij. A small clay tablet that was used for recording purposes was also retrieved. Accompanying the tablet was a stone cylinder seal used to personalize business transactions. Cylinder seals were made of stone and engraved with geometric designs. Such geometric patterns are typical of the third millennium BC.

Agricultural goods were stored or shipped in large sacks or jars sealed with clay; cylinder seals were then rolled over the clay while it was still wet. The resulting impressions in the wet clay served as identifying marks or signatures since at that time most people could not actually write their own names. At the smaller site, where the inhabitants once lived, a number of stone formations were uncovered; they were used as wharves or mooring facilities for small grain-carrying boats. Even though no traces of actual boats have been found, a small clay representation of a boat has been recovered. The clearest evidence that boats were in common use at Tell 'Atij comes from a number of stone anchors that were found at the site. These anchors consisted of triangular-shaped stones into which three holes had been drilled. One of the holes would have had a rope passed through it that was attached to a boat, while the other two holes contained long sharpened pegs that would have held the anchor firmly to the river bottom. Marine traffic on the Khabur River is rare today, but 40 or 50 centuries ago it was common.

A pedologist (soil specialist) from Laval University accompanied the team of archaeologists each season and carried out research on the types of soils around Tell 'Atij. He was able to determine that the Khabur River was deeper in ancient times than it is today, and served as a transportation artery for boat traffic. In addition, he discovered that at the time the principal tell was occupied, Tell 'Atij was actually an island in the middle of the Khabur River. Centuries later, the river silted up and a land bridge formed between its east bank and the island tell.

Why did ancient peoples choose Tell 'Atij as a grain storage depot? The tell was situated on the edge of a vast grain-producing area that did not depend on irrigation for agricultural production. By studying the meagre plant remains left on the floors of the silos, a paleobotanist (a specialist in ancient plant remains) was able to determine that grains which grew naturally in the vicinity were collected and stored in silos on the island site. Tell 'Atij, and the area further to the north, received sufficient annual rainfall (25–50 cm) for crop production. In addition, it was located at an elevation of 290 m above sea level, which meant that it was slightly cooler than the agricultural regions at lower elevations to the south. Further south, in the river valleys of Sumer and Akkad, rainfall agriculture was impossible and farmers had to rely on a sophisticated irrigation system to ensure crop production. In times of famine, when the yearly harvests had not been sufficient, and the city-states of Sumer or Akkad needed additional grain to meet their needs, they sent agents north to the Khabur river valley to purchase or barter grain supplies to alleviate the threat of starvation. In times of food shortage the contents of the silos at Tell 'Atij (and other towns in the area as well), would have been loaded on to small boats and sent down the Euphrates River to the city of Mari, as well as Sumer and Akkad further to the south.

A stone cylinder seal decorated with a linear design impressed on clay, third millennium BC.

Stone anchor.

Written evidence

There is no written evidence of trade between Tell 'Atij and the cities of Sumer and Akkad during the third millennium BC. However, there are documents a few hundred years later from the second millennium BC that indicate that kings from the south did indeed procure food supplies from the Khabur River region. Texts from the city of Mari indicate that food expeditions frequently travelled to the "Upper Country," meaning the region of the Khabur river valley. Texts written during the reign of King Zimri-Lim (18th century BC) indicate that he was not always able to bridge the gap between harvests and was forced to seek additional supplies of grain outside his own kingdom. These texts speak of caravans consisting of as many as a thousand donkeys capable of carrying up to 100 tonnes of grain, making the voyage north to bring back food supplies. Mentioned in addition to land caravans are river expeditions that transported as much as 350 tonnes of grain in a single voyage. Archaeologists have established that the great city of Mari was founded about 2800 BC as an economic and administrative centre. Mari was strategically situated at the middle region of the Euphrates River to exploit the grain-producing areas of Khabur and other tributaries of the Euphrates River.[22] Evidence seems to indicate that Tell 'Atij was part of a vast food supply network created to meet the needs of the large urban areas further to the south.

The end of Tell 'Atij

Tell 'Atij functioned as a grain storage and distribution centre for about a thousand years. Then, for some reason that is still unclear, it ceased operations and was abandoned for many centuries until the Romans came and spent a few decades at the foot of the mound, which they used as a cemetery. Three Roman burials from the second century AD have been discovered near the tell and this comes as no surprise since Tell 'Atij lies only a kilometre north of the large Roman town of Tuneinir. A military outpost, Tuneinir was occupied by the Romans 2000 years after the original inhabitants had abandoned Tell 'Atij. After the Romans, the site was used sporadically as a burial area. During the third millennium BC the site was surrounded by an oval defensive wall, half of which has been eroded away by the river over the centuries. The wall would have been about 250 m in circumference, creating an enclosure about 80 m long by 45 m wide. The wall was 2.5 m thick and 6 m high, indicating that enemies and intruders were certainly known to the inhabitants of Tell 'Atij, and undoubtedly outsiders coveted the food supplies that were stored within the town. At some point the Khabur River then silted up on the east side of the tell, making it vulnerable to attacks by intruders. However, it does not appear that the small community met a violent end since the archaeological record shows no evidence of war or conflict. Instead, Professor Fortin believes that with the establishment of the Akkadian Empire around 2350 BC (see Ch. 4), a new trading strategy was developed in the south that no longer included storage depots like Tell 'Atij. This change in trading patterns ultimately forced the inhabitants to abandon the site.

Even though much has been learned during the six seasons of excavation at Tell 'Atij, not all the questions about who the people were or what happened to them will be answered. Starting in the late 1990s the waters of the Khabur River began to back up behind the large dam situated downstream and, within a few months, they submerged forever the last remains of this small, fortified town.

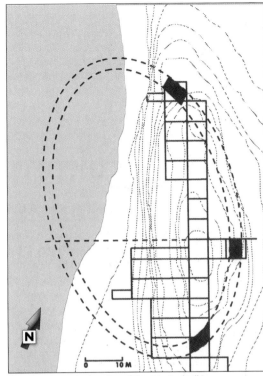

This plan shows the location of the principal tell in relation to the Khabur River. The dotted lines indicate the original location of the town wall, now washed away by centuries of erosion. Each square measures 6 m × 6 m and indicates an excavated area.

2 Agriculture and the origins of civilization

What is civilization? What do we mean when we say that an individual or group is civilized? In the context of this book no moral or ethical sense will be attached to the word civilization, nor will it be used to judge people's behaviour as being either good or bad. Instead, the word civilization will be used to indicate a number of technological developments and social changes that appeared in Mesopotamia, and neighbouring Egypt, more than 50 centuries ago.[1] Agriculture was the first of the great changes that enabled civilizations to develop. What is agriculture? Agriculture,[2] the domestication of certain plants and animals, resulted in radical economic, social, and technological changes for ancient peoples. Domestication means the development of a mutual dependence or "symbiotic relationship" between people and specific groups of plants and animals.[3] Once domestication occurs, all three are dependent upon each other for their collective survival. After agriculture was established the stage was set for changes and developments that led to the rise of civilization. The principal elements of civilization are:[4]

- **Cities**. A city may be defined as any group of people living in an urban environment with a population of 10 000 or more.[5] The social conditions created by cities required specialization of tasks for each member of society, resulting in differences in wealth, and creating an inequality among community members that was previously unknown.

- **Monumental architecture**.[6] Building projects, such as fortification walls, temples, or pyramids, required the large-scale effort on the part of most or all of the members of a community.
- **Writing**.[7] Writing is the act of communicating transactions, events, or ideas through a mutually understood set of symbols or characters inscribed on paper, clay, stone, or some other substance.

Evidence indicates that agriculture, combined with the elements of civilization, came together for the first time in human development in the regions of the Tigris and Euphrates Rivers, about 3100 BC. At the same time similar developments were taking place in Egypt, but evidence for cities like those found in Mesopotamia is still lacking.

THE ORIGINS OF AGRICULTURE

Before people became farmers and herders and began to live in villages and cities, they sustained themselves by hunting and gathering.[8] This method of obtaining foodstuffs is referred to as a "hunting and gathering economy", and the people who practised it are called hunter–gatherers. In this type of economy, animals such as wild goats or gazelle were hunted for their meat and skins, and cereal grains, such as emmer wheat and barley, were gathered as food sources. In the ancient Near East, most of the hunter–gatherers' diets consisted of the wild grains that grew naturally in the foothills away from the Nile and Tigris–Euphrates river valleys, since these valleys were too hot and dry for them to grow. Before 10 000 BC, small tribes of hunter–gatherers roamed the foothills near the Tigris and Euphrates Rivers, following the herds of wild goats, sheep, and gazelle, killing the animals as they needed them, and supplementing their diets with cereal grains and other plants that could be found growing naturally. People were not the only ones who ate the wild cereal grains; the herd animals also depended on them for survival.

Until about 12 000 years ago, people survived by hunting animals with stone-tipped spears or bows and arrows, and gathering quantities of cereal grains and other kinds of plants by hand. Then, rather suddenly, between 10 000 and 5000 BC, there were some remarkable changes in their economy and lifestyle. Starting at this time there is evidence for the domestication of both plants and animals,[9] and permanent human settlements began to appear. Human beings, and closely related human ancestors, had been hunter–gatherers for several million years prior to the development of agriculture. Why did they change their methods of obtaining food?

It is unlikely that in the distant past some very intelligent and farsighted individual simply woke up one morning, reflected about his or her situation as a hunter–gatherer, and decided to improve life by inventing agriculture.[10] Some have speculated that women, not men, first understood agricultural processes by watching seeds grow into plants around the campsite. Since women did not partake in the hunt, proponents of this theory reasoned that they would have had the time to observe the secrets of planting and harvesting, and would then have used their new discoveries to augment and improve the food supply. But there is no evidence that would indicate that one of the sexes was more inclined than the other towards the development of agriculture. The change from hunting and gathering to agriculture took thousands

of years and cannot be considered as a discovery by a single person. Nor is it likely that pre-agricultural people were ignorant of the connection between seeds and the growth of plants from them. It has been established that wild grasses, fruits, nuts, berries, roots, and cereals had been a part of human diet for thousands of years prior to the time the first steps towards agriculture were taken. Although it was known that food-bearing plants grew from seeds, hunter–gatherers did not consider it necessary to plant them because they grew naturally, in the wild.

Some of the earliest attempts at agriculture were made about 11 000 BC in the coastal areas of Israel, Lebanon, Jordan, and Syria. This period of early agricultural development is referred to as the Natufian period (10 500–8500 BC). During this time small bands of 50–100 hunter–gatherers lived in circular huts and practised intensive gathering of wild grains, and may have attempted the domestication of some herd animals. Eventually, the climate began to dry out and agriculture in this region never developed beyond a very rudimentary level. Later, the major phases of agricultural innovation occurred further east and north in the highlands of Anatolia and in the Zagros mountains, in what are now the countries of Turkey, Iran, and Iraq.

Three hypotheses on the origins of agriculture

1. The oasis hypothesis

The change people made from hunting and gathering to food production was one of the most momentous events in all of human evolution. More than any other change in the previous two or three million years, agriculture not only changed how people obtained their food, but it changed social relationships between them, and how they related to the planet. Agriculture has resulted in massive and lasting modifications to

A farmer in eastern Turkey harvesting grain with a handheld sickle. Early farmers in the Near East used similar methods.

the physical environment of earth, and a substantial increase in the number of its inhabitants. It has only been since the 1920s that a concerted effort has been made to better understand the problems stemming from the changes from a hunting and gathering economy to one based on agriculture. One of the pioneers in this area was the historian V. Gordon Childe. His ideas about the origins of agriculture are referred to as the "oasis hypothesis". Childe believed that climatic changes at the end of the last Ice Age had a great effect on subsequent human development. According to Childe, until about 12 000 years ago much of the Near East, including Iraq, Palestine, Egypt, and Turkey, had been fertile and well-watered before the great ice formations began to dry out and withdraw towards the northern regions of the planet. When the glaciers melted and disappeared, rivers stopped flowing from them and the great grasslands of the Near East turned to deserts. As a consequence, hunter–gatherers, who had traditionally exploited the vast herds of game animals in the open countryside, were forced into the shrinking wet areas along the banks of the Nile, Tigris and Euphrates Rivers, or around oases that still managed to survive in the increasingly hot and dry deserts.

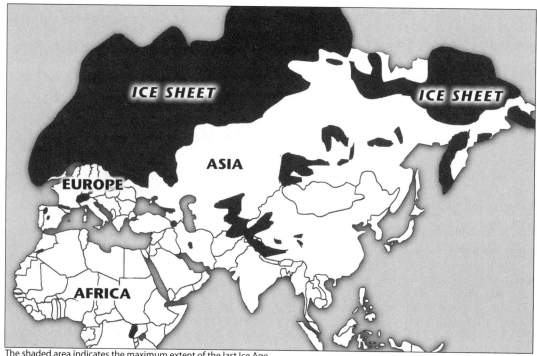

The shaded area indicates the maximum extent of the last Ice Age.

circumstances would want to take up agriculture. Childe assumed that people were naturally progressive and over the centuries had attempted to improve their living conditions by developing new and better techniques of obtaining food. But, putting people and animals together in close proximity would not in itself have led to domestication. Instead, it probably would have served only to reinforce hunting activities, since if the people knew that the animals could no longer stray very far from their water sources, the hunters would not have been obliged to follow after the animals to hunt them down; they could have simply waited by any riverbank or water hole until their prey came in search of the ever-diminishing water supply and killed them. Following Childe's reasoning, there would have been no need to start penning up the animals, since they would have come by necessity to the hunters who lived near sources of water, instead of the hunters being forced to seek them out. Childe's hypothesis does not satisfactorily explain how or why humans made the shift from hunting and gathering to agriculture, but it does emphasize the importance of climatological change when considering the origins of agriculture.

According to Childe, once people and animals were confined to smaller areas, their close proximity to each other provided a stimulus for them to adopt new food-producing techniques.[11] Stimulated by this new closeness to their food sources, hunter–gatherers moved beyond their traditional methods of obtaining food and made the very progressive step towards agriculture. As the water supply diminished through the desiccation of the environment, people, plants, and animals, all dependent on stable water sources, were forced into a closer contact with each other. This closeness or "juxtaposition",[12] as Childe called it, enabled people to observe animals firsthand and led to their domestication. It also required peo-

ple to abandon their nomadic lifestyle and settle in one place to ensure that they and their newly domesticated animals would always be close to reliable water sources.

Childe's hypothesis dominated thinking on the subject for several decades until research by paleoclimatologists (people who study ancient climatic conditions) showed that even though there was a slight climatic change about 9000 BC, the great climatological change Childe spoke of at the end of the last Ice Age did not occur in the Near East the way he said it did.[13] Although Childe's hypothesis succeeds in bringing plants, animals, and people together, it does not explain why people in these

2. The nuclear zone hypothesis

In response to Childe's oasis hypothesis, two British anthropologists, Harold Peake and Herbert Fleure, argued that agriculture began not in the lowland river valleys or oases but in the highlands of Turkey and the foothills adjacent to the Tigris–Euphrates river valley. Wild cereal grasses such as wheat and barley grew naturally in these regions, and did not depend on human intervention for their growth and survival. No one was able to test either Childe's oasis or Peake and Fleure's foothills hypotheses until the late 1940s. At that time an American anthropologist, Robert Braidwood, organized an archaeological expedition to a small village in Iraq called Qalat Jarmo expressly to determine the origins of agriculture.[14] Qalat Jarmo was located in a unique ecological zone that met certain requirements for the development of agriculture. This zone, called the "nuclear zone", was located in an area 300–1800 m above sea level, far from the river valleys of Egypt and Mesopotamia, where temperatures were too harsh to allow wild wheat and barley to grow naturally. Nor was the nuclear zone so high in the mountains that the wild cereal grains would die from the cold temperatures found at elevations above 1800 m. The nuclear zone was located between two temperature extremes that were neither too hot, nor too cold.

The nuclear zone was situated inside a region where the average rainfall was 25–50 cm each year (see map). If the rainfall had been higher, forests would have grown up in the area and covered the space needed for wild wheat and barley grains to grow. Likewise, in areas where the annual rainfall was less than 25 cm the wild grains would have died out from lack of water. Braidwood excavated for five seasons, searching for the first signs of primitive agriculture. To carry out his research he assembled a team of specialists that included archaeologists as well as a botanist, a zoologist, and a geologist to help study and analyse the very diverse types of data that were needed to substantiate his hypothesis.

About the same time, hoping to prove Childe's oasis hypothesis, a British archaeologist named Kathleen Kenyon mounted an expedition to the ancient city of Jericho, known from the Old Testament of the Bible for the story about its walls supposedly being knocked over by the force of loud trumpet blasts. Unlike Qalat Jarmo, Jericho is located outside the nuclear zone in an area 250 m below sea level, and receives little rainfall. It is, however, located next to a copious spring. Even though Jericho was older than Qalat Jarmo, the dates for both showed that the two villages were already active 9000 years ago.

For some time a debate raged between scholars as to which hypothesis, the nuclear zone or the oasis,

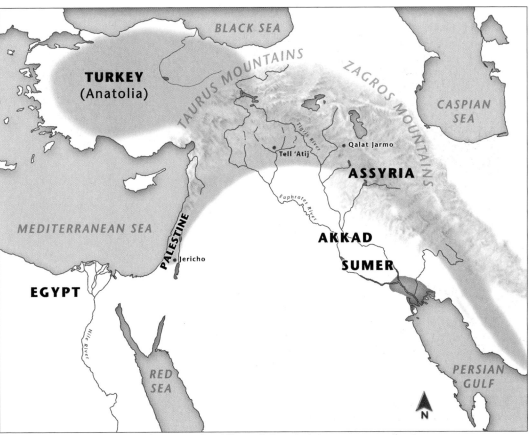

Annual rainfall. Shaded areas received 25–50 cm of rainfall annually. It was in these same areas, at elevations 300–1800 m above sea level, that the first steps towards agriculture were taken during the Neolithic period.

was correct. Several decades of research have shown that the inhabitants of Jericho were traders who exchanged salt from the nearby Dead Sea for food products,[15] but they also grew some food themselves. It seems that Jericho was both an ancient trading centre and an early agricultural village. Since the Jericho excavations in the 1950s, many early farming villages have been found, most located in the nuclear zone, but only two other early agricultural sites, Mureybet and El-Kown, have been located near rivers or oases. Evidence indicates that after the initial impetus in Syria-Palestine, the first steps towards agriculture and the domestication of animals took place in the nuclear zone in the foothills of the ancient Near East, and not near oases, nor in the Nile or Tigris–Euphrates river valleys.

Through pioneering research, Braidwood and others had been successful in establishing where agriculture originated, but they were never able to explain fully why agriculture occurred.[16] After all, it was argued, if hunting and gathering had been a successful economy for thousands, even millions of years, why change? We are sometimes tempted to think that people are naturally innovative and want to continually improve their circumstances by developing new time- and labour-saving techniques. However, because modern people of the 21st century view their own lifestyles and environment in this way does not mean that prehistoric peoples shared their ideas concerning progress. Anthropological research has shown that some primitive hunter–gatherers who existed until recently in remote regions of the earth, did not devote more than 8–12 hours a week hunting and gathering food.[17] The rest of the time they spent with their families, talking, telling myths and stories, repairing their weapons and clothes, or just taking it easy. Contrary to the popular belief that hunting and gathering was a bleak and terrible existence, studies show that some hunter–gatherers spent less time obtaining food than the average North American or European factory worker. One might ask: if hunting and gathering was such an easy and agreeable life, why take up farming? Farming is hard work and often requires tremendous effort and dedication to clear and prepare the land, fight off diseases and predators, and build irrigation canals, before finally bringing in the harvest. Furthermore, with agriculture one is permanently tied to the land with little or no chance of ever leaving it to find new adventures or to meet new peoples. Compared to farming, hunting is an exciting and stimulating activity that challenges hunters as they stalk their prey. For millennia generations of farmers in the Near East were born, lived out their lives, and died without ever travelling beyond the next village, without ever knowing what was over the next hill.

3. The population pressure hypothesis

Even though by the late 1960s it was becoming clear where and when agriculture began, the catalyst that actually caused people to begin the whole process of plant and animal domestication was still poorly understood. Childe, as well as Braidwood, had said essentially that once people were in close proximity to the right kinds of animals and plants, things began to happen and eventually agriculture developed. But hunter–gatherers had always been in close contact with plants and animals, the same ones that would one day be domesticated, and yet nothing had happened before. Why, about 12 000 years ago, did people begin to change the way they obtained their food?

Following the work of American anthropologists Lewis Binford and Kent Flannery, Canadians Philip Smith and T. Cuyler Young Jr. introduced a new element into the search for the origins of agriculture.[18] Smith and Young hypothesized that because of a slight warming of the climate (but not the kind of climatic change proposed by Childe), the living conditions of hunter–gatherers slowly improved, resulting in a very gradual increase in population. This increase continued for many centuries until food resources became too scarce to maintain the population by hunting and gathering alone. When this critical point was reached, about 10 000 years ago, people were faced with a major food crisis. To avoid starvation, people living in the nuclear zone had little choice but to intervene actively with plants and animals in an effort to increase food production.[19]

Coping with the food crisis

One method of intervention consisted of breaking the ground with sticks, making it easier for seeds to germinate and take root. This would in turn serve to extend the growing season by protecting the seeds from the cold, and would ensure that fewer seeds were lost to birds and rodents. Another method of intervention was the selective hunting of game animals. By killing only the males or older females beyond the age of reproductive fertility, a steady supply of meat would be maintained without diminishing the size of the herd.[20] People began watching over the herds to make sure that other predators such as lions and wolves did not eat too many of the wild goats, sheep, gazelle, or cattle destined for human consumption. Leading the flocks to fresh grazing areas and drinking water also helped to ensure that the animals remained healthy and productive. These procedures were some of the first steps away from hunting animals towards actually taking care of them, and eventually would lead to the domestication of sheep and goats by 7000 BC, followed by pigs and cattle between 6500 and 6000 BC Unlike previous interpretations, the population pressure hypothesis provided a reason why people took up agriculture: they were forced to do so.[21] Accordingly, had a population increase not occurred it is questionable whether

Chronology of ancient Mesopotamia: early periods (all dates BC)

Stages of civilization	Period	Dates
Hunters and gatherers	End of Upper Paleolithic	15,000
End of the last Ice Age and the beginning of agriculture	Epi-paleolithic	12,000–7000
Early farming communities	Neolithic	8000–4000
	Hassuna (North)	6000–5300
	Samara (South)	7000–5300
	Halaf	6000–5000
	Chogi Mami	5400–5100
	Ubaid	5000–3800
	Early Uruk	3800–3500
Bronze Age begins	Middle Uruk	3500–3200
Formation of early cities	Late Uruk	3200–3100
Development of writing	Jemdet Nasr	3100–2900
	Early Dynastic I	2900–2700
	Early Dynastic II	2700–2500
	Early Dynastic III	2500–2350

the domestication of plants and animals would have ever taken place. Once people began to intercede actively in the development of edible plants, cereal grains began to increase in size as well as expand their range outside the nuclear zone. This took place through a natural process called "hybridization", whereby through mutations or cross-breeding, living organisms change their structure or behaviour. Cereal grains, like wheat and barley, began to produce more and bigger grains, but at the same time they also lost some of their ability to plant themselves in the ground with their old efficiency. When this happened, cereal grains had to depend more and more on the intervention of human farmers to assure their survival. This mutual dependency is a good example of the *symbiotic relationship* that developed between people and their newly domesticated food sources. To help their crops survive, farmers started removing unwanted plants that were in competition with their food sources, a practice referred to today as "weeding". Eventually, farmers began to devise dykes and ditches to supplement the water supply to their fields of grain. In reaction to human intervention, the new hybrid wheat and barley strains were able to adapt to the hotter temperatures of the great river valleys far from their original home in the nuclear zone. Once this happened the real potential of massive river irrigation could be combined with the newly developed wheat and barley strains. From that moment on, the way was open for the greatest economic, social, and technological changes ever to take place since people had first appeared on earth. In the entire span of our existence on the planet, no development has had a more lasting impact on people than the development of agriculture. All that we now call "modern civilization" is the result of the agricultural revolution. By about 5000 BC, small farming villages were beginning to appear in the Tigris–Euphrates river valley and shortly thereafter in the Nile river valley. These early villages were inhabited by people who had up until that time been hunter–gatherers, roaming the land in search of wild plants and animals for their survival. The gradual shift from a hunting and gathering economy to an agricultural one took about 5000 years. If we consider that people and human ancestors had been on the earth for four, or perhaps five million years, then this time period is extremely short, and it is for this reason that V. Gordon Childe called this period of rapid change the "agricultural revolution".

Map showing the location of some early farming villages.

A multidimensional approach to the origins of agriculture

The three hypotheses presented all maintain that there was one major cause behind the origins of agriculture.[22] In the case of the oasis hypothesis it was a great climatic change; for the nuclear zone hypothesis it was a certain set of conditions that created a special ecological region where agriculture could occur; for the population pressure hypothesis it was the increase in human population. Now, researchers realize that all three of these factors had a role in the development of agriculture. In the case of the oasis hypothesis, it has been established that there was some kind of climatological change in northern Africa and southwestern Asia that must have driven people out of the desert areas towards water sources. This may have been an important factor in the development of agriculture, but climatological change alone did not cause people to take up agriculture.

Childe believed that agriculture developed around river valleys, while Braidwood showed that the region where most agricultural innovations originated was where wild cereal grains (and the animals who ate them) grew naturally in the nuclear zone. The nuclear zone was indeed the area where edible cereal grains occurred naturally, but this factor alone is not sufficient to explain the origins of agriculture.

The major drawback of the population pressure hypothesis is that there are no census figures from this period, and no way has yet been devised to verify accurately prehistoric population figures. Nevertheless, proponents of the population pressure hypothesis point out that the number of early agricultural sites did increase in the ninth millennium BC, and this seems to imply that there was a gradual increase in population as well.

To better comprehend the origins of agriculture in the future, all three hypotheses will have to be employed in varying degrees to understand how the agricultural revolution came about. It now appears that during different periods of prehistory, in different areas, diverse groups of people took up agriculture for a number of different reasons, in accordance with the needs and environmental conditions throughout the different areas of the ancient Near East.

Agriculture and urbanization: from farming villages to cities

Once the agricultural techniques of plant and animal domestication became indispensable to human existence, the nomadic lifestyle necessary to follow the herd animals gradually gave way to a more sedentary lifestyle. It is often believed that "settling down" is some kind of instinctive form of human behaviour. However, it has never been proved that people have any natural or innate desire to settle in towns or villages. They probably only did so as a result of the growth of agriculture or, as in the case of early villages like Jericho, because they were situated on trade routes and had commodities such as salt and ochre that could be traded for foodstuffs. The establishment of small, permanently inhabited settlements, numbering from a few dozen to perhaps 200 people, occurred in the foothills area of the Zagros mountains by about 8000 BC. Even though earlier pre-agricultural villages are known, most begin to appear, along with evidence for early domestication of plants and animals, after 7000 BC. Agriculture was not universally adopted in all early villages, and hunting

villages continued to exist alongside agricultural villages for a considerable length of time. By 6000 BC, small agricultural villages begin to appear outside the special environment of the nuclear zone. Villages such as Hassuna, in northern Iraq, receive only 20 cm of rainfall annually and are outside the limits of rainfall agriculture. This means that some kind of irrigation must have been used to ensure crop growth.

The movement away from the nuclear zone continues to be verified through archaeological research. The village of Chogi Mami (5400–5100 BC) was located only 137 m above sea level, far below the limits of the nuclear zone, and shows clear evidence of irrigation canals. This means that its inhabitants were no longer strictly dependent on rainfall to water their fields. The site also yielded a large number of fully domesticated plants and animals, and had a mud-brick tower, possibly used to defend the village from enemies.

In the sixth millennium BC, evidence of increased human conflict begins to appear in the archaeological record. South of Hassuna, at the village of Sawwan, a wall and a large ditch were constructed around the village complex, which seem to indicate

Left: A farmer digging an irrigation ditch in northern Iraq. Right: A farmer threshing grain using a sledge pulled by two cattle, eastern Turkey.

that the inhabitants were increasingly concerned with defence.[23] Despite this, most villages from this period had no fortifications of any kind, which may indicate that, in general, things were fairly peaceful.

Villages like Chogi Mami and Sawwan had larger populations than the earlier agricultural villages situated in the nuclear zone. It is possible that as many as 1000 people inhabited Chogi Mami by 5100 BC. Buildings in this period were built with cigar-shaped mud bricks, which allowed larger and even multi-storeyed structures to be constructed. There is also clear evidence that social stratification and craft specialization were occurring in more complex forms. This represented a shift away from social organization based on hunting and gathering to one based on agricultural production. In response to their new food production methods, human groups created new forms of culture that corresponded to agricultural technologies.

The first urban centres

In what is called the Ubaid period (5000–3800 BC), people living in the southern reaches of the Tigris–Euphrates river basin made a number of changes and innovations that led directly to the development of the first cities. During the period of formation of early villages, the northern part of Mesopotamia was at the forefront of technological innovation. Starting early in the fifth millennium BC, the situation was reversed somewhat, and larger towns and cities began to appear in the southern part of Mesopotamia. There were few permanent settlements in southern Mesopotamia until the Ubaid period. The Ubaid period (see chronological chart, p. 24), was a transitional period that witnessed the change from villages and small systems of irrigation agriculture to cities and large systems of irrigation agriculture. In the south, irrigation agriculture was practised from the very beginning since rainfall alone in this region is

insufficient to sustain farming activities. Without additional water supplied through irrigation, grain farming would have been impossible. By about 4000 BC, the villages and towns in this region were as large as those further north, some covering as much as 4 hectares (40 000 m²) in area. By 3800 BC the site of the town of Eridu covered 10 hectares and had an estimated population of 2000–4000 people.

As the size and population of farming communities increased, so did the complexity of their social structures. Not only were there farmers living in or around these settlements, but there were also potters and basket-makers, various kinds of merchants, leather-workers, and labourers. To meet the communities' spiritual needs, full-time priests and their assistants maintained the growing number of temples. Southern Mesopotamia was ideal for the development of irrigation agriculture because the region was flat and located between two large rivers. But it also had a number of drawbacks. First, because southern Mesopotamia was formed from alluvial silt (soil transported and deposited by water), there was no naturally occurring stone of any kind in the area, and the whole flood plain, over 300 km long and half as wide, contained no hardwood trees; oak, pine, and cedar timbers had to be imported from great distances. Stone and wood, which were necessary for construction projects and the production of many luxury goods, had to be sought outside Mesopotamia at great cost. This lack of essential natural resources created a demand for raw materials, which served to stimulate trade and turned Mesopotamia into a great trading region. Although long-distance trade of small quantities of goods had existed in the Near East for thousands of years, it was only with the development of agriculture and cities that what archaeologists call the "Uruk expansion"[24] occurred in the middle of the fourth millennium BC. This phenomenon brought together a number of professional traders and merchants in a vast pan-Mesopotamian import–export network, which was created around

3600 BC and lasted for several hundreds of years. The organization and administration of such a trade network required a recording system and scribes, who could read and write business transactions. Even though the first true writing does not appear until the very end of the fourth millennium BC, in the Ubaid period, the recording of various business transactions was already taking place.

THE DEVELOPMENT OF WRITING

Like agriculture, no single individual invented writing, nor was writing developed so that people could write down their histories. Starting about 8000 years ago, the earliest forms of writing were developed to record business transactions. As trading and agricultural activities increased it became difficult to keep track of who owed how much to whom. As a result, sometime in the Neolithic period, about 6000 BC, small clay objects called "tokens" began to appear in the archaeological record. Tokens were made in various shapes such as discs, oblongs, and cones. Often the tokens had simple designs such as crosses or dots inscribed into their soft clay surfaces before they hardened. For many years the meaning of these tokens was unclear. However, in the 1970s Denise Schmandt-Besserat,[25] following her teacher, Pierre Amiet, proposed that these small bits of clay were actually counters used to represent various objects such as sheep, goats, or measures of grain. In essence one token stood for one object.[26] For instance, one cone-shaped object stood for one measure of grain, one oval stood for one jar of oil, and one circle with a cross stood for one sheep.

The purpose of the tokens is now clear; they were used as mnemonic (memory) devices to help remind merchants and traders of simple business transactions they made during the early phases of agricultural development. In the fourth millennium BC, merchants and traders began to place the tokens into a sealed clay envelope shaped like a ball. A number of these balls have been recovered, and when broken open they may contain up to four dozen tokens of various shapes and sizes. The clay balls sometimes had the names of the people involved in the sale impressed on the outside. Since at this time there was no fully developed form of writing, each individual of any importance possessed a personalized stone seal, called a cylinder seal (illustrated p. 31), with a design inscribed on it that would indicate the name of a particular person. This "name" seal was rolled on the outside of the clay envelope, and if there was ever a need to check the business transaction the owner of the envelope could be identified. If necessary, the envelope could be broken open and the tokens verified. This was an effective way of recording things, but each time a transaction needed to be verified the clay envelope had to be broken open, examined, and then a new envelope had to be made and resealed. In some instances tokens were perforated and a string was passed through them and its ends tied together. To make sure that no one tampered with the string, or removed any of the tokens, a small lump of clay was placed over the knotted portion of the string and the cylinder seals of both parties were rolled over the wet clay. This method incorporated both security and visibility of the tokens, but was abandoned in favour of an even more efficient method of recording transactions.

Pictographs and cuneiform writing

Some time later, in the fourth millennium BC, instead of being placed inside the clay envelopes, the tokens were simply pressed into the envelope's outside while it was still moist. This left an impression of the token that could be read. The problem with this method was that pressing the tokens into the clay did not always leave clear images. Eventually the tokens were completely abandoned, and instead of pushing them into the wet clay, their shapes were drawn or inscribed

Tokens and counters found at Tell 'Atij, Syria.

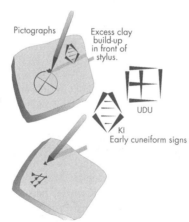

Early cuneiform sign formation.

From tokens to writing. Various stages in the development of writing from early tokens on the left, about 6000 BC, through the Sumerian period, 3000 BC, to Neo-Assyrian, 700 BC.

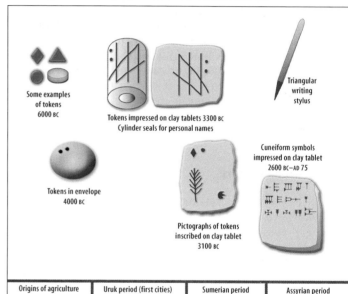

Origins of agriculture 8000 BC	Uruk period (first cities) 4000–3100 BC	Sumerian period 3rd millennium BC	Assyrian period 1st millennium BC
		KI	matum
		LU	immeru
		ÂB	arhu
		NINDA	akalum

on the outside of the envelope with a sharp reed. Symbols such as these are called "pictographs". The first pictographs were simply drawings of tokens[27] and they constitute the earliest form of writing. Specialists of ancient writing systems agree that late in the Uruk period, about 3100 BC, the first evidence of pictographic writing appears. Several centuries later, during the Early Dynastic II period (2700–2500 BC), another important change took place. Originally pictographs had been written on clay using a sharpened section of reed, perhaps 20–30 cm long and about the thickness of a pencil. But during the third millennium BC the pointed writing instrument was exchanged for a triangular-shaped one that changed the pictographs into wedge-shaped or cuneiform signs. With this innovation, instead of drawing simple pictures of objects, the wedge-shaped end of the reed was pressed into the clay lump, then withdrawn rapidly. This motion produced the groups of wedges in the cuneiform writing system that was used first by the Sumerians, and then by subsequent peoples in Mesopotamia for nearly 30 centuries.[28]

The word "cuneiform" comes from Latin and means "wedge form" writing. It should be remembered that cuneiform was not a language, but rather a writing system used to express a number of Near Eastern languages.[29] Cuneiform characters were a faster way of making stylized renderings of pictographs. Some cuneiform signs represented individual things or concepts, while others represented syllables that could be combined to form words. Written in cuneiform, pictographs became more abstract and stylized and no longer resembled pictures of the objects they were originally intended to represent. The sign for "man", *lú*, no longer looked like a human form

but instead was written

By the Early Dynastic III period (c. 2500 BC), most cuneiform symbols were no longer pictographs since they no longer constituted picture writing. Originally, pictographic writing was really a form of "noun" writing. Each object or thing had a pictograph that described it. A cow was drawn in the form of a cow, a man in the form of a man (or a deity), and a star in the form of a star. The pictographs numbered in the hundreds, one for each object recorded. However, as the number of objects represented by pictographs increased, so did the number of pictographs that had to be memorized. Imagine, for a moment, that when one learned to write English it was necessary to learn hundreds or even several thousand symbols instead of the 26 that are contained in the alphabet.

Early in its development a major conceptual change occurred in the cuneiform writing system; the pictographs began to represent the different syllables or sound parts of individual words instead of simply being pictures of objects. When this happened the

Cuneiform tablet containing "liver omens" (see Ch. 9), Middle Babylonian period. (Redpath Museum, McGill University)

number of symbols was greatly reduced and instead of having to memorize thousands of signs, scribes only had to learn a few hundred. Because pictographs are pictures of objects identified by their shapes, pictographs constitute a visual writing system. But when the cuneiform symbols began to stand for sounds the nature of the writing system was transformed into an auditory writing system. Of course, the writing system was still read or visualized with the eye, but the cuneiform symbols represented sounds and only occasionally objects. For example, in the earliest forms of writing the pictograph

meant "star" or "heaven" and was pronounced *an*. In cuneiform script the same pictograph was written

It retained the meaning star, and was still pronounced *an*. However, if the same symbol occurred as part of a complete word it was pronounced the same way, but instead of meaning the thing "star", it meant the sound *an*. This concept can be more easily understood by examining the Akkadian word *antalum*, which means "eclipse". In this word the cuneiform symbol for *an* occurs once again

but when combined with other signs *an* is simply one syllable in a polysyllabic word that no longer represents a picture of a thing. Once early forms of writing were in place in southern Mesopotamia, the idea of writing seems to have influenced the development of writing in Egypt to the west and Elam to the east.[30] The archaic Elamite script is to a large extent still undeciphered, but the pictographic signs indicate that much of their writing system was borrowed from Mesopotamia.

Writing in Egypt

As in Mesopotamia, much of the impetus for early writing in Egypt was for record-keeping and accounting.[31] The earliest representations of Egyptian writing were inscribed on storage jars found at the city of Abydos. These inscriptions appear about 3150 BC and by 3080–3040 BC there were several hundred signs of one, two or three consonants used to communicate whole words. The ancient Egyptians referred to these signs as the *medu netcher*, "the gods' words". Since the fourth century BC, this system has been called hieroglyphic or "sacred" writing. From that time on the word "hieroglyph" was used by the Greeks to refer to Egyptian writing. Because Egyptian writing was essentially pictographic, scribes, at least those who inscribed stone monuments, became artists as they learned to draw the figures used to write. Hieroglyphic writing was considered a form of representational art, and Egyptian art and writing developed many close ties over the centuries.[32] Most texts were written on papyrus or wood using a small brush. Black ink was used for the body of the text and red ink for titles and important passages. Many inscriptions were also incised into the stone walls of temples, palaces and public buildings.[33] In the Middle Kingdom (2040–1640 BC) there were about 750 signs. This number increased to several thousand

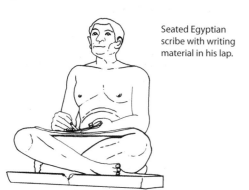

Seated Egyptian scribe with writing material in his lap.

during the Graeco-Roman period (332 BC–AD 395). Along with the hundreds of hieroglyphic signs or pictures there were also 24 "alphabetic" signs, which never developed into a true alphabetic system.[34] Hieroglyphs could be used in two different ways. First, as pictures or, more precisely, pictograms to depict things such as

for owl

for mouth or

for seated man.

The second way was to express sounds. For example, the sign for mouth, usually accompanied with a vertical line

was the sound for *r*. The sign

depicts a simple plan of a house and was used to write the word

pr, which means "house". There is another word that makes use of the same two sounds *p* and *r*

but when accompanied by another sign, ⋀, called a "determinative", it tells the reader that the combination of signs is to be read as the verb "go out". Determinatives are signs placed after words to clarify their meaning. The determinative man

following a word means man and his occupations. The determinative sun, ☉, relates to the sun, time and light. The determinative ⊗ means a town, village or geographical location.[35]

The grammatical structure of Egyptian and Sumerian is very different. Egyptian belongs to the Afroasiatic group of languages which includes Semitic, Chadic, Berber, and Cushitic. Sumerian did not belong to any known language group. Although some signs are similar, Egyptian and Sumerian pictographs did not come from the same source and are not interchangeable. Egyptian pictographs are definitely drawn from the culture of the Nile river valley, while those of Mesopotamia come from the cultural tradition of the Tigris–Euphrates river valley. Both writing systems used determinatives to help the reader understand the meaning of the signs, and both used pictures to convey the meaning of objects as well as ideas and concepts. But here the similarity ends since Sumerian, and later Akkadian, lost their pictographic values early in their history. For the most part, hieroglyphic Egyptian remained pictographic throughout its long history, while early in the third millennium BC, Sumerian pictographs ceased to look like the objects they represented and appear as groupings of wedge-shaped signs. In addition, both Sumerian and Akkadian used syllables made up of combinations of vowels and consonants as the building blocks for many words. Egyptian hieroglyphs used groups of one, two or three consonants to form words. Hieroglyphs were not used to write vowels and, for the most part, they were not expressed in ancient Egyptian.

Normal hieroglyphic writing was used in official documents and on monumental inscriptions, and remained in use for more than three millennia until the beginning of the Christian era. Alongside hieroglyphs, a second, faster form of writing also developed. This cursive script (a kind of long-hand), used to write religious and administrative texts, is called "hieratic". A third type of writing, which was even faster since it did not involve drawing tiny pictures, was called "demotic" and appeared in the seventh century BC. Demotic was used for writing the everyday language of accounts, administrative texts, letters, and contracts, and was used until the fifth century AD. In the final period of Egyptian history (700 BC–AD 500) all three forms – hieroglyphics, hieratic and demotic – were used concurrently. Long after ancient or pharaonic Egypt had ceased to exist, elements of ancient Egyptian language and writing survived in Coptic, the language of Christian Egypt. Whereas hieroglyphs and hieratic are two different scripts of the same language, demotic, and later Coptic, have their own grammatical structure. Using a combination of the Greek alphabet and half a dozen demotic signs, Coptic was widely used in Egypt until it was superseded by Arabic in the ninth century AD. One of several Coptic dialects still survives today in the liturgy of the Coptic Church.

Unlike in Mesopotamia, clay was rarely used as a writing medium in Egypt, and was never adopted on a large scale. Early forms of Egyptian writing show signs of Mesopotamian influence in the form of cylinder seals for personal identification, similar to those found in Mesopotamia, which appeared in Egypt but with Egyptianized pictographs.

Writing appears in Egypt during the Naqada III period (3200 BC) with little evidence of prior development.[36] But in Mesopotamia early writing developed over a period of several thousand years and went through various stages of tokens and envelopes before fully fledged writing finally appeared. During the fourth millennium BC there is evidence of Mesopotamian influence on early Egyptian civilization in the areas of art, architecture, and pottery. Such Mesopotamian influences seem to indicate that the Egyptians, at the end of the fourth millennium BC, were in contact with, and inspired by, the creative forces that were rapidly developing in the southern Tigris–Euphrates river valley. The Egyptians did not borrow the Sumerian writing system, but it seems that they may have borrowed the idea of writing from them, which they then Egyptianized and made their own.[37] Like several other innovations the Egyptians received through their contacts with Mesopotamia, Egyptian scribes quickly adapted writing to their own needs and circumstances. The Egyptian hieroglyphic and Sumerian–Akkadian cuneiform writing systems remained in use for thousands of years despite the fact that they were complicated and contained hundreds, even thousands, of signs that took years of schooling to master. Because of this, the profession of scribe was very prestigious, even magical to most of the population, who did not attend school or know how to write. Scribes who knew how to write were very much in demand. Throughout much of Mesopotamian history, to be legal the sale of goods between two people required a written record of the transaction, otherwise it was considered theft. Events like marriages had to have written contracts or they were not legally binding (see Ch. 5). Nearly everyone had to occasionally use the services of a scribe, and scribal services always came at a price. Egyptian scribes thought their profession was above all others and claimed that there was no better job on earth than being a scribe. Because scribes were so powerful they were eager to protect their profession, and changes that could have simplified writing to make it more accessible to others were slow to come. However, changes did come from outside Egypt and

Mesopotamia, where the scribal guilds were weaker and less firmly implanted in the everyday operations of society.

The development of the alphabet

The Sinai alphabet

Along with hundreds of hieroglyphs, the Egyptian writing system also contained an alphabet, even though Egyptian scribes never used these signs as such independently. The earliest evidence for a true alphabet was found in the region of the Sinai peninsula, and evidence of this system has also been found in the desert regions to the west of the Nile River. The first traces of this alphabet were left by miners labouring in the copper mines of the Sinai desert for their Egyptian masters. They were discovered in 1905 by William Flinders Petrie, the legendary British archaeologist, and may date back to as early as the 12th Dynasty (1991–1783 BC).[38] The Sinai alphabet shows clear Egyptian influence since many of its symbols are similar to pictographs used in Egyptian writing. However, unlike previous Mesopotamian and Egyptian writing systems, these pictographs were not used to represent objects, but instead, to represent the consonants that made up an alphabet.[39] For example, the symbol for head,

or *rosh* indicated the consonant *r*, while the symbol for ox,

or *aleph*, indicated the letter *a*, and

stood for house or *bet*, indicating the consonant *b*,

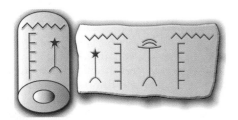

A Mesopotamian style cylinder seal inscribed with Egyptian hieroglyphs.

and so on for some 30 consonants. The principle used in this alphabet is known as the "acrophonic principle" and is reminiscent of the child's nursery rhyme:

A is for apple, B is for ball,
C is for cat, and D is for doll.

If we add a simplified drawing of a tree for the letter T then we can imagine a child writing the word "cat" using a drawing of a cat, an apple and a tree to spell out C-A-T, using only the first letter of each drawing.

The Canaanite, or cuneiform, alphabet

One of the earliest alphabets comes from the ancient Canaanite town of Ugarit, which was located on the Mediterranean coast of Syria. Initial discovery of Ugarit was made in 1929 by a French team of archaeologists led by Claude Schaeffer. In the first season of excavations archaeologists recovered some 2000 clay tablets, which were written in a highly simplified alphabet made up of 30 cuneiform characters. Although written with cuneiform signs the writing system is not the same as the one used to write earlier Mesopotamian Sumerian and Akkadian. The signs of the cuneiform alphabet are simplified, but some of them nevertheless resemble Akkadian signs. Evidence indicates that around 1500 BC the Canaanites combined elements of the Semitic alphabet that had developed in the region with cuneiform symbols written on clay tablets.[40] This alphabet seems to rely on knowledge of the earlier Sinai alphabet, and was used widely in Syria-Palestine. To date about 2000 tablets, most of them concerned with Canaanite religion and mythology, have been recovered and translated. Around 1200 BC, the ancient city of Ugarit and its innovative alphabet were swept away by invaders known as the Sea Peoples (see Ch. 16), but the idea of the alphabet did not perish with its

founders. By this time a number of peoples in the area were beginning to use some kind of alphabet. The Sinai and Canaanite alphabets were similar since they were both used to write Semitic languages. However, the Sinai alphabet used symbols drawn from the Egyptian hieroglyphic tradition while the Canaanite alphabet used symbols drawn from the cuneiform tradition of Mesopotamia.

The alphabet is based on the concept that human speech consists of a certain number of basic sounds. These sounds, called "phonemes" by linguists, are the building blocks of all words, either spoken or written, and consist of both consonants and vowels. Since all languages have a limited number of sounds or phonemes, these can be symbolized by a small number of signs or letters, which form an alphabet. As mentioned above, writing systems using cuneiform signs used syllables that consisted of vowels and consonants and in the case of Egyptian, signs with consonants only. The key to the success of early alphabets was their use of consonants only, vowels being dropped entirely. Using only consonants to write is not as complicated as you might think. With practice, most people can read vowel-less phrases with little difficulty; you can probably read "th dg rn aftr th cr" as "the dog ran after the car".

The alphabet was one of the most impressive and lasting achievements of the First Civilizations. The original concept was Egyptian and it reached its true form with important innovations from the cultures of Syria-Palestine. The alphabet simplified written communications as never before and made writing available to merchants, businessmen, traders, farmers, and

Ugaritic alphabet written with cuneiform signs.

craftsmen while distancing it from the closed circles of professional scribes, who previously had dominated written communications.[41]

The spread of the alphabet

Simplified writing systems based on the alphabet, which were easy to learn and use, quickly spread to other regions in the Near East. Alphabetic Aramaic became more and more widely used in the administration of the Assyrian Empire (1000–614 BC) in place of the traditional, and more complex, cuneiform script consisting of nearly 800 signs. The use of Aramaic continued through the Neo-Babylonian (612–539 BC) and Persian periods (525–332 BC) and it became one of the official languages of the vast Persian Empire. Aramaic dominated all other writing systems in the western provinces of the Persian Empire including Egypt and Anatolia, and remained in use in Palestine into the early centuries of the Christian era. During the same period, in Syria-Palestine, groups of scribes including Phoenicians, Hebrews, Amorites, and Moabites, began developing local forms of alphabetic writing. The alphabet also spread along the Mediterranean coast and was adopted by other cultural groups in the area. By 800 BC the Phoenicians had expanded their trading activities into the western Mediterranean Sea, founding harbours and colonies on the shores of North Africa and in southern Europe. The Phoenicians, and later the Hebrews and the Greeks, helped to spread the alphabet all through Europe, North Africa, and the Near East. Consequently, the Phoenician alphabetic script came into use all around the shores of the Mediterranean Sea. Finally, five centuries ago, European explorers and settlers brought languages using this simplified writing system, consisting of just a few dozen letters, to the Western hemisphere where it is now the dominant writing system, as it is in many other parts of the world.

The continuing development of cities

Creating an agricultural system based on irrigation, which is sometimes called a "hydraulic civilization", required intensive organization of labour and much innovation to build and maintain.[42] During the Ubaid and Uruk periods, farmers worked the land close to villages, which were usually in the centre of a particular farming area. Work had to be organized in different, often complex ways. Certain tasks were given to individuals or groups who had specialized knowledge to ensure that the system operated smoothly and that maximum harvests were obtained. Overseers had to be chosen to ensure that canals were maintained in good order and that water ran freely to all of the cultivated areas, even those that were located some distance from the rivers. Dykes had to be built and maintained to keep water from destroying newly planted fields during times of flooding. Irrigation was simplified because the Tigris and Euphrates Rivers separate into numerous small rivers and streams, which provided water to a large area of southern Mesopotamia. Additional canals and dykes were sometimes required because the land was near sea level, and in close proximity to the waters of the Persian Gulf. Because the level of the flood plain was only a few metres above sea level, tides could rise in a few hours and damage farm land and destroy the harvest with salt water from the sea. In ancient times, storms from the south could cause waves of sea water to be carried inland for many kilometres, causing severe crop damage. Furthermore, because the clay soil in this area is extremely hard it drains poorly, causing the formation of large pools of stagnant water. If these pools were allowed to stand for long periods of time, excessive salinization (salt build-up) would destroy the crops and render farming areas useless.[43]

The temple and the formation of early cities

Archaeological and written evidence points to the temple[44] as the focal point of secular and divine power throughout Sumerian history and prehistory. Each small farming village had its own god or goddess who ensured the success of the crops and the welfare of the community. Settlements in this period are sometimes referred to as "temple villages" or, later, when their population increased, temple towns. From the Ubaid period, archaeologists have found evidence of religious beliefs in the form of statuettes, usually in the shape of animals or people. A number of these statuettes have been found in small temples. Some temples were painted with ritualistic scenes involving people and animals. Offerings were made on a daily basis to the town god, who lived in the temple in the form of a statue. The land of a particular town was thought to belong to the deity of that town, and the people worked to feed themselves and the god who ensured their success and well-being. The temple was the religious and cultural centre of all early Near Eastern societies. Usually elevated slightly above the other buildings in the town, the temple was the focal point of community activities, where people could worship their gods and partake in religious activities and celebrations. Religious activities were not restricted exclusively to prayer and spiritual reflection, but were often the chief source of entertainment for the population. Religious feasts and holidays were accompanied with music, feasting, and dancing, and on some occasions the statue of the god was taken out of the temple precinct and paraded around the city for all to see and admire. Music, incense, and costumes accompanied with much pomp and ceremony were of great importance to the people and played a key role in their lives. The temple was a symbol of spiritual stability and security for the population. It was in the temple complex with its sacred halls and chambers, and its towering ziggurat (see Ch. 4), that the priests were able to communicate with the spirit world and ensure the well-being and good fortune of everyone. Throughout much of the fourth and fifth millennia BC, the lower Tigris–

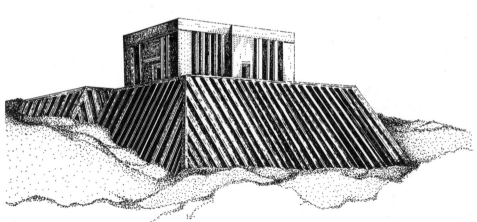

A reconstruction of Eanna, "the house of heaven", at Uruk, built on a raised platform made of mud bricks. Dedicated to Anu, the sky god and Inanna, the goddess of sex and war.

Euphrates river valley must have been one of the most prosperous, fertile, and, at the same time, seemingly peaceful and stable regions of the ancient world. It is, perhaps, this time in prehistory that the ancient myth-makers were referring to when they spoke of a paradise or "Garden of Eden"[45] somewhere in the area just north of the Persian Gulf. In fact, the Book of Genesis in the Old Testament speaks of four rivers that are said to water the biblical garden of Eden. Two of these are specifically named the Euphrates and Tigris Rivers.[46]

Natural resources

The southern region of Mesopotamia, particularly the land of Sumer, was a flat and treeless expanse of land ideal for irrigation agriculture. In a good year Sumerian farmers could produce abundant crops with plenty of food left over. However, the region lacked many of the natural resources essential for continued development, and this paucity of natural resources was one of the major factors behind the unique development of Sumer and the nations that grew up in the Tigris–Euphrates river valley. Because the inhabitants were forced to trade their agricultural surpluses for much-needed natural resources, the Sumerians, Akkadians, Babylonians, and Assyrians became traders and merchants who opened up and maintained trade routes with their resource-rich neighbours as far away as Egypt, India, and Afghanistan.

The influence of trade was particularly noticeable in the development of cities. Cities were the ideal locations to store and receive goods, and served as natural centres for the development of the secondary industries and services that tend to grow in a healthy trading environment. Even though other factors were important in stimulating the growth of cities, trade was the single most important factor in urban growth in Mesopotamia. According to Guillermo Algaze,[47] the maintenance of a reliable trading network dictated the formation of political and religious institutions and policies that served to maximize the export of grain surpluses in exchange for raw materials. Once raw materials reached Mesopotamian cities they were consumed or turned into manufactured goods, which served to stimulate the creation of employment for craftsmen and labourers. To keep track of the numerous transactions and exchanges of goods, scribes and bureaucrats were needed to record the thousands of business transactions essential to a trading economy. Maintaining reliable sources of raw materials became the most important aspect of political policy-making, and those who did not wish to trade with the cities of Mesopotamia often had to face the threat of military takeover. In turn, the wealth created by the Sumerian cities made them prime targets for groups seeking quick riches through military conquest. Defence against invaders forced cities to establish well-trained, well-equipped armies and take other measures to defend themselves, such as constructing massive fortification walls. With the increase in farming activities more food was produced and, since there was a large amount of uninhabited land available, it was relatively simple to bring larger and larger areas into food production. When food production increased, population increased. When population increased, more land was brought into production to feed the additional people. It seems that this cycle continued for centuries until at some point there were more people than there was available land for food production. When the irrigated land of one town became so enlarged that it encroached on the land of another town, conflict between neighbouring groups of people was inevitable.

Increased human conflict

Even though there is evidence for human conflict as far back as the Late Paleolithic period (22 000–8000 BP), an increase in organized violence between groups of people is evident by around 3000 BC. This trend continued, becoming full-scale wars in the early centuries of the third millennium BC. Evidence for increased violence can be found in the archaeological record. The city of Uruk contained the large temple complex of Inanna, which covered 9 hectares, and the White Temple of Anu, which stood on a raised platform and measured more than 20 m on a side. These temple complexes were situated in cities that had as many as 10 000 inhabitants and yet there were no fortification walls around them. Therefore, it seems unlikely that warfare, at least on a large scale, was a major problem in the period before 3000 BC. However, by 2700 BC the population of Uruk had risen dramatically to 50 000 inhabitants, an increase of 500 per cent in three centuries.[48] It was during this same period that the great defensive walls, 8 km in length and possibly 8 m high, were built to defend the city. Most small- and medium-sized villages and towns could not defend themselves successfully because they lacked the manpower to construct walls thick enough and high enough to hold off raiding armies. It was only in the larger cities, where there was an abundance of human power that could be organized in an effective manner to undertake such construction projects, that defensive walls of sufficient strength could be built. Some of the earliest examples of monumental architecture were fortification walls. Once cities began to build defensive fortifications, the residents of smaller villages moved to the cities in large numbers, seeking protection behind their great mud-brick walls. This demographic shift drove up the population of a few large cities while it emptied many villages in the surrounding countryside. One important archaeological study of village and city remains in southern Mesopotamia in the vicinity of the city of Uruk shows that in the Late Uruk (3200–3100 BC), and Jemdet Nasr (3100–2900 BC) periods, the number of small towns and villages reached their peak at 123 sites.[49] This same study shows that there was only one city, Uruk, that covered more than 50 hectares, but there were over a hundred villages that were 6 hectares or less in area. Several centuries later, in the Early Dynastic II and III periods, the number of small villages of 6 hectares or less had dropped to only 15. At the same time the number of cities with an area of 50 hectares or more had increased to eight, showing a dramatic shift away from villages to larger cities and the protection they afforded their inhabitants.

Innovations in leadership

In Mesopotamian mythology, cities and towns were considered creations of the gods. Accordingly, the city-state was the private property of a divine family and the main god who, along with his wife and children, controlled the capital city.[50] Outlying towns and villages were owned by lesser deities. The most powerful divine families of each city-state formed a large extended family headed by the god Enlil (Lord Air), whose temple was located in the city of Nippur. Enlil was the chief god of all of southern Mesopotamia, and he served as judge and arbiter in the many border conflicts between neighbouring city-states. Political events often took on a spiritual meaning and conflicts were seen in terms of gods struggling between themselves for control of the region. Even though there was a pronounced spiritual element in city-state leadership, city-states also needed rulers who were concerned with political or secular activities too. In many instances, rulers acted in both capacities to meet the new and unprecedented challenges of war. Sometimes the spiritual leader of the temple, who was often the leader of the entire town or city, was given the title *en*, meaning "lord". However, there was no single term or title for a ruler used by all city-states. Other leaders were given the title of *ensi*. They served as the head priest or representative of the god of the city-state on earth, and performed both sacred and secular duties. At the city of Umma the ruler used the title *sanga*, in general meaning "priest". These temple leaders headed a growing group of priests whose duty it was to feed, care for, and maintain the cult and statues of the local gods and goddesses. They were peacetime leaders who were chosen each year by an assembly, and their principal tasks were to take care of the spiritual needs of the population.

Part II: Mesopotamia

3 The Early Dynastic period and the formation of the first city-states

By around 3100 BC the techniques of irrigation agriculture, based primarily on the exploitation of the cereal grains wheat and barley,[1] had been successfully put in place in Mesopotamia, and the region had been transformed into the world's first great agricultural production zone. The historical period of human development began at about the same time near the southern end of the Tigris–Euphrates river valley where different groups of people, among them the Sumerians, had settled in the region just north of the Persian Gulf. The name Sumer signifies the southern part of Mesopotamia from approximately the city of Nippur south to the Persian Gulf. In the Sumerian language this area was called *Kiengir* or sometimes *Kalam*: "the Land". Although there was a distinct Sumerian language it is more difficult to identify the Sumerians as a distinct people.[2] The origins of the Sumerians and their ethnic make-up have not yet been determined. Some scholars believe that the Sumerians were already living in southern Mesopotamia by the fifth millennium BC, while others have argued for a later date in the middle of the fourth millennium BC.[3] At present there is insufficient evidence to indicate whether the Sumerians were outsiders who migrated into southern Mesopotamia, or whether they had always lived there.[4] During much of the fourth and third millennia BC, Sumerian speakers intermingled with groups who spoke languages unrelated to Sumerian such as Akkadian and Amorite. In the earliest periods of history, Sumerian was the common written language of southern Mesopotamia for a thousand years, but it eventually died out in the second millennium BC and was replaced by Akkadian.

Although they had few raw materials or natural resources to work with, the Sumerians were an innovative group of people who dominated southern Mesopotamia for more than a millennium. They were talented builders, artists, and writers, and their works of art and literature bear witness to the depth and importance of their civilization. Shortly after 2400 BC, they lost their dominant position for about 200 years to the Akkadians (see Ch. 4) before making a brief comeback around 2100 BC. This Sumerian Renaissance (Ur III period, 2119–2004 BC) lasted for about a century before the Sumerians disappeared as a political and cultural force and were eventually absorbed by other groups in the region.

The city-state

The city-state was the system of political organization used in the southern part of the Tigris–Euphrates river valley during much of the third millennium BC. The city-state originated during the Uruk period around 3500 BC,[5] and consisted of an urban centre with as many as 50 000 inhabitants,[6] which served as the administrative, economic, and cultural core for the surrounding region. The city-state was encircled by a number of smaller towns and villages and would have been about the size of a county in the United Kingdom. A typical city-state controlled a land area

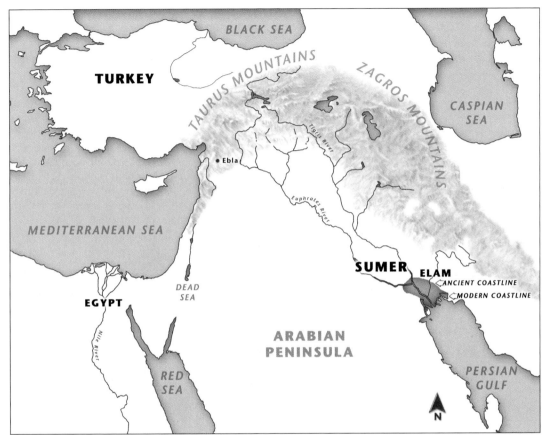

Map of Sumer and southern Mesopotamia.

within 5–10 km[7] of the core city. There were several dozen[8] such city-states in southern Mesopotamia early in the third millennium BC, and sometimes they engaged in local warfare over territorial boundaries, control of irrigation waters, or the trade of raw materials.

The leaders of city-states took the title *en* (lord) and later *énsi* (priest-king)[9] and they carried out both religious and secular duties. The *énsi* functioned as the city god's representative on earth and was chosen from among the citizenry of the city-state each year. Another title associated with the leaders of city-states was *lugal* (great man), who is usually interpreted as a military leader called upon to defend cities and towns from their enemies in times of crisis. Towards the middle of the Early Dynastic II period, a number of city-states fell under the power of a single ruler from the city of Kish,[10] who used the title *lugal kish* (King of Kish). Later, in the Early Dynastic III period, the centre of political power moved to other cities, but the title *lugal kish*[11] was maintained by rulers to indicate control over southern Mesopotamia. In assuming the title *lugal kish*,[12] the ruler of one city-state asserted control over the entire land of Sumer and other city-states were subject to his authority.

Chronology of the Early Dynastic period (all dates BC)

Early Dynastic I period	2900–2700
Early Dynastic II period	2700–2500
Early Dynastic III period	2500–2350
King Enmebaragesi of Kish	
King Mesalim of Kish	
Ur-Nanshe of Lagash	
Eannatum	2450
Eannatum I	
Uru-inimgina	2350
Lugalzagesi	2300

The city of Kish, with mud-brick walls.

The temple and the city-state

The temple was the principal spiritual and cultural institution of Sumerian society and, as in earlier periods, it continued to play a key role in the development of urban life and was instrumental in bringing about the social changes necessary for the formation of early Mesopotamian society.[13] The temple was the god's house, where the god's statue was fed and cared for by priests. Texts make it clear that the cult of the deity was perceived by the population to be an expression of the community's solidarity.[14]

The temple owned large tracts of land and functioned as a centre for the redistribution of food and other agricultural products. Large sections of the population worked as temple employees tending animals, raising crops, or working in other temple enterprises as weavers, potters, and bakers.[15] The temple engaged in trading activities and texts indicate that unfortunates such as the handicapped, orphans, and widows found employment there as field hands, labourers, or weavers. The economic, commercial, and religious activities of the temple generated the need for a bureaucracy, and a writing system more sophisticated than simple tokens, to handle the increasing amount of communication between different levels of government controlling the economy, and the city-state's trading enterprises.[16] At one time it was believed that the temple controlled the entire economy, and everyone worked on temple land as sharecroppers for the temple. But recently it has been argued that even though the temple may have controlled up to half of the available agricultural land in some city-states,[17] powerful families and private individuals also played an important role in the economic life of the inhabitants of southern Mesopotamia. Most people who worked the lands were not slaves, but citizens who had fewer legal and political rights than those at the top of the social ladder. As in most societies in the third millennium BC, slaves played only a minor role in the economy of ancient Sumer.

The Early Dynastic I period (2900–2700 BC)

The earliest stage of Mesopotamian history is called the Early Dynastic period and is divided by modern scholars into three parts, each about 200 years long. Together they cover the first six or seven centuries of the third millennium BC, from about 2900 BC to 2350 BC. The word "dynasty" implies that there were various ruling families, but leadership was not always dynastic. Instead, in the Early Dynastic period most leaders were chosen by members of the community, who selected one of their peers to be the leader of their city-state.[18] True dynastic succession only became commonplace in the Early Dynastic III period, after 2500 BC.

The great flood

A number of Sumerian literary sources from the Early Dynastic I period refer to a great flood[19] that nearly destroyed all the people on earth (see Ch. 8). The flood story was centred around the city of Shuruppak, and tells of a king who survived a devastating flood in a great boat and was rewarded with immortality by the gods. It is not surprising to find flood stories originating in an area situated between two major rivers, each flooding at a different time of the year. Nor is it unreasonable to imagine that someone was sufficiently knowledgeable of the rivers' behaviour to gather his farm animals and family into a boat and ride out the devastation of some great deluge while his fellow citizens perished. The pervasiveness of the flood myth has found its way into as many as 68[20] ancient mythologies.[21] But, interestingly enough, there is no similar flood story from Egypt, the other great river civilization of the ancient Near East. The hero of the flood story was named Ziusudra (in Akkadian versions, Utnapishtim), meaning "he who has eternal life". The flood story makes up one of the episodes in the

greatest of all stories from Mesopotamia, the *Gilgamesh Epic* (see Ch. 8).

In the story, Utnapishtim, along with his family and flocks, survived a flood that lasted seven days and seven nights (the later Akkadian version of the story states that the flood lasted only six days and six nights). When the flood subsided, Utnapishtim's massive boat came to rest on top of a mountain. The Old Testament story of the flood, which has been linked to Mesopotamian sources,[22] has Noah's vessel, carrying him and his sons' families and two of every kind of animal (Genesis 6:19) plus seven pairs of "clean" animals for sacrifice (Genesis 7:2–3), coming to rest in the mountains of Ararat, located in Turkey. Many people mistakenly believe that Noah's vessel came to rest on a single mountain peak, but the passage in Genesis[23] clearly gives the name of an entire range of mountains, and not the name of a single mountain.[24] The fact there now exists a mountain in southern Turkey called Mount Ararat (Agri Dagh) has led many ark enthusiasts to the region in search of pieces of Noah's vessel. None have been found. It is safe to say that no one will ever find Noah's vessel, if it ever existed. Alleged wood remains supposedly found on Mount Ararat have been dated to the seventh century AD using the carbon-14 method.[25] This corresponds to the same time that Christians began to consider the mountain as the resting-place of Noah's vessel and started building structures on it.

A flood that would have covered the earth with the 4–5 km of water necessary to cover the mountains of this region is physically impossible. There is simply not enough water anywhere on earth (or under it), to produce the volume necessary to reach the tops of mountains. Even if the polar ice caps melted there would only be a 50–100 m rise in the sea level of the entire planet, and this is far too little to enable a boat to land on any mountaintop anywhere on the planet.

However, a flood on a much smaller scale may very well have taken place.[26] During the 1920s, a British archaeologist, Sir Leonard Woolley, actually found what was considered by some scholars of the day to be evidence of a great flood.[27] While excavating at the Sumerian city of Ur, Woolley found a layer of silt (water-borne earth and sand), that was over 3 m thick. He reasoned that such a massive layer of flood debris must have been the result of some kind of catastrophic flood. Woolley dug through the layer and beneath it found the remains of earlier inhabitants from the Ubaid period (see chronology, p. 24). It appeared to Woolley that this thick silt deposit was evidence that the people of the Ubaid period had been destroyed by a great flood and were later replaced by people from the Uruk period.

There are several problems with Woolley's flood evidence. First, the layer of silt that was supposed to provide physical proof of a great flood is five or six centuries older than the time indicated in the Mesopotamian flood story, which specifically refers to people who lived in the Early Dynastic I period, about 2900 BC.[28] Next, if Woolley's evidence had indicated a vast flood that covered a large area of Mesopotamia, then we would expect to find similar silt layers from the same time period at cities in other parts of Mesopotamia. In fact, this is not what the archaeological record indicates.[29] There are no silt layers that match the one found by Woolley anywhere else in southern Mesopotamia. Even at the town of Eridu, only a few kilometres from Ur, there was no evidence of a similar silt layer produced by flooding.[30] Further north, at the city of Shuruppak, there is some evidence for a much smaller flood. At Shuruppak a modest flood deposit was found between the two stratigraphic layers that marked the end of the Jemdet Nasr period, and the beginning of the Early Dynastic I period (2900 BC). These deposits may well be evidence of a local flood (not one that covered the entire planet) that was later perpetuated in stories and myths. The fact that flood evidence was

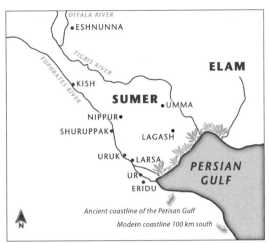

Map of Sumer and the principal city-states in southern Iraq.

found at the city of Shuruppak, exactly where the story specifically states that a large flood took place, supports this location and time period for a flood that inundated southern Mesopotamia. It appears that early in the third millennium BC, a flood did occur, one whose memory was embellished and perpetuated by myth-makers and storytellers of the time. The story proved so popular that it became part of the standard Sumerian and Akkadian literary repertoire. Eventually, it found its way into the mythology of a number of ancient peoples, and into the Old Testament of the Bible.[31]

The Early Dynastic II period (2700–2500 BC)

The Early Dynastic II period was an era of increasing conflict. Military clashes were small by later standards and were fought between modest armies that numbered in the hundreds, or at most a few thousand soldiers. Despite their small scale, such conflicts caused great hardship and suffering for their victims.

During this period, the temple of the city's god remained the centre of power, but the power of the military leaders eventually grew to rival the power of the temple and its spiritual leaders. Nevertheless, archaeological evidence for the existence of separate palaces distinct from temples is difficult to discern in the early phases of Sumerian history.[32] The increase in military conflicts is reflected in a number of myths and stories that concern heroic characters and warriors like Gilgamesh of Uruk and Emmebaragesi, the *en* (priest-king) from the city of Kish. Although the actual texts date from the Old Babylonian period many centuries later, they reflect the threat of war that existed in Early Dynastic times. One text claims that Gilgamesh led his army against Kish and captured the bodies of its seven legendary heroes. It also recounts in poetic fashion that Gilgamesh stamped on Lord Emmebaragesi as though he were stamping on the head of a snake. Epic tales that tell of the deeds of mighty warriors from this period show the persistence of military conflicts in Mesopotamia. The first tablet of the *Gilgamesh Epic* indicates this situation when the narrator states that the walls of Uruk were made of burnt mud bricks and that their foundations "were laid by the Seven Sages", the wise men of old. The archaeological record supports this claim and excavations at Uruk have revealed the remains of a great wall 8 km in length, built entirely of burnt mud bricks. Increased military activity is also shown in the artwork of the period. Cylinder seals (see Ch. 2) show frequent representations of contests and struggles between animals and warriors.

In order to keep their power, leaders had to maintain good relations with the gods and this involved much ritual and cultic activity on their part. They also had to maintain the internal peace and prosperity of the city and the surrounding countryside.[33] This encouraged leaders to broaden and strengthen their leadership concerns. Soldiers were used in peacetime for digging canals and building or repairing the city walls. At the same time there were a number of cities that retained the title, *en* and later *énsi*, which was more closely associated with the temple.

The Early Dynastic III period (2500–2350 BC)

By about 2500 BC, writing had reached the point where it could be used to communicate complex stories, myths, and religious concepts, instead of only recording business transactions or lists of kings and gods. It was during this period that the standard writing system of much of the ancient Near East, based on the use of cuneiform symbols, reached a full and sophisticated level of development.

Ruling families

A few dynasties or ruling families are known in the Early Dynastic II period, but after 2500 BC hereditary kingship was widely established in southern Mesopotamia. Kings of the Early Dynastic III period claimed that their power was given to them by the gods and that this right remained in the king's family, and could be passed on to one of his relatives. The heir to the throne was chosen during the lifetime of the king, quite possibly by divination or fortune-telling (see Ch. 9). It was believed that the son of the king was born of a sacred marriage[34] between the king and the high priestess of the temple. This special birth gave him the privilege and status to rule by divine right, and kings may have been inclined to make large donations to the temple. This created a relationship of mutual dependence between the king and the priests: the religious and political elements of early Mesopotamian society.

The king's role as leader of his people meant that he had to defend his subjects from outside enemies as well as from the rich and powerful members of his own city-state.[35] It is for this reason, and for propaganda purposes, that one of the last kings of Lagash,

Urakagina (Uru-inimgina) (c. 2350 BC), restored to the citizens of that city many of the rights and privileges that had been taken from them by wealthy landowners and nobles. After describing how Urakagina rebuilt the temple, the palace, and the canals of the city, a Sumerian text tells us that the head boatman would seize the boats and the head shepherd would seize all of the donkeys, while the head man of the fisheries would seize the fish, and so on for wool, beer, and other commodities. All of this Urakagina managed to rectify in a just manner for the citizens of Lagash. The reforms of Urakagina[36] are the earliest preserved of many legal codes and proclamations from various Sumerian, and later Babylonian, leaders that were recorded to defend the weak, and maintain social and economic stability.

Unification

In the Early Dynastic I period, the centre of political power was located in the north at the city of Kish, and even though the Sumerians were never totally unified, it does appear that there was a measure of unity established under the control, or hegemony, of Kish. In order to avoid constant military conflicts, a mutual defence agreement[37] was reached between the various city-states. The formation of this union enabled the city-states to unite on religious and cultural grounds, since the people of Sumer shared the same land and traditions, and worshipped many of the same gods. In the Early Dynastic II period, the centre of Sumerian political and cultural unity moved from Kish to the city of Nippur. Nippur was not a powerful city-state but a religious centre, the home of the powerful god Enlil who wielded great spiritual and political influence in southern Mesopotamia.

Urban development in the north

Southern Mesopotamia depended almost exclusively on intensive irrigation agriculture.[38] It was criss-crossed by canals, marshes, and swamps. Not all the land in the south could be exploited for agricultural purposes because land far from the water supplied by rivers or canals could not be used. In contrast, the northern portion of the Tigris–Euphrates river valley was a few hundred metres higher, slightly cooler, and received more rainfall.[39] Even though rainfall was meagre, agriculture did not always require irrigation, and most of the land not used for grain production could be used for grazing cattle, goats, and sheep. While a number of city-states were developing in southern Mesopotamia during the Uruk and Ubaid periods in the fourth millennium BC, a few city-states were also developing on the periphery of the Tigris–Euphrates river valley in the north. Halfway between the upper Euphrates region and the Mediterranean Sea, the city of Ebla[40] began forming, probably as a result of the borrowing of some cultural and technological concepts during the "Uruk expansion" in the late fourth millennium BC. However, the earliest occupation of Ebla and the flowering of the large urban centre that developed later, are separated by several hundred years. Ebla had a long history and was destroyed and rebuilt on several occasions over the centuries. It was sacked by one of the Sargonid kings, possibly Naram-Sin,[41] in the late third millennium BC, and later by the Hittite king, Murshili I, on his way to Babylon around 1600 BC. Although the city continued to be occupied until the seventh century AD, its most important period of occupation covered a thousand-year period from the middle of the third to the middle of the second millennium BC. In the Early Bronze Age (c. 2500 BC), Ebla covered 56 hectares and was the major trading emporium for northern Syria. The site is surrounded by a thick rampart made from earth and stones about 15 m tall and 60 m thick. Four gates, whose surviving remains date from the Middle Bronze Age about

1600 BC, penetrate the rampart. The economy[42] of the city was controlled by the palace,[43] although the temple may have also played an important role too.

Italian researchers began excavating the site of Tell Mardikh (the Arabic name of the site of Ebla) in 1964.[44] After a number of years, they located a collection of some 10 000 cuneiform tablets originally stacked neatly on shelves in a large secular building, located in the centre of the city, called Palace G by the excavators. The discovery of the Ebla tablet archive in the 1970s came as a surprise to historians and archaeologists, who had previously believed that areas outside the south were culturally backward and lacked writing. The scribes of Ebla wrote in Sumerian but some of their tablets were written in Eblaite, a Semitic language closely related to Akkadian. The scribes of Ebla adopted the cuneiform writing system for their language using a number of Sumerian terms in their accounting practices while also developing their own local terms. When the tablets were first discovered, exaggerated claims were made linking the names of biblical characters, such as the ancestors of the patriarch Abraham, the towns of Sodom and Gomorrah, and the name of the Old Testament deity Yahweh, to the city-state of Ebla. These claims, which were made by outsiders and not the excavators, have since proved to be false, and there are no known connections between Ebla and the Bible.

After several decades of careful study of the cuneiform documents, much is known about the nature of the economy, administration, and kingship of the city-state and its surrounding regions. It is believed that Ebla was a city of 15 000–20 000 people at the centre of a large and active economic network, part of which was controlled and administered by a central palace authority.[45] Farming products included emmer, wheat, and barley, while herds of sheep and goat, sometimes numbering over 67 000 animals, were at the centre of a vast wool production industry that brought wealth to the inhabitants of Ebla and the neighbouring region.

Palace and administrative areas at Ebla (Middle Bronze Age).

Remains of the gate and earthen rampart at Ebla (Middle Bronze Age).

The Elamites

During the Ubaid period, Sumerian culture, with its writing, cities, trade, and architecture, spread along the southeastern shores of the Persian Gulf into the land of Elam. After the middle of the third millennium BC, the Elamites began taking control of Sumerian cities situated in the flat alluvial plain near the Persian Gulf. To counter the Elamite threat the Sumerians depended on the strong frontier cities of Umma and Lagash, situated on the eastern edge of the rich farmland facing Elam. Eventually, Umma and Lagash fought not only against the Elamites, but also against each other, and they even formed alliances with other Sumerian cities in an attempt to dominate the area. One of the earliest representations of a Sumerian battle, complete with formations of uniformed soldiers, is a low-relief sculpture called the Stele of the Vultures. This limestone stele (a standing block or slab of stone), 1.88 m high, was erected by King Eannatum of Lagash to commemorate the victory of his forces over those of the city of Umma led by King Enakalle. Only about half of the stele has survived, but these fragments give a good indication of the type of warfare waged between city-states in the third millennium BC. On the obverse side of the stele, Eannatum can be seen leading a formation of foot soldiers into battle. The soldiers are shown actually marching over the corpses of their defeated adversaries. On the bottom register of the stele, Eannatum is shown in his war cart with his men following behind him, their spears raised in the air. This second type of posture may indicate that the battle was over since their weapons are in an upright position.

On the reverse side of the stele the god Enlil, the patron deity of the city of Lagash, is shown holding the soldiers of Umma in a huge net. In his right hand the god holds a stone hammer with which he is preparing to smash the heads of his captives. The context of the whole scene would lead us to believe

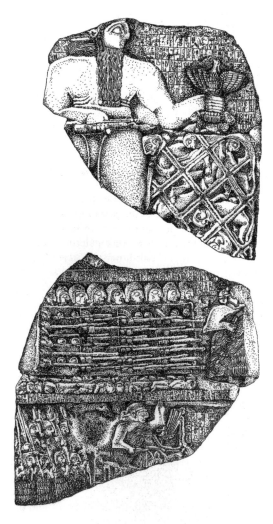

that the victim of the first hammer blow was none other than Enakalle, the leader of the losing forces of Umma. It is not the victorious king who is shown smashing the heads of his enemies, but the city god, Enlil, to whom they owe their victory. The inscription on the stele indicates that the god Enlil instructed Eannatum to cast a great net over the armies of Umma and heap up their dead bodies into great piles. The survivors of the massacre fell down on their hands and knees and wept, begging for their lives.

Despite the many conflicts portrayed in Mesopotamian art, there were also periods of peace and stability. One such period occurred towards the end of the Early Dynastic III period under King Mesannepadda. This period of peace saw the construction of many canals and temples as well as expanded trade and economic activities.

The Victory Stele of Eannatum of Lagash, also known as the Stele of the Vultures, showing the god Enlil about to smash the heads of his victims with a stone mace or hammer. Below his soldiers march over the corpses of his enemies. Limestone, low-relief sculpture, height 1.88 m. (Louvre Museum, Paris)

Fragment of the Victory Stele of Eannatum of Lagash, also known as the Stele of the Vultures. Vultures eat the dismembered bodies of victims. (Louvre Museum, Paris)

Sumerian archaeology

Explorers, archaeologists, and historians from many different countries contributed to the rediscovery of the ancient civilizations of the Tigris–Euphrates river valley. Some of the greatest discoveries in Mesopotamia were made by Leonard Woolley, a man of unique talents.[46] He was not only a skilled archaeologist, but also a good writer and speaker who could thrill his readers and lecture audiences with fascinating accounts about life on an archaeological excavation in the Near East. Woolley started his career as an excavator in the Sudan, south of Egypt. In 1911 he went to Syria to lead the British excavation at the great city of Karkamish (Carchemesh) situated on the upper Euphrates River. Before the outbreak of World War I, there was a great deal of archaeological activity in the Near East, partly because of genuine scholarly interest, but also for spying and intelligence gathering. Since archaeological teams were equipped with cameras and surveying equipment, they were used by various nations for intelligence work.

Most archaeologists of this period were only interested in doing their research and were not gathering intelligence for their governments. But the politics of the Near East were different in the early part of the 20th century from those today, and when some nations felt that their interests were threatened, they resorted to using whatever means they considered necessary to obtain information about the activities of their adversaries. At the beginning of the 20th century, German archaeologists were also very active in the Near East, carrying out some of the most important excavations ever attempted in this area. The German emperor, Wilhelm II, had a personal interest in the excavations going on at the ancient cities of Babylon and Ashur. German archaeological projects were large and well-funded, and produced outstanding results. The Germans made a number of contributions that helped to improve the reliability of data gathered during an excavation, as well as refining and improving many archaeological techniques. They were, however, doing more than just archaeology in the area; they were also building a railway to connect the Persian Gulf to the Turkish capital at Constantinople (now Istanbul). By doing this they hoped to open up new markets and trade routes that would enable German business interests to compete with other European nations for markets in the Far East. On its way to the Mediterranean Sea, the German railway ran from the Persian Gulf, up the Tigris River to Mosul, from there across the Syrian desert to Karkamish, and then on into Turkey.

The British began excavating at Karkamish and made a number of interesting discoveries. But, the Karkamish excavations also served as a pretext for intelligence gathering about the German railway construction project. The excavators could note the positions of key bridges, culverts, and other important features that could help the British army should they find it necessary to do battle with the Germans for control of the area. In the end, the intelligence work was futile; the railway was not completed before the outbreak of World War I in 1914.

The royal tombs of Ur

After the war, Woolley was asked to head the British excavations at the city of Ur,[47] one of the oldest and most powerful cities of the ancient Sumerians. Woolley dug at Ur from 1922 to 1934, and one of the most noteworthy achievements of his 12 seasons of work there was the discovery of a large cemetery, which contained more than 2000 burials, some dating back to the Early Dynastic period. The scale of the cemetery excavations was staggering. It was four years before Woolley opened even a single royal grave because his workers needed time to gain the proper digging experience required to undertake such a massive and technically difficult project. Once his team was properly trained, they spent another four

years clearing 2000 commoners' graves and 16 royal burials, which contained some of the most beautiful artifacts ever found in the Near East. Like all archaeology, most of the work was dull and monotonous. Because the area was used as a cemetery for thousands of years, two-thirds of the graves had been robbed in antiquity. Corpses of common people were wrapped in reed matting or placed in wooden or clay coffins. The bodies were invariably laid on their sides with the legs flexed upwards near the chest while the hands were arranged in front of the breast. Grave goods generally consisted of a few beads, pins, and perhaps a dagger or other personal belongings, along with some food offerings.

The first royal burial contained the remains of *lugal* Meskalamdug. His grave was a plain earth pit containing a wooden coffin and a small chamber large enough to hold numerous personal objects. At the head of the grave there were a number of spears stuck into the ground, points downward. On three sides of the coffin, now totally rotted, lay vases made of clay and alabaster along with 50 copper bowls, the remains of a shield, two gold daggers, copper daggers, chisels, tools, bowls of silver, copper jugs, plates, and more. The bones of the body were almost completely decayed, due to the high level of acid in the soil. Around what had once been the waist was a decayed silver belt on which hung a gold dagger and a lapis lazuli whetstone fixed on a gold ring. In front of the waist was a solid mass of lapis lazuli and gold beads, and between what were once the hands of the deceased was a gold bowl with the inscription "Meskalamdug hero of the good land". Later, in another tomb, a cylinder seal was found which confirmed his rank as *lugal*. Meskalamdug was both king and warrior, and along with his grave goods were found a battle-axe and mace, both made of a gold and silver alloy called electrum.

One of the most interesting objects found in the grave of Meskalamdug was his helmet. It was made of beaten gold in the form of a wig with locks of hair

formed in low relief. This technique is called "repoussé" and is achieved by hammering out a design in the metal from the reverse side.

In the royal burials the dead were laid in tombs built of stone and burnt bricks. To construct a burial chamber, a pit was dug about 10 m deep, 10 m wide, and 15 m long. In the bottom of the pit a tomb chamber was built with a vaulted roof and an entrance on one side. A long sloping passage, perhaps 20 m long, served as a ramp down which the body of the deceased ruler and the funeral entourage could approach the tomb. In one of the royal tombs, Queen Shudi-ad was placed on a wooden platform, and three of her female attendants were placed next to her. Since the interior of the chamber was very small, only 4.5 m × 2.75 m, conditions must have been somewhat cramped for its occupants. Once the queen and her attendants were placed inside, the entrance was sealed with bricks. According to Woolley, it is probable that her servants were killed

Gold helmet of Meskalamdug (about 2500 BC), Early Dynastic II period. (Iraq Museum, Baghdad)

or drugged before being sealed in the tiny tomb.[48] Once the door to the tomb chamber had been blocked, the second phase of the burial ceremony could commence.

Down into the empty pit, whose walls and floor were covered with coloured matting, marched a procession of the members of the deceased queen's court. Her entourage included soldiers and body-guards, plus male and female servants, dressed in their finest garments of red wool. On their heads they wore ornaments and decorations made from finely crafted gold, silver, lapis lazuli, and carnelian. Soldiers with the insignias of their rank, along with musicians strumming their harps and lyres, were followed by an ox-drawn wagon accompanied by a driver and attendants for the animals. Everyone took their assigned places in the great death pit, and each at the proper time placed a small stone cup to their lips and drank a poisonous potion, which hastened them to the underworld. Once they were in the underworld they could continue to serve and please their masters. The tomb of Shudi-ad was connected to another larger and more lavish tomb believed to have belonged to her husband, a king (his name is not known), who died and had been buried some years before her. His burial was much the same as his queen's, with retainers, servants, musicians, and soldiers and large amounts of gold, silver, carnelian, and lapis lazuli. The king's tomb contained 59 bodies, mostly women, two wagons pulled by six oxen, and four musical instruments.

Musical instruments

Lyres (harp-shaped musical instruments) were among the most important objects recovered at Ur. They consisted of a sounding box made of wood and bordered with a mosaic design of carnelian, ivory, and lapis lazuli. Attached to the sounding box was the head of a bull made of beaten gold over a wood

One of the 11 musical instruments found by Woolley at Ur, and later restored using new wood. Gold leaf appliqué and inlay mosaic. (British Museum, London)

frame. On several of the instruments the bull had a beard of gold or lapis lazuli. One sounding box had a mosaic showing a hero figure (possibly Gilgamesh) wrestling with two bulls, while in another scene jackals, bears, and donkeys are depicted in a kind of mythical animal band playing musical instruments.

The Standard of Ur

A rare glimpse into Sumerian life was unearthed in the tomb of the king with the discovery of a wood and mosaic object known as the Standard of Ur. Like a giant jigsaw puzzle, the Standard of Ur consisted of hundreds of pieces of ivory, lapis lazuli, jasper, and carnelian set in bitumen (a tar-like substance), and then attached to two wooden panels. Each panel contained a scene, one of war the other of a banquet, divided into three registers. When Woolley found the Standard of Ur the wooden background was entirely decayed and only the tiny mosaic pieces remained buried in the dirt. Over the centuries the mosaic pieces had kept their form in the soil and the scenes were still visible to the excavators. By carefully uncovering small sections, about 3 cm^2 at a time, and immediately covering them with wax, Woolley's archaeologists were able to remove all the mosaic pieces while still maintaining their original designs. Later they were glued on to new wooden panels and placed on display in the British Museum in London.

The Standard of Ur represents an imperfect, but extremely valuable, time capsule from the world of the Sumerians. Each register on the Standard represents a story or event. On the side of the Standard depicting war scenes we see in the top register a group of victorious soldiers presenting prisoners of war to a person portrayed larger than everyone else. It is tempting to interpret this individual as an important leader, perhaps the *lugal*, or "great man". Next to him, one of his grooms attends his war cart. On the second register a formation of uniformed spearmen are shown taking prisoners, presumably to present as booty to the leader or king in the register above. On the lower register there are four Sumerian war carts, not chariots, pulled by small, donkey-like animals called "onagers". In each war cart there is a driver and a spearman. A basket of spears is located at the front of each cart. The driver would manoeuvre the cart into position so that the spearman could throw his missiles at the enemy. The onagers are shown leaping over the cadavers of dead enemy soldiers. This should not be taken as a representation of a factual occurrence, but instead as an artistic motif representing the defeat of the enemy. It would have been nearly impossible to get the onagers to leap over human cadavers, even though in battlefield conditions it may have occasionally happened by accident. Since there was no suspension system on the carts, striking an object like a human body would probably have turned the cart over, throwing its human occupants to the ground: a rather dangerous and embarrassing occurrence, particularly during the confusion of battle.

On the opposite panel of the Standard, the peace or banquet scene shows the *lugal* in the top register (it is tempting to think that the registers were arranged in a hierarchical order according to social class), drinking beer with his soldiers, and the important farmers and merchants of the city. The drinking scene, like the war carts rolling over enemy soldiers, became a standard motif in Near Eastern art and was used time and again in artistic representations, outlasting its creators by many centuries. Below the drinking scene we see a register showing prosperous herders of cattle, goats, and sheep, as well as fishermen, while on the bottom register there are labourers carrying bundles and packages. This was probably a representation of the lowest strata of Mesopotamian society. The exact purpose of the Standard is not really known. It contains no inscriptions or other clues, and may simply have been some kind of decoration or a part of the furniture.[49]

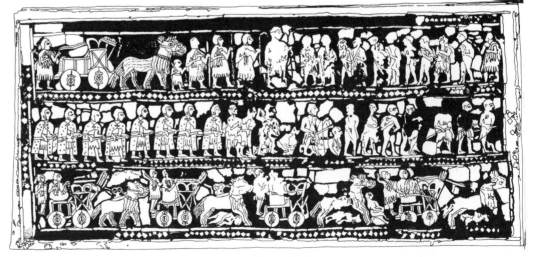

The Standard of Ur from the Early Dynastic II period showing scenes of war and peace; see photograph overleaf. (British Museum, London)

Standard of Ur, banquet scene.

those who were killed or committed suicide belonged to the king's or queen's retinue and were considered part of their personal belongings, much like their carts, musical instruments, or clothing. The burial attendants were probably not poor slaves who were dragged against their will and forcefully interred with their crazed rulers.[52] It is conceivable that it was an honour and privilege for the servants to accompany their rulers to the grave, since the afterlife that awaited them in the company of the king and queen would have been far better than anything that they could have hoped for had they been forced to fend for themselves in the underworld.

Ideas about death and the afterlife (eschatology)

The people of Mesopotamia had a pessimistic eschatology.[53] Their concept of the afterlife was one of gloom and darkness, no matter what social class they belonged to or how good or bad they had been during their lives on earth. American Sumerologist Samuel N. Kramer translated a broken passage from the *Gilgamesh Epic* that speaks of a man being buried with his wife, his son, his mistress, and his musician. This passage may be alluding to exactly the same kind of situation that was found in the Ur burials. Another passage, written several centuries after the Ur burials, describes how musical instruments called the "harps of mourning" were placed on the ground, and when their songs began to play, the people were ready to die.[54] The same passage also refers to boats that travelled to hostile shores, perhaps referring to the underworld. This imagery could be alluding to harps like those found at Ur (11 in all). The references to boats and a hostile shore are also intriguing since there were model boats made of silver and copper found at Ur, and the mention of the hostile shore could be referring to the fact that Sumerian myths mention that the dead had to be ferried across "the

Entrance to a royal tomb at Ur, mud-brick construction.

The royal burials of Ur bring to light in one archaeological discovery an amazing cross-section of ancient Mesopotamian society that reveals important clues about their art, architecture, and music, as well as social structure, warfare, and religion. But what about the burials themselves? What do they mean and what do they tell us about ancient concepts of the afterlife? In addition to preserving hundreds of pieces of artwork that testify to the outstanding level of Sumerian craftsmanship, the cemetery of Ur gives us a unique glimpse into beliefs concerning their fate when they died and went into the underworld.[50] Although there is ample evidence at Ur for the entombment of kings, servants, and animals, there are no accompanying inscriptions that might explain why such things were practised.[51] Mass burials are also known in Egypt from about the same time and, like the tombs at Ur, the Egyptians left no clues that would indicate why they practised such things. All of

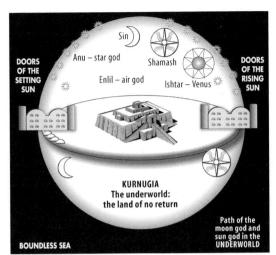

Mesopotamian cosmology.

and prepare for death, and accompany their rulers into the afterlife. According to Woolley, for a brief period of time in the Early Dynastic period, a few Sumerian rulers considered themselves to be at least partly divine. Such semi-divine kings were accompanied by their retinue of servants and attendants into the underworld where they would share in a special afterlife with their sovereigns that was not accorded to other people.

Some have argued that because dynastic kingship was new, and had only become a common practice at about the same time as the mass burials at Ur, the new king had to bury all of the wealth of the previous ruler before taking office. This custom is known to have existed in other societies and was believed to increase the ruler's status.[55] Even though the eschatological beliefs of the ancient Sumerians are still not completely understood, one thing is certain: the discovery of the royal tombs of Ur remains one of the most impressive archaeological discoveries ever made in Mesopotamia. In the archaeology of the Near East, the royal tombs of Ur are as impressive as the discovery of the tomb of the Egyptian pharaoh Tutankhamun (see Ch. 15).

waters of death" to the underworld by a boatman called Urshanabi. This seems to indicate that when the high priestess began to sing the song of death, the servants and musicians of the palace had to assemble

4 The Akkadians and the Ur III Dynasty

PART I: THE AKKADIANS

The term "Akkadian" refers to Semitic-speaking peoples who occupied the regions of the Tigris–Euphrates river valley north of the cities of Nippur and Sippar. It may derive from Akkade, the name of the main city of the Akkadians located somewhere in central Mesopotamia. Throughout much of Near Eastern history the term "Akkad" meant the geographical region where predominantly Akkadian speakers lived. Later this region would be called Babylonia. Like the Sumerians, the Akkadians[1] practised agriculture, lived in cities dominated by large temples, and shared similar lifestyles. Much of Sumerian and Akkadian religion, art, and architecture were also similar, but probably the most important cultural element they shared was the cuneiform writing system. Not having a writing system of their own, the Akkadians adapted cuneiform signs to their own language, which was still in use 2000 years after the Sumerians had ceased to be the dominant power in southern Mesopotamia. Even though the Sumerians and the Akkadians shared many common cultural traits, there was at least one major difference between them. The Akkadians spoke and wrote a Semitic[2] language related to modern Hebrew and Arabic, while the Sumerians used a language unrelated to any of the other languages of the Near East. Along with Eblaite, Akkadian is the oldest written Semitic language and differs from Sumerian in structure, grammar, and syntax. Some of the Semitic languages used in the ancient Near East are listed below:[3]

- East Semitic: Akkadian, first written texts appear in the 26th century BC. The spoken form of the language probably appeared earlier.
- Later dialects of Akkadian: Old Babylonian and Assyrian around 2000–1500 BC; Middle Babylonian and Assyrian 1500–1000 BC; and Neo-Babylonian and Neo-Assyrian 1000–600 BC.
- West Semitic languages: Ugaritic and Canaanite, 14th century BC.

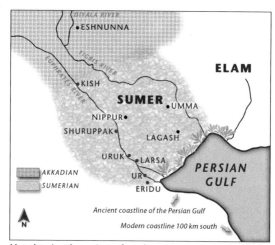

Map showing the regions of southern Mesopotamia where the Sumerian or Akkadian languages were dominant.

Chronology of the Akkadian and Ur III periods (all dates BC)

Akkadian period (2334–c.2160)	
Sargon I	2334–2279
Rimush	2278–2270
Manishtushu	2269–2255
Naram-Sin	2254–2218
Shar-kali-sharri	2217–2193
(Six minor kings)	c.2160
Ur III period (2119–2004)	
Utuhegal	2119–2113
Ur-Nammu	2112–2095
Shulgi	2094–2047
Amar-Sin	2046–2038
Shu-Sin	2037–2029
Ibbi-Sin	2028–2004

- Phoenician, and Hebrew, tenth century BC, and Aramaic, which also appeared in the tenth century BC and was eventually spoken throughout much of the Near East.
- Nabatean, a language close to Arabic, which appeared in the third century BC; classical Arabic, fourth century AD.
- Modern Arabic, which has been the dominant language of the Near East since the seventh century AD.

When southern Mesopotamia became politically weakened about 2350 BC, an Akkadian named Sargon seized political power in the Tigris–Euphrates river valley, and eventually became one of the legendary kings of the ancient Near East.

Akkad, Sumer, and Assyria.

Sargon of Akkad (2334–2279 BC)[4]

The birthplace of Sargon is unknown, but according to legend, he was a peasant, or water carrier, who worked on an irrigation project for Ur-Zababa, the *lugal* of the city of Kish. Stories about Sargon state that he was the "son of a nobody", and emphasize that he was a commoner and not a member of any ruling family. Somehow, Sargon managed to work his way up to the prestigious title of "cup bearer"

for Ur-Zababa. Eventually, he managed to overthrow Ur-Zababa and take the title "King of Kish". It was also at this time that he took the name Sargon, *sharru-kin*, meaning "legitimate king". This leads historians to believe that he was not supposed to be the king, but was in fact a usurper. He then gathered up an army, marched south against the Sumerian king, Lugalzagesi of Uruk, and defeated

him. Sargon brought Lugalzagesi back to Kish in a wooden neck stock and displayed him, like an animal, in front of the city's main gate.[5] In the period that followed, Sargon attacked and defeated a number of cities in the south, including Ur, Lagash, and Umma. Sargon claims he was victorious in every battle he fought and soon conquered all of southern Mesopotamia.

The myth of Sargon

In the ancient world, myths and fantastic stories were often created to embellish the lives and exploits of important rulers.[6] Stories about kings and queens who were conceived by some miracle, or who had a unique birth or childhood, are well-known. Rulers such as Alexander the Great, Cyrus the Persian, Queen Hatshepsut of Egypt (see Ch. 13), and Sargon of Akkad had mythical tales woven into the historical fabric of their lives.[7] The myth of Sargon describes his birth, his humble beginnings, and his early life up until the time he became king. Sargon's story is reminiscent of another legendary person from the Near East: Moses.[8] Sargon was famous in ancient history and scribes wrote of his conquests and exploits for nearly two thousand years after his death. Students and scribes retold and embellished the stories of Sargon well into the first millennium BC and in the eighth century BC an Assyrian king, Sargon II (721–705 BC), took his famous name as his own. The story of Sargon recounts that his mother was a priestess, and that he did not know the identity of his father.[9] This may indicate that he came from humble origins and was perhaps a man of the people. His mother gave birth to him in secret but could not keep him. She placed him in a basket made of reeds and sealed it with bitumen (tar) so that it would not sink. Then she set the basket adrift on the Euphrates River. Eventually it was found by Akki, a wealthy landowner, who took in the infant Sargon and raised him as his son. Later, Akki appointed Sargon as the overseer of his vast estates. One day, Ishtar, the goddess of sex and procreation, granted him her love. As a result, Sargon was given kingship over all of Mesopotamia for 56 years.

The conquests of Sargon

Early in his reign, Sargon chose Akkade, a small city north of Kish, to be the capital of his new kingdom.[10] The city of Akkade has not yet been located but it is believed to be situated somewhere near modern Baghdad. Some scholars argue that Sargon formed the world's first empire,[11] and it is clear that he did make a number of fundamental changes in the political system of Mesopotamia. Instead of relying on the centuries-old city-state system, Sargon expanded his control over all of Mesopotamia, into Iran, Syria, and the regions around the Persian Gulf. Under Sargon power shifted away from the temple and was concentrated more in the hands of his family and allies. For a period of several centuries, political power was transferred from southern Mesopotamia further north to around the city of Akkade.

At the beginning of his political career Sargon was content with the title "King of Akkad", meaning he was the ruler of the immediate area around the city, but as his power grew and his empire expanded he took the more traditional title of "King of Kish".[12] Sargon formed a professional army that written sources claim numbered 5400 men.[13] Once Sargon had conquered the southern portion of Mesopotamia he made a symbolic gesture that was charged with meaning and was repeated by other kings for centuries afterwards: he washed his bloodied weapons of battle in "the Lower Sea", that is, the Persian Gulf.[14] He then turned his armies to the northwest and continued up the Euphrates to conquer the city-states of Mari, Ebla and the land of Lebanon, and a place called "the Silver Mountain", somewhere in the far-off Taurus mountains of Turkey. After conquering all the lands between the Persian Gulf and the Mediterranean Sea, Sargon was no longer content with the old title "King of Kish", and as a reflection of his greatly expanded kingdom he took the title "King of the Lands",[15] a title more suited to the grandeur of his newly formed empire.

Changes in kingship

Not only did Sargon take a new and exalted title for himself, but he broke with tradition by abandoning the city of Kish as the centre of political power. During his reign a new emphasis was placed on the Akkadian language at the expense of the older Sumerian, which was pushed into the background. Despite these changes, Sargon respected ancient traditions and did not suppress them. Sargon's daughter, Enkheduanna,[16] an accomplished poetess who wrote in excellent Sumerian, was appointed to the position of *entum*, or high priestess, of the moon god Nanna at the city of Ur. The moon god played a key role in religion throughout the long history of Mesopotamia. More than 1500 years later, the Babylonian king, Nabonidus (see Ch. 7) would revive the worship of Nanna. Enkheduanna became the high priestess and human wife of the moon god, as well as the high priestess of the sky god, Anu, at Uruk. This placed an Akkadian woman in the highest religious position in two of the most venerated religious centres in the Sumerian-speaking regions of southern Mesopotamia

The kingdom of Akkad

The Akkadians were successful merchants, traders, and craftsmen. Their capital city, Akkade, was a thriving commercial centre and in its harbour ships from Magan (Oman) and Dilmun (Bahrain) in the Persian Gulf, 800 km from Akkade and even from far-off Meluhha on the Indian sub-continent,[17] could be found loading and unloading goods. Since the Early Dynastic period an extensive trade network had existed between southern Mesopotamia and what is now India. Ships from Mesopotamia carried their goods 2000 km along the shores of the Persian Gulf, all the way to the Indus river valley and the regions of the great Harappan civilization. One text boasts that in the city of Akkade one was jostled by monkeys, huge elephants, water buffalo, and beasts from distant lands. In its harbour there were so many ships from so many places that citizens of Akkade were constantly astonished and astounded. People from many groups, including the Amorites and the Shubartu from northern Mesopotamia and the western reaches of Syria, along with others, came in great numbers, "like pack asses" carrying trade goods to Akkade.

Sargon's widespread military campaigns were largely economic. He was more interested in securing safe overland trade routes and reliable sources of raw materials for his new capital city, Akkade, than in territorial expansion. Trade routes along the Euphrates River were an important link with the Mediterranean Sea and the markets of Syria, Anatolia, and Egypt.[18] To the east lay the markets and resources of Elam and Parsumash on the Iranian Plateau, and further still was the newly emerging Harrapan civilization in the Indus river valley some 2000 km from Akkade. Through conquest and trade, Sargon expanded Akkadian interests far beyond the boundaries of the previous Sumerians. The booty from distant campaigns and trading enterprises was brought back to Akkade and filled the king's treasury. It was then redistributed in the form of gifts to temples, members of the king's family, and favoured subjects. Since Sargon both created wealth and handed it out, he was able to maintain control over all aspects of society and keep his enemies from gaining power. This new system of gaining and redistributing wealth led to the increasing importance of the king and the office of kingship. The king controlled the centre of power, was responsible for military success, and was seen as someone of extreme importance, far more so than other members of society.

The bronze head of Sargon

One of the most interesting archaeological discoveries from the Akkadian period is a magnificent copper head that many scholars believe to be a representation of King Sargon himself.[19] The hollow head, 37 cm high, was found preserved in a rubbish heap in the ancient Assyrian city of Nineveh. It depicts the king wearing an ornamental coiffure that resembles the style of the wig-helmet worn by Meskalamdug from the royal cemetery of Ur, and that of Eannatum on the Stele of the Vultures (see Ch. 3). The hair is reminiscent of a Sumerian art form, but the realistically modelled beard, moustache, and facial expressions go beyond the older styles and techniques. The eyes, which were probably made of precious stones, have been gouged out and the flattened nose is a result of the head having been dropped.

Bronze head of a king, possibly Sargon of Akkad. (Iraq Museum, Baghdad)

The dynasty of Akkad

Two of Sargon's sons followed him in their turn on the throne and, like their predecessor, their chief concerns included keeping trade routes open and maintaining reliable sources of raw materials. Occasionally, tribal peoples on the fringe of the empire would close down access to vital resources such as copper and tin. These two metals were extremely important since both were necessary for the manufacture of bronze, the hardest and most sophisticated metal of the time. When its resources were cut off the state had two choices: it could look elsewhere for new sources, which were usually further away and more costly, or it could take existing supplies by force.

The Victory Stele of Naram-Sin

When such a choice was presented to Naram-Sin, the fourth king of Akkad, he decided to take the raw materials by force. One such incident against a group of fierce mountain dwellers, known as the Lullulbi, has been recorded on a limestone slab 2 m tall known as the "Victory Stele of Naram-Sin".[20] Erected about 2250 BC in the city of Sippar, the stele depicts Naram-Sin much larger than his soldiers. This was in keeping with the earlier artistic tradition that the king's size was commensurate with his importance. At the top of the stele Naram-Sin is shown in front of a stylized mountain, standing on the bodies of two of his defeated enemies. The two celestial objects over his head represent the sun and the planet Venus. There may have been other celestial objects in the upper left-hand section of the stele, which is lost. In front of him and on the lower right we see his enemies making gestures of submission such as breaking their spears or raising their hands. One of the unfortunate enemy soldiers is realistically shown with a spear sticking out of his neck as he falls backwards from the force of the weapons wielded by the mighty king. Below Naram-Sin, on his left, his own soldiers are shown, but it is only the king who actually inflicts harm on his enemies. Once again this serves to emphasize the king's role as a great warrior. The original Akkadian inscription has almost completely disappeared. But another inscription written in Elamite was added 1000 years after the time of Naram-Sin when the Elamite king, Shutruk-Nahhunte, took the stele as war booty to his own city of Susa.

Like his Akkadian predecessors, Naram-Sin took the normal titles of kingship, including the lofty title "King of the Universe".[21] But, unlike his predecessors, Naram-Sin also took another, even grander title: "God". He placed the symbol of a star, the determinative placed in front of the names of all gods, in front of his own name and became *il Naram-Sin*: the "God Naram-Sin".[22] A temple was then built in Akkad to glorify the new god-king, and Naram-Sin was the first Mesopotamian ruler to be referred to as "God" in his own lifetime. In Sumerian and Akkadian works of art, gods were shown with a crown of horns on their heads; the more horns the more important they were. On the Victory Stele, Naram-Sin is shown wearing a helmet with one pair of horns, meaning his divine status was much lower than that of most other gods, but he was still considered superior to people. The practice of deifying kings during the Akkadian period reflects the growing importance of the king. It appears that the king's supporters were sufficiently impressed by their king and his conquests that they raised him to the level of a minor deity, and built a temple where he could be worshipped like other gods.

Victory Stele of Naram-Sin, Akkadian period. Limestone, low-relief sculpture, height 2 m. (Louvre Museum, Paris)

Even though a number of Akkadian and Sumerian kings (see below) claimed divine status, the practice of deifying kings never really caught on in Mesopotamia as it did in Egypt, and by the beginning of the second millennium BC divine kingship was abandoned. In Mesopotamia it was accepted that kings were above their fellow citizens and were the god's servants on earth, but they were not welcomed into the realm of the gods as Egyptian kings were.

The end of Akkad

Naram-Sin was the last great monarch of Akkad. His successors faced growing pressure from both inside and outside the kingdom. For generations the Akkadians had relied heavily on military might to extend and maintain their political power, but shortly before 2200 BC things began to fall apart. The Elamites, their rivals from the east, turned against them, there were revolts in Sumer, the nomads in far-off Syria attacked them, and savage mountain peoples known as the Gutians,[23] along with their old enemy the Lullubi, rose against them too. The last Akkadian king, Shar-kali-sharri, whose name ironically means "King of all Kings", attempted in vain to prevent his kingdom from collapsing, but eventually he was killed in his own palace during a revolt.

The Akkadian period lasted about 170 years (2334–2160 BC) and left a lasting impression on the political, religious, and economic development of Mesopotamia.[24] Its geographical horizons had been enlarged as never before, and the period of small city-states gave way to large, centralized kingdoms that held control over extensive trading networks and vast expanses of territory. Centuries later kings would look back to the Akkadian Dynasty in search of guidance and inspiration, sometimes repeating the same formula that had made the kingdom of Akkad the most formidable power to develop in Mesopotamia during its early historical period. Even though the

Sumerians would temporarily regain control over the region, their days as the dominant people of Mesopotamia were numbered and they were eventually absorbed into the cultural landscape of the Tigris–Euphrates river valley.

According to later textual sources, the land of Akkad was overrun by the Gutians.[25] The city-dwelling Akkadians despised the Gutians and maligned and ridiculed them, portraying them in their writings as sub-human barbarians, savages with the bodies of people but the faces of apes and the brains of dogs. Texts from the Old Babylonian period indicate that Enlil, seeking revenge, decided to punish the Akkadians because they had become filled with pride and ignored the needs of the people. To that end he brought the Gutians out of their homeland in southwestern Iran and allowed them to sweep over the land of Akkad like swarms of locusts,[26] laying waste to Akkad and its great empire. The Gutian invasion brought a temporary end to the long process of change that had taken place over the previous millennium.

At the end of the Akkadian Empire there was a 50-year period of intense inter-city rivalries between a number of city-states. Around 2200 BC, as the centralized political power of the Akkadian Dynasty began to slip away, power was once again divided among a number of local rulers. Cities such as Uruk, Lagash, and Kish became local centres of power as they had been under the city-state system of government. Just before the final collapse of the Sargonid Dynasty, the city of Lagash broke away from the Akkadians and became an independent kingdom. In the following years a number of other cities would do the same. Historians call this the Lagash Dynasty, and its most famous king was Gudea of Lagash. A prodigious builder, he rebuilt 15 temples in the nearby city of Girsu, which became an administrative centre. Gudea took the title of *en*-priest of the temple of the chief god of Lagash, Ningirsu, a god of vegetation and war. Except for campaigns against Elam and Anshan, Gudea did not undertake many military campaigns during his reign, but then his territory was far less extensive than that of the previous Akkadian Empire. To build so many temples Lagash must have been a very prosperous city and its wealth came from trade not conquest. Over a century ago, 15 statues portraying the likeness of Gudea were recovered by French archaeologists and most of them are now housed in the Louvre Museum in Paris. Their fine workmanship attests to the skills of the artists of the time.

The Third Dynasty of Ur and the Sumerian revival

According to the Sumerian king list, Utuhegal, king of Uruk, reigned for seven years. He was responsible for driving the Guti out of the land, and restoring kingship in Sumer.[27] Afterwards, his brother Ur-Nammu, took the reins of kingship and made the city of Ur the new capital of a reunited Sumer. Ur modelled itself on the successes of Akkad and became the dominant power in the region for more than a century. The Third Dynasty of Ur, also called the Ur III period, was dominated by several important kings, among them Ur-Nammu. After gaining control of the city of Ur, Ur-Nammu, "Warrior of Nammu", took the title "King of Ur, King of Sumer and of Akkad", and founded a brief but brilliant period of Mesopotamian history. Not only did he and his successors recreate part of the previous Akkadian Empire they had inherited, but they also gave southern and central Mesopotamia a period of relative peace and stability while restoring the Sumerian language and culture to pre-eminence.

Tens of thousands of economic and administrative texts have survived from this period, providing scholars with a good idea about the workings of the Sumerian economy. Following the Sumerian tradition, the economy was mixed between the king, the temple, and private families, with the temple maintaining its importance as one of the economic centres of the kingdom. Several things distinguish this period from the preceding Akkadian period: geographically the Third Dynasty of Ur was smaller in area and population, Sumerian once again became the primary language of administration and bureaucracy, and the military was not used to extend political control to the far corners of Mesopotamia as it had been under the Akkadians. Although there was a renewed emphasis on Sumerian culture, the new dynasty also maintained cultural traditions that were uniquely Akkadian. To that end, like Sargon and his successors, Ur-Nammu appointed his daughter Ennirgalanna *entum*-priestess of the moon god Nanna at Ur and one of his sons *en*-priest of the goddess Inanna (see Ch. 8), in the city of Uruk. He arranged the marriage of another son to the daughter of the king of Mari, the powerful kingdom on the middle Euphrates. There is little evidence to suggest that he waged war on his neighbours; instead he emphasized diplomacy to bring others under his influence.

The Laws of Ur-Nammu

From this period, perhaps promulgated by Ur-Nammu himself,[28] comes a collection of legal prescriptions – the "Laws of Ur-Nammu" – which called for the re-establishment of harmony and justice in the land. With a lofty moral tone, the prologue makes it clear that these laws were enacted to banish evil, violence, and injustice in the land, and to protect widows, orphans, and the poor from the greed and rapaciousness of the rich and powerful. Crimes such as sexual assault against both citizens and slaves were no longer permitted and could result in the death penalty for the aggressor. However, despite the official propaganda, women continued to be exploited by the temple and rulers and were paid far less than male workers.[29]

Defamation, false testimony, and a number of bodily injuries were not punished by death as they would be later under Hammurabi (see Ch. 5) and later Hebraic law. The Laws of Ur-Nammu stipulate that bodily injuries such as cutting off a foot or a nose, knocking out a tooth, or breaking a bone, would result in a fine paid in silver metal, the amount varying according to the severity of the crime. Not only did he proclaim the re-establishment of order in Sumerian society, but Ur-Nammu also undertook programmes to help develop agriculture, by digging or clearing out the vast network of canals, and rebuilding the destroyed or damaged fortifications of Ur, and building or rebuilding a number of temples. To create a stable atmosphere for trade, Ur-Nammu established uniform weights and measures, which reassured traders and merchants that transactions would be equitable in the local marketplace as well as across the land. These changes resulted in a century-long period of economic growth and political stability.

Sumero-Akkadian architecture

The most significant architectural structures created by the peoples of ancient Mesopotamia were the mud-brick towers called "ziggurats".[30] In at least one sense, ziggurats were to Mesopotamia what the pyramids were to Egypt: monumental symbols of a great civilization. But the similarities end there; ziggurats and pyramids were built for entirely different reasons and were in no way connected to each other. George Roux and others[31] have suggested that Sumerian architects may have been inspired by the Egyptian pyramid builders, but this is doubtful. In its earliest form, the ziggurat consisted of a terrace of trodden clay and mud bricks that served as a raised platform for elevating temples. Elevated temple platforms situated under existing ziggurats were built one on top of the other over many centuries. With each new addition they grew in size, leaving earlier stages

Ziggurat of Ur, mud-brick construction, Ur III period.

The remains of the ziggurat at Dur-Kurigalzu, Kassite period.

Stairs leading to the second stage of the Dur-Kurigalzu ziggurat, Kassite period. Layers formed by reed mats placed at intervals are still visible after 35 centuries.

buried under later enlargements. Although individual Egyptian pyramids usually went through some modifications during their construction, in most cases they were built for a single king, and new pyramids were not built over the remains of older ones.

A ziggurat is essentially a series of mud-brick platforms of diminishing sizes built one on top of the other. Early ziggurats had three levels, later expanded to seven. Pyramids were tombs, but no one was ever buried in a ziggurat. A number of pyramids contain chambers and passageways, unlike ziggurats, which were completely solid and devoid of any passages or chambers. Ziggurats had wide exterior ramps and stairways leading to a small temple at their summits. Pyramids had no exterior stairways or ramps, were never meant to be climbed by people, and had no temples or other kinds of structures at their summits. Finally, and perhaps most important of all, pyramids were built out of stone, while ziggurats were made using mud bricks.

The largest ziggurats were those in the cities of Babylon and Dur-Untash in Iran. They measured up to 105.2 m on a side and rose an estimated 52.6–90 m in height.[32] Ziggurats were not as durable as pyramids, and most of them are so badly deteriorated that archaeologists can only estimate their original size. The base of the ziggurat of Ur measures 62.5 m × 43 m and Leonard Woolley determined its original height to be 16.7 m. The plan of a sixth-century BC ziggurat drawn on a clay tablet from the city of Babylon shows a structure that measured 90 m on each side, had seven stages, and was 90 m high. If it was ever constructed it would have been the highest and most impressive ziggurat ever built.[33] Unfortunately, very little of this mud-brick structure remains today and it is difficult to determine how large it really was. The largest pyramids are much better preserved, primarily because they were built of stone blocks and not mud bricks. The Khufu Pyramid at Giza (see Ch. 11), measures 230 m on a side and still towers 141 m above the desert floor, although it originally rose to a height of 146 m. The base of the Khufu Pyramid covers 53 000 m², while the largest ziggurats cover only 10 000 m²: less than one-fifth the size. Dimensions such as these indicate more than just size; indirectly they reveal a great deal about the societies that built them and the raw materials available to their builders.

Since there was no stone for building projects in Mesopotamia, mud brick was used. Mud for brick-making was available everywhere in Mesopotamia. One had only to scoop up a few handfuls of earth, add some water and straw, and then place the mixture in a brick mould to produce an endless supply of bricks. Despite the availability of this cheap building material, ziggurats were always considerably smaller than pyramids. This may have been because the Sumerian city-states were smaller and could not assemble either the manpower or the wealth required to build pyramid-size structures.[34] Later, when the Assyrians had a vast empire that included Egypt, ziggurats were still small in comparison to Egyptian pyramids. This was probably due to several factors. The central core of most ziggurats was made of unbaked, sun-dried bricks and it was covered with an outer shell, up to 15 m thick, of baked bricks. In the core of the ziggurat, reed mats (visible in the photographs opposite) were laid and layers of bitumen were added to prevent water from penetrating to the core. Even with these precautions rainwater from the rare yet devastating cloudbursts that sometimes occurred in the region, did occasionally leak into the interior of the structure, causing its unbaked core to expand, bulge, and crumble. All kings of Mesopotamia had to face the constant task of rebuilding crumbling mud-brick structures such as palaces, temples, fortification walls, and ziggurats. Structures rarely lasted a century without major refurbishment.

The Egyptians did not have this problem. Although many domestic structures were built of mud bricks, they built their principal monuments in stone, which required little or no maintenance, and their structures have lasted into modern times. Like stone, baked mud bricks are practically indestructible and will last for millennia. Why, then, were ziggurats not built entirely out of baked bricks instead of just their exterior walls? If they had been, they could have withstood the ravages of time and their kings would not have been obliged to repair them every few years.

As is so often the case, environmental factors may have dictated the quantity of burnt mud bricks used in large structures. There were very few trees in Mesopotamia, and the Sumerians, Babylonians, and Assyrians lacked the necessary fuel to bake the millions of bricks required for large structures. Most of the wood and straw fuel available was used for cooking fires in private homes and could not be spared for brick-making. Another factor that contributed to the demise of ziggurats was size of the bricks used to make them. Mud bricks are smaller and lighter than the great stones used in pyramid construction and long after they were abandoned, peasants in search of easily available building material found ziggurats to be a convenient source of bricks for constructing houses and other domestic buildings.

The purpose of Egyptian pyramids is clear: they were tombs for their deceased kings. But if ziggurats were not tombs then what was their purpose? Early explorers naively thought that they were used by Babylonian and Assyrian priests to escape the mosquitoes.[35] Some maintain that the first small ziggurats were simply raised platforms where the village grain supply could be kept dry during the annual flood.[36] As early as the fourth millennium BC temples were built on raised earth and mud-brick mounds and ziggurats may have been a further development of this type of construction.[37] The most widely accepted explanation is that ziggurats were meant to be climbed. Ziggurats always had several stairways leading to their summits and it seems clear that their primary purpose was to elevate the priests closer to the realm of the gods in the heavens. In the city of Sippar the ziggurat was called the "The Staircase to

The eroded remains of the ziggurat at the city of Ashur in northern Mesopotamia, Late Assyrian period.

Holy Heaven",[38] and offerings were made to the gods from a small temple at the summit of the ziggurat.[39] In this way, ziggurats formed an important spiritual link between people on earth and the sacred realm of the gods in the heavens.

In the early days of Assyriological research it was claimed that ziggurats were built as celestial observatories where astronomers could have studied the stars without city buildings obstructing their view.[40] It is likely that on some occasions celestial observers climbed to the top of ziggurats to observe the night sky, recite prayers to the gods of the night, and make offerings to the celestial gods.[41] It should be kept in mind that, since the moon and planets would still appear to be the same size, climbing a few metres to the top of a ziggurat would not give an observer a significantly closer or better view of celestial objects. It is doubtful that ziggurats would have been of much use to astronomers and calendar-makers, but they would have elevated priests and celestial observers into the higher spiritual realm that was such an important element of their religious world. Nevertheless, not once in the hundreds of Assyrian and Babylonian astronomical and astrological texts do astronomers ever mention that they climbed to the top of a ziggurat to observe the heavens.[42] Originally, ziggurats were not built to be observatories, although on occasion, after they were built, they may have been used as such.

The most widely known reference to a ziggurat outside Mesopotamia occurs in the Old Testament[43] in the story of the Tower of Babel. The story may have been borrowed by the Hebrews from the Babylonians[44] during the first millennium BC, or it may just have been a well-known story in the ancient world. The Old Testament writers were impressed by the great temple structure dedicated to the chief Babylonian god, Marduk, and its towering ziggurat, which they called the "Tower of Babel". The word "Babel" is the Hebrew form of the Akkadian *Bab-ilim*, meaning "gate of god".[45] The word Babylon is the Greek form of the same name. The ziggurat at Babylon was called *é-temen-an-ki*, meaning "the temple foundation of heaven and earth". The god Marduk commanded the builders to make the base of the tower in the underworld and build its summit so high that it would reach the heavens. The ziggurat was so spectacular that the summit of the tower was called the "rival of heaven". In the Genesis story people wished to build a great city and become famous. To accomplish this they began to build a huge tower that would be so tall that it would reach into the heavenly realm. This kind of activity was so disquieting to the Old Testament God that he caused the people to speak in different languages. The humans were confused by their inability to communicate with each other and thus scattered in all directions, taking with them the world's many languages.

5 Mesopotamia in the second millennium BC: the Babylonians and the Kassites (2000–1600 BC)

Periodically, the kingdoms of the Tigris–Euphrates region were taken over by outsiders. The wide-open expanses of land from the Zagros mountains in the east to the Taurus mountains in the west were the homelands for numerous groups of people who invaded or migrated into the lands of Mesopotamia. One such group was known as the Amorites, whose name means "the Westerners".[1] The Amorites were Semites who spoke a language related to Akkadian. Semi-nomadic herders and labourers, they began moving into Mesopotamia at the end of the third millennium BC, where they often worked for sedentary families as domestics, farm hands, or menial labourers before establishing themselves as propertied members of society. Although many Amorites began as migrants, over the years they were able to work their way into the rich and prosperous centres of southern and central Mesopotamian society and eventually take them over. The last of the Mesopotamians overrun by the Amorites referred to them as uncouth desert dwellers who lacked any traces of civility. The Sumerians claimed that the Amorites had no knowledge of farming, and did not live in houses or towns, but roamed the mountains living on roots and raw meat. When they died they were not even buried in the ground. To fortify themselves against the Amorite threat, the inhabitants of southern Mesopotamia built a long and massive structure, or perhaps series of fortresses, called "The Amorite Wall",[2] stretching between the Tigris and Euphrates Rivers.

The Sumerians fought a long battle for survival against the Amorites, who raided villages and attacked travellers and merchants. Around 2000 BC the Amorites broke through the system of defences and pushed south towards the Persian Gulf. The next two centuries witnessed a return to the more traditional city-state form of government. No one person or group could take firm control of the region, but by 1800 BC the descendants of the Amorite invaders were themselves living in what had once been the heartland of Sumer and Akkad. They adopted many of the ways and customs of the people they had only recently conquered and became successful farmers, merchants, and traders. Once they became established city dwellers and farmers, the Amorites abandoned their nomadic lifestyle and willingly absorbed the religion, lifestyle, and other cultural elements of their Sumerian, Akkadian, and Ur III predecessors. In addition, a few of them learned Akkadian and the cuneiform writing system, mastered the bureaucratic functions necessary to maintain long-distance trading networks, and developed the complex forms of government required to rule a large territory.

Hammurabi and the First Babylonian Dynasty

One of the most remarkable ruling families in the long history of the Near East was the First Babylonian Dynasty,[3] which lasted from the 19th to the 16th centuries BC, and for a brief period of time dominated southern Mesopotamia. Its most famous king, Hammurabi,[4] was a distant descendent of the very Amorites who in previous generations had taken power from the rulers of southern Mesopotamia. Hammurabi (1792–1750 BC)[5] inherited a small kingdom from his father, Sin-muballit, about 100 km long and 50 km wide.[6] During the early years of his reign, Babylon was one of many small city-states dotting the Tigris–Euphrates river valley. However, by the end of his 42-year reign he had extended his control over much of Mesopotamia, from the upper Tigris–Euphrates river valley to the Persian Gulf. Because the political scene in Mesopotamia was so fragmented, in the early years of his reign Hammurabi concentrated on economic and administrative matters in his small kingdom. After several decades of skilful leadership, Hammurabi's kingdom grew stronger than the rival kingdoms around him. Having built up a position of strength, in the thirtieth year of his reign Hammurabi went on the offensive and within a few years had taken control of much of Mesopotamia. Around 1760 BC he defeated the combined forces of Assyria, Eshnunna, and Elam, and the following year he captured the capital of King Rim-Sin at Larsa. Once southern Mesopotamia was secured he turned on his one-time ally, King

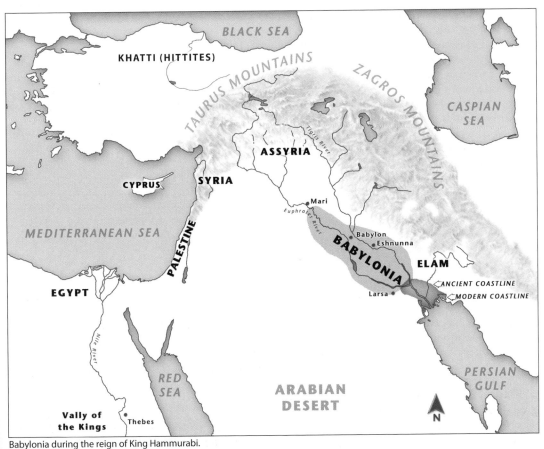

Babylonia during the reign of King Hammurabi.

Chronology of the First Babylonian Dynasty (all dates BC)

Sumu-abum	1894–1881
Sumu-la-El	1880–1845
Sabium	1844–1831
Apil-Sin	1830–1813
Sin-muballit	1812–1793
Hammurabi	1792–1750
Samsu-iluna	1749–1712
Abi-eshuh	1711–1684
Ammiditana	1683–1647
Ammisaduqa	1646–1626
Samsu-ditana	1625–1595
Hittite sack of Babylon	1595

Zimri-Lim of Mari, a powerful and prosperous kingdom to the north.

Mari: a kingdom on the middle Euphrates

The great kingdom of Mari[7] was centred around the city of the same name on the middle Euphrates River, halfway between the Persian Gulf and the Taurus mountains, about 50 km north of the present Syrian–Iraqi border. Mari was a large urban centre founded about 2900 BC, at the beginning of the Early Dynastic I period. Although not much is known about Mari during the third millennium BC, archaeological evidence – including the statues of the singer Ur-Nanshe, the surveyor Shibum, and King Lamgi-Mari – indicates that the kingdom was clearly influenced by the culture of southern Mesopotamia. During the Akkadian period of the later third millennium BC, and for a period of nearly 300 years afterwards, the sovereigns of Mari were designated with the title *shakkanakku*, a term that meant either "governor" or "king".[8] This was a period when the city and surrounding kingdom of Mari were very powerful both economically and politically. The last years of Mari's history were dominated by King Zimri-Lim (1779–1757 BC) and his family.

The city of Mari was ideally situated to control traffic on the river as well as overland trade between northern Mesopotamia, Syria, and the Mediterranean coast. Less than half of its site remains today, since much of it has been eroded away by the Euphrates River. The remaining portion of the city forms a semicircle about 900 m wide and 1.9 km long. The original city of Mari was organized on a circular plan nearly 2 km in diameter.[9] The modern bed of the Euphrates River is found more than 2 km from the site, and it puzzled archaeologists for some time why the city was located so far from the river. At first, it was believed that the river simply changed its course, as so often happens in Mesopotamia. But, geo-morphological studies have shown that the original city walls were laid down at some distance from the river, and a canal was cut from the river into the centre of the city.[10] It seems clear that a large system of canals existed that facilitated the transport of goods to and from the city, particularly from northern Mesopotamia.

The discovery of the city of Mari was one of the most important archaeological discoveries of the 20th century.[11] The first traces of Mari were uncovered by accident in August 1933 when a local man, digging stone out of the ancient mound of Tell Hariri, struck a large statue that had been buried for nearly forty centuries. The statue was brought to the attention of a French military officer, who went to the site and examined the headless statue with a cuneiform inscription covering part of it. Realizing the importance of the find, the officer took the statue back to the nearby town of Abu Kemal and contacted authorities. Soon word reached Assyriologists at the Louvre Museum in Paris, and by Christmas 1933 a team of French archaeologists were in the field excavating the site. More than 70 years later, researchers continue their investigations, currently under the direction of Jean-Claude Margueron.

The site of Mari is immense, and was home to perhaps as many as 50 000 people. The main palace measures 120 m × 200 m on a side, covered 2.4 hectares, and contained 260 rooms and courts. It must have been a visual marvel and was famous even among the ancients. In some places the walls were 4 m thick, and rose 4–8 m high. The royal chambers of the king and queen were large and sumptuous and, unlike the vast majority of the population, they had running water and toilets as well as terracotta baths. The site has produced a number of statues that adorn museums in Damascus and Paris along with an extraordinary mural painting that shows King Zimri-Lim in the palace sanctuary of the goddess Ishtar. But perhaps the most important discovery at Mari was the unearthing of scribal archives

Chronology of Assyria and the kingdom of Mari (all dates BC)

Assyria	
Ila-kabkabu	(dates uncertain)
Shamshi-Adad I	1813–1781
Ishme-Dagan	1780–1741
Mari	
Yaggid-Lim	(dates uncertain)
Yahdun-Lim	(dates uncertain)
Yasmah-Adad	1796–1780
Zimri-Lim	1779–1757

Painted wall scene from the palace at Mari.

that so far have yielded more than 20 000 complete cuneiform tablets. These clay documents have been studied and published since the 1930s, bringing to light many interesting aspects of the kingdom of Mari and the sometimes difficult relations with neighbouring kings, including Hammurabi of Babylon.

Written in a dialect of Akkadian called Old Babylonian, the tablets provide a precious glimpse into the day-to-day activities and inner workings of the kingdom of Mari and the political and social events of the time. Most of the tablets are economic texts, ration lists, personnel lists, legal decisions, and audits. There is also a small group of letters and literary texts, palace intrigues, and anecdotes about the lives and events of the people in the court. One group, the "Harem Texts", sheds light on the status and duties of the large number of women kept in the palace. These included the daughters of the king and members of the royal family, as well as those of lower ranks such as singers (perhaps also concubines), and the lowest rank, the domestic workers who maintained the palace and its kitchens. Because of these texts, Old Babylonian Mari is one of the best-documented palace compounds in the long history of the ancient Near East.

Shamshi-Adad, King of Mari

Shamshi-Adad[13] was an Amorite who ruled the region of Assyria in northern Mesopotamia for about 33 years. During the early part of his life, he lived in exile in Babylonia (southern Mesopotamia) since his ancestral home in the northern Tigris–Euphrates region was occupied by Dadusha, king of Eshnunna. Dadusha ruled a kingdom that covered the north-eastern part of Mesopotamia and controlled the river and overland trade routes in the Tigris–Euphrates river valley. It also controlled Shubat-Enlil, Shamshi-Adad's home city. Shamshi-Adad slowly fought his

way back to his homeland, gradually taking back the important cities of Ashur and Ekallatum (which means "Palaces") and, most important of all, the great city of Mari. Shamshi-Adad was also successful in his westward expansion and even set up a victory stele somewhere near the Mediterranean Sea on the coast of Lebanon. After he won back his homeland from Eshnunna, he divided the region into three parts. In a sense, it was a single kingdom ruled by King Shamshi-Adad and his two sons: Shamshi-Adad ruled the northernmost region, called Shubartu, from its capital, Shubat-Enlil (Tell Leilan, Syria); the elder son, Ishme-Dagan, ruled the land east of the Tigris from the city of Ekallatum ; his younger brother, Yasmah-Adad, controlled the western part of the kingdom from the city of Mari after Shamshi-Adad had driven out the local rulers who fled to the west.

From their letters[14] we get some interesting insights into the characters of the three rulers. Written accounts indicate that Shamshi-Adad was a wise, hard-working ruler who overcame many hardships and fought difficult battles to regain his homeland. In contrast to his father, Yasmah-Adad was fond of good wine, enjoyed the company of the palace women, and was reluctant to fulfil administrative duties. In one letter his father criticizes him for being immature and for failing to carry out his religious duties and make sacrifices, as well as for not making important appointments to his court. He even accuses him of being a child with no beard like a real man. His brother Ishme-Dagan, on the other hand, emulated his father and carried out his duties as an active and effective ruler. He was a brave warrior whose armies conquered enemy cities and defended the kingdom from marauders. In another letter, Shamshi-Adad complained that while Yasmah-Adad lay about with the women in his palace, his brother was out making conquests, and inflicting defeats on their enemies. After the death of his father, Ishme-Dagan wrote to his brother assuring him that as long as he was alive they would both keep their respective

thrones. Such was not to be the case, however, and they were both overthrown a few years after the death of their father.

Before Shamshi-Adad rose to power in Assyria, Mari had been a strong kingdom ruled by a king named Yahdun-Lim whom Shamshi-Adad had driven out of the city of Mari. Yahdun-Lim had a son named Zimri-Lim, who lived in exile in the western kingdom of Yamhad, around modern Aleppo. When Shamshi-Adad died, Zimri-Lim fought his way back to Mari and deposed Yasmah-Adad, the son of Shamshi-Adad, and once again established his family's control over the city. During much of his reign, Zimri-Lim's chief ally had been Hammurabi, king of the small kingdom of Babylon, further south down the Euphrates River. Over the years the two kings cooperated with each other through the exchange of envoys and ambassadors. They also shared important political and military information, and on occasion sent soldiers to help one another against mutual enemies. However, despite their long association, in the thirty-second year of his reign, 1760 BC,[15] Hammurabi attacked and subdued Mari. Zimri-Lim was defeated and disappears from the historical documentation. Zimri-Lim's palace at Mari was looted and burned, the tombs of earlier rulers beneath the throne room were pillaged, and then the palace was demolished. Finally, the walls of the great city were torn down, rendering it defenceless. With the Babylonian defeat the glory days of Mari were over. For some time it remained under Babylonian control and never fully recovered its greatness. During the Assyrian period it was little more than a small town, and by the end of the first millennium BC it was a mere village overlooking the wide expanse of the Euphrates River. In consolidating his hold over Mesopotamia, Hammurabi put an end to one of the great cities of the ancient Near East, and as a result of his conquests, for the first time since the reign of Sargon of Akkad, Mesopotamia was once again under the control of a single ruling family.

Social classes during the time of Hammurabi

Class structure in Mesopotamia during the second millennium BC was based primarily on economic differences between people. Society was divided between those who owned the land, herds of animals, or property, and those who owned little or nothing at all.[16] The Laws of Hammurabi distinguished three basic social classes: the *awilum*, the *mushkenum*, and the *wardum*. The word *awilum* simply means "man",[17] and over the years it has been given a number of different translations such as "freeman", "full citizen", or "gentleman".[18] In this chapter, the term "free citizen" will be used to refer to the *awilum*: propertied citizens with full legal rights who formed the upper levels of Babylonian society.

In the Old Babylonian period the term *mushkenum* denoted a member of a group whose rights were limited in comparison to those of the *awilum*.[19] The *mushkenum* were required to give some kind of military or civilian service to the state in return for certain legal and economic rights. In this chapter the term "commoner" will be used to refer to the *mushkenum*: those who possessed little wealth or property and had fewer legal rights than the *awilum*.[20] Both the *awilum* and the *mushkenum* could speak in the assembly, or *puhrum*, which was made up of freemen from the community who made important decisions and judged legal cases.

The lowest class of people in Old Babylonian society were the *wardum* or slaves. Slaves were taken partly from prisoners of war and their descendants and partly from *awilum* and *mushkenum*, who were forced to sell themselves or members of their families in order to pay their debts. Slaves who were taken as captives or prisoners of war usually remained slaves for their entire lives. Debt slaves could only be held for three years, after which time they regained their former free status. Once handed over to their creditors the slaves were shaved and branded with a distinctive mark. Slaves were considered the property of their masters and could thus be disposed of as their owners saw fit. Both palaces and temples owned slaves, but very few private citizens could afford such luxuries.[21] Slaves performed domestic duties on private estates or, if they belonged to the palace or one of the temples, they were used to construct roads, dig canals or erect fortification walls. They also worked as agricultural labourers tilling the lands.

The average price of a slave at the time of Hammurabi was about 20 measures or shekels of silver although it could go higher. By way of comparison, the average wage paid to a labourer was only 10 shekels of silver a year. It was cheaper to hire workers than to own slaves outright, particularly for agricultural work. A slave owner had to feed, clothe, and house his slaves, and pay for the medical expenses if the slave became ill. In contrast, if one hired a worker for 10 shekels of silver a year, the worker paid for his own needs from his earnings, and if he fell ill another worker could quickly be found as a replacement. Instead of agricultural slaves, the system was based on tenant farmers who received seed, animals, land, and implements, which they paid for by giving a percentage of the harvest to the landowner when the crops were in.

In Babylonia, as in most ancient societies, men held a privileged place in society compared to women. The father of a family held the highest position and his decisions were seldom challenged. Because of his position of authority, the head of the family considered his wife (or wives, since there was no limit to how many women a man could marry) and children to be subject to his will. At the time of Hammurabi, women had few liberties and were essentially bearers of children. However, despite their lower status, women did have some rights and privileges. They could own property and manage their own businesses; something that was denied women in a number of other ancient societies. One special occupation reserved for women was that of tavern keeper or alewife (*sabitum*) involved in the preparation and sale of wines and beer. The tavern keeper or alewife also engaged in various business ventures, and was a small commodities broker who arranged the sale of cereal grains and manufactured goods while keeping a percentage of the transaction as her fee for having arranged the sale. This was a good business arrangement because a tavern was the logical place for merchants with boatloads of produce to meet prospective buyers when they first arrived in a major city like Babylon. The *sabitum* brought buyers and sellers together along with alcoholic beverages, food, and entertainment while business deals were discussed and transacted.

Laws before the time of Hammurabi

At one time it was thought that the Laws of Hammurabi were the oldest in history, but it is now known that there were several older collections of laws written a few centuries before his time such as the Laws of Ur-Nammu discussed in Chapter 4.[22] Before laws and legal decisions were written down, human beings did not exist in a state of lawless chaos. People had accepted patterns of proper behaviour (unwritten laws) for many thousands of years before the advent of writing. Because early societies were unable to write down their laws does not mean that there was no order or respect for human rights and property. No group of peoples can live together without some sort of an understanding concerning acceptable forms of behaviour. Despite the numerous wars and social upheavals throughout history, people have been, for the most part, law-abiding creatures.

THE LAWS OF HAMMURABI

In Mesopotamia the rendering of justice to citizens was always a royal task, although the king usually delegated the judgement of legal cases to a group of professional judges.[23] In the Old Babylonian period, when kings first took power, they usually issued something called a *mêsharum*-act, which was the king's proclamation of justice to the population. The *mêsharum*-act covered a number of things such as cancelling debts and obligations, freeing debt slaves, and fixing the prices of commodities to ensure economic stability. Hammurabi made such a *mêsharum*-act in the second year of his reign when, as he states, "he established justice in the land". During his reign some laws were altered to respond to changing customs and conditions, and the king had these new laws inscribed on an upright stone, or stele, and put on public display. Thus, the Laws of Hammurabi are not a true "Code",[24] or codification of laws, but a collection of important royal decisions and verdicts[25] made by the king. These were then added to the already existing unwritten, or "common laws" of Old Babylonian society. The Stele of Hammurabi does not record these common laws. Nevertheless, the royal verdicts that are recorded on his stele give an interesting and revealing look at some aspects of the Babylonian legal system and what kinds of behaviour were considered to be just or unjust.

The Stele of Hammurabi

The Laws of Hammurabi are inscribed on a stele 2.25 m high made of polished black basalt; 282 legal decisions or laws are inscribed in vertical columns. The top portion of the stele contains a low-relief sculpture showing Hammurabi with one hand raised in an attitude of prayer typical of this period, standing before Shamash, the god of justice, who is seated on a throne. The throne is portrayed in the shape of a temple, and is situated on top of a range of mountains. Since Shamash was also the sun god, flames and rays of sunlight are shown issuing from his shoulders. In his right hand he holds a circle, or large ring, and a rod.[26] After its completion, in the twenty-first year

The upper portion of the Stele of Hammurabi. Basalt, total height 2.25 m. (Louvre Museum, Paris)

of Hammurabi's reign, the stele was set up in a public place, perhaps in front of the temple of the sun god Shamash, and could be consulted by any person who could read (most could not). The epilogue of the Hammurabi *mêsharum*-act invites any wronged person involved in a lawsuit to go before the statue of the King of Justice (the Stele of Hammurabi)[27] and have the words of the king read out so that the accused would know their legal rights and obligations and be at ease. In the epilogue Hammurabi tells the reader that his purpose in setting up his stele was to prevent the strong from oppressing the weak and to give justice to widows and orphans. In the 12th century BC the Elamite king, Shutruk-Nahhunte, conquered the city of Babylon and part of the booty that he took back to his capital at Susa was the King of Justice stele containing the Laws of Hammurabi. Three thousand years later, in AD 1901, French archaeologists rediscovered the stele and took it to the Louvre Museum in Paris.

Lex talionis

One legal concept found in the Laws of Hammurabi is the wronged person's "right of retaliation". In the Old Testament this concept is rendered as "an eye for an eye, a tooth for a tooth". This right of retaliation, *lex talionis*, probably reflects traditional Amorite customs since this form of punishment was largely unknown in earlier Sumerian legal texts. Among the Amorites, the father was considered the absolute head of the family and his word was law. The same held true for the larger Amorite tribes; one man, or *sheikh*, ruled the tribe by decree, and his decisions were supported by a group of elders. Even a casual reading of the laws reveals that the punishments dealt to the guilty were often extremely harsh. But the reason the laws were so strict and punishments so severe was to avoid blood feuds among families. If a member of one family killed a member of another family, and the punishment for such a crime was not severe enough to appease the injured family, acts of revenge between the two could escalate and result in armed conflicts, causing injury to innocent people and disrupting the community. To avoid this, Amorite custom demanded quick and severe punishment of the guilty corresponding to the nature of the crime committed. This custom was still respected long after the Amorites had taken control of southern Mesopotamia and is reflected in the Laws of Hammurabi. Thus we read in Laws 196 and 197 that if a free citizen has put out the eye of an another free citizen, "they shall put out his [the offender's] eye", and "if he breaks the bone of a free citizen, they shall break his bone". The same type of retaliation is seen again in Law 200, which states that if a free citizen knocks out the tooth of another free citizen equal to himself (of the same social class) then, "they shall knock out his [the offender's] tooth". In the interest of social peace and harmony, leaders believed that it was necessary to formulate laws that saw a life paid for with a life, and bodily injury paid for with bodily injury.

Accusations of murder and witchcraft

The Laws of Hammurabi begin by addressing the problem of citizens making false accusations against each other. By punishing false accusations, Hammurabi attempted to ensure truthfulness when legitimate accusations were made. In Law 1, if one free citizen accused another free citizen of murder, but was unable to prove his case or substantiate his accusations, "the one who made the accusation would be executed".

In Old Babylonian society, belief in witchcraft, demons, and supernatural powers was commonplace, and as a result the problem of false accusations went beyond the confines of the natural world. Because just about everyone believed in magic and supernatural forces, accusations of sorcery were frequent, so

Law 2 attempted to curtail widespread accusations of witchcraft among the citizenry. In this law innocent citizens were protected against false charges of sorcery, but they still had to go through a dangerous and possibly fatal "ordeal by the river god" to prove their innocence. Law 2 states that if a free citizen charges another with sorcery, but is unable to prove his case, the person charged with sorcery has to plunge into the "holy river": the Euphrates River. If the accused drowned, he was considered guilty and his accuser would take possession of his property; "but, if the river has shown that the free citizen was innocent and he has come out of the river safe, the one who brought forth the charge of sorcery against him will be put to death, while the one who threw himself into the river shall take possession of the estate of his accuser".

Enforcing the law

It is not known where the actual law cases were tried, but since the sun god Shamash was the god of justice it is probable that some trials took place in front of his temple.[28] Other cases may have been heard in the courtyard near the main city gate, the traditional place where people gathered and where things of importance to all citizens transpired. In the Old Babylonian period there was no equivalent to a modern police force or public prosecutor. If citizens could not settle things satisfactorily among themselves then they would bring their case before the judges in the assembly. In cases of corporal punishment the family of the aggrieved was allowed to inflict the punishment on the guilty person. In other cases an officer of the king carried out the penalty. The methods of punishment for capital offences included drowning, burning, and probably decapitation.

The penalty for theft was usually death and anyone who knowingly accepted stolen goods received the same punishment. The section of the

laws concerned with theft (hubtum) indicates that in some instances the citizens themselves dispensed justice at the scene of the crime without consulting the judges or the assembly. Law 25 makes it clear that if a fire breaks out in a free citizen's house and another free citizen helping to extinguish the fire begins stealing goods from the owner's house, "that man shall be thrown into that fire".

An interesting aspect of the Laws of Hammurabi concerned the compensation of victims. If the king and the god of justice could not protect a citizen's home or business from theft then the citizen would be compensated for his losses by the mayor of the city. Law 23 states that if a citizen is robbed and the thief is not caught the citizen can formally declare his losses "before a god (in the temple of Shamash), and the city and the mayor in whose territory or district the robbery was committed shall replace whatever the free citizen lost".

Agriculture

Agriculture was of primary importance to the Babylonian economy since it provided food for the people and any surpluses were exported in exchange for much-needed raw materials. Because of its importance the state played a major role in ensuring that the land was utilized intelligently and that irrigation ditches and canals were properly maintained to maximize animal and crop production. In much of the Tigris–Euphrates river valley, land that was not cultivated quickly returned to its natural state, making it useless for agricultural production. Farmers had to exercise constant care to keep the land from reverting to desert or marshy wasteland. If a man rented a field for cultivation but had not raised grain on it, he was required to pay to the owner of the land the amount of grain the field would have produced under normal conditions. Law 43 states that if a free citizen lets a cultivated field go to waste, "he shall give grain corresponding to [the crops raised by] his neighbours to the owner of the field". He also had to plough the field and return it to its owner ready for planting.

There were also provisions to protect the farmer if bad weather made it impossible to bring in a good crop. If, after the harvest had been gathered and the rent had been paid, damage was done by the god Adad (the weather god), or if a flood had carried away the topsoil of the field, any damage had to be cleaned up and repaired by the tenant farmer. But if the flooding came before the harvest, and as a result the crop yield was very poor, then the owner and the tenant divided whatever was left according to a percentage previously agreed upon. If the loss was so great that the tenant had not even covered his costs, the owner of the land had to let the tenant use the land the following year free of charge so he could recover his losses. In Law 48, if the tenant had borrowed silver to buy seed but because of the disaster was unable to pay it back, then in that year he did not have to pay interest on what he had borrowed. The tenant was released from the written agreement with the landowner by soaking in water the clay tablet on which the contract was written, causing it to dissolve into nothing. This act effectively annulled the contract until the tenant was in a better situation to repay his debt.

The maintenance of irrigation canals was of utmost importance for Babylonian farmers. Law 55 states that if a farmer does not maintain canals, ditches, or dykes passing through his land on the way to the fields of other farmers, he is liable for any damages caused to neighbouring fields. He would be obliged to "pay grain corresponding to the amount of the crop of his neighbour".[29]

Trade and commerce

Certain members of Babylonian society engaged in business and private enterprise, and a number of laws concerned trade and commerce and the people engaged in entrepreneurial activities. Merchants (*tamkarum*) or their agents (*shamallum*) travelled around Mesopotamia selling grain, wool, oil, and other goods, trying to get the best prices for their merchandise. Like modern business people, they had to avoid the risks and pitfalls of anyone engaged in business, maintain a sufficient profit margin, reduce transportation costs, and ensure product availability. Along with the challenges of commercial enterprise, there was the constant threat of robbers on the open road while the merchant or his agent travelled from one town to the next. Law 103 states that if an agent of a merchant has been robbed, "the agent shall swear his innocence before a god and then he shall go free". While on the road the agent was required to keep good records of his expenses and to deduct them from the capital he had been provided with by the merchant. Without records and receipts, business deals were considered invalid, and Law 105 states that if the agent has been careless and has not obtained a sealed receipt for the money that he paid to the merchant, the money (silver or grain) cannot be credited to his account. If the agent returned home safely to the city of his merchant partner and they had been successful and had made a profit, the agent had to give the merchant who financed the enterprise double the money lent to him. The agent was permitted to keep the remainder for himself.

Taverns and brothels

Taverns and brothels were often frequented by robbers, cut-throats, and other unsavoury characters, and tavern keepers were required by law to report such undesirable persons to palace authorities. So, according to Law 109, if robbers were gathered together in a tavern of a woman beer seller (*sabitum*) and she did not inform the palace authorities so the criminals could be apprehended, "that woman beer seller will be put to death". Some women tavern keepers apparently cheated their customers and did not always give them the quality alcoholic drinks they paid for. In Law 108, if a *sabitum* was caught "watering down" the beer or wine and charging an unfair price for it, her customers could "convict that beer seller and throw her into the river". It is not clear who would convict the *sabitum*, but it might have been done on the spot by the beer drinkers she had cheated. The law does not make it clear what would happen to the woman if she survived being thrown in the river, but it is possible that if she managed to swim back to shore she was allowed to live.

Family laws

The longest section of the Laws of Hammurabi contains 68 clauses concerned with family matters such as marriage, divorce, the status of wives and children, marriage contracts, and the inheritance of property.[30] Underlining the importance of written documents and contracts, no marriage was valid without a written contract and, as stated in Law 128, any male citizen who married a woman, but "has not drawn up a contract for her, that woman is not a wife". If a man could not repay his debts the lender could seize one of the man's dependants, such as his wife or one of his children, to work off the amount owed. Law 117 makes it clear that debtors were often forced to give their wives or daughters as payment of their debts. In such cases the wife or daughter had to work in the house of the lender for three years, and "at the end of the third year their freedom shall be re-established".

The purpose of marriage, at least so the men claimed, was to produce male offspring. A famous section in the twelfth tablet of the *Gilgamesh Epic* (see Ch. 8)[31] illustrates the prevailing attitude of male domination by explaining that the fewer sons a man had, the more difficult would be his sojourn after death in the underworld. When the hero of the story asks his friend what the conditions are like in the underworld, he answers that the man with only one son "lies under the wall weeping bitterly", while men with more sons have increased status and more wealth. A man with two sons "lives in a brick house and eats bread". One with three sons "drinks fresh water" and the one with four sons "his heart rejoices!" The man with seven sons is "like a man close to the gods". Male domination and a preoccupation with male offspring are omnipresent in the section of the Laws of Hammurabi concerning marriage and the family. However, despite the wife's lower status, when the marriage contract was drawn up she could have a clause added to it that protected her from ever being sold for debt service.

Law 129 makes it clear that adultery between a married woman and another man is punishable by death, and those caught in such circumstances were tied together and thrown into the river. The reason why the man is punished in this case is not for adultery, since adultery was not considered a criminal offence, but because he had trespassed on another man's property by having sex with his wife. Thus he was treated as a common thief. The penalty for theft, remember, was execution. In this instance both adulterers were drowned. However, if the husband wished he could allow his wife to live: "If the lord (or master) of the wife lets her live, then the king shall let his servant live." This seems to mean that just as the king has the power of life and death over his subjects, the husband has the same powers over the adulterers and can permit them to live.

Marriage in Babylonia was a civil affair, and no religious ceremonies or sanctions were attached to it.

Before a marriage, the future husband would approach the father of the girl with an offer of a bridal gift: either a sum of money or its equivalent in goods. This bridal gift (*tirhatum*) has been interpreted as a "bride price" by some scholars, while others see it only as a form of financial compensation to the bride's family, since in losing her they would be losing the labour and services of one person.[32] If the offer was accepted, a contract (*riksum*) was drawn up and a marriage feast was held with food provided by the bridegroom. When the marriage arrangements were completed the bride brought with her a dowry (*sheriqtum*) consisting of grain, silver, and household goods. If the woman was wealthy, her bridal contract could include one or more female slaves as her personal maids. These slaves served as more than just personal servants for their mistress; if the wife was barren the maids could be used to produce offspring by the husband. This would prevent him from taking another wife, while serving to protect the woman's status and the dowry she had brought to the marriage. Since the principal purpose of marriage was to produce children (especially male children) a woman who was divorced (*ezébum*) because she was barren was an embarrassment to her family and had little chance of ever finding another husband. The main cause of barrenness in women in Mesopotamia was malarial fever. In the marshy areas of the many rivers and canals in Babylonia this was a fairly common occurrence, and it is for this reason that a law concerning barrenness was included in the Laws of Hammurabi. Therefore, Law 138 states that if a free citizen wishes to divorce his chosen wife because she has not borne him sons, "he shall give her silver equivalent to the value of her bridal gift and shall make good to her the dowry which she has brought from her father's house and so divorce her". Barrenness was not the only reason a man could use to divorce his wife. Law 141 indicates that if a wife behaves in a manner considered unacceptable to the husband such as persistently "behaving foolishly

wasting her wealth and belittling her husband", her husband can divorce her, and "nothing shall be given to her as a divorce settlement". The law continues, stating that if the husband did not wish to divorce her, he could keep her in his house as a slave while he was free to marry another woman. This kind of law would have served to keep women at home where they could perform their household duties and avoid any conflict or risk any accusations of improper behaviour from neighbours. No equivalent law existed concerning men. The Babylonians were polygamous and men could have concubines, or slave girls, as sexual partners without social stigma or legal reprisals from their wives. If a wife found her husband an unfit partner (Law 142) she had no legal recourse except to refuse to have sexual relations with him saying "you may not have me", and thus divorce him. But in order to do this she had to go before the all-male assembly or city council, and only if they found that she had been a good woman, had otherwise obeyed her husband, and was without blame, could she take her dowry and return to her father's house. She received no financial compensation for being wronged, as men did, and there is no mention of returning her bridal gift, but only her dowry, which was hers to begin with. A divorce was very easy for a man to obtain in ancient Mesopotamia. An earlier Sumerian law tells us that a man could divorce his wife at any time by pronouncing the formula "You are not my wife", and paying her ½ mina (about 250 grams) of silver. Similar laws were still in effect at the time of Hammurabi.

A number of laws deal with the rights of children in relation to their parents, and again the favoured place of male heads of families is emphasized. For example, if a man was caught having sexual intercourse with his daughter he was banished from the city (Law 154). But, if a son was caught with his mother they were both burned (Law 157). Normally, family property was divided equally among its male and female members. The father could choose one son as his favourite and give him a larger share of the inheritance, leaving the remaining wealth to be divided equally among the other children. The wife also had a share of the family wealth for her maintenance in the event that her husband should die before her. The amount was determined when she married into the family. Daughters' share of the inheritance was given to them in the form of dowries but this wealth left the family when they married. This loss was offset by sons, who received dowries and brought wealth into their family when they married. The more sons a family had, the more wealth in the form of dowries came into the family. Respect for one's elders was an absolute necessity in Babylonian society, as is shown in Law 195, which states that "If a son strikes his father, they shall cut off his [the son's] forehand."

Class distinctions and the Laws of Hammurabi

The next section of the Laws of Hammurabi illustrates how society in the Old Babylonian period was divided into different classes. Each class was subject to essentially the same laws, but the penalties differed depending on whether one was a free citizen, a commoner, or a slave. Because the free citizen was of a higher class, some laws did not apply to him, but those that did cost him more when it came time to pay fines. As indicated above, if a free citizen put out the eye of another free citizen or broke one of his bones he would receive the same bodily injury as punishment. However, if the person were of a lower class the punishment was reduced and the free citizen was allowed to give some kind of monetary compensation to an injured person of a lower class. Thus, in Laws 198 and 199, "If he (a free citizen), has put out the eye of a commoner or has broken the bone of a commoner, he shall pay 1 mina (about 500 grams) of silver." But if a free citizen put out the eye

of a free citizen's slave or broke one of his bones, he was only required to pay half the price or value of the slave.

Several of the laws indicate that some free citizens were more important than others and held higher ranks.[33] Law 200 stipulates that "If a free citizen struck the face of another free citizen who is more important than he, he shall be whipped with an ox-tail sixty times in front of the assembly." If a commoner struck another commoner (Law 204) he was not beaten but had to pay a fine of 10 shekels (about 90 grams) of silver. If a slave ever dared to strike a free citizen in the face his ear would be cut off.

If a free citizen struck the daughter of another free citizen and caused her to have a miscarriage (literally, "lose the fruit of her womb") the fine was 10 shekels of silver. If the daughter died as a result of the blow, then they had the right to kill the guilty man's daughter. However, according to Law 211, if a free citizen struck a commoner the punishment was less severe and he was only obliged to pay 5 shekels (45 grams) of silver. But in Law 212: "If that woman dies he shall pay ½ mina [250 grams] of silver".

The fine was less if it involved a slave girl. If a free citizen struck a slave girl belonging to another free citizen, (Law 213) and caused her to "lose the fruit of her womb", he had to pay 2 shekels (about 20 grams) of silver. But in Law 214, if the slave girl died, the free citizen had to pay the owner "⅓ mina [about 165 grams] of silver."

It should be stressed that the written laws were often more severe than those actually practised in everyday affairs. Not every man jumped at the chance to make a slave out of his wife or disinherit his sons. If a boy struck his father in a moment of youthful rage this did not mean that he immediately lost his hand. Even though the punishments described in the Laws of Hammurabi were severe by modern standards, most husbands and wives cared for each other and their children, both sons and daughters, and wanted them to have happy and prosperous lives.

Wage and price controls

The final section of the Laws of Hammurabi deals with wage and price controls, which regulated prices for goods and services, and provided fines and punishments for those who practised their crafts carelessly. Farm labourers and ox herders were paid 750–1000 litres of grain a year for their services. Numerous laws regulated the prices charged for hiring all kinds of draught animals, as well as for hiring wagons, barges, boats, and galleys for river transport and the men required to operate them. There were even laws to regulate the prices that surgeons could charge their patients for certain operations. These laws indicate that even though the lower classes had fewer civil rights they also paid less for many services. Thus, Laws 215 to 217 stipulated that if a surgeon made a deep incision[34] in the body of a free citizen with a bronze knife and saved the man's life or if he opened a fleshy lump in the eye of a free citizen and saved his eye, the surgeon would be paid 10 shekels (about 90 grams) of silver. However, if the patient was a commoner, he paid only 5 shekels (about 45 grams) of silver. If the patient was the slave of a free citizen then the owner of the slave paid only 2 shekels (about 18 grams) of silver to the surgeon. If the surgery failed (Law 219) and the patient died, then "they shall cut off his [the surgeon's] hand". This probably did not happen very often since Babylonian doctors probably knew very little about surgery and rarely attempted complex surgical interventions. Also there would have been a great shortage of surgeons in Babylonia if every time someone died while they were being treated the surgeon's hand was cut off (or there would have been a large number of one-handed surgeons). Furthermore, very few new surgeons would have entered into surgical training if they knew that they ran a high risk of losing their hands every time their treatment failed.

The laws concerning architects and shipbuilders operated on the same principle but appear to have been applied more often. Laws 228 to 232 state that if a builder builds a house for a free citizen, but because of shoddy workmanship the house collapses and causes the death of the householder, "that builder shall be put to death". If the collapse caused the death of the free citizen's son then "they shall execute the builder's son". However, if it caused the death of a slave then the builder had only to replace the slave with one of equal value. The same principle also applied to shipbuilders who built leaky ships.

Although the Laws of Hammurabi are not as old, and are less original, than once thought, they still give a unique insight into Babylonian concepts of justice and illuminate many of the diverse aspects of an ancient society getting to grips with the antisocial behaviour of its citizens. Towards the end of his reign, Hammurabi could look back over the years at his numerous achievements and claim that he had rooted out the enemies of Babylon, put an end to war, promoted the welfare of the land, and made the people rest in friendly habitations.

THE END OF THE FIRST BABYLONIAN DYNASTY

The Hittites: the people of Khatti-land

While the Amorites were establishing the First Babylonian Dynasty (1900–1600 BC), and gaining control of central Mesopotamia, hundreds of kilometres to the northwest, in Anatolia, a new group of people, the Hittites, were creating a powerful kingdom that would be drawn into the sphere of both Egyptian and Mesopotamian politics and economics.

By the middle of the second millennium BC, the Hittites had become one of the strongest and most influential kingdoms in the ancient Near East, second only to Egypt. Starting around 2000 BC, Mesopotamia and Egypt can only be understood against the background of international politics, and the ever

growing power of the kingdoms in the regions surrounding the Tigris–Euphrates and Nile river valleys. From this point onwards, the horizon of Near Eastern politics and culture expanded at an increasing rate to eventually include southern Europe, Anatolia (Asia Minor or Turkey), North Africa, the Arabian peninsula, and regions as far away as the Indus river valley.

The Hittites were Indo-Europeans, ethnically and linguistically distinct from the Sumerians, Akkadians, and Amorites. Hittite is the oldest member of the family of written Indo-European languages, which includes ancient Greek and Latin. The living members of the family include English, French, German, and the Slavic languages of eastern Europe, as well as ancient Sanskrit from India.[35] The origins of these languages are unknown, but early Indo-European speakers may have come from somewhere north of the Black Sea. During the third millennium BC they settled mainly in southern Europe and Anatolia and later moved into many parts of northern Europe.

From the Neolithic period (7000–4000 BC), Anatolia was divided into small, fortified political units that controlled the surrounding areas. By the end of the fourth millennium BC, the period of "Uruk expansion" (see Chs 2 and 3), there was an increasing prosperity brought about by the growing need for natural resources in Mesopotamia, particularly metals, such as tin, silver, and gold, which were lacking in the south. The main stimulus to the central Anatolian economy was the presence of Assyrian merchants from the city of Ashur in northern Mesopotamia.[36] Starting early in the second millennium BC, city-states, such as Kultepe Kanesh, began to appear in Anatolia. Assyrian activity in the region is carefully documented in the thousands of economic texts recovered by archaeologists. Written in Assyrian, a dialect of Akkadian, these texts reveal a large Assyrian trading colony operating in southeastern Anatolia between 2000 and 1750 BC. This created a complex trading network between Anatolia, Syria,

and Mesopotamia that was bound up in the web of international politics. Early in the second millennium BC the pattern of life in Anatolia was based on independent city-states engaged in international trade. Several centuries later this system was no longer workable. By 1750 BC a new power structure was in place that used a mixture of trade and conquest, and which was similar to the short-lived "empires" of Naram-Sin and Sargon a few centuries earlier.

The Hittite Old Kingdom (1650–1500 BC)

The first king and founder of the Hittite kingdom was King Khattushili I, "man of the city of Khattusha". He established his capital at Khattusha (Boghazköy) in central Anatolia, and subdued many of the cities that lay between his capital and his trading partners to the south and east. His grandson, Murshili I, continued this expansion to include the important city of Halab (Aleppo) in Syria. The most daring exploit of this early period of Hittite history took place in 1595 BC, when Hittite forces sped south under the leadership of Murshili I and sacked and burned Babylon, the city made famous two centuries earlier by Hammurabi. Even though the Hittites were too weak to hold on to the city, the last king of the First Babylonian Dynasty, Samsu-ditana (1625– 1595 BC) fled before the troops of Murshili I and never returned to power. Little is known about the raid, and Babylonian sources are lacking. Hittite texts tell us that the statues of Marduk, the chief god of Babylon, and his consort, Sarpanitum, were taken from the city's temple. As successful as the Hittite raid had been, they had over-extended themselves and were forced to withdraw closer to their homeland, Khatti. The Hittite attack on Babylon put an end to one of the longest ruling dynasties in the ancient Near East, and showed their rivals that they were a vigorous political power to be reckoned with. For the next century the Hittites faced many political problems, but managed to hang on to their power until the last half of the 15th century BC, when a new and vigorous leader emerged in the land of Khatti and established a true Hittite Empire.

The Hittite Empire (1430–1200 BC)

Suppiluliuma I and his successors ushered in the longest period of Hittite domination, nearly 150 years, and for a period of time the Hittites were the most powerful political force in the ancient Near East.[37] King Suppiluliuma I came to the throne around 1370 BC and ruled until 1330 BC. During his 40-year reign he enlarged Hittite territories and laid the foundations for a period of Hittite greatness. During his early years, Suppiluliuma I consolidated his power base through the skilful use of diplomacy and military might to maximize his gains. Given the extent of Hittite power and influence it was inevitable that the Hittites would clash with the great African kingdom of Egypt. During this period the political fortunes of the Hittites and the Egyptians, under the rule of Akhenaten, become entwined (see Ch. 14). Part of Suppiluliuma I's diplomatic strategy was to arrange political marriages for his sister and two of his daughters to cement political alliances. He married a Babylonian princess, and attempted to marry his son, Prince Zannanza, to the widow of the Egyptian king, Tutankhamun. However, what could have been a stroke of diplomatic genius turned to tragedy (see Ch. 16), and ruined Egypto-Hittite relations for decades.

At the same time difficulties were compounded when the Hittite king died of the plague brought back by his soldiers from their wars in Syria.[38] The clash between Egypt and the Hittites continued and, a century later, after suffering heavy losses at the battle of Qadesh (see Ch. 16), Pharaoh Ramesses II and King Khattushili III signed a peace treaty favourable to the Hittites in which Egypt gave up many of

Hittite fortifications and stone revetments at Khattusha (modern Boghazköy), Late Bronze Age (about 1350 BC).

Segmented city wall at Khattusha, Late Bronze Age (about 1350 BC).

The Lion Gate at Khattusha (see also colour photograph).

King's Gate at Khattusha, time of Tudhaliya III or Suppiluliuma I (about 1350 BC). High-relief sculpture of a god dressed as a warrior with helmet, dagger, and battle-axe.

its holdings in northern Syria. Hittite power came to an end early in the 12th century BC when the land of Khatti, like so many others in the ancient Near East, succumbed to invaders known as the Sea Peoples (see Ch. 15).[39]

The Kassites (1600–1154 BC)

After the Hittite raid there was a political vacuum in southern Mesopotamia. The Hittites were too weak to hold the city, the members of the First Dynasty of Babylon had fled or were killed, and the door was open to any group strong enough to take possession of the city and its environs. A group of people known as the Kassites[40] (*galzu* in Kassite, *kashushu* in Akkadian) happened to be in a position to move in to fill the void. The Kassites probably came from the central Zagros mountains of Iran and over the centuries immigrated, or fought their way, into the Babylonian heartland. After the dissolution of the First Dynasty of Babylon the Kassites took over southern Mesopotamia for more than four centuries,[41] and were one of the longest ruling groups in the history of the Near East. During his reign, King Agum II Kakrime seems to have recovered the statues of Marduk and Sarpanitum, which had been stolen by the Hittites, and returned them to Babylon. From that time the Kassites chose Marduk as one of their gods, made Babylon their religious and ceremonial capital, and adopted or emulated Babylonian traditions. Over the years they built or restored a number of temples dedicated to Mesopotamian gods in the southern Mesopotamian cities of Ur, Eridu, and Uruk. The economy was maintained through international trade, by building temples and palaces, digging drainage canals, expanding cities, and providing infrastructure through public works projects.

The Kassite administrative capital, Dur-Kurigalzu, was situated 90 km north of modern Baghdad and named after the then reigning king, Kurigalzu II (1332–1308 BC). The city contains a number of impressive structures, which bear witness to the greatness of the Kassite or Third Dynasty of Babylon. The immense palace of King Kurigalzu II measures 300 m on a side and covers 9 hectares. Nearby were temples dedicated to the gods of the Mesopotamian divine family: Enlil and Ninlil (Lord and Lady of the Air) and their son, Ninurta. Other structures include the still-visible remains of a ziggurat that still stands 57 m high (see Ch. 4). Over their four centuries of rule the Kassites fought various wars and are known

to have defeated the Assyrians, the Elamites, and other peoples in the region. The century-long period from the reign of Kurigalzu II to Kashtiliash IV (1332–1225 BC) marked the high point of Kassite domination over southern Mesopotamia. During the reign of Burna-Buriash II (ruled c. 1359–1333 BC), Babylonia ranked as one of the great powers of the ancient Near East. He was referred to as "Great King" and accorded the same status and respect as the kings of Egypt and Khatti.

More than 12 000 cuneiform[42] texts dating from the Kassite period have been recovered, and although most of them are limited to the realm of economics, they nevertheless give some interesting glimpses into Kassite culture. Some scholars have argued that there was a linguistic connection between Kassites and Indo-Europeans, but this is difficult to determine since the written sources in the Kassite language are scarce and do not include complete sentences. One of the most informative sources is a text written in Akkadian, which contains a number of Kassite words concerning horse breeding,[43] and training and chariot technology. Although horses were domesticated in the Eurasian steppes and Ukraine region by the fourth millennium BC, and were mentioned in Sumerian cuneiform sources as *anše.kur.ra* (donkey of the mountains), the Kassites were the first people in Mesopotamia to breed horses successfully.[44] The arrival of the horse in Mesopotamia coincides with the introduction of the chariot in the Near East, and

the principal use of the horse in the middle of the second millennium BC was for chariots and chariot warfare.[45] To be useful in battle, horses and chariot drivers required rigorous training for quick battlefield manoeuvres. Evidence for this kind of training has been preserved in a document written by a man called "Kikkuli of Mitanni". Written in Akkadian with many terms in Kassite, this unique text was a kind of training manual, and contained advice on the culling, diet, and exercise necessary for training chariot horses. This text seems to indicate that the Kassites were responsible for the introduction of horses and chariots in the ancient Near East.

Although the Kassites were not great innovators, and created little that was new in the realm of architecture and culture, they nevertheless guarded and maintained Mesopotamian culture throughout the second half of the second millennium BC. It was during the Kassite period that Akkadian writing was standardized, and numerous myths, stories, and treatises were written down in their definitive forms, which were then passed down to later generations of scribes. Many later Babylonian scribes traced their ancestry back to their predecessors who lived during Kassite times. After the collapse of the Kassite Dynasty many of the Kassite people stayed in the region they had ruled and eventually became totally assimilated. Others are known to have settled further east in Iran, where they maintained their independence for many centuries until the Hellenistic period.[46]

6 The Assyrians

The rise of Assyria

Although the northern kingdom of Assyria[1] had previously been strong under the leadership of kings such as Shamshi-Adad,[2] during much of the second millennium BC Mesopotamia was controlled by powers to the south in Babylonia with its powerful Amorite and Kassite dynasties. By the tenth century BC the traditional powers of the Near East were in a state of disarray. Babylonia was weak and being infiltrated by Arameans,[3] a new group of Semitic-language speakers. Further west, Egypt was in decline and ruled by immigrants of Libyan descent[4] (see Ch. 16). This situation enabled Assyria, a small nation of farmers and herders on the upper Tigris River, to move on to the centre stage of Near Eastern history.[5] Assyriologists refer to the period 1000–612 BC as the Late or Neo-Assyrian period, when for four centuries Ashur (the land of Ashur) was one of the most powerful and well-organized empires the ancient world had ever seen.

Assyrian warfare

The early part of the first millennium BC was a time of political and social turmoil. In order to survive the numerous battles and full-scale wars, punctuated with migrations of thousands of homeless people[6] in search of new lands, a nation had to fight or perish. It is against a backdrop of political and social insta-bility that the ancient Assyrians became mighty fighters whose reputation as the most violent and warlike people in the ancient Near East lived on long after they had ceased to exist as a nation. The Assyrians developed an economy based on war and military conquest that required acts of violence against conquered peoples. However, the legendary brutal-ity of the Assyrians was, in most instances, no worse than any other nation of the time. The Assyrians were simply more efficient at war and conquest than everyone else. In addition, the Assyrians appear more brutal than their neighbours because they used both written and visual art forms extensively, and accu-rately, to dramatize their military might.[7] All civiliza-tions are remembered for the things they leave behind them. Egyptians are remembered for pyra-mids and mummies, the Greeks for the writings of their great thinkers like Plato and Aristotle, the Romans for their accomplishments in building aque-ducts, roads, and structures like the Coliseum. Like-wise, the Assyrians are remembered through written accounts of battles and scenes of slaughter and conquest that have left a reputation of violence as their principal legacy. But the Assyrians were more than just fighters and it would be unfair to mention only their military exploits while ignoring their other achievements.[8] They were also great builders and administrators. They produced beautiful and finely crafted works of art and built some of the most impressive cities in the ancient world. Like other peoples in the ancient Near East, the Assyrians went to war for economic, strategic, and religious reasons. Military campaigns took place in the spring and summer almost every year. After the harvest was safely stored, the king would gather up his army, made up mostly of farmers, and strike out against the neighbouring lands.[9] The main reason for military raids was economic. Often, war was nothing more than a form of organized national theft where one nation systematically robbed another. Once a year the Assyrians would organize a military raid or razzia, a kind of annual "hold-up" of their weaker neighbours, to obtain what they called *mandattu* (tribute) or *shallatu* (loot or booty).

Economic gain was not the only reason for war. It made good strategic sense to attack and destroy one's enemies before they had a chance to destroy the home country, and this was often the reason for military action in the ancient world. Had the Assyrians not struck out against their rivals on a number of occasions, it is likely that they would have been overwhelmed. The third reason the Assyrians waged war was religious. Even though the Assyrians believed in many gods, they did have their own supreme god, Assur, god of the Assyrian nation.

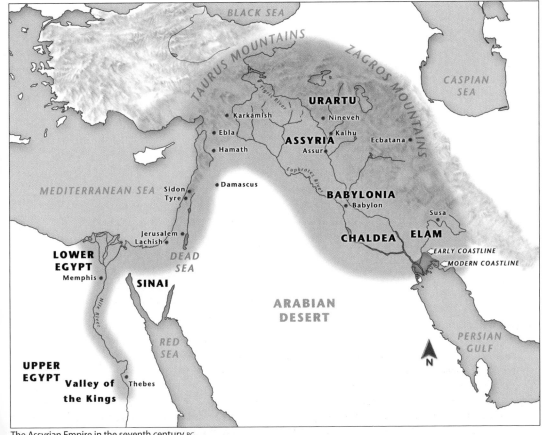

The Assyrian Empire in the seventh century BC.

Assyrian chronology: early kings in the first millennium BC (all dates BC)

Adad-Nirari II	911–891
Tikulti-Ninurta II	890–884
Assurnasirpal II	883–859
Shalmaneser III	858–824
Shamshi-Adad V	823–811
Adad-Nirari III	810–783
Shalmaneser IV	782–773
Ashur-Dan III	772–755
Ashur-Nirari V	754–745
Tiglath-pileser III	744–727
Shalmaneser V	726–722

Soldiers of Tiglath-pileser III carrying away the statues of gods of a captured town.

Assur was the chief deity of the city of Ashur, and originally a local god whose influence was limited to the city of the same name. The god Assur began as a deified rock in the middle of the city, but, as the political power of the Assyrians expanded so did his prestige and importance. The Assyrian king was Assur's representative on earth and therefore, along with his many political tasks, functioned as the god's high priest as well.[10]

The Assyrians did not wish to convert people to the religion of Assur, but they did believe that their enemies worshipped inferior gods, and that it was acceptable to force them to recognize the might of the great god Assur.[11] Sometimes Assyrian leaders were commanded by their gods to destroy their enemies. Warfare was the chief occupation of the Assyrian king and the Assyrian nation was organized to make war and live by its profits.[12] The Assyrians' military expertise was formidable, and subsequent empires found Assyrian tactics and organization so efficient that they modelled their own armed forces on them. The total strength of the Assyrian army may have numbered as many as 100 000 men[13] if all reserves were called up, although forces numbering 10 000–20 000 were more common.[14] Sennacherib claims to have fielded an army of 208 000, but this figure may include support personnel.[15] The commander in chief of the army was called the *turtanu*. The various fighting units were divided into groups or *kisru* (knots), of 200–1000 men. A smaller unit consisted of 50 fighting men under the direction of a captain or *rab hanshe* (chief of fifty).[16] Most troops were infantrymen and were backed by chariotry, cavalry, and engineers. Engineering units built and operated siege engines and battering rams, and were responsible for building bridges out of timbers or making rafts for crossing rivers, as well as cutting roads and removing obstacles so the army could keep moving even in difficult terrain.

Battering rams were large, wheeled vehicles that were pulled up to the edge of the city walls by animal power and then manoeuvred into position by soldiers. Inside these wagon-like machines was a long, metal-tipped log the size of a telegraph pole that could be crashed against the wall with great force until it weakened and collapsed. Siege towers were large wooden structures, perhaps as much as 10 m high, covered with some kind of armour; these provided archers with a vantage point for firing volleys of arrows as covering fire for soldiers attempting to scale city walls. Because of their great size, siege towers had to be floated into position and could only be used against cities situated near rivers.[17] Weapons common among foot soldiers were the spear, the bow and arrow, and slings for throwing stones, as well as swords and, occasionally, battle-axes. Assyrian bows were either of the simple type made out of a single branch of wood or the more sophisticated composite bow that was fabricated of layers of wood and bone. The bow and arrow was effective to perhaps 150–250 m.[18] Arrows were generally fitted with points made of iron and feathers from birds of prey such as eagles or vultures. Groups of archers are

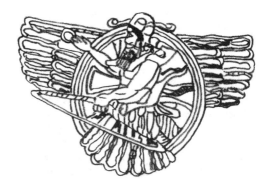

The Assyrian god Assur shown holding a bow and encircled by a winged disc.

Assyrian battering ram smashing down a city gate. Soldiers are shown much larger than actual size.

shown accompanied by shield-bearers holding large wicker shields with curved tops that extended back over the head of each archer, protecting him from enemy fire. In some cases archers were also shown accompanied by a spearman for extra protection. To protect themselves most soldiers wore some kind of armour or heavy clothing. In the lower ranks the poorer soldiers wore simple leather or cloth garments while in the higher ranks clothing with scale armour, made up of small pieces of metal sewn on to the fabric, served as a protective barrier against blows and cuts received in battle.[19]

The Assyrians used various types of two-wheeled chariots as mobile weapons-firing platforms. These were made from light materials such as wood, wicker, and leather, and were pulled by two horses. Chariots usually had a driver and an archer, but later a shield-bearer was also added. Horses were essential for chariotry and cavalry as the principal means of fast, manoeuvrable battlefield transportation, and were highly prized as booty when taken in raids against enemy forces. Cavalrymen generally carried a short bow and a short sword as weapons. Sometimes there were two men on a horse, the second man again being a shield-bearer to protect the mounted archer. Later the use of shield-bearers was discontinued. Even though Assyrian horses were smaller than modern animals, the task of a cavalryman must have been very dangerous because they rode bareback, stirrups being unknown in this region until many centuries later. Staying astride a horse at full gallop while firing a bow and arrow surely resulted in numerous accidents, both in training and on the battlefield. The raising of troops was the responsibility of the captains.[20] Each captain had at his disposal a number of villages and towns that served as a pool for potential recruits. The captains were required to fill quotas set by the governors of each province, and in turn each province had to contribute a certain number of troops to maintain the army of the king. Native Assyrian troops recruited in the homeland filled key

positions around the empire since they could be counted on to look after Assyrian interests more faithfully than non-Assyrians. Assyrian citizens were most often given positions of leadership in the military organization and they made up most of the chariotry and cavalry. The infantry consisted mainly of non-Assyrians. Early on, foreigners were employed in peacetime for guard duty after an area had been conquered by the regular Assyrian army. By the end of the eighth century BC many foreigners, including Arameans, Greeks, and Philistines appear in infantry units, while prisoners of war were often grouped together to form distinct fighting units.

Before embarking on a military campaign, priests and diviners performed sacrifices and examined sheep livers in search of favourable omens to determine whether the campaign would be successful. The army was led by priests[21] bearing standards and emblems (banners representing the gods) followed by the chariotry, cavalry, infantry, and their long trains of baggage and paraphernalia. Prior to battle the king inspected the formations of troops that, in many instances, he would lead into battle himself. The army carried a daily ration of barley for each man. In addition, city leaders and provincial governors were required to provide food for troops passing through their regions. Sometimes food had to be obtained by living off the land, which often meant whatever the soldiers could steal or frighten local people into giving them. The Assyrians became the undisputed masters of siege warfare and their methods and tactics, which they perfected after many years of practice, were subsequently adopted by other ancient nations. Sieges did not take place very often. At the sight of the Assyrian army many cities just gave up and handed over large amounts of treasure to the Assyrians in exchange for their lives. Sieges were very expensive and tied up thousands of troops for up to several years at a time. If the Assyrians were forced to besiege a city it usually meant that when the city fell it would be looted, its officials tortured and

murdered, and its citizens deported to some distant region of the empire. When a successful campaign was completed the downtrodden hostages and the booty taken from them was carried back to Assyria and paraded through the streets of the capital before cheering citizens.

Assurnasirpal II

The most important Assyrian ruler of the Late or Neo-Assyrian period was King Assurnasirpal II, who reigned from 883 BC to 859 BC. After he ascended to the throne he gathered his army and struck out against the hill people of northern Mesopotamia. Then he moved to the southwest against a vassal city on the lower Khabur River, called Suru, home of the Bit Halupe. The king's description of his attack on the city illustrates in vivid detail the power and cruelty of the Assyrian leaders. This type of text was one of the first of many that would become the standard format for war propaganda used to strike fear and terror into the hearts of the enemies of Assyria.[22] After having attacked and conquered the city the king records how he treated the vanquished inhabitants, whom he calls "rebels", by skinning all the leaders of the rebellion and covering a pillar with their skins. He continues his description by reiterating that he cut off arms, legs, noses, ears, and fingers of some, while others were burned to death, and ends by boasting that he hung their heads in the trees all around the city.[23] Clearly such acts were meant not only to punish those who had revolted, but to frighten the leaders of other cities and regions who might have been contemplating withholding their annual tribute from the soldiers of the great god Assur. In one of his campaigns Assurnasirpal II crossed the mountains of Lebanon and travelled all the way to the Mediterranean Sea. There he re-enacted a ritual that all great conquerors of the ancient Near East had performed since the time of Sargon of Akkad (see Ch. 4); he washed his weapons in the waters of the Mediterranean, made sheep offerings to the great gods, and took tribute from a number of coastal cities.[24] This important penetration set a precedent for future Assyrian kings, and eventually saw the whole Mediterranean coast drawn into the growing sphere of Assyrian influence.

Hunting wild animals[25]

Like most ancient Near Eastern monarchs, Assurnasirpal II hunted wild animals such as bulls, lions, and elephants. Lion hunting in particular was considered a royal sport, as well as a good character-building exercise for kings, who were ultimately responsible for leading their troops into battle. Assurnasirpal II tells us that during one hunt he trapped 30 elephants, killed 257 wild oxen, and brought down 370 lions with hunting spears from his chariot. It was the king's duty to protect his subjects and their farm animals from such dangerous creatures. Often, poor farmers living out in the hinterlands had neither the training nor the weapons to rid themselves of dangerous beasts such as lions, and had to call upon the king, or one of his soldiers, to come to their aid.[26] The practice of lion hunting was not new to the Assyrians, but known already in the fourth millennium BC, and the tradition continued in the Near East for centuries afterwards.[27] Not all lion hunting by Assyrian monarchs occurred in the wild. Some hunts took place in closed areas inside cities, such as parks. One sculptured lion-killing scene shows King Assurbanipal holding a lion at arm's length with his left hand while he plunges a sword into the animal's chest with his right hand. Although this sort of feat may appear to be an unlikely form of exaggerated royal propaganda, killing lions this way was entirely possible since the Mesopotamian lion (subsequently hunted to extinction) was slightly smaller than African lions. Up until the last century there are well-attested stories of young Arab men proving themselves by seeking out lions and killing them using essentially the same method shown in the low-relief sculpture below.

Assurnasirpal II did not spend all his time at war or extracting tribute from subject cities and kingdoms too weak to repel his powerful armies. He also built a new and strategically located city, Kalhu, on the east bank of the Tigris River and adorned it with a great palace. In addition he dug a great canal, called the *patti hegalli* (the stream of abundance), to water the surrounding plain for farmers and serve as a protective moat for the new city. When the city and its great palace were finally completed, the king held an enormous banquet, the menu of which was recorded in detail, to feed all the workers and citizens of the new city as well as ambassadors from many nations. The banquet boasted 70 000 guests and lasted for ten days, during which the people feasted, drank, bathed, and were anointed with sweet-smelling oils. In the

King Assurnasirpal II (883–859 BC) depicted in religious ceremonial dress as the chief priest of the god Assur.

King Assurbanipal (668–627? BC) killing a lion. Low-relief sculpture. (British Museum, London)

closing lines of the stele that commemorates the event, Assurnasirpal II is shown to us in a different light, that of the good and generous king who loved and cared for his people and when the festivities were over, he sent his subjects home in peace and joy.

Civil war and decline

After Assurnasirpal II's reign, Assyria went into a period of decline, and for years the land was troubled by serious internal problems. Some years later one of his grandsons, Assur-dannin-apli, instigated a revolt, and during a four-year period (827–824 BC) Assyria was in the throes of civil war. This revolt was led by minor princes from the cities of Nineveh, Ashur and Arba'ilu (Erbil), and free citizens, who were not receiving their share of benefits from the flow of tribute into the country. What the rebels wanted was a king who would give them their fair share of the booty from wars they helped to fight, plus a share of the profits from the enterprises and investments that accompanied the thriving Assyrian economy. However, the rebels were crushed and no changes in the system were made. Assyria continued to decline for the next 80 years while its enemies grew stronger and threatened the weakened nation. North of Assyria a new group of people was forming in the area between Lake Van and Lake Urmia, called Urartu.[28] Excavations have shown that the Urartians built cities of stone and mud brick enclosed behind massive walls and defensive towers where food and water were stored in anticipation of war. Urartian artisans were expert metallurgists, and most of the nation's wealth came from exploiting the copper and iron mines located in what is now eastern Turkey, modern-day Armenia, and Azerbaijan. The emergence of such a large and powerful country on Assyria's northern borders had a decisive influence on future events.

Administrative reforms under Tiglath-pileser III (744–727 BC)

If the Assyrians were going to survive the menace of Urartu, and the growing threat of other powers in the area, they would need a leader with sufficient political skill and foresight to recognize the demands of certain groups in Assyrian society, and to reorganize the political structure of the country. In 744 BC just such a person came to the throne: Tiglath-pileser III.[29] Although his family background and origins remain a mystery, there is good reason to believe that he was a usurper who took advantage of the unrest of the time to stage a palace coup d'état and take the Assyrian crown for himself. Tiglath-pileser III was an intelligent and vigorous man who was able to evaluate the situation correctly and move into action. The new king made a number of fundamental changes to the organizational and administrative structure of Assyria that enabled it to become a powerful military and economic force. Many of his reforms and institutions would be perpetuated by the Babylonians and Persians, and later authors falsely credited many of these reforms to them, although they were created by the Assyrians. Under the previous kings, large areas of conquered land were given as governorships to various Assyrian officials. These governors became nearly as powerful as the king. They began to act as petty kings who made their positions hereditary and passed their rule on to their children, who ignored the king and acted as independent rulers. Tiglath-pileser III abolished these governorships and divided the land into many small provinces, none large enough or strong enough to challenge the authority of the king. These provinces were ruled by a district lord (*bel-pihati*) or a governor (*shakkanakku*), who was responsible only to the king. By increasing the power of the king, Tiglath-pileser III was able to give new strength to the land of Ashur. To make sure that the appointed provincial governors did their job properly, overseers (*qepu*) were placed in each

province to report to the king. If a governor failed in his duties the king would be notified by the overseer, and the offending person would be admonished or removed from office. He also instituted the practice of making the young crown prince the administrator of the kingdom and its affairs while the king was away campaigning with the army. This helped to legitimize the heir apparent as the next king and reduced the number of disputes over the throne when a king died. To ensure that the king could be quickly informed about the activities of his governors and their territories, a system of roads and posting stages was established. Mounted riders could carry letters and communications from most parts of the empire to the capital at Nineveh within five to seven days, which was a dramatic improvement over previous systems of communication. Strategically placed posting stages provided mounted messengers (*mar shipri*) with fresh horses and extra rations of food as they rode across the land carrying small sacks of letters and dispatches written on parchment or clay tablets.[30] Many of the principalities and kingdoms conquered by Assyria were incorporated into the empire as provinces, and came under the direct control of the king and the central administration. After the Assyrians defeated an enemy, they usually left the old ruler in control of the conquered area as their vassal. If he revolted, or refused to pay tribute, he was defeated again, his kingdom abolished, and an Assyrian governor placed in power. Even though the conquered territories usually suffered much during their conquest and lost their independence in the process, when the Assyrians finally took them over they gained a certain amount of internal peace, security, and, in some cases, economic benefits.

It is, perhaps, best to remember that when the Assyrians conquered a country, their invading armies were not overthrowing governments that had been democratically elected by their citizens. At this time no country embraced the modern principles of democracy or individual rights and freedoms that are known in many parts of the world today. The local rulers displaced by the Assyrians were, in many cases, as brutal and greedy as the Assyrians themselves. In these circumstances, unless they were directly under attack by the Assyrian army, ordinary citizens may not have noticed any changes in the quality of their lives or living standards from one ruler to the next. Under the leadership of Tiglath-pileser III the army was completely restructured. Soldiers had better weapons and military leaders employed better tactics than before. The era of simple raids was at an end; under Tiglath-pileser III the army became large, full-time, and permanent. The old conscription army was replaced by contingents levied from conquered provinces. As a result the size of the Assyrian army increased dramatically but its reliability was reduced, since a large number of foreign elements in the army replaced the traditional sons of Assyria, who were more patriotic and willing to make sacrifices for their homeland. Tiglath-pileser III's predecessors had always considered the Euphrates River as the boundary of greater Assyria in terms of direct rule, but Tiglath-pileser III went beyond it and incorporated a number of former vassal states into the Assyrian fold and made them provinces. This development continued under subsequent rulers, and served to enlarge the empire until the middle of the seventh century BC. As the empire grew larger the boundaries and frontiers it had to defend also grew, which in turn required more and more soldiers to defend them. To avoid military pressure from outside their borders, the Assyrians surrounded the empire with vassal kingdoms, that is, kingdoms who were independent of Assyria but maintained friendly relations with the forces of Assyria and refrained from attacking it. Even though Tiglath-pileser III made many necessary and important changes in Assyria, some problems remained unsolved. One of these was the land of Urartu on the northern frontier of Assyria. Both Urartu and Assyria wanted control of the region around the upper Euphrates River and the Mediterranean coast. Control of this area meant access to vital supplies of timber, metals, and horses. Vassal states in this area proved to be unreliable at times since they could play Urartu, Assyria, and even distant Egypt against each other while striving to get the best possible arrangement for themselves.

To avoid the possibility of future revolts against Assyrian control, Tiglath-pileser III implemented the policy of mass deportation[31] to deal with the citizen populations of defeated countries. Thousands of conquered peoples were displaced from one part of the empire to another to meet the needs and goals of Assyrian political and military strategy. The Assyrians believed that by uprooting rebellious groups and moving them to far-off lands unfamiliar to them, feelings of regional pride and identity (patriotism) would disappear as deportees struggled to adapt to the rigours of making new lives. Deportation cut off potential troublemakers from their former allies, leaving them alone and friendless in a new land. By deporting their enemies and making them start their lives anew, the Assyrians eliminated any potential for revolt.[32] In many instances, for example in the reign of Tiglath-pileser III, deportation appears to have achieved its goal. Between 742 and 741 BC, 30 000 inhabitants from the region around the city of Hama were sent to the Zagros mountains on the opposite side of Mesopotamia, while 18 000 Arameans were sent from the Tigris region to northern Syria. In other years, 65 000 people were displaced in Iran, while in another mass deportation operation 154 000 people in southern Mesopotamia were affected. It has been estimated that up to 1.2 million people were deported from their homes during the Late Assyrian period.[33] A number of low-relief sculptures depict masses of men, women, and children with their belongings and farm animals marching pitifully to some new, but unfamiliar destination. Some of the deportees must have died on the long marches across the hundreds, even thousands, of kilometres of countryside. However, those who survived were not always badly treated. In some instances they found waiting for them abandoned homes or farms in their new land that had belonged to other people who had also been deported.[34] Although it must have been demoralizing and difficult, many deportees made a new and successful start and after some time were absorbed into Assyrian society.

Tiglath-pileser III mounted a number of campaigns against the forces of Urartu in the Levant and eastern Anatolia, winning many victories and expanding the empire. He was successful in holding off the Urartians, making major gains against them, but he was never able to defeat them. This would be done only by his successors. However, he did stabilize and solidify Assyria's position in the north and west, which was a very important phase in the overall Assyrian strategy. Despite this, it was to the south, in Babylonia and southern Mesopotamia, that the principal threat to Assyrian stability still existed.

Problems in the south

One of the major problems for Tiglath-pileser III, and all subsequent Assyrian kings, was their southern flank bordering on Babylonia. Babylonia existed as an independent kingdom under Assyrian control and was a centre for religion, art, literature, mythology, and other cultural traditions that the Assyrians shared with the peoples who lived in the Tigris–Euphrates river valley. The city of Babylon was the intellectual centre of greater Mesopotamia, a kind of university town where erudite men (there is little written evidence for educated women at this time) carried on a tradition of learning and scholarship. The Babylonians were the inheritors of the Sumerian and Akkadian culture passed down to them by great kings such as Sargon of Akkad and Hammurabi. Most Assyrians held the land of Babylonia in high esteem and considered it the home of much of their own culture. Despite this, the relationship between Assyria and Babylonia was often strained. Sometimes

Babylonia stood with Assyria and added unity and strength to the empire, while at others Babylonia withdrew and cast the whole of Mesopotamia into turmoil and war. The temple of the Babylonian god Marduk was located in the city of Babylon, and every year the New Year's festival (*akitu*) took place there (see Ch. 7). The whole city and surrounding regions took part, at which time the king of Babylon "took the hand of Marduk" as the most important moment of the ritual calendar. Like the Babylonians, the Assyrians also held the god Marduk in high esteem and the New Year's festival was an important event in their own religion. The Assyrians revered Babylon to the extent that on several occasions when the city was being attacked by outsiders, the Assyrians sent their armies to help the Babylonians.

Along with the Babylonians there were two other groups who also caused the Assyrians numerous problems in the south: the Chaldeans and the Elamites. In the ninth century BC, a new people who spoke Aramaic moved into Babylonia and settled as far south as the swampy marshlands where the Tigris and Euphrates Rivers emptied into the Persian Gulf. The Kaldu or, as the Greeks and Romans knew them, the Chaldeans,[35] succeeded on several occasions in overthrowing Babylon and installing one of their own people on the throne. In 732 BC the Chaldean Mukin-zeri took Babylon and occupied the throne. The Assyrians did not want this and tried to convince the citizens of Babylon to revolt and overthrow the new king. However, this strategy did not work and so the Assyrians attacked the city and drove the Chaldeans out. Mukin-zeri fled south into the marshes; Tiglath-pileser III put Babylon under direct Assyrian administration, and had himself crowned king. At the New Year's festival, Tiglath-pileser III, like other Babylonian kings before him, "took the hand of Marduk" to signify the start of a prosperous New Year and also to indicate that he, too, accepted Marduk as a great god to be respected in ritual and deed. Babylon was not the only problem on Assyria's

southern flank. The long-time enemy of Mesopotamia, Elam, once again began to intervene in the political affairs of the region. The Elamites had been causing problems for the various rulers of the southern Tigris–Euphrates river valley since the third millennium BC. During the reign of Tiglath-pileser III, the Elamites conspired with the Chaldeans to gain more power and wealth in the south, and these two

King Sargon II. Low-relief sculpture. (Museo di Antichità, Turin)

groups were to be a major source of problems for the Assyrians until the end of their rule in the Near East.

After a successful reign of 18 years, Tiglath-pileser III left Assyria in a position of great strength. He had reorganized the country's administration and army, and had established a complex and efficient empire. He had taken Assyrian soldiers further than ever before in conquest. At his death Assyrian power stretched from Judah on the Mediterranean coast of Syria-Palestine up into eastern Anatolia, north up to the territory of Urartu, and south to the Persian Gulf.

THE SARGONID KINGS (721–612 BC)

After the death of Tiglath Pileser III in 727 BC, there was a period of several years of instability and an insurrection out of which emerged a new king who took the long-honoured name of an ancient Akkadian predecessor: Sargon. This second "legitimate king", as Sargon II called himself, probably took power in a palace coup. He claimed to be a son of Tiglath-pileser III,[36] and like him proved to be an able and powerful ruler who continued Assyria's policy of expansion on all fronts in the Near East. To solidify his power base at home he offered tax exemptions to the citizens of the capital city of Ashur, and to all the temples of Assyria. The revolt that put Sargon II on the throne also served as a signal for vassals and conquered territories unhappy with Assyrian rule to revolt and re-establish local rule. Such was the case in Babylonia, where Elamites and Chaldeans formed an alliance that enabled them to overthrow their Assyrian administrators and put a man named Merodach-Baladan on the throne. Sargon reacted by sending his armies south along the Tigris River to cut the Elamite and Chaldean forces in half, and retake Babylon. However, with Elamite support Merodach-Baladan was able to hold off the mighty Assyrian army, and managed to stay in power for ten years. Under the rule of Merodach-Baladan, Babylonia prospered. He maintained and repaired temples, kept the provincial bureaucracy functioning, and built bridges, roads, and canals. For the next decade an uneasy peace existed between Assyria and Babylonia.

Meanwhile, on the other side of Assyrian territory in Syria-Palestine, another more threatening revolt broke out that saw a number of city-states and small kingdoms form a coalition that attempted to throw off Assyrian rule. Their attempts failed and the combined armies of Hamath, Arpad, and Samaria were beaten by superior Assyrian forces. Even though both of these events occurred at opposite ends of the empire they were not unrelated, but were the consequences of the expansionist policies of the former king, Tiglath-pileser III. Because of his incursions east into Iran and southwest into the Levant, Tiglath-pileser III had cut off the important trade routes vital to Elamite survival. In particular, his conquest of the Levant had taken away many of Elam's important clients in Egypt. Egypt on one flank of the Assyrian Empire, and Elam on the other, could not be expected to sit passively by and take no action to regain lost trading partners and markets.[37]

Both the Egyptians and the Elamites were weak and could not take on Assyrian forces by themselves. Over the following decades they devoted much time and effort working with smaller kingdoms and city-states to stimulate local revolts and confusion in attempts to weaken the Assyrian Empire. This was done with the hope that someday they would be able to take control of the areas and peoples they had

previously ruled, and once again have access to their old trading partners. As with Tiglath-pileser III, Sargon II's most pressing problem when he first ascended to the throne was his close and dangerous neighbour to the north, Urartu. In 714 BC, in the eighth year of his reign, Sargon II launched a great campaign against the forces of Urartu, which left them seriously weakened and no longer a threat to Assyria.[38] After a few more years of successful campaigning in other parts of the empire, the Assyrian position was consolidated, and by the beginning of the year 710 BC, Sargon II was victorious everywhere. The whole of Syria-Palestine was firmly in Assyrian hands; to the east the Medes were made vassals, Urartu was no longer a threat, and the Egyptians had a new king, friendly to Assyria.

But Babylon remained under Merodach-Baladan and was still a threat as well as an embarrassment to Assyria. The Assyrians, the greatest military power in the ancient Near East, could conquer a variety of enemies far from their homeland and yet were never capable of a total victory over the weaker Babylonians so close to home. When the armies of Sargon II marched against Babylon, the forces of Merodach-Baladan responded with a skilful defence that exploited their local environment. They took advantage of the swampy terrain of the marshlands, in what had once been the old city-state kingdoms of southern Mesopotamia, to make hit-and-run raids against the Assyrians, retreating back to the safety of the marshes where Assyrian forces could not be effectively used against them. Sargon II's operations against Babylonia were costly and hazardous and lasted for three years, until 707 BC. With the defeat of Babylon, Sargon II consolidated his conquest by deporting 108 000 Arameans and Chaldeans to various regions in the west. With most of the rebels gone he released some local citizens taken prisoner under Merodach-Baladan, extended tax exemptions to numerous cities, and then entered the capital city of Babylon and had himself crowned king. For the next

five years Sargon II ruled Babylonia and was recognized as its rightful king by most of its people. After restoring order and stabilizing the south, Sargon II died while on campaign against some tribal peoples in the north.

Sennacherib and Babylon

Sennacherib ruled from 704 to 681 BC. Although he was not Sargon II's first-born son, he was brought up in the *bit rimki* (the "house of succession"), a special place where future kings were prepared to be rulers of Assyria. He appears to have spent his early years as a soldier and administrator in the northwest, where he learned to know and understand the Urartian situation firsthand. The Urartians had suffered heavily at the hands of his father, and now were preoccupied with the menace of another group of people known as the Cimmerians, who lived on their northern flank. Because of Urartu's own difficult political situation it was in no position to harm Assyria, but could serve as an effective buffer zone, a kind of geopolitical shock absorber, between the Assyrians and possible dangers from the north. In the light of this new situation Sennacherib made peace with Urartu, greatly reducing his problems in that part of the empire. With this accomplished he set about building a great capital for himself and his empire.

Nineveh at the time of Sennacherib

Nineveh was an extraordinary city.[39] Positioned in the heartland of Assyria in a fertile agricultural zone, Nineveh was a major trading centre at the crossroads of the major east–west trade routes to Syria and the Mediterranean Sea, and the north–south trade routes from Anatolia to the Persian Gulf. Established at the confluence of the Tigris and Khosr Rivers, the site of Nineveh has been occupied for at least 6000 years. At the time of Sennacherib, the city sprawled over 750 hectares and its walls were 12 km in length, 25 m high; it had a population of perhaps as many as 150 000 inhabitants.[40] The circuit wall, wide enough, according to legend, for three chariots to be driven side by side at the summit, was pierced by 15 gates with roads leading out of the city in all directions.

The city of Nineveh had wide streets and public squares. Around the palace was a large park and botanical garden containing many species of plants, flowers, and trees imported from the south around Chaldea. Other sections of this vast garden contained specimens including myrrh plants, and many kinds of vines and orchards. To water this great garden Sennacherib built special canals to trap fresh water flowing from springs and streams 50 km away from Nineveh. At one point he built a tremendous aqueduct, over 300 m long and 22 m wide, to carry the water over another stream flowing below it through a small valley.[41] Situated in the middle of this garden was the king's royal residence, "The Palace Without Rival". It was 500 m long and 200 m wide, and was one of the marvels of Near Eastern architecture.[42]

Soon after his construction projects had started, Sennacherib was obliged to send his armies into the field to put down several revolts. Once again the question of Babylon and its status within the empire came up. How much independence, if any, should it have? Who should be king? There were pro- and anti-Babylonian advisers in the Assyrian court and at different times Assyrian kings would favour one or the other groups.[43] Sargon II had treated Babylon gently and tried his best to keep order and peace without granting outright independence; Sennacherib would be less than gentle with the ancient capital and its surrounding kingdom. In 703 BC, Merodach-Baladan once again organized the Chaldeans and Elamites in a coalition that raised a revolt in Babylon and the surrounding countryside. Sennacherib led his armies south and tried to put down the rebellion; with the approach of the Assyrian army, Merodach-

Lamassu. High-relief sculpture, Nineveh.

The great walls of Nineveh (eighth century BC).

Nergal Gate, Nineveh (800–600 BC). Baked mud-brick construction.

Baladan fled south into the marshes. In order to break the spirit of the rebellion, Sennacherib swept through Chaldea in a devastating campaign that destroyed or captured over a hundred walled cities, and deported 208 000 Chaldeans[44] to Assyria. He practised a scorched-earth policy, allowing his troops to either eat or burn the crops, fields of grain, palm groves, and orchards of the local residents.

As soon as Sennacherib had defeated the Chaldeans he was obliged to turn his armies around and march for many weeks until he reached the western vassal states, so he could put down a revolt in Judah and the surrounding regions on the Mediterranean coast. King Hezekiah of Jerusalem[45] had joined an anti-Assyrian coalition of coastal cities backed by Egypt. The organizer of this western revolt was none other than Merodach-Baladan.[46] Just before the arrival of Assyrian troops, Merodach-Baladan's agents had been sent to see the king of Jerusalem and ask him about his "health". It seems likely that their conversations had more to do with the political and military situation in the region than health matters. But despite their plans and preparations, Sennacherib's army over-ran the coast of Palestine and defeated the coastal cities, chased out the Egyptians, and put Jerusalem under siege. Sennacherib's account of the affair tells us that he besieged and captured 46 of Hezekiah's "strong walled towns" and numerous small villages. Then, using ramps of trodden earth built against the walls of Jerusalem, he brought up battering rams and siege engines, and even dug tunnels under the walls to weaken them. He boasts that he shut Hezekiah inside his city "like a bird in a cage". Despite this, Hezekiah did not capitulate to the Assyrian army, probably more out of luck than military skill. But he did not come away from his encounter with the Assyrians without paying a heavy price for having provoked the king of the land of Ashur. He was forced to pay as tribute 30 talents of gold (one talent equals about 30 kg), 800 talents of silver, and all kinds of treasures, plus his daughters, his harem, his male and female musicians, and several of his cities.

Three years later Merodach-Baladan was again involved in anti-Assyrian activities but they were only of minor importance, and after 700 BC he packed his court and his family gods into ships and fled into the swamps of Elam, and was heard of no more. Thus ended the career of one of the most interesting kings ever to have ruled in Babylonia. Over a period of 30 years of political involvement Merodach-Baladan tried, and at times succeeded, in making the kingdom of Babylonia the legitimate homeland of his people. The struggles of Merodach-Baladan were not forgotten, and about 75 years after his death Babylonia did manage to gain control not only of southern Mesopotamia, but of Assyria and its empire as well.

To protect Assyrian interests in Babylonia, Sennacherib placed his own son, Assur-nadin-shumi, on the throne of Babylonia, hoping that with this gesture he could bring order to the southern portion of Mesopotamia. This arrangement worked well for several years. However, in 689 BC things finally boiled over when the Babylonians, with the help of Elam, rose again in revolt against Assyria and kidnapped and murdered Sennacherib's son. A shocked and enraged Sennacherib reacted by destroying the city of Babylon, the ancient religious and cultural centre of Mesopotamia: "the gate of the gods", a city so pow-

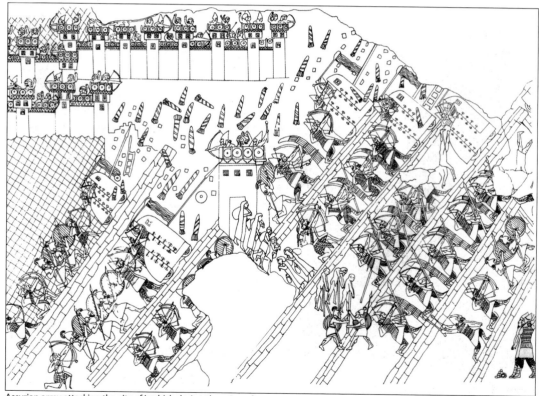

Assyrian army attacking the city of Lachish during the reign of Sennacherib (701 BC). Low-relief sculpture. (British Museum, London)

erful and revered that it was known to its citizens as "the bond of heaven and earth". The years of patience and respect shown by previous kings gave way to revenge as Sennacherib attacked the city "like a hurricane", and filled the streets with the corpses of its citizens. To ensure that the city would cause the king no problems in the future, he claims he flooded it and turned the once bustling city into a meadow. He certainly did ravage the city, but since it survived and was later revived (see below) much of this narration must be hyperbole.

Lamassu. A protective spirit used to protect the doorways and entrances of palaces and temples. Composite human-headed creature with the body of a bull and the wings of a great bird.

Sennacherib's destruction of Babylon was perhaps understandable since he lost his beloved son to the rebels, but from a religious perspective it was not very wise. His devastation of the great city was so complete that he even destroyed the temple of Marduk, the great god of Babylon, the god of Hammurabi, who had been worshipped for centuries by the people of Mesopotamia. Many feared that with the loss of the cult centre of such a great god all manner of evil, such as plagues, famines, and wars, would be inflicted on the land of Assyria, bringing years of hardship in revenge for such a reckless and impious act. However, following the sack of Babylon no great calamities befell the Assyrian people. Instead, eight years after the attack, in 681 BC, Sennacherib was murdered. One unlikely story claims that the king was crushed by one of the great *lamassu* (winged bulls), which was pushed on top of him while he was at prayer in the temple.

A more likely reconstruction of events has been developed through some clever historical detective work by Finnish Assyriologist Simo Parpola, who discovered a tablet indicating that the murderer was one of the king's own sons, a man named Arad-Millissu.[47] Arad-Millissu somehow escaped punishment for his crime and fled north to the land of Urartu. The fact that the murderer of a great Assyrian king was not punished for his crime but allowed to get away may indicate that Assyrians were not too upset by the king's death.

Another of the murdered king's sons, Esarhaddon, succeeded his father, and once in power devoted considerable resources in an effort to rectify the physical and spiritual devastation his father had caused the city of Babylon. Initially, the gods were said to have cursed the city for 70 years, during which time no activities could take place there. However, the new king found a way to get around this magical interdiction by simply transposing the numbers (perhaps by turning the tablet upside down), so that the integers were reversed. Instead of 70 (written as 60 + 10 = 70 or

in cuneiform) the merciful god Marduk, eager to return to his temple in Babylon, allowed the priests to interpret the figures as (10 + 1 = 11),

shortening to only 11 years the period of forced sterility on the city. Once this magical and religious problem had been solved the way was open for the restoration of the ancient capital. The reconstruction of Babylon and the repatriation of its citizens began in the first year of Esarhaddon's reign in 680 BC.

The conquest of Egypt

With the reconstruction of Babylonia underway and the rest of the empire momentarily stable, Esarhaddon[48] was free to embark upon the ultimate extension of the Assyrian Empire: the conquest of Egypt. In the spring of 671 BC, Esarhaddon led his armies into Syria-Palestine and crossed the Sinai desert. After considerable hardship, which, according to the cuneiform inscriptions, included the appearance of "two headed serpents", and the cutting open of their camels' bellies to find water to drink, Assyrian forces crossed into the green lands of the Nile Delta. Esarhaddon's account of the campaign claims that the conquest of the city of Memphis took only two weeks. However, because Egypt was so vast and far from the Assyrian heartland it proved difficult to control, and was never fully integrated into the Assyrian Empire like other conquered areas closer to home. The Assyrians were able to raid Egypt, but they were never able to hold on to it and make it part of their empire. Two years later the pharaoh, Tarqu (Taharqa in Egyptian, see Ch. 16), who had fled to southern Egypt during the Assyrian attack, returned and recovered his capital at Memphis and led a rebellion against the Assyrian occupation army. Upon hearing of the revolt, Esarhaddon gathered his armies once again, and set out to re-establish Assyrian control over the Egyptians. However, the king died on the way to Egypt and two of his sons, by a pre-arranged succession agreement, took the thrones of both Assyria and Babylonia.

Esarhaddon divided the kingship of the empire between the two of them to ensure that Assurbanipal would rule in the north and Shamash-shum-ukin, would rule in the south. With this arrangement he hoped to establish peace and security throughout Mesopotamia. But even though in principle the two rulers were equal, it was Assurbanipal, the king of the north, who had most of the power.

Assurbanipal 668–627? BC: the zenith and collapse of Assyria

When Assurbanipal ascended the throne of Assyria in 668 BC he inherited one of the greatest empires the world had ever known, yet by the end of his reign Assyria would be near collapse and would not survive to the end of the seventh century BC. At the beginning of his reign Assurbanipal's greatest concern was the reconquest of Egypt, which had temporarily slipped away from Assyrian control. Shortly after he took the throne, he sent a large army to the Nile Delta and again captured Lower Egypt and a number of important cities, including Memphis. But once again the Egyptians regained control of their land after the main Assyrian army had left. When the Assyrians attacked, the land of Egypt was actually under the control of the Kushites[49] (see Ch. 16): people from the far south of Egypt who had taken control of most of the Nile river valley in the middle of the eighth century BC. In 663 BC Assyrian forces were again in Egypt, but this time they did not simply take the northern capital and then return home. They marched their armies all the way to the southern

capital at Thebes and delivered a devastating blow to the region. Temples and palaces were burned and looted, and Egyptian leaders and citizens were rounded up and deported to Assyria.

The sack of Thebes and the Assyrian penetration into southern Egypt mark the maximum extent of Assyrian expansion. The Assyrian Empire had reached its logistical and technological limits, and over the following few decades it would begin to shrink in size. Despite their victory, the Assyrian foray into Egypt was short-lived. After they defeated the Egyptians, the Assyrians appointed a man named Psamtik (see Ch. 16) to be the senior administrator of Egypt. Several years after Assurbanipal's attack on Egypt, Psamtik formed an army, and by 650 BC the Egyptians had driven the Assyrians from their land once and for all. A few years later Psamtik declared himself pharaoh of Egypt, and brought an end to the Assyrian interlude.

Maintaining their hold on Egypt, the Assyrians faced the same problems that stopped many empires in similar circumstances: they had over-extended their resources. The Assyrians had to defend themselves against a dozen nations, and numerous small principalities and tribes, along a vast border that extended for thousands of kilometres from the Persian Gulf to the Mediterranean Sea and into Anatolia. Assyria had reached the point where its resources were too meagre and its adversaries too numerous to retain its power over all of them. The Assyrians had no choice but to let Egypt slip away for, once again, problems with the Elamites and Babylonians resurfaced in the south. Assurbanipal had come to realize that stable relations with his neighbours and partners in the southeast would be beneficial to trade and commerce. So, when a famine struck Elam, the new Assyrian king sent much-needed assistance that helped to save the lives of many Elamites. But, afterwards, despite Assyrian aid, the Elamites took advantage of Assyria's preoccupation in Egypt to launch an attack on Babylon in 665 BC. The Elamites' lack of

gratitude and hostility towards Assyria would not be forgotten by Assurbanipal.

The great revolt

The double monarchy in which the kingship of greater Mesopotamia was shared between Assurbanipal and Shamash-shum-ukin worked for nearly 17 years. But eventually, Shamash-shum-ukin grew tired of this arrangement and wanted to assert Babylonian might as he saw fit. In 652 BC he started a great revolt against his royal brother. Shamash-shum-ukin put together a vast coalition of anti-Assyrian forces that included Elamites, Chaldeans, and Arabs and engaged Assyria in a bloody four-year struggle. Assurbanipal finally defeated the Elamites and recorded his victory on several low-relief sculptures, which are now housed in the British Museum in London. In the mid-640s Assurbanipal returned to the southeast and in a rampage of hatred and vengeance struck a terrible blow at Elam. The Assyrian army marched through the land, destroying its major cities and capturing and looting the capital, Susa. Assurbanipal's troops showed no respect for the Elamites or their gods. After centuries of conflict between the two regions, the hatred of Assyria for this small but powerful nation that had on so many occasions caused problems and hardship for kingdoms in Mesopotamia was unleashed on the people, cities, and temples, and even the dead of Elam. Assurbanipal tells us that he destroyed the ancient tombs of their kings, who had not worshipped the gods Assur and Ishtar, took their bones away to Assyria and "put restlessness on their ghosts", and deprived them of their all-important food offerings.

The remaining civilian population was to a large extent deported west to Samaria, north of Judah, on the Mediterranean coast.[50] The Elamite troops were incorporated into the Assyrian army, and the remaining human and animal populations were taken to

Assyria as spoil. Once again in his exaggerated style, Assurbanipal claimed he devastated Elam and left it "empty of human voices", but it was not completely destroyed, and would recover a few years after the Assyrian attack. With the defeat of Elam and his withdrawal from Egypt, Assurbanipal had cut his losses and consolidated his forces. As a result the land of Ashur should have been stronger and better prepared to face its enemies, but in reality Assyria had been seriously weakened during the civil war and was dangerously close to collapse.

Assyria on the defensive

After the great rebellion, things were temporarily quiet in the south. The kingdom of Elam had been defeated, and Babylon and its allies had been drained by seven years of bloody warfare. But in Assyria proper things were not going well. For the period after 640 BC we have very little documentation about Assyrian activities, which indicates that things were coming apart. After the rebellion Assyria did not embark on major exterior campaigns but had to change tactics and go on the defensive against its enemies.[51] In the years that followed there were widespread disturbances in many parts of the empire, another indication that central authority was breaking down. By about 630 BC Assurbanipal's son, Assur-etil-ilani, became king, and he and his father ruled conjointly until the older man died in 627 BC. In 626 BC a Chaldean prince named Nabopolassar, perhaps a relative of Merodach-Baladan, defeated the Assyrian army at Uruk and took the throne of Babylon. It is from this time, 23 November 626 BC, that scholars mark the beginning of the 13th or Neo-Babylonian Dynasty in southern Mesopotamia.

Feeling confident after having established their own dynasty, the Babylonians engaged in continuous warfare with the Assyrians, which ultimately led to the capture of the Assyrian capital. Alone, the Babylonians were not powerful enough to defeat the still mighty Assyrians, so they formed coalitions with their usual close neighbours plus the Medes, new migrants who had established themselves on the Iranian Plateau (see Ch. 17). The Medes had previously been vassals of the Assyrians and had paid tribute to them, but over the years the Medes had grown stronger, were on the offensive, and no longer paid tribute. In 614 BC the Medes independently attacked Ashur, the religious centre of Assyria. When the Babylonians heard about this they mobilized their armies in an effort to take advantage of the situation. It was under the walls of the city of Ashur that Nabopolassar, the new king of the Babylonians, and Cyaxeres, the king of the Medes, established an alliance to fight together until the Assyrians were defeated. From this moment the fate of Assyria was sealed and two years later, in 612 BC, the combined armies of the Medes and the Babylonians besieged the great Assyrian metropolis of Nineveh. After a three-month siege the city fell and was sacked and burned. Nabopolassar boasted that he "slaughtered the land of Assyria" and turned it into "heaps and ruins". The Assyrians, who had dominated the whole of Mesopotamia, Syria-Palestine, and, briefly, Egypt, were vanquished by a coalition of forces who had suffered greatly under Assyrian domination. Although remnants of the Assyrian royal family continued to hold out at Harran until 609 BC, with the fall of Nineveh the era of Assyrian domination had ended.

The library of Assurbanipal

Assurbanipal's treatment of his enemies could be vengeful and brutal, but there was another side to the Assyrian king that should be mentioned. He was one of the few Assyrian kings who could actually read and write. He had great respect for the written word, and collected thousands of tablets from all over Mesopotamia to create one of the world's most famous and oldest libraries.[52] Although the number of texts he collected would be considered small by modern standards, he managed to gather several thousand tablets (the exact number is not known because many of them are fragments of a single tablet, but estimates vary from 5000 to 25000). They were stored in a special archive room where they were discovered about 150 years ago during the early days of exploration of the city of Nineveh. This collection of tablets consisted of important clay documents including letters, contracts, and historical inscriptions, as well as religious and literary texts, myths, and scientific works. The king's scholarly interests are enhanced by the fact that many of the texts were copies of older Sumerian and Babylonian texts, which were made at

Two Assyrian scribes. One is shown writing on a clay tablet while the other is writing on parchment. Painting on plaster.

Siege of Gaziru. Low-relief
sculpture from Nimrud.

his request. This indicates that Assurbanipal had a genuine desire to preserve the literary, religious, and cultural heritage of ancient Mesopotamia for future generations. In one of his letters he writes to his governors asking them to be on the lookout for all manner of texts. If they see something interesting, he orders them to send it to him for his library at his capital, Nineveh. The discovery of the tablets in the 19th century by British explorers, and their retrieval and storage in the British Museum in London, has provided a significant source of information for the greater understanding of ancient Assyria.

The collapse of Assyria

With the collapse of Assyria the northern domination of the Tigris–Euphrates river valley came to an end. There is no single reason why the Assyrian Empire fell, but two important contributing factors deserve to be mentioned.[53] The first concerns the use of foreigners in the Assyrian military. Like many armies the Assyrians engaged large numbers of non-Assyrians from conquered territories as soldiers in their armed forces. Their payment was often only a daily ration of food, the promise of adventure and travel, and, occasionally, the right to some unrestrained looting of a conquered city. Swelling its ranks with large numbers of non-Assyrians surely weakened the resolve of the army to fight effectively and with a spirit of commitment and love for the homeland.[54] The second reason was economic. Prosperous regions conquered by the Assyrians initially brought in great wealth, which subsequently diminished substantially. Conquered merchants and farmers who had been producers of wealth could not be expected to continue to produce at the same level since any profits they made would have been taken from them.[55] The more prosperous a region was, the more desirable it was to the Assyrians. Thus, for local peoples it was better not to appear to be too affluent in order to avoid attracting their attention. As a result of this short-sighted policy of resource appropriation, regions that originally served as sources of wealth were quickly exhausted, and the forces of Ashur had to go further and further from their homeland in search of new areas to exploit for loot and other kinds of material goods. It seems never to have occurred to the Assyrians that by their oppressive measures they were destroying the very basis of their prosperity. Over the years, as they used up one region after another, they were caught in a vicious circle: the more countries they conquered and drained the more new regions they had to conquer to maintain their standard of living. The Assyrians eventually over-extended themselves, while all the time depending more and more on non-Assyrians to protect and ensure the functioning of the empire. During the reign of Assurbanipal this system collapsed, and the Babylonians moved in and took over the Assyrians and their empire and made it their own.

7 The Last Babylonian Dynasty

After the death of Assurbanipal, King Nabopolassar took the throne of Babylon in southern Mesopotamia while in the north the Assyrian Empire continued its decline. Nabopolassar represented a vigorous new ruling family that with help was able to destroy the hated Assyrians, take over their empire, and establish the kingdom of Babylonia[1] as the major power in the Near East. The new king began his reign by consolidating his forces and mounting a ten-year struggle that drove the Assyrians out of southern Mesopotamia and freed Babylonia once and for all from the Assyrian yoke. Never again would the forces of the god Assur enter Babylonian territory. After 609 BC the Assyrians are heard of no more and no one seems to have mourned their passing. The Medes, who helped to bring about the Assyrian defeat, took their share of the booty and went back to their homeland on the Iranian Plateau. They were more interested in concentrating their efforts in the north, towards Armenia and the rest of Anatolia, than in Mesopotamia.

Chronology of the Last Babylonian Dynasty or Neo-Babylonian period (625–539) (all dates BC)

Nabopolassar	625–605
Nebuchadnezzar II	604–562
Amel-Marduk	561–560
Neriglissar	559–556
Labashi-Marduk	556–
Nabonidus	556–539
Persian conquest	539

Egypt returns to Syria-Palestine

With the defeat of the Assyrians, the Egyptians were in a position to dominate the entire Mediterranean coast of Syria-Palestine from the Nile Delta to the southern reaches of Turkey. They hoped to bring this area under Egyptian control and re-establish their power over lands they had ruled during the New Kingdom. But the Babylonians could not allow Egypt to control the rich provinces of the west. The coastal areas of Syria-Palestine were rich in raw materials and trade, and strategically too vital to Babylonian survival to allow anyone else to take control of them. The Egyptians proceeded with their plans to bring the region under their control and although they almost succeeded, their plans were foiled by the military skills of Nebuchadnezzar II, the son of Nabopolassar. Nebuchadnezzar II[2] was a skilled general who was given command of the Babylonian army when his ageing father became too ill to lead another campaign. Nebuchadnezzar II caught the Egyptian army by surprise and annihilated it in the spring of 605 BC at Karkamish, on the great bend of the Euphrates River in upper Syria.[3] This battle was one of the most important in the centuries-long struggle (see Chs 14 and 15) between Egypt and Mesopotamia for supremacy over Syria-Palestine, and the Egyptian defeat gave Babylon control of the area.[4] Ironically, less than a century after the battle of Karkamish, neither Egypt nor Babylonia would be independent kingdoms.

Nebuchadnezzar II, King of Babylon

A few months after the battle of Karkamish, King Nabopolassar died in the city of Babylon. The great king who had succeeded where so many others had failed, and who had driven the Assyrians out of Babylonia, "had gone to his fate" and was no more. Nebuchadnezzar II[5] would prove to be just as competent as his father and would make the land of Babylonia greater than it was even during the time of Hammurabi. Upon hearing of the death of his father, Nebuchadnezzar II raced back to the capital to be crowned king, and then immediately returned to the western front to continue his struggle against the Egyptians to protect his possessions in the west. In 601 BC, Nebuchadnezzar II marched against Egypt, hoping to add the Nile river valley to his empire as the Assyrians had done nearly a century earlier. To his surprise he met with strong Egyptian resistance; both armies suffered heavy casualties, and he was forced to return to Babylon in order to re-equip his forces. Although he was an excellent general, Nebuchadnezzar II was never able to conquer Egypt.

The conquest of Judah

Seven years later, the small kingdom of Judah[6] sided with Egypt and refused to pay tribute to Babylon. Nebuchadnezzar II could not tolerate this kind of rebellious behaviour and laid siege to the Judean capital, Jerusalem.[7] On 15/16 March 597 BC[8] the city fell to the forces of Nebuchadnezzar II. The young king of Judah, 18-year-old Jehoiakin, and more than 3000 of his subjects[9] were deported to Babylon. Much tribute was also taken from the city and from the temple of the god Yahweh. Plundered objects included sacred temple vessels, consisting of great brass cauldrons, which were taken to Babylon and placed in Esagila, the temple of Marduk. The Babylonians then placed Zedekiah, another member of the Judean royal family, on the throne. Initially, Zedekiah looked after Babylonian interests for Nebuchadnezzar II but after several years he too rebelled. Believing that the Egyptians would come to their aid and help them expel the Babylonians, a number of the city-states of Syria-Palestine, including Jerusalem, appear to have formed a coalition against Babylon. Despite the many warnings from the prophet Jeremiah, Zedekiah went ahead with his plan to break free from the Babylonians, and Nebuchadnezzar II once again attacked Jerusalem. Zedekiah appealed to the new Egyptian king, Apries, for help, but the Egyptians sent only a small force of soldiers that could not affect the outcome of the battle.

The siege of Jerusalem was very costly, lasting 18 months and tying up thousands of Babylonian troops far from home, and Zedekiah and his city paid dearly

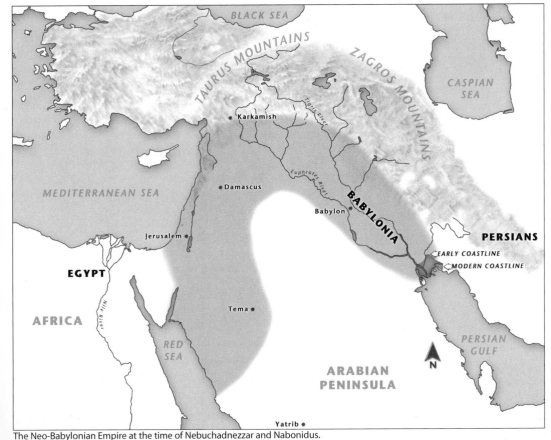

The Neo-Babylonian Empire at the time of Nebuchadnezzar and Nabonidus.

for refusing to submit to Babylon. The walls were breached on 25 August 587 BC[10] and archaeological evidence indicates widespread destruction of many buildings and traces of a great conflagration that swept through the city at the time of its capture. When Jerusalem capitulated it was looted, its walls were broken down, and the great temple of Solomon that had been the pride of all Judah was destroyed. Many of the inhabitants of the city who had not starved to death during the siege were deported to Babylonia. After Zedekiah was captured, the Old Testament Book of Kings recounts that he was brought before Nebuchadnezzar, judged, and found guilty. The last thing the king of Judah saw before having his eyes put out was the death of his sons: "And they slew the sons of Zedekiah before his eyes, and put out the eyes of Zedekiah, and bound him with fetters of brass, and carried him off to Babylon".[11]

The great city of Babylon[12]

The wealth gathered by Nebuchadnezzar during his various campaigns was used to rebuild and glorify Babylon.[13] According to R. W. Koldewey, the German archaeologist who excavated the city in the years before World War I, Nebuchadnezzar used more than 15 million standard-sized baked mud bricks measuring $33\,cm^2$ by 7 cm thick in his building projects.[14] The Babylonian king rebuilt and enlarged Esagila, the temple of Marduk and the ziggurat, Etemenanli, the highest mud-brick tower ever built (see Ch. 4), as well as many other smaller temples and shrines. In addition, he built 8 km of city walls of baked mud bricks, and the city gates were covered with glazed mud bricks that sparkled in the sunlight. Outside the walls the city was surrounded by a deep moat. The greatest city in antiquity before classical times, Babylon had perhaps 250 000 inhabitants.[15] It was the centre of learning and culture and the arts,

Wall detail showing the mythical snake-headed *mushushshu* moulded into the mud bricks along the main processional way, Babylon.

Arched entrance with crenellated wall, Babylon.

and was the most sophisticated and glamorous city in the ancient world before the rise of Alexandria and Rome, hundreds of years later. It contained one of the seven wonders of the ancient world: the so-called "hanging gardens of Babylon".[16] This vast and spectacular botanical complex was built for Amytis, the wife of Nebuchadnezzar, apparently so she would not be homesick for the mountainous terrain of her native land.

In Babylon scholarly men[17] discussed, conversed, and wrote about religion, literature, mathematics, and astronomy, and left a legacy of learning that was passed down through the centuries. They made lists of plants, stones, and gems, along with drugs and potions used for the treatment of diseases; they composed and copied magical and religious texts, dictionaries, and word lists, and recorded the thousands of economic transactions of the business community;

Akkadian and cuneiform writing, which had been the foundation of written expression in Mesopotamia and much of the rest of the Near East for nearly three thousand years, vanished until it was rediscovered by European explorers, and deciphered in the 19th century AD.[18]

The palace coup of Belshazzar

Nabonidus, the last native king of Babylonia, ruled from 556 to 539 BC. He, his centenarian mother, Adad-Guppi, and his shrewd and greedy son, Belshazzar, make up one of the most interesting families ever to rule in the ancient Near East.[19] Nabonidus came to power in a palace coup that saw the overthrow of the young King Labashi-Marduk, who, because of his youth and apparent lack of powerful friends, was deposed and murdered. Before assuming the role of king, Nabonidus had been a palace official in Babylon and served both King Nebuchadnezzar and a minor king, Neriglissar, whose reign lasted only about three years. According to one of his own inscriptions, Nabonidus claims that he had no intention of becoming king, and was unaware that the perpetrators of the coup were going to make him the new ruler of Babylon. Afterwards, his fellow conspirators carried him to the palace and prostrated themselves before him, kissing his feet as a sign of subservience. Nabonidus was troubled by the idea of being king and wanted to concentrate his efforts in the new dynasty on religious matters. Only after consulting with the gods did he reluctantly accept the kingship of the land.

In 556 BC the young King Labashi-Marduk succeeded his father, Neriglissar, on the throne of Babylon. He ruled for only a few months before being removed from the throne. Accusations against him, that he neglected to make offerings to his deceased ancestors, or that he was a poor general, were fabricated by the conspirators, no doubt in

Reconstructed palace building, Babylon. Mud-brick construction.

Ishtar Gate, Babylon (seventh century BC). Glazed and baked mud-brick construction, height 14.73 m. (Staatliche Museen, Vorderasiatisches Museum, Berlin, Germany)

and they studied and recorded celestial movements, solved mathematical problems, and ran schools to train young scribes. Recorded on clay tablets, much of this information was copied by scholars and students who passed it on to future generations. Centuries after the fall of Babylon, the scholars of Greece and Rome acknowledged the academic greatness of the Babylonians, and took directly from them copious amounts of material that had a profound affect on their own scholarly tradition. After the city had been abandoned as a political centre in 275 BC, a school of astronomers remained there and continued to make celestial observations and calculations in a city that was losing its cultural and political importance with the passing years. By 500 BC, Akkadian had slipped into obscurity as a spoken language, and was used only by a handful of scholars in written form. The last dateable cuneiform tablet was an astronomical text written in Babylon in AD 75. Afterwards, order to justify their illegal actions against the legitimate heir to the Babylonian throne.[20] The leader of the plot to overthrow the king was probably Belshazzar, the son of Nabonidus. Economic texts show that shortly after the coup, property and estates previously belonging to the royal family found their way into the possession of Belshazzar, and that afterwards his financial situation improved dramatically. It appears that the principal reason for the takeover was the economic scheming of Belshazzar and his circle of friends, who wanted to become rich and powerful. Not only was Belshazzar the leader of the plot against the legitimate king, but he probably wanted the kingship for himself as well. However, he could not claim kingship as long as his father was still alive. By putting his father on the throne before him he accomplished two things: he ensured himself the kingship when his father died; and he established the beginnings of a new dynasty that would give him and his heirs the future crown of Babylonia.

Adad-Guppi: the mother of Nabonidus

One of the most interesting and influential women of this period was Adad-Guppi, the mother of Nabonidus and the grandmother of Belshazzar. She was born in 649 BC, in the twentieth year of the reign of King Assurbanipal, at the city of Harran in northwest Syria, about 600 km from Babylon. She died in the ninth year of the reign of her son Nabonidus, in 547 BC, which made her 102 years old.[21] After the Assyrian defeat (see Ch. 6), the new king of Babylonia, Nabopolassar, brought Adad-Guppi and her son back to Babylon as captives. She would have been 39 years old at the time and her son was probably a young adult. Once in Babylon she was given some kind of influential position working with the Babylonian royal family. In one of her inscriptions she states that she was treated with great respect, as if she were one of the king's own daughters, and that while she was in the palace she introduced her only son to both King Nabopolassar and his successor, Nebuchadnezzar. In total she worked in the palaces of Harran and Babylon for about 70 years, from the age of 23 until well into her 90s. Adad-Guppi and Nabonidus were both devoted followers of the moon god, Sin of Harran. She states that she was a "seeker" after Sin for 95 years of her life.[22]

The religion of the moon god

When the Medes and Babylonians attacked the Assyrian-held city of Harran in 609 BC, they unwillingly destroyed Ehulhul (the "House of Joy"), the great temple of the moon god. Afterwards, the great shining house of the moon god lay in ruins and many people, particularly the Babylonians, were distressed and repentant for the terrible destruction they had wrought on his sacred house. In Mesopotamia people believed that if a temple was destroyed, it was a sign that their god had become angry with his people and had abandoned them. Only when his temple had been rebuilt would the god and his beneficial acts return once again. After the temple of the moon god had been destroyed, the Medes continued to occupy the city of Harran and would not give it to the Babylonians, who were too weak to take the city by force. Nabopolassar managed to bring the statues of Sin to Babylon and provided a temple for them in which Adad-Guppi continued to worship the moon god and maintain his cult. To show her concern and devotion to the moon god, Adad-Guppi refused to wear fine clothes or jewellery of silver and gold; nor did she sprinkle herself with sweet-smelling perfumes. Instead, she went about dressed in torn garments and a coat of sackcloth while doing everything in her power to glorify the moon god.

A religious interpretation of Assyro-Babylonian history

Babylonian historians interpreted political events differently from modern historians, and it is often impossible to draw a firm line between religion and politics. In the ancient Near East, political occurrences were interspersed with religious beliefs and interpreted as a continuing drama that involved both humans and gods. For Nabonidus the central idea[23] that dominated his perception of events, and determined the actions he undertook during his reign, was the divine struggle taking place between the moon god, who had been driven from his temple, and the Medes, who were still occupying the city of Harran where the god's temple was located. Accordingly, Nabonidus believed that it was his duty to drive the Medes out of Harran and restore the god's temple. Once this was accomplished, he believed, the moon god would return and peace and order would be re-established throughout the land.

Reconstruction of the Ziggurat of Babylon.

The celestial dream of Nabonidus

At the beginning of his reign Nabonidus had a dream in which the moon god Sin, glowing brightly in the night sky, and Marduk, who shone in the heavens as the planet Jupiter, appeared to the king and instructed him to rebuild the temple at Harran.[24] In the dream Nabonidus reminded the two powerful deities that the city of Harran still lay in the hands of the Medes, who did not wish to give it up. Because of this, there was no way he could rebuild the temple of the moon god. But Marduk in his wisdom provided another human agent to destroy the Medes; his name was Cyrus the Persian (also called Cyrus the Great). Cyrus was the young and energetic leader of a powerful new kingdom that was developing on the Iranian Plateau and would soon take control of the entire Near East. Three years after Nabonidus took the throne, Cyrus marched against the Medes and was victorious. Once the Medes were defeated, Harran came under Babylonian control. At last Nabonidus could begin the restoration of the temple of the moon god, a project that would last for much of his reign.

Nabonidus not only wanted to rebuild the temple of the moon god, but he also wanted to make Sin the most respected and powerful deity in all of Babylonia. The worship and veneration of the moon god was nothing new in Mesopotamia. The moon had been a major deity for several thousand years before Nabonidus came to the throne, but no one before him had ever attempted to elevate the moon god above all the other Mesopotamian deities. Sin had been an important deity throughout much of Mesopotamian history and his fortunes and importance rose and fell with the passage of the centuries. In the third millennium BC, the Sumerians worshipped and made offerings to the moon. Several Akkadian kings went so far as to incorporate the name Sin into their personal names. Naram-Sin (Beloved of the moon god) and Warad-Sin (Servant of the moon god) are two examples. In the first millennium BC the moon was still considered a great deity. Assyrian kings such as Sennacherib ("the moon god has replaced the brothers for me") showed their respect to the lunar deity, like many kings before them, by using his name as an element in their own names.

Shortly after Nabonidus took the throne he attempted to reduce the power and importance of the chief god, Marduk, and elevate Sin to the top of the pantheon. This move backfired and the people of Babylonia revolted. Many important cities turned against Nabonidus and his god, most of their citizens rejecting Sin in favour of their long-time deity, Marduk. Although Nabonidus and Belshazzar were both co-conspirators in the overthrow of Labashi-Marduk, they were not of one mind when it came to religious matters. Belshazzar was a traditionalist who wanted the god Marduk to remain at the head of the pantheon, but his father wanted to change the hierarchy of gods and create a new religious order. After his failed attempt at religious reforms it was probably at his son's insistence that Nabonidus left Babylon for Arabia for an extended stay.[25]

Nabonidus in Arabia

In the spring of the third year of his reign, Nabonidus gathered his armies, left the kingdom in the hands of his son, Belshazzar, marched west through Syria-Palestine, and then turned his armies towards the Arabian Peninsula. He continued south along the Red Sea, conquering a number of cities and towns on the coast, before finally settling in the city of Tema, located in the northwestern corner of Arabia, many weeks' march from Babylon. Amazingly, he stayed in the region for ten years before returning home, and the reasons for his long absence have always puzzled historians. It has been argued that no reasonable king would have exiled himself for ten years so far from his centre of power, deep in the sandy wastes of the Arabian desert, and during that time not take part in the religious and political life of his own country, unless he suffered from some kind of illness, was strange, or just plain mad.[26] But on closer examination Nabonidus's conquest of this area was perhaps not such a foolish move after all.

Tema and the surrounding area were the home of the Arabs who had come into contact with the kings of Mesopotamia long before the time of Nabonidus. The Arabs were not a poor people and Arabia was not an empty desert wasteland, as some might think. The Arabs had vast flocks of herd animals, and the area was rich in spices. In addition, they mined for gold, and carried out long-distance trade through their Red Sea ports. In the eighth century BC, Tiglath-pileser III reported that during one of his campaigns he took as booty 30 000 camels, 20 000 sheep and 5000 bags of spices, plus gold and other precious stones. Other Mesopotamian kings plundered similar wealth from the Arabs and Nabonidus was drawn to the area for the same reasons: the promise of great wealth and the control of trade routes that connected Mesopotamia, Africa, and the Mediterranean regions in a profitable trading network. The importance of Tema lay in its geographical location (see map, p. 91) since it was situated on the main caravan trade route between Damascus and Yatrib (Medina). The Assyrians waged numerous campaigns against the Arabs of the region in the seventh century BC, and Nabonidus followed the same strategy in his operations, which paid off in economic and strategic gains for Babylonia. Thus, his move into Arabia was not a strange or irrational act at all, but simply a continuation of the imperialist policies practised by the previous kings of Mesopotamia.

Nabonidus knew that since his son was in control of the capital, he could stay in Arabia and continue his policy of expansion. In light of the growing power of the Persians in the north and the east, the Babylonians, if they wished to maintain some kind of power base, had little choice but to expand into Arabia, an area that was relatively easy to conquer and rich in material goods. Nabonidus and his advisors understood that many of the lands traditionally exploited by the Babylonians (northern Mesopotamia, Turkey, and Iran), were under the control of the more powerful Persians, and that if the Babylonians were to maintain their power,[27] they had to establish control over new lands in a part of the Near East that was beyond the reach of their powerful rivals.

The *akitu* (New Year's) festival

During the time Nabonidus was absent from Babylon he did not participate in an important religious ritual known as the *akitu* or New Year's festival.[28] The king's role in the festival was essential; it could not take place if he was not present. The *akitu* festival was celebrated in the spring of each year over 11 days in March/April, the Babylonian month of *Nisanu*. This length reflected the fact that the lunar year (see Ch. 9) was 11 days shorter than the solar year. Lesser deities and their attendant priests and followers from nearby cities came to Babylon to take part in the festival, and it was a time of great feasting and celebration. The first few days were spent reciting prayers and incantations and making animal sacrifices. On the fourth day the *Enuma Elish*[29] (the Babylonian creation myth) was recited in front of the statue of Marduk. The story describes how in the beginning order was brought out of chaos when the god of fresh waters, Apsu, was separated from the goddess of salty waters, Tiamat. Later, one of the Babylonian gods killed Apsu. This enraged Tiamat, who took revenge on the murderer. With an army of demons and monsters, commanded by the evil Kingu, Tiamat attacked the gods and threatened to destroy them. Just when all seemed lost, a brave young god named Marduk volunteered to go out on the battlefield and fight Tiamat.

The chief god of the Babylonian pantheon, Marduk, in the reign of King Marduk-zakir-shumi (854–819 BC). Engraved lapis lazuli.

The gods agreed that if Marduk defeated Tiamat he would become the chief god and all the other gods would be subservient to him. Marduk engaged Tiamat in a great struggle in which he managed to overpower and kill her. He then split her great carcass in two halves; with one half he made the earth under his feet, and with the other half he made the vault of heaven on which he placed the stars, the sun and the moon. Then, with the blood of the evil Kingu mixed with earth, he created people to work the fields and feed the gods through sacrifice. Thus liberated from agricultural work, the gods were free to live a life of leisure.

On the fifth day of the festival the king entered the temple of Marduk and took part in a special ritual where he was reduced to the status of an ordinary citizen. The king was stripped of his royal insignia, his sword, and sceptre, and then the chief priest slapped his face, pulled his ears, and made him prostrate himself before the statue of Marduk. During this festival the king was required to "take the hand of Marduk". This refers to the king playing the role of the god and his sacred marriage[30] to a high priestess. The sacred marriage symbolized the agricultural cycle of planting and harvesting of grain, and was a spiritual metaphor for the renewal of life and the forces of nature. The statues of all the gods were then transported in chariots to the north end of the city to the special *akitu* temple. Here great gifts, sometimes consisting of tonnes of silver and gold, were given to the gods. On the last day of the festival, all of the celebrants went back to the temple of Marduk for a great banquet before returning once again to their respective cities. Failure of the king to take part in the *akitu* festival was a bad omen, and seen as an act of great impiety against the gods. The people of Babylonia lived in fear that floods, famine, and war would befall them as a result of the king's neglect of his religious duties.

Belshazzar

During Nabonidus's absence in Tema, Belshazzar remained subordinate to him and it seems there were no major problems between the two men concerning the sharing of power and the day-to-day functioning of the government. In his father's absence Belshazzar never used the title king to refer to himself, nor did he ever take his father's place in the *akitu* festival. Nabonidus never gives any indication that he was concerned that his son would take the throne while he was in Arabia. Proof of this can be seen in the fact that Nabonidus left Belshazzar in control of the army to use as he saw fit. Surely, if Nabonidus had any suspicion about his son's loyalty he would not have put an army at his disposal, since he could have turned it against him. Belshazzar ignored the moon god in his father's absence so that religious and political stability could be maintained in the land.

After ten years Nabonidus left Arabia and returned to Babylon. Based on favourable astronomical omens, it was decided that the appointed time had arrived, the moon god was satisfied with the situation in Babylonia, and Nabonidus could return home and resume his duties as king. Nabonidus returned to Babylon in October, the 13th year of his reign. There seem to be two reasons why he returned at this time: work on the temple at Harran was progressing well and it was imperative that he be present to celebrate its completion; and he was getting old (he was probably already in his early 70s), and thus he had to take action to implement the religious reforms he hoped to bring about. Shortly after his return he set in motion the necessary changes that would enable Sin to become chief god. His second attempt to make the moon god the supreme deity of the land seems to have met with short-lived success.

Ehulhul, the "House of Joy"

Nabonidus had maintained while he was in Arabia that the reason why he refused to participate in the New Year's festival was because the temple of the moon god had not been rebuilt. Work on the temple was finally completed about a year after his return. It is known that the decision to rebuild Ehulhul was one of the earliest taken in his reign, but it took much longer to complete than originally planned. Before the temple Ehulhul was completed, the king's mother, Adad-Guppi, died at the age of 102. It must have been a great disappointment to her that she never actually saw the moon god's statue returned to its rightful place. However, she must have been aware that its reconstruction was progressing, and that her son was doing everything in his power to restore the sacred structure to its original greatness.

On his return to Babylon, Nabonidus resumed the king's traditional role in the *akitu* festival. In the last year of his reign, just as some stability seemed to be returning to the land, the king seized Esagila, Marduk's main temple in Babylon, and replaced his symbol, a stylized spade, with a lunar crescent, the symbol of the moon cult. Nabonidus went so far as to refer to Marduk's temple as "the dwelling place of Sin". The citizens of Babylon were outraged by his actions. Marduk had been the great god of the Babylonian people for over 1000 years, and for the second time in his reign Nabonidus had attempted to usurp the greatest of all Babylonian deities. In their anger some groups were possibly plotting against Nabonidus,[31] seeking to replace him with a new king who would be more respectful to the ancient gods of Babylon. The discontented priests and followers of Marduk resented the imposition of the moon god and many must have interpreted his actions as a betrayal of the people by the king.

The end of Babylon

Despite Nabonidus's attempts to enlarge his empire in Arabia, and implement his religious reforms at home, his days as king were numbered. The Persians were growing stronger and the menacing threat of their power hung over the Tigris–Euphrates river valley. The end came quickly in the autumn of 539 BC, when the armies of Babylon were defeated in a bloody and costly battle at the city of Opis. The defeat was overwhelming, the Babylonian army was shattered, and Belshazzar was killed. A few days later the capital city's defences collapsed, and in October of that same year the Persian army, under the command of General Gubaru (Gobryas), marched into Babylon unopposed.[32] A few days later, when things had calmed down, King Cyrus himself entered the city.

Despite his unpopular attempts at religious reform, many people still supported Nabonidus as king,[33] while a few may have welcomed Cyrus as a liberator. Texts relate how Cyrus marched into the city with the god Marduk as his spiritual companion, and how the people welcomed the Persian king with smiling faces, jubilation, and rejoicing.[34] It is possible that some of the priests of Marduk were pro-Persian since they knew that Cyrus would re-establish the Marduk cult if he was allowed to take control of the city. Among those with good reasons to welcome the Persians were the priests of the god Marduk,[35] and various groups, such as the Jews, taken captive some fifty years earlier during the rule of King Nebuchadnezzar. Some of the residents of Babylon were so opposed to Nabonidus that, after 17 years of his rule, they would have welcomed anyone who could rid them of him and his moon god, even if it was a foreign king. Cyrus must have been aware of the religious conflict between Nabonidus and the followers of Marduk, and surely these difficulties figured in his overall plans for the conquest of Babylon. Cyrus had probably been in contact with the priests of Marduk, whom Nabonidus had greatly offended, and it may have been due to their efforts that the Persian army had relatively few problems entering the city. In addition, it is likely that some supporters inside the city helped to hasten the city's collapse by helping the invaders gain easy access to the city.[36]

Interpreting these events in religious terms, the priests saw Cyrus as an agent of the god Marduk, who used the Persian king to restore the traditional chief deity of Babylon once again to his rightful place in his temple, Esagila. But before giving all the credit to pro-Persian elements within Babylonia, it should be remembered that the Babylonian army had been defeated only a few weeks earlier, and the people may have simply given up hope and let the invaders enter the city. In his first year as king of Babylonia, Cyrus arranged for many captured peoples to be returned to their homelands. He also arranged for the return of the statues of the various gods that Nabonidus had brought to Babylon to protect the city, as well as the restoration of their temples. There is evidence that he improved the material well-being of the inhabitants of Babylon and the surrounding cities, and that his style of rule was less oppressive than that of many previous kings. Cyrus was an intelligent leader who won the goodwill of those he conquered by leaving their religion and political institutions intact, while posing as a liberator instead of a conqueror, and these traits made him very popular throughout the Near East.[37]

For example, after Cyrus entered Babylon, he freed the Jewish exiles taken by the Babylonians, and returned their temple treasures. The liberated Jews hailed him as their "messiah",[38] a term usually reserved for the kings of Israel such as David and Solomon.

Even though the worship of Marduk triumphed at this time, it would die out later and be replaced by other gods. In the centuries that followed, moon worship would continue as an important form of religious expression, gaining in popularity, while the city of Harran continued to be the centre of moon worship for the next thousand years. In the seventh century AD, when the religion of Islam swept over the Near East, all idols and religious icons of the previous civilizations were destroyed or discarded by the followers of Allah as objects of worship; all, that is, except for two ancient vestiges of Mesopotamian celestial beliefs, which became the symbols of Islam – the symbol of a star and the crescent moon, the old symbol of the lunar cult of Sin.

The Persian conquest marks the end of Mesopotamia as an independent political entity. After the Persians no more great kingdoms were created by people native to the Tigris–Euphrates river valley. The age of the great empires of Mesopotamia was over, and no longer would the kings of Assyria and Babylon be able to claim that they were the "kings of the four quarters" or the "kings of the lands".

Part III: Religion, science, and medicine

8 Mythology and religion in Mesopotamia: the story of Gilgamesh and Enkidu

The formation of the *Gilgamesh Epic*

The *Gilgamesh Epic* is one of the oldest and most interesting stories to come out of the ancient world.[1] Centuries older than the Bible, or the works of classical writers such as Homer or Virgil, the Gilgamesh story is an exciting tale peopled with legendary heroes, mythical beasts, and lusty gods and goddesses. The two major characters of the story are Gilgamesh and his friend, Enkidu. The underlying theme is a universal one that connects modern readers with the past and helps them identify with the main theme of the story: the age-old question of death and the fact that all humans must eventually come to terms with their own mortality. The story is probably based on a real, but much embellished person, Gilgamesh, the *en* or ruler of Uruk, who lived around 2700 BC.[2] Although the origins of the *Gilgamesh Epic* are much earlier, the first known copies of the story were not written down until the end of the Ur III period, about 2000 BC. At that time rulers who wrote in Sumerian once again took control of southern Mesopotamia, and it became fashionable for kings to glorify their ancestors and recall their past deeds. King Shulgi claimed that the early gods and kings of the land were his ancestors, and he commanded his scribes to write stories about them and their amazing exploits to enhance his own power and prestige. Shulgi's scribes wrote hymns that claimed Shulgi was the son of Ninsuna and Lugalbanda, the mother and father of Gilgamesh, making

Gilgamesh his own brother.[3] For many years tales and stories about Gilgamesh and Enkidu circulated separately in Mesopotamia. Around 1800 BC, shortly before the time of King Hammurabi, the first versions of the complete epic based on earlier Sumerian Gilgamesh tales were composed. A number of fragments of these original Gilgamesh stories still exist today. The Old Babylonian authors of the first complete versions of the text combined many of the previously existing Gilgamesh episodes into a complete cycle of stories, with a structured storyline and plot, and created an epic: a story of sweeping or national proportions concerning the exploits of a heroic character. Around 1300 BC, the Old Babylonian version of the epic was reworked by a scribe from Uruk, Sin-leqi-unninni; with minor modifications, the story remained the same from then on. The *Gilgamesh Epic* appears to have been widely known in the ancient Near East, and copies of it have been found all over Mesopotamia and as far away as Anatolia, Syria, and Canaan. However, unlike the Egyptian story of Osiris and Isis (see Ch. 12), the *Gilgamesh Epic* was never translated into Greek or Latin, and as a result the story was neglected and eventually forgotten when the civilization of Mesopotamia came to an end. The epic contains about 3000 lines of text and was written on 11 clay tablets.[4] Tablets recovered around Mesopotamia over the past 125 years have produced many incomplete copies of the epic. Most copies were found in the library of King Assurbanipal at Nineveh. Although evidence is lacking, the story may have been sung or accompanied by music,[5] as were many other stories in the ancient world.

Nature against civilization

The story opens by praising Gilgamesh as the "one who has seen the source", meaning he has been granted great knowledge and wisdom. The opening lines of the first tablet extol his many accomplishments, particularly the building of the great circuit wall of the city of Uruk. The story boasts that the mighty wall was built entirely of burnt mud bricks and that the Seven Sages, mythical wise men of Mesopotamia, laid out the plans for Gilgamesh's city. This element is particularly interesting when we recall that the Early Dynastic II period was a time of great urban expansion brought on by an increase in military activities, to the detriment of smaller villages. The city was divided into four sections, including a great garden of palm trees, open spaces of low-lying land, an area for the city's many temples, and the inhabited city proper. At the time of the real King Gilgamesh, Uruk may have had a population of 50 000 people. The first tablet continues by revealing that Gilgamesh was very handsome. He was two-thirds god and one-third human, and thus far superior compared to other humans. Still, he was not quite a god. He was very tall and very strong and he walked around like a wild bull, and no man was his rival. The other men of the city were afraid of him and stood at attention waiting for his orders. He dominated them, never giving them a moment's rest. He had his way with the women of the city and took them from their husbands and lovers to his bed. The citizens of Uruk complained to the gods and asked them to create an equal, or counterpart, to Gilgamesh, someone who would divert his energies elsewhere so the city dwellers could live normal lives in peace.

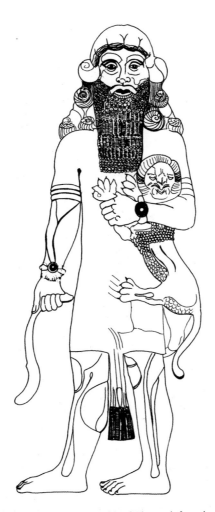

High-relief sculpture, possibly of Gilgamesh, from the palace of Sargon II at Khorsabad (721–705 BC). Height 4.70 m. (Louvre Museum, Paris)

At their request Aruru, the goddess of creation, carefully washed her hands and then pinched off some clay and threw it into the wilderness from whence sprang the wild man Enkidu, the counterpart and future companion of Gilgamesh. Enkidu was the opposite of Gilgamesh. He was more animal than human, a bull man,[6] his body covered with shaggy hair. The hair on his head was "like a woman's", he wore the skins of wild animals for clothing, ate grass like the gazelle, and drank with them and other animals at the watering holes. The wild animals of the steppes were his only friends; he had no contact with people. When local hunters attempted to trap wild animals that destroyed their crops, Enkidu would tear up the traps and free his animal friends. The trappers were afraid when they saw Enkidu. Neither they, nor any of the other farmers or villagers, could hope to catch this wild man of the steppes.

But there was a way to capture Enkidu without resorting to the traps used to catch wild beasts. One particular trapper went to the temple of the sex goddess, Ishtar, found a beautiful young woman named Shamhat, and brought her back to the wilderness. The trapper and Shamhat waited by the watering hole and when Enkidu approached to drink, she removed her clothing and showed him her naked body. Enkidu was quick to respond and sexually engaged the young woman for six days and seven nights.

After he was satiated with her charms, he attempted to return to his animal companions but they ran away from him and he could no longer keep up with them. Sex had made his limbs weak, and his strength was gone. By coming in contact with humans Enkidu had lost his special relationship with the animals and they no longer wished to associate with him. But at the same time his understanding and knowledge had greatly increased. The young woman told him that he was beautiful and now that he knew the pleasures of sex he was like a god. She told him to forget about his former animal companions and come with her to Uruk. In the great city there were festivals and parties every day. In the city of Uruk people dressed in fine clothes, there was always music playing, and young women stood about laughing and teasing the men with their voluptuousness. Shamhat continued her transformation of Enkidu by introducing him to other elements of civilization. She gave him a piece of her garment to clothe himself and taught him how to eat bread and drink beer and wine. She commanded him to rub sweet-smelling oil on his body so that he would not smell like an animal. When he did his body hair disappeared and he turned into a human. The local sheep and cattle herders called on Enkidu to help them protect their flocks from predators, and Enkidu began to hunt down the wolves and lions that attacked the livestock. Enkidu had now come full circle; he no longer ran with the wolf and the lion, but hunted them down. He was no longer part animal, he was fully human.

The first part of the epic is concerned with the characters of Gilgamesh, who was two-thirds god and one-third human, and Enkidu who was mostly animal and only slightly human. Gilgamesh represents civilization and Enkidu represents nature.[7] In their first encounter (see below), Gilgamesh (civilization) defeats Enkidu (nature). Through sex and by consuming human food and drink, wearing clothes, and following the customs of the land, Enkidu becomes civilized. The conflict between civilization and nature forms one of the key elements of the story. The division between the civilization of farmers, who tilled the land and lived in houses grouped together in villages or cities, and herders, who lived in tents and followed a nomadic way of life, impressed the authors of the story. The difference between those who practised a highly developed form of agricultural civilization and those who still lived on its periphery as non-farmers was eminently clear to the people of the Tigris–Euphrates river valley.[8]

The quest for fame

Once Enkidu was "civilized" and had abandoned his animal ways, the woman Shamhat took him to Uruk, the city of Gilgamesh. The people of the city were very impressed by the strong and handsome stranger and realized that he was the equal to Gilgamesh. The first encounter between Enkidu and Gilgamesh involved Gilgamesh's right to have sex with the city's young brides before their husbands on their wedding nights. This meeting quickly turned into a confrontation and they began boxing and fighting with each other. Eventually Gilgamesh won the fight, but declared that he had great respect for the wild man from the steppe. The two men kissed and embraced each other and became lifelong friends.

They soon became bored with the tranquillity of city life. Gilgamesh desired fame. Fame would make a man immortal, because long after his death people would speak of the great man's deeds and accomplishments. Enkidu also desired fame so, after having great weapons forged for them, they set out to kill a terrible monster called Humbaba (or Khuwawa), the guardian of the Sacred Cedar Forest, who lived in a mysterious land located far to the west. Even the great gods feared Humbaba, whose mouth was fire, whose breath was death, and whose roar was so violent it could ravage the land like a flood. When Gilgamesh and Enkidu reached the Sacred Cedar Forest they engaged the monster in a battle and managed to overpower him. At sword point Humbaba begged for mercy and said that he would become Gilgamesh's slave. But Enkidu reminded Gilgamesh of the great fame he would achieve if he killed the monster. He convinced him to slay Humbaba quickly, before the gods found out what they intended to do and became angry with them. Before his death Humbaba uttered a curse against Enkidu and was then dispatched by the two men.

Afterwards they fashioned a raft of cedar trees from the Sacred Cedar Forest and floated down the Euphrates River on it, holding up the head of Humbaba for all to see. When they reached Uruk they were hailed as heroes. Gilgamesh put on his finest robe and crown and marched through the streets of the city. He was now so famous and attractive that the goddess Ishtar proposed marriage to Gilgamesh. She told him that in addition to the pleasures of the flesh that he was sure to enjoy with her, she would also make him very rich. She sweetened her marriage proposal by offering him a beautiful chariot of lapis lazuli and gold, harnessed to four powerful mountain mules. But Gilgamesh refused her proposal and reminded her of the way she had treated her previous husbands and lovers. For example, after she had her way with him, she had banished to the underworld the young shepherd Dumuzi, the lover of her youth; after her affair with a small bird she broke its wing, so that it constantly cried out *kapi, kapi*, "my wing, my wing"; after she seduced the mighty lion she caused hunters to dig deep pits for it so they could catch the great beast; and after she loved the horse she ordained for him the whip and the lash and made him run great distances carrying his human riders. Gilgamesh continued by reminding her that after she seduced the shepherd Ishullanu, who made great sacrifices to her every day, she turned him into a wolf so his fellow shepherds were on the lookout for him and even his own dogs chased after him. Gilgamesh continued naming the lovers and husbands mistreated by Ishtar. Not wishing to be subjected to the same fate, Gilgamesh scorned Ishtar and refused to marry her.

Ishtar was furious. No one had ever refused her before. She was a goddess and not accustomed to rejection. To get revenge on Gilgamesh she went up into the highest heavens and asked her father, Anu (the sky god), to give her a creature called the "Bull of Heaven", a starry monster represented in the heavens by the constellation Taurus, the bull. Ishtar brought the monster down out of the sky and took it to Uruk to kill Gilgamesh. The Bull of Heaven was so powerful that one snort from his nose blasted a huge hole into the ground and blew 100 valiant men into it. A second snort ripped an even larger hole into the ground, and 200 more men fell in. Faced with such a powerful creature, Gilgamesh and Enkidu were in big trouble. However, the two heroes managed to grapple with the bull and, while the former wild man controlled it by twisting its tail, Gilgamesh plunged his sword into the beast's neck and killed it. Then they ripped out its heart and presented it to the sun god, Shamash, as an offering. This act of bravado shocked and astounded Ishtar and she went up on the great walls of Uruk and began moaning and wailing at the loss of the Bull of Heaven. Then she uttered a mighty curse against Gilgamesh. When Enkidu heard the curse he ripped off the bull's hindquarters and flung it in Ishtar's face.[9] At the sight of the beast's hindquarters Ishtar assembled all the women from her temple, and they began mourning and weeping over the hindquarters of the Bull of Heaven.

Meanwhile, Enkidu and Gilgamesh washed the blood of the bull from their hands in the Euphrates River and marched triumphantly through the streets, where they called out to the great crowd of people assembled there, "Who is the bravest of all the men of Uruk?" To which the multitude answered, "Gilgamesh is the bravest of all the men." They continued their march through the city and the people of Uruk sang the praises of Gilgamesh over and over again. Then the heroes retired to the palace of Gilgamesh for a great victory celebration.

Later that night Enkidu had a terrible dream in which he saw his own death. Because of their mighty deeds, he and Gilgamesh had indeed attained great fame and their names would be repeated in stories and legends long after their deaths. But in an attempt to attain immortality through fame they had committed brazen deeds that had violated the accepted limits of human behaviour. The killing of Humbaba and the Bull of Heaven angered the gods, who decreed that

one of the two, Enkidu, would have to pay for such audacious acts. Shortly thereafter Enkidu fell ill and began to die. As his sickness overtook him he cursed the trapper and the woman Shamhat, who had tricked him and brought him out of his pristine and natural state in the wilderness and led him into the world of humans, whose actions were judged by the gods. He asked the sun god Shamash to impoverish the trapper, causing him to be hungry and destitute. For Shamhat,

he asked that she live the life of a lowly prostitute, always standing in the shadows of the city wall looking for customers. He beseeched the sun god to cause her to suffer greatly, for her drunk and sober customers to slap her cheek, and for the drunk to vomit on her clothing. He asked that she reject her own children, and that she dwell in the rubbish dumps of Uruk. But the sun god did not carry out Enkidu's curses; instead he argued that Enkidu should not

Solar disc representing the sun god Shamash shown suspended on an altar in front of the Babylonian king, Nabû-apla-iddina (c. 870 BC). The disc commemorates the restoration of the Temple of Shamash in the city of Sippar.

curse the trapper and Shamhat because, thanks to them, he was able to enjoy the fruits of civilization. Because of them he knew the joys of sex, the food and wine of kings, beautiful clothes, and the friendship of the great Gilgamesh. After hearing the sun god's defence of the trapper and Shamhat, Enkidu realized his errors and retracted his curses, and blessed the two who had brought him to civilization.

Before Enkidu died he had another dream, which enabled him to glimpse the underworld; a place called *kurnugia*, "the land of no return", the place where everyone went when they died. In a number of modern religions there are two distinct places to which a deceased person can go after death: a pleasant place, heaven, and a terrible place of suffering and torture, hell. In Mesopotamia there were no such options for the deceased; everyone went to the same place regardless of their position in society, or how they had behaved. According to Enkidu's dream the realm of the dead was not a very pleasant place to go, and life on earth was happy and gay by comparison. *Kurnugia*, Enkidu recounted, was a place bereft of light from which there was no escape. In *kurnugia* the dead ate clay and drank filthy water, everyone wore garments made of feathers like birds, and dwelt in darkness. All people, no matter what rank they had attained in life, were destined to go to *kurnugia* when they died. In the land of no return Enkidu saw great kings waiting on the tables of the gods, humbly serving them cooked meats and sweets and pouring them water. Although *kurnugia* was dark and dreary and certainly not a pleasant place to be, it was nevertheless unlike the later New Testament dwelling places of the dead and it was certainly not hell, where the damned endured all manner of eternal pain and suffering. In *kurnugia* the dead were in a kind of dark and dusty limbo, as if they were "put on hold" for eternity.

When Enkidu first entered the underworld in his dream he saw in one corner a pile of discarded crowns left there by former kings who, like the lowliest paupers of Uruk, ended up in *kurnugia* when their lives ended. The Mesopotamian underworld was in sharp contrast to the widely accepted Egyptian vision of the realm of the dead (see Chs 11 and 12), which reflected the Egyptian desire to see life on earth continued after death, but without the nagging problems normally associated with human existence. In most representations of Egyptian afterlife there was no sickness, and no want. Egyptian tomb paintings depict the tomb owner and his family enjoying a leisurely afterlife dressed in fine clothing and surrounded by an abundance of food and servants. They were usually depicted enjoying a carefree afterlife, much as a modern person might envision an early and well-planned retirement. The Egyptian afterlife is more reminiscent of a pleasant beach holiday in the Caribbean than any kind of frightening post-mortem existence. All eschatological beliefs evolve over the centuries, and this was certainly true in Mesopotamia. For this reason we occasionally read about glimpses of the Mesopotamian afterlife that are not quite as negative as the ones presented here. But in general, throughout three millennia of Mesopotamian civilization, a negative and pessimistic view of the underworld prevailed in the minds of the people who lived in the Tigris–Euphrates river valley.

The death of Enkidu came as a great shock to Gilgamesh. He was stricken with grief and held his dead companion in his arms for seven days and seven nights, refusing to let go of him until maggots began to fall from his face. In his grief Gilgamesh tore out his hair and threw off his fine robes. Finally, he was forced to accept the reality of his friend's death. Enkidu was given a great funeral and all the people of the city of Uruk mourned his passing. He was mourned as well by his old friends, the animals. Bears, panthers, tigers, wild bulls, water buffalo, ibex, lions, and all the many creatures from the wilderness mourned the death of Enkidu. After his funeral Gilgamesh had his artisans make a great statue of gold, copper, and lapis lazuli in his friend's memory.

With the death of Enkidu, Gilgamesh began to question his own immortality, saying, "Will I not die? Am I not a mortal like Enkidu?" No longer was it evident to Gilgamesh that the fame the two heroes had established for themselves would be sufficient to calm his heart and rid him of his fear of death. Even if unborn generations would tell of the mighty deeds of Gilgamesh and Enkidu, this was no longer enough to satisfy his heart. Like the gods, he wanted real immortality: Gilgamesh wanted to live for ever.

The quest for immortality

Determined not to meet the same fate as Enkidu, Gilgamesh began his quest for eternal life. There were only two people who had ever gained eternal life: a man named Utnapishtim and his wife. They lived in a distant place called "the source of the rivers", located at the end of the earth. To get there Gilgamesh had to travel to Mount Mashu, a mountain so high that it reached up to the celestial vault and guarded the place where the sun god emerged from beneath the earth every day. When he reached the foot of the mountain he encountered the Scorpion people, who did not want to let Gilgamesh pass to Mount Mashu. As with others before him, they tried to discourage Gilgamesh in his quest, but he convinced them to let him pass so he could continue his journey. From Mount Mashu he crossed into a world of darkness, the path that the sun took when it set at night and travelled below the flat disc of the earth through the underworld. Under the earth it was so dark that Gilgamesh could see nothing. He travelled for many days in complete blackness, groping along somewhere under the surface of the earth. Finally he emerged into the light of day once again and found himself in a magical kingdom called the "Jewelled Garden". In this garden trees were made of precious stones, their foliage was of emeralds and lapis lazuli, and they bore carnelian as fruit. Passing through the Jewelled Garden, Gilgamesh encountered a most interesting woman named Siduri, a tavern keeper who lived far from civilization, somewhere near the end of the earth.

Carpe diem

Siduri is one of the most important characters in the Gilgamesh story. It is Siduri who explains the Mesopotamian philosophy of life and death to Gilgamesh, and her message gives us much insight into how the people of Mesopotamia viewed themselves and their relationship to the gods and the universe. Siduri asks Gilgamesh, "Why are you wandering about so?" She explains that Gilgamesh will never find the eternal life he is seeking because, "When the gods created people they allotted death to them and eternal life they held back in their own hands". She advises Gilgamesh to eat and drink his fill and be happy every day and every night, and make every day a day of rejoicing. Instead of worrying about his fate at death Gilgamesh should keep his body washed, wear clean clothes, enjoy dancing, enjoy sex with his wife, and attend to the welfare of his children. Taking care of the basics, says Siduri, is the lot of mankind.

This simple philosophy represents the essential pragmatism and down-to-earth approach to life of the people of Mesopotamia: live your life today to the fullest and be happy with it. Period. This simple *carpe diem* (Latin meaning "seize the day") outlook contains no complicated philosophical arguments or concepts concerning human nature, but only a few thoughts about how to get through life while at the same time getting something out of it. At this point the story is essentially over; Gilgamesh might as well go back home to Uruk and pick up the pieces of his life. But he refuses to give up his quest for eternal life. He decides to make one more attempt to find immortality, and continues his search for Utnapishtim[10] and his wife.

The *Abubu*, or the great flood

In the mythical past, humans and gods lived together in cities. The humans were noisy and boisterous, crashing about making wars, haggling in the marketplaces, and living in a loud and disturbing manner that prevented the gods from getting any rest. Enlil, the most powerful of all the gods, decided to exterminate the humans by sending a great flood that would drown them all and put an end to their noisy behaviour. However, the god of wisdom, Ea, warned Utnapishtim, one of the citizens of the city of Shuruppak, of the impending disaster. Ea told him to tear down his house, build a great ship, and bring his family and a few animals with him in order to survive the flood.[11] The vessel he was commanded to build was not really a boat or ship, but more like a huge cube that measured about 60 m on each side. It has been suggested that the cubic form may have represented some kind of theological allusion to the ziggurat of Shuruppak.[12] According to the story, Utnapishtim gathered about him all of the craftsmen necessary for the task and built the structure. When the huge craft was finished a celebration was held for his family and all the workers. He then loaded the ship with his farm animals, his family, and the craftsmen, and they waited inside for the great flood to begin.

The flood began when Nergal, the god of the underworld, pulled out the masts that supported the heavens above the earth, and caused the water-laden heavens to fall from the sky. More water was released when Ninurta, the god of war, caused the canals and dykes to overflow. Then, the gods of the assembly lifted up their lightning torches, illuminating the earth and the skies, and the land was shattered "like a broken pot". The story recounts how everyone on land was caught in the torrents of water and perished. The force of the flood storm was so powerful that even the gods themselves fled into the upper reaches of the sky, and cowered like frightened dogs as the storm raged on. As the noisy human beings perished the gods realized the seriousness of their mistake and were sorry for what they had done. Feeling great remorse, they wept together. After seven days and nights the flood stopped and all was quiet. Utnapishtim looked out from his boat and saw that all of humankind "had turned to clay".

According to the story, as the waters subsided the boat came to rest on Mount Nimush, somewhere in the Zagros mountains. The boat rested on the mountain for seven days before Utnapishtim sent out a dove to test the land and determine if it was suitably dry to descend from the boat. But finding no place to land the dove came back. Next he sent out a swallow, but the swallow also returned to him. Finally, Utnapishtim released a raven, which found food and did not return. At this point he released all the animals and offered a sacrifice to the gods. When the gods smelled the sweet savour of burning animal flesh "they gathered over it like flies", because they were very hungry. Originally human beings had been created to feed the gods, freeing them from work, so that they could enjoy a life of leisure and not have to toil for their food. When the gods killed all the people in the great flood, their food offerings stopped. The gods were glad that a few people had survived the great catastrophe, since they still had human servants who could once again make food sacrifices to them.

It is obvious that there are a number of similarities between the story of the great flood in the *Gilgamesh Epic*, and the story of Noah[13] and the Ark found in the Bible in the Book of Genesis. Both stories state that the divine powers were unhappy with the behaviour of human beings, and wanted to destroy them. In each story one man and his family were commanded to construct a large vessel of wood that could withstand the coming deluge. According to their descriptions, neither the biblical boat (ark) of Noah, nor the boat of the *Gilgamesh Epic* appear to have been very seaworthy, particularly when compared to other ancient sailing craft. In the Noah story it rained for 40 days and 40 nights, while in the Gilgamesh story the flood lasted seven days and nights. Both boats land in mountainous regions: Noah's in the mountains of Ararat (Urartu), and Utnapishtim's on Mount Nimush. Both Noah and Utnapishtim made sacrifices after leaving their respective vessels. One of the most interesting points of comparison between the two stories is the bird episodes. Utnapishtim sent out a dove, a swallow, and a raven, in that order, before descending from his ship. Noah first sent a raven, which did not return to the ark. Then, at seven-day intervals, he sent out three doves before determining that the post-diluvian conditions were hospitable enough to descend from the ark. Scholars have known for some time that many of the stories in the Old Testament of the Bible were borrowed from, or in some way influenced by, non-biblical sources, and the flood story from the *Gilgamesh Epic* is a clear example of this. This is not to say that the Old Testament writers copied the flood story from the epic word for word. But the *Gilgamesh Epic* was widely known in the ancient Near East and parts of it were integrated into the Old Testament some time during the first millennium BC

Because they survived the great flood, Utnapishtim and his wife were ordered to kneel down in front of the great god Enlil, whereupon he touched their foreheads and bestowed upon them eternal life. From that time on they were allowed to dwell far away at "the source of the rivers". It was there that Gilgamesh encountered them and said that he, too, wanted immortality. But Utnapishtim explained that he was not a god, and could not make Gilgamesh immortal. Gilgamesh had no choice but to give up his quest and return home. Just as the dejected Gilgamesh was casting off in his boat for his return voyage to Mesopotamia, Utnapishtim's wife pleaded with her husband to give Gilgamesh something for his effort, so his search would not have been in vain. So it was that Utnapishtim told Gilgamesh of a magical plant at the bottom of the sea that he could

eat when he was old, and it would restore him to youth once again.[14] So Gilgamesh went to the sea, plunged down into the waters and retrieved the plant. At last he had something to show for his effort. He placed the magic plant in his pouch and began the long, dusty walk back towards the city of Uruk. On the way home Gilgamesh stopped to bathe in the cool waters of a spring. He removed his pouch and clothing, and while he was splashing about in the water a serpent smelled the fragrance of the plant, stole the plant from the pouch, and swallowed it. Too late, Gilgamesh discovered the theft, and as the serpent slithered away Gilgamesh saw it slough off its old skin and become young once again.

Now Gilgamesh had nothing from his quest. Or did he? Even though the chance to obtain immortality had slipped away from him, he had gained much valuable experience and knowledge about the world. Now he was older and wiser and had been forced to come to terms with life and death. His quest for immortality through fame had backfired. He may have performed great and notable deeds, but he also angered the gods and lost his friend in the process. His quest for true immortality, like that of the gods, was an even more daring and audacious undertaking; it defied human nature itself. To be human is to be mortal: to have a beginning and an end to our time on earth. Any attempt to modify things only offends the gods and brings down their wrath. In the end Gilgamesh accepted the finite limits of his life and turned his energies to the lasting things he could do in his role as the king of Uruk. This is symbolized in the story by Gilgamesh's greatest accomplishment – the massive and enduring wall of Uruk, 8 m high and 9 km long – to which the story returns. In the final lines, Gilgamesh is advised to go up on the wall of the mighty city, to examine its foundations, and inspect its brickwork. Even the core of the wall was made of burned brick; it was a marvel of construction technique and engineering. After all, the story asks, "Did not the seven sages of old lay its foundations?"

9 Science and technology: astronomy and medicine in Mesopotamia and Egypt

PART I: ASTRONOMY

While Egypt has many spectacular stone monuments and beautiful tomb paintings that still dazzle the modern viewer, Mesopotamia cannot boast the same spectacular material remains. Mesopotamian civilization did indeed produce many fine works of art and architecture, but the statues and paintings, and the beautiful glazed-brick ziggurats that once dotted the countryside are now only dusty ruins. However, the Mesopotamians excelled in the realm of celestial knowledge, and although a number of ancient civilizations, such as China,[1] also had an interest in astronomy, Mesopotamia was the birthplace of scientific astronomy, the oldest of all the sciences, as well as astrology, one of humanity's oldest religious beliefs. Even though the validity of astrology has been rejected by the Western scientific community in recent centuries, one of the most important vestiges of ancient Near East civilization that still survives in the modern world can be found in any daily newspaper: the horoscope. Astrology has changed over the past three millennia, but what is known today as "astrology" would have been recognizable to an educated person living in Babylonia or Assyria hundreds of years before the time of Jesus or Julius Caesar. The basis of much of astrology was established some 2500 years ago, and the earliest astrological elements can be traced as far back as the second millennium BC.

Celestial divination

The word divination comes from the Latin *divinatio* and means "to guess". In English, divination is often referred to as "fortune-telling". Divination offers some revealing insights into the thoughts of ancient Mesopotamians and it represents one of the high points of intellectual development in the ancient Near East.[2] In Mesopotamia it was believed that the gods left signs in nature as a way of warning their human subjects about what they were planning to do in the future. By analysing flights of birds, or by studying the patterns of drops of oil poured into water, clues concerning the future behaviour of the gods could be obtained.[3] One of the most popular ways of divining the future was by examining the livers and intestines of sacrificial sheep (see illustration opposite). The *barú*, a priest who specialized in divination, would remove and examine the liver of a sheep, and attempt to find signs concerning the future by looking for abnormalities on it. Over many centuries fortune-tellers developed a specialized terminology to refer to all the important parts of the sacrificial animal, and recorded and stored thousands of omen texts concerning their divinatory investigations in temple libraries throughout Mesopotamia.[4] The divination priests were not interested in any modern scientific reasons why the sacrificial animal's liver or intestines were abnormal or sick, or why one part was swollen or discoloured or in the wrong location. Instead, they believed that such things were

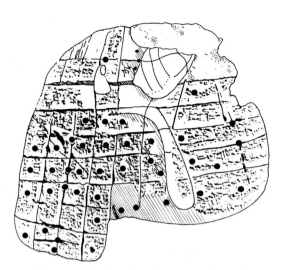

Model of a sheep's liver inscribed with omens and magical formulae for use by diviners, Last Babylonian Dynasty. Clay, 8 cm × 13 cm. (British Museum)

placed on the animal's internal organs by the gods to provide signs for them so that they could know the future and perform the proper religious rituals to avoid any unwanted consequences.

There were a number of things that divination priests could observe and interpret. The observation of thunder and lightning, clouds, flights of birds, bright spots on the lungs of a sacrificial sheep, or the birth of malformed animals, such as a two-headed lamb with eight legs, were unexpected signs from the gods that were charged with meaning. There was one other form of divination that was known by the First Dynasty of Babylon, around the 18th century BC, and became widespread by the beginning of the first millennium BC: celestial divination – looking at the heavens for signs from the gods.[5] If sheep entrails, storm clouds, and deformed animals contained clues about the future, then surely the stars must contain their share of insights into the future as well. Celestial divination had a long and interesting history in

Mesopotamia, and somehow (this remains unclear to Assyriologists) it developed into an early form of astrology. Astrology may be defined as the pseudo-science that pretends to enable people to understand the influences of the sun, moon, and stars on earthly affairs and predict future events.[6] Two types of astrology developed in Mesopotamia: an early form called omen astrology that was practised from about 1800 BC, and a later, more sophisticated form called horoscopic astrology that developed after 500 BC.[7]

Omen astrology: writing in the heavens

Only a few celestial observation texts are known from the beginning of the second millennium BC. One of the oldest divinatory texts based on celestial observations comes from the Old Babylonian period and explains that if the north wind blows across the face of the sky before the new moon then "the wheat will grow abundantly". Or, if the lunar calendar does not begin on the first day of the month because of a miscalculation then what the texts refer to as "shaking" (some form of epilepsy) will descend upon the land.[8] The structure of this passage adheres to the standard formula "if such and such a thing is seen in nature, then such and such a thing will happen in the future". All divination texts, whether they were used to observe the livers of sheep, interpret dreams, or look at the heavens, used the same formula. First, something strange or extraordinary, such as an eclipse or the birth of a deformed animal, shocked the observer and warned of impending danger. After observing such an event the diviner would consult one of the lists of omens to determine its meaning. Collections of omens (the word is Latin for "warning") served as reference works for diviners attempting to understand what they had observed and which predictions they should make. The *Enuma Anu Enlil* was the major celestial divination collection; it contained over 7000 omens, and served

as the principal reference work used by celestial fortune-tellers.

Even though diviners made predictions based on celestial objects and phenomena, they were not, in the strictest sense of the word, astrologers. In fact, there was no word in Akkadian to designate either "astrologer" or "astronomer". Instead, those who practised celestial fortune-telling were designated "scribes of the *Enuma Anu Enlil*", meaning scribes of celestial divination omens. Omen astrology was not concerned with the lives of individuals, but with the general welfare of the king, the land, and its people. Wars, plagues, and the state of the harvest were the primary concerns of omen astrologers.[9]

In the Late Assyrian period, after 750 BC, omen astrology was practised by a select group of men who received special training for the task and worked for the king.[10] The Assyrians established a large and well-organized network of celestial observation posts that operated in about a dozen cities in Assyria and Babylonia (see map of centres of celestial observation and divination, overleaf). Each observation post had a team of ten men who "kept watch" for eclipses, halos around the moon, conjunctions of planets, meteorites, and so on. Once something important was seen, celestial observers searched through the *Enuma Anu Enlil* to find similar occurrences in the past and the omens that accompanied them. This information was then recorded on a small clay tablet and sent to the capital, where court scholars and divination specialists informed the king of the omens and discussed their meanings with him. The men who made the observations were highly educated *ummanu* (masters) of the divinatory discipline. By today's standards they would be considered academics, the equivalent of research scientists or university professors.

For their work they were paid a few measures of silver a year, and given a plot of land, a few servants, and some farm animals. Practising the diviner's art was not always easy and the masters sometimes criticized each other for making bad observations or faulty interpretations. One celestial diviner writes to the king that an omen sent by one of his colleagues was "nonsense" and that the king should ignore it.[11] There appears to have been fierce competition between celestial diviners, since the one who could impress the king with the most accurate predictions would rise to a position of power and influence. Even though omen astrologers did not live in the palace complex of the Assyrian king, they were, nevertheless, near the centre of political power and had great influence on the king and the decisions he took.[12]

Centres of celestial observation and divination in the ancient Near East from the Old Babylonian period to the Neo-Babylonian period (1800–539 BC).

The substitute king ritual

The Assyrian king had numerous religious duties and functions that he had to fulfil as the representative of the people before the gods. If something terrible was predicted by the celestial diviners, the king was required to make special sacrifices or prayers to avoid evil consequences for the land. An eclipse of the moon could be very dangerous for the king and the nation. In order to avoid the consequences of an evil eclipse the king was sometimes temporarily removed from the throne and replaced by a substitute until the danger had passed.[13] This was called the *shar puhi* (substitute king ritual), and in it the legitimate king and a temporary substitute king exchanged roles. The substitute was generally someone who was expendable, a prisoner of war, a criminal, or a political enemy of the king. Once the real king had been removed from the throne he lost his kingly status, was referred to as a "peasant", and withdrew from his official duties for a period of 3–100 days.

The substitute king was dressed in the king's robes, provided with a queen, and seated on the throne. Various measures were taken once the substitute was on the throne to make certain that all the evil effects of the eclipse would fall on him and his queen. This included writing down the eclipse omen and making sure it was recited by the substitute. In some cases the omen tablet was even attached to the hem of his robe, to ensure that the evil that was originally destined for the true king was directed towards the substitute. When it was considered that the danger was past, the substitute and his queen were killed, taking with them the evil effects of the eclipse. Afterwards, the real king was returned to the throne.

For a long time the substitute king ritual had to be performed after an eclipse had taken place, since the celestial diviners did not know how to determine when lunar eclipses would occur. But by the eighth century BC, celestial diviners had devised arithmetical schemes that enabled them to know the months when an eclipse was possible, and thus predict lunar, but not solar, eclipses. Such knowledge would have greatly increased the prestige of a celestial diviner, who could warn the king and have him removed from the throne before the eclipse took place.[14]

The lunar calendar

Throughout its long history the principal Mesopotamian calendar was based on the moon. There are three good reasons for choosing the moon. First, the moon is easily visible in the night sky and its light is much gentler to look upon than that of the sun. Secondly, the moon changes its shape every day, always expanding or contracting. With a little practice anyone can determine what day of the month it is simply by looking up into the night sky. Thirdly, after each lunar cycle the moon disappears for one or two days. This means that there is a clear break between each lunar period when the moon is absent from the sky and only the stars and planets are visible.

In Mesopotamia the calendar was based on 12 lunar periods (moons), or months. Even though the lunar calendar is very convenient to use, it has several serious shortcomings, which puzzled calendar-makers and celestial observers for centuries. The first of these is that the lunar month can vary in length, and it is difficult to determine when it will be 29 or 30 days long. Secondly, 12 lunar months make a year of only 354 days, 11 days short of the solar year, which is slightly less than 365¼ days long. Since the solar year and the lunar year are not the same length, after three years a lunar calendar would have been more than one month ahead of the solar year. If this discrepancy were to be allowed to continue, the seasons and the agricultural cycle of ploughing, sowing, and harvesting would be noticeably behind that of the lunar calendar. Such a shifting calendar was not very practical, and some kind of system had to be developed to synchronize these two cycles and bring

them into harmony. The problem was overcome by adding an extra month to the calendar every three years. The extra months were called the second *Ululu* or a second *Adaru* depending on what time of the year they were added to the calendar. In the first millennium BC a more refined system was developed in which seven intercalary lunar months were added over a period of 19 solar years.[15]

In the Babylonian calendar days were not named (Monday, Tuesday, Wednesday, etc.); instead, each day was numbered. There was no designation for week, and nor were there any calendrical units longer than one year.

Understanding the lunar month

To be practical, a month must contain a whole number of days, and each day must begin and end at the same time. Since the lunar month can be either 29 or 30 days in length, the major problem for Mesopotamian calendar-makers was determining when months would begin and end. The only way to know when the new month began was to observe the moon's first crescent after its monthly period of invisibility. In most civilizations in the Mediterranean and ancient Near East, with the exception of Egypt, the first day of the month began in the evening with the appearance of the thin lunar crescent, as it became visible in the west shortly after sunset. Locating the moon on the first day of the month was not always easy. At first visibility the moon shows a thin crescent that is often close to the horizon, where clouds, dust storms, and fog can obscure the sky, making it difficult, or impossible, to see.[16] Because the Mesopotamian calendar was based on the observation of the first lunar crescent, someone had to go out and look for the moon and verify that it was actually visible. Observing the lunar crescent and establishing the first day of the month was of critical importance in maintaining the calendar. It was for this reason, as well as

Observing the first lunar crescent on the western horizon just after sunset permitted celestial observers to determine the first day of the month.

divination, that celestial diviners watched the skies for a glimpse of the slim lunar crescent to verify that the new month had indeed begun. If the crescent moon was seen at the right time it was a good omen, but if they missed seeing it on the first day, the calendar would be off, causing confusion for the country's religious and commercial activities. Numerous astrological reports written to the Assyrian court mention with joy that the crescent moon was seen on the first day of the month, while others mention that the moon was not seen on the first day, an unlucky situation.[17]

The ideal month

The moon was not just a calendrical object; it was also a major deity who was worshipped and venerated. The name of the moon, Sin, was written with the number 30; and the ideal month also contained 30 days. Along with the irregular lunar calendar the people of Mesopotamia created another calendar that was not based on any celestial objects such as the sun or the moon. This "ideal calendar" contained 12 months of 30 days each, thus corresponding to the mystical number of the moon, while at the same time avoiding the inability to understand the complexities of lunar motion. This calendar did away with the inconsistencies that hindered and confused the business community, but it never replaced the lunar calendar as the principal time-keeping system of Mesopotamia. After many centuries of use, Mesopotamian calendar-makers were able to understand lunar motion and created a calendar that could be synchronized with the seasons. Still, their calendar was always difficult to keep in step with the seasons and the solar year, and it remained cumbersome and erratic for much of their history.

Naming the constellations

The rising and setting of constellations at different times of the year may have helped farmers to determine the best time to plant their crops as far back as the sixth millennium BC, and perhaps even earlier. Star formations such as Leo, represented by a lion, or Taurus in the form of a bull (see Ch. 8), were known by the same animal shapes and names in the third millennium BC as they are today. It is indicative of the importance of the celestial legacy of ancient Mesopotamia that not a single constellation name from ancient Egypt survives on modern star charts, but numerous star formations can be traced back to their Mesopotamian origins.[18] Although there are good reasons to believe that they named a number of individual stars and constellations, Egyptologists are able to identify only a handful of star formations from original Egyptian sources.[19] In comparison, the night sky is dotted with numerous star formations whose original forms, names, and even their religious or mythological meanings, were assigned to them by star-watchers along the Tigris and Euphrates Rivers thousands of years ago.[20] We know that sky-watchers in ancient Egypt also had a keen interest in watching and naming the stars and planets, and used them for time-keeping, and calendrical and religious purposes. But what caused the people of Mesopotamia to eventually develop astrology and astronomy?

The zodiac and astrology

Throughout the more than 1000-year period that omen astrology was practised in Mesopotamia, celestial diviners did not identify the zodiac, the band of 12 zones represented by constellations that form the background of stars through which the planets, the sun, and the moon appear to move. The zodiac is a major element in the kind of astrology that is practised today, and includes astrological signs such as Aries, Taurus, Gemini, and so on. The zodiac (which is Greek meaning "little animals") was first used for divination purposes in Mesopotamia sometime after 500 BC, along with a form of astrology that emphasized the individual instead of the king and national affairs.[21] A small number of basic and somewhat primitive horoscopes recorded on clay tablets have been found in Mesopotamia. The earliest of these can be dated to 29 April 409 BC.[22] This text is similar to a modern horoscope in a number of ways. It gives the time of birth of the individual, and the location of the planets and the moon in the constellations of the zodiac. It concludes by indicating to the newborn infant that "things will be good for you": an optimistic, if not very detailed prediction for the infant's start in life.

Horoscopic astrology

Fully developed "horoscopic astrology" did not exist until ideas about celestial divination from Mesopotamia were influenced by Greek philosophical ideas in the fourth century BC.[23] True horoscopic astrology is actually a mixture of Assyro-Babylonian astrology and a number of Greek philosophical concepts.[24] The Greeks thought that the heavenly spheres above and the earth below interacted with each other creating a cause-and-effect relationship. This is not to say that all Greek philosophers knew about, or believed in, astrology, but certain ideas they expressed about the nature of the universe were necessary before horoscopic astrology could fully develop. In this new type of astrology there were a number of subtle changes and refinements. The major difference between Mesopotamian astrology and later Greek astrology was that the stars and planets no longer gave signs or warnings about future events; instead, they actually caused them to take place.[25] It is this new concept of cause and effect that so dramatically separates the old Near Eastern astrology from the astrology of the Greeks. This new form of "astral determinism" eventually made its way west, where it was widely practised in Rome, and later in Christian

Ancient constellations. Details from two tablets from Uruk (third century BC). Top left: Pleiades; centre: man in the moon; right: Taurus. Bottom: Leo and Hydra.

Europe. It also spread eastwards to India, where it had a profound influence on the development of astronomy and astrology on the Indian subcontinent.[26]

Babylonian astronomy

While astrology attempts to understand the supposed influence of heavenly objects on human behaviour, astronomy is the scientific study and measurement of celestial objects and phenomena. In the ancient Near East, no clear distinction was made between the two. The worshipping of sky gods, the naming of constellations, and the ability to distinguish the planets from fixed stars, does not constitute scientific astronomy. Astronomy may be defined as "that science which provides a mathematical description of the motion and behaviour of celestial objects". Because astronomy provides mathematical models for determining the motion of celestial objects, astronomers can predict where they will be located at any time without recourse to observation. This means that by using a mathematical formula, an astronomer can determine the location of celestial objects even on cloudy nights when the skies are covered, or during daylight hours when only the sun is visible.

The application of scientific astronomy is evident in the solution to the problem of the length of the month, and predicting when the new crescent moon would appear. Sometime after 500 BC, the Babylonians devised arithmetical schemes that calculated the motion of the sun, the moon, the planets, and the constellations, and recorded them on tables that could be consulted by astronomers. This enabled them to accurately determine the length of the month, predict lunar eclipses, and find any planet in any zodiacal constellation in the heavens. After a centuries-long tradition of celestial observation in the Tigris–Euphrates river valley, scientific astronomy and a sophisticated form of zodiacal astrology appeared.

The reasons why these two developed are not entirely clear, but one thing seems certain: Babylonian mathematical astronomy is the cornerstone of all other forms of modern scientific enquiry, and is one of the most important achievements of Mesopotamian civilization.[27]

Astronomy and astrology in Egypt

Although many popular books over the past century have repeatedly claimed that the Egyptians possessed a highly developed astronomy and astrology, these claims are incorrect. Compared to Mesopotamian civilization, Egyptian accomplishments in the area of celestial knowledge were important, but somewhat less impressive.[28] Nevertheless, they did make use of their observational knowledge of astronomy during the construction of the pyramids (see Ch. 11) to align the four sides of these great burial structures on true or celestial north, and the cardinal points of the compass. To accomplish this feat, pyramid builders used the northern, or circumpolar, stars to determine the location of the celestial north pole.[29] They did this centuries before the invention of the magnetic compass, which, in any case, would have been less accurate than the measurements made by the pyramid builders. However, historians of science have tended to view this technique as being less sophisticated than other forms of astronomical knowledge, arguing that using the stars to determine true north required only a familiarity with the circular movement of the stars in the northern portions of the heavens, and not a highly developed knowledge of mathematics nor any advanced theories of stellar motion. What was required was to note the rising point of one of the northern stars and its subsequent setting point some time later. Bisecting the angle between the rising and setting points yields celestial, or true north. Wooden instruments called a *bay* and a *merqet*, that could have been used for this purpose

have been found.[30] Although many temples were dedicated to celestial deities in Assyria and Babylonia, there is no clear evidence that celestial objects were ever used, as they were in Egypt, to orient structures towards true north or any of the other cardinal directions.

Pyramid shafts

The claim that some of the shafts in the Khufu Pyramid (see Ch. 11) were used as "tunnels" that were aimed at the polar star so that the shape and angles of the structure could be maintained by the builders during construction is likewise unsubstantiated by the evidence.[31] Since the 19th century one of the most widely believed legends about the pyramids has been that the star Alpha Draconis (Thuban) was used by Egyptian architects to align the pyramids on true celestial north. It was imagined that architects would position themselves at the bottom of the descending passage, deep in the Khufu Pyramid, and when looking up they could see the star Thuban and use it as a kind of celestial reference point to help them control the shape of the pyramid structure. But research using sophisticated computer programs that can recreate the positions of the stars in the sky at the time the pyramids were built, has shown that the descending passage pointed to no important star that could have been used for alignment purposes.[32]

The pyramids were built with great precision. Casing stones were fitted tightly together with great care, and the exterior angles were highly accurate. But fitting stones together properly and chiselling them to smooth and precise angles has more to do with good planning by the architects and correct deployment of skilful stonemasons than it does with the stars. There can be little doubt that circumpolar stars were used to orient the pyramids towards true north, but all other talk of alignments is open to question or simply unfounded. Some over-eager pyramid enthusiasts still

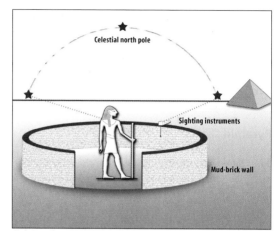

Sighting the rising and setting points of a star on the horizon using a low wall and the *merqet* and *bay* instruments to determine true celestial north.

insist that these great stone structures were store-houses of astrological and astronomical knowledge. However, royal pyramid building ended in Egypt around 1800 BC, more than 1000 years before the zodiac was developed, and long before the birth of either horoscopic astrology or mathematical astronomy. Nevertheless, during the Pyramid Age the Egyptians did have a keen interest in the heavens. They worshipped the sun as the god Re, and they believed that the deceased king accompanied the sun god on his daily voyage across the skies. Sometimes the deceased king was perceived as a rower in the solar boat helping to row the sun across the heavens, while at other times he is seen as the captain of the boat. Religious passages called the *Pyramid Texts*, inscribed in the burial chamber of 5th Dynasty King Unas, speak of the king as becoming one of the northern stars in the afterlife.[33] But worshipping celestial deities does not constitute either astronomy or astrology, any more than worshipping the Nile River would have made the Egyptians hydraulic engineers. This level of

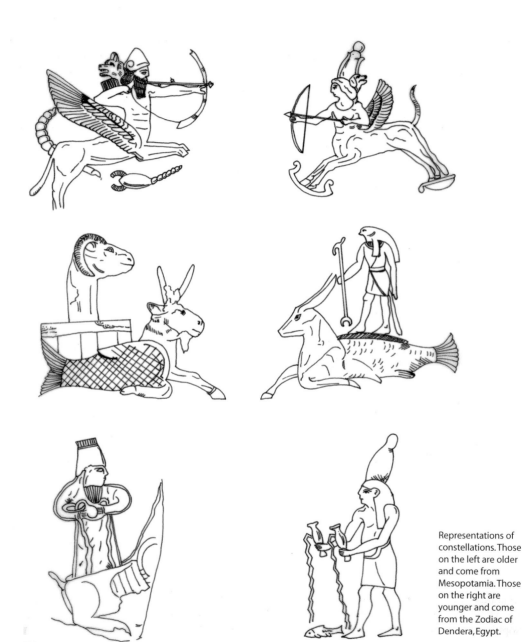

Representations of constellations. Those on the left are older and come from Mesopotamia. Those on the right are younger and come from the Zodiac of Dendera, Egypt.

interest in the heavens corresponds to what historians of science refer to as "shepherd's astronomy", practised to some extent by many ancient civilizations around the world, but it did not constitute any kind of exact science. Despite their relatively modest understanding of the heavens, ancient Egyptian sky-watchers were skilled celestial observers who fulfilled a number of important and useful functions in Egyptian society,[34] and their calendrical and time-keeping legacies are with us to this very day. Even though the Egyptians developed a solar cult, and the star Sirius and the moon were important deities, the planets had neither the same religious importance they had in Mesopotamia, nor temples devoted to them.

The Egyptians seem to have had less interest than the Mesopotamians in cataloguing and recording the movements of celestial objects. Few celestial observation texts are known from Egypt before the third century BC, and there is little evidence of the earlier type of celestial divination known as "omen astrology", similar to that of Mesopotamia, until the second or third century AD.[35] The Egyptians eventually adopted astrology after the Persian and the Greek conquests. Most astrological texts from Egypt are from the Roman period.

The earliest writings of an Egyptian astronomer and astrologer come from a nobleman and scribe named Harkhebi, who lived around 250 BC. Harkhebi wrote that, "clear-eyed", he made regular observations of the unerring stars to determine the future. Much of what he says shows a clear Mesopotamian influence. The famous low-relief sculpture of the zodiac found at the Temple of Dendera, which was once thought to contain ancient Egyptian astronomical wisdom, was fashioned about 30 BC, three centuries after the Greeks conquered Egypt. While it contains authentic forms of Egyptian astronomy, the signs of the zodiac are Egyptianized copies of Babylonian and Assyrian zodiacal figures, some of which were known in Mesopotamia as early as the second millennium BC.

In their writings the Egyptians made numerous references to the sun, the moon, and the stars, but they left the names of only a few identifiable constellations, the five planets visible to the unaided eye, and lists of 36 decanal stars used for telling the time. Unlike Mesopotamia, there is no indication that the moon and planets were systematically observed and recorded over long periods of time, or that there existed a network of celestial observation posts in the Nile river valley staffed by trained observers. In addition, collections that contained the technical terms necessary for specialized knowledge of the heavens that could be consulted for reference purposes were unknown in ancient Egypt.

Why the Egyptians showed less interest than the Mesopotamians in astrology and astronomy is unclear, but it may be because, unlike the peoples of Mesopotamia, the Egyptians were less interested in divination or fortune-telling. The underlying concept of divination, which maintained that the gods placed messages and warnings in natural phenomena that could then be detected and understood by trained divination specialists, was not a well-developed concept in Egyptian religion. Instead, the Egyptians seem to have placed more emphasis on rites performed in the temples by highly skilled priests, who, according to at least one Egyptologist, were primarily interested in repeating the orderly past, and not in searching out answers concerning the future.[36]

The calendar and astronomy

For centuries, celestial observers and calendar-makers in Mesopotamia attempted to understand the mysteries of lunar motion, and how the lunar calendar could be synchronized with the seasons and the solar year. The need for a better understanding of the lunar calendar and knowing when to add an extra month so the calendar would be in line with the solar year may have led to a more sophisticated mathematical understanding of lunar motion.[37] In contrast, the Egyptians relied on their 365-day civil calendar and placed less emphasis on developing a system on

The Zodiac of Dendera showing a number of the signs of the zodiac (some signs are not shown), Dendera, Egypt.

intercalary months to bring the lunar calendar in line with the solar year and the season.

The civil calendar

The Egyptians had several calendars. Two of the most important were the lunar calendar and the 365-day civil calendar. The Egyptians avoided the problems of attempting to calculate the lunar year and bring it in line with the solar year by creating a "civil calendar", which some have claimed was the most intelligent calendar ever made.[38] The civil calendar was composed of 12 months of 30 days each, plus five additional ("epagomenal") days that were added on at the end of the year, making a 365-day calendar. This made it just one quarter day short of the length of the solar year (365¼ days). Even though the civil calendar was the principal business and administrative calendar in use throughout their history, the Egyptians kept the lunar calendar to regulate religious functions such as festivals and ceremonies.

The lunar calendar

The oldest Egyptian calendar was based on the moon. Like the calendar-makers of Mesopotamia or any society that used a lunar calendar, Egyptian calendar-makers occasionally had to make certain adjustments to keep the lunar calendar synchronized with the cycle of the seasons. As in Mesopotamia, the Egyptians found a solution to this problem by using the bright star Sirius to help them determine when the lunar cycle had fallen behind and when it was time to add an extra month. Sirius was a very convenient and meaningful celestial object for the Egyptians since it appeared just before sunrise each year about the same time the waters of the Nile River began to rise prior to its annual flood (illustrated p. 5). When the first dim light of Sirius began to emerge in the pre-dawn light

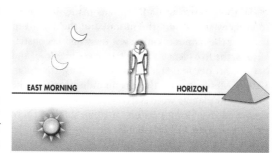

EAST MORNING   HORIZON

The disappearance of the lunar crescent just before sunrise marked the beginning of the Egyptian lunar month.

of the sun it signalled the beginning of the New Year, and the Egyptians referred to Sirius as "the opener of the year; the inundation". They also realized that if the last lunar month, called *wep-renpet*, occurred before the New Year, the lunar calendar was still accurate. However, if the calendar had already slipped into the first month of the New Year, it was time to add an extra month to the calendar.

Unlike other lunar calendars in the ancient Near East, the Egyptian lunar month began after the disappearance of the last thin crescent of the waning moon in the eastern sky, just before sunrise.

Thoth and Khons

The moon was associated with a number of Egyptian deities, the most prominent one being Thoth, the god of scribes and learning. Thoth had a cult centre at the city of Hermopolis in Middle Egypt, and was usually represented in paintings and sculptures as a man with the head of an ibis bird or as a seated baboon with a lunar disc on his head. The moon god Khons (or Khonsu) was represented in art as a young man in the form of a mummy. On his head he wore a crown shaped like a crescent moon, which held a complete lunar disc. The name Khons means "trav-

eller," referring to his monthly journey across the sky as the ever-changing moon. Khons was a god of lesser importance than the great Egyptian deities Amun or Osiris. His lower status is perhaps reflected in the fact that few large temples were ever built for him. Unlike Sin, their Mesopotamian counterpart (see Ch. 7), the followers of Thoth and Khons never attempted to overthrow the established hierarchy of gods. Three of the most important days in the lunar month were the day Khons was conceived, the day he was born, and the day he reached maturity at the full moon. These may be interpreted as the day when the moon is invisible in the sun's bright light, the evening of the first crescent visibility, and the day of the full moon when it reaches its maximum size.[39]

Egyptian interest concentrated on the early morning rising of celestial objects on the eastern horizon.[40] Egyptian religious beliefs maintained that the east was the direction of birth and resurrection, while the west was the direction of disappearance and death. The sun, the stars (including Sirius), and the planets rose in the east and were reborn. Anything that set below the western horizon met its end and died. This belief is reflected in the location of mortuary complexes on the west bank of the Nile River. Because the east was the direction of rebirth in the Egyptian calendar, the lunar month began when the last crescent of the waning moon disappeared in the east just before sunrise. This is the opposite of the Mesopotamian calendar, which began with the sighting of the first lunar crescent in the west, just after sundown. The Egyptian day began at dawn while the day in Mesopotamia began at twilight. Unlike the Mesopotamian calendar, where the days were only numbered, each day of the Egyptian month had its own name.

Star clocks

The ancient Egyptians developed an ingenious way of telling the time using the stars.[41] This practice came into use in Egypt during the Old Kingdom in the third millennium BC.[42] As the earth continues its annual journey around the sun, new stars become visible. Like Sirius, when it becomes visible in the sky just before sunrise, other stars also appear on the eastern horizon just before sunrise every few days. Using the appearance of such stars, the Egyptians divided the year into 36 ten-day periods called "decans". Charts of these decans were drawn up and used to tell the time at night and to help ensure that nocturnal religious activities were performed at the proper times.

Such lists of stars are referred to as "star clocks". Star clocks are divided into 36 columns, each representing a period of ten days.[43] The five additional days at the end of the year had their own special section at the end of the star lists. The Egyptians divided the night into 12 night hours as the stars passed across the heavens overhead. The night hours were not all the same length. The winter night hours were longer than those of summer because winter nights are longer and it stays dark longer, and the hours in the summer were shorter because the nights are shorter.

The Mesopotamians had a similar system of using the stars to tell the time of the year and the time of night. The calendar stars were called "the three stars each",[44] meaning that there were three stars for each month, and they functioned in a similar manner to those used by the Egyptians. Again, like the Egyptians, the Mesopotamians used rising and setting constellations, called "*ziqpu* stars", as they crossed the meridian or midpoint of the heavens to tell the time of the night and establish the night watch.

The legacy of Near Eastern celestial knowledge

Both Egypt and Mesopotamia made important and lasting contributions to our knowledge of the heavens and the way we keep time. The Egyptians gave

us the 24 hour day and, with some modifications, our 365-day year, which was borrowed from the Egyptians by the Romans during the time of Julius Caesar. This "Julian calendar" was used for over 1500 years before it was reformed during the reign of Pope Gregory in AD 1582. The Gregorian calendar, with a few refinements, is the calendar we still use today. Egyptian celestial knowledge was passed on to other cultures as well, and Greek scholars such as Eudoxus (fourth century BC) and Oenopides (fifth century BC) studied and seem to have learned their astronomy from the Egyptians.

Mesopotamian astronomy and astrology made a significant impact on the celestial knowledge and beliefs in many parts of the ancient world. As early as the Vedic period (1400 BC), there is clear evidence of a Mesopotamian influence on the Indian calendar.[45] The great astronomer Claudius Ptolemaeus, a Roman citizen living in Alexandria in the second century AD, based his calculations on eclipse observations made in the city of Babylon centuries before as the basis for his work *The Almagest*, the most important astronomical treatise from the ancient world. Numerous Greek, Roman, Indian, and Arab histori-

Egyptian cosmology. The sky goddess Nut with stars covering her torso. She represents the celestial vault and is held aloft by the air god Shu. The earth god Geb reclines below.

ans and astronomers referred to the works of Mesopotamian celestial observers and acknowledged their debt to them. Most importantly, historians of science have established that Mesopotamian, in particular Babylonian, mathematical astronomy was the common ancestor of modern scientific enquiry.[46]

PART II: MEDICINE

Disease – the absence of health – has been one of the foremost challenges of human existence. Since earliest times human beings have suffered from sicknesses and injuries that have stricken them, and maintaining health has been a difficult struggle, particularly before the advent of modern, scientific medicine. The mystery of why seemingly healthy people suddenly fall ill due to some disease has baffled and terrified people since ancient times. Although there is little evidence from prehistoric times of attempts to cure or treat the sick, once the first civilizations begin to record their activities and leave material artifacts, evidence of attempts to understand and treat diseases and injuries begin to appear in the archaeological and historical record.

Disease and the rise of civilization

In the Upper Palaeolithic period, tens of thousands of years ago, people may have known the healing properties of some herbal remedies and probably practised therapeutic or healing rituals in an attempt to cure the sick.[47] By the Neolithic period, 10 000 years ago, evidence of trephination, drilling holes in the skull with a hand-powered tool, appeared in the Levant. It seems this was done to relieve pressure from tumours inside the cranial cavity, or to allow what were interpreted as evil spirits to escape. The real medical value of this procedure is questionable.[48] Hunter–gatherers living in Palaeolithic times would have been infected with diseases borne by the animals they hunted, but these were a minor danger to their overall health.[49]

With the development of plant and animal domestication people were required to settle in one place, and this sedentariness encouraged the spread of many diseases. Although permanent houses and the formation of villages and towns provided shelter from the elements, living in permanent dwellings also encouraged mice and rats to live in close proximity to humans and increased the incidence of rodent-borne diseases such as bubonic plague. With the domestication of animals there was an increase in certain kinds of diseases common to domesticated dogs, cattle, pigs, and sheep.[50] The long-term, close-contact care such as feeding, milking, brushing, and shearing domestic animals helped spread their diseases to humans.[51] Living indoors also cut off sunlight, one of the most effective disinfectants known.[52] Living in houses reduced air circulation, which facilitated the transmission of air-borne diseases. The influenza virus, which is easily maintained inside houses, does not readily survive outdoors. Urban living also substantially increased garbage, sewage and other forms of human waste, which served as breeding grounds for a wide variety of diseases, including tuberculosis.[53] By the middle of the fourth millennium BC, there were large concentrations of people living in urban areas in southern Mesopotamia, and in one or two cities in Egypt, without proper sewage systems or clean drinking water. These concentrations of humans helped spread diseases at a much faster rate than in prehistoric times when hunter–gatherers had much less contact with neighbouring groups of people. Contagious diseases spread as the search for raw materials widened. The introduction of larger trading networks, and military campaigns, meant diseases could be spread by merchants and invading armies at a rate previously unknown. Even though the lot of humans improved with domestication and sedentariness, the costs of civilization to human health and quality of life were

high. This is reflected in the life expectancy of some early farmers, which was noticeably lower than that of the hunter–gatherers who came before them.[54]

Medicine in Mesopotamia[55]

The causes of disease

People in ancient Mesopotamia surely knew that some illnesses were caused by such things as over-exposure to cold, heat, and dampness, and rotten or spoiled food, or by over-eating or drinking too much alcohol. But modern concepts of diseases being transmitted by micro-organisms only began about two centuries ago. The people of the first civilizations believed that diseases were caused by supernatural agents, such as gods and demons, or the ghosts of departed relatives. If a living relative neglected to make mortuary offerings the ghost of the dead could persecute the offender,[56] and the "hand of a ghost" was sometimes blamed as the cause of sickness. One text, the *Ludlul bel nemeqi*,[57] warns of the ever-present Lamashtu demon,[58] who invaded the body and caused great pain and mental depression. The Lamashtu was a dreadful swamp demon with eagle claws for feet and hairy armpits. She loved human blood, fed on rotten meat, and pursued pregnant women preying on their babies. She cast spells on mothers, and counted the days until they delivered their infants so she could take them.

Deeply rooted in Mesopotamian thought was the concept that disease was visited upon humans as punishment by the gods because the sick person had committed an offensive act. Prayers indicate that people lived in fear of unknowingly offending the gods and causing themselves harm. In their prayers people beseeched the gods not to take offence at their activities and they took precautions against punishment through disease. One text from the city of Mari speaks of a certain woman, Shimatum, who

was guilty of gossiping against her master. He complained to the gods who in turn punished her with mangled fingers and epileptic seizures.[59] But despite being the cause of diseases, the gods could also take mercy on sufferers and heal them.

Magic by sympathy and contagion

Sorcery could take place if a witch or sorcerer took some of the victim's body parts or clothing – something that was very personal and in close contact with the intended victim – and used it to cast a spell. If a small sample of the intended victim's semen, fingernails, spittle, or a lock of hair had been acquired a sorcerer could work magic on that sample, which would then affect the intended victim.[60]

Gods and demons were not the only causes of disease. It was believed that some diseases were physically contagious and could be passed from one person to another. A letter from Mari mentions a woman infected with something called the *simmum* disease. The writer makes it clear that it was known that the disease was very contagious and that to avoid contagion those around the woman should not drink from the same cup, sit in the same chair, or sleep in her bed.[61]

The treatment of diseases in ancient Mesopotamia

In Mesopotamia healers of one sort or another do not appear in cuneiform texts before the Ur III period, about 2050 BC;[62] threats to public health such as unclean water, urban epidemics, and famine are also found in texts from this time. Marduk, Ishtar, and Ea were the gods of healing, along with the popular goddess Gula, who was associated with dogs. No hospitals or sanatoriums were known, but the temple of Gula may have served as some kind of health centre since the priests of Gula were probably also physicians.[63]

Medical texts frequently refer to two different approaches to healing: an empirico-rational approach and a magico-religious approach. The first, called *asûtu*, depended on empirical observation and rational means to diagnose and treat illness. *Asûtu* used herbs, salves, ointments, and physical manipulation as the principal therapies. It had a practical, hands-on element to it, even though, from a modern perspective, the medicines and treatments employed were probably not very beneficial to the patient. The *asu* was the main practitioner of this method and his title means roughly "physician" or "healer". The word may have originally referred to a "knower of the healing properties of water". The therapeutic texts used in this type of medicine usually describe the patient's complaint and give a list of ingredients to treat the problem with instructions on how the *asu* was to prepare and administer them. *Asu* healers carried with them a leather bag or a box for their pharmaceuticals, and a small charcoal brazier to use when preparing concoctions and herbal remedies.

Texts treating herbal pharmacology are among the main sources for understanding medicine in Mesopotamia. Therapeutic texts followed the standard formula for describing the problem, such as "if the sick person has such-and-such symptoms, then the *asu* should prepare such-and-such ingredients and administer them in a prescribed way". This procedure indicates that the *asus* examined their patients, and then prescribed what they believed to be effective and appropriate herbal cures for them. Thus in some small way they were like modern physicians, except that the drugs they administered were probably not very effective.

Much of the *asu*'s activities probably consisted of treating injuries such as cuts, broken bones, and dislocated shoulders from falls and farming accidents. These would require them to bind wounds, set broken bones, and suture wounds closed with needle and thread, implying a certain level of knowledge about bones, joints, and how to stop wounds from bleeding. A composition of three tablets called the *Uruanna: mashtakal* lists several hundred herbs and animal parts used to heal the sick. Ingredients included common herbs, roots, stems, leaves, and fruits that were used either fresh or dried, or sometimes ground up or pulverised, and often mixed with milk, beer, wine, honey, or vinegar.[64] Other ingredients included milk, fat, tallow, blood, or the hair of a black dog, or a shred of a soiled menstrual rag. Sometimes the ingredients had to be harvested at a specific time of day or night or they had to be grown in a special location, such as near a grave. In addition, sometimes a prognosis was also given announcing that the patient would recover from their illness. In other circumstances the texts state that the sick person would not recover.

Even though there were two basic types of medical treatment available in Mesopotamia, the division between the two was not always clear. Often both the magical and the physical treatments would be used on the same patient and there was little distinction made between them by medical practitioners. Despite the empirico-rational approach of the *asu*, Mesopotamian medical practices did not lay the foundations for later scientific medical practices.[65]

Surgery

It is doubtful that physicians could undertake complex surgical interventions. Most surgery consisted of minor incisions to lance boils, remove cysts, or perform bloodletting. In many parts of the ancient world physicians believed that "bad blood" sometimes made its way into the body and caused illness. The solution was to "drain off" a certain amount of this bad blood to restore health. This was a dangerous procedure since the patient risked infection, and the resulting loss of blood pressure could bring on cardiac arrest. Although bloodletting was performed in Mesopotamia, the practice does not seem to have been widespread. Some simple types of surgery were performed but it is unclear whether healers possessed powerful anaesthetic agents to calm their patients during surgery other than beer and wine, which are inadequate for the task. Some researchers have argued for the use of pain-relieving substances such as opium, in Mesopotamia called *azallu* (the "plant of forgetfulness"), while others believe that drugs like opium were not used there.[66] However, such pain relievers may have been used in ancient Egypt from the 18th Dynasty[67] or earlier. Opium poppies are clearly depicted in some tomb paintings, and many hundreds of examples of *bilbils*, small bottles in the shape of the opium plant, which are believed to have contained opium in a liquid solution, have been found throughout the Near East. These forms of evidence indicate that some kind of opiate was available for pain sufferers, at least in certain locations.

Several of the Laws of Hammurabi (218–220) describe how the *asu* made: "a deep (serious) incision with a bronze knife on a man and has caused the man's death, or has opened out a man's eye socket and destroyed the man's sight". The exact nature of these interventions is puzzling. The eye surgery mentioned was probably minor and only involved some kind of scarification on or near the eye.[68]

Despite the limitations, it is probable that in some instances a surgeon had no alternative, and attempted risky surgery to relieve pain and give the patient a chance to survive. The problems associated with surgery were increased because ancient physicians did not understand the blood circulation system and had only the most rudimentary means of controlling bleeding or infection. Drugs such as penicillin only became available in the 20th century. Before that time little could be done to combat infections that resulted from open wounds and surgical procedures. Other medical procedures that required manipulating exposed body organs or open fractures (broken bones that penetrated the skin) would also have been difficult to perform without pain-controlling agents, but in these extreme cases the healer would have had no choice but to do whatever he could to relieve the suffering of the patient.

Mesopotamian healers probably augmented their knowledge of bones and bodily organs from the slaughter of animals.[69] Law 224 of the Laws of Hammurabi speaks of a veterinarian or the "*asu* of cattle and donkeys". Since the laws make no clear distinction between healers of animals and people it is possible that these were the same *asus* who healed people. There is no evidence that either trephination or circumcision were practised on either males or females.

The Mesopotamian medical tradition made no attempt to understand the various parts of the body or the function of bodily organs by performing dissection or autopsies. Because physicians in Mesopotamia could not investigate medical problems and diseases inside the body without risking further damage to the patient, many cures involved using existing orifices – such as the mouth, nose, and anus – to introduce herbal cures and potions into the body. This may explain why so many prescriptions required taking various concoctions orally, breathing in their vapours, or by enemas and suppositories inserted or injected into the anus. Cleansing the body of evil spirits and toxic substances was one of the principal strategies of medical treatment in the ancient Near East.

Magico-religious healers

The second type of medical treatment was magico-religious in nature and concentrated on the non-physical and spiritual aspects of healing. The *ashipu* was a "diviner physician",[70] a fortune-teller–healer, who treated illnesses, but performed other, non-

medical tasks as well. The *ashipu* relied on magical incantations and spiritual intervention by the gods to help heal the patient. An expert in magic,[71] the *ashipu* was a kind of witch-doctor[72] whose treatments emphasized magical, ritualistic and spiritual methods of treating diseases with less emphasis on drugs and ointments.

The *ashipu* was also an exorcist who drove demons out of the afflicted person's body by using incantations and the recitation of magical rituals. The whole concept of this type of medicine, from cause to treatment, was based on the idea that the patient's illness was caused by supernatural forces that had been angered by the sick person and had entered their body as a form of punishment. There is no indication which type of treatment, the empirico-rational or the magico-religious, was more widely practised. Healers and patients considered both to be legitimate ways of curing the sick. It was the job of the *ashipu* to find the correct magical formula or perform the correct ritual so the demon or spirit would leave the body of the afflicted person and health could be restored. As an exorcist and magician the *ashipu* carried out priestly as well as medical functions and was usually not a full-time healer. In addition to healing, the *ashipu* cleansed temples or practised divination; some were sky-watchers[73] or performed tasks that had nothing to do with treating the sick.

Training

Nothing specific is known about the training of either the *asu* or the *ashipu*. Since the *ashipus* were priests, diviners, and exorcists they spent time as students studying religious and magical texts, learning all the spells to rid the sick of the demons and evil forces that had taken control of their bodies. Outside the large cities it is likely that doctors, exorcists and midwives received no formal training but relied on some kind

of apprenticeship to learn their craft. There were no officially recognized medical standards for practising the healing arts in the ancient Near East. Standardized training in accredited medical schools and medical examination boards are almost purely modern institutions.

Childbirth, midwives, and infant mortality

In ancient Near Eastern societies women were meant to marry and bear children (see Ch. 8). If a woman was childless her husband could take another woman in order to have children. Adoption was also practised as a way to bring children and heirs into a family. Many babies were adopted immediately after delivery when they were still wet with blood and water. During pregnancy the mother and unborn child were protected from the ravages of the demon Lamashtu (see above) by wearing protective amulets: small charms such as stones, objects of metals, or plants, sometimes inscribed, which were worn as protection from disease caused by demons or ghosts. Pregnancy and childbirth were dangerous for both the mother and the baby, and many texts speak of problems for women during and after childbirth. The *shabsutu* (midwife) assisted women during childbirth and there is no indication that either the *asu* or *ashipu* was present or helped during delivery.

There are no statistics on infant mortality rates from the first civilizations, but evidence from cemetery analysis indicates that in early urban societies mortality rates were very high. Perhaps as many as 10–30 per cent of babies died soon after birth and 30–50 per cent of young children before the age of five years.[74] Given the level of medical technology and the often unsanitary living conditions of the time, these estimates probably reflect the situation with a high degree of accuracy. It is unclear if any methods of birth control were known or used, but texts indicate that breastfeeding, which could have limited pregnancies, continued until the child was about 3 years old.

Abortion

Textual evidence indicates that abortion was rare in ancient Mesopotamia, but it is clear that in at least one instance, mentioned in a text from Babylonia, a concoction of herbs was to be ingested to induce abortion.[75] In at least three law collections, the Lipit-Ishtar Laws, the Laws of Hammurabi and the Middle Assyrian Laws[76] there are clauses that speak of men striking women and causing them to miscarry. These do not constitute abortions, but were common acts of violence against women. None of them involved either a surgical procedure or herbal mixture administered specifically to produce an abortion. Nevertheless, it is clear that abortions did take place, and any woman caught attempting an abortion was subjected to impalement, a horrible and degrading form of punishment. Clause 53 of the Middle Assyrian Laws[77] states that any woman, "who by her own action loses her foetus … will be impaled and they shall not bury her". Impalement meant that humiliation and shame would be heaped on the victim's family, while her decomposing cadaver would be picked clean by birds, and her spirit would spend eternity as a wandering ghost.

Medicine in ancient Egypt

Like Mesopotamia, Egypt also had empirico-rational and magico-religious methods of healing the sick and treating the injured[78] and, as in Mesopotamia, the ancient Egyptians would probably not have considered one approach more valid or effective than the other. In all pre-scientific societies empirical knowledge and magical acts were both equally valid ways of understanding and controlling situations in the real world. Most healers, from the most famous court physician to the humblest village witch-doctor, probably knew something about both systems and used them when they treated the sick. To many people, both ancient and modern, it is perfectly rational to bind wounds, administer herbs and recite prayers when treating a patient.

Healthcare, healers, and physicians in ancient Egypt

According to tradition the first, and most famous, physician in Egypt was Imhotep, chief vizier and architect of the step pyramid (see Ch. 11) of the 3rd Dynasty king, Djoser. Two thousand years after his death Imhotep was deified as the god of medicine, wisdom, and learning, and he was also identified with Asclepius, a Greek god, who filled a similar capacity. His fame as a healer god reached its peak during the Graeco-Roman period (332 BC–AD 395). Healers who administered drugs and emphasized the empirico-rational approach to treatment were called *swnw* (conveniently pronounced "soonu") in Egyptian. As in Mesopotamia, there are no Egyptian words that correspond exactly to our words for physician or doctor, and it is perhaps more accurate to employ the terms "healer" or "health practitioner" when referring to the *swnw* of ancient Egypt.[79] It seems clear that there were female physicians or healers as well.[80] Priests were called *w'bw* (pronounced "wabu") and emphasized prayers while *s'w* (pronounced "sau") emphasized magical aspects such as amulets. Healers were also known as the "priests of Sekhmet", a goddess depicted in art as a lion-headed woman, who possessed the powers of healing, and was the patroness of physicians and veterinarians.

Most *swnw* were probably sons of healers who followed in their fathers' footsteps and carried on the tradition and healing practices of their elders. As in Mesopotamia, there is no evidence that healers acquired any formal training in medical schools, and it seems likely that medical knowledge was passed on from father to son during a long period of apprenticeship. However, there was one institution situated close to some temples called *per ankh* (the "house of life"), which may have been a place of learning and repository for medical texts.

Dental health, teeth, and "toothers"[81]

The practice of healing was institutionalized in Egypt from around 3000 BC, and the first healers to appear in texts were dentists, called "toothers".[82] The ancient Egyptians had few dental caries or cavities, probably due to their diet, which contained no refined sugar.[83] Throughout the entire 30-century span of Egyptian history teeth show extreme attrition[84] from the fine grit that made its way into the bread consumed by everyone. Flour for making bread had to be ground between stones and, as a result, minute particles of stone were transmitted into the daily bread of the entire land, and caused severe wear on the teeth, often wearing them down to the gums. Evidence from well-preserved mummies indicates that caries (cavities) were rare, but tooth abscesses were common and few people died with all of their teeth still intact. Abscesses of a few sufferers were relieved by drilling holes into the jawbone (mandible) near the root of the infected tooth to drain off accumulated pus deposits.

In Mesopotamian texts complaints about aching and infected teeth are common, and both therapeutic and magical treatments are prescribed. One text from the Late Babylonian period recounts how the god Ea allowed a type of blood-sucking worm to live among the teeth and gums. This explanation of the cause of dental problems is followed by instructions to the dentist to seize the root of the tooth with an unidentified tool and pull it out. The incantation ends with a mighty curse against the tooth worm.[85]

Causes of disease

Unlike in Mesopotamia, the concept of contagion, the touching or contact with a sick person or contaminated object as a means of spreading diseases, seems to have been unknown in ancient Egypt.[86] It was thought that diseases were caused by occult or magical forces, sorcery, or immoral behaviour; another cause, seemingly unique to Egypt, was "foreign women", who could cast spells on unsuspecting local men. One Egyptian text speaks of disease being caused by the "breath" of a god, which brings to mind the Babylonian idea that diseases were caused by the "hand of a ghost" (see above). Although Egyptian concepts about the causes of disease were in many cases on the same level of sophistication as those of other pre-scientific societies, they also developed what was probably the first empirical theory of the causes of diseases.[87]

The Egyptians believed that putrefaction and rotting were associated with death, disease, and infection. One of the major causes of disease was the food consumed by humans. It exited the body either as faeces, urine, or some other form of decay. Intestinal decay was the result of *whdw* (pronounced "wekhedu"), and one way to improve or restore health was to rid the body of *whdw*, which would stop putrefaction and disease. *Whdw* could either develop inside the body or it could invade it from the outside. Once in the body *whdw* could attach itself to some form of putrefaction such as faeces or pus, and then travel throughout the body via a series of tubes. As the *whdw* spread through the body it left behind dental abscesses, suppurating sores, intestinal cramps, eye infections, fevers, and other maladies. Because *whdw* caused disease, it was only reasonable that the cure was to rid the body of toxic waste materials, and healers often prescribed laxatives to clean out the body's system. Medical texts repeatedly advise healers to prescribe remedies that will expel waste or disease from the body, or empty the stomach of

disease. Removal of *whdw* meant that much care and attention had to be placed on the anus. Proper evacuations would remove harmful amounts of *whdw*, and were believed to be basic for the suitable maintenance of health.[88] Nearly every surviving medical papyrus deals with the anus, and many prescriptions involved enemas or purges. There were even men called the "Shepherds of the anus", whose task it may have been to administer enemas and release excess amounts of *whdw*.

Along with enemas, purgatives, and expectorants, which were commonly used to cleanse or rid the body of offensive substances, both spitting and vomiting were thought to rid the patient of disease. In some cases it was believed that *whdw* was caused by parasitic worms in patient's stools. By examining mummies modern researchers have determined that worms were a persistent problem among the ancient Egyptians. Guinea worms, roundworms, tapeworms, and hookworms[89] have all been found in the mummified remains. Parasitic worms were probably observed by Egyptian *swnw* and their patients, who deduced that these worms were the cause of *whdw*.

Although the ancient Mesopotamian healers from Sumer, Babylonia, and Assyria recognized some non-spiritual causes of disease, they had no comprehensive theory based on physical causes that attempted to account for the origins or treatment of ailments. The situation seems different in the case of Egyptian medicine. Egyptologist Robert Ritner has argued convincingly that the Egyptian idea of *whdw* as the cause of illness constituted the first empirical and comprehensive disease theory in history.[90] Accordingly, the concept of *whdw* offers a physical explanation for the onset of disease, as well as ageing and death. The concept of *whdw* as a way of explaining disease in a purely physical manner was a major departure from the more traditional ideas about disease and sickness known in places like Mesopotamia.

Anatomical knowledge

Egyptian anatomical knowledge is reflected in the more than 200 anatomical terms that refer to parts of the body and specific organs. Despite this large number of technical terms, organs such as the kidneys and some individual bones are not mentioned. It was traditionally believed that Egyptian knowledge of anatomy, and medicine in general, came from mummification, the treatment of battlefield wounds by physicians who accompanied the pharaoh's armies into the field, or at construction sites, where the *swnw* would have observed and treated broken bones and severed limbs.[91] It has been argued that mummification was important for learning about the body, because much knowledge of anatomy would have been acquired by removing internal organs and preparing the cadaver for burial. This interpretation is, however, open to question, since the mummifiers who prepared the dead for burial were considered unclean outcasts, and it is doubtful that the *swnw* would have had much contact with them.[92] Nevertheless, mummies have proved an important tool for modern medical researchers, helping them to understand the nature and extent of a number of medical problems encountered by the ancient Egyptians. By examining some of the thousands of mummies in ancient Egypt, a number of illnesses have been identified. Since peoples in other parts of the ancient Near East did not preserve corpses to the same extent as they did in Egypt, this valuable means of studying past illnesses (palaeopathology) is unavailable to medicine outside Egypt.

Although there was no special term for veterinarian in ancient Egyptian, it has been argued that much anatomical knowledge came from the practice of veterinary medicine, and that the treatment of human and animal medical problems was not as clearly defined in ancient times as it is today.[93] This argument may have merit because farmers and herders often had to slaughter animals and would quickly learn about their organs and bone structure.[94]

A number of Egyptian medical texts (papyri) were straightforward, hands-on manuals on how to deal with medical problems. In the second half of the first millennium BC, increased trade with the outside world expanded the range of medicinal plants used to treat illnesses, and at the time Egyptian healers were considered among the best in the world. From the Persian period onwards, Egyptian medical knowledge did much to prepare the way for advances in later Graeco-Roman medicine.

Medical papyri

Much of our knowledge about Egyptian medical practices has been preserved on a number of papyri housed in museums and private collections around the world. Medical papyri, such as the *Ebers Papyrus*, containing 877 prescriptions for largely herbal remedies, and the *Papyri Ramesseum IV and V*, dealing with contraception, birth, and neonatal care, have survived the ages and offer important clues to understanding ancient Egyptian medical practices. One of the most informative of these, the *Ebers Papyrus*,[95] indicates that the healers knew about the beating of the heart and blood vessels that went to all the limbs and extremities of the body. The healer was instructed to place his hands in various places on the body to pick up the beating of the heart. The text explains that the heart "speaks out" of the vessels that go to the arms and legs and other bodily extremities. The vessels were thought to be tubes of some kind that carried blood, sperm, air, urine, tears, and even faeces, to the various parts of the body. The *Ebers Papyrus* mentions that there are four blood vessels to the nose: two contain mucus and two contain blood. Four vessels give blood to the temples and the eyes. Another four vessels go to the anus and when they overflow with faeces the excess

finds it way to other bodily extremities, causing medical complications.

Surgery and the treatment of traumatic injuries

The *Edwin Smith Surgical Papyrus*,[96] is a well-preserved section of a medical text containing instructions on how to deal with traumatic injuries. The appearance of the word "surgery" in the modern title is somewhat misleading since no actual surgical incisions are mentioned in the original papyrus document; complex surgery was probably only attempted in extreme cases in pre-scientific medicine. For example, there is no evidence that more radical forms of surgery such as amputations and trephination were practised in ancient Egypt.

Although the *Edwin Smith Surgical Papyrus* never mentions surgery, it does refer to sewing wounds closed. Other than a suturing needle and a tool for cauterizing or burning wounds to close them, no other tools are mentioned. Along with a few magical incantations, the text contains instructions for many sound medical practices recognizable by modern physicians.[97] Written in simple language, with clear descriptions of actual cases, it has been argued that the text was a training manual for apprentice physicians, or a first-aid manual for "medics" employed in first-aid work on construction sites or on the battlefield.[98] This interpretation is supported by the fact that in a number of instances the text refers to a "teacher" who seems to be giving on-site instructions to students. It may be that on the battlefield the healers were not *swnw*, but simply soldier-medics. Another indication that the *Edwin Smith Surgical Papyrus* is a teaching text is shown by the rather basic language, which would not have been employed if the text has been written for experienced physicians. In simple terms, skull fractures are said to be like breaks in a pot, exposed brain tissue is said to resemble molten copper, and counting pulse beats is said

to be like counting quantities with the fingers. The text contains 48 cases, systematically divided into sections on injuries to the cranium, the forehead, the nasal bones, the cheeks and upper jaw, and the spine, dislocated and broken bones, abscesses, and others.

Even though the text is written in simple language, it contains a large amount of sophisticated medical knowledge. The healer is instructed to observe the patient and determine his condition, then proceed with the steps necessary to treat the wound and ameliorate the situation. This is clear in one case where the *swnw* must set a broken arm. He is instructed to lie the patient down with something to spread the shoulders so the two parts of the broken arm can fall into place. Then he has to place a splint over the break and bind it for support.

The text divides cases into two categories: those which can be treated with a good possibility of being cured, and those that cannot be cured due to the severe nature of the injury. One section of the *Edwin Smith Surgical Papyrus* gives detailed descriptions of a number of open wounds to the head. One clause explains that if a man has a head wound that fractures his skull and exposes the brain, the wound should be palpitated or massaged, to better observe and understand the nature of the wound. If the head wound is severe and the victim bleeds from the nose and the ears, it states that this type of wound cannot be treated or cured.[99] One symptom that shows up a number of times with head wounds is stiffness of the neck. This, again, is a symptom that accompanies head wounds and is known to modern medical practitioners.

Other injuries to the head mention a shuffling walk and the dragging of the feet, indicating the patient had suffered damage to that part of the brain controlling movement.[100] Still other injuries include brain damage that causes spasms of the limbs, as well as loss of control of some limbs and shoulders. These severe injuries are among those that cannot be treated. As a result of skull injuries caused by falling on the head, the text mentions cervical vertebra crushed together, resulting in the patient's inability to speak. This type of accident could also cause paralysis in the arms and legs. Accidents of this kind came into the category of injuries that could not be treated by Egyptian healers. The fate of the untreated patient is not given, but it seems they were to be stabilized as much as possible. It is doubtful they were deserted or abandoned to their fate without at least being made as comfortable as possible under the circumstances.

Sanitary conditions

Even though Greek authors such as Herodotus, writing in the fifth century BC, claimed that the Egyptians practised scrupulous hygiene, archaeological evidence does not support this. Latrines existed as far back as the 2nd Dynasty, but excavations at Amarna (Akhetaten, see Ch. 14) and elsewhere indicate that even upper-class residences were surrounded by piles of rubbish, and open sewers were the norm.[101] Nevertheless, houses at Amarna contained showers and latrines that drained into the ground, and some were even equipped with sit-down-type toilet seats.[102] Such amenities were, however, rare and most homes had only minimal or no fixed sanitary facilities. There is good evidence that portable toilet seats were used, and this may account for the seeming lack of permanent toilet facilities[103] in some upper-class houses, where such amenities were to be expected. Many of these same homes were equipped with shower or bathing facilities where water could be poured over the bather who stood on a stone floor slab with a hole for draining away excess water. Along with dumps and waste piles, the Nile River served as a very convenient sewer for waste and rubbish disposal.

Pregnancy, childbirth, and abortion

The *Kahun Papyrus* is the earliest text to discuss pregnancy and contains 17 cases of which some are concerned with the problems with fertility.[104] It recommends that in order to conceive a woman place a clove of garlic in her vagina. If the next day her breath smells of garlic then she will conceive. Another instructs the healer to verify if the muscles of the woman's breasts are firm: if they are she will conceive, but if they are soft she will have difficulty conceiving. Another case study claims that a diagnosis for fertility can be made by smelling the woman's urine. Details of how this was to be done are unclear. Another pregnancy test requires the woman to urinate in a container filled with emmer wheat. If the seeds sprout the woman is pregnant; if the seeds die she is not. The *Berlin Papyrus* tells healers how to determine if a woman is pregnant and how to determine the sex of the baby while still in the womb. Both the *Kahun Papyrus* and the *Berlin Papyrus* contain a measure of sound medical knowledge mixed with much folklore. The *Ebers Papyrus* also has advice on contraception; a woman not wishing to become pregnant was instructed to place a mixture of acacia leaves, honey and some kind of moist cloth into the vagina.

Impotence seems to have been a problem in both Egypt and Mesopotamia. Lack of potency was usually attributed to sorcery. If the sorcerer's spell could be broken through incantations and rituals, sexual power could be restored. One Egyptian treatment for impotence was to wrap the penis in a concoction of fruit juices, fats, and salt mixed with sawdust. In Mesopotamia there are a number of texts that refer to the "lifting of the heart", meaning the man was suffering from erectile dysfunction. To remedy the situation a potion made from parts of sexually charged or excited animals, including bats and birds, was consumed, and incantations recited. Other remedies required rubbing potions on the genitals.

The medical tradition of ancient Mesopotamia and ancient Egypt

Throughout its long history, the medical knowledge and practices of ancient Mesopotamia remained at the level of folk medicine. To a large extent the same thing can probably be said about ancient Egypt, but with some notable exceptions. Both ancient Mesopotamia and Egypt knew about the existence of the pulse, but the Egyptian medical papyri indicate that they had a rudimentary idea about the circulatory system of vessels or tubes centred at the heart and radiating to various organs and extremities of the body.[105] Although many historians dismiss Egypt's famous reputation as a centre of medical knowledge and innovation, particularly in later Classical and Renaissance literature and medical lore, it may in fact, be well deserved.[106]

There is no indication that Mesopotamian healers ever explored the inside of the bodies they attempted to heal. The body was considered inviolable and they rarely or never experimented with dissection as later Greek physicians would. Interestingly, dissection was first practised in Alexandria, the great city built in Egypt on the edge of the Mediterranean Sea. The Greek physician, Herophilus, one of the recognized pioneers in experimental medicine, lived in the city of Alexandria. It is likely that Herophilus was able to experiment with dissection and autopsies because the tradition already existed. Egypt was the only place in the ancient world where such things were permitted, and the practice of mummification carried over into dissection.

It appears that the ancient Egyptians were responsible for initiating several important innovations that prepared the way for further advances in medical knowledge in the Graeco-Roman period. These included autopsies, an outgrowth of mummification, which enabled healers to better understand the physical components of the body, and *whdw*, a concept that provided an empirical theory about the causes of diseases and their treatment.

Along with these Egyptian innovations, healers in Mesopotamia and Egypt practised a mixture of empirico-rational and magico-religious treatment of the sick, and healers in both countries believed that ghosts, demons, and gods were the causes or cures of many diseases. Notwithstanding their many limitations, Mesopotamian and Egyptian healers were able in some ways to treat and comfort the sick and injured, and over the centuries they helped generations of people face, and sometimes overcome, the diseases and wounds they suffered.

Clockwise from top left: view across the Euphrates River near the city of Ashur; family home constructed of marsh reeds, southern Iraq; man holding cobra, Upper Egypt; girl filling water containers on the Khabur River, northeast Syria; the Nile River at Luxor (Thebes), Upper Egypt.

Clockwise from above: excavations at Tell 'Atij, Syria; mud-brick palace walls with low-relief figures, Babylon; the Sphinx, known as "Horus of the Horizon"; mud-brick walls with arched entryway, Babylon; workers receiving their weekly pay at Tell 'Atij, Syria.

Clockwise from above: stone walls with crenellations, Nineveh, northern Iraq; Khufu Pyramid (4th Dynasty) with village in the foreground, Giza Plateau, Egypt; step pyramid of King Djoser (3rd Dynasty), Saqqara, Egypt; Djeser-Djeseru, Temple of Hatshepsut (18th Dynasty), Deir-el-Bahri, Upper Egypt; Valley of the Kings, Upper Egypt.

Clockwise from top left: rampart with stone revetment (13th century BC), Khattusha, central Anatolia; the New Kingdom Temple of Amun at night (18th Dynasty), Upper Egypt; pair of statues of Ramesses II, Luxor Temple (19th Dynasty), Upper Egypt; Lion Gate (13th century BC), Khattusha, central Anatolia; stairway to the summit of the ziggurat at Aqar-Quf, central Iraq.

Part IV: Egypt

10 Egypt: the Black Land

The common name for ancient Egypt was Kemit, meaning the "Black Land". Unlike some societies, where black was considered the colour of death and sinister forces, for the ancient Egyptians black was the colour of life and fertility. When the rich soil of the Nile river valley was watered it turned a dark, blackish-brown colour and produced rich and abundant crops. The modern name "Egypt" is a Greek word derived from the Egyptian *hikuptah*, used by the ancient Greeks to refer to the Egyptian city of Memphis. Egypt was also referred to as the "Two Lands", or the "Land of the Pharaohs", terms that will be used, along with Egypt, in the following chapters.

Egyptian craftsman fabricating alabaster bowls, Upper Egypt.

Ancient Egypt, situated in the northeast corner of the African continent, made up part of a vast desert region that stretched from the West African coast, through the modern countries of Morocco and Algeria, across the top of the continent through Libya and on to the shores of the Red Sea. Most of Egypt receives little or no rainfall, and large-scale agriculture would be impossible if not for the Nile River, one of the world's longest and most important rivers. For this reason the Greek historian Herodotus called Egypt "the gift of the Nile". Without such an important water source the area would have remained sparsely populated, and one of the great civilizations of the ancient world would never have developed there.

The riverine systems of Egypt and Mesopotamia

The Nile river valley is quite different from the Tigris–Euphrates river valley. In ancient times the Nile River usually began to rise in June and flooded in August. Most importantly, it flooded before crops like wheat and barley were planted in October. Because of this favourable timing, the Nile river valley was a more reliable ecological zone for irrigation agriculture than the Tigris–Euphrates region. While the Nile River originates in equatorial Africa, the Tigris River and Euphrates River originate in the highlands of Turkey. Even though the two rivers flow through the plains of Mesopotamia and empty into

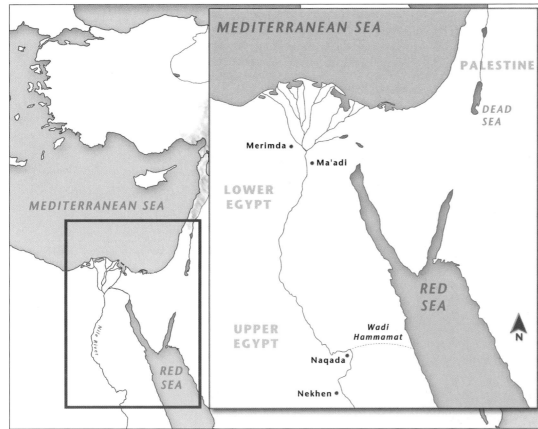

Map of Egypt.

A village in Lower Egypt
near the Nile River.

Top: Farmer in the Nile Delta using a primitive
shaduf or water-lifting device to irrigate his
fields. Bottom: Rich croplands in the Nile Delta.

the Persian Gulf, they are in many ways quite dissimilar. The Euphrates River is snow-fed and nourished by winter snowfalls in the Taurus mountains, which melt and run off into the Persian Gulf. In contrast, the Tigris River is rain-fed, receiving water from the many tributaries that drain from the Zagros mountains. Because the Tigris River receives most of its water from rainfall it is very unreliable, and after a major rainstorm it can rise quickly and cause devastating floods. In contrast, the Euphrates River has a tendency to hold its frozen moisture and release it all at once in the spring. Another important difference between the two river systems is that the Tigris River and Euphrates River flood in the spring,[1] just as the crops are about to be harvested, and even though they are essential for agriculture, the two rivers are also a major threat to the crops and farmers who depend on them for their survival.[2]

The Nile River,[3] with its source in Lake Victoria, flows from equatorial Africa to the Mediterranean Sea, crossing 35 degrees of latitude. Its head waters are below the equator in the Southern Hemisphere and flow north for over 6800 km to the Mediterranean Sea. The annual flooding of the Nile River was caused by spring and summer rainfall occurring in the East African highlands, thousands of kilometres to the south of Egypt. The first flood waters reached Lower Egypt in late June and had a distinct greenish colour caused by algae suspended in the fast-moving current. Later in the summer additional flood waters arrived and flooding continued into September. By this time the algae had begun to decay and turned reddish-brown. Vast quantities of silt, rich in important fertilizing agents such as calcium, magnesium carbonates, and sodium chloride, were deposited by the flood waters. The annual flood brought water, fertile soil, and fertilizers to Egyptian farmers, making it a truly bountiful river;[4] little wonder that the Egyptians worshipped it as a god.

In ancient times, the Nile river valley was quite narrow and restricted the size of irrigated farmland

so that it seldom reached more than 3–4 km on either side of the river.[5] Beyond the area that was in contact with the river lay only the dry desert sands where nothing grew. The desert area was called *Desheret*, "The Red Land", and was symbolic of death.

Geography and climate

Egypt can be divided into northern and southern sections near what is now the modern city of Cairo. About 150 km before the Nile River reaches the Mediterranean Sea, it branches out into a triangular-shaped area called the Nile Delta. In such close proximity to the Mediterranean Sea, the Delta has a different climate from the rest of the Nile river valley. The Delta receives 10–20 cm of annual rainfall; areas south of the Delta receive less than 10 cm. Such a small amount of moisture is totally insufficient for agriculture, and farming was only possible in Egypt because of the Nile River. Rainfall south of the Nile Delta is sporadic and some areas rarely receive rain at all. When it does rain, after dry periods that can last several years, downpours are violent but of short duration, turning wadis (dry riverbeds) into raging torrents.

Transportation on the Nile River

The Nile River not only provided water and fertilizer for crop production, but it was also an excellent river highway for transporting goods, which helped unify the people of the Two Lands. The northernmost 850-km stretch of the river has no rapids, allowing boats to float with the current from one end of Egypt to the other. Since the prevailing winds blow in the opposite direction, from north to south, they can be used to propel sailing boats up-river against the current. This provided an ideal natural transportation system that existed in few other places in the world. Because the

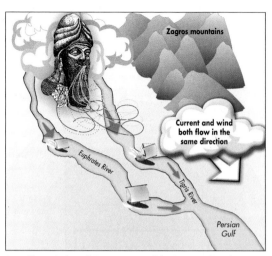

Prevailing winds and river currents of the Tigris and Euphrates rivers.

Egyptian Predynastic chronology (all dates BC)

Lower Egypt: Nile Delta and northern Nile river valley		Upper Egypt	
Faiyum	5230–4450	Badarian	4500–4000
Merimde	5200–4100	Naqada I (Amratian)	4000–3600
Ma'adi	3700–3300	Naqada II Gerzean	3500–3300
		Naqada III	3300–3000

Nile River flows towards the Mediterranean Sea, one speaks of going *down* the river to Lower Egypt even though Lower Egypt is actually on the *upper* part of modern maps; when one goes *up* the river to Upper Egypt, in other words against the current, one is heading in a southerly direction. In Mesopotamia the currents of the Tigris and Euphrates Rivers and the prevailing winds move in the same direction, making river travel more difficult than in Egypt.

Besides being called "the Black Land", Egypt was also called *Tawy*, the "Two Lands", meaning Upper

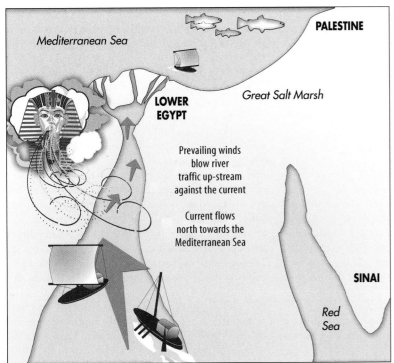

Prevailing winds and current
direction of the Nile River.

greater emphasis on gathering edible cereal grains. This led to the development of early forms of agriculture, and a subsequent decrease in the importance of hunting and gathering. Most tools in the Predynastic period were made of stone, although there were a few copper implements. Granaries, partially submerged into the ground and lined with matting or basketwork, were used to store surplus grains. By the middle of the fourth millennium BC, during the Naqada II period, the Nile river valley experienced an increase in small communities of agriculturists who supplemented their diets either by hunting the decreasing population of wild game, or by practising animal husbandry and herding domesticated animals. Even though the early Nile river valley dwellers may have taken some steps towards plant and animal domestication, evidence indicates that early agriculture was an innovation that came to Egypt from Syria-Palestine sometime around 5000 BC.[9] The domestication of herd animals like sheep, long known in the Near East, occurred in Egypt after 5000 BC.

Archaeological evidence from the Badarian period (4500–4000 BC) indicates that people in some parts of Upper Egypt led a semi-sedentary life. Badarian villages consisted of simple huts covered with brush or thatch. People fished in the Nile River and grew wheat, barley, and chickpeas, and relied to some extent on hunting. Clothing was either woven from linen or made from animal skins. Remains at Merimde[10] (5200–4100 BC) in Lower Egypt lead us to believe that it consisted of scattered huts that served as shelters and wind-breaks. Most of the dwellings were so small that they could not have been occupied by more than one person, or at most a woman and a small child. People still practised hunting and gathering but they stayed closer to their villages, where they grew cereal grains, which they processed for consumption. Pottery consisted of both coarse wares and polished wares; pottery with an incised herringbone pattern closely resembles ceramic wares found at Neolithic sites in Palestine.

and Lower Egypt. This is an important geographical as well as historical division because the ancient Egyptians marked the beginning of their own history with the unification of Upper and Lower Egypt. Throughout their history the ancient Egyptians referred to their rulers as being the "kings of Upper and Lower Egypt".

The development of early Egypt

The period preceding the beginning of Egyptian history, about 3050 BC, is referred to as the Predynastic period.[6] From about 7000 BC to the end of the third millennium BC the climate of North Africa was wetter than it is now, and this additional moisture allowed small trees and grasses to grow in areas that today are only desert.[7] This permitted hunter–gatherers to live away from the Nile river valley and practise a mixture of pastoralism and hunting and gathering. The hilly regions adjacent to the Red Sea had tree cover and grazing land, which supported animals such as deer, ibex, gazelle, antelope, and wild asses. In addition, there was a substantial population of other types of wild animals normally associated with regions further south in Africa including elephants, rhinoceros, and giraffes.[8] By the sixth millennium BC, increasing human population placed a

Tools were largely made of bone plus a variety of lithic types used for arrowheads, sickles and axes.

Later village complexes, such as Ma'adi (3700–3300 BC), show evidence of both cereal agriculture and herding, with much less emphasis on hunting. At Ma'adi there was a marked increase in craft specialization, with copper being used to make stone tools and weapons. Ma'adi was part of a trading network that extended from Upper Egypt in the south, through the Sinai Peninsula, and into Palestine in the north. Throughout much of its prehistory, Egypt remained a land of small farming villages, and scattered along the Nile River were bands of people who lived by a mixture of fishing, farming, herding, and some hunting and gathering. This type of economy worked well for many years, but by the fourth millennium BC game was becoming scarce, and people continued to settle into small farming villages, working their fields and tending small flocks of sheep, goats, and cattle.

Agricultural communities made up of small farms alongside rivers may not lend themselves well to the development of cities. Unlike Mesopotamia, which was known for its many cities, Egyptian society was not as markedly urban throughout much of its early history. Only a few cities developed along the Nile River before the first millennium BC.[11] However, by the middle of the fourth millennium BC, Egypt had at least two large towns: Nekhen and Naqada, the larger of the two. The town of Nekhen (which the Greeks later called Hierakonpolis, "City of the Hawk King") developed on the west bank of the Nile River in Upper Egypt. It is possible that by 3300 BC it had a population of 2000 inhabitants,[12] and in the centuries that followed this figure was certainly higher. Nekhen may not have had as large a population as contemporary cities in Mesopotamia, but it had many of the characteristics of a metropolitan centre. The town was entered through a great gateway and was surrounded by a high fortification wall that was up to 9.5 m thick in some places. Like Mesopotamian cities

from the same period, there was an enclosed area in the centre of the city for a temple precinct that was set off by a large *temenos* wall. At Nekhen an important deposit of art objects was found that show the high level of craftsmanship that had been reached in Egypt by the end of the fourth millennium BC, giving a fascinating glimpse into the formation of the early Egyptian state. A few of these objects show a distinct Mesopotamian influence.

The Mesopotamian connection

A number of factors that indicate the Predynastic culture of Egypt received some form of stimulation from the emerging city-states of Mesopotamia, particularly during the Uruk period late in the fourth millennium BC.[13] Signs of Mesopotamian contact and influence have been found throughout the Nile river valley, not only at Nekhen, but in the north, in the Nile Delta region, and in Nubia to the south. Evidence consists of palettes, mace heads, cylinder seals, and artistic motifs of interlacing long-necked serpents and men wrestling with large beasts. Clay "nails", or cone-shaped wall decorations typical of the Uruk culture of southern Mesopotamia, were found at the town of Buto in the Nile Delta. Additional architectural evidence consists of new types of building techniques that were previously only known in Mesopotamia,[14] but were used by Egyptian builders to create structures of truly monumental size.[15]

Given the evidence for Mesopotamian influence, scholars have asked why people from Mesopotamia, or at least people familiar with elements of Mesopotamian culture, would go to Egypt, and how they got there. How did people from distant lands travel to Egypt at a time when transportation technology was in its infancy? In the late fourth millennium BC, ships were small, and navigation techniques primitive. Horses and camels had not been domesticated, the wheel had only recently been invented, and road

systems were undeveloped or non-existent. Nevertheless, such voyages could have been undertaken. If ships stayed within sight of land and found safe harbours at night they could have crossed the Red Sea or used the Mediterranean Sea to get from Syria-Palestine to the Nile Delta.[16] But it would not have been necessary to travel by water since donkeys[17] could have made the overland trip provided they had sufficient food and water, or people may have simply walked from Mesopotamia to Egypt. But why did they go? The answer most often given is that traders from Mesopotamian city-states were looking for gold[18] or trading opportunities. In historic times, the city of Naqada[19] located 75 km north of Nekhen was called "the Golden Town",[20] and the region was known for its deposits of gold. Most scholars believe that a northern land route[21] was used to get to Egypt. Traders and explorers could have followed the Euphrates River north, and then turned west and continued down the coast of Syria-Palestine to the Nile Delta. But there is some evidence for sea travel as well in the form of numerous representations of boats, similar to those known from Mesopotamia, which are portrayed in rock carvings in the Wadi Hammamat,[22] the most direct route from the Red Sea to Naqada in Upper Egypt.

Scholarly consensus has long maintained that there was significant Mesopotamian contact and influence on Egypt in the fourth millennium BC. However, some Egyptologists are questioning[23] the long-held idea that Mesopotamian traders spread the idea of writing[24] to Egypt. Excavations of the cemetery complex at the city of Abydos have revealed a number of subterranean burial chambers containing early forms of Egyptian writing[25] from the Naqada III period to the Early Dynastic period[26] in the late fourth millennium BC (3300–3000 BC). This is writing in the form of inscribed jar labels found in these tombs, contemporary with the early city-states in southern Mesopotamia. This evidence seems to indicate that early forms of writing appeared at the same time in both Egypt and Mesopotamia. Since the two writing systems are so different, it has been argued that writing may have developed independently in Egypt.[27]

Even though there was a period of contact between Mesopotamia and Egypt, Egyptian civilization did not develop only as a result of Mesopotamian influence. Before contact with Mesopotamia, Egyptian civilization was already forming on the banks of the Nile River, so whatever influence Mesopotamia had on Egypt only facilitated its emergence. At the end of the fourth millennium BC, the period of contact between Egypt and Mesopotamia temporarily came to an end, and whatever was borrowed from the Tigris–Euphrates region took on a distinctive flavour that was wholly Egyptian.

The rediscovery of ancient Egypt

The story of the rediscovery of ancient Egypt is one of the most fascinating episodes in the recent history of the ancient Near East.[28] The glories of ancient Egypt had been almost totally forgotten after the fall of the Roman Empire in the late fifth century AD. A few European travellers had ventured into Egypt during the Middle Ages and the Renaissance, and had returned with tales of magnificent monuments and fabled cities. Since political conditions were sometimes unstable, visitors usually did not venture much further south than Alexandria and Cairo. The only information about ancient Egypt came from classical historians like Herodotus and Diodorus, who had written accounts of Egypt in ancient times. Renewed interest in the land of the Nile was greatly stimulated by Napoleon Bonaparte's invasion of Egypt in 1798. At that time Britain and France were at war, and Napoleon wanted to establish a base in Egypt so he could cut off Britain's trade routes to India and the Far East. But Napoleon was not only interested in conquering Egypt; he also wanted to record and

study the lands of the ancient Pharaohs.[29] Before his invasion, Napoleon created the Commission des Arts et Sciences, which consisted of scholars who were to study Egypt while Napoleon's soldiers conquered it. When Napoleon left the port of Toulon in 1798, along with the 38 000 soldiers and 328 ships of his invasion force, he took with him 175 scholars or *savants*. This intellectual contingent of Napoleon's invasion force had a large library, plus crates of scientific measuring equipment to be used by chemists, geologists, cartographers, and other scientists to make a thorough study of Egypt.

Having drawn his troops up in front of the pyramids of Giza, Napoleon exhorted his men to fight valiantly, declaring to his soldiers "forty centuries are looking down on you", referring to the towering stone tombs that formed the background of the battle scene. The battle was of great historical importance because it was the first conquest of a Muslim country by Europeans since the time of the crusades of the Middle Ages, centuries earlier. The Egyptian defenders were led by Murad Bey, who commanded an army of 90 000 against Napoleon's smaller force of 25 000. But the outcome of the battle was never in doubt. Napoleon commanded a highly disciplined, modern army with cannons and rifles with bayonets. The Egyptian warriors, armed only with scimitars (curved swords) fought bravely, but after two hours of battle, and thousands of casualties, the Egyptian forces left the field in defeat. The glory of Napoleon's conquest of Egypt was short-lived for, a few weeks after the battle of the pyramids, the British fleet, under Admiral Nelson, caught the French invasion flotilla at Abukir Bay and destroyed most of the French ships. In 1799, a year after an impressive beginning to his Egyptian campaign, Napoleon was forced to leave Egypt, his invasion a failure. Although Napoleon's invasion was a military disaster, the scholars who had accompanied him made a number of important, even startling, discoveries that gave birth to the science of Egyptology. One of the men who

accompanied Napoleon was the talented artist Dominique Vivant Denon. Denon travelled throughout Lower and Upper Egypt, drawing in great detail the hundreds of monuments and temples whose ruins were still visible above-ground. When Denon returned to France he published a popular book entitled *Travels in Upper and Lower Egypt* (1803) and Napoleon made him director-general of the museums of France. A few years later the *Commission des Arts et Sciences* published the results of their work in a lavishly illustrated 21-volume work entitled *Description de l'Égypte* (1809–1828).

The Rosetta Stone

Among the discoveries that the *savants* made was a stele of heavy black basalt called the Rosetta Stone (1.14 m × 0.74 m × 0.28 m), which contained a bilingual inscription written in three different scripts: the top portion was written in the traditional hieroglyphic or pictographic style; the middle section was written in demotic, a cursive form of Egyptian writing; and the bottom section was written in ancient Greek. The top two sections of the stone were unreadable, but ancient Greek was a well-known language for many scholars.

Plaster casts of the Rosetta Stone were made and sent to Paris, but as part of the surrender terms when the French troops capitulated to the British, the French were obliged to give the precious relic to their conquerors. It was taken to Britain after the hostilities, where it remains today in the British Museum in London. From that moment the race was on to see who would be the first to decipher the mysterious script and open the doors to ancient Egypt; the Rosetta Stone was the key to deciphering ancient Egyptian writing. The first major progress in understanding it was made by the English scientist Thomas Young (1773–1829), although he never actually deciphered the text of the Rosetta Stone.

The Rosetta Stone, which has a trilingual inscription. (British Museum, London.)

That difficult task was accomplished about 20 years later by Jean François Champollion. As a child Champollion (1790–1832) was exceptionally talented and spent his early years studying at the *lycée* in the town of Grenoble. He began studying ancient Hebrew when he was 11 years old, and was already proficient in Latin and Greek. One day he saw a plaster cast of the Rosetta Stone in the home of a family friend and asked if anyone could read it. The answer at that time was no, for ancient Egyptian was still a mystery. Upon hearing this, the young Champollion is said to have declared that some day he would decipher the writing on the stone; 20 years later he did exactly that. At 13 he was reading Arabic and Coptic, the last form of the ancient Egyptian language, and he studied Chinese to see if it was related to ancient Egyptian. When he was 17 years old he decided to further his studies in Paris and used another book he had written, *Egypt Under the Pharaohs*, as his entrance exam essay. His professors were so impressed they embraced him, and made him a member of the Grenoble teaching faculty on the spot.

Champollion went on to study in Paris where he immersed himself in Persian, Sanskrit, and more Coptic, the key to understanding hieroglyphs.[30] He was so poor while studying in Paris during the troubled days of the Napoleonic Wars that he nearly starved to death on a number of occasions, and yet, despite numerous hardships, it was during this time that he began working on deciphering the hieroglyphs.[31] Two years later, the 19-year-old returned to Grenoble and took up his position as a professor at his former school. In 1822 he published his now famous *Lettre à M. Dacier*[32] explaining some of the basic aspects of the ancient Egyptian writing system. Champollion's work was quickly recognized as a scholarly masterpiece and shortly thereafter he was appointed head of the Egyptian section of the Louvre Museum, and the first professor of Egyptology at the Collège de France in Paris. In 1828 he led an 18-month expedition to Egypt, where he discovered buried temples, deciphered unknown inscriptions, and confirmed many of his theories. He died aged 41, three years after his return to Paris. As a result of Champollion's work the language of one of the world's most ancient and venerable civilizations came to life once again.

Egyptology

After Napoleon's Egyptian campaign, and the eye-opening discoveries made by the *savants*, an increased awareness and interest in Egyptian culture swept over Europe. By the middle of the 19th century excavators, from Germany, Britain, France, and other countries, were combing the Nile river valley, copying inscriptions and recovering precious objects. Reports of new discoveries were published in newspapers and books, which reached a growing audience of people who desired to learn more about the ancient kingdoms along the Nile. By the beginning of the 20th century, museums in Europe and North America were displaying thousands of artifacts from Egypt, while a growing number of scholarly and popular books brought a greater awareness of this ancient land to the public. Specialized journals of Egyptian history and archaeology published by scholarly organizations began to appear in the 19th century along with dictionaries of the Egyptian language. This initial period of discovery was highlighted by the discovery of the tomb of Tutankhamun (see Ch. 14) by Howard Carter in 1922. Beginning with Napoleon as part of a military enterprise, today Egyptology is a well-established field of research that seeks to further the understanding of one of the world's most beautiful and fascinating civilizations.

The unification of Egypt

Egyptologists traditionally mark the beginning of Egyptian history with the unification of Egypt under the rule of a single king, Narmer.[33] It is now generally agreed that Egypt had achieved some kind of political and cultural unity in the Naqada III period, but Narmer's role in this is still debated. Before unification, Egypt was made up of a number of small political districts ruled by strongmen or tribal chiefs. Gradually, the southern rulers (Upper Egypt) expanded their power and influence into the Nile Delta region in the north (Lower Egypt) until eventually the whole Nile river valley was conquered by forces from the south.[34] Lower Egypt was called *ta-*

Map showing the regions of Upper and Lower Egypt.

The red crown of Lower Egypt and the white crown of Upper Egypt. The combined crowns are shown on the right.

mehu, and encompassed the Nile Delta to its apex near the ancient capital of Memphis.

Upper Egypt, called *shemau*, started at the First Cataract (the word "cataract" refers to the rapids or cascades of the Nile River) and went as far as the city of Memphis 700 km to the north. After unification, the kings of Upper Egypt were designated *ny-swt*, meaning "one who belongs to the sedge plant". The characteristic headdress of these kings was a tall white crown, the *hedjet*. The kings of Lower Egypt bore the title *bity*, which perhaps means "one of the bee", and was represented by the hieroglyph of a bee. The official headdress of the king of Lower Egypt was a red crown, the *deshret*, made of wicker with a high back and a curved element protruding from the front. The unification of Egypt was accomplished when one individual managed to wear the crowns of both regions. The first person shown wearing the two crowns on the same artifact was Narmer, whose name means something like "deadly or baleful catfish", about 3000 BC. This act marks the unification of Upper and Lower Egypt and the beginning of Egyptian history and dynastic kingship.

Egyptian history has been traditionally divided into dynasties since the third century BC, when Manetho, an Egyptian priest, wrote a treatise on history and chronology and divided Egyptian history into 30 ruling families or dynasties.[35] Although Manetho's system contains some errors, modern historians still follow his basic divisions. Beginning in the 19th century AD, Egyptologists began to divide Egyptian history into larger blocks of time containing a number of dynasties such as the Old Kingdom, the Middle Kingdom and the New Kingdom, interspersed with periods of social and political decline referred to as the First Intermediate, Second Intermediate, and Third Intermediate periods (see chronological chart, overleaf). The first three dynasties, the Early Dynastic period, lasted from about 2920 BC to 2575 BC. There are no written documents that refer directly to the unification of Upper and Lower Egypt,[36] thus one of the most important events in Egyptian history has gone unrecorded. However, an artifact known as the Palette of Narmer in the Egyptian Museum, Cairo, provides some interesting information concerning the early political history of the Two Lands.

The Palette of Narmer

Exactly when and how Egypt became unified is not fully understood, but clues to its formation can be found on artifacts such as the Palette of Narmer.[37] The Palette is a flat, shield-shaped object made of slate that was supposedly used to grind eye paint and cosmetics. Each side is divided into registers containing various scenes and symbols sculpted in low relief. At the top on both sides the goddess Hathor is shown as a human-faced cow. Between her representations the name of the king is inscribed inside a *serekh*, a rectangular frame that contains the king's name and represents the palace where he lived. His name is written with the hieroglyphs for "catfish" and "chisel", which are read "Narmer". The centre register of the obverse side shows Narmer wearing the white crown, the *hedjet*, of Upper Egypt. With his raised arm he is preparing to strike the king of Lower Egypt, whom he holds by the hair. Behind Narmer stands a servant, holding his sandals and carrying a jar in his right hand. Narmer is seen wearing a kilt, some kind of animal tail, and an artificial tuft of hair strapped to his chin. These elements were adopted by later kings as part of their royal attire. The combination bird and human head symbol to the right represents the emblem of the hawk god, Horus, presenting victory to the king, who has subdued his enemy and restrains him with a string through his nose. On the bottom register are two dead enemies of the king defeated by the mighty Narmer.

On the reverse side, the second register shows the king visiting a battlefield where his enemies have been

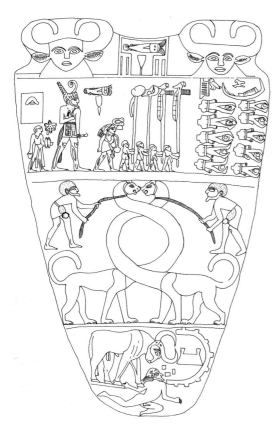

Palette of Narmer, obverse. Slate, height 64 cm. (Egyptian Museum, Cairo.)

Palette of Narmer, reverse. (Egyptian Museum, Cairo.)

Chronology of major historical divisions in Egyptian history (all dates BC)	
Late Predynastic period	3300–3200
UNIFICATION	
Early Dynastic period	2920–2575
Old Kingdom	2575–2134
First Intermediate period	2134–2040
Middle Kingdom	2040–1640
Second Intermediate period	1640–1532
New Kingdom	1532–1069
Third Intermediate period	1069–664
Late period	664–525
Persian period	525–332
Hellenistic period	332–30

known if the Palette represents the actual unification of the Two Lands or only one of the many conquests that took place as part of the general process that brought Upper and Lower Egypt together as a single nation around 3000 BC. Nevertheless, the Palette of Narmer gives some interesting insights into the formation of the early Egyptian state.

The Early Dynastic period (2920–2575 BC)

After Egypt was unified, dynastic kings ruled the Nile river valley and Egyptian civilization flowered and prospered for many centuries. The Egyptian state was considered to be not a political organization constructed by humans, but a creation of the gods at the beginning of time. From the very beginning Egyptian kings were considered to be divine beings sent to rule the earth: the divine sons of a human female and the ancient sky god, Horus, a god in the form of a great hawk with outstretched wings that covered the sky, whose eyes were the sun and the moon. Horus was also the son of Osiris, the god of the underworld (see Ch. 12). Several generations before the kings Narmer and Aha, the name of the god Horus was incorporated into their names and this tradition continued throughout Egyptian history.

slain. The enemy corpses have their heads neatly tucked between their legs, and are laid out in two rows of five headless bodies. Standing before them are standard-bearers carrying the symbols of various local tribes. The king is shown wearing the *deshret*, the red crown. The chisel and catfish hieroglyphs are once again clearly visible, indicating that the same person is wearing both crowns in two different scenes. The middle register of the reverse side con-

tains two mythological creatures whose long, intertwined necks form the circular area in which cosmetics were crushed. Their necks are tethered by ropes held by servants. In the lower register a bull, representing the king, tramples an enemy while knocking down an enemy fortress. Most Egyptologists interpret the Palette of Narmer as a representation of the king of Upper Egypt subduing the king of Lower Egypt or perhaps one of his other enemies. It is not

Later kings were also considered to be divinely connected to the sun god Re, the source of life, light, and power.

The king was sometimes referred to as the "perfect god", and his unique status allowed him to act as a mediator between his human subjects and the gods. In theory, only the king could approach the gods since he was the son of a god.[38] The political nature of kingship, and the everyday tasks of ruling the country, were mixed with religious beliefs and mythology and the king, who was called the "benevolent shepherd" of the land, kept things in smooth working order. To rule properly and justly, the king was obliged to act according to *ma'at*, the concept of truth and justice that served as the moral foundation on which the state was built. The concept of *ma'at* was so important that many kings even incorporated the word *ma'at* into their Horus names.[39] To the ancient Egyptians, everything was chaos and confusion without the king, but once he was on his throne, order and good government could be maintained in the Two Lands. In matters of administration the reigning king's sons and other close relatives were given important positions as priests, viziers (administrators), and the head of the all-important treasury. However, apart from the names and titles of kings and a few important family members, little is known about the history of the day-to-day events of this period, or why some dynasties lasted longer than others.

One of the chief functions of the king was to maintain the unity of Upper and Lower Egypt. This can be seen in the distinctly symbolic clothing worn by the king with symbols from both regions of Egypt, such as the crowns of Upper and Lower Egypt. The centralized government under the king redistributed food surpluses during times of need to make sure that there was enough for everyone. The king also used manufactured goods to engage in trade with outsiders. With the resources of the palace at his disposal, the king could control the most lucrative forms of trade, since he controlled more wealth than any single individual. Archaeological evidence indicates that by the Naqada III period and the 1st Dynasty, Palestinian goods were being included in Egyptian royal tombs and, conversely, Egyptian goods have been found in Palestine during the same period, making it clear that there was active trade between the two regions. It is also evidence of Egyptian settlement in Palestine.[40]

By the 2nd Dynasty there is little evidence of continuing direct trade with Mesopotamia, but trade did continue with Palestine. After unification, the use of copper increased and larger construction projects using wood, mud bricks, and small amounts of stone were undertaken. In the Predynastic period the Egyptians were familiar with softer precious metals like gold and silver, and they continued to work with copper as they had in earlier times, although many of their tools and implements were still made of wood or stone. By the Early Dynastic period a few inscriptions on stone or other durable materials begin to appear, but no written documents on papyrus have survived from the early centuries of Egyptian history. As a result, scholars tend to emphasize artifacts and archaeological discoveries in their attempts to understand the formation of early Egypt. Non-written sources of information such as temples, funerary complexes, and their accompanying artwork have revealed much about the religion, politics, and everyday life in the early phases of Egyptian history, and will be emphasized in Chapter 11.

11 The Old Kingdom or the Pyramid Age (2575–2134 BC)

About four centuries after King Narmer, Egypt entered into the historical period called the Old Kingdom. Also known as the "Pyramid Age",[1] the Old Kingdom is a term used to refer to the time period covering the 4th to the 7th Dynasties, although some Egyptologists include the 3rd Dynasty too. The Old Kingdom was a time of consolidation and development of the state and represents a major flowering of Egyptian civilization. During the Old Kingdom, Egypt experienced a long and uninterrupted period of economic prosperity and political stability that was a continuation of the previous Early Dynastic period, which saw the unification of Egypt into a single state ruled by a king who was elevated to a semi-divine status. Old Kingdom Egypt was administered by a literate elite, who developed a centrally administered state that could guarantee prosperity and stability for its leaders and inhabitants.

The social hierarchy of the Old Kingdom has been likened to the other great innovation of the period: the pyramid. At the summit of the social pyramid was the king and immediately below him were his family members, many of whom held important positions within the governing elite. The king entrusted his relatives with the highest positions in the administration, and many of the most important positions in temples, which were also centres of political and economic power, were held by family members.

By the Old Kingdom, Egyptian society was unified and highly organized. The capital of the Two Lands remained at Memphis, south of the Nile Delta,

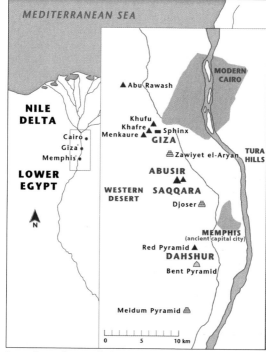

Lower Egypt showing the locations of the major Old Kingdom pyramids.

where Upper and Lower Egypt join together. Although many great architectural structures of the period remain, little is known about the size and layout of the capital itself, and few Old Kingdom historical or administrative texts have survived. As a result, knowledge of this period is incomplete and, as for the previous Early Dynastic period, few political events are actually known. Despite this, scholars know the names and the lengths of the reigns of almost all the kings of this period, including the famous pyramid builders of the 4th Dynasty, as well as lesser-known kings of the 5th and 6th Dynasties. The 6th Dynasty King Pepi II was the last important ruler of the Old Kingdom. He came to power as a child at the age of 6 and ruled for an incredible 94 years. By his time there was increasing friction between Upper Egypt and the newly emerging states of Nubia to the south.

Chronology of the Early Dynastic period, Old Kingdom and Middle Kingdom (all dates BC). The reigns of some individual kings are included.

Early Dynastic period (Dynasties 1–3)		
1st Dynasty		2920–2770
2nd Dynasty		2770–2649
3rd Dynasty		2649–2575
	Djoser	2630–2611
	Huni	2599–2575
Old Kingdom (Dynasties 4–8)		
4th Dynasty		2575–2465
	Snefru	2575–2551
	Khufu	2551–2528
	Khafre	2520–2494
	Menkaure	2490–2472
5th Dynasty		2465–2323
6th Dynasty		2323–2150
7th/8th Dynasties		2150–2134
First Intermediate period		
9th/10th Dynasties	2134–2040	(Herakleopolis)
11th Dynasty	2134–2040	(Thebes)
Middle Kingdom		
11th Dnasty		2040–1991
12th Dynasty		1991–1783
13th/14th Dynasties		1783–c.1640

Surviving economic and administrative documents make it clear that people, animals, and crop yields were counted on an annual basis, so the people could be taxed. There was no money at this time so people paid with agricultural goods.[2] Egyptian society was roughly divided into three groups directly under the king: the most powerful group was composed of literate men who wielded authority granted to them by the king; then there were minor officials connected to palaces and temples such as doorkeepers, soldiers, and quarrymen; and then the vast, illiterate peasantry who made up most of the population. Ideally, the king was the sole proprietor of the entire country and all its industries and natural resources.[3] Trade and crafts were owned by the king and were directly under his control. He had total control over the entire population of the country including the lower portion of the social pyramid; the rural agricultural population, who had the status of serfs, farmed land they did not own and paid a portion of their harvests to people higher up the socioeconomic ladder. Yet although the palace and the state controlled much of the economic activity there is ample evidence for private ownership of land[4] and the free exchange and bartering of goods. Agricultural resources divided into three categories: the crown, which had vast land holdings; religious estates, which maintained shrines and temples dedicated to the deceased and endowments for their cults; and private individuals.

The state was also concerned with the administration of law and justice and the maintenance of ma'at throughout the land. During the Old Kingdom there were law courts staffed with permanent officials with titles such as "overseer of the court", or "master of the secrets of judgements in the court", who specialized in legal matters, and had the power to deal with criminal cases.[5] Unfortunately, the ancient Egyptians left no collections of laws or law codes[6] similar to those of Mesopotamian kings such as the First Babylonian Dynasty king Hammurabi,[7] so little is

known about the actual functioning of Old Kingdom law courts.

Egypt's economy was based on the production of agricultural goods and their redistribution.[8] The state and temples were the major landowners, and they collected part of what the peasants raised each year and used it to feed and maintain royalty, the temple, and their employees. The remainder was stored to be used in times of famine. In order to properly administer the 1000-km kingdom, Egypt was divided into smaller administrative units called "*nomes*", and each *nome* had a governor or *nomarch*, who took orders from the king. Towards the end of the Old Kingdom, *nomes* ignored the central authority of the king and attempted to operate like small, independent polities. In fact, one of the major themes throughout much of Egyptian history was the struggle between the centralized control of the king and *nomarchs* to increase their own power. Nevertheless, there were times, such as the Old Kingdom, when the king held absolute power over the land and was able to utilize the country's natural resources on an unprecedented scale, allowing him to embark on massive mortuary construction projects such as the pyramids. One of the clearest manifestations of Old Kingdom wealth and stability were the large and costly projects undertaken in the middle years of the third millennium BC. The Early Dynastic period saw the first widespread use of stone as a building material, and by the Old Kingdom Egyptian masons were the undisputed masters of stone architecture, preparing the way for Egypt's most enduring and impressive creations: the pyramids.

Concepts of the afterlife

It is sometimes believed that the ancient Egyptians were preoccupied with death and had a morbid fascination with dead bodies and tombs.[9] To some extent this may be true, but they were probably no more concerned with death than any other civilization, ancient or modern.[10] Several Old Kingdom texts emphasize this with the opening words, "Oh you who love life and hate death." The Egyptians may appear more interested in death and the afterlife because so many of their tombs and so much of their funerary art has lasted into modern times. Even the most casual visitor to Egypt cannot help noticing the many spectacular tombs and mortuary structures, both above and below ground, scattered the length of the Nile river valley. Art history books and museums in Europe and North America are filled with examples of artwork created for funerary purposes and never intended to be put on public display. Some of the finest examples of Egyptian art buried with the dead were crafted strictly for religious and magical purposes. Carefully burying art objects such as statues, personal effects, and tomb paintings ensured that some of the most precious art objects ever created would survive long after their civilization had vanished. Even though most tombs were looted in antiquity by the Egyptians themselves, small amounts of their art have escaped detection by tomb robbers over the millennia. But even when emptied of their precious contents by thieves, hundreds of scenes of religious rituals and episodes from daily life depicted on tomb walls have managed to survive in remarkably good condition. Underground burial not only protected art objects from thieves, but it also protected them from wind, dust storms, and the destructive rays of the sun. Because some of their art has survived, it is possible for us to conjure up images of the ancient Egyptians, and recycle them in our own traditional and popular forms of art. In a very real sense, Egyptian art has made them immortal.

Concepts of the soul

Unlike many modern religious beliefs, the ancient Egyptians believed that an individual had more than one "soul" that survived after death. The soul was non-physical and was divided into three principal entities; the *ka*, the *ba*, and the *akh*.[11] The *ka* was created for each person at birth and has been considered variously as the person's twin, or double, or as a kind of "guardian angel". Some Egyptologists have seen the *ka* in psychological terms[12] as representing the personality, temperament, or vital force. The word also seems to mean fortune or position. Whatever the exact nature of the *ka*, it is clear that the deceased person and his *ka* had a close association after death. The king is referred to as going to his *ka* at death, and religious writings known as the *Pyramid Texts*[13] mention that the *ka* occasionally acted as a guide to the afterlife for the dead. Sometimes the *ka* and the king are referred to as being in the tomb together. The tomb was called "the house of the *ka*", while the priests responsible for its maintenance were called the "servants" of the *ka*.[14]

The *ka* was represented as either a bearded human figure with a wig and two upraised arms, or as two upraised arms bent at the elbow. Even though the *ka* was of a non-physical nature, it had to be fed like any other living being. Indeed, the plural of the word *ka* means "sustenance", clearly linking it with food. Sustaining the *ka* after death was of prime importance to the Egyptians, and this is why many of their funerary rites were devoted to food and drink offerings, and why so many burials from the Predynastic period to the end of the Pharaonic period contained chambers where large amounts of food could be stored.

The second aspect of the soul was the *ba*.[15] The *ba* was represented as a human-headed bird that was free to leave the confines of the tomb and visit places that had been enjoyed by the person during his or her lifetime. The word *ba* means "animation" or "mani-

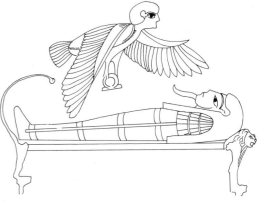

The *ba* as a bird hovering over its mummified remains. (*Book of the Dead.*)

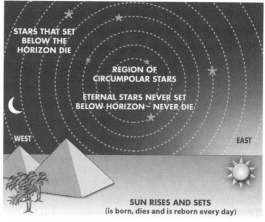

The stars of the circumpolar region of the heavens.

"estation" and referred to the spirit that the Egyptians believed lived on after a person died. Even though the *ba* was free to move about, it could not survive outside the tomb for an extended period of time. When darkness came, the *ba* had to return to its own tomb for the night. If the *ka* was not fed and sustained the *ba* had nowhere to return. For the *ka* and the *ba* to survive, the body had to be preserved, food and drink offerings had to be made, and the tomb had to be protected against the ever-present danger from tomb robbers in search of gold and treasure.

The third, more rarefied, aspect of the soul, called the *akh*,[16] could be either benevolent or evil. Normally translated as "spirit", the *akh* played a special role serving as an intermediary between the living and the dead. Living people could ask the *akh* of a deceased relative to intervene for them against other *akhs* who were causing them problems.[17] The *akh* was also that part of the soul incorporated into the universe, which became one of the eternal stars, an immortal beacon floating in the night sky. The Egyptians believed that celestial bodies such as the sun, the moon, or the stars that set below the horizon effectively died and were reborn at their next appearance. Thus, the sun died each night in the west and was reborn the next morning at sunrise in the east. The same fate awaited all humans who were buried, or in essence went below the horizon, at death. However, there is one group of stars, known as the circumpolar stars, that do not set below the horizon because they are clustered around the north celestial pole above the earth. Familiar stars in this area include the Big Dipper (Ursa Major) and Little Dipper (Ursa Minor).[18] Because these stars never set below the horizon, to the Egyptians they never died. Becoming one of the circumpolar stars at death ensured the deceased eternal life as a visible manifestation of the departed for those on earth to see. Several shafts in the Khufu Pyramid (see below) face north, which has led some scholars to speculate that they were oriented towards the area of the circumpolar stars and served to guide the deceased towards the region of the eternal stars. The *Pyramid Texts* inscribed inside the pyramid of the 5th Dynasty king Unas and 6th Dynasty pyramids refer to the dead king as a star among the eternal or circumpolar stars, who rose in the east, and sat among the stars in the northern skies.[19] There are numerous references to the king as a star living in the sky, but at the same time he was still magically connected to his earthbound *ka* and *ba*, who were confined to the environment in and around the tomb.

Pit graves

Like most peoples, the ancient Egyptians believed in the post-mortem (after death) survival of some kind of spirit or soul. Egyptian concepts of the afterlife were influenced by the climate and environmental conditions that prevailed in the Nile river valley. The low relative humidity, meagre amounts of rainfall, and general aridity combined to make Egypt one of the driest regions in the Near East. Predynastic Egyptians of the fifth and fourth millennia BC buried their dead in shallow graves referred to as pit burials or pit graves. The dead were buried lying on their sides with their knees drawn up against their chests, and their hands folded before their faces. Heads of the deceased were oriented to the south with faces towards the west, the direction of the setting sun.[20] Grave goods included pots for food and drink as well as objects of personal adornment such as combs and pins. In some instances corpses were covered with animal skins or coarse matting, or placed inside baskets made of woven twigs.

Pit graves were often covered by a pile of sand or stones: a tumulus. This made it easier for the relatives of the deceased to find the burial site in the desert and return to make food offerings. The tumulus also protected the deceased from wild dogs, which often destroyed burials looking for food. The sparse grave goods from the Predynastic period offer few clues concerning post-mortem beliefs, but food and personal belongings are a clear indication of a belief in some kind of an afterlife. Most pit graves were oval and quite small, a little over 1 m long and half as wide. Due to the hot, dry climate, the body was often naturally preserved, and no artificial means were required to preserve it. Many naturally preserved cadavers have been recovered from most regions of Egypt and from different historical periods. On numerous occasions desert burial grounds have yielded the dried-out remains of some long-forgotten individual, buried thousands of years ago, whose shrivelled corpse is still covered in an envelope of dried skin, with hair and fingernails in place, and the shrunken, ghoulish face discernible. On occasion, the Egyptians must have seen previously buried corpses dug up by animals, or perhaps accidentally uncovered while digging other graves. Observing that the dead were preserved in a dried-out condition, they incorporated the idea of physical preservation of the body into their beliefs about the afterlife. The early Egyptians probably did not know why the bodies were

Predynastic pit grave, fourth millennium BC. The deceased was buried facing west, covered with reed matting. The burial contained food offerings, beads, and household objects.

preserved in their desiccated form, but they held to the belief that the body had to be preserved for the soul to survive in the afterlife.[21]

The Egyptians had a very physical eschatology. Concepts that deal with preserving, provisioning, and protecting the dead dominate their attitudes about death and the afterlife throughout all periods of their history. If the body rotted, the chances for a happy eternal life were diminished or eliminated. To survive, the body had to be fed, protected, and provided with food and drink.[22] This is shown clearly in the graves where large quantities of pots for food and drink provisions have been recovered dating from the Early Dynastic period. The body also had to be secured from thieves, wild animals, and sand storms. If the body was disturbed in any way, the post-mortem existence of the deceased would be terminated forever. It is perhaps for an extra measure of security that the in-ground burials at Abydos, a town in Middle Egypt containing a number of royal burials, were surrounded by thick mud-brick walls sunk into the ground.

During the 1990s the German Archaeological Institute excavated a number of these enclosed pit graves, which at one time contained the burials of three 1st Dynasty kings: Iri-Hor, Aha, and possibly Narmer.[23] The pit burial of Aha consists of three mud-brick-lined chambers plus evidence of several large wooden shrines. To the east of these chambers excavators found a series of 33 smaller, brick-lined burials which contained the remains of male servants of Aha, between 20 and 25 years old, who were killed or perhaps committed suicide, and were buried with him. All other 1st Dynasty burials at Abydos have subsidiary burials that contained people who were interred at the time of royal burials. It is unclear whether those buried in the subsidiary tombs were priests, high-ranking officials, or domestic servants who were to serve the king in the afterlife. The 1st Dynasty was the only period in Egyptian history when humans were sacrificed in such circumstances;

the practice was abandoned afterwards in following or later dynasties.[24] After the formation of the Egyptian state the amount of wealth amassed by the king and the ruling elite increased. This new-found wealth was used during the king's lifetime to build palaces and temples and, in preparation for his death, for the construction of tombs and funerary complexes.[25]

Changes in Early Dynastic funerary structures

In the 1st Dynasty, the *mastaba*, a new type of above-ground burial structure, appears in some burials. The word *mastaba* means "bench" in Arabic and the structure resembles the low benches often found outside modern-day Middle-Eastern homes. Early *mastaba*s were made of mud bricks and were shaped like the houses of kings and members of the ruling elite. *Mastaba*s were built directly on top of in-ground burials and some had a small mortuary chapel attached to the east side. The mortuary chapel served as a place where the living could come and make food offerings and prayers to the deceased. First Dynasty *mastaba*s were equipped with large storehouses for food, which was magically consumed by the dead throughout eternity. The *mastaba* of Queen Neithhotep at Naqada had a superstructure containing 20 above-ground chambers used for food storage.[26]

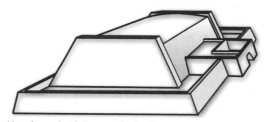

Mastaba tomb, 4th Dynasty, third millennium BC.

Like all Egyptian funerary monuments, the design of the *mastaba* underwent constant changes and modifications to improve its function and to make it correspond structurally to the religious beliefs and needs of the dead. Later *mastaba*s had up to 45 above-ground chambers containing stone and pottery vases, copper tools and vessels, wooden and ivory furniture, weapons, cosmetic and toilet articles, and even board games. Smaller burial complexes were provided for lesser officials, while the graves of the poor had not changed significantly from the pit graves of Predynastic times. The practice of having chambers both above and below ground continued until the middle of the 1st Dynasty, around 2900 BC.

In response to the growing problem of tomb robbery the number of above-ground chambers diminished while the number of underground chambers increased. This trend continued until above-ground chambers were abandoned altogether. Underground storage areas consisted of a long central passage with chambers branching out on either side. The *mastaba* structure proper no longer contained any storage chambers and was completely filled in with rubble to form a solid trapezoid-shaped mass.

During the early phases of Egyptian history, vessels for holding food and drink provisions were the most numerous objects found in tombs. This is in sharp contrast to the Old Kingdom, when the amount of food provisions had diminished in importance and more attention was given to precious objects, elaborate coffins, and non-edible goods. It is also in the Old Kingdom that the size of the burial chambers and the vast amount of goods contained in them were reduced. For sheer numbers of objects the Early Dynastic period is unsurpassed. The tomb of the 3rd Dynasty king Djoser has yielded 40 000 stone vessels and more chambers still await excavation.[27] Most of the vessels probably did not contain food or drink, but served to provide provisions for the afterlife magically. One of the most popular types of food offering consisted of choice cuts of beef that were to be magically consumed by the deceased. Some *mastabas* contained chambers devoted to the storage of meat only, particularly cuts from the rib sections of the animal. Other *mastabas* contained brick granaries containing large amounts of grain for making bread. Besides meat and bread, liquid refreshments were provided by vast numbers of pottery jars filled with wine. In one instance during the 2nd Dynasty, a meal was set out in a tomb on fine stone and pottery dishes, providing nourishment for the deceased for all eternity. The ingestion of food was always magical, and as long as the food remained uneaten it would always be there for the hungry tomb occupant. To ensure that the king or high-ranking person would enjoy a life of leisure, servants and attendants were sometimes buried in *mastabas* attached to the tomb of their master, or they were buried near it (but not in it, as in Mesopotamia) in their own smaller *mastabas* arranged in rows outside the sacred precinct.[28] They were probably buried at the same time as their masters, but it is not known how they died.

The step pyramid of Djoser

The 3rd Dynasty king Djoser made a number of innovations in funerary architecture, which can be seen in the vast complex he constructed at Saqqara,[29] of which his step pyramid forms the centrepiece and is one of the most outstanding examples of Egyptian architecture. Much of the credit for this remarkable structure is probably due to the king's chief architect, Imhotep, who later was reputed to have been a great healer, architect, and astronomer. If we can believe the ancient stories, his healing powers were so proficient that he was deified and worshipped as a god after his death. Whether he was ever an astronomer is not known, but in architecture it appears Imhotep was an innovator who achieved great things.

For his funerary complex, Djoser chose a location on the west bank of the Nile River, next to a 2nd

Dynasty royal cemetery, and the capital city of Memphis. He began by building a traditional *mastaba* with a number of underground storage chambers, as had been the practice for centuries. The core of his monument was a structure made of locally available soft limestone, covered with a layer of higher-quality limestone quarried on the opposite bank of the Nile River at Tura, about 20 km away. The original *mastaba* measured about 8 m high by 63 m on each side. The structure was oriented, more or less, towards the four cardinal directions (north, south, east, and west), but its base does not appear to have been laid out using the observation of celestial objects. The orientation of the structure may have more to do with the north–south direction of the Nile River than the stars.

At this point in its construction, a layer of stone less than a metre thick was attached to the exterior surface of the *mastaba*. Then, for some reason, it was enlarged again. An additional 9 m was added to the base on the east side, giving the tomb an oblong shape. Before these modifications were completed, a radical new plan was introduced. The base of the *mastaba* was extended again by another 3 m on each side, and then three smaller *mastabas* were built on top of the original structure. Once again the plans were changed and the entire mass was enlarged a third time, surpassing the previous structure in height and breadth. Finally, after some additional modifications, the structure was increased from four to six stages, and this remained its final form. The completed step pyramid, covered with polished limestone, rose 60 m high and measured 140 m × 118 m at its base. It was certainly one of the most dazzling architectural showpieces ever created by people up to that time.

King Djoser's tomb was different from previous burial structures. Unlike earlier *mastabas* built mainly of mud bricks, Djoser's was built entirely of stone. The stones were small in comparison to later mortuary structures, but the step pyramid of Djoser

Step pyramid of King Djoser and section of the outer wall.

Step pyramid of King Djoser and a section of the outer wall.

contained a massive amount of material compared to earlier single-stage *mastaba*s. What is less evident, and yet very important for understanding the uniqueness of this structure, is how a sufficient number of workers were organized, housed, and fed so that such a project could be brought to successful completion. Previously, the building of a large, single-storeyed *mastaba* could have been completed with local workers from the surrounding area. But, there were not enough labourers in the area around Memphis to undertake such a large project and additional workers would have been needed from other parts of the kingdom. The step pyramid of Djoser was thus an innovation in both the uses of stone, and the organization and use of labourers, and

it changed the way royal building projects were undertaken for centuries afterwards.[30]

King Djoser was buried under the structure at the bottom of a 28 m-deep vertical shaft. The burial chamber consisted of a cavity 3 m long by 3 m high and 1.7 m wide. It was constructed of pink granite slabs, and sealed at the top by a granite plug that weighed three tonnes. Since the tomb was robbed in antiquity, no coffin or precious objects have been found in the burial chamber. After the king was buried, the shaft leading to the burial chamber was filled with rubble in an attempt to keep thieves from entering the tomb. Djoser's burial complex was one of the most spectacular architectural achievements of the ancient world. His much-modified structure

demonstrated a willingness to make changes and experiment with new building techniques.

In addition to the step pyramid, Djoser's funerary complex consisted of a number of other elements, most of which were previously unknown. The step pyramid and sacred precinct were surrounded by a *temenos* wall made of high-quality Tura limestone that stood 10 m high and stretched 1.7 km long. Inside the sacred precinct were a number of buildings and temples used by priests to supply and cater to the needs of the king in the afterlife. Other than the step pyramid, the most important structure in the complex was the mortuary temple: a standard feature of all large burial complexes that originated in the Predynastic period and was in use throughout most of ancient Egyptian history. The function of the mortuary temple was to provide a place where offerings could be made, and hymns and rituals in honour of the dead king could be sung and performed. In one corner, where the mortuary temple joined the *mastaba*, a special room called the *serdab* was located. The *serdab* consisted of a small, completely sealed chamber that contained a lifelike statue of the king. The statue was probably intended to serve as a focal point for offerings and as a substitute for the king and his mummy in case they were destroyed. Djoser's *serdab* was pierced by two holes, which allowed the king to look out, and meant the smoke of incense and food offerings could enter the chamber. At Saqqara, the mortuary temple was built adjoining the north side of the step pyramid. Later, in the 4th Dynasty, mortuary temples were built on the east side, the direction of the sunrise, and the Nile river valley, which reflected a growing interest in the cult of the sun god, Re.[31]

Step pyramid or stage *mastaba*?

The term "step pyramid" is used to refer to a small number of mortuary structures from the 3rd Dynasty. Although the term is somewhat imprecise, its use is firmly entrenched in Egyptological terminology and is unlikely to be abandoned. Even though these structures are composed of a number of layers or stages, in one sense it is incorrect to refer to them as "steps" since they were never meant to be climbed by *living* people. However, the layered shape may have represented some kind of "stairway to heaven" that enabled the king to spiritually, or magically, reach the afterlife. One of the magical spells in the later *Pyramid Texts* seems to be referring to the step pyramid when it mentions a staircase to heaven laid out for the king so he could climb up to the heavens.[32] But if the step pyramid served as a stairway to heaven for the dead king, it was never meant to be used as such while the king was alive. The step pyramid of Djoser contains no stairways or ramps for climbing to its summit. Moreover, the Djoser structure, and those similar to it, are not pyramids, as a quick look in any geometry textbook will verify.

Attempts have been made to find a link between Egyptian pyramids and large stone ceremonial structures found in Central America, which some people erroneously believe is proof that Egyptians travelled to the New World many thousands of years ago (see illustration). In fact there is not a single pyramid-shaped burial structure known in Central America. There is abundant evidence that the Mayan or Aztec civilizations built large stone structures, but they were never shaped like true pyramids and it is pointless to compare Egyptian pyramids with the structures of Mayan or Aztec civilizations. The shape of step pyramids most closely resembles Mesopotamian ziggurats, but the evidence indicates that *mastaba*-shaped structures in Egypt predate ziggurats by hundreds of years, and there seems to be no relationship between them (see Ch. 4). Perhaps it would be better to refer to the layered funerary structures of this period as "stage *mastaba*s" (some German scholars use the term "*Stufen mastaba*", which means the same thing) instead of step pyramids, since this term

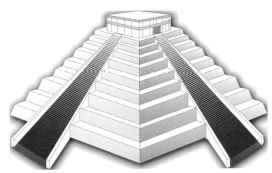

The structural similarities between the step pyramid, the ziggurat and a Meso-American temple. Top: Egyptian *mastaba*; middle: Meso-American staged structure; bottom: Mesopotamian ziggurat.

describes more accurately their shape and function. Several other 3rd Dynasty kings built step pyramids. These include the complexes of King Sekhemkhet, which measured 120 m on a side, and a massive structure that belonged to King Kha'ba, located at Zawiyet el Aryan, which was never completed. But the step pyramid design was not destined to have a long history, and its popularity gave way to further experimentation at the beginning of the 4th Dynasty.

The development of the true pyramid

Located 50 km south of the ancient capital at Memphis is the heavily damaged funerary structure known as the Meidum Pyramid.[33] Like the step pyramid of Djoser, the Meidum structure did not attain its final form until it had gone through a number of structural transformations. The structure currently appears as a square, three-storeyed tower about 70 m high, emerging from a pile of rubble and broken stone, and at first glance it is difficult to determine its original shape. Constructed in the 4th Dynasty, the Meidum Pyramid was explored and excavated in the early part of the 20th century by a number of archaeologists, including Gerald Averay Wainwright.[34] By tunnelling into the centre of the structure Wainwright determined that its earliest discernible form was an eight-layered *mastaba* or step pyramid similar to those of the previous 3rd Dynasty. This tower-like building was composed of a rough-cut stone core over which was applied the now traditional Tura limestone casing. The eight-stage structure was meant to be the final phase of its construction, but for some reason, as in the earlier Saqqara step pyramid, yet another layer was added to the entire structure, and it was finished a second time in Tura limestone. This second layer was also meant to be the final phase of construction. Then the structure was altered for a third and final time. The monument was given yet another layer of stone and the steps, or levels, were filled in, transforming it from a step pyramid to a true pyramid. Originally, each side of the Meidum Pyramid measured 147 m long at ground level, and it reached a height of 93.5 m. The entrance to the pyramid was located 18.5 m above-ground on the north side. The Meidum Pyramid was an impressive structure, and represented a major architectural achievement by Egyptian architects, masons, and engineers. Stones used in the pyramid were much larger than those of the Djoser step pyramid and indicate that the builders had more confidence in their stone-working capabilities. By the time the Meidum structure was completed the Egyptians had become the greatest builders of the ancient world, and possessed the technological and organizational skills that would enable them to undertake even greater building projects in the future.

The puzzle of the Meidum Pyramid

Because it was built of high-quality stone, the Meidum Pyramid has been used by the local population as a source of building material for houses, bridges and other types of buildings for thousands of years. Evidence from later excavations indicates that it was probably first exploited for its supply of stone as early as the 19th and 20th Dynasties of the New Kingdom.[35] The size of the blocks and the convenient location of the structure have ensured its continued use as a source of inexpensive stone even in modern times. After his own excavations in 1892, Flinders Petrie reported that village stonemasons could cut up one of the 6 tonne casing stones in a matter of minutes and turn it into tombstones to be sold to local inhabitants. Earlier, European explorers reported a stairway up the side of the structure to facilitate quarrying operations.[36]

In 1968 the distinguished Oxford University physicist Kurt Mendelsshon advanced the theory that the Meidum Pyramid collapsed due to structural weaknesses and design flaws.[37] His interpretation gained widespread acceptance among the public and some Egyptologists, and made its way into many popular accounts of Egyptian history and architecture. However, a recent study by a team of Egyptian archaeologists led by Ali El-Khouli has reaffirmed older interpretations that the present appearance of the structure is due entirely to centuries of quarrying, and not because the pyramid collapsed from structural miscalculations on the part of the ancient engineers.[38]

The pyramid shape

British Egyptologist I. E. S. Edwards[39] suggested that the pyramid shape represented the rays of the sun as they descended towards earth, forming a celestial path or stairway to heaven. There is much to support this interpretation since the priests of the sun god used a pyramid-shaped stone as one of the central cult objects in their worship of the solar deity.[40] The solar influence on the pyramid shape is echoed in the *Pyramid Texts* as well, which speak of the king as ascending to heaven on the sun's rays.[41] However, choosing the pyramid shape for their funerary structures may have had more to do with construction techniques than religious considerations. By building these

The remains of the core structure of the Meidum Pyramid.

Core remains of the Meidum Pyramid.

The descending shaft leading to the burial chamber of the Meidum Pyramid. The electric lights, handrails, and wooden ramp are modern additions.

structures in stages that were progressively smaller as they rose higher, the builders provided themselves with sufficient work space and manoeuvring room for hauling and placing the large building blocks. This is why large burial and ceremonial structures, not only in Egypt but also in many parts of the ancient world, were built in diminishing proportions, and it is probably for this reason that ancient civilizations did not build massive tombs in the form of cubes or spheres. Regardless of why the pyramid form was chosen, the Meidum structure was, at the time of its construction, a pyramid. Now it is only a rugged stone structure standing alone in the desert.

The shape of the structure was not the only innovation in the Meidum Pyramid. The burial chamber was placed inside the pyramid instead of beneath it, and was approached by a passageway built in the masonry on the north side. The narrow entrance to the tomb is 57 m long, and is inclined at an angle of 28 degrees to the horizon, pointing towards the region of the circumpolar stars. The burial chamber measures 6.5 m × 2.75 m, and its roof is made entirely of overlapping layers of limestone forming a corbelled vault.[42] The first archaeologist to enter the tomb was Gaston Maspero in 1882. However, he found no traces of the king or his sarcophagus. Nor did he find any treasures or precious objects.

The layout of the buildings at the Meidum Pyramid complex was followed by later pyramid builders for much of the Old Kingdom,[43] and consisted of the *main pyramid* and, later, up to three auxiliary pyramids nearby. Abutting the pyramid on the east side was the *mortuary temple*, which continued to serve as the cultic centre for sacrifices and prayers necessary for the well-being of the deceased king. This entire grouping was surrounded by a long *temenos wall*. Leading away from the pyramid was a massive stone *causeway*, which connected the pyramid complex to the *valley temple*, located adjacent to the Nile River.

No royal inscriptions bearing the name of the builder of this first true pyramid have been found at

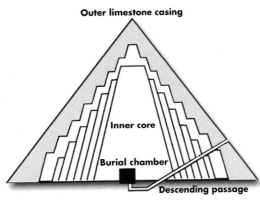

Section drawing showing the core and outer portions of the Meidum Pyramid.

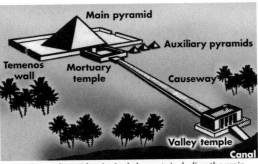

Pyramid complex with principal elements including the main pyramid, the auxiliary pyramid, *temenos* wall, mortuary temple, causeway, and valley temple.

the site. However, a graffiti scribbled on the walls of the mortuary temple by Egyptian visitors, who went to the site 1000 years after it was built, indicate that it belonged to King Snefru, the first king of the 4th Dynasty. The graffiti would seem to indicate that Snefru was the tomb's builder. But another pyramid, the Red Pyramid, located 50 km north at Dashur, can definitely be attributed to him. Another pyramid at the Dashur site belongs to him as well. This would make Snefru the builder of three pyramids, more than any other Egyptian king,[44] which is quite impressive given the estimated 3.7 million tonnes of stone, and the labour required to build three such structures.[45] It is known that, for a short time in the Early Dynastic period and the beginning of the Old Kingdom, some kings had two funerary monuments: one representing the south, located in Upper Egypt, and the other representing the north, located in Lower Egypt. Nowhere is there any precedent for more than two funerary structures per king at any time in Egyptian history.

Some Egyptologists do not think that the Meidum structure was built by Snefru.[46] It has been proposed that the structure was built by an earlier 4th Dynasty king named Huni. How, then, can the graffiti referring to Snefru found in the Meidum structure be explained? Either the visitors, 1000 years after the fact, were mistaken and scratched the wrong name on the Meidum Pyramid, or King Huni died before his pyramid was completed, and his son Snefru completed it for him. These interpretations correspond well with the facts and would explain why Snefru's name is associated with three pyramids, even though one of them belonged to his father.

The Bent Pyramid at Dashur

One of the strangest-looking pyramids is the so-called "Bent Pyramid" at Dashur, built by Snefru. The Bent Pyramid is not really a pyramid at all, but

The Bent Pyramid at Dashur.

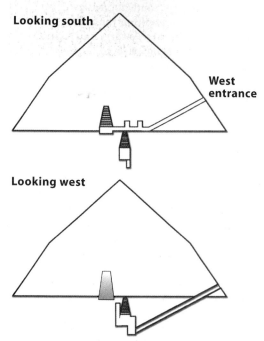

Section drawing showing the Bent Pyramid from the west and south.

a rhomboid. The structure measures 183.5 m on a side and rises to a height of 105 m. Snefru was no doubt not attempting to create a new shape for funerary structures when he chose this bent or truncated configuration. It probably took this unusual form because of certain structural problems encountered by the builders. Unlike other pyramids, the base of the Bent Pyramid was built directly on the soft desert sands. Fearing that the base would not be able to support the massive weight of more than a million stones, halfway through the construction project the engineers decided that they would have to reduce the weight of the upper part of the structure. They accomplished this by reducing the exterior angle of the casing stones from 54 degrees to a flatter 43 degrees in an attempt to keep the great mass of stones from collapsing. Whatever their reasons for changing the angle of the structure, the ancient engineers made a wise choice, and the structure still stands today with its odd-looking bend, 45 centuries after it was built.

The pyramids at Giza

Pyramid development reached its peak in the 4th Dynasty with the construction of the giant funerary structure of King Khufu ("Cheops" in Greek), located on the Giza Plateau, west of modern Cairo.[47] The ancient Egyptians emphasized the solar aspect of this massive structure by naming it "The horizon (of Khufu)". The Khufu Pyramid (also called the Great Pyramid) is an overwhelming structure to behold. To see its massive structure rising above the Giza Plateau, shrouded in mist at sunrise or by the light of the full moon, is an unforgettable sight. It is built with an estimated 2.3 million limestone blocks, most weighing about 2 tonnes each, but some weighing as much as 50 tonnes. The structure originally measured 146.6 m high, and although part of its upper portion is now missing, it still rises to 138.75 m. The base measures 230 m on a side and covers 5.3 hec-

tares. The difference between the length of the four sides is a meagre 4.4 cm.[48] Furthermore, each side was quite accurately oriented to the four cardinal points, deviating only slightly from perfection. Considering the age of the structure and the basic, but nevertheless adequate, measuring and surveying tools the ancient Egyptians possessed,[49] the accuracy of the Great Pyramid is phenomenal. Although from a distance the Khufu Pyramid gives the impression of being substantially intact, upon closer examination this is not the case. The top courses of stone are missing and the structure is no longer pointed at the summit, but instead forms a platform large enough for about a dozen people to stand on, with room left over for a small, red aircraft warning light.

Like the Meidum Pyramid, and many other funerary structures, the Khufu Pyramid was exploited as a quarry site in ancient and medieval times. Towards the end of the 12th century AD, during the reign of Sultan Saladin (AD 1174–1193), the exterior casing stones were stripped and used in the construction of the great Citadel mosque and bridges in Cairo. In AD 1356 the city of Cairo suffered an earthquake that resulted in a great loss of life and the destruction of much of the city. The Great Pyramid and a number of other structures on the Giza Plateau had their outer layers of valuable limestone removed and used in the reconstruction of the Citadel and the bridges of the devastated city. It is not known exactly when thieves first broke into the Khufu Pyramid in ancient times, but Stadelmann believes it happened during the Middle Kingdom,[50] and that the stone of the causeways and temples was used by the kings of the later 12th Dynasty for their own construction projects. According to Muslim stories the tomb was entered in the 9th century AD when the caliph of Baghdad, Al Ma'mun, forced his way into the structure.[51] But it is probable that the tomb had been violated before Al Ma'mun, since the Roman period historian Strabo (first century BC), recounts that he saw people go in and out of the pyramid with ease

Left to right: The Khufu Pyramid, with two smaller "Queen's pyramids" in the foreground, 4th Dynasty, Giza Plateau, Lower Egypt. North side of the Khufu Pyramid showing the original descending passage entrance above and below, where people are standing, the entrance cut into the pyramid face by Al Ma'mun. The lower or so-called "Queen's Chamber" located in the interior of the Khufu Pyramid. It probably contained a special statue of the king's *ka*. The Grand Gallery, 8.74 m high × 46.7 m long, located at the end of the ascending passage. Corbelled arch construction.

through a kind of tilting door on the north side. A notion that was always popular, and no doubt true at the time of its construction, was that the pyramid contained gold and other treasures.

Mysteries of the pyramid

Throughout the ages people have been fascinated by the pyramids, and travellers came to Egypt from far and wide to visit them and marvel at their grandeur. The Greek historian Herodotus visited the Giza Plateau in the fifth century BC, and wrote at length about these structures. It was Herodotus who put forth the well-known, and often repeated, estimate that it took 400 000 men (100 000 men working in shifts of three months each), 20 years to complete the structure.[52] There is no evidence to support these estimates, and they are probably exaggerated. Recent research indicates a much smaller total workforce of 25 000 to 35 000 stoneworkers and labourers: only a small percentage of the population.[53] Because of their overwhelming size and grandeur it is not surprising that ancient visitors fabricated stories about how and why they were built. Arab writers from medieval Cairo claimed that they had been constructed by an ancient king as repositories for all wisdom and scientific knowledge, so that when the biblical flood took place (see Chs 3 and 8) such knowledge would not be lost. The late Roman historian Julius Honorius quoted a legend that claimed the pyramids were the granaries of the Old Testament in which the patriarch Joseph stored grain for the lean or famine years.[54] This legend was still being retold centuries later in the narrative of the Englishman Sir John Maundeville, who supposedly visited Egypt in the 14th century AD. His narrative claimed it was common knowledge that the pyramids were originally granaries, but contained only snakes when he visited them.[55]

Explorers of the 18th and 19th centuries AD were responsible for the well-known, but unfounded, ideas that the pharaonic Egyptians had developed a secret and highly advanced science, and that they were experts in mathematics and astronomy. For the past two centuries all manner of wild and impossible claims have been made about the pyramids: everything from the assertion that they emit rays that enable people to reach greater levels of spiritual consciousness, to claims that they can cure diseases, sharpen razor blades, and improve the performance of hockey players.

In 1859 John Taylor argued in his book, *The Great Pyramid: Why Was It Built, and Who Built It?*, that the Khufu Pyramid was not simply a royal tomb, but was built with divine inspiration, and within its design and measurements were secret coded messages from God concerning the nature of the universe. The ideas of Taylor greatly impressed Charles Piazzi Smyth, professor of astronomy at the University of Edinburgh. Smyth spent months in Egypt, living in an abandoned tomb and making many measurements of the Khufu Pyramid, which he claimed had been built using a unit of measurement he called the "pyramid inch". Since Smyth was a British subject it is not surprising that his pyramid inch equalled one British or Imperial inch. He also claimed that the builders of the Khufu Pyramid used another unit of measurement called the "sacred cubit", which equalled about 25 inches. Smyth believed the sacred cubit was the same unit of measurement used by Moses to build the *tabernacle*,[56] the portable religious sanctuary of the ancient Hebrews containing the Ten Commandments, as well as Noah's Ark. Armed with these two units, Smyth measured the baselines, passageways, and chambers of the Khufu Pyramid and came up with all kinds of supposed relationships between the dimensions of the Great Pyramid and the earth and the solar system. He claimed to have discovered a direct correlation between the pyramid and the diameter of the earth, the number of days in the solar year, and the distance between the earth and the sun.[57] But such numerology really proves nothing about the way the pyramid was built, or the level of astronomical sophistication of the Egyptians. Scholars know that the ancient Egyptians never had a unit of measurement that resembled the "pyramid inch", and that this imaginary unit was created by Smyth to fulfil his unfounded prophetic calculations;

the standard unit of measure in ancient Egypt was the "royal cubit" of 52.5 cm. Such numerical relationships could be found just as easily almost anywhere on earth. By creating some arbitrary unit of measurement one could obtain the circumference of the earth from the number of steps on the Lincoln Memorial in Washington, D.C., or the distance to the sun or number of days in a year using the number of street lights in Toronto.

Smyth was devoutly religious and, like John Taylor before him, believed that the Great Pyramid represented the Bible written in stone. In one of his influential books, *Our Inheritance in the Great Pyramid* (1880), Smyth used pyramid measurements to chart the major events in biblical history and to predict the end of the world, which was supposed to happen in the year 1881. The fact that this date came and went and the world did not end did not deter Smyth and his followers. They simply recalculated the dates, still using the "pyramid inch", of course, and pushed the date forwards to 1928, then 1936, and finally 1953.

On closer examination, the notion that the Great Pyramid was built according to a divine plan becomes untenable. Originally, the architects prepared the king's burial chamber deep under the structure. For some reason this plan was abandoned and another chamber was built above ground level in the centre of the pyramid.[58] Once again the architects changed their plans and moved the burial chamber to an even higher area in the pyramid. But it seems reasonable that if the design of the pyramid were divinely inspired it would have been built correctly the first time, and subsequent design changes would have been unnecessary.

By the 20th century, many theories denied outright that the pyramids were tombs at all, and indeed, no complete mummies or cadavers had ever been found in any of them. The tombs had been robbed of their rich contents long before modern times, and the thieves left no remains for archaeologists. Others

went so far as to deny that the Egyptians themselves had anything to do with their construction. One author claimed that the pyramid builders came from the area of the Euphrates River or perhaps somewhere else in Asia. More recently, a whole new set of beliefs has emerged that not only deny that the Egyptians were capable of building such structures, but deny that anyone on earth was responsible for their construction. These notions come from ancient astronaut enthusiasts, who claim that pyramid construction was undertaken at the instigation of creatures from outer space. Twentieth-century pyramid ideas reflected a growing awareness of space travel as humans began to take their own first steps into space. People in the 19th century, before manned flight and space travel, did not create notions about space visitors building the pyramids. To explain their pyramid fantasies they created so-called "races" of superhuman beings (which reflected their beliefs in their own racial superiority), or attributed pyramid construction to divine inspiration. Despite many reported sightings and claims of actual abductions by extra-terrestrials, there is no scientific confirmation that travellers from other parts of the universe have

The Sphinx, or Hor-am-akhet, "Horus of the Horizon", situated directly east of the Khafre Pyramid.

ever visited the earth. Even if they did visit the earth at some time in the distant past (and it must be emphasized that there is no evidence for this), there is no indication of any kind that extra-terrestrials were in any way involved in pyramid construction.

Who built the pyramids?

Since the time of Herodotus it has been claimed that slaves were used for pyramid construction,[59] but there is no evidence that Egyptian citizens were ever reduced to slavery as pyramid builders.[60] Holding, feeding, and maintaining large numbers of slaves was economically impractical during the Old Kingdom. It was only during the first millennium BC that slavery became a profitable, large-scale social system in the ancient world.[61] By that time pyramid construction had been abandoned in favour of other forms of funerary architecture. During the Old Kingdom there were some domestic slaves attached to the king and his court, and the 4th Dynasty king Snefru brought back 7000 prisoners of war[62] from his campaign in Nubia. These captives may have been used as slaves on one of the king's pyramid projects, but they never constituted the bulk of the workforce required for pyramid construction.

It is sometimes believed that Hebrew slaves from the time of Moses were responsible for building the pyramids, but there is no evidence for this often-repeated assumption. Exactly when the Hebrews first appeared in the Near East is a subject still debated by scholars,[63] but it is clear that there were no Hebrews in Egypt until at least 1000 years after the time of pyramid construction.

In order to maximize crop production the Egyptians depended on the efficient use of the Nile flood waters for irrigation. Early in their history local bureaucracies were established to organize the population to construct and maintain systems of irrigation canals. Egyptian citizens owed the state a certain number of days of work every year to maintain this community effort.[64] Beginning early in their history the Egyptians had learned how to organize and maintain large irrigation systems, and this expertise proved useful when applied to organizing the construction of large-scale funerary monuments.[65] From August to early October, much of the farmland was inundated by the Nile floods and many of the peasants were forced to abandon their farms. During this period the otherwise idle farmers were conscripted to work on royal building projects in exchange for rations of food. Throughout the long and rather precarious period of flooding, when family grain reserves no doubt ran low, the king may have taken on the role of the provider for his people, and they in turn helped their god-king to prepare for his afterlife. While the bulk of pyramid workers would have been made up of peasants conscripted for handling the large stones, there was also a core of professional craftsmen that included stone cutters, masons, and architects who carried out the more technical work, as well as directing the project to completion. The majestic pyramids did not rise from the desert solely from the efforts of masses of conscripted labourers. Religious duty and the well-being of the land were important factors behind pyramid construction. The Egyptians believed their king to be the embodiment of *ma'at*, order and harmony, which resulted in the well-being of everyone. The only way *ma'at* could be maintained was through the king, and the king had to be properly buried if he was to continue to serve and protect his subjects. Therefore, it was considered to be in everyone's best interest to contribute to the construction of the king's final resting place.

Pyramid construction

It is not possible to estimate reliably the time necessary for pyramid construction. Herodotus is responsible for the estimate that it took 20 years to build the Great Pyramid,[66] but it should be remembered that he was no building expert and visited the pyramids at Giza two thousand years after they were built, long after royal pyramid building had ceased altogether. However, there is an intriguing piece of information concerning the length of time required to build a large pyramid at Dashur. While exploring the Red Pyramid at Dashur, which has a base of 4.84 hectares and is almost as large as the Khufu Pyramid, German Egyptologist Richard Lepsius discovered that one of the casing blocks at the base of the structure was inscribed with a date from the 21st year of the reign of King Snefru. Another block located halfway between the summit and the base was dated the following year.[67] Extrapolating from this, the Red Pyramid could have been completed in three years and the Khufu Pyramid in perhaps as little as six years.[68] It should be emphasized that these numbers are still estimates and have not yet been confirmed.[69]

From 2630 to 1640 BC the ancient Egyptians built about 35 large pyramids and another 50 smaller ones. Some pyramids were built with large blocks and solid limestone cores, while others were filled with rubble, gravel, or a combination of mud bricks and stone. Since pyramid builders changed their plans and experimented with new methods, no single building technique was used to make all of them. What puzzles most people is how the larger pyramids were constructed; the question most often asked is how were the massive building stones cut, moved from their quarries, and raised to such heights?

Choosing and preparing the site

Construction sites were chosen for practical reasons such as the availability of good stone, a solid base, and the proximity to religious and political centres. Before the actual placing of stones could begin, a large flat surface had to be levelled to serve as the base for the structure.[70] Some have argued that water was

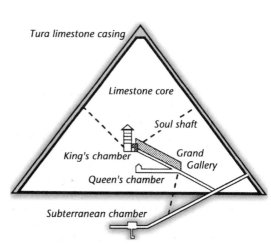

Interior of the Khufu Pyramid showing passages and chambers.

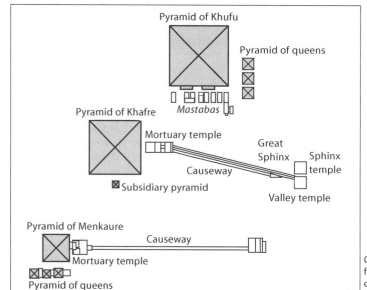

Overview of the Giza complex showing from lower left to upper right the pyramids of Menkaure, Khafre, and Khufu. The Sphinx, Hor-am-akhet, is on the middle right.

channelled through a series of ditches over the base of the pyramid and acted as a natural means of determining which areas protruded above or below the water line.[71] Others maintain that the Egyptians used a simple square level and plumb line, sighted on a rod or pole similar to those used by modern surveyors, to ensure a flat surface. The square level method is supported by recent field tests which demonstrated that it was accurate to within a centimetre over a distance of 40–45 m.[72] Regardless of which system was used, the Khufu Pyramid was levelled so accurately that there is a difference of only 2 cm between the elevation of the north and south sides.[73] Once the area had been levelled, the next step would have been to determine the four cardinal directions.

Passages

The Khufu Pyramid is placed so precisely that each of its four sides faces one of the cardinal points of the compass. The accuracy of pyramid alignment in relation to the four cardinal points is impressive: the Khufu Pyramid is accurate to less than one-twentieth of a degree (3'6"). The cardinal points were probably determined by marking the rising and setting points of a northern star and then bisecting the angle between the two points to determine celestial north.[74] The other three directions could then be determined easily. Alternatively, the pyramid may have been oriented by using the shadow of the sun cast by a long pole, or *gnomon*. Either method would have worked quite well, although it has been argued that the solar method is more accurate.[75] Badawy and Trimble have argued that air shafts were unknown in

other pyramids so they must have been cut into the pyramid structure for some other reason.[76] The two researchers found that the northern shaft pointed towards the upper transit of the star Thuban, while the southern shaft pointed towards two stars, Alnitak and Mintaka, in the belt of the very striking constellation of Orion. However, it is highly unlikely that the so-called "air shafts" of the Khufu Pyramid ever served as any kind of astronomical function since both passages bend horizontally just before they reach the burial chamber, making it impossible to see anything by looking through them.[77] Although they served no astronomical function, they may have had some religious significance since the Egyptians believed that the king became one of the circumpolar stars at death.[78] Therefore, it is possible that the northern shaft was constructed to represent this purpose symbolically. Likewise, the southern shaft pointing towards Orion may have had some religious significance since the constellation Orion represented Osiris, the Egyptian god of death and resurrection.

Moving the stones

Once the surface was levelled and the directions were established, stoneworkers could begin to cut and haul the more than two million blocks used to construct the larger pyramids such as those of Snefru, Khufu, and Khafre. Most of the soft limestone that makes up the inner core of the Khufu Pyramid was quarried within 500 m of the building site.[79] Using copper chisels (many have been recovered), small holes were cut into the unquarried stone. Then, wedges of wood or copper were pounded into the holes, which cracked the stones along nearly straight lines. The stones were then manoeuvred on to sledges and dragged to the pyramid. Flinders Petrie estimated that a team of eight men would have been sufficient to move a 2.5 tonne block from the quarry to the building site and up the ramps leading to the summit.[80] Even though the Egyptians were familiar with the wheel, it is most likely that wheeled vehicles pulled by oxen or other traction animals were probably not used extensively in pyramid construction. Feeding and caring for a multitude of these beasts may have created major logistical problems for the pyramid builders.[81] People can look after themselves, follow complicated instructions, and would have been able to manoeuvre more easily in crowded work areas far above the ground. Scenes from tombs as late as the 18th Dynasty, more than 1300 years after the Great Pyramid was built, clearly indicate that heavy objects were still being moved on wooden sleds pulled by gangs of men. An illustration from the 12th Dynasty (c.1991–1783 BC) shows an alabaster statue of Djehutihotep that weighed an estimated 60 tonnes being pulled on a sled by a team of 172 men. Water or oil is shown being poured on the ground in front of the sled to reduce friction, while a beater strikes together two blocks of wood to create a marching rhythm for the work gang.[82]

Construction techniques

The outside casing stones of the Great Pyramid were quarried from the harder, high-quality stone found at Tura, on the opposite side of the Nile River about 20 km away from the building site.[83] Moving the

Pyramid-shaped entrance to a New Kingdom tomb near the Valley of the Kings, western Thebes, Upper Egypt.

casing stones this distance could have presented a major land transportation problem but, fortunately, when the Nile River flooded, it rose to within a few hundred metres of the Giza Plateau, enabling boats loaded with Tura stone to manoeuvre close to the construction site and unload their cargoes. Some of the stone used in pyramid construction was a very hard form of granite, but granite represented only a tiny fraction of the total amount of stone used in the Khufu Pyramid, and most other pyramids contained only small amounts of granite.

Unlike limestone, granite is produced by geological processes that heat the rock to a very high temperature and make it much harder than limestone. Because it is harder it is much more difficult to quarry, and tools made out of copper, which is soft, will not cut granite. But the Egyptians had other ways to cut granite. There is ample evidence from quarries near Aswan in Upper Egypt that workers used grapefruit-sized balls of dolerite, an extremely hard stone, to pound away at the quarry face until the blocks of granite came free. Some of the granite in the King's Chamber clearly shows marks that appear to have been made by the teeth of some kind of saw. It has been suggested that the pyramid builders used copper saws with diamond teeth set into them, but the Egyptians did not have diamond saws capable of cutting granite. It is most likely that sand, which contains large amounts of very hard quartz, was used as an abrasive powder, which was rubbed on pieces of granite for long periods of time until they were rendered into usable slabs of stone. In a technologically oriented society such as ours, it is sometimes difficult to imagine great stones being moved without the help of cranes or pulleys. But in ancient Egypt these problems were solved with simple technology and an abundance of manpower. It helps to remember that labour was cheap and plentiful, and what the Egyptians lacked in technology they made up for with a large labour force and plenty of time to complete the task.

Raising the stones

Once the blocks were cut and transported to the building site they had to be raised up and incorporated into the structure. This posed one of the most perplexing problems in pyramid construction: how were the stones raised?[84] The most likely solution is a system of ramps that wrapped around the pyramid and led to the summit of the structure. There are different ramp theories.[85] According to one, a main ramp was built facing the east side of the pyramid, while an alternative theory proposes that there were four ramps, one starting at each corner of the structure, built against the core blocks and rising parallel to the sides of the structure. The only remaining archaeological evidence for ramps points to the single ramp theory. Despite the lack of solid evidence, many Egyptologists accept the wrap-around ramp theory, maintaining that a ramp that enclosed the four sides of the pyramid would have been disassembled after construction was completed, leaving no clues of its existence. The gradient, or rate of incline, for ramps varied from 1:8 to 1:12; that is, the ramp went up 1 m for every 8–12 m of length. A papyrus from the 19th Dynasty, now in the British Museum in London, speaks of a ramp that was 380 m long by 29 m wide, with a height of 32 m: a 1:12 gradient. A single ramp high enough to reach the summit of the Khufu Pyramid using the same 1:12 ratio would have been over 1750 m long and would have been a building project almost as ambitious as the Great Pyramid itself.

The legacy of the pyramids

No structures symbolize ancient Egypt more than the pyramids, by far the most impressive monuments from the ancient world.[86] Research shows that they are not the products of superhuman or extra-terrestrial intelligence, but the result of good design, efficient organization, and hard work by the Egyptian people. To deny that the Egyptians built the pyramids would be the equivalent of denying that the Americans made the first manned voyage to the moon. Those who refuse to acknowledge that the Egyptians built the pyramids are guilty of a kind of cultural theft, taking from the Egyptians one of their greatest achievements by claiming that they were not intelligent enough to undertake such a project. Conversely, those who claim that the pyramids contain fantastic powers, or that the Egyptians possessed some kind of super intelligence, exaggerate Egyptian accomplishments in an attempt to force their own 21st-century technological view of the world on to the pre-industrial society of the Nile river valley. The pyramids were tombs for Egyptian god-kings, and demonstrate what humans can achieve when their collective talents and creativity are focused on a single project. Although the builders of the pyramids are long gone, their great structures still stand, and remain an inspiration to all those who see and appreciate them.

12 Funerary practices, rituals, and mummification

Pyramid complexes, with their accompanying temples, towns, workers and priests, constituted a vital element of the economy and social structure of Old Kingdom Egypt. But, even though the pyramids were the most stately and impressive forms of funerary architecture in the ancient world, in some ways they were unsuccessful.[1] First, they did not help to preserve the body, but hastened its decomposition (see Mummification, p. 163). Secondly, they did not protect the body from tomb robbers, but instead, stood as giant advertisements to thieves, crying out that hidden inside them was the wealth of kings.[2] A few Egyptologists have argued that pyramid construction seriously diminished the human and agricultural resources of the land.[3] In her study of the pyramid workers at the town of Kahun,[4] Egyptologist Rosalie David has argued that building and equipping vast pyramid complexes was a sizeable drain on community assets that led to an economic decline and brought an end to the Old Kingdom.[5] It is known that during the 5th Dynasty whole villages and large tracts of land were dedicated to pyramid complexes, to maintain the deceased king and the high officials and priests of his cult.[6] During the 6th Dynasty, King Pepi I decreed that two villages be exempted for eternity from any work other than supplying labourers for the two pyramids of Snefru, a king who lived three hundred years earlier. As the number of pyramids increased over the centuries, along with the number of people required to maintain and repair them, more land and goods were needed to provide for the deceased.

Although mortuary complexes and their dedicated offerings may have contributed to the economic problems in the Old Kingdom, there were other factors at work as well.[7] Foremost among these was the loss of power by ruling families and the central government as priests and high officials began taking larger shares of goods that originally had been reserved for the temples and cultic activities of the royal family. As wealth shifted away from ruling families, estates and villages in the outlying regions became more independent, and Egypt became politically fragmented.

Egypt in the Old Kingdom was a centrally planned and administered state. Besides its important symbolic and religious role, its main function was organizational. By collecting a portion of the annual harvest and storing it in the capital, it could prevent famines on a local basis by redistributing surplus food resources to the affected areas.[8] The central government also regulated conflicts, and imposed order by serving as an arbitrator in local disputes in the outlying areas.[9] Such functions ensured peace and stability for much of the Old Kingdom, particularly during the 4th and 5th Dynasties. In the *nomes* or outlying areas of the Nile river valley local leaders were appointed to collect taxes and ensure the good administration of regional activities. To maintain their authority, *nomarchs*, or provincial leaders, increased their powers by taking larger shares of resources destined for the king and the central authority in Memphis. The outlying areas began to act more independently and, increasingly, the king had to send payments of goods and resources to them, and release them from certain taxes in order to maintain their allegiance. In the 5th Dynasty a new office was created called the "Overseer of Upper Egypt". Such titles reflect the growing power of regions like Thebes, which became richer at the expense of the capital.[10] The strengthening of the *nomes* continued in the 6th Dynasty as local rulers built more shrines and temples dedicated to local gods with donations provided by the king.

The First Intermediate period

By the 6th Dynasty, *nomarchs* had expanded their power at the expense of the king and increasingly considered their positions as hereditary. They formed militias, named their sons as their heirs, and built small but elaborate funerary structures. Eventually provincial rulers drifted away from the traditional form of rule by a single monarch, and for more than a century the Two Lands struggled through a period of instability and social unrest. In addition to the breakdown of political and social order, climatological factors were also an element in the decline of Egyptian fortunes at the end of the third millennium

BC. After 2250 BC reduced rainfall across northern Africa caused a series of low Nile floods that resulted in food shortages and famine conditions in the Nile river valley.[12] Egypt's decline is also reflected in the literary and religious texts of the period, which speak of the disintegration of law and order and a loss of respect for the old ways. *The Admonitions of Ipuwer*[13] bemoan the fact that the rich and high-born were dressed in rags, while their servants and slaves went about dressed in the stolen belongings of their former masters. To make matters worse, the tombs of their ancestors were violated, and commerce with foreign lands was disrupted or halted. Together, these factors combined to bring about a century (2134–2040 BC) of social and political unrest that Egyptologists refer to as the "First Intermediate period".[14]

The Middle Kingdom

Popular perceptions of ancient Egypt are dominated by the Old Kingdom with its pyramids and royal statuary, and the New Kingdom with the Theban temples at Karnak and Luxor and the numerous burials with their wealth of funerary art, the Amarna statuary, and the military kings of the Ramesside period. Sandwiched between these two, and overshadowed by them, was a period called the Middle Kingdom.[15] Although the Middle Kingdom did not produce architecture on the grand scale found in the Old and New Kingdoms, in later periods the Egyptians considered it their golden age.[16] The Middle Kingdom produced some of the most notable works of art and literary compositions to come out of ancient Egypt.

The Middle Kingdom began when the ruler of the southern city of Thebes, Nebhepetre Mentuhotep, referred to as "the Ancestor", brought to an end the civil war against leaders from the north, and became the sole ruler of a united Egypt. The Middle King-

dom lasted for four centuries and ended when Semitic peoples from Syria-Palestine, called Hyksos, took control of the Nile Delta region of Lower Egypt and the country was once again divided for over a century.

Mentuhotep, meaning "The god Montu is content", referring to the war god Montu, spent much of his 50-year reign waging war on the north, but once peace had been established he turned his energies to peacetime activities throughout the Two Lands. These included large building projects such as his funerary temple in western Thebes, just outside the area that centuries later would become the Valley of the Kings. Such enterprises required expeditions to mines and quarries to procure the necessary building materials, and a competent bureaucracy under the control of the king and his administrators to oversee such activities. In addition, roads were secured and traditional trade routes were re-opened, implying that the political situation was stable and people felt confident in the newly established order. Not only did Mentuhotep succeed in reuniting Egypt into a single kingdom, but he also built one of the most original funerary structures in ancient Egypt. Unlike Old Kingdom rulers, Mentuhotep did not build a traditional pyramid as his final resting place. Instead, he took some of the elements of the pyramid com-

Chronology of major historical divisions in Egyptian history (all dates BC)

Late Predynastic period	3300–3200
UNIFICATION	
Early Dynastic period	2920–2575
Old Kingdom	2575–2134
First Intermediate period	2134–2040
Middle Kingdom	2040–1640
Second Intermediate period	1640–1532
New Kingdom	1550–1069
Third Intermediate period	1069–664
Late period	664–525
Persian period	525–332
Hellenistic period	332–30

Chronology of the Later Old Kingdom, First Intermediate period and Middle Kingdom (all dates BC)[11]

The Later Old Kingdom		
5th Dynasty	2465–2323	(Wenis, *Pyramid Texts*)
6th Dynasty	2323–2150	(Pepi II, reigns 94 years)
7th/8th Dynasties	2150–2134	(Numerous minor kings)
First Intermediate period		
9th/10th Dynasties	2134–2040	(Herakleopolis)
11th Dynasty	2134–2040	(Thebes)
Middle Kingdom		
11th Dnasty	2040–1991	
12th Dynasty	1991–1783	
13th/13th Dynasties	1783–c.1640	

plex and fashioned them into a new form of funerary architecture that was less expensive and time-consuming to build, but maintained much of the grandeur of the earlier pyramids.

Later forms of funerary architecture

Centuries before the time of Mentuhotep, priests, bureaucrats, and other wealthy citizens who could not build pyramids began to fashion rock-cut tombs for themselves. At Thebes these tombs were cut into the soft limestone cliffs on the west bank of the Nile River opposite the city of Thebes, the first capital of Egypt during the Middle Kingdom. Mentuhotep decided to build in the same area, and for his mortuary temple he selected an area at the base of a steep cliff, called Deir el-Bahri, where towering limestone formations rose abruptly to a height of about 150 m above the adjoining terrain. His structure was composed of two columned terraces, a lower one covered with a porch or portico in front, and an upper one consisting of another portico which surrounded a *mastaba* (see photograph) or pyramid form[17] built in the centre. This central structure was small when compared to earlier *mastabas* and pyramids: only about 18 m on a side.[18] The entire mortuary temple rose perhaps 15–20 m above the desert floor. During successive excavations archaeologists found the remains of numerous tamarisk and sycamore trees that had been planted in front of the structure. A causeway, 47 m wide and nearly 1000 m long, led away from the complex towards the Nile River. The back of the structure abutted directly against the face of the cliff and contained additional porticoes and a columned temple. The king was not buried in the central *mastaba* structure; its function appears to have been only symbolic. Instead, the tomb builders cut an inclined passage 160 m long in front of the terraced complex that ended in a small chamber. Inside the chamber an empty wooden coffin and a life-sized limestone statue of the king were found.

The entrance to a second tomb, reached by an even longer passageway, was cut at the back of the complex behind the central *mastaba*. It descended beneath the hypostyle shrine (a covered, flat-roofed structure supported by columns) at the base of the cliff and ended in a small chamber with granite-lined walls. Most Egyptologists believe that this second chamber, actually cut into the mountainside, was where Mentuhotep was buried. Like most royal tombs in Egypt this one, too, had been robbed in antiquity.

Deir el-Bahri was such an impressive burial location that, 500 years later, the pharaohs Hatshepsut and Thutmosis III (see Ch. 13) would build mortuary structures close by, inspired by Mentuhotep's architectural masterpiece.[19] Although little remains of Thutmosis III's temple, enough remains of Hatshepsut's structure for a team of archaeologists from Poland to undertake the long and complicated process of restoring it.[20] Hatshepsut, like Mentuhotep, was buried in the mountain behind her temple, but there is a difference between the two burials: the

A model reconstruction of the mortuary temple of King Mentuhotep at Deir el-Bahri, 11th Dynasty.

entrance to Mentuhotep's burial chamber was directly connected with his mortuary complex to the limestone cliffs behind (even though it was later covered over and hidden). But there was no direct link from Hatshepsut's mortuary temple to her burial chamber. She chose to have the location of her burial chamber kept secret, and was buried in the desolate valley several hundred metres behind her mortuary complex.

Two other kings named Mentuhotep followed, with successful reigns that continued the Middle Kingdom tradition of trade as far south as modern-day Ethiopia and perhaps Eritrea. However, the reign of Mentuhotep III lasted only six years and this may be indicative of some kind of trouble. Then, the 11th Dynasty mysteriously collapsed and a new ruling family, still within a united Egypt, came to power. It is known that a vizier named Amenemhet, from Upper Egypt, controlled an expedition force of 10 000 soldiers. Amenemhet had the same name as the first king of the following dynasty and it seems likely that he overthrew the last Mentuhotep[21] and established himself as king of the Two Lands.

Although little is known about the origins of the 12th Dynasty, it seems clear that the new royal family was made up of usurpers from Upper Egypt. The new king, Amenemhet I, took the designation "Repeater of Births" to indicate that with his reign there was a new beginning, a rebirth, for Egypt. To promote his legitimacy he erected a number of monuments linking him to the previous dynasty and alluded to ancestry as far back as the 1st Dynasty king Aha and kings of the 6th Dynasty.[22] He moved the capital to a new city, called Itj-tawy, which he founded in Lower Egypt. Little is known of the new capital, including its location, but it was probably located between the cities of Memphis and Meidum, and near the pyramids of the 12th Dynasty which survive to this day. The new capital was close to the great burial complexes of the Early Dynastic and Old Kingdoms, where venerable rulers such as Djoser and Khufu had built their pyramids. The new rulers reinforced their links with the traditions of the Old Kingdom by returning to the traditional pyramid form of burial, although on a less grandiose scale than those of the 4th Dynasty. By building their capital and funerary structures near the Old Kingdom capital of Memphis, which was probably still a thriving city, the 12th Dynasty sought legitimacy by being close to the ancient seat of power. There is another reason why the capital was moved to the north; it seems that raiders were threatening from Libya and Syria-Palestine, and the king wanted to be closer to potential trouble spots.

The kings of the 12th Dynasty reinforced their claims to power through the use of literature as a form of political propaganda.[23] One such composition, *The Prophecy of Neferti*,[24] actually fabricates an Old Kingdom wiseman who predicts the appearance of the founder of the 12th Dynasty; Amenemhet I. Another example is *The Story of Sinuhe*,[25] one of the classic pieces of Egyptian literature.

The Story of Sinuhe is a fictional autobiography that recounts the adventures of Sinuhe, a courtier who fled to Syria-Palestine to escape the political tumult in Egypt after the death of Amenemhet I. The story contains a section that praises the 12th Dynasty king Sesostris I (Senwosret), recounting what a good and wise king he was. At the end of the story King Sesostris I did not forget his faithful servant. When Sinuhe returned home the king welcomed him back to Egypt and he was richly rewarded.

Another important source of information concerning Egypt's relations with neighbouring countries was a group of writings known as the "execration texts".[26] Essentially, these texts condemned people who were deemed undesirable to the Egyptians. This widely practised activity dates back to at least the 6th Dynasty. With their accompanying rituals, execration texts were inscribed on pottery jars or anthropoid figurines to prevent, by magical means,[27] plots, conspiracies and acts of rebellion against the Two Lands. The curse was then read out and afterwards the figurines or clay jars were smashed.[28] Middle Kingdom evidence for these types of curses mention enemies from Syria-Palestine in the northeast, Nubia in the south, and Libya in the west, as well as internal enemies.

An important and lasting political innovation of the Middle Kingdom was the practice of co-regency, which was instituted during the reigns of Amenemhet I and Sesostris I.[29] Their ten-year co-regency may have come about to ensure a smooth transition from one king to another. In practice, co-regency allowed the heir apparent the chance to learn the ins and outs of kingship by ruling jointly with the older, more experienced, king. As was often the case, when the older king died there was a chance that a revolt would break out as competing families fought each other to gain access to the throne. Despite these precautions, Amenemhet I was assassinated. In a remarkable literary work, *The Instructions of King Amenemhet I*,[30] Amenemhet I makes a post-mortem appearance and explains how through treachery and deceit he was killed in his palace, and warns his son, Sesostris I, to trust no man. Even with their new capital, co-regency, propaganda, and sound political manoeuvering, the early kings of the 12th Dynasty still had to contend with powerful *nomarchs* who ran their *nomes* like independent fiefdoms, with nearly complete autonomy. In order to manage those families, who were a threat to the power of the Crown, kings had to compromise some of their control of the Two Lands by allowing some families to keep their privileged positions and a share of the tax revenues they collected. In exchange for these privileges they were allowed to run their own courts and maintain small militias. Still, *nomarchs* had to provide workers for royal building projects and other royal enterprises. This power-sharing system seems to have worked well for some time but by the reign of Sesostris III the central government managed to consolidate its strength over the *nomarchs* which reinforced the domination of the later 12th Dynasty kings.

Trade and international relations

Middle Kingdom rulers maintained vigorous trading relations with their neighbours, particularly with the port of Byblos in Syria-Palestine, Egypt's principal source of wood for building projects. Relations between Egypt and Byblos were always strong, and evidence of Egyptian influences in art and culture became commonplace during the 12th Dynasty. It is clear that the Egyptians participated in trading enterprises in the eastern Mediterranean and the Aegean as well, since Egyptian trade goods have been found among the ruins of Minoan sites on the island of Crete and Minoan goods have been found in Egypt. In contrast, the situation was different in the south, where the Egyptians not only traded with the Nubians and Kushites below the Second Cataract, but actually brought much of the region under direct control through military conquest, as archaeological excavations and texts indicate.[31] In the south, Egyptian territorial gains were protected by a series of trading posts and forts between the First and Second Cataracts.[32] The Egyptians worked hard to maintain trade relationships while at the same time maintaining closed borders in an attempt to keep foreigners out of the Two Lands.

Building and reclamation projects

By the reign of Sesostris III, Egypt had complete control of much of the southern portion of the Nile river valley beyond its late Old Kingdom borders and had put in place a strong centralized government in the rest of the country. Towards the end of the 19th century BC, King Amenemhet III ruled for at least 46 years, and was able to undertake the construction of two vast and impressive pyramid complexes, one at Dashur and the other at Hawara.[33] Although the size and quality of construction of Middle Kingdom pyramids did not match Old Kingdom structures, they are still impressive. Both structures built by Amenemhet III were made of brick with reinforced stone walls, and measure over 100 m on a side. The Dashur Pyramid rose 81.5 m above the ground, but suffered structural problems, which forced builders to abandon the project and build another,[34] smaller pyramid, 58 m high, beside a huge religious and cultic complex at Hawara in the Faiyum. Pyramid builders during the Middle Kingdom did not use the same methods employed by earlier Old Kingdom pyramid builders. For the pyramids of kings Sesostris I, Amenemhet I and Sesostris II, masons constructed special internal reinforcing walls, which ran from the core in the centre of the structure and radiated outwards towards the four corners. Between these walls the empty spaces were filled with field stones and mud bricks.[35] The outer stone casing gave the impression of pyramids built of solid stone. Middle Kingdom pyramids placed a great emphasis on the security of the burial chamber of the king that surpassed anything previously known in pyramid construction. Unlike earlier pyramids, the entrance to the Hawara Pyramid was located on the south side. This was probably done to fool tomb robbers, although it went against traditional religious ideas. The descending passage from the south entrance gave robbers the impression that it led to a small room and a cul-de-sac. Actually, the passage was covered with a sliding roof, which led to two other passages on a higher level. One was a false passage leading north, while the other turned east towards the burial chamber. Some portions of the passage ran at right angles, which doubled back ending up near their starting point. The plan worked because there is plenty of evidence that tomb robbers spent much energy trying to cut through the false passage. But, despite these complex security preparations, thieves eventually managed to penetrate the burial chamber and loot it.

The Faiyum

The Faiyum or "Southern Lake" (She-resy)[36] as it was known to the ancient Egyptians, was a large natural lake to the west of the Nile River surrounded by marshes and agricultural land. The lake was fed by a branch of the Nile River and Graeco-Roman writers claim that during his reign Amenemhet III undertook a vast land reclamation project to increase agricultural production.[37] The lake may have served as a reservoir where surplus waters were held until needed during the dry season. South of Amenemhet's pyramid stands a large mortuary temple known by classical authors as the "Labyrinth".[38] As described by the ancient historians Herodotus and Diodorus Siculus,[39] Amenemhet III was the builder of a vast complex of covered halls that were considered to rival the famous labyrinth of King Minos at Knossos on the island of Crete, and, according to the historian Strabo, the 4th Dynasty pyramids themselves. The surrounding structures were so vast that it was claimed that no one could find their way through them without an experienced guide.

The legacy of the Middle Kingdom

Amenemhet III was one of the great kings of ancient Egypt. He was not a great conqueror as later kings would be, but he left his mark through beautiful art objects and many building projects. The kings of the Middle Kingdom managed to reunite the divided kingdom and re-establish peace and order in the Two Lands. They provided prosperity for their people and, over time, restored power to the central government and overcame the threat of divisive *nomarchs*. During this period Egypt controlled much of the area south of the First Cataract, and was content to keep trading relations with its neighbours, concentrate on building programmes, and maintain stability.

The end of the Middle Kingdom and the Second Intermediate period

In the years following the reigns of Sesostris III and Amenemhet III the Two Lands remained stable and prosperous. However, a few years later a woman, Queen Nefrusobek (1787–1783 BC) took the throne; a woman reigning usually indicates that there were no male heirs available and that the dynasty was dying out. For the next century and a half, during the 13th Dynasty, some 70 kings of little account ruled in the Two Lands. Egypt remained prosperous and stable until around 1640 BC when outsiders, called the Hyksos, took control of northern Egypt. Elsewhere in the country it appears that the 14th Dynasty continued to rule in different parts of the Nile river valley. As a result of outside pressure and internal instability there was a breakdown of central rule, and Egypt once again slipped into a period of social and political decline: the Second Intermediate period.

THE FATE OF THE DEAD

The myth of Osiris

Osiris was the ancient Egyptian god of fertility and the underworld.[40] Osiris represented the cycle of birth, growth, and death that determined the fate of all living things, and his own death and resurrection assured his followers eternal life.[41] Primarily a god of vegetation, Osiris personified the rebirth of plants that provided Nile river valley dwellers with food. During the summer months the land became parched and dry and the hot Egyptian sun, sometimes blazing at 50 °C, turned the Nile river valley into a burning wasteland. In midsummer, during the hottest period of the year, the Nile River flooded, and its precious waters renewed the land, crops grew, and all life flourished again. Once the crops were harvested, the land dried out and seemed to die. This cycle of birth, fruition, and death was associated with Osiris, and the return of vegetation after the Nile flood was seen in religious terms as the triumph of life over death. A clear representation of this concept was found in the tomb of the famous 18th Dynasty king Tutankhamun. Included with the king's burial equipment, the excavators found a shallow wooden dish, or planter box,[42] shaped like the silhouette of Osiris, and filled with earth and barley seeds. The dish was watered and placed in the tomb alongside the mummified remains of the king in the burial chamber. A few days after the tomb was sealed the seeds sprouted, and then dried out and died.[43] The germinating seeds symbolized the resurrection of the fertility god, and showed the close parallel in the minds of

the Egyptians between the rebirth of plants through seeds planted in the soil, and the rebirth of humans buried in the earth after death. This concept is expressed in a passage in the *Coffin Texts*[44] entitled "The spell for becoming barley", which explains that at death a special "plant of life" grows from the body of Osiris that enables the dead to live again.

In the myth of Osiris the Egyptians blended their ideas about fertility and eschatology into an interesting and exciting story that expressed some of their most important and fundamental religious beliefs. Since no complete version of the story written in Egyptian has survived, the principal source of the myth comes from the Greek author and philosopher Plutarch.[45] He recorded one version of the story[46] in the second century AD, although the story existed in

some form perhaps as far back as the Early Dynastic period.[47]

According to Plutarch, Osiris was an ancient Egyptian king who abolished the practice of cannibalism and introduced Nile river valley dwellers to the elements of civilization: farming, the domestication of animals, and the first law code. As a result, Osiris was loved by everyone and Egypt prospered and flourished. However, Osiris's successes made his brother, Seth, jealous and he decided to assassinate Osiris. Seth and his gang of conspirators organized a banquet for King Osiris, and built a wooden chest (or coffin), that conformed to the exact measurements of Osiris's body. The chest was brought to the banquet hall and once the drinking and merriment were well advanced, Seth playfully declared that he would give the ornate chest to whoever could fit into its cramped dimensions. All the guests tried it, but no one could fit into it. When it was his turn, Osiris lay down in the box and fit into it perfectly. Once inside, Seth and his conspirators slammed the lid on the chest, nailed it down, and sealed it with molten lead. Then they threw the chest into the Nile River. At this point, Isis, the wife of Osiris, began wandering the banks of the river in search of her missing husband. But the chest containing Osiris was not to be found since it had been carried down the river and out into the Mediterranean Sea. Eventually it washed up on the beach in far-off Syria. Here a great cedar tree grew up on the spot where the chest landed and engulfed the chest within its thick trunk, with Osiris still inside it. One day the king of Syria saw the beautiful tree, and decided to cut it down and use it as one of the pillars for the new palace he was building; he did not know that the Egyptian king was imprisoned inside the tree trunk.

Word of her husband's whereabouts finally reached Isis. She journeyed to Byblos to be near him, but she had no idea how to get him out of the pillar. Isis, who was really a great and powerful goddess in disguise, eventually made friends with some of the

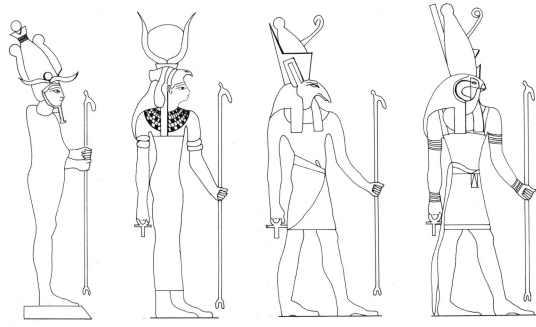

The principal deities of the myth of Osiris: Osiris, Isis, Seth, and Horus.

maid servants of the Syrian queen. She braided their hair and by breathing on them imbued them with an aroma that surpassed any earthly perfume. When the queen saw how beautiful her servants were and smelled their perfume she enquired as to the source of their beauty. Upon learning of this remarkable stranger who made women so attractive, the queen soon had Isis working for her as a beautician and nursemaid to her infant son. Since Isis was a goddess she did not need to nurse the queen's baby boy at her breast, but simply gave the child her finger to suck. While nursing the child Isis decided she would do the youngster a favour and make him immortal. This required that she hold him over an open flame to magically burn off the impurities of human mortality. One night the boy's mother happened to look in on her son and nursemaid and found Isis holding him over a flame, while the various mortal parts of his body burned vigorously. Not surprisingly, the queen was quite upset by this and began shrieking and carrying on since she believed that her son was being roasted alive by his nursemaid.

At this point Isis was forced to reveal her true identity, which she did by manifesting herself in her full godly splendour, which dazzled and impressed the child's mother. When the Syrian queen realized that Isis was a goddess and meant her son no harm, she asked why a great Egyptian goddess was working "undercover" as a nursemaid in her palace. Isis then recounted the story of her husband Osiris, the party given by his brother Seth, and the wooden chest with her husband inside it that had floated down the Nile River and had been taken up into the tree that was now one of the pillars of the queen's palace. After explaining her situation, Isis demanded the pillar and her husband. The queen of Syria gladly assented to the wishes of the Egyptian goddess and arranged for the immediate removal of the pillar. Once her husband was liberated from the pillar Isis took him by boat back to Egypt. Even though Osiris was near death, Isis did manage to revive him long enough to

conceive a child. They named him Horus and eventually he grew up and avenged his father's death by killing Seth.

Horus the Avenger

The battle between Horus and Seth was a long and bloody affair. At one point during the fight Seth tore out one of Horus's eyes, while Horus returned the favour by tearing off Seth's testicles. Finally the gods judged that Horus should be the new king of Egypt and ascend the throne of his father, while Seth was relegated to a shadowy existence in the desert. Once Horus was on the throne his father was revived in the underworld and ruled the post-mortem realm, while his son ruled the living in the Two Lands. When Osiris was revived, so too were the forces of nature; grain grew in the fields, animals were born, people had children. Osiris and his wife and son, Isis and

Horus, were worshipped in Egypt for nearly 30 centuries and they outlasted many other forms of religious belief in the ancient world. The worship of this sacred family spread beyond the borders of Egypt and was well known in Greece and the Roman Empire.[48] Isis eventually surpassed her husband in popularity and shrines dedicated to her were found as far north as Hadrian's Wall in England, as well as in Germany and in the Danube region.[49]

Osiris as judge of the dead

By the Middle Kingdom there was a strong emphasis placed on correct moral behaviour as a prerequisite for entry into the afterlife. Osiris became the judge of the dead and, along with the assembly of gods, judged whether a person had behaved properly in his or her lifetime before they were allowed into the afterlife. From the New Kingdom and later, many

The conception of Horus. Isis is shown as a sparrow hovering over her husband, Osiris, who lies on a lion-headed bed.

Osiris, Egyptian god of the afterlife, shown here in the typical mummiform stance.

The weighing of the heart ceremony. The heart of the deceased is on the left-hand side of the scale while the feather of *ma'at* is on the right. The goddess Ma'at stands on the right.

copies of the *Book of the Dead*[50] show scenes of the weighing of the heart ceremony, in which the heart of the deceased was placed on one side of a scale, and weighed against the feather of truth and justice, *ma'at*, on the other side of the scale.[51]

If the person had behaved correctly during their lifetime then they would enter into the afterlife. If that person had behaved improperly they would be eaten by a creature that was part crocodile, part hippopotamus, and part lion, known as Ammit, "the eater of the dead".[52] Once it had been determined that a person had lived a just and righteous life, they had to appear before the assembly of gods and declare that they had not committed forbidden acts such as murder and incest. Finally, when it had been determined that they were truthful and just, they were allowed to enter into the realm of Osiris in the underworld.

The myth of Osiris was closely associated with the royal family.[53] The living king of Egypt was identified with Horus; every king was given a special Horus name, which indicated that he was indeed the living king of Egypt. The queen was identified with Isis, the first lady of the Two Lands. She was the symbol of female fertility and produced many children. Isis was the perfect wife and mother, and served as a role model for all Egyptian women to follow. Finally, Osiris was the living king of the underworld, the overseer of the realm of the dead. This most ancient sacred family outlived the Egypt that produced it, and survived into the early Christian period. It was so popular that it posed a threat to early Christianity and was ordered to be abolished by the Roman emperor, Theodosius, in the fourth century AD. When the cult of Osiris finally disappeared, it was replaced by a religion that also had a saviour-god who was killed by his enemies and then rose to life again: Christianity.[54]

MUMMIFICATION AND THE PRESERVATION OF THE DEAD

Early attempts to preserve the dead

Ensuring that the body did not decompose was always a major concern for the ancient Egyptians (see Ch. 11).[55] In the Predynastic period most cadavers that were placed directly into the hot desert sands dried out rapidly and remained essentially intact.[56] In the Early Dynastic period and Old Kingdom, when the Egyptians began to build larger funerary structures, and the body was placed in the cooler and less arid *mastabas* and pyramids, the desiccating process was halted and the cadavers decomposed.[57] By providing their dead with larger and more prestigious tombs the Egyptians unwittingly created the conditions for the complete destruction of the body. During the 1st Dynasty they began to take steps to overcome this problem by preserving the cadaver through artificial means. Their first attempts consisted of wrapping the corpse in layers of linen bandages, which had virtually no effect in stopping the process of decomposition. Bandages continued to be the main form of preservation through the 2nd and 3rd Dynasties, and a few fragments of wrapped body parts have been recovered by archaeologists.[58] When it was realized that they could not preserve the flesh simply by using linen strips, the Egyptians began soaking the bandages in resin so they could at least reproduce the outer appearance of the body, particularly the facial and genital areas. When the resin dried, it hardened and formed a kind of shell or cocoon around the body that reproduced bodily features and appeared lifelike. Despite this treatment, inside the resin-coated shell of linen bandages the decomposition process continued. Since decomposition produces heat, some of the inner bandages were heated to such high temperatures that they were actually blackened and charred. The process of wrapping the corpse with bandages of linen was not really mummification since it did not use preservatives, and did nothing to stop the decomposition of the corpse. Instead, it was merely a superficial or cosmetic treatment applied to the exterior of the body only.[59]

By the 4th Dynasty new methods were being used to preserve the corpse that involved the removal of the large internal organs, which were placed in separate containers. The liver, lungs, intestines, and stomach were each wrapped in linen and stored in special recessed areas in the floors or walls of the tombs. The organs of Hetepheres, the mother of Khufu, may have been stored in a square alabaster box with four compartments, one for each of her major internal organs. By the 5th and 6th Dynasties internal organs were being stored in special limestone containers called Canopic Jars. Even though this procedure improved the chances that both the body and the major organs would have a chance to dry out before they were placed in the tomb, it did little to preserve the body itself. Removing organs from the body might appear to pose serious eschatological problems, since it will be remembered that the Egyptians had a very physical concept of the afterlife. How could the body survive if its key organs have been removed? What good would it do to provide food offerings for a body that was missing important internal organs such as the stomach? This posed no problems for the Egyptians since the body and its missing parts would be magically reunited in the afterlife and would continue to function as before, receiving food offerings, and living happily in the otherworld.

Starting in the 6th Dynasty bodies were buried fully extended instead of being contracted as in earlier periods.[60] A fully extended body facilitated cutting open and removing the internal organs. Wrapping the body in painted, resin-soaked strips of linen remained the standard form of funerary preparations until the Middle Kingdom. Despite the fact that mummification techniques were not very effective, plenty of attention was expended on increasing the lifelike details of the mummy. A woman from the

Two views of the mummy of Djedmaatesankh, ninth century BC.

6th Dynasty was found covered with a long dress on the outside of her linen body wrappings. Beneath the dress the body had been wrapped and padded to reproduce the shape of the woman's figure, particularly the breasts. Instead of resin, the linen wrappings of some mummies were covered with thin coats of plaster. This enabled them to recreate the deceased in a much more lifelike manner, even reproducing such details as wigs, moustaches, and facial features. Throughout the Early Dynastic period and the Old Kingdom the emphasis was on preserving the exterior features of the deceased, while not actually being able to stop the decomposition process. By the end of the third millennium BC corpse decomposition was still a problem after hundreds of years of burials away from the drying effects of the desert sands. Peasants and others who could not afford the costly burials of the rich continued to bury their dead in the traditional way in the hot desert sands, and as a result many of these humble burials have survived into modern times.

Natron and true mummification

What was needed to truly preserve the body was some kind of drying agent that could take the place of the desert sands, and at the same time replicate their desiccating attributes. Just such an agent was found in the form of a mineral called "natron". A combination of sodium carbonate and sodium bicarbonate,[61] natron is a naturally occurring substance that was readily available to the ancient Egyptians. It is not known when natron was first used for complete mummification, but it was employed in a few instances as far back as the 4th Dynasty, and was in widespread use for general mummification practices by the 18th Dynasty. The classic style of mummification appears in the New Kingdom (1550–1069 BC), and with the introduction of natron chances were greatly increased that the body could be preserved.

Some of the best-preserved mummies come from the 18th Dynasty. Mummification reached its peak in the 21st Dynasty,[62] after which it remained the standard burial practice in Egypt, even after the Greek and Roman conquests, continuing to be practised up until the fourth century AD.

It was during the 12th Dynasty that the removal of the brain began.[63] This was done by breaking the ethmoid bone, which allowed entry via the nose cavity into the cranium. The brain was then drawn out with a hooked instrument, or allowed to decompose enough so that it was in a partially liquid state; then, probably by flushing with water or oil, it was removed or drained out through the nostrils. According to Herodotus,[64] who is not always very reliable, the corpse was soaked in a liquid solution of natron for 70 days, the internal organs were removed through incisions in the abdomen, and then the body was wrapped in linen bandages before being entombed. It is now known that the corpse was not soaked in natron but simply covered with it in its dry form for about 40 days until the moisture was drawn out of the body. Prior to being placed in their tombs a number of additional steps were taken to improve the appearance of the deceased. Embalmers might weave human hair into the skulls of balding people. Others had body cavities as well as arms, legs, and necks stuffed with packing material to maintain the natural contours of the body, in an attempt to eliminate the sunken and dehydrated appearance that regularly occurred through mummification. By the 21st Dynasty plumped bodies, and faces with packed cheeks, were common among the wealthy. Artificial eyes of stone were sometimes inserted along with other cosmetic touches such as human-hair eyebrows, which usually disappeared because of the harsh effects of the prolonged exposure to natron. More cosmetic refinements were made during the Greek and Roman periods. Mummies sometimes had fingernails gilded with gold, and some women even had their nipples gilded. In rare cases the entire head might be covered with a thin layer of gold. For the facial area this gilding may have been done as much for magical purposes as for cosmetic ones; since gold is immutable and never decays, its magical properties were perhaps applied to the more important areas of the body. Late in Egyptian history, bitumen, a tar-like substance, was introduced as a preservative for the dead. Known in Arabic as *mumiya*,[65] the origin of the word mummy, this substance was used freely in the mummification process and rendered corpses a dark colour while making them very heavy. In Europe during the Middle Ages and the Renaissance, crushed or ground-up mummy remains were highly valued for their supposed medicinal and curative powers. Actually, they had no real medicinal value, and probably caused more harm than good to the sick and infirm who drank concoctions of ground mummy and alcohol prepared by the doctors of the time.

Although usually known to the public only through Hollywood horror films, mummies provide Egyptologists with an interesting insight into the religious beliefs of the ancient Egyptians. In archaeological and medical research mummies have been useful in helping scholars determine the kinds of illnesses and injuries the Egyptians suffered as well as their diet and some of their work habits. By using modern X-ray techniques, the age of mummies can be determined, which helps to identify royalty, and

The opening of the mouth ceremony,[66] from the *Book of the Dead* belonging to the nobleman Hunefer, 19th Dynasty, Valley of the Nobles. The scene shows Anubis, god of mummification, holding the mummy of Hunefer. In front stands "the son whom he loves", his eldest son, who restores sight, hearing, and breathing to his deceased father. Hunefer's son is shown twice, performing these tasks. On the left stands a priest in front of a food offering.

their age at death. This information can be used to verify the length of their reigns and determine family relationships.[67] With the advent of sophisticated scanners, which are non-intrusive and do not require the removal of bandages, a whole new realm of research is opening up that promises to give new and interesting insights into the lives of the ancient Egyptians.

The Valley of the Kings

The most important development in funerary practices of this period took place early in the 18th Dynasty, when King Thutmosis I decided to be buried in a dry and desolate valley *behind* the cliffs of Deir el-Bahri, in the Valley of the Kings.[68] Ineni, Thutmosis's master-builder in charge of constructing the king's tomb, was deeply concerned about secrecy and wanted to ensure that the king's tomb was not discovered by robbers. He wrote that he supervised the excavation of the rock-cut tomb of his majesty in great secrecy, with no one seeing or hearing about their building activities. Compared to earlier periods

of Egyptian history, secrecy, and keeping the location of the tombs from being discovered, became more important to later Egyptian kings. The emphasis on secrecy represented a move away from the overwhelming grandeur and ostentation of the Pyramid Age centuries earlier.

In the New Kingdom and afterwards, once the king was buried inside the tomb in the Valley of the Kings, it was covered with sand and rock so that the entrance could not be found by tomb robbers. Mortuary temples,[69] where prayers and food offerings were made to the deceased, and which were originally connected to the tomb, were separated from the actual burial site by a distance of between a few metres and several kilometres.[70] This was a clear departure from the feeding and care of the dead in the Early Dynastic period, when the deceased was either surrounded by food, or had access to food offering areas via shafts and doors leading from the burial chamber to the mortuary temple.[71] The new arrangement required that food offerings and prayers be transmitted magically to the deceased. A good example of this separation is the tomb of the 19th Dynasty king Ramesses II. His tomb was located in the Valley of the

Wall painting from the tomb of Nahkt, western Thebes. Reign of Thutmosis III.

The Valley of the Kings was the principal burial location for kings and queens during the New Kingdom.

Painted tomb scene, 19th Dynasty, Valley of the Kings.

Female musicians and singers. Detail from a banquet scene in the tomb of Nebamun, an agricultural official from the time of Amenhotep III, 18th Dynasty.

Kings, about 2.5 km from his mortuary temple, which was some distance outside the Valley of the Kings.

Despite the fact that burials were completely isolated from mortuary temples, and that tomb builders did their best to camouflage important burial locations, tombs were still robbed on a regular basis. The *Abbott Papyrus*, a text from the time of King Ramesses IX (1126–1108 BC), records many interesting details about a group of tomb robbers who looted the tombs of one king, Sobekemsaf of the 17th Dynasty, and a number of nobles in the nearby Valley of the Nobles. Eventually the thieves were caught and found guilty. A few were put to death for their crimes but at least one managed to bribe his way to freedom. A few years later, during the reign of Ramesses XI, looting of royal tombs in the Valley of the Kings became widespread and an indeterminate number of tombs were robbed.[72]

13 The Hyksos period and the New Kingdom

The end of the Middle Kingdom

During the 13th Dynasty the glory of the Middle Kingdom began to diminish, and Egypt was once again weakened and went into a period of decline. By the end of the dynasty the principle of hereditary succession was being ignored while various regional families jockeyed for power at a local level.[1] Dynastic problems tended to erode the power and prestige of kingship, particularly because it was perceived that kings could no longer ensure the welfare of their subjects on a large scale. As the situation worsened, the traditional centralized form of government collapsed and was replaced by a fragmented political system dominated by weak rulers, some of whom claimed to be kings.[2] As royal authority eroded, defensive forces diminished, fortresses fell into ruin, and Lower Egypt was left open to domination by outsiders.

The Hyksos period

Early in the 17th century BC, parts of northern Egypt were taken over by people from Syria-Palestine who were culturally and linguistically related to the Amorites (see Ch. 4),[3] a similar people who had taken control of the southern portions of Mesopotamia several centuries earlier at the beginning of the second millennium BC.[4] This group was already filtering into Egypt during the 12th Dynasty and they increased their activities during the 13th Dynasty. Writing nearly 1400 years after the fact, the Egyptian historian, Manetho, recorded that for some unknown reason Egypt was struck by invaders of obscure origins. He recounts how these low-born brigands burned down temples and treated the Egyptians with cruel hostility, massacring some and enslaving others.[5] Manetho called these invaders the Hyksos; after the collapse of the Middle Kingdom they formed the 15th Dynasty and ruled Lower Egypt for a little more than a century. The Hyksos established their capital in the city of Avaris located in the northeastern Nile Delta, between their new possessions in Lower Egypt and their traditional homeland in Syria-Palestine. At the same time the 17th Dynasty, comprising native Egyptians, ruled Upper Egypt from the city of Thebes. This Theban Dynasty continued to rule southern

Chronology of the Middle Kingdom and Hyksos period (all dates BC)

Middle Kingdom	**2040–1640**	
11th Dynasty	2040–1991	
12th Dynasty	1991–1783	
13th Dynasty	1783–c.1640	
14th Dynasties		Minor kings contemporary with the 13th and 15th Dynasties
Second Intermediate period	**1640–1532**	
15th Dynasty	1640–1532	Hyksos, Lower Egypt
16th Dynasty		Additional Hyksos rulers contemporary with 15th Dynasty
17th Dynasty	1640–1550	Thebes, Upper Egypt

Egypt as vassals of the Hyksos, paying tribute or taxes to them.[6]

The Hyksos never took direct control of the entire land of Egypt, and the two dynasties coexisted for a little more than a century. The Hyksos were related to the Amorites[7] and Canaanites;[8] and although they wrote their Semitic names in hieroglyphic script, for the most part they kept their own cultural traditions, in particular their own form of Amorite kingship and the worship of Anath and Ba'al, the traditional female and male deities of Syria-Palestine.[9] The Hyksos appear to have been immigrants who infiltrated Lower Egypt, and then, when traditional Egyptian leadership weakened, took control of the land with a minimum of warfare and established one of their own people as king. Despite their non-Egyptian origins the Hyksos adopted some aspects of the older Egyptian culture, such as Egyptian royal dress and royal titles, and worship of the sun god Re.

Immigrants and invaders

People from Syria-Palestine had been migrating into Egypt since the late third millennium BC and by the 13th Dynasty they had become quite numerous, particularly in Lower Egypt. These immigrants were referred to by the Egyptians as the 'aamu[10] (Asiatics), meaning people who spoke a west-Semitic language and came from southwest Asia, probably southern Syria and Palestine. Manetho mistakenly translated

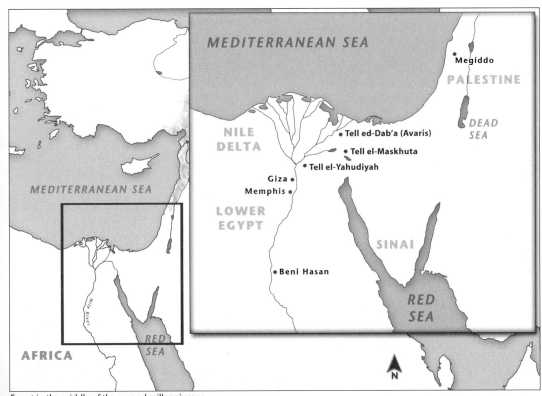

Egypt in the middle of the second millennium BC.

Asiatic or 'aamu traders from Palestine from the tomb of Khnumhotep, 11th Dynasty, Beni Hasan, Middle Egypt.

Hyksos as "Shepherd Kings", but this etymology is incorrect. It appears that these wandering people were not invaders but simply herders seeking pasture for their flocks, merchants trading their goods, or unskilled labourers looking for work.[11] The tradition of wandering peoples seeking a better life in the Nile river valley was well known in ancient Egypt and is referred to in the literary text called *The Prophesy of Neferti*.[12] The Egyptians seem to have readily accepted these Asiatics into their land since a papyrus text[13] from the late Middle Kingdom lists 45 men, women, and children with Semitic names and of Syro-Palestinian origin working in a single household. There were probably many such households throughout Egypt at this time.

The tomb of Khnumhotep (c.1900 BC), the provincial governor, at Beni Hasan displays a wall painting showing a band of 37 *'aamu* bringing *stibium*, the famous black cosmetic eye paint, to be traded in the Two Lands. The group is led by their sheikh, named Ab-sha (Abishel), who is specifically designated as a *hika-khoswet*, or "ruler of a foreign land". Somehow, the Egyptian word *hika-khoswet*, which was the title given to a ruler or king, became understood as the name of a whole group of people and was used as such by Manetho in historical writings as "Hyksos". In the remainder of this chapter the people misnamed by Manetho as the Hyksos will be referred to by that name, even though the ancient Egyptians did not refer to them as such.

Rulers of foreign lands

Who were the rulers of foreign lands? William Flinders Petrie, a pioneer British archaeologist, excavated the Nile Delta site of Tell el-Yahudiyah in the 1880s and discovered two pieces of evidence that for a long time were considered as typical examples of Hyksos material culture: one was a new type of pottery, the other a special type of fortification enclosure.

Petrie also believed that the Hyksos possessed two weapons that were unknown to the Egyptians: the horse-drawn chariot[14] and the composite bow. The composite bow was made of several layers of wood and bone that were glued together, giving it a greatly increased range that made it a clear advancement in the weapons technology of the day. The horse-drawn chariot was a fast, mobile, weapons-firing platform popular with armies of the time, although its battlefield effectiveness has been debated.[15]

According to Petrie, the compound bow and the horse-drawn chariot were the hallmarks of Hyksos material culture. With these advanced weapons the Hyksos were able to defeat the native Egyptians through military force, just as Manetho had said. But Petrie's interpretation of the Hyksos did not withstand the rigours of later archaeological research. In 1936 the German (later Swiss) Egyptologist Herbert Ricke showed that Petrie's fortification enclosures actually[16] belonged to temples and had no defensive value.[16] Later, in 1951, a Swedish Egyptologist, Torgny Säve-Söderbergh, demonstrated that the horse and chariot and the compound bow were being used in other parts of Asia at the time of the supposed "Hyksos invasion", and their invention could not be directly attributed to them.[17] Over the years some of Petrie's interpretations had to be abandoned as elements that had been attributed to Hyksos material culture had to be reassessed in the light of new discoveries.

The Hyksos capital

For nearly a century the location of the Hyksos capital city of Avaris,[18] mentioned in Egyptian texts, remained unknown. In the 1960s, a team of Austrian Egyptologists, under the direction of Manfred Bietak, was able to locate the lost city of Avaris in the Nile Delta at a site now known by the Arabic name of Tell ed-Dab'a.[19] Not only were the Austrians able to locate

Donkey burial from Tell el-Maskhuta situated in front of a Middle Bronze Age (2000–1550 BC) tomb similar to those found in Palestine.

the ancient Hyksos capital, but they were also able to determine that certain strata uncovered at Avaris belonged to the Hyksos period and contained artifacts and structures that belonged to the Syro-Palestinian Middle Bronze Age (2000–1500 BC). This indicated that the Hyksos had the same material culture as neighbouring Syria and Palestine, and were part of the same cultural group.[20] These discoveries were reinforced by excavations undertaken at other nearby sites, such as Tell el-Maskhuta,[21] which showed a number of similarities with the material culture found at Tell ed-Dab'a.[22]

Again, the strata belonging to the Hyksos contained the same material culture as those at Tell ed-Dab'a.[23] The migrant interpretation has been strengthened since neither Tell el-Maskhuta nor Tell ed-Dab'a contained evidence that they had been destroyed by fire or military conflict by the Hyksos in a time when cities were set on fire as a way of punishing defeated enemies.[24] These pieces of evidence undermine the idea that there was any kind of military invasion of Egypt by foreign invaders. It is more likely that in the 13th Dynasty, as Egypt weakened, groups from Syria-Palestine grew in power and sophistication and were able to take control of Lower Egypt.

During this same period Syria-Palestine reached a level of material and cultural wealth that was unmatched until the Roman period some 1500 years later. It has even been suggested that the roles of Egypt and Syria-Palestine were actually reversed during this period.[25] Northeastern Egypt fell under the strong influence of the expanding Syro-Palestinian culture, which gave Egypt a large number of new immigrants and a new royal family while at the same time enriching it with new elements in its material culture. The weakening of centralized rule in Egypt at this time is reflected in the southern Nile regions of Upper Nubia as well, since the Kushites were also enjoying a period of greater prosperity and expansion north into Upper Egypt.[26] For more than a century, while Egypt declined, its neighbours both in the north and in the south gained in power and for a time controlled much of the Nile river valley.

The Hyksos period was a turning point in Egyptian history. Before this time the Two Lands had been somewhat insulated from outside intrusions by natural barriers such as the great deserts and seas that formed its borders. To a certain extent it remained cut off from much of the bloodshed and turmoil that plagued so many other parts of the ancient world. However, after the Egyptians succeeded in ridding themselves of foreign rulers they struck out against neighbouring countries and conquered them one after another, becoming more aggressive and imperialistic in the centuries that followed.[27]

The expulsion of the Hyksos

About 1550 BC, Kamose, the last king of the 17th Dynasty, launched a war of liberation against the Hyksos. Kamose led an attack against the north and reached the capital at Avaris, although he was unable to conquer it. The task of the conquest of the Hyksos stronghold was left to his successor, perhaps a younger brother, Ahmose (1550–1525 BC), who succeeded him and drove the Hyksos rulers out of Egypt. As well as freeing Egypt of outside forces, Ahmose also had the distinction of being the founder of the 18th Dynasty, one of the most powerful ruling families in all of Egyptian history. Ahmose was succeeded by Amenhotep I and then by Thutmosis I, one of Egypt's great warrior kings. He was able to pursue the Hyksos and their allies into Palestine and pushed the frontiers of Egyptian influence deep into Syria all the way to the Euphrates River at Karkamish (Carchemish). Once this was accomplished he turned his armies to the south against the Kushites and re-established Egyptian control in Upper Egypt, pushing upstream as far south as the Third Cataract.[28] The region of Kush, which was rich in gold and other minerals and trade goods, was then turned into an Egyptian colony and ruled by a viceroy directly responsible to the king.

THE NEW KINGDOM (1550–1069 BC)

The New Kingdom[29] was one of the greatest periods of Egyptian history. In the New Kingdom, Egyptian power and influence spread beyond the Nile river valley to encompass much of Syria-Palestine, reaching

Map of Lower Egypt and Upper Egypt and the kingdom of Kush in Upper Nubia.

Chronology of the New Kingdom and Third Intermediate period (1550–664) (all dates BC)

New Kingdom	
18th Dynasty	1550–1307
Ahmose	1550–1525
Amenhotep I	1525–1504
Thutmosis I	1504–1492
Thutmosis II	1492–1479
Thutmosis III	1479–1425
Hatshepsut	1473–1458
Amenhotep II	1427–1401
Thutmosis IV	1401–1391
Amenhotep III	1391–1353
Amenhotep IV/Akhenaten	1353–1335
Smenkhkare	1335–1333?
Tutankhamun	1333–1323
Aya	1323–1319
Horemheb	1319–1292
19th Dynasty	1292–1196
20th Dynasty	1196–1069
Third Intermediate period	**1069–664**

(Amarna period bracket spans Amenhotep IV/Akhenaten through Horemheb.)

all the way to the borders of Mesopotamia on the banks of the Euphrates River. The three dynasties of the New Kingdom spanned five centuries and produced some of the most interesting and creative characters in all of ancient history. It is during the New Kingdom that the title "pharaoh" comes into use. The word originally meant "great house", but during the reign of King Thutmosis III it began to be used to refer to individual kings.[30] The 18th Dynasty shows a marked change from previous periods of Egyptian history. Royal pyramid construction projects had long since ceased, the Valley of the Kings became the preferred burial site for royalty, and Egypt had become a conquering, imperialistic power that attacked and looted weaker kingdoms.[31] With its new-found wealth it became the richest and most powerful kingdom on the African continent.

Hatshepsut, the female king of Egypt

During the New Kingdom queens and female members of the upper classes were much more visible in Egyptian society and appear to have played an increasingly important role in the affairs of the Egyptian state.[32] Three women of the 18th Dynasty are of particular interest: the powerful Queen Tiye, wife of Amenhotep III; Nefertiti, the wife of the controversial Akhenaten; and the most remarkable female of the dynasty, Hatshepsut,[33] meaning "Foremost among the noble ones", who ruled Egypt for nearly 20 years.[34] Once Egypt was re-established within its own pre-Hyksos borders, a complex and unusual series of events took place. King Thutmosis I and his principal wife, Ahmose, only had a daughter, Hatshepsut, who was married to her half-brother, Thutmosis II, one of the king's sons by a lesser wife. Upon her marriage to Thutmosis II, Hatshepsut became the "King's Great Wife" and filled the traditional role of the king's chief royal spouse. Nothing indicates that she conducted herself in a manner dif-

ferent from that of royal wives who had preceded her. Her husband and half-brother, Thutmosis II, seems to have had a short and rather unremarkable reign. He was neither a great conqueror nor a great builder like his father. The most profound effect he had on Egyptian history was to die without leaving a male heir to the throne to make a smooth transition of power from father to son. He did have a son by a lesser wife, Aset, and this son was again given the name Thutmosis. This third Thutmosis was only about 8 years old when his father died: too young to rule alone. Therefore, his aunt and stepmother, the widowed Queen Hatshepsut, took control of the land and served as its ruler.

So far the succession had been conducted according to tradition and in keeping with *ma'at*, the concept of universal order and harmony. When similar situations had arisen previously, if the young king was not old enough to rule alone then an older family member took control until the youngster gained sufficient experience. A passage from the tomb of the high official Ineni reveals that in the early years of their shared reign, Hatshepsut and Thutmosis III ruled together in harmony. The passage states that when Thutmosis II died and went up into the heavens to join the gods, his son took his place and was crowned king of the Two Lands, while Hatshepsut actually governed the land as she saw fit.[35]

At first Hatshepsut conducted herself as though she were a normal Egyptian queen and took the usual royal titles of previous queens, but things suddenly changed some time around the seventh regnal year of the young King Thutmosis III.[36] She abandoned the pretext of being a temporary ruler waiting for the real king to grow up, and proclaimed herself to be "king" of Egypt. She began to refer to herself using the masculine form of her names and titles, had herself portrayed wearing masculine royal clothing, and was even depicted wearing the ceremonial beard like ancient King Narmer (see Ch. 10) and other male predecessors. After she had taken the royal titles

traditionally reserved for the king, artistic renderings show both Thutmosis and his stepmother together, but she is given precedence over him. In spite of her acknowledged superiority over her nephew, contemporary records in no way indicate that any conflict existed between them. Nor is there any evidence that would indicate that the young Thutmosis III was exiled to some far-off country[37] as some historians have argued, while his supposedly "wicked stepmother" illegally ruled the Two Lands.

Perhaps Hatshepsut would never have gained the recognition and fame that surrounds her memory if she had simply kept her traditional royal titles and ruled Egypt as a queen, fulfilling all the duties necessary to keep the Two Lands functioning properly. Even though it may have been considered somewhat unusual for a woman to rule Egypt instead of a man, most officials and commoners could probably have lived with this arrangement if it meant peace and stability. However, she must have caused quite a commotion when she declared herself to be king. Taking all of the kingly titles, and wearing male clothes, has prompted a number of Egyptologists to interpret her actions as those of an ambitious and power-hungry woman not willing to share her power with the younger Thutmosis III.[38] But there is another, more plausible way to explain why Hatshepsut went to such extremes with her royal titles and dress. The highest-ranking women in the court were referred to by such titles as "Chief Royal Wife", "King's Daughter", and "King's Sister", and there was no way to feminize the king's titles because they were in the masculine form of the Egyptian language. Since Hatshepsut had no husband and was not married to Thutmosis III, she could not be his "Chief Royal Wife"; nor could she call herself "King's Daughter" because she was already a mature woman. It was perhaps for these reasons that she decided that if the titles did not fit her then she would change her dress and physical appearance to fit the titles. We do not know if she actually wore male attire in her eve-

Top: Hatshepsut kneeling in front of the god Amun-Re, who extends his hands towards the *khepresh* ("blue crown"), detail from her fallen obelisk, Amun-Re Temple, Karnak. Granite, incised low-relief sculpture. Bottom: Column from Hatshepsut's temple in the form of the goddess Hathor, Temple of Hatshepsut, Deir el-Bahri.

ryday life, if she just had herself portrayed on official monuments in this type of clothing, or wore male clothing only at official state functions.[39]

In the early years of her reign statues clearly show Hatshepsut wearing a dress that reveals breasts and other feminine physical features. A few years later she is depicted wearing the very masculine kilt traditionally worn by Egyptian kings, but with only a thin, gilet or T-shirt above the waist. Sometimes she is shown wearing the male ceremonial royal kilt, unclothed from the waist up, without feminine features and appearing very much like a man. In some low-relief sculpture she is portrayed virtually identically to Thutmosis III.

Divine conception and birth

Kingship in Egypt was a not only a political function, but also a religious one, and the religious nature of Egyptian kingship presupposed that the office of king was to be held by a man.[40] All of the mythology, costumes, and titles were created for a man. But after she assumed the title of king, Hatshepsut modified traditional creation myths concerning the divine conception of the king to suit her own set of circumstances, and contrived a story about her own divine parenthood and birth. In her version of the myth, the god Amun disguised himself as Hatshepsut's father and visited her mother as she slept, leaving her pregnant. The text makes it very clear that, just like kings, Hatshepsut was the daughter of a god and not a mere mortal. Generally only kings were immortal and their lesser wives were not, although the king's chief royal wife did share some divine principles with her godly husband. After she was conceived the god Amun declared to Hatshepsut's mother that she was now pregnant with a daughter whose name was Hatshepsut, who was destined to be the future ruler of Egypt.

There has been a tendency to portray Hatshepsut as a domineering, power-hungry woman determined to wrestle the throne of Egypt from its rightful owner, the young and innocent Thutmosis III. Throughout most of this century she has been portrayed in both scholarly and popular literature as a kind of wicked stepmother.[41] More recently scholars have interpreted the reign of Hatshepsut as a reaction to a dynastic crisis[42] in which Egypt was left with no suitable heir to the throne. To prevent potential usurpers from taking royal power from Hatshepsut's family, thus losing the wealth and privileges of royalty, Hatshepsut took on the role of king until the crisis passed and a new king was again firmly established on the throne.[43] Accordingly, Hatshepsut was a woman willing to take extraordinary measures so Egypt could maintain its stability. Only a few decades earlier Egypt had re-established its power after taking back Lower Egypt from the Hyksos, and certainly the memories of foreign domination were very fresh in the minds of the leaders of the Two Lands. Hatshepsut herself reminds her subjects of this, and in one of her inscriptions states that she restored things that had been ruined by the Hyksos and destroyed all traces of them. Wishing to avoid the kind of instability that had allowed the Hyksos to take control of Egyptian interests, Hatshepsut and her supporters adapted to the extraordinary circumstances of her time. This does not mean that Hatshepsut was lacking in ambition or desire for the throne of Egypt.[44] No timid person, male or female, would have been able to challenge centuries of tradition and authority as Hatshepsut did without plenty of talent and a good deal of ambition. Hatshepsut was certainly not meant to stay in power as long as she did. It seems that once she had a taste of power early in her reign while Thutmosis III was still a young boy, she grew to like the role of leader of Egypt and decided to maintain it for as long as she could.[45]

Queens before Hatshepsut

Hatshepsut was not the first woman to rule over the Two Lands in the place of a king.[46] On several occasions in Egyptian history, when a ruling family ran out of male heirs, a woman was chosen as interim ruler until a suitable male heir could be found, or until the old dynasty was replaced by a new ruling family. This seems to have happened as early as the 1st Dynasty, when the task of leadership passed to Queen Merit-neith.[47] It has been suggested that she was the wife of King Djet who died before their son, Den, was old enough to take the throne. It seems that Merit-neith ruled until her death, after which her son took over and continued the family line. Since the written evidence is scarce, it is difficult to reconstruct many details of the life of this early queen, but her tomb in the Cemetery of Kings at Abydos was as rich as any of her male contemporaries. She even had some servants interred with her, indicating that she had attained a very high and respected status among her peers. Later, a similar situation occurred again in the 12th Dynasty. As with Hatshepsut, it seems there was no male heir to carry on the dynastic line and Princess Sobeknefru[48] struggled to hold on to the throne for perhaps as long as four years before she disappeared, along with her family line, which had ruled Egypt for around 200 years. In the case of Sobeknefru, as in the 1st Dynasty, the ruling family was threatened by the lack of a male heir, and as a last resort the wife of the deceased king was placed on the throne (undoubtedly with the support of the other family members) to avoid the inevitable struggle for the throne that always ensued in these circumstances.[49] The long and successful reign of Hatshepsut was exceptional in Egyptian history. Men, not women, were meant to rule the Two Lands; women were chosen to step in and take control of power only when there were no male heirs available. During its 3000-year history Egypt had several hundred kings, and yet there were

at most a handful of women, perhaps five, who ruled the Two Lands.[50]

Djeser-Djeseru: Hatshepsut's mortuary temple

One of the most remarkable structures in ancient Egypt is Djeser-Djeseru, the mortuary temple Hatshepsut built on the west bank of the Nile River across from Thebes.[51] Made of limestone, this temple is approximately 100 m wide by 160 m long, and consists of three massive columned terraces with long, sloping ramps connecting each level. Her temple was

Djeser-Djeseru, Hatshepsut's mortuary temple at Deir el-Bahri.

Hatshepsut's temple seen from the summit of the western escarpment.

clearly influenced by another remarkable example of Egyptian architecture, the temple of Mentuhotep, and is situated only a few metres from it (see Ch. 12). Hatshepsut was not buried in a subterranean burial chamber behind the temple, like the 11th Dynasty king, Mentuhotep, centuries earlier, but in a rock-cut tomb (KV 42)[52] completely separate from the temple in the Valley of the Kings. Inside the covered terraces of Djeser-Djeseru there are a number of painted low-relief scenes of Hatshepsut's career as ruler of Egypt.[53] On the north wall of the middle terrace the episode of her divine conception and birth is presented, while a series on the south wall recounts the expedition to Punt that took place during her reign.

Trading mission to Punt

A distant and mysterious land, Punt (Pwenet), was located somewhere southeast of Egypt, near the Red Sea. Punt was important because it had exotic luxury items fancied by the Egyptians such as incense, myrrh trees, ivory, ebony, leopard skins, and gold. Painted low-relief scenes show the people of Punt living in round thatched huts elevated on stilts and surrounded by animals associated with tropical Africa, such as giraffes, hippopotamuses, and apes. Other scenes show five large Egyptian ships leaving for the southern land where they are greeted by the prince of Punt, Parehu, and his huge, arch-backed wife, Eti. As the expedition arrives some of the chiefs are shown prostrating themselves before the queen's divine emblem (she did not accompany the mission herself), and they refer to her as the "King of Egypt" and call her the "female sun".

Obelisks

Another important series of scenes at Djeser-Djeseru shows the transportation by boat of two giant ob-

elisks, each 29.5 m long and weighing around 325 tonnes.[54] Obelisks were long, gently tapered pieces of granite that terminated in a small *ben-ben* or pyramid form at the top. They were made of a single piece of granite that came only from the area around the First Cataract of the Nile River at Aswan, 200 km south of Thebes. Obelisks (Greek for "little skewer") are fascinating objects inscribed with hieroglyphic signs and dedicated to one of the gods. Sometimes the upper portions of obelisks were painted or covered with electrum. Many obelisks were taken from Egypt in ancient times and ended up in the cities of Rome and Istanbul. In AD 1833, during the reign of the French king, Louis-Philippe I, an obelisk belonging to Ramesses II was erected in the Place de la Concorde in central Paris. Later on in the 19th century Egyptian obelisks were set up in London and New York.[55]

Hatshepsut could not have risen to power and maintained her position for 20 years without the help of family members and allies in the court.[56] One of her officials, Senenmut,[57] rose through the ranks and held numerous important positions at court. He attained the title "Steward of Amun", meaning that he had control over the vast wealth of the temples and sacred precincts of Amun-Re, the most important god in Egypt. Some historians and novelists have maintained that Senenmut and Hatshepsut were lovers. If this is true, their story would make an interesting and romantic tale, but there is no real evidence that would indicate that they had anything other than a professional relationship.

Senenmut was in charge of procuring obelisks for Hatshepsut, as well as constructing many of her temples and buildings. He even prepared two burial

Left: Obelisk of Ramesses II. Height 22.5 m, Place de la Concorde, Paris. Centre: Uninscribed obelisk with cross. Height 25.37 m. This obelisk originally stood in Alexandria, Egypt, but was moved in 1586 by Pope Sixtus V to the Piazza di San Pietro, Vatican. Right: Obelisk of Hatshepsut. Height 29.56 m, Amun-Re Temple, Karnak, Thebes.

chambers for himself, one of them within Hatshepsut's great mortuary temple precinct. Both tombs were entered and badly damaged in antiquity, and his quartzite sarcophagus was smashed to pieces. About the 16th year of Hatshepsut's reign, Senenmut, for unknown reasons, disappeared from the royal scene. Perhaps he died, or fell out of favour with Hatshepsut.

The reconstruction of the Two Lands

Hatshepsut has been portrayed as a pacifist[58] who shunned military conquest in favour of great building projects and trading missions to exotic lands. Although she was a great builder and interested in trade, she was no pacifist. Warfare was a minor element of her foreign policy, used only when other methods of dealing with enemies were unsuccessful. However, she was interested in military matters and launched several small campaigns, and may have even taken to the battlefield herself.[59] Hatshepsut had a plan for the reconstruction of Egypt in the post-Hyksos period, and to implement it she needed a peaceful and stable environment that would allow her to undertake building projects and trading expeditions.[60] In a number of inscriptions she emphasized the need for peace so that she could restore Egypt to its former greatness, and she characterized her reign as being the years of peace. All evidence indicates that in this she was successful. During her reign there is evidence that much of Egypt's former prosperity was restored, and the uncertainty and confusion of earlier times diminished. In the final years of her reign, after about 20 years of successful rule, the ageing queen may have been ailing and in decline, and her nephew, Thutmosis III, was anxious to take sole control of the Two Lands. In the 22nd year of his reign Prince Thutmosis III took full control of the throne of Egypt, and Hatshepsut, the female king of Egypt, died and was buried peacefully and with full honours in the Valley of the Kings.

Thutmosis III, the warrior king

It has been suggested that Hatshepsut somehow suppressed Thutmosis III[61] for nearly two decades until he finally grew strong enough and bold enough to overthrow her rule, perhaps murdering her in the process. But there is no need to resort to such violent and radical explanations in order to understand the relationship between the two rulers. Hatshepsut and Thutmosis III had some kind of power-sharing arrangement, and even though his stepmother dominated the early years of their reign together, as he grew older he became more powerful and eventually ruled Egypt for a total of 54 years (1479–1425 BC), including the 20 or so years he shared with Hatshepsut. The arrangement of royal power-sharing surely caused some tensions between the two rulers. But even though Thutmosis controlled the army, he never used his military power to overthrow his stepmother's rule. From all appearances, Hatshepsut's reign was necessary to ensure dynastic stability in a time of uncertainty, and Thutmosis III himself was probably very aware of this fragile situation.

After the death of Hatshepsut, Thutmosis III spent most of his reign in wars of conquest and he was to a large extent responsible for the establishment of the Egyptian Empire that took form during the New Kingdom.[62] During his independent reign of 33 years plus the additional 26-year reign of his son, Amenhotep II, who was also a military man, the Egyptian Empire was able to maintain the territorial gains made in the earlier reigns of Thutmosis I and Amenhotep II. This period of expansion and conquest was due in part to the large and efficient military organization that Egypt had developed, and the presence of competent generals who were able to lead the soldiers of the Two Lands to victory in many battles.[63]

During the last years of Hatshepsut's reign, the city-states and small kingdoms of Syria-Palestine

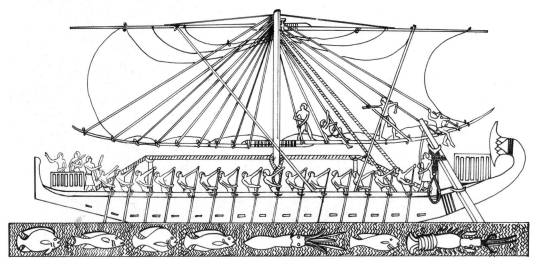

New Kingdom boat from the time of Hatshepsut. (Egyptian Museum, Cairo)

attempted to throw off the yoke of Egyptian oppression imposed upon them by Thutmosis III's grandfather, Thutmosis I. In the last year of Hatshepsut's reign, Thutmosis III marched into Gaza and attacked people he called "rebels", meaning those who refused to pay tribute to Egypt or allow outside control of their cities and lands. One inscription tells how the king left Egypt near today's Suez Canal on a campaign to overthrow Egypt's enemies and extend the boundaries of the Two Lands in accordance with the command of his father, the god Amun. The first goal of this campaign was to capture the city of Megiddo, which was the centre of a loose coalition of kings and princes fighting against Egyptian domination. The details of this campaign were recorded by a scribe named Tjenen and, although there is much boasting in favour of the Egyptians, his account seems to be an essentially truthful rendition of Thutmosis III's first major military engagement.

A combination of luck and good leadership enabled the Egyptians to get very close to Megiddo without being detected. When the king's forces attacked, the enemy troops stationed outside the city were easily defeated and fled before the armies of the Two Lands. The Egyptians chased the enemy forces from the field, and they could even have smashed their way into the city and taken it as well had it not been that, in the middle of the attack, the pharaoh's forces broke ranks and began looting the abandoned weapons, horses, and chariots left on the field of battle by their enemies. This disciplinary breakdown gave the defenders of Megiddo a chance to get inside the city's walls to safety. The description of the campaign recounts that the fleeing soldiers of Megiddo were hoisted up over the city walls by their garments while the army of the king went about looting the goods of its enemies. This costly error forced the Egyptians to lay siege to the city for seven months before it finally capitulated. The wait, however, was worth it, for when Megiddo fell, along with it went more than 350 towns and villages.

After the campaign was over, scenes of the capture and destruction of Megiddo were inscribed on the walls and pylons of the temple of Amun at Thebes, which Thutmosis III had extended to honour the gods who had brought him victory. High on the walls of the temple precinct, in painted low-relief carvings, were the names of the towns and cities captured by him, each one represented by a prisoner with his hands bound behind his back.

Even though the city of Megiddo had been captured, the struggle for Syria-Palestine was not over. From the 23rd to the 39th years of his reign, Thutmosis III fought up to 17 military campaigns in an attempt to control the area. In the captured city-states and small kingdoms, Thutmosis III placed governors and princes drawn from the local population. To keep them loyal after his armies had returned to Egypt, Thutmosis took their brothers and children with him back to Egypt as hostages. While in the Two Lands they were educated in the ways of Egypt and when they grew older and were sufficiently indoctrinated with Egyptian ideas and culture, they were sent back to their homelands to serve as faithful rulers for the king.

Perhaps Thutmosis III's greatest military accomplishment was the crossing of the Euphrates River

Chariot panel showing battle scenes, from the tomb of Thutmosis IV, 18th Dynasty, KV 43. (Egyptian Museum, Cairo)

into the land of Naharin, meaning "River Land". This entailed the transportation of boats over 400 km from the port city of Byblos to Karkamish, where they were used to traverse the Euphrates River.[64] The boats were built in Egypt, sailed to Byblos, and then transported across the countryside on wagons pulled by oxen. Crossing the Euphrates River represented the furthest northern extension of Egyptian power and hegemony, placing them on the borders of one of the other great powers of the time, the kingdom of Mitanni.[65]

At the other end of the empire in Upper Egypt, Thutmosis III had consolidated Egyptian presence as far south as the Fourth Cataract region on the Nile River at the provincial capital of Napata. During his reign Egyptian control stretched from the great bend in the Euphrates River near Karkamish, roughly 1400 km north of Thebes (actual land and sea route distances would have been much greater) to over 1000 km to the south. Even though the Egyptian presence and outright control of the south in the areas known as Wawat and Kush (Lower and Upper Nubia) remained strong for many centuries, Egypt's control of northern regions was always tenuous and began to slip away almost immediately. During the New Kingdom much of Egypt's resources and foreign policy were concentrated on the struggle to maintain control of Syria-Palestine. Both Thutmosis III and Thutmosis I had extended Egyptian hegemony to the Euphrates River, but subsequent kings were forced to gradually withdraw over the years, giving up parts of the northern empire to the Mitanni or the Hittites.

The fruits of conquest

With the conquest of new territories came revenues for the king, the religious organizations, and the people of the Two Lands. Some of this new-found wealth was used to enhance and enlarge the temple of Amun at Karnak, in the religious quarter of the capital. There Thutmosis III added the sixth pylon to the main temple structure, on which he recounted his military campaigns including the battle of Megiddo, as well as several ceremonial gates and chapels and two obelisks, in addition to his own massive mortuary structure, which he built just a few metres from Hatshepsut's at Deir el-Bahri, on the west bank of the Nile River. He also enriched Egypt's religious life by instituting new religious festivals and holidays in which the entire country participated. The temple was one of Egypt's main land-owning institutions and possessed tremendous wealth, which it used to employ local peoples. It was also the main depository for foreign slaves taken in military campaigns.

Later in his life Thutmosis III took his son, Amenhotep II, as his co-regent. There were many stories about the strength and athletic prowess of this vigorous king, who continued the policies of conquest of his father. According to legend, he was a great archer and his bow was so strong that no one else could draw it. After a long and solid reign he was followed by Thutmosis IV, who, like his father and grandfather, was active in the same areas of Syria-Palestine in the north and around Napata in the south. By this time Egypt had a well-established empire, and although it had to struggle constantly to maintain its possessions, it was the strongest power in the ancient Near East.

There was a marked change in the style of kingship when Amenhotep III (1391–1353 BC) came to the throne.[66] Benefiting from the hard-won accomplishments of his predecessors, Amenhotep III ruled Egypt for 38 years at the apex of its imperial power. Unlike some of the previous kings of the 18th Dynasty, he did not spend much time on military campaigns but left this aspect of his rule to his generals and professional soldiers. While the army was out in the field protecting Egypt's interests, Amenhotep III was occupied with his building projects. At Karnak he made additions to the Amun temple and built a new temple to the god of war, Montu. The fact that the Egyptians emphasized the war god at this time perhaps indicates how important and profitable war had become, and how important it was to keep the war god's favour. In addition, he built a huge family mansion and what was probably the largest mortuary temple ever built in Egypt, complete with its own harbour. The family temple was quarried for its building stone later in the 18th and 19th Dynasties and almost nothing remains of it today except two large statues of the king. By the reign of Amenhotep III, Egypt was at the peak of its power and prestige. Slaves and booty taken in battle from Egypt's weaker neighbours poured into the Two Lands, while foreigners and mercenaries serving in the armies of the pharaoh clogged the cities and towns along the banks of the Nile River. At this key moment, the great stage of Egyptian history was set for one of Egypt's most interesting and enigmatic kings, Akhenaten.

14 Akhenaten and the Amarna period

The 18th Dynasty king Akhenaten (1353–1335 BC) was one of the most controversial people to ever rule ancient Egypt and has provoked more debate among historians, archaeologists, novelists, art historians, and even psychiatrists, than perhaps any other king from the ancient Near East. In the past scholars have either praised him as a visionary or condemned him as a fanatic. J. D. S. Pendelbury called Akhenaten "a religious maniac", while H. R. Hall thought he was "mad" or at least "half insane".[1] The father of psychoanalysis, Sigmund Freud,[2] wrote a book in which he advanced the theory that Akhenaten inspired the Hebrew patriarch Moses to accept monotheism: the belief in one god. Freud argued that Moses was an Egyptian and went so far as to claim, incorrectly,[3] that one of the names of the Hebrew god Adonai was actually a derivation of Aten, the name of Akhenaten's god.[4] A century ago the influential American Egyptologist James Henry Breasted called Akhenaten "the first individual in history",[5] while more recently Akhenaten specialist Donald Redford called him a "totalitarian", and his regime "tiresome".[6] The diversity of opinions[7] about Akhenaten demonstrates the many different ways historians can interpret the same person.[8]

Traditional views of Akhenaten

Traditional views of Akhenaten are due in part to the work of Breasted, whose interpretations found their way into a number of popular histories of Egypt and gained a large audience among the public through historical and biographical novels based on his ideas. According to Breasted, Akhenaten took the throne when Egypt was at the peak of its power and its empire extended from Syria-Palestine, in the north, to far up the Nile River to Kush in the south. During the reign of his father Amenhotep III, Egypt was strong and secure with wealth and tribute pouring into the country from conquered lands. Since a large amount of this wealth was given to the priests of the Amun-Re cult, who offered it to the gods as a sign of appreciation of their help in Egypt's success, the temple amassed great wealth and power. This enhanced power allowed the priests to challenge the political power of the king himself.

Re was the old sun god who gained prominence during the reigns of Djoser[9] and later Snefru and Khufu, the great pyramid-building kings of the 4th Dynasty. With his major shrines and temples, Re dominated Egyptian religious thought during the Old Kingdom, and for the remainder of Egyptian history the sun god was always a major force in

Chronology of the Amarna period (all dates BC)

Amenhotep III	1391–1353
Amenhotep IV/Akhenaten	1353–1335
Smenkhkare	1335–1333?
Tutankhamun	1333–1323
Aya	1323–1319
Horemheb	1319–1292

religion. In the Middle Kingdom, the northern cult of Re was combined with the southern cult of Amun, "the hidden one," an air and fertility god, to form the Amun-Re cult with its spiritual centre located at Thebes. This religious organization wielded great political power, and it was to offset this power, and restore power to the pharaoh, that Akhenaten turned away from the Amun-Re cult and sought to establish a new solar deity and priesthood

that he could control. The friction between the Amun-Re priests and the new king became intolerable and, in a bold and revolutionary gesture, Akhenaten denounced the cult of Amun-Re and replaced it with a new god symbolized by the solar disc called the Aten. Since they were both sun gods, in many ways the Aten was similar to Re. The king changed his name, Amenhotep IV, which meant "the god Amun is satisfied",[10] to Akhenaten, which

contained the element "Aten" and meant "spirit of the Aten".[11]

To promote his new god and make him the supreme deity of Egypt, Akhenaten deposed the priests of Amun-Re as well as other religious cults, and closed down their temples, leaving them to fall into ruin. At the same time he sent his agents throughout the land to chisel out the names of the other gods, even obliterating the plural form of the

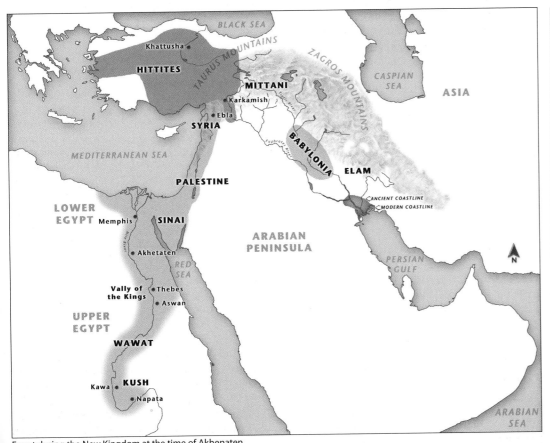

Egypt during the New Kingdom at the time of Akhenaten.

Akhenaten, Amarna period. (Egyptian Museum, Cairo)

word "god" from monuments and shrines. Five or six years after he had ascended to the throne Akhenaten moved his family, court, and religion to his newly founded capital city, known today by the Arabic name El-Amarna,[12] but which he named Akhetaten, "the horizon of the Aten". The new capital, which Akhenaten vowed never to leave, was situated in Middle Egypt about 250 km north of Thebes. In his new city he became preoccupied with spiritual matters and spent most of his time writing poems and hymns to Aten. One of his hymns, which he may have written himself, is the beautiful "Great Hymn to the Sun", which extols the virtues of the Aten sun disc and its beneficent light and life-giving rays.[13] The Great Hymn praises the Aten for giving light, chasing away the darkness, and giving life to all plants, animals, and humans. According to the traditional view, because Akhenaten had essentially disconnected himself from the practical, everyday aspects of running Egypt's hard-won empire, the country began to suffer and go into decline. Some scholars erroneously thought they had found evidence for this neglect in a number of unanswered letters requesting military and financial assistance.

The Amarna Letters

In 1887, farmers ploughing their fields near a village in Middle Egypt called El-Amarna uncovered some hardened lumps of baked clay, which looked as if they might have some value on the antiquities market. These objects eventually made their way into the hands of scholars, who recognized them as letters written on clay tablets in cuneiform script. Known as the Amarna Letters,[14] these texts reveal that in the 14th century BC a diplomatic communications network existed in the Near East that stretched from Egypt into Mesopotamia and Turkey (Anatolia). Ambassadors carried dispatches to the Egyptian capital at Akhetaten from the distant lands of Mitanni,

Khatti, and Assyria, and even from as far away as the kingdom of Babylon. A number of these letters were sent by rulers of petty kingdoms located in Syria-Palestine,[15] which frequently engaged in wars with Egypt's main enemies, the Hittites and the Mitanni. To sustain such military activity required men and equipment and the wealth to pay them. The Egyptian allies thought that the pharaoh of Egypt would send them copious amounts of gold since they believed that "gold was as plentiful as dust in the land of Egypt". The belief that Akhenaten neglected the empire[16] was based on the readings of a number of the Amarna Letters that contained pleas for help, asking the king to send reinforcements to beleaguered vassals of Egypt struggling against the enemies of the Two Lands. Some of the letters addressed to the king from his vassals portray them as faithful servants trying desperately to hold on to the crumbling pieces of the empire while the king foolishly refuses to send help, or even acknowledge their difficult situation.[17]

More recently it has been realized that the Amarna Letters must be read with caution and that the messages in these texts cannot always be taken at face value. Often, the cries for help were only thinly disguised pleas for the pharaoh's gold to enable the writer to promote some personal project of his own, which had little to do with the safety or well-being of the Egyptian Empire. Even before the time of Akhenaten, Egyptian rulers had grown accustomed to such pleas for help and tended to ignore them. Thus, not acting upon such requests does not necessarily suggest that Akhenaten neglected the workings of his empire.[18]

Akhenaten and monotheism

In terms of Akhenaten's religion, the traditional view maintained that he made a clean, sharp break from existing religious beliefs. Breaking with the past, the

young king conceived the idea of monotheism,[19] the belief in one god, as opposed to polytheism, the belief in many gods. Egypt had hundreds of gods and countless shrines, altars, and temples dedicated to them. Then, almost overnight, Akhenaten forcibly replaced them all with his brand of solar monotheism. Some commentators have given him the title of "heretic king" because he destroyed Egypt's long-standing religious traditions; others have seen him as a great religious reformer who, centuries before the Old Testament prophets, advanced human spirituality by concentrating all religious beliefs into one supreme godhead, and even advancing the concept of a "trinity" of gods.[20]

Living in *ma'at*

It was important that the king live in accordance with *ma'at* (truth and justice) to ensure that truth and order prevailed, and that natural disasters and foreign invaders did not ravage the land. Akhenaten qualified his name with the phrase "Living in *ma'at*." He also took the concept of *ma'at* one step further than his predecessors, and in artistic representations had himself portrayed not as an idealized god-king like previous pharaohs, but instead as he really appeared: a misshapen, effeminate-looking man whose bizarre appearance has seldom been matched in the ancient world. Akhenaten was depicted with a long neck, lantern jaw, and oddly shaped body, which included a distinct "pot-belly", and with feminine hips and thighs, and even breasts.

Because the kings of Egypt influenced fashion trends and dress codes, family members and courtiers were disposed to emulate the way their rulers dressed. Artistic representations of the time show people other than the royal family wearing the same style of clothing and with the same misshapen appearance as the king. According to the traditional interpretation, the fact that he chose to have himself represented truthfully, according to *ma'at*, has led some scholars to interpret him as a man more interested in truth than tradition, and believe him to have been a true revolutionary in art as well as religion. Considering Akhenaten's supposed withdrawal from Egyptian political life and consequent neglect of the empire, and his distaste for war and military matters, it is not difficult to see how many years ago Egyptologists came up with an Akhenaten who was a monotheistic pacifist. These elements, combined with his preoccupation with religious poetry and theological concepts, helped to create the impression of a king who was more concerned with his solar god and his beautiful wife and family than with governing the empire and making war. Then, tragically, this "flower-child" king was pushed aside or murdered by jealous priests and generals who wanted to re-establish the old order.

With this summary of some of the traditional ideas about Akhenaten serving as an introduction to his life and times, let us examine the more recent discoveries concerning the Amarna period[21] and its central character.

New evidence and revised interpretations

Akhenaten was not supposed to be the pharaoh of the Two Lands. Instead, his older brother, Prince Thutmosis, was the heir apparent. Originally, Akhenaten had been kept in the background and was not shown with his father on any of his monuments as a child. Perhaps this was intentional because the young prince suffered from some kind of congenital disease that made him "hideous to behold".[22] But Thutmosis died, and Akhenaten ascended the throne of Egypt in about 1353 BC. As a child, Akhenaten was probably in poor health and could not partake in the more warlike activities such as hunting, archery, and chariotry that were traditionally engaged in by young Egyptian royalty. Some interpreters believe it is likely

that he preferred the arts such as painting, sculpture, and poetry. His chief sculptor, Bek, claimed that it was the young prince himself who taught him the art of statue making.

The word Aten, the name of Akhenaten's god, was an ancient word known already in the Old Kingdom, and simply meant "solar/sun disc". During the reign of Akhenaten's grandfather, Thutmosis IV, the sun disc was given credit for victory in battle and his royal palace was called the "Mansion of the Disc". During the reign of Akhenaten's father, Amenhotep III, the Aten sun disc acquired divine status and became a fully fledged god who was master over all the lands illuminated with its warm, life-giving rays. Akhenaten's father called himself the "dazzling sun-disc", and gave the Aten additional prestige when he attached the word "Aten" to his royal barge, his palace, and some of the members of the royal family. It is clear that the Aten was growing in popularity before the reign of Akhenaten. Thus it cannot be said that he alone was responsible for the Aten's rise to power. However, once Akhenaten was king he did forge ahead with reforms that for a short time made the Aten the most powerful deity in all Egypt. When Akhenaten came to the throne one of his first official acts was to build a temple to the Aten in the centre of the Karnak temple complex at Thebes, the city that was the principal home of the god Amun. Known as the "Mansion of the Aten", it was situated only a few hundred metres from the Amun temple. The priests of Amun must have been angered by this affront to their ancient god, whom they considered to be the most important in all Egypt. It was probably during the building of this temple that the young king realized that no matter how impressive he made his new temple to the Aten, Thebes was the home of Amun and had been for nearly a thousand years. Trying to outshine this mighty god in his own city was futile.

In the fifth year of his reign Akhenaten founded a new city 250 km north of Thebes in an area that had

not previously been inhabited. He named his new capital "Akhetaten", and a year later moved his family and court there. At the same time he changed his name from Amenhotep IV to Akhenaten and declared the god Amun a public enemy of all the people of Egypt. It was during this time that agents obliterated the name Amun wherever it appeared on the walls or columns of temples, palaces, or tombs. The element "Amun" was even eliminated from the name of Akhenaten's own father, who may have still been alive at the time. Other gods, some more ancient and venerable than Amun, suffered a similar fate, including Osiris, the popular god of the afterlife. After his sixth year in power the plural "gods" is never seen again during the reign of Akhenaten. From this time until his death the people of Egypt, at least officially, had no gods to worship except the Aten. The new solar monotheism was followed by the king, his court, and close followers, and there were, no doubt, a number of true believers who were sincere adepts of the religion of the Aten.

Outside the capital it is uncertain whether the new religion had many followers. Ordinary people who lived away from the centres of power seem to have clung to their old beliefs[23] and Akhenaten never made an effort to convert them to his teachings. Akhenaten changed a number of traditional funerary practices and eschatological beliefs that had been in use for centuries. The afterlife was no longer a pleasant place to spend eternity, and enjoy the cool breezes that blew along the Nile River while living amidst food and luxury. Instead, it was simply another vantage point from which the deceased could worship the blazing sun disc.

The suppression of Osiris,[24] the peoples' favourite god, compelled the priests of the new religion to retain many of the elements of the traditional funerary beliefs. Mummification, grave goods, anthropoid coffins, and Canopic Jars were all maintained. In Akhenaten's religion the deceased were dependent on the Aten, and not Osiris, to safeguard them in the afterlife.[25] Instead of going to the pleasant Fields of the Blessed, souls remained in their local neighbourhoods. In the morning, when the Aten rose, the dead came out of their tombs and partook of some kind of spiritual existence. They returned to their tombs in the evening at sunset. Both the living and the dead went to sleep at night, the living safe in the comfort and security of their homes, and the dead deep in the safety of their tombs cut into the cliffs of the limestone hills. Both the living and the dead accompanied Aten to his temple to share in the food offerings that were made there.

The key elements of Egyptian eschatological beliefs, which for centuries had played a major role in Egyptian religion and culture, were modified or greatly reduced. Akhenaten took the beautiful and colourful religion of the Two Lands that had been the spiritual lifeblood of the Egyptian people for centuries, and stripped it of much of its magic and beauty. In return, he left the people with little to believe in or to comfort them in their moments of religious need except a harsh, blazing sun disc. Akhenaten's new religion, "Atenism", was characterized by the god's remoteness. Traditional myths were pushed aside, and there was little to replace them. There were no myths or stories about the Aten and his life, and in place of the natural elements that the Egyptians had always recognized as divine, Akhenaten only honoured one force: the light of the sun. In addition, Atenism lacked essential elements like love and compassion, which would have made it more appealing to ordinary people, and although Aten was the creative force that brought all things to life, even foreigners and animals, the needs of the poor and downtrodden were never addressed.

Akhenaten and the military

The long-held notion that Akhenaten was anti-military and a pacifist is no longer tenable. In the art of the "beautiful child of the sun-disc", as Akhenaten called himself, scenes showing the army appear in many places. At no time in its history had the military ever been more evident in Egyptian art than during his reign.[26] The capital city, Akhetaten, was an armed camp and Akhenaten's state barge and temples show scenes of him in the traditional pose, slaughtering the enemies of Egypt. Enemy captives appear in heraldic motifs and in scenes of the king and queen appearing before their subjects. At important festivals, princes who were held as hostages of conquered foreign lands are shown presenting gifts and tribute to the king. Foreign rulers who had been subdued by previous Egyptian kings continued to send tribute to the king by land caravan and by boats from the distant lands of Kush, Syria-Palestine, and the far-off Aegean. Akhenaten, like his ancestors, continued sending settlers to Kush to colonize the land, and a temple to Aten was built at Kawa, 1000 km south of the capital in Upper Nubia. Akhenaten promoted his image as a war leader and even enjoyed some military success in Kush, although he did not actually accompany his army on its campaigns. Having been informed about certain rebellious tribes in the south, the king ordered one of his lieutenants to move against the region of Akita, where 361 cattle were captured and 145 Kushites were taken captive, some of whom were impaled on stakes. The effectiveness of these policies was reflected in a number of passages that declare that there were no rebels in the time of Akhenaten, or that the king's war cry was like a "flame of fire in pursuit of all foreign lands". Such statements do not reflect the character of a pacifist or "Christ-like" figure, as some traditionalists once maintained.

The political and military situation in Syria-Palestine was more complex than in Kush, and Akhenaten fared poorly as a result. It was unfortunate for him to have ruled at a time when the empire was facing many challenges and was beginning to unravel. Had he been a more skilful politician he might have been able to outmanoeuvre his adversaries and take advantage of the rapidly changing situation between the Hittites, the Mitanni, and the numerous small kingdoms situated between them and Egypt. Instead, he hesitated, misread the situation, and then blundered his way through a number of political crises that cost Egypt much of its power and prestige. Why Akhenaten did not act more effectively is difficult to understand, but his failure in the political arena was not due to his excess of mysticism, but to his lack of political skill and determination to win.[27]

Queen Nefertiti

Almost as famous, and at the same time mysterious, as Akhenaten was his wife, Nefertiti, whose name means "The beautiful one has come". A painted bust, recovered by German excavators in 1912, shows her to have been a woman of great beauty. In low-reliefs and paintings (Amarna art) she appears regularly with her husband, and in one important temple, "The Mansion of the *Benben* Stone", she was actually represented as often as Akhenaten and was even shown worshipping the Aten disc without the king.[28] The extent of her power is emphasized in one scene that shows the queen smashing the heads of her enemies with a club; in another, bound Asiatic and Kushite slaves are shown kneeling before her throne.[29] The head-smashing motif was usually reserved only for kings such as Narmer (see Ch. 10).

It appears that Nefertiti shared with her husband the love and devotion to the Aten, since she is shown with the king performing ritual and cultic duties in the presence of the sun disc.[30] Some popular novels based on her life tend to stress the apparent romantic love that existed between the royal husband and wife, and indeed it does seem that they had a special relationship that emphasized their family. The artistic record shows them mainly in official or religious scenes, but several reliefs show the royal couple

Akhenaten and Nefertiti offering to the Aten disc. To the left is one of their daughters. The rays of light emanating from the Aten disc end in hands extending ankh signs, the symbol of life, to the king and queen. Incised low-relief sculpture, height 1.05 m (Egyptian Museum, Cairo)

playing with their children. Once Nefertiti is seen sitting on her husband's lap and in another scene they are shown kissing on the lips.

Egyptologists are unclear about Nefertiti's fate later in the reign. Cyril Aldred maintains that in the 14th year of Akhenaten's reign Nefertiti disappeared from the court scene at Akhetaten, and probably died at that time.[31] Redford believes that Nefertiti was not dead, but was displaced by the royal couple's eldest daughter, Meritaten.[32] Accordingly, Akhenaten took Meritaten and elevated her to the position of "favourite" and "mistress"[33] of his house. At this point reliefs show the father with his daughter performing cultic acts in front of the sun god, and in a diplomatic letter from the king of Babylon, Burna-Buriash, she is mentioned as "the mistress of your house", a term that was used to refer to the woman who had the highest status in the kingdom.

As Nefertiti began to fade into the background, Meritaten was portrayed as larger than the other women of the court, and in some reliefs Meritaten's figure was actually incised over the figures of other royal women. It was during this time that Akhenaten chose one of his close male relatives, a boy about 14 years old, as his co-regent. This new "apprentice pharaoh" was named Smenkhkare, meaning "He whom the Spirit of Re has ennobled". He married his cousin, Meritaten, and the young rulers were supposed to be the heirs of Akhenaten and Nefertiti. It is not clear whether Smenkhkare and Meritaten ever reigned independently, but the young Smenkhkare died aged about 17 after he and Meritaten had one child, which died in infancy. After the death of Smenkhkare another of the king's nephews, or a son by one of Akhenaten's other wives[34] (he was probably not the son of Akhenaten and Nefertiti since they seem to have had only daughters), was chosen as Akhenaten's co-regent and married his next eldest daughter, Ankhesen-pa-aten.

Even though this second candidate for the throne of the Two Lands would die after having ruled for only ten years, he was destined (at least in the 20th century AD) to become one of Egypt's most famous kings. Although he was the legitimate king, Tutankhaten was too young to rule the country himself, and the real political and religious decisions were made by a group of adults who worked behind the scenes representing the old guard. Under the reign of Tutankhaten, the Amun-Re cult was reinstated to its former position of power, the capital was moved back to Thebes, and a great programme of temple restoration and reconstruction was begun. To symbolize a return to the normal state of affairs, the boy-king eliminated the element "Aten" from his name and replaced it with the traditional "Amun". Thus, when, his tomb was discovered by Howard Carter, in 1922 AD, the world came to know him by his traditional name: Tutankhamun.[35]

Although some interpretations of Akhenaten claim that later in his reign he was so unpopular with the priests and the army that he was murdered, there is in fact no evidence for this. It is most likely that he died peacefully in the 17th year of his reign, and was buried near his capital in a royal tomb with all the wealth and ceremony that was due to a great king. The fate of Akhenaten's wife, Nefertiti, still remains unclear. It is not known if she lived on after his death, or if she, too, died about the same time. For some time, it was believed that after his death the king's city of Akhetaten was sacked and destroyed and his tomb was violated. But it is now known that these activities took place much later, between 15 and 40 years after Akhenaten's death, mainly during the reign of the general-king Horemheb,[36] and that at the time of his death there was no great outcry of hatred and emotion against him or his reign.[37]

Akhenaten's physical appearance

Why did Akhenaten look so strange? In works of art Akhenaten was represented in such a bizarre fashion

that the 19th-century French scholar Eugène Lefébure speculated that Akhenaten was a woman like Hatshepsut, masquerading as a man on the throne of the Two Lands.[38] Auguste Mariette imagined that Akhenaten had been castrated by his enemies while on a military campaign. Mariette argued that castration would account for the king's effeminate features.[39] When looking at representations of Akhenaten as he appears in reliefs, paintings, and sculptures, we notice his long neck and face, and his effeminate waist, thighs, and breasts. Considering that he was supposed to be a fertility symbol for male Egyptians and that he was given the title "Strong bull, beloved of the Aten", alluding to the bull's reproductive powers, Akhenaten's physical characteristics do not seem to fit with the idealized god-king of the Two Lands.

To understand Akhenaten's portrayal in sculpture and painting it is important to remember that Egyptian art was not portrait art, and ancient artists did not attempt to produce photographic likenesses of their subjects.[40] In retrospect, early travellers and Egyptologists were naive for thinking him to be a woman, based on his physical traits. Some have even suggested that he was homosexual,[41] which supposedly explains his effeminate appearance and choice of clothing. However, the apparent portrayal of the king's imagined or real sexual preferences explains nothing about Akhenaten's possible physical abnormalities.

The medical hypothesis

To explain his appearance many Egyptologists and art historians generally rely on one of two hypotheses: a medical condition and artistic representation. The first of these is centred around a medical condition called Fröhlich's Syndrome,[42] which is a disorder of the endocrine system that results from the malfunctioning of the pituitary gland. Males who suffer from

this disorder often exhibit physical abnormalities similar to those that are shown in artistic representations of Akhenaten. In male patients with Fröhlich's Syndrome, the genitalia fail to develop at puberty. Fat distribution typical of young females occurs in young males, causing them to develop enlarged breasts, thighs, buttocks, and abdomens. In addition, fat deposits in the pubic area can in some cases engulf the penis and testicles, hiding them from view. Fröhlich's Syndrome may also cause the skull to swell, a condition called hydrocephalism, as well as excessive growth of the jaw, a shrill or high-pitched voice, and the absence of body hair. Given this description, Fröhlich's Syndrome seems to provide an explanation for Akhenaten's physical appearance.[43]

But there are a number of problems with this medical hypothesis. First, males who suffer from this condition are sterile, leaving no way to account for the king's children, including the six daughters he had with Nefertiti. Arguing that he was not their father is not very convincing because it does not take into account the scenes of intimacy that show the king playing with his daughters. If someone else fathered them we would expect the king to have less interest in them. Secondly, Egyptologists critical of this interpretation maintain that even though Akhenaten's representations may appear to show the symptoms of Fröhlich's Syndrome, a medical doctor cannot make a physical examination of a statue or painting, and unless the mummy of the king is found this explanation is questionable. Interestingly, a number of Egyptologists maintain that the king's mummy has been found in the Valley of the Kings.

Tomb KV 55

If King Tutankhamun's tomb is the most famous in the annals of Egyptology, then the tomb designated KV 55 (Kings' Valley 55) is surely the most controversial. Over the years a number of Egyptologists have maintained that it contained the mummified remains of Akhenaten. The tomb was excavated in 1907 by an amateur, Theodore Davis,[44] who was not a trained archaeologist and knew little about proper excavation procedures. Despite his lack of experience he was given a concession to excavate, somewhat unsuccessfully, the same piece of ground that a few years later would reveal the tomb of Tutankhamun. Edward Ayrton and Arthur Weigall, both professional archaeologists, accompanied Davis. Tomb KV 55 presented the excavators with some very challenging technical problems, and Davis and his team managed to produce one of the worst excavation reports on record, criticized repeatedly for being sloppy and unprofessional. The excavators thought the remains they had discovered were those of an older person. Davis was convinced that he had found the remains of Queen Tiye (and titled his official account of the excavation *The Tomb of Queen Tiyi*), but Weigall thought they must be those of Akhenaten. Since the two excavators could not agree on the identity of the tomb's occupant, they called on a professor of anatomy, Grafton Elliot Smith, to settle the question of whether the skeletal remains were those of a man or a woman. To everyone's surprise Smith identified the remains as those of a young man in his early twenties. He also concluded they were the remains of none other than Akhenaten.[45] This conclusion seemed impossible since the "heretic king" was supposed to have lived into his late 40s or early 50s. In 1931, Max Engelbach, who concluded that they belonged to Smenkhkare, husband of Akhenaten's oldest daughter, Meritaten, conducted a new study of the skeletal remains. Subsequent examinations by another anatomist, D. E. Derry, tended to support Engelbach's conclusions. The debate is still going on today, nearly a century after the discovery of Tomb 55, but the most widely held view is that the remains are those of Smenkhkare. In the near future scientists may be able to resolve the problem by using new DNA identification techniques. For the time being

the location of the mummy of Akhenaten is still unknown, and the question of whether he suffered from Fröhlich's Syndrome remains unanswered.

The artistic interpretation

Critics of the medical solution maintain that the bizarre and exaggerated artistic renderings of the king appeared early in his reign, and after a few years gave way to more conventional methods of representing the human form that were nearer to those traditionally used in Egyptian art.[46] Proponents of the artistic interpretation maintain that Akhenaten's strange appearance reflects the artistic style used by the sculptors and painters of the time, and was never meant to be interpreted as an anatomically correct rendering of the king's physical features.[47] If his appearance reflects an artistic style it would explain why members of his family and a number of his courtiers had strangely shaped bodies like the king, since it would be impossible to imagine that the entire royal family had Fröhlich's Syndrome. This so-called "expressionist style" used to represent the king was simply copied by everyone else who was close to the king at court. Throughout history there are instances of nobles and commoners who emulated the dress and hairstyles of their king in order to win favour with the royal house, or just to be in fashion. If the artistic interpretation is correct, then the problems some scholars have associated with Akhenaten's unconventional appearance seem much less problematic.

To perhaps better understand the impact artistic styles can have we need only to imagine archaeologists several millennia in the future discovering a number of paintings by one of the well-known modern artists such as Pablo Picasso. Anyone who is familiar with Picasso's work knows that the famous Spanish artist often did not draw or paint people as they actually appear in life. Various parts of the anatomy are stuck in the wrong places, heads are

misshapen, and eyes and noses appear where normally we would expect arms and legs. Think of the fantastic theories scholars of the future would invent if they tried to rely on these works of art as true representations of how 20th-century people actually appeared!

If the king looked odd then his strange appearance may have been an asset in his attempts at religious reform. Jean Yoyotte has argued that since Akhenaten was rendered "in the likeness of the Aten", by showing both male and female characteristics, he may have been representing himself as both the mother and father of creation.[48] In some instances ancient peoples believed that hermaphrodites (having both male and female sexual organs) were fertility symbols, and accorded them special status in society. It is possible that Akhenaten's physique was considered to be an indication of his unique religious character and actually worked in his favour towards promoting the religion of Atenism.

The legacy of Akhenaten

Ideas and opinions about the "heretic king" have changed substantially since evidence of his reign first came to light over a century ago. It is now known that Akhenaten was no more a pacifist than he was a eunuch. His supposed effort to unify his empire under a single solar deity is no longer taken seriously, and his political and social innovations have been denied. Despite this, he is recognized as the first, albeit short-lived, monotheist by many Egyptologists and historians of religion. It appears that Akhenaten was a patron of the arts, and perhaps he was a poet or skilled in painting or sculpture. In the realm of foreign affairs Akhenaten appears to have been a "bungler" whose failure to understand the complex political situation of his time was matched by his inability to act decisively. If his art is any indication of what he looked like and was the standard of excellence his courtiers tried to emulate, then the impression we are left with is that Akhenaten and his courtiers had abandoned the physically active life for one of sloth and inactivity. In painting after painting we see men and women with bloated bellies slouching on cushions and pillows looking like 18th Dynasty "couch potatoes".[49] In religion he was certainly an innovator and reformer. Yet, many of his ideas about monotheism and the uniqueness of his belief in a single deity died with him. As original as he was, he was unable (or unwilling) to establish a network of disciples who would carry on his teachings when he was gone. Religious teachers like Jesus and Buddha spent years walking the length and breadth of their respective lands, teaching and preaching their ideas and beliefs to their followers. But Akhenaten never engaged in such activities, and as a result never developed a popular following for his ideas. The concept of monotheism, so highly prized in the later religious traditions of the West, died with Akhenaten and had to be reinvented centuries later. Ultimately, his contribution to religion was only a brief momentary flash that was buried with him at his capital Akhetaten, "the horizon of the Aten".

THE RE-ESTABLISHMENT OF THE OLD ORDER

After the momentous reign of Akhenaten the land of Egypt was politically weaker, the empire was smaller, and the temples of many of Egypt's most powerful cults were abandoned and in shambles.[50] At Akhenaten's death Smenkhkare took the throne, but only for about two years.[51] With both Akhenaten and Smenkhkare dead, there was no adult male to assume the throne of the Two Lands. The heir to the throne, Tutankhaten, was only 10 years old at the time of his accession at Amarna but he was king in name only. It seems that he had no living relatives left; his mother Kiya, his stepmother, Nefertiti, and his elder

stepsisters were all deceased. The real power behind the throne was in the hands of older and more experienced members of the ruling elite, particularly a senior civil servant called Aya.[52] He was assisted by another highly placed official and family member, Horemheb, meaning "Horus is in jubilation", who was a skilled general and competent administrator. Horemheb was married to the sister of Nefertiti, Mutmodjmet,[53] and thus related to the royal family. His close ties with royalty allowed him to move with ease in the small circle of powerful people who ran the country. Aya, and later Horemheb, were practical rulers who put the country under the control of the army, reinstated power to the priests of Amun-Re, and took steps to return the country to its pre-Atenist power and stability.

At about the age of 9 Tutankhamun was married to a woman four or five years older than himself, named Ankhesen-pa-aten, who already had a child by her own father, Akhenaten. As soon as Tutankhamun was installed on the throne the royal house and all of Egypt changed back to the old religious traditions of the pre-Amarna period. At the same time Tutankhaten, meaning "living image of the Aten", dropped the theophore (divine element) "Aten" in his name and replaced it with the traditional Amun, becoming Tutankhamun, "living image of Amun", the name by which he is known to the modern world. His wife, no doubt like many other people at court, did the same and changed her name to Ankhesenamun.

Tutankhamun left the city of Akhetaten and moved the capital of Egypt back to Memphis. While the young king officially wore the crowns of Upper and Lower Egypt, Aya and the priests of Amun re-opened the temples and shrines of Amun-Re and the many other gods whose worship had been abolished during Akhenaten's 18-year reign. Under the influence of his older advisors, Tutankhamun issued decrees that restored the rights of the old ruling elite and the priests of numerous temples that

had stood unused for years. He also formally acknowledged the errors of his predecessor.[54] The restoration was recorded on several great stelae; they recount how the old religion once again became the official religion of the state and its people. Throughout his reign a number of building projects were undertaken to restore or rebuild the temples at Thebes, which had been neglected during the reign of Akhenaten. Towards the end of Akhenaten's reign senior members of his court had probably realized that things could not continue as they were, and had made plans for a return to more traditional ways of the past.

The discovery of Tutankhamun's tomb

The discovery of the tomb of Tutankhamun[55] is one of the greatest stories in archaeology. Not only did the tomb contain gleaming golden coffins and fabulous works of art of unsurpassed beauty, but behind the discovery lies one of the most fascinating, yet frustrating, stories in all of Egyptology. The discovery was so big, so spectacular, that it could not be separated from the political events that were unfolding in Egypt at the same time.

Since the completion of the Suez Canal in 1869, the British had a keen interest in Egypt, which served as a vital link to Britain's main colony, India, and other possessions in the Far East. In 1882 the British took military control of Egypt and the ancient Land of the Pharaohs became a British colony in all but name. By the beginning of the 20th century there was a growing nationalist movement among the Egyptians, who wanted to see an end to British dominance. In the late 19th and early 20th centuries, just about anyone with sufficient money and a few contacts inside the Service des Antiquités, the French-dominated antiquities department, could obtain the right to excavate in Egypt. One such person was George Herbert, the Fifth Earl of Carnarvon, a wealthy Englishman who grew up at Highclere, his family's beautiful estate in central England. The young Lord Carnarvon was apparently witty and charming, but had no real goals in life. He flunked out of various schools, including the prestigious Eton, and abandoned his studies at Trinity College, Cambridge after two years. His only interests were travel and sports. But after a serious automobile accident in which he suffered broken bones, burns, and a concussion, and which left him partially handicapped, his life changed; he wanted to accomplish something important in life. Following the advice of his doctor, he began to spend time in the dry climate of Egypt, and it was there that he developed an interest in Egyptology. Although he knew nothing about archaeology, in 1906 he obtained permission to excavate a site near the Valley of the Kings. By the end of his digging season he had come to the realization that he would need to employ an experienced archaeologist for the long term if he was going to accomplish anything worthwhile in his new-found career as a "digger". Carnarvon was a treasure hunter, uninterested in academic archaeology, and he had little patience with recording stratigraphy or pottery types.

Howard Carter was the complete opposite. Carter was a dour and temperamental man who made few friends during his life. His origins were humble. Like many people of the poorer classes in Victorian England, he had no formal education. His father was a draughtsman and portrait painter and taught his son his craft. In 1890, quite by chance, the well-known Egyptologist Percy Newberry was looking for an experienced draughtsman to copy some Egyptian objects housed in the British Museum. Carter got the job. After working for three months in the museum, Carter was promoted and became a junior member of the prestigious Egypt Exploration Fund,[56] the premier Egyptological research organization in Britain. That same year he accompanied the legendary Sir William Flinders Petrie to Egypt. From 1890 to 1898

Howard Carter worked with some of the most respected Egyptologists of his day, and received a solid grounding in Egyptology through his years of on-the-job training. In 1903 his services were terminated, and for the next four years Carter lived by selling his watercolours to tourists and conducting tours to the Valley of the Kings.

In 1906 he met and joined forces with Lord Carnarvon. For the next few years Carter and Carnarvon excavated a few sites on the west bank of the Nile River, as well as at Luxor and Karnak, but they found little of interest. They wanted to excavate in the Valley of the Kings, where Carter believed the tomb of Tutankhamun lay undisturbed, but the excavation concession for the Valley of the Kings belonged to Theodore Davis. Like many excavators and treasure seekers before him, Davis (see Ch. 14) was a dilettante who dreamed of finding an undisturbed tomb of a pharaoh. After years of work Davis had found the tombs of the pharaohs Thutmosis IV, Hatshepsut, and Horemheb, all of which had been robbed in ancient times and contained no treasure. Davis had also found some objects that he thought were of little importance, but which turned out to be remnants of the burial ceremony of Tutankhamun left in a pit not far from where his lost tomb would one day be rediscovered. Davis believed that the pit containing the burial goods was the tomb of Tutankhamun, while Carter reasoned that the real tomb entrance was near the tomb of a later pharaoh, Ramesses VI. In the end Carter would be proved right. Having searched the area for years, in 1914 Davis gave up his concession, convinced that there was nothing of value left to find there. At last, Carter and Carnarvon had permission to excavate in the Valley of the Kings, but before they could begin working World War I broke out.

During the war years Carter worked as an intelligence officer for the British and all excavation work was suspended for next three years. Carter and Carnarvon eventually started their first season of

excavation in 1917. They decided to dig everything to bedrock in a triangular area formed by the tombs of Ramesses II, Ramesses VI, and Merneptah. After five seasons of costly work they had still found nothing, and by 1921 Carnarvon wanted to end the project, but Carter convinced him to fund one more season. In their final attempt Carter decided to excavate the remains of some huts used by workers during the construction of the tomb of Ramesses VI, a pharaoh who ruled about two centuries after Tutankhamun. As it turned out, the workers' huts were built right on top of the entrance stairway to Tutankhamun's tomb.

Work progressed steadily and then, on 4 November 1922, Carter's workers discovered a step, the first of 16, that formed a stairway leading down into the earth. The stairway was about 6 m long and blocked by a door bearing mud plaster stamped with seals containing cartouches inscribed with "Nebkheperure", the throne name of Tutankhamun, one of several special names given to Egyptian kings. Evidence indicated that the tomb had been robbed in ancient times, and that the passageway had then been re-filled with rubble and resealed. Beyond was a passage another 10 m long by about 2 m wide. It was sealed at the far end by another mud-plaster wall. When the blockage was removed Carter and Carnarvon realized that they had discovered an intact tomb of the little-known pharaoh Tutankhamun. The tomb contained four chambers filled to the ceilings with precious objects of stunning beauty. There were four disassembled chariots, chests, beds, couches of ivory and ebony, chairs of bronze and gold, and a host of other belongings. The burial chamber contained a catafalque (a canopy used in funerary ceremonies) consisting of four gilded wooden shrines overlaid with gold enclosing a red quartzite sarcophagus. Inside the sarcophagus there were three coffins of diminishing sizes, one inside the other. The innermost coffin was made of solid gold, the outer two of gilded wood inlaid with semi-precious stones and coloured glass. Inside the smallest coffin was the king's poorly preserved mummy. To Carter and Carnarvon his state of preservation was of little importance. What mattered was the parade of new and beautiful objects that attracted dignitaries, tourists and curiosity seekers by the thousands to the Valley of the Kings. Newspapers around the world ran front-page stories nearly every day about each new find. "King Tut" was the biggest, most exciting media event since the end of the war.

But behind the scenes things were in turmoil right from the start. Egypt was changing; there was growing resentment against the British, who no longer had the power and prestige they once enjoyed. Foreign excavators had previously divided their finds with the Egyptian antiquities department. Only the contents of intact tombs had to stay in Egypt. Most other finds were divided evenly, with half going to the excavators and their private collections or sponsoring museums, and the other half going to the Egyptians. But to a growing number of Egyptians this was no longer acceptable; they wanted all objects to remain in Egypt. To make matters worse, Carnarvon had sold *The Times* newspaper in London exclusive rights to all news stories and photographs. The rest of the world's papers had no rights to enter the tomb, and had to purchase their stories from *The Times*. Egyptian newspapers were particularly angry because they had to buy stories and photographs about events in their own country from a British newspaper. They asked why foreigners should be allowed to mine Egypt's treasures and ran stories about secret plans to steal the king's mummy and take it to England. At one point riots broke out in Cairo, and the police and the army had to be called in to restore peace. Carter was stubborn and unsympathetic to Egyptian demands, and insisted on keeping things the way they had always been.

Halfway through the first season, Lord Carnarvon became ill from an infected mosquito bite and died in Cairo. This was a blow to Carter who was already having great difficulty dealing with the publicity and the hundreds of tourists who flocked to the site each week. Meanwhile, newspapers around the world were filled with stories of a "curse"; according to them the ghost of Tutankhamun had taken revenge on Carnarvon for violating his tomb. This false story was probably started by journalists who had been denied access to the tomb, and it mattered little to the newspapers that there were no inscribed curses to be found anywhere inside the tomb. For Carter, the real curse was all the attention he was receiving. If this was not enough, things were not going well between Carter and the antiquities authorities in Egypt. When they asked for a bigger role in the project, Carter refused to even discuss it. Bowing to popular pressure the Egyptian government insisted that all objects must remain in Egypt. Carter was furious and went on strike. He pulled his staff out of the tomb, locked the iron doors at the entrance, and refused to do any more work until the government backed down. Much to his surprise, the Egyptian government moved in with its own guards, changed the locks on the doors, and locked Carter out. In 1924 Carter went on a very successful lecture tour of the United States and Canada, where he thrilled his audiences with illustrated lectures of his discovery.

A year later Carter was finally allowed back in the tomb, but only after he agreed in writing to finish recording and removing the thousands of objects, and to give up all claims on them. It took Carter until 1932 to empty the tomb of its contents. He and his team spent nearly a decade clearing and cataloguing everything in the tomb. After excavating the tomb of Tutankhamun, Carter did not engage in further archaeological fieldwork. His time in the Valley of the Kings left him drained, and he returned to London where he lived out his final years as an art dealer. He died in 1939. The discovery of Tutankhamun's tomb changed how archaeological research was carried out in Egypt, and contributed to the formation of international laws that protected each nation's cultural heritage. Despite the wealth of objects discovered,

Carter never published a scientific study of the objects, and many of them remain unknown and unstudied to this day. But even after the discovery of rooms full of treasure, not much is really known about the young king. Scholars cannot reconstruct much of his story except that he was surrounded with beautiful things and died young. Forensic examination of his skeletal remains puts his age at death at about 17 or 18 years, meaning he probably died during the tenth year of his reign. There is no positive evidence from his mummy as to the cause of his death.

Many archaeologists believed that after Tutankhamun's tomb there was nothing more of great importance to be found in the Valley of the Kings, but in the 1990s American Egyptologist Kent Weeks[57] discovered a whole series of tombs belonging to the sons of Ramesses II, just across the road from the tomb of Tutankhamun. It seems there are still wonders to be found in the Valley of the Kings.

In search of a husband

Tutankhamun was married to one of Akhenaten's daughters, Ankhesenamun (formerly Ankhesen-paaten), at an early age and the young couple hoped they would have many healthy male heirs to continue their family line. The young king appeared to have a long life ahead of him, but as he reached the end of his teens he still had not produced a son to wear the red and white crowns of Upper and Lower Egypt. Then, at about age 20, Tutankhamun died and Ankhesenamun[58] was left alone to fend for herself. Ankhesenamun was a strong-willed woman[59] who wanted to continue ruling Egypt with a new husband. But since there were no more Egyptian men of royal blood left to marry, she faced the possibility of being deposed as queen. The fact that she was a daughter of the now-hated Akhenaten and a member of a royal family that had fallen into disrepute, did not help her as she searched for a solution to her problem. To avoid losing the throne, Ankhesenamun[60] resorted to a clever but dangerous strategy: she sent messengers with a letter to the Hittite king, Suppiluliuma, asking to marry one of his sons.[61] By marrying a Hittite prince, Ankhesenamun could bring new, albeit foreign, royal blood to the throne of Egypt while solidifying her own position as queen. Such a marriage would assure that she and her children continued to rule Egypt, while strengthening relations between the two countries. An Egyptian–Hittite marriage would have created the most powerful military and political alliance in the Near East, and would have helped Egypt to maintain its conquered territories in southern Syria and Palestine.

In her letter, Ankhesenamun explained that her husband was dead, she had no sons, and did not want to marry a commoner. She also mentioned that she was afraid, no doubt indicating that her situation was precarious, and her life may have even been in danger. When the king of the Hittites received the queen's letter he was sceptical about the sincerity of the request.[62] Before sending one of his sons, the king sent ambassadors to verify the story. When the offer proved to be genuine, the king agreed to send one of his sons to Egypt to marry the royal widow. While Ankhesenamun waited for the Hittite king to make up his mind, events were unfolding quickly in the Two Lands. Aya, by now a man advanced in years, took the throne for himself, and, according to Egyptian religious custom, buried Tutankhamun in a hastily completed tomb in the Valley of the Kings. After a long and successful political career, Aya had no intention of giving up the throne to a foreigner. When he

Gold death mask of Tutankhamun. Gold and inlaid blue glass. On the forehead are perched the vulture Nekbet and cobra Wadjit, fashioned of gold and inlaid with blue faience, glass, carnelian, and lapis lazuli. (Egyptian Museum, Cairo.)

Painting on limestone from a tomb in western Thebes showing a group of female musicians, 18th Dynasty.

found out that a Hittite prince was on his way to Egypt to marry Ankhesenamun, he had the young man, named Zannanza, executed.[63] Ankhesenamun's actions were no doubt considered treasonous[64] by the Egyptian ruling elite. After her failed attempt to find a new king she either disappeared or, as some scholars have suggested, was forced by Aya to marry him, possibly against her wishes since he was her grandfather. If this marriage ever took place, it would have increased Aya's power and status within the royal family, and Ankhesenamun would have stayed on as queen. It is unclear why Aya murdered the Hittite prince; he could have simply sent the young man back home instead of killing him, and avoided incurring the anger of the Hittite nation. Instead, the Hittite king was outraged by the murder of his son, and in revenge immediately attacked Egypt's remaining possessions in Syria. In the battles that followed he caused much damage and took many Egyptian prisoners back to his capital city. A short time later, old Aya died after ruling Egypt for only four years. Because of his involvement in the murder of the Hittite prince, it would be 75 years before stable relations would be established between the Hittites and the Egyptians.

The end of the 18th Dynasty

Horemheb was a commoner who was a talented career officer in the Egyptian army, and served with distinction for many years. During the rule of Tutankhamun he was appointed King's Deputy, making him the second most powerful man in the kingdom. Horemheb was probably in his mid-40s when Aya died. After Horemheb buried Aya in the Valley of the Kings, he declared himself king of Egypt and once again the Two Lands had a strong military man to run the country. His marriage to Nefertiti's sister provided him with the necessary link to the royal family, and he faced no opposition when the crowns of Upper and Lower Egypt were placed on his head. Horemheb ruled for the next 27 years (1319–1292 BC) and managed to continue the restoration of the land. Even though Akhenaten was dead and his religion in decline, a number of his temples remained open to a diminishing number of worshippers. It was Horemheb who finally shut them down and put an end once and for all to the cult of the Aten. A few years into his reign Horemheb undertook a number of major building projects, including the enlargement and embellishment of the great Temple of Amun at Karnak. He was also responsible for the destruction of the hated temple of the Aten, located close by. Horemheb dismantled the temple, built during the early years of the reign of Akhenaten, and used the stones as building material for his own construction projects. Part of Akhenaten's principal temple at Akhetaten ended up forming the foundation layer for one of Ramesses II's temples 27 years later. It was also at that time that the systematic destruction of Akhenaten's old capital, Akhetaten, was undertaken, along with the progressive erasure, especially under Seti I, of his name from all monuments and inscriptions. The destruction at Akhenaten's city was so complete that all monuments and shrines were levelled, and not a single stone wall was left standing. To ensure that the "heretic" king's reign would be forgotten, Horemheb dated all of his own monuments from the death of Amenhotep III, Akhenaten's father. By skipping the reigns of Akhenaten, Smenkhkare, Tutankhamun, and even Aya, Horemheb eliminated more than 30 years of Egyptian history, and ensured that the memory of those kings who had been touched by Atenism would be forgotten. Through his rewriting of the history of this period, later generations would know nothing about the religion of the Aten disc, and the effects it had on the Two Lands. Horemheb's revision, along with those of Seti I and Ramesses II, who were also involved in revising the events of the Amarna period, proved effective since the kings of the Amarna period remained unknown for over 3000 years, until they were rediscovered in the 19th century AD. Even though Horemheb ruled Egypt with a steady hand and practical policies for nearly three decades, like many Egyptian kings before him he failed to leave an heir to the throne. Since he had no sons, during his years as pharaoh Horemheb nurtured and trained one of his aides, a man named Pramesse, to take the throne when he died. Horemheb chose Pramesse (later his name was altered to Ramesses) because he was a trusted leader, and because he had a strong, healthy son who was a commander in the chariot corps. In this man, the ageing Horemheb saw not only a competent potential leader, but also a family and the beginnings of a dynasty.

Horemheb was the last king of Egypt's most successful, and certainly most interesting dynasty. Spanning 250 years, from the wars against the Hyksos to the empire of Thutmosis III, from Hatshepsut to the religious upheaval of Akhenaten, the 18th Dynasty produced some of Egypt's greatest achievements in art, architecture, and politics, and it undoubtedly produced its most stimulating and controversial characters.

15 The 19th Dynasty and the Ramesside kings

During his reign Horemheb, the last king of the 18th Dynasty (see Ch. 14), prepared for himself a large and sumptuous tomb in the Valley of the Kings. The man who oversaw these preparations and served as the chief official at this burial was Pramesse, the king's faithful deputy. When Pramesse took the throne, he changed his name to Ramesses I, meaning "Re has fashioned him", a name that would be used by a total of 11 kings during the 19th and 20th Dynasties, which spanned nearly two centuries.[1] Although Ramesses I founded a new dynasty, he ruled for only about 18 months before he died. He was succeeded by his son Seti I, meaning "Man of Seth", who, like his father, had served in the military and was determined to regain Egypt's lost possessions in Syria and Palestine. His achievements included building one of the most beautiful temples in all of ancient Egypt, dedicated to the god Osiris and all the principal gods of Egypt. Built at the town of Abydos,[2] this unique structure had seven chapels dedicated to the major Egyptian gods: Osiris, Isis, Horus, Amun, Ptah, Re-Harakhty, and the deified king himself. In his military campaigns, Seti I managed to move across what is now Lebanon and retake Damascus. Eventually, he managed to take much of the coast of Syria-Palestine, including the rich coastal cities of Tyre, Sidon, and Byblos, all previously Egyptian colonies or vassals. Such activities brought Seti I into conflict with Egypt's old adversaries, the Hittites. During his reign Seti I even managed to retake the city of Qadesh, which had traditionally been Egyptian, but had been lost during the reign of Akhenaten.[3] To commemorate his victory, the Egyptian king erected a stele proclaiming his victory inside the city. However, the victory was short-lived and the Hittites soon drove the Egyptians out of the area under their own vigorous and talented king, Muwattallis, who was not willing to see further Egyptian incursions into his territories.

Ramesses II

During his reign, Seti I formally proclaimed his son, the younger Ramesses, crown prince and future heir to the throne. A few years later, the second Egyptian king to bear the name of Ramesses[4] became co-regent with his father, and under his guidance learned the arts of warfare and statesmanship.[5] After 11 years of rule, Seti I died and his son, by now a seasoned and experienced ruler, became the sole occupant of the throne of Egypt. Ramesses II ruled for a total of 67 years (1279–1213 BC),[6] and left a legacy of military conquest and great building projects.

Chronology of the 19th Dynasty (1292–1186 BC) (all dates BC)

Ramesses I	1292–1290	
Seti I	1290–1279	
Ramesses II	1279–1213	
Merneptah	1213–1204	
Seti II	1204–1194	
Amenmesse	1194–1194	(less than one year)
Siptah	1194–1188	
Twosret	1188–1186	

The Egyptian army

By the 19th Dynasty, the Egyptian army was a highly organized and well-trained fighting force.[7] Previously, the army had been made up mostly of native Egyptians. But with the capture of many prisoners of war taken in Egypt's frequent campaigns beyond its own borders, an increasing number of foreigners were forced to fight for the pharaoh and the Two Lands. Some of the contingents in the army were hired soldiers, or mercenaries, who would fight for whichever army would pay them the most. These new elements increased the ranks of the pharaoh's troops, but their loyalty to Egypt was sometimes doubtful. Egyptian fighting forces were made up mostly of infantrymen: foot soldiers who were armed with swords, spears, shields, and bows and arrows. Spears were not thrown but were used as handheld thrusting weapons. Swords were used for cutting and thrusting, along with battle-axes for close hand-to-hand combat, which occurred when two armies crashed together on the battlefield. Archers used both the simple bow and the compound bow, and their airborne missiles could rain down a hail of death on their enemies at distances of 160–175 m.[8] Foot soldiers carried the brunt of attack responsibility and were supported by a highly trained and skilful

Ramesses II seated on his throne. Black granite. (Turin Museum.)

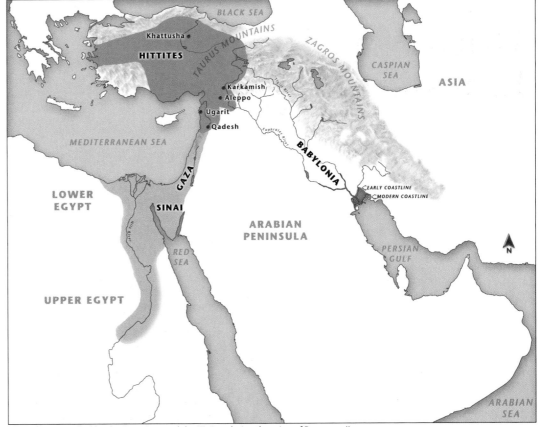

Territories controlled by the Egyptians and the Hittites during the reign of Ramesses II.

chariotry.[9] It is difficult to say how many chariots the Egyptians actually possessed, but they probably had no more than 500–1000 chariots at their disposal during the reign of Ramesses II.[10]

Ramesses II and the Hittite wars

Early in his reign one of Ramesses' priorities was the reconquest of Syria-Palestine. His first attempt in the fourth year of his reign had ended in failure, with the Egyptian forces being driven out. A year later Ramesses II was ready to undertake a second major campaign for the reconquest of Egypt's lost possessions in Syria.[11] To accomplish this he would have to reconquer the important city of Qadesh.[12] In the spring of 1274 BC, the Egyptian army, composed of Egyptian and foreign contingents, left from the northern capital of Pi-Ramesses in the eastern Nile Delta. With the king riding at the head of his army in his chariot, the army moved quickly through Gaza and Palestine and on towards the Bekah Valley region, known as Amurru, and the targeted city of Qadesh. The battle of Qadesh is one of the most famous military clashes in Near Eastern history. It is special because the whole battle was recorded in great detail, in lengthy literary and visual compositions, which are sometimes exaggerated, on the walls of the Temple of Amun-Re at Karnak and the Ramesseum, Ramesses II's own cultic temple on the west bank of

The colossal statue of Ramesses II as "Re of the Rulers", from the first court of the temple at Luxor.

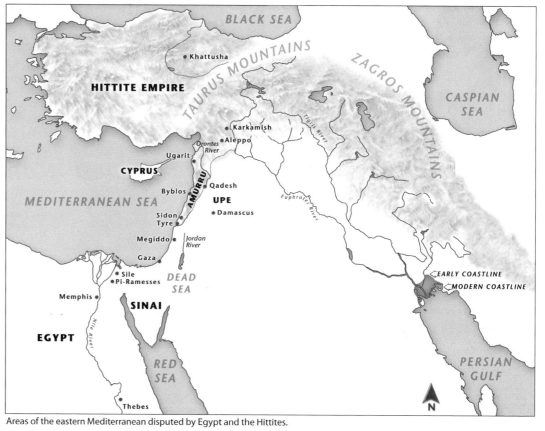

Areas of the eastern Mediterranean disputed by Egypt and the Hittites.

the Nile River in western Thebes. Events are presented as a great Egyptian victory, when in fact the Egyptians suffered heavy losses and, as soon as the Egyptian forces left the region, the area once again returned to Hittite control. Despite Egyptian claims of victory, the battle of Qadesh left the Hittites in control of the region around Damascus, which had formerly been the border between the two powers.[13]

The pharaoh's army was divided into four divisions, each one named after an important Egyptian god, and in total perhaps numbered 15 000–20 000 foot soldiers. The king led the Amun division, accompanied by his own personal bodyguard, and a number of members of the royal family. The Amun division was followed by the Re, Ptah, and Seth divisions, which were several hours' march behind. As Ramesses II proceeded into the Bekah Valley another Egyptian army, the Ne'arin, marched up the coast of Palestine about 30–40 km away, covering the main army's left flank. As the main army passed through the Labwi forest, a few hours' march south of Qadesh, two wandering herdsmen were captured by Egyptian scouts. The two men claimed to be deserters from the Hittite army who wanted to fight on the side of the Egyptians.

They were brought to Ramesses II for questioning and revealed that Muwattallis, the Hittite king, and his army were nowhere near Qadesh. Muwattallis, they explained, was afraid to fight the mighty Egyptians and had taken his army 200 km north to Aleppo. Ramesses II was overjoyed by the flattering news that Muwattallis was afraid to do battle with him, and it appeared that victory was easily within his reach. Believing that the gods were on his side, he hurried ahead of the main force of his army. With only his household guard and immediate staff, Ramesses II crossed the Orontes (Arantu) River and set up camp about 3 km from the towering walls of the great city of Qadesh. Once the camp was set up and preparations were underway for what Ramesses II and his general staff thought would be an easy victory, another pair of Hittite spies, who by stealth had infiltrated the Egyptian ranks, were captured. After being beaten, they confessed that they were indeed spies for the Hittite king, who they explained was not at Aleppo, but only across the Orontes River just outside Qadesh where he had hidden his vast armies in a nearby forest. The news of Muwattallis's whereabouts was a shock to Ramesses II. How naive he had been. He admonished his intelligence agents for their sloppy work and prepared to make the best of what appeared at the time to be a precarious situation.

Ramesses II immediately sprang into action. It was imperative that he contact the rest of his army, so he sent scouts to inform the Ptah division, which was just coming out of the Labwi forest, of his situation. Then he arranged for the royal family to be hastily ushered out of camp and away from immediate danger. These measures were barely completed when rows and rows of Hittite chariots charged across the river and smashed through the right flank of the Re division, which was hurrying to reach the king. The charge took the foot soldiers by surprise and they were cut to pieces as their ranks broke up

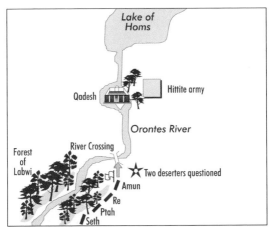

Ramesses II leads the Amun division of his army followed by the Re, Ptah, and Seth divisions.

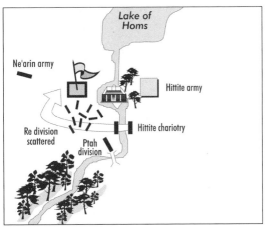

The Re division is scattered by Hittite chariot forces.

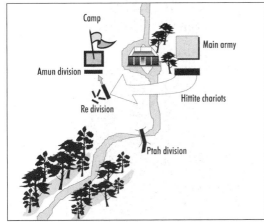

Hittite chariots sweep towards the camp of Ramesses II. He rallies the Amun division and counterattacks. The Re division is scattered, but attempts to regroup.

and were chased by Hittite chariot forces. As the Re division caught up with the Amun division protecting Ramesses II, many soldiers panicked and scattered in all directions. Very quickly it appeared that all was lost for Ramesses II and the armies of the Two Lands.

The year before, Ramesses II had managed a few easy victories in the west and had become overconfident. His naive acceptance of the Hittite agents had clouded his thinking and caused him to act foolishly. As things collapsed around him and his soldiers were driven from the battlefield in disarray, Ramesses II made a quick and fervent prayer to the most powerful god in all Egypt, Amun, asking for help in his hour of need. According to his version of events, Ramesses II seized his weapons, summoned his chariot driver, organized a few of his panic-stricken troops, and began a counterattack. The inscriptions that record the battle claim that everyone, except the king, panicked and tried to flee the oncoming Hittite forces. But showing greater strength and

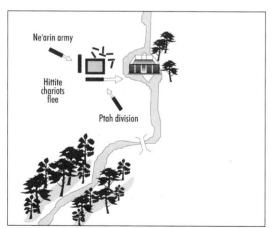

The Ne'arin army arrives at the scene of the battle. The Hittites are caught between the Ptah division and the Ne'arin army and are forced to flee.

courage than all the others, Ramesses II jumped into his chariot and set about pouncing on the Hittite troops like a falcon, slaying them in great numbers. In a few minutes, so Ramesses II's version of the story tells us, the young pharaoh had single-handedly turned the tide of the battle and his revived armies went on to defeat the Hittites and deal them a crushing blow.

Ramesses's furious counterattacks and charges momentarily slowed down and confused the attacking Hittite troops and probably saved the day by giving the Egyptians a few precious moments to regroup. It was then that the great god Amun seemed to answer the king's prayer, because suddenly the Ne'arin, the troops covering Ramesses's western flank, appeared on the scene and rushed directly into the thick of the battle. Now, the Hittites were caught between Ramesses's charges from the east and the Ne'arin forces from the west. Within minutes, the tide of the battle turned. Ramesses II now had enough time to rally his troops in greater numbers, picking up stragglers who had earlier fled the field of battle. With fresh reinforcements Egyptian troops attacked and threatened to surround the Hittite chariotry. The Hittites wisely withdrew in order to regroup for a second attack, but Ramesses's infantrymen forced the charioteers back across the battlefield and right into the Orontes River.

One can only imagine the Hittite king, Muwattallis, as he gazed out in dismay at the battle, which had gone so well for him in the beginning. Muwattallis had been preparing his forces for months, and had put together an army of perhaps 35 000 foot soldiers and hundreds of chariots capable of striking a crippling blow to the young and inexperienced Ramesses II, thus ridding the land once and for all of Egyptian invaders.[14] Because of his superior planning and strategy, Muwattallis deserved to win. He had thought of everything, from the spies he had planted to mislead Ramesses II to the careful concealment of his forces behind the city. Then, suddenly, the tide of

the battle turned against him; his troops were abandoning their weapons and chariots, and swimming for their lives in the middle of the Orontes River.

At the end of this first engagement the Egyptians held the field and the Hittites were forced to retreat back to Qadesh. What had started as an Egyptian rout had been turned to their advantage. As both armies took time to regroup and gather their dead and wounded, more of the scattered troops of the Amun and Re divisions, chased from the field during the initial attack, began to drift back into camp. Ramesses II admonished those who had deserted under fire as weak-willed and cowardly. In recounting the difficult moments of the battle, Ramesses II thanked no one except his shield-bearer, Menna, and the pair of horses who pulled his chariot in and out of the bloody foray while he single-handedly destroyed his adversaries. Ramesses II went so far as to mention their names, Victory-in-Thebes and Mutis-content, and said that in the most desperate moments of the battle it was only his horses who chose not to abandon him. To show his appreciation, he declared that from then on he would personally feed the two beasts every day. Both sides suffered heavy losses during the battle. The Hittite chariot corps was beaten and they lost a number of important leaders and allies. Muwattallis lost two of his brothers, two of his shield-bearers, his secretary, four leading charioteers, and six generals in the fight.[15] The Egyptians had two badly mauled infantry divisions, the Re and the Amun and, although the rest of the army was intact, the number of dead and wounded must have been very high.

The next morning the armies fought again, but neither had the strength to subdue the other. Wisely, the Hittite king sought to end the dispute the same way he had done with Ramesses's father 15 years earlier. He proposed a truce in which each side would accept a territorial status quo that would leave Amurru and Qadesh under Hittite control, and allow the Egyptians to keep their possessions in the south.

The generals and high-ranking officers in the Egyptian army urged the young king to accept the Hittite offer. It is clear that they wanted to sign the treaty and return home without incurring any additional losses. But Ramesses II refused to sign. He still dreamed of coming back some day, taking Qadesh and the land of Amurru, and putting them under Egyptian control. No sooner had Ramesses II left Amurru and returned home to the Nile Delta, than Muwattallis marched his armies south and took a large portion of Egypt's possessions in Syria, including the city of Damascus and the prosperous province of Upe. The older and more experienced Muwattallis decided to make the young, headstrong Ramesses II pay for his refusal to sign a peace treaty that would have benefited both powers. From inscriptions Ramesses II had cut into the walls and pylons of a number of his temples, it appears that the Egyptians fought the Hittites to a draw at Qadesh. However, Hittite sources, which are probably more reliable, paint a different picture of the outcome of the battle. From their perspective, the Hittites viewed themselves as the winners at Qadesh since they managed to maintain control of the city, and conquer additional Egyptian territories.[16] With nothing but casualties to show for his efforts, Ramesses II had no choice but to gather up his wounded, and return to the Two Lands. After the battle of Qadesh it was clear that the Egyptians had lost the first round of the Hittite wars, but Ramesses II would be back.

Ramesses II returns

As he promised, four years later, in the summer months of the ninth year of his reign, Ramesses II was indeed back in Syria, taking a number of cities along the coast. His victories, however, were only temporary for no sooner had Ramesses II left his conquered areas than the Hittites moved in again and put their own supporters back in power. In the

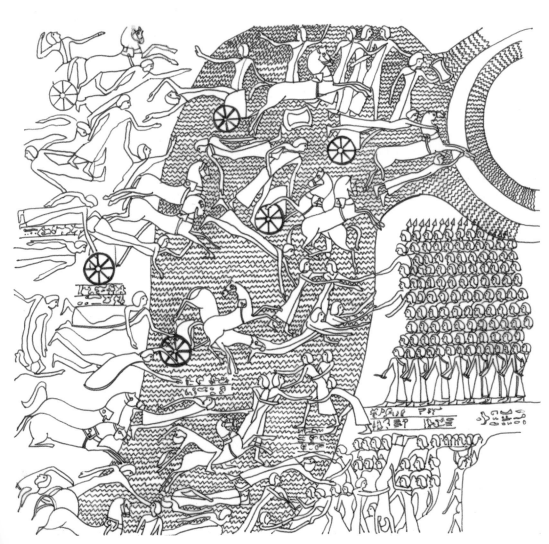

Hittite soldiers swimming the Orontes River, fleeing from the counterattack by Egyptian forces.

Egyptian attack on the fortified city of Dapur in Syria-Palestine. Hittite forces are shown in confusion as Egyptian soldiers scale ladders and take the helpless city.

following year he returned to set up a stele near the Nahr el-Kalb (the Dog River), claiming dominion over all the surrounding territories. But his claim was hollow and once again, after Egyptian forces had left the conquered areas, the Hittites re-established control of the region. Finally, after coming to the realization that he could not hold the northern part of Syria, the pharaoh stopped campaigning beyond the old boundaries, the same ones that Muwattallis had proposed to Ramesses II after the battle of Qadesh. From the 11th to the 17th years of his reign, no more wars were waged in Syria, no more stelae were set up with grandiose claims of sovereignty over territories that could not be held, and for eight years there was relative peace in the land of Amurru.

Troubles in Khatti

At the beginning of the reign of Ramesses II, the Hittites were probably the most powerful nation in the Near East. But within a few years their power began to decline rapidly.[17] Among their problems was one that was all too familiar to the Egyptians: no clearly established heir to the throne. Although Muwattallis had ruled for 24 years with great vigour from about 1306 BC to 1282 BC, his only son was by a secondary wife who was not of royal blood. Muwattallis's brother, Khattushili, finally gained the upper hand in the situation after he staged a palace coup and took control of the country. But the uncertainty of succession weakened the kingdom while two pretenders to the throne, Khattushili III, and Urhi-Teshub, the nephew of Muwattallis, who took the throne name Murshili III, fought with each other for the right to rule.[18]

After Khattushili III finally won the struggle and had consolidated his power, he made an offer of peace to Egypt that would protect his country's southern flank and free much-needed soldiers and resources to hold off other enemies in the region.

Thus, in the 21st year of the reign of Ramesses II, Hittite emissaries arrived at the northern capital, Pi-Ramesses, with a peace treaty engraved in cuneiform script on a glittering silver tablet. Even though the original treaty has long since disappeared, copies of the document written on clay tablets have survived. The treaty was also incised on the great stone pylons at the temple of Amun in Karnak, so historians have versions of the treaty from each of the participating

Osiride statues with folded hands holding staff and whip, from the 19th Dynasty funerary temple of Ramesses II, western Thebes.

Fallen colossal head of Ramesses II lying in the courtyard of his mortuary temple, western Thebes. Granite.

Mortuary temple of Ramesses II seen from the west, western Thebes.

The Hall of Pillars in the mortuary temple of Ramesses II.

East pylons of the funerary temple of Ramesses II, the Ramesseum.

countries to study and compare.[19] In the Egyptian version, Ramesses II referred to Khattushili III as his "brother", and each ruler vowed never to trespass on the territory of the other. They also agreed to a mutual defence pact, which stipulated that if a third power were to attack either Egypt or the Hittites, each would go to the other's aid. In addition, each nation pledged to safeguard and respect the royal succession of the other. With the signing of the treaty, Ramesses II gave up any hope of ever retaking Amurru and Qadesh and becoming a great conqueror like his distant predecessor, Thutmosis III of the 18th Dynasty. With the signing of the treaty an era of stability settled over much of Near East and led

to a peaceful renaissance, which lasted until about 1200 BC.

If the Egyptian king could not conquer others, he at least had the chance to build great monuments to honour himself and his gods. The Egyptian–Hittite treaty was a success, and a few years later Khattushili III offered his eldest daughter in marriage to the middle-aged Ramesses II. Thus, in the 34th year of the reign of Ramesses II, the Hittite king sent his daughter and her entourage, with many splendid gifts that included gold and silver, spans of horses, slaves, cattle, and other splendid gifts to seal the marriage. Nefertari, queen of Egypt and chief royal wife of Ramesses II, even wrote to and received letters

from the chief wife of the Hittite king, Pudukhepa, in an attempt to build a closer relationship. The era of good relations between the Hittites and Egypt continued until the end of the 67-year reign of Ramesses II. The Egyptian–Hittite treaty freed Ramesses II from military concerns and allowed him to undertake some of the most extensive building programmes in Egyptian history. Ramesses II built, or enlarged, the great temples at Karnak, Abydos, the Valley of the Kings, and far to the south in Kush at Abu Simbel. If Ramesses II could not fight his way to fame and immortality, then he would build his way into the memory of future generations.

In Egyptian history Ramesses II was a giant. He dominated the 13th century BC, and his reign was more stable than most and lasted longer than that of any of his contemporaries. During his long reign the leadership of the country was not called into question once, while during the same period the Hittites and other nations suffered through leadership changes every few years that sometimes led to civil wars or palace revolts. The reign of Ramesses II also coincided with a period of timely floods and abundant harvests, which made for a stable and prosperous economy. These factors made Egypt a happy and stable land during much of the 13th century BC. Ramesses II, often called "Ramesses the Great", certainly deserves the title. He came to power perhaps around age 25 and ruled for 67 years, making him close to 92 years old when he died. Few Egyptian kings built as many great monuments, obelisks, or statues as he did, and no one sired as many children. When the old king died he was mourned by the citizens of the Two Lands, and laid to rest in a lavish tomb in the Valley of the Kings.

16 Egypt in the late second and first millenniums BC

The Kushites, Libyans, and Assyrians

Even though the first thousand years of ancient Egyptian history were free of any major foreign invasions, about halfway through its 3000-year history Egypt's geographical boundaries could no longer keep foreign invaders out of the Nile river valley. Beginning with the Hyksos in the 18th century BC, and then the Libyans and the so-called Sea Peoples a few centuries later, Egypt was repeatedly subjected to periods of foreign immigration and invasion.[1] This tendency continued during the first millennium BC, when the Kushites temporarily gained control of the Two Lands, followed shortly thereafter by two Assyrian invasions in the seventh century BC. Whatever security natural boundaries may have given the Nile river valley earlier in its history was now gone,[2] and by the first millennium BC, Egypt was subjected to unprecedented foreign domination and exploitation.

For several centuries during the period of the New Kingdom (1550–1069 BC), economic and military equilibrium had been maintained by the Egyptians and the Hittites over much of the ancient Near East and eastern Mediterranean. From the 15th to the 13th centuries a long period of relative stability and prosperity had endured in the region. This period came to an end with the collapse of the Hittite Empire (Khatti), about 1200 BC. Although Egypt and the Hittites fought the occasional war, as we saw in Chapter 15, neither was able to completely domi-nate the other.[3] To promote their own well-being they maintained order by controlling bandits on land and pirates at sea, keeping trade routes safe and prof-itable, and making sure that smaller powers did not destabilize things. The balance created by the two great powers was always fragile and at times uncer-tain, but it worked well for more than two centuries. However, with the loss of the Hittites, Egypt alone was incapable of controlling the situation, and the political stability and profitable trading networks

Chronology of the later 19th Dynasty and the 20th Dynasty; the end of the New Kingdom (all dates BC)[4]

19th Dynasty	1292–1186	
Merneptah	1213–1204	(Libyans and Sea Peoples)
Seti II	1204–1194	
Amenmesse	1204–	
Siptah	1194–1188	
Twosret	1188–1186	
20th Dynasty	**1186–1069**	
Sethnakhte	1186–1184	
Ramesses III	1184–1153	(Libyans and Sea Peoples)
Ramesses IV	1153–1147	
Ramesses V	1147–1143	
Ramesses VI	1143–1136	
Ramesses VII	1136–1129	
Ramesses VIII	1129–1126	
Ramesses IX	1126–1108	
Ramesses X	1108–1099	
Ramesses XI	1099–1069	
Third Intermediate period	**1069–712**	

disappeared.[5] For a long period after the collapse of the Hittites, Egypt had to abandon its dreams of an empire, and was forced to go on the defensive.

The Libyans

During the New Kingdom there was increased contact between the Egyptians and the Libyans, a people who came from an area along the Mediterranean coast up to 1200 km west of the Nile River. The dominant tribes in this area were the Libu, hence Libyans,[6] and the Mashwash. Evidence suggests that the Mashwash were coastal dwellers and the Libu were pastoralists who lived in the hinterland. Both tribes were separated from the Nile river valley by a vast expanse of sparsely populated desert. There are no specific references to conflict between Libyans and Egyptians in the 18th Dynasty, but contact between the two groups did intensify during that time. References to Libyans in the 19th and 20th Dynasties are more frequent. Both pharaohs Seti I and Ramesses II fought with the Libyans, and in addition, Ramesses II built a string of forts and storage areas from the western Nile Delta along the Mediterranean coast to help defend against Libyan encroachment.[7] Some of the Libyans were pastoralists since the Egyptians indicate that they captured large numbers of cattle, sheep, and goats that belonged to the Libu and Mashwash peoples; others lived in towns and villages. They were not poor people since some of them possessed gold, silver and bronze, as well as swords and chariots.[8] These kinds of goods indicate a level of material culture above that of a strictly pastoral society. By the 19th Dynasty the Libu and Mashwash had settled along the western border of the Nile river valley, and they used this area as a base for extensive raiding activities against other parts of Egypt. During the time of Merneptah (19th Dynasty)[9] and Ramesses III (20th Dynasty)[10] the Libu and Mashwash spread into the Nile Delta and threatened the important city of Bubastis. About 1210 BC, the Egyptian king, Merneptah, fought off a substantial Libyan invasion whose forces were dominated by the Libu tribe. Merneptah was warned that the Libyans were moving along the coast and were approaching the western regions of the Delta.[11] The Libu were accompanied by their allies, the Sherden, Teresh, and Sheklesh.[12] For six hours the two armies fought each other near the town of Buto in the northwest Delta. As was the usual practice, the Egyptians concealed their own losses, but it is clear that the battle turned into a rout and the invaders were driven from Egyptian soil. Merneptah boasts that he killed 9300 Libu and their allies. But even though Merneptah had dealt the Libyans a crushing blow, this single defeat was not the end of the Libyan menace. Several decades later the Libyans were back with more allies and a great invasion fleet of ships.

Egypt and the Near East at the beginning of the first millennium BC.

The Libu and Mashwash and their geographical location in relation to Lower Egypt.

disciplined army.[14] Artistic representations from Ramesses III's temple at Medinet Habu show substantial numbers of women and children on foot and in ox-drawn carts, and large numbers of farm animals, accompanying formations of attacking soldiers.[15] In some scenes the soldiers, their families, and their farm animals are shown jumbled together in apparent disorder.

The Sea Peoples

In later Libyan attacks the forces defeated by Merneptah included people who did not come from North Africa. These additional peoples were called the Sherden[16] and the Sheklesh, and they appear to have come from the islands of Sardinia and Sicily, across the Mediterranean Sea.[17] Still others who joined them were called the Ekwesh and the Denen, groups who may be correlated with the Achaean and Danaean Greeks of the *Illiad*, and the famous story of the Trojan War. Collectively the Egyptians called these groups the "Sea Peoples".[18] The Libyans and the Sea Peoples had joined forces a few years earlier, and around the eighth year of the reign of Ramesses III, about 1180 BC, two groups of them attacked Egypt in the Delta region. Some of the invaders moved down the coast of Palestine on land, while others came by sea in a large flotilla of "long ships". They joined forces with the Libyans (Libu and Mashwash) who were approaching the Delta from the western desert. As the two armies converged on the Delta region in a pincer movement, the Two Lands faced what was certainly one of the greatest threats to its independence during its long history. Ramesses III recorded the event in detail on the walls of his temple at Medinet Habu on the west bank of the Nile River opposite the town of Thebes. He recounts that the Sea Peoples formed a federation in their islands, probably the Greek isles in the Aegean Sea off the coast of Turkey, and then swept through

The coming of the Libyans

People living in North Africa 1200 km from the Nile river valley would not have travelled such great distances to attack one of the ancient world's most powerful nations unless they had some very compelling reasons to do so. Food shortages caused by drought are the most probable reasons for such invasions, and the 19th Dynasty king Merneptah (1213–1204 BC) specifically mentions famine as the cause of the invasion of 1210 BC.[13] But increased population may have been a factor as well, since the invasion during the time of Ramesses III had the character of a kind of armed migration of desperate and homeless people, and not strictly an invasion by an organized and

The plumed headdresses of Sea Peoples' warriors shown as bound prisoners. Detail from Medinet Habu, mortuary temple of Ramesses III, western Thebes.

the lands of the Hittites (Khatti) and continued down through southern Turkey, into the lands around Karkamish, Amurru, and the island of Cyprus. Ramesses III's depiction includes details of the kinds of clothes and battledress worn by the invaders, many of whom are shown wearing a plume protruding from their helmets. It has long been realized that the plumed headdress is remarkably similar to depictions of battledress in the graphic art and literature of Late Bronze Age Greece.[19] These feathered helmets, along with kilts, shields, and the shape and decoration of their fighting ships, are of Mycenaean (early Greek) origin.[20]

There is some consensus[21] that around 1200 BC a loose coalition of Mycenaean states[22] attacked Troy, the famous city of legend, whose story was told by the poet Homer in the *Iliad*. In the years after the defeat of Troy, some of the warriors joined up with people along the west coast of Turkey and moved slowly eastwards towards the land of Khatti, and on to Syria and Cyprus. The last Hittite king, Suppilu-liuma II, recorded that he fought on several occasions with ships from Cyprus manned by Sea Peoples. At the same time, raiders were threatening the city-state of Ugarit on the Syrian coast. Ugarit was a wealthy city that maintained a fleet of 150 fighting ships to defend it. But while the main battle fleet was away fighting one contingent of Sea Peoples, another attacked the undefended city. Clay tablets from Ugarit depict a desperate situation; 'Ammurabi, the king of Ugarit, sent an urgent message to his allies in Cyprus asking for help, saying that the city was un-defended and that terrible things were being done to the citizens.[23] But help never came and the belea-guered city was razed to the ground and disappeared from memory for more than 3000 years. For some time no nation was able to withstand the forces of the Sea Peoples. In quick succession, well-established kingdoms like the Hittites and Ugarit fell, and were not heard of again until they were rediscovered by archaeologists in modern times.

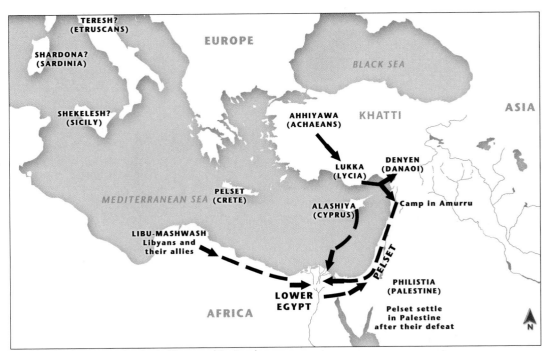

Possible migration routes taken by the Libyans and Sea Peoples.

The Sea Peoples moved into the land of Amurru (western Syria) where they rested for a time and regrouped. From Amurru the Sea Peoples moved down the coast of Syria and into Palestine, their women, children, and animals remaining on land while the warriors manned their ships a short distance offshore. To defend the Two Lands from the approaching invaders, Ramesses III set up a defen-sive barrier in Palestine, along the coast near Gaza. Further south and west, he placed a wall of fighting ships, cargo ships, and smaller boats, to block access to the mouth of the eastern branch of the Nile River. Although some invading ships did manage to break through the river defences, the soldiers of Ramesses III caught them and sank them, set them ablaze, or dragged them to shore, where they were destroyed. The battle must have been long and costly to both sides, but in the end the invaders were defeated. Ramesses III claims to have killed 28 000 Libu and 2175 Mashwash, while taking another 2052 captive.[24] Unable to penetrate the Egyptian defences, the Sea Peoples were forced to disperse, give up their conquering ways, and settle permanently in the lands around the eastern Mediterranean Sea.

The aftermath

After the defeat of the Sea Peoples and the Libyans, many of the attackers managed to stay on and settle in special camps set up for them in the Delta region, and within two centuries after their defeat they were producing kings and forming their own royal houses in Egypt. After the great battles mentioned by Ramesses III and Merneptah, other groups who had accompanied the Sea Peoples went on to settle in Anatolia and Palestine. The Tjeker settled around Haifa, on the coast of Palestine, while the remainder of the coast was settled by the Peleset and later that region became known as Philistia to the writers of the Old Testament, Palestina to the Romans, and Palestine in modern times.[25] By the middle of the 12th century BC the Sea Peoples had dispersed to diverse regions around the Mediterranean and had disappeared into the fabric of Mediterranean society. By the end of the reign of Ramesses III (1184–1153 BC), Egyptian presence in Syria ended and the Sea Peoples, having lost in their attempt to invade the Two Lands, settled in Egypt's former Syrian possessions. Large numbers of Libyans, who had formerly been invaders, were funnelled into the Egyptian army and formed the basis of a soldier class. The chaos and destruction caused by the Libyans and Sea Peoples were important factors in the decline of Egypt but, despite their defeat, the descendants of the Libyans would rise again several centuries later and make their presence known in Egyptian affairs.

Egypt at the end of the New Kingdom

External forces such as the invasion of the Libyans and the Sea Peoples were not the only factors at work weakening Egypt at the end of the New Kingdom.[26] Inside the Two Lands a series of weak kings, economic problems, and a decline of centralized government made it increasingly difficult to maintain internal stability. With the loss of Egyptian possessions in Syria and Palestine there was a drop in tribute and booty as well as foreign trade.[27] The amount of land owned by the king diminished, while land

Attack of the Sea Peoples. Pylon of the mortuary temple of Ramesses II, western Thebes.

holdings of temples and military personnel increased. Abuses in the collection and distribution of food rations to workers and artisans are documented. The situation was complicated by a period of drought, which reduced river levels causing food shortages and famine. In addition, the workmen preparing the tomb of Ramesses III were forced to demonstrate and go on strike because they had not received their food rations.[28] This indicates clearly that there was a decline in the economic conditions of the time, and that the king was unable to manage effectively the operations of the state. Egyptian kings after Ramesses III reduced their travels around the land and distanced themselves from the administration of the kingdom. As their personal involvement with the functioning of the kingdom lessened, their personal influence with those who ran the country decreased as well. High officials, priests, and some commoners, took more control of the affairs of the Two Lands. The priests of Amun increased their land holdings, and one priest even had his image depicted as being equal to that of the king. For the first time high priests began to form dynasties, and were no longer dependent on the king. The priests of Amun gradually gained control of Upper Egypt and formed their own ruling dynasty, which rivalled that of the king. In retrospect, Akhenaten's fears of the growing and potentially dangerous powers of the priesthood appear to have been justified.[29]

The Third Intermediate period

Like the previous two intermediate periods of Egyptian history, the Third Intermediate period[30] was a time of disintegrating centralized power and the fragmentation of the Two Lands into competing groups struggling among themselves for the leadership of the country. During the 20th Dynasty, Egyptian rulers, whether the priests of Amun in the south or the kings of the north, lost control of their holdings in Kush

south of the First Cataract of the Nile River. The influx of foreigners in the previous centuries also left its mark on Egyptian affairs. In the centuries following their defeat by Merneptah and Ramesses III the Libyans had found a place for themselves in the fabric of Egyptian society and became part of the ruling elite. At the beginning of the first millennium BC the kings of the 21st Dynasty ruled the north from the city of Tanis (see map, overleaf) in the eastern Nile Delta. Their control of Lower Egypt extended from the Mediterranean Sea south to the Faiyum. Meanwhile Upper Egypt was ruled by a series of military commanders and high priests of Amun who had established themselves at Thebes. This Theben branch of the 21st Dynasty still acknowledged the Delta kings of Lower Egypt, and even married into their families, yet remained independent of them. With one exception, the priests of Amun did not claim to be pharaohs, but they ruled Upper Egypt as if they were.[31]

One of the pharaohs of the 21st Dynasty, Osorkon, bears a Libyan name. Osorkon belonged to

Chronology of the Third Intermediate period 1069–664 (all dates BC), and kings mentioned in this chapter

21st Dynasty	1069–945	Tanis
Osorkon (Libyan descendant)	984–978	
22nd Dynasty	945–715	Tanis
Sheshonq I	945–924	
Osorkon I	924–889	
Takelot I	889–874	
23rd Dynasty	818–715	Tanis/Thebes
Iuput I	804–878	
24th Dynasty	724–711	Sais
Tefnakhte	724–717	
25th Dynasty	760–656	Napata
Kashta	760–747	
Piye	747–716	
Shabaqo	716–702	
Taharqa	690–664	
Tantamani	664–656	

the same group of Libyan warriors who were defeated by Ramesses III at the beginning of the 20th Dynasty. Unlike some foreigners in Egypt, the Libyans kept their traditional names, old titles, and forms of tribal government.

By the end of the ninth century the centre of Egyptian power was no longer fixed in one location, and for a time the cities of Tanis, Sais, and Bubastis in the north, and Thebes in the south, all claimed to be the Egyptian capital.[32] Egypt had become a patchwork of chiefdoms and petty kingdoms, and must have presented a very disunited and disorganized image to the other major powers of the surrounding regions.

Egypt under Libyan rule

Early in the first millennium BC, Sheshonq I, a man of Libyan descent, established in the Delta city of Bubastis a new ruling family, the 22nd Dynasty, which ruled Egypt for the next two centuries. One of the new king's titles was "Great Chief of the *Ma*",[33] short for Mashwash, which reflects the persistence of the tribal traditions of the Libyans and predates Sheshonq I by several centuries. Sheshonq I was a capable ruler who successfully centralized political, military, and religious power and brought a new era of stability in the country. To accomplish this he reimposed royal control over Upper Egypt, and to offset the power of the priests he made his son, Iuput, high priest and governor. By taking control of the principal levers of power, Sheshonq I created a stable power base at home that left him, and his successor, Osorkon I, free to take back some of Egypt's former possessions in Palestine.

Egypt returns to Asia

In the middle of the tenth century BC the kingdom of Israel was in turmoil and Sheshonq seized the opportunity to exploit Israelite disunity to loot the region,[34] if not regain some of Egypt's lost territory.[35] The armies of Sheshonq penetrated into Palestine as far north as the city of Megiddo, and he is usually acknowledged to be the "King Shishak", who attacked Jerusalem during the reign of Rehoboam. Sheshonq I took his armies up the coast of Palestine and plundered the region, taking much gold and booty. He renewed contacts with Byblos, one of Egypt's traditional trading partners since the middle of the third millennium BC, and re-established a presence in the region that Egypt had lost earlier. For a short period Egypt could dream of the past glories of its once great empire. Plunder from Sheshonq's campaigns financed some major restorations on the temple of Amun at Karnak. Sheshonq I inaugurated a 50-year period of peace and prosperity in Egypt, but his successors, Osorkon I and Takelot I, were not such capable leaders. In a few years Egypt's hard won gains had been lost once again as the country weakened, and progressively splintered into numerous ruling factions.

Since so many positions of power were not dependent on personal competence, but family affiliation, and heredity, the political system in Egypt at this time can be compared to the feudal states of Europe during the Middle Ages.[36] At the time any small-time leader who had local support could claim to be the king of Egypt. The clearest indication of the divided situation in Egypt can be seen in the confusion of ruling families by the end of the eighth century BC. For several decades, the 22nd, 23rd, 24th and 25th Dynasties all ruled various regions of the country from four different cities simultaneously.[37] The principal centres of power in the 22nd (or Libyan) Dynasty, were at Tanis in Lower Egypt, but at the same time the 23rd Dynasty was in control of Thebes in Upper Egypt. Also, the 24th Dynasty ruled a small principality in the western Delta region of Lower Egypt from the city of Sais. To the south, the 25th Dynasty was composed of a line of kings who

TANIS   21st Dynasty and Libyan capital city
TANIS/THEBES   23rd Dynasty capital city
SAIS   24th and 26th Dynasties capital city

Principal cities of the Third Intermediate period during the eighth century BC.

were centred in the city of Napata in Kush or Upper Nubia.[38]

Kush and Assyria: the struggle for Egypt

While Egypt remained fragmented with no central government to unite it, far to the south another power, the Kushite kingdom, was manifesting strength, unity, and vision. The Kushites[39] were a people who lived in the area around the city of Napata, 2000 km south of the Nile Delta (see map, opposite). Kush, also known as Nubia, the land up-river from Egypt, was divided into two regions: Wawat and Kush. Wawat was the region closest to

Egypt, and was settled with farmers scattered along the Nile River, and occasionally with towns and villages with substantial populations. The capital, Napata, was located in Kush proper. Since the end of the New Kingdom, Kush and Wawat had existed as separate and independent regions.

The economy was essentially agrarian, producing grains such as barley, sorghum, and sesame, as well as flocks of herd animals such as sheep and goats. Natural resources included gold, copper, iron, and precious stones. Egypt had traded with the Kushites for many centuries, and Kush was rich in gold, copper, semi-precious stones for jewellery, and quality stone for statues. Trade goods from equatorial Africa passed through Kush on their way to the rich

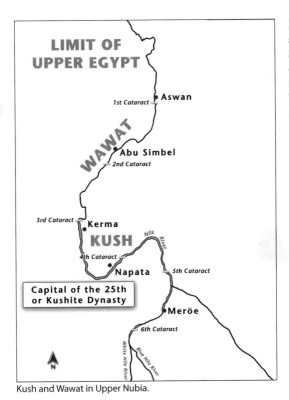

LIMIT OF UPPER EGYPT

1st Cataract • Aswan

WAWAT

• Abu Simbel
2nd Cataract

3rd Cataract

• Kerma

KUSH

Nile River

4th Cataract

• Napata   5th Cataract

Capital of the 25th or Kushite Dynasty

• Meröe

6th Cataract

White Nile River

Blue Nile River

N

Kush and Wawat in Upper Nubia.

markets in Egypt. These goods included ebony logs, giraffe tails for fly whisks, leopard skins for priestly garments, monkeys, baboons, eye paint, incense, spear shafts, ivory, and ostrich feathers, along with animal skins, exotic woods, and aromatic resins and gums.[40] Kush was strategically placed on the Nile River, had abundant resources, and was economically and politically important to Egypt.

The Kushites were black Africans who built *mastaba* and pyramid-shaped tombs, had a centralized form of government, and adopted Egyptian hieroglyphic script for their writing.[41] During the New Kingdom the Kushites were vassals of the Two Lands, had absorbed Egyptian culture and religion, and were faithful worshippers of the god Amun. Starting in the 18th Dynasty, Egyptian kings selected one of their sons to rule over Kush for the king, and they were given the title "The king's son of Kush". The Kushites copied many earlier Egyptian works of art, using them as the standard against which their own were measured. The ruling classes copied the artistic styles of the Old, Middle, and New Kingdoms, which recalled the glorious achievements of former days.[42] As the Kushites conquered and settled areas further north in Egypt, their respect increased for the former periods of greatness when Egyptian monuments displayed a grandeur and sophistication that was missing in their own time.[43] Their love of the past accompanied them into the post-mortem world. The Kushites practised mummification, filled their tombs with sumptuous goods, and in some instances had their teams of horses buried with them. One Kushite king, Piye, was buried in a pyramid-shaped tomb, while other Kushites were laid to rest close to the great funerary monuments of bygone days in the cities of the dead at Saqqara, and near the pyramid complex at Giza.[44]

In reaction to the deteriorating political situation in Upper and Lower Egypt, Kushite kings began to take a greater interest in activities to the north. In the middle of the eighth century BC, the Kushite king Kashta marched north and brought all of the Nile river valley down-river to Thebes under his control. The Kushites viewed this and subsequent campaigns into Egypt not only as invasions for economic and strategic gain, but also as sacred missions to restore the old ways of *ma'at*, and protect the supremacy of the god Amun.[45] In Thebes the Kushite king took great care to attend to religious matters and spent time making offerings and assisting in religious ceremonies. Piye (Piankhy) succeeded his father, Kashta, and declared himself king of Egypt, taking the traditional royal titles that had been used by Egyptian kings for centuries.

Late in the eighth century BC, Egypt had four different dynasties ruling simultaneously, including the 25th (or Kushite) Dynasty, which ruled from both Napata and Thebes. In the north the Libyan ruler of the 24th Dynasty, Tefnakhte, formed a small rival kingdom and headed south with his army, threatening Kushite holdings. Tefnakhte used the title "Great chief of the *Mashwash*",[46] recalling his Libyan ethnic background. Piye made an attempt to regain control and sent his armies north to the Delta, bringing all the petty kings and princes under his control. As Piye extended his dominion along the Nile River, Egypt was once again united, at least on the surface, and in a position to take on the role of a powerful rejuvenated nation. In his inscriptions Piye explained that the petty kings of the north had misbehaved like naughty children, and it was his duty to bring them into line. After their defeat he treated them with leniency, and installed many of them as governors in regions they already ruled. Tefnakhte surrendered like everyone else, but then fled north and regrouped his forces. Piye almost succeeded in reuniting Egypt, but the fact that he did not eliminate Tefnakhte undermined his nearly successful attempt to bring Egypt once again under the control of a single powerful ruler. Like most Kushite rulers, Piye chose to stay far to the south at Napata instead of moving north to Thebes or Memphis to more closely administer the Two Lands, which may have contributed to his inability to truly reunite the country.

The Kushite domination of Egypt lasted nearly a hundred years, and created an interesting set of political circumstances in North Africa and the ancient Near East. The traditional centres of power in Upper and Lower Egypt, such as Memphis and Thebes, were caught between the growing power of the Assyrians from Mesopotamia, and the Kushites from the Middle Nile region of Central Africa. But at the end of the eighth century BC, as the Assyrians gained strength in Syria-Palestine and moved towards the Nile Delta, the Kushites under their new leader,

Shabaqo, reunited the Two Lands and, temporarily at least, kept the Assyrians out.

Assyria in Egypt

As the Assyrians moved closer to Egypt[47] the small states of Palestine, such as Judah, Samaria, and Gaza, looked desperately to Egypt for help to avoid being conquered. The Egyptians were only too eager to help the smaller states remain strong, since if they fell there would be nothing between the Egyptians and Assyrian forces. Combined Egyptian and Kushite forces fought in Palestine with the kings of Judah against the Assyrians on a number of occasions, and in some instances they managed to keep the Assyrians at bay.[48] But the armies of the Two Lands suffered a major defeat at Eltekeh while going to the aid of a coalition of small kingdoms and princes during the reign of Hezekiah, king of Judah.[49] About 25 years later the Assyrians, under the leadership of King Esarhaddon, swept through all of Palestine and invaded Egypt in 674 BC. Somehow, Egyptian forces managed to repulse the Assyrian invasion armies at the northern border town of Sile. Unfortunately for the Egyptians, three years later, in 671 BC, Esarhaddon was back, and this time he managed to conquer the Delta region and the ancient capital of Memphis. With this defeat Egypt was obliged to pay a heavy tribute to Assyria. The Kushite king, Taharqa, wisely fled south to avoid being captured. The Assyrian defeat was costly, but did not last long. Taharqa reconquered Memphis and Egypt two years later, after the Assyrians had returned home leaving only a small garrison of soldiers and some Assyrian-appointed Egyptians to look after their newly acquired interests. When Esarhaddon received news in 679 BC that his Egyptian power base had been overthrown by the upstart Taharqa, he rushed back to reconquer Egypt, but on the way he died, and the counterattack was cancelled.

The intrigues of Taharqa's successor, Tantamani, who attempted to sabotage Assyrian control in Egypt, brought massive and vengeful Assyrian retaliation under the last great Assyrian king, Assurbanipal. On two more occasions the Assyrians marched on Egypt, once in 667 BC and again in 664 BC. After the campaign of 667 BC, Assurbanipal left a small garrison of soldiers and some supposedly sympathetic native Egyptians in control of the Two Lands. But once again, when the Assyrians had left Egypt in the hands of their appointed overseers and returned home with their loot, Tantamani, the Kushite king, drove out the Assyrians and their sympathisers. This enraged Assurbanipal and in 664 BC he returned and plundered the entire country, causing widespread death and destruction. The second time the Assyrians sacked the ancient city of Thebes far to the south in Upper Egypt. Tantamani wisely fled south out of harm's way at the approach of the Assyrians, while the country was ravaged and plundered.

This was a low point for Egypt under the leadership of the Kushite kings and what had been, until then, their successful domination of the country. But the losses the Kushites had suffered under the Assyrians, and the daunting task of controlling a divided land that was the constant prey of the world's most powerful army, seems to have dampened Kushite interest in Egypt. Some time after the Assyrian sack of Thebes, the Kushites abandoned Egypt and returned south to the safety of their pre-expansion borders.[50] In 652 BC the Assyrian occupation came to an abrupt end. The Shamash-shum-ukin revolt broke out in Babylonia, and Assyrian forces were needed urgently at home. For the next four years Assurbanipal was preoccupied with a long and costly civil war. Afterwards, because of growing problems, the Assyrians were unable to free their armies from the defence of the homeland for a return campaign, and never threatened Egypt again. Because the Assyrians were caught up in their own domestic problems, Tantamani's rival, Psamtik, took

Chronology of the Late period 664–525 (all dates BC)

The 26th (Saite) Dynasty	664–525	Sais
Necho I	672–664	
Psamtik I	664–610	
Necho II	610–595	
Psamtik II	595–589	
Apires	589–570	
Amasis	570–526	
Psamtik III	526–525	

control of an Egypt that was free of foreign conquerors for the first time in many years.

The 26th (or Saite) Dynasty,[51] was one of the last significant dynasties of the Two Lands ruled by native Egyptians. The Saite kings ruled from their capital city of Sais in the eastern Nile Delta for 140 years. When the Saites took control of Egypt they inaugurated a century of social and political order and economic progress[52] that is often referred to as the Saite Renaissance.[53] When Psamtik I succeeded his father, Necho I, in 664 BC his kingdom consisted of a small portion of territory in the eastern Delta and around Memphis that was still nominally under Assyrian control. When he died 54 years later, he left behind a united and healthy Egypt that could take its place among the great nations of the ancient Near East. When he first took the throne it appeared that Egypt might once again return to its previous divided condition. But Psamtik was a man of many talents, and he put an end to the long period of instability caused by fragmented forms of government in the Third Intermediate period. The first task facing Psamtik[54] was to bring under his control the various ruling princes and unify the country under his rule. Many local rulers were left in place, but Psamtik made them abandon their titles of "King", "Great Chief", or "Army Leader", and they finally became incorporated into a centralized form of government.[55] He accomplished this in part by opening up trade and business relations with the wealthy and dynamic trading peoples to the north, particularly the Greeks and the Phoenicians.[56] The wealth created by trade quickly began to enrich his coffers and enabled Psamtik to engage mercenary troops, mostly Greeks from Ionia and Carians, to serve as the principal elements in his army. The bulk of the Egyptian army still comprised native Egyptians and some Kushites. By engaging mercenaries with new fighting skills and equipment, who had no allegiance to anyone in Egypt but themselves, he quickly conquered the princes of the Delta and took control of Lower Egypt. In Middle and Upper Egypt he was able to use diplomacy to eventually bring these areas on side and after the first decade of his rule the country was united. With the task of unification behind him he was able to embark on a national construction programme, which stimulated the economy and helped reinforce a sense of unity in the population.

The Saites were very interested in business and trade[57] and ruled as merchant kings (royal businessmen) seeking out new and profitable trade routes and trading partners for Egyptian goods. It was Psamtik who set the precedent for exporting Egyptian grain and wool,[58] which helped to stimulate economic growth. Egypt had many products and goods to offer her trading partners, including grain, textiles, ox hides, dried fish, and papyrus, which was the cheapest and, at this time, most widely used writing material. The Saites entered into business arrangements with the powerful Greeks who were one of the emerging trading powers of the Mediterranean world. However, not all Egyptians were in favour of such close contacts with the Greeks. Large numbers of Greeks began to immigrate to the Delta region and settle in their own communities in cities they founded. Favouritism shown to Greek traders, plus the large number of Greek soldiers in the army, aroused jealousy among certain segments of the population. There were other irritants too. Certain Greek religious practices were allowed, and wealthy Greek merchants began to marry Egyptian women instead of Greeks. The Egyptian population occasionally showed their disapproval of these policies of favouritism by revolting against their leaders. The long-term effects of these tactics were eventually felt across the land by both the Egyptians and the Greek immigrants. Because the Greeks were seen to be too powerful and exploitative of the country's wealth at the expense of native Egyptians, the Persians had less trouble invading the country and putting it under their control in 525 BC.

Necho II: the "Sea King"

Necho II[59] was a king who expressed interest in the sea and projects related to maritime activities. One of his areas of maritime interest was the great canal-building project, which linked the Nile River with the Red Sea.[60] The construction of such a canal indicates a well-defined naval policy that required easy access to the Mediterranean and Red Seas. But even though Necho II initiated the 85-km canal project, some scholars do not believe that he ever finished it.[61] They maintain instead that it was only completed after the Persian conquest, when Darius I undertook the project once again (see Ch. 17). The purpose of such a canal may initially have been military, but trade was certainly an important factor in its conception. Herodotus[62] stated that the canal was abandoned after the loss of 120 000 lives during its attempted construction. These figures are most certainly exaggerated although, given the nature of such a vast project, there was probably a significant loss of life during its construction.

With the growing power of Babylon and, later on, Persia, Necho II, like Nabonidus of Babylon 50 years after him (see Ch. 7), may have deemed it necessary to abandon his colonial interests in Syria-Palestine in favour of lands to the south along the Red Sea coast of Africa, in the areas of present-day Ethiopia that opened up during the reign of Hatshepsut in the 18th Dynasty. During the sixth century BC, as Persian power and domination increased throughout southwest Asia (Iran, Mesopotamia, Anatolia, and Syria-Palestine), the weaker powers like Babylon and Egypt showed an increased interest in the lands adjacent to the Red Sea, which were temporarily beyond the reaches of Persian power.[63] The second element of Necho II's maritime policy was the construction of a large fleet of triremes, the most advanced fighting ships of the day. The fleet in the Mediterranean was placed there for military purposes since the Mediterranean was the scene for many battles between navies representing the various kingdoms in the region. The ships were built by Greek artisans, probably in the city of Naucratis, which had been established as a Greek trading colony in the Nile Delta at the end of the seventh century BC. The ships were probably manned by Greek sailors, not Egyptians, and were used against pirates operating in the Red Sea who preyed on Egyptian shipping in the area.

The third element of Necho II's maritime policy concerned a voyage around the continent of Africa. The other great sea power of the time, the

The possible route of the Egyptian–Phoenician voyage around the continent of Africa.

Phoenicians, had a well-established maritime empire in the western Mediterranean and knew the southern coast of Europe and the northern coast of the African continent. The Phoenicians were renowned as skilled sailors and explorers, and it would have been in the interests of both countries to undertake an expedition around the African continent, not for scientific reasons, but to discover new trade routes and markets. The joint expedition was under Phoenician command, and it took three years for them to circle the continent returning through the Straits of Gibraltar. The sailors were obliged to interrupt their voyage twice, in order to grow crops and replenish their food supplies.[64] Even though there is some scepticism that such a voyage actually took place, the story is credible since the sailors reported, correctly, that the sun shone from the north, on their right, as they rounded the Horn of Africa.[65]

Foreign policy in Syria-Palestine

Half a century of stable and prosperous rule by Necho II's father, Psamtik I, achieved such a resurgence in the land that Necho II was able to commit the necessary resources required to once again embark on a policy of expansion in Syria-Palestine. As Assyria weakened and lost control of its empire in southwest Asia, the Egyptians hoped to rush in and take control of the area. This policy met with initial success and the Egyptians were able take their armies as far as the Euphrates River during the period of Assyrian disintegration (see Ch. 6). The armies of the Two Lands went to the aid of the Assyrians, their long-time enemies, in an effort to stop the rapidly expanding Babylonians, who were in the process of taking over all of Mesopotamia. The Egyptians attempted in vain to help the Assyrians after the fall of Nineveh and Harran. The *Babylonian Chronicle* records that in 610 BC the Assyrian king, Assur-uballit, along with an Egyptian army, abandoned

Harran as the advancing armies of the Babylonians approached the city.[66] Egypt's chances to rebuild an empire in Syria-Palestine came to an end when the Babylonians, under Nebuchadnezzar, defeated the Egyptian forces in 601 BC at the battle of Karkamish on the Euphrates River.

In effect, Necho II, like so many pharaohs before him, lost Syria-Palestine for Egypt, but he did manage to hold off the Babylonians and keep them from conquering the Two Lands. Even though over the years one or two more unsuccessful attempts were made to re-establish an Egyptian presence in Syria-Palestine, with Necho II's defeat, the entire region was lost to Egypt for a long time.

The last great pharaoh

Ahmose II (570–526 BC), or Amasis II,[67] was one of the last notable pharaohs of Egypt. Despite the continued encroachment of foreign powers on Egyptian borders, inside the Two Lands classical historians leave the impression that during the rule of Amasis II the country was very prosperous. A number of documents have survived that confirm this. The vast building programmes that were going on at this time could not have been undertaken without a solid base of economic resources to finance them.[68] Amasis II was a general who came to power in a revolt. His most notable policy was the treatment of Greek traders and colonists, who had become very powerful in Egypt. Amasis II was sympathetic to Greek interests and promoted the Greek city of Naucratis in the western Nile Delta as an emporium for Greek trade. One of the principal reasons for the establishment of Naucratis was to keep Greek commercial activities confined to a single area away from the heartland of the country, and out of sight of the population.[69] But this strategy was not always successful, and served to intensify the growing distrust between Egyptian citizens and Greek colonists. Late in the sixth century

BC, Egypt and Babylonia, who had traditionally been enemies, began to draw closer together as allies in the face of the increasing might of the Persians, a new and growing power in Iran. By 539 BC the Persians (see Ch. 17) had taken control of the Iranian Plateau, plus Mesopotamia and Anatolia. Egypt was now alone with few allies, except the disunited Greeks, to help it in its struggle against this new and vigorous power from the east.

The death of King Amasis II

King Amasis II ruled Egypt for 45 years and died in 526 BC. Shortly after his death Egypt was in the hands of the Persians under the leadership of Cambyses. In 525 BC the Egyptians lost the all-important battle of Pelusium on their northeastern border, and Egyptian resistance collapsed in the face of the Persian onslaught. The Egyptians might have been able to give a better account of themselves on the battlefield had they not been betrayed by their allies and friends. The leaders of the Greek mercenary contingents of the Egyptian army went over to the Persians just before the battle and revealed vital military information to the enemy.[70] The Arab tribesmen of Gaza served as guides and provided water for the thirsty Persian soldiers as they crossed the desert, while the Phoenicians provided ships to supply the invading army with provisions. On the home front there was collusion with the invaders on the part of some of the Egyptian high officials, particularly one man named Udjahorresnet, who some believe was the chief of naval operations.[71] After the army was defeated and the conquest completed, a Persian official was appointed *satrap* (governor) of Lower Egypt while Cambyses continued his conquest to the south, eventually taking Kush.

The Persian conquest must have been a terrible blow to the Egyptian ruling class and entrepreneurs and business people, particularly since the country was enjoying a good deal of political stability and economic success. How much it affected the lower classes – the peasants, farmers, and craftsmen – is difficult to determine, but their lives probably did not change in any appreciable way. It is possible that few of them realized that the long line of native Egyptian rulers had finally come to an end, and in the future, except for a few brief periods, outsiders would rule the Two Lands for many centuries to come.[72]

Part V: Mesopotamia and Egypt under Persian rule

17 The Persians

For centuries, outsiders viewed the rich river valleys of Mesopotamia and Egypt with envy and, on occasion, attempted, sometimes successfully, to take control of the region. The Kassites (see Ch. 5) were outsiders who migrated into southern Mesopotamia, and managed to place one of their own on the throne in Babylon. During the second millennium BC the Kassite Dynasty ruled southern Mesopotamia for more than four centuries, from the beginning of the 16th century until the beginning of the 12th century BC.[1] Even though they controlled the physical region of Babylonia, the Kassites adopted many aspects of the Babylonian way of life and, in many ways, it was Babylonian culture that conquered the Kassites. During the second millennium BC, with the invasions and migrations of the Hyksos and the Sea Peoples,[2] the security of Egypt was seriously threatened (see Ch. 15). Yet even though these new peoples occupied Lower Egypt, for the most part they never managed to impose their own cultures on the Two Lands. In fact, once they had taken possession of the land, most foreign conquerors made an effort to imitate the art, architecture, and religious practices of the Egyptians or the various people of Mesopotamia. By the middle of the first millennium BC things were different. A new group from the east wrested power away from the locals, and for two centuries rulership of both Mesopotamia and Egypt was in the hands of the Achaemenids, the ruling dynasty of the Persian Empire.

The Medes and the Persians

The Iranian Plateau,[3] homeland of the Medes and Persians, is a vast highland region roughly three times the size of France that stretches from the Tigris River in the west to the Indus River in the east.[4] Much of this geographical region falls within the borders of the modern state of Iran. The Iranian Plateau lies between two large bodies of water, the Caspian Sea to the north, and the Persian Gulf to the south. Although archaeological research for the earliest periods of the history of the region is still in its infancy, evidence indicates that hunter–gatherers, using Acheulean style hand-axes, inhabited the Iranian Plateau as early as the Palaeolithic times, 75 000 years ago.[5] By the Neolithic period (10 000–5000 BC), the western Iranian Plateau was at the forefront of the agricultural revolution, which saw the domestication of goats, the cultivation of cereals, and the establishment of early agricultural villages.[6] Susa, one of the ancient capitals of the Elamites, was founded in the plains of Khuzistan in south-southwestern Iran around 4200 BC, and was followed by the flowering of the Elamite kingdom, which lasted from 2700 to 1500 BC.[7]

The Medes and the Persians originated in Central Asia or the Caucasus mountain region about 1000 BC.[8] During the first half of the first millennium BC the Medes and Persians, along with other ethnic groups, began to move into the Iranian Plateau and the fertile valleys of the Zagros mountains east of the Tigris River.[9] The Medes and the Persians were linguistically associated, since they were both Indo-Iranians[10] who spoke related languages.[11] By the end of the seventh century BC the Medes were the dominant force in the region. They settled northeast of the region of the old kingdom of Elam, north of the Persian Gulf, around what would later become Fars (Parsa in Old Persian, and Persis in Greek), the heartland of Persia.

Neither the Medes nor the Persians spoke any of the Semitic languages of Mesopotamia, such as Akkadian or Aramaic, nor were they part of one of the traditional cultural groups, such as the Sumerians, Babylonians, or Assyrians, who had ruled ancient Mesopotamia in the past. Very little is known about the Persians before 550 BC, except that they moved into the region traditionally occupied by the

Elamites. Seventh-century BC texts from Assyria and Babylonia refer to Persians living in the capital city of Susa at that time. The first kings of Persia took the title "King of Anshan", the name of one of the ancient cities of Elam. The land of Persia and its king submitted to Assurbanipal after his victories over the Elamites (see Ch. 6), and the Persian ruler sent his son as a hostage to the Assyrian king to ensure his

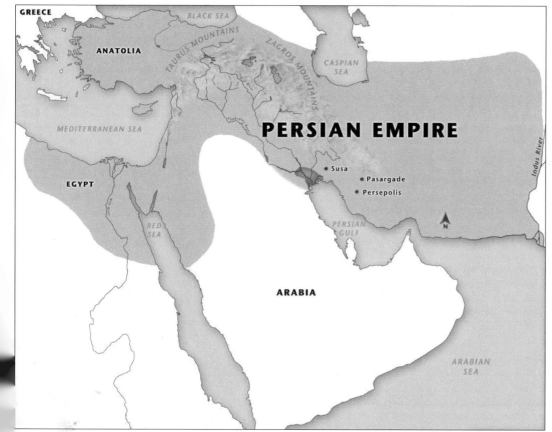

The Persian Empire, encompassing Egypt and Mesopotamia, about 500 BC.

Procession of life-sized Persian archers. Glazed bricks from the façade of the Palace of Darius I, Susa.

loyalty. Later, Cyrus I (c.620–590 BC) and Cambyses I (c.590–559 BC) were followed by Cyrus II, "the Great" (559–530 BC). Despite their well-known military campaigns, scholars know little about the politics and social organization of the Persians and their leaders when they first began their period of expansion and conquest in the ancient Near East.

The Greek historian Herodotus[12] recounts that the Medes were originally village dwellers who made a certain Deioces their king. He established his capital at the city of Ecbatana, and ruled over them for 53 years. How much of this story is true is debatable, and at least some aspects of it seem to be more legend than truth.[13] Beginning in the middle of the ninth century BC and continuing to the middle of the seventh century BC, Assyrian sources give a somewhat clearer picture of the Medes as a culturally and socially diverse people spread throughout the central Zagros region.[14] Assyrian texts speak of many non-Iranian peoples in the region in the early eighth century BC but a century later the Medes had gained strength, and were one of several groups – including the Babylonians, the Lydians, and the Egyptians – manoeuvring for control of Mesopotamia. The Medes[15] appear in Assyrian texts in the middle and late ninth century BC,[16] and sources speak of Median tribes which later formed a unified state in the seventh century BC. The Medes and Babylonians formed a military alliance that brought an end to Assyrian domination of Mesopotamia in 612 BC, and the collapse of Assyrian power by around 610 BC. The Medes profited from the riches taken in the sack of the city of Nineveh, and with the Assyrian collapse they filled much of the political vacuum left in the north. By late in the seventh century BC, a Median state had formed under the leadership of King Cyaxeres, who extended his power all the way to the kingdom of Lydia on the west coast of Anatolia. Some time during his 40-year reign Cyaxeres also conquered the Persians, who occupied the southeastern portion of the Iranian Plateau. By around 600 BC

Median hegemony stretched from the Halys River in Anatolia all the way to northeastern Iran.

The Medes and their culture had a strong and lasting influence on the broader culture of the region, but Median political control of the Persians did not last long. In 550 BC the Median king, Astyages, attacked Cyrus,[17] king of the Persians, but at one point the Median army refused to fight and handed King Astyages over to Cyrus. At that moment Cyrus (Kurush in Old Persian)[18] became the political and military leader of both the Medes and the Persians. As soon as he had taken power Cyrus marched to the Median capital of Ecbatana and took all the wealth of its treasury back to his own capital at Pasargadae (see map, p. 219).[19] By overthrowing the Medes and

taking control of their vast territories, Cyrus II had suddenly thrust the Persians to the forefront of world power.

Almost overnight, the Persians took control of a vast kingdom that stretched over much of southwestern Asia. Cyrus II cemented the legitimacy of his reign to the traditions and history of Persia's past by claiming he was the son of Cambyses, the grandson of an earlier Cyrus, and a distant descendant of a half-mythical king named Teispes. By 547 BC Lydia was under the authority of the Persians. The armies of Cyrus II, commanded by Lydian generals, were sent further west to subjugate the Greek coastal cities and the islands of Ionia, Caria, and Lycia on the eastern shores of the Mediterranean Sea. Once Cyrus II had

Chronology of the Persian period with significant events (dates BC except where indicated)

Early kings	(dates uncertain)		
Teispes (Chispish)	c.650–620		
Cyrus I (Kurash)	c.620–590		
Cambyses I (Kambuziya)	c.590–559		
Cyrus II the Great	559–530	Conquest of Babylon	539
Beginning of the Achaemenid (Persian) Dynasty	c.550		
Cambyses II	529–522	Conquest of Egypt	525
First Persian period in Egypt: 27th Dynasty	525–404		
Bardyia	522		
Darius I	522–486		
Xerxes I	486–465		
Artaxerxes I	465–424		
Xerxes II (short rule)	424		
Sogdianos	424–423		
Darius II	423–405		
Egyptian Independence: 28th Dynasty	405–343		
Artaxerxes II	405–359	29th Dynasty (Persian)	399–380
Nectanebo II	359–343	30th Dynasty (Egyptian)	380–343
Second Persian period in Egypt : 31st Dynasty	343–332		
Artaxerxes III	359–338		
Artaxerxes IV	338–336		
Darius III	336–330	Alexander the Great (III) conquers Egypt	332
Period of Hellenistic domination in Egypt	332–30	Alexander the Great (III)	332–323
		Seleucid period in Mesopotamia	311–146
Period of Roman domination	30 BC–AD 395		

consolidated his control of former Median territories he turned his armies towards the heartland of Mesopotamia, and the Babylonian Empire of King Nabonidus. In October 539 BC, Cyrus II marched into the city of Babylon (see Ch. 7),[20] effectively putting an end to native Mesopotamian rule over the region.

Cyrus the Great

When Cyrus II entered Babylon, his own texts claim that the people of Babylon received him as a benevolent liberator. Because Cyrus II put an end to Nabonidus's attempts to raise the moon god Sin to pre-eminence over the traditional god Marduk, the citizens of the great city bowed down to him, or so the written accounts claim, and kissed his feet and their faces were "shining with happiness". It is questionable if the Babylonians really wanted to be taken over by a foreign power, and there is undoubtedly a strong element of Persian propaganda woven into these joyful greetings.[21]

Once in power Cyrus restored the city of Babylon and the cult centres at Nineveh, Ashur, Uruk, and a number of other cities, and brought the statue of the god Marduk back to Babylon. Cyrus was known for his religious toleration; he was careful to present himself not as an outsider and conqueror, but as a new king who respected the traditional gods and traditions of ancient Sumer and Assyria. Cyrus II's reputation for tolerance in ancient texts was enhanced after his conquest when he freed peoples held captive in Babylon, including a number of Jews taken prisoner by the Babylonian king, Nebuchadnezzar. The Old Testament writers hailed him as the saviour and "messiah" of the Jews,[22] a few thousand of whom had been held in the city of Babylon for more than 50 years since the capture of Jerusalem (see Ch. 7). Even though Cyrus was tolerant of the religions of the countries he conquered, the liberation of the Jews

and their eventual return to Judah was probably carried out for sound political reasons as well. The Persians needed faithful allies in Syria and Palestine if they were to protect their western flank and eventually conquer Egypt.

Textual sources indicate that in his actions and projects Cyrus ruled wisely and with an even hand.[23] In diplomacy he kept taxes low and his new capital city at Pasargadae[24] was modest when compared to other capitals in the Near East. Construction work at Pasargadae was carried out by Lydian craftsmen from the western extremities of the empire, since it seems likely that the Persians, who had previously been herders[25] and did not have a tradition of living in cities, did not possess the necessary building skills to undertake such a project. Cyrus died while fighting against nomadic Massegetai tribesmen in central Asia, and was buried in a modest tomb. Unlike so many previous dynasties, which suffered conflicts over succession at the time of their founder's death, the rule of the Persian Empire passed peacefully into the hands of Cyrus's son, Cambyses II in the summer of 529 BC.

Cambyses II and the conquest of Egypt

The conquest of Egypt in 525 BC marked another great turning point in the history of the ancient Near East, and was one of the largest territorial expansions in Persian history.[26] Egyptian forces, already weakened by the loss of important allies, were defeated by the battle-hardened Persian army, which swept over them at the Nile Delta town of Pelusium. The inexperienced Pharaoh Psamtik III, who had been betrayed by one of his chief officials, fled the scene, but was eventually captured and sent to the Persian capital at Susa. Like the Egyptian pharaohs, King Cambyses II (Kambuziya) and three of his successors wrote their names using hieroglyphs enclosed in sacred cartouches, and following Egyptian tradition, they formed the 27th (or Persian) Dynasty of rulers in

Egypt. But even though the new rulers Egyptianized their names, they were still conquerors who ruled from Persia and forced unwanted changes and taxes on the people of Egypt. Starting with Cambyses II, Egypt was no longer the "Two Lands", or "Upper and Lower Egypt". Instead, the whole Nile river valley was amalgamated into a single great province of the Persian Empire.

Propagandistic accounts of Cambyses claimed that he was an uncouth barbarian. Herodotus states that Cambyses killed the sacred Apis bull, one of the most revered religious symbols in ancient Egypt.[27] This would have been a grave crime, since the Apis bull, the *ba* or soul of the great god Ptah, was a very popular sacred animal, worshipped in the city of Memphis in Lower Egypt. The symbolic fusion of characteristics of the bull with the king, combining fertility, sexuality, and aggressiveness, was an ancient concept in Egypt.[28] The sacred bull was adorned with special markings on its hide and was portrayed with a sun disc between its horns. Bulls were also considered sacred for a number of other Egyptian gods, including Mnevis, Bukhis, certain manifestations of the sun god Re, and the war god Montu.[29]

Apis bulls were selected and raised in special precincts, and when they died, instead of being eaten and having their by-products tanned or processed for human consumption, they were mummified and buried by the whole community with great respect and ceremony. Contrary to Herodotus's account, archaeological excavations at the Serapeum of Memphis tell a different story about Cambyses's treatment of these sacred animals. Excavations there have located the place where the sacred bulls were buried, and accompanying stelae display Cambyses II, the King of Upper and Lower Egypt, dressed as the Egyptian god Horus, performing the burial rituals of the Apis bull himself in 524 BC.[30] It is clear that such a false episode of anti-Persian propaganda against Cambyses II was written by his enemies and does not represent a reliable account of the events. Instead of destroying or desecrating the sacred bulls, Cambyses II actually worshipped and respected them. Additional archaeological evidence indicates that the new Persian ruler was respectful of many other Egyptian beliefs and traditions too.[31] When Cambyses II was crowned pharaoh he took the position seriously and acted like an Egyptian ruler, and not just a conqueror. He was even very conscientious about performing the religious rites that were part of the duties of a pharaoh of the Two Lands. Inscriptions indicate that he restored some existing temples, had the temple of the warlike goddess Neith at the Delta city of Sais cleaned up and cleared of squatters' houses, and was even inducted into the rituals connected with the cult of Neith. Such acceptance would not normally have been granted to an outsider.

There are several reasons why Cambyses II was tarnished with such a bad reputation in later traditions, the most likely being that he reduced the amount of wealth going to the priests and the temples. Reducing the power of the priests and the temple was something previous Egyptian pharaohs had attempted, with varying degrees of success, going back at least to the time of Akhenaten. Once Cambyses II cut the funding of the Egyptian religious establishment, the priests were sure to propagate negative stories about him, which found their way into the histories of the Persian period.

Even though there had been major changes in the upper levels of rulership, under Persian domination life in Egypt continued much as before. The old gods were still worshipped, religious festivals were still celebrated, and temples were maintained on a regular basis. The cycle of planting and harvesting, always in harmony with the annual cycle of the Nile floods, continued as always. During much of the Persian period the Egyptians were governed under their own laws, which the Persians had codified. In the first years following the Persian conquest the Egyptians no doubt suffered some losses as a result of Persian domination. Nevertheless, there was still a good

measure of prosperity. Stone quarries were opened, numerous temples were built or repaired, and the life of the average peasant may have even improved slightly.

Cambyses II only ruled Persia for seven years. After his conquest of Egypt he only stayed in the Nile river valley for three years, before dying in Syria on his way back to Persia to put down a series of revolts that had broken out. Along with his two sisters, he was the only living descendant of Cyrus II, the architect of early Persian expansion and conquest. As was often the case in the ancient Near East, when the reigning king died, plots were hatched by family members and their followers, and revolts broke out as competing groups fought for the throne, and the power and wealth that accompanied kingship. The story of this struggle for the throne of Persia, or at least one version of it, was recorded by Cambyses's successor.

Darius I (522–486 BC)

The death of Cambyses II and the subsequent succession of Darius I[32] (Daryavush in Old Persian) was recorded in a massive trilingual inscription written in Elamite, Old Persian, and Akkadian. The inscription and accompanying low-relief sculptures were cut into the side of a tall, twin-peaked rock face called Bisitun, or Bagastana,[33] meaning "Land of the gods". The peaks are located in a mountain pass in the Zagros mountains, which rise dramatically above the surrounding plains. The southern face of the mountain falls almost vertically, and there, 100 m above the old Baghdad–Hamadan road, Darius I inscribed the story of his struggle to take the throne of Persia.

Before his reign the Persians had no written form of their language. Most written communications were done in Aramaic or Akkadian. Darius realized that the dignity of the king and his imperial subjects required their own writing system, and ordered the creation of a syllabic cuneiform script that consisted

of 43 signs. Darius claims to have created a different kind of writing system that did not exist before, and "according to the will of Ahura-Mazda", the chief god of the Persians. This writing system was used to write "Old Persian", the court language of the Achaemenid Dynasty.[34] Because of its small number of signs, and close relationship with Aramaic, it was one of the earliest ancient scripts to be deciphered in the 19th century.

The Bisitun inscription relates that while Cambyses II was in Egypt, a priest named Bardiya usurped his throne and took the title "King of Iran and Babylonia". But, on his way back to Persia to regain control of his kingdom, Cambyses II died, and when the news of his death reached home seven Persian princes rebelled against Bardiya and a civil war broke out between all the royal pretenders. According to the Bisitun inscription, the responsibility to restore the true ruling family to the throne fell on Darius I. The young king suppressed the rebellion and took power with, once again he informs us, the help of the god Ahura-Mazda. Depicted in the form of a winged solar disc, Ahura-Mazda was the chief god of the Persians, who over the years became increasingly popular throughout the empire.[35]

This account, too, is propagandistic, and the real story of the struggle for succession will probably never be known. However, what details can be distilled from the circumstances indicate that Darius I was probably not next in line to become king since he mentions that both his father and grandfather were alive when he took the throne.[36] This would indicate that he was not in the direct line of succession, but was probably one of several usurpers, and he may have even murdered Cyrus's son, Bardiya, to get the throne.[37] Once on the throne of Persia, like so many other kings before him, he justified his rule by tracing his ancestry back through previous generations of rulers, claiming that his family had been providing kings to the Persian people since Achaemenes (Hakhamanish), the founder of the Achaemenid

Twin bull's head capital and pillar from the Palace of Darius I, at the Persian city of Susa. (Louvre Museum, Paris.)

experience necessary to match the efficiency of existing systems of the conquered peoples. By the reign of Darius I, the Persians had managed to develop their administrative and bureaucratic skills and had instituted their own system based on smaller units or provinces called *satrapies*. This system seems to have a number of similarities with the older Assyrian administrative system put in place by Tiglath-pileser III (see Ch. 6). Each *satrapy* (from the word *khshaçapavan*, meaning "protecting the kingdom"[38]) was ruled by a governor, who was usually a close relative or associate well-known to the king and his advisers. Darius I also instituted economic and legal reforms, and established a regular system of taxation and tribute.

The administrative capital of his empire was located at Susa,[39] the old Elamite capital, which had been occupied since the fourth millennium BC. It was from Susa that the Elamite armies ravaged Mesopotamian kingdoms, and it was Susa that the enraged Assyrian king Assurbanipal destroyed in the seventh century by burning the city and its temples and ploughing salt into the fields to curse the city and the surrounding region with barrenness. Ironically, a little more than a century after Assurbanipal, Susa was at the centre of the mightiest empire the world had ever seen.

Successful administration depended on a reliable and fast communication system that could send messages from the fringes of the empire to the capital in the shortest possible time. Only with good communications could armies be sent to trouble spots to fight off enemies and put down revolts. Herodotus[40] gives a good description of the royal road from Susa all the way to Sardis, 2000 km away in western Anatolia. Some sections of Persian roads in Iran have survived into modern times. In most places the roads were not paved but were simply dirt tracks on the bare ground. Nevertheless, they would have been well marked and maintained and, most importantly, patrolled by soldiers who would have kept them safe

Dynasty. As an additional measure of security, and to ensure there would be no other pretenders to the throne born to the surviving daughters and granddaughters of Cyrus II, he married all of them. Although revolts broke out in opposition against him, within a year Darius I had eliminated his enemies and he ruled the Persian lands for the next 36 years. Like Cambyses II before him, Darius I continued his plans for expanding the boundaries of the empire, both to the east as far as India and to the west in Europe.

He began by occupying parts of Thrace in southern Europe and campaigning in the west against the Scythians across the Danube River. In the east he added the province of India to his holdings. Although things went well in the east, the Persians suffered a number of defeats in the west. In the first decade of the fifth century BC the Persians attempted to expand their control into southeastern Europe

only to meet stiff resistance from the Greeks, particularly the city-state of Athens. In 492 BC the Persian general Mardonius led a campaign against the Greek mainland. After landing successfully the Persians were defeated by a smaller Greek force at the famous battle of Marathon in 490 BC. Then, after failing to take the city of Athens, the invasion was called off. But a decade later the Persians would return with one of the largest combined naval and land forces ever seen in the ancient world.

Administering the empire

When Cyrus II took power he was content to simply take over the existing administrative system he had inherited from his subjects. He probably did this because the Persians did not have the bureaucratic for travellers.[41] The roads were used for royal communications and for dispatching armies to troubled areas. They were also the lifelines of trade and were used by merchants for transporting goods; the more freely and safely merchants could travel to carry out their business and trade, the more prosperous the country would be. The road system was established by determining how far a horse and rider could travel in a day. Rest houses or posting stages were built at regular intervals along the road with grooms and supplies to maintain the riders and their horses, plus a place for them to eat and rest. Like their administrative system, the Persian road system used and expanded the royal road system originally put in place by the Assyrians two centuries earlier[42] (see Ch. 6). A number of permanent bridges were also built, spanning the great rivers such as the Tigris, Euphrates, Diyala, and the Greater and Lesser Zab Rivers, as well as the Halys River in distant Anatolia. The exact nature and type of construction of the bridges is unclear, but they were probably pontoon bridges consisting of a number of boats tied together over which a roadway was constructed. For economic and political stability, Persian rulers understood they had to build and maintain roads and canals as well as repair city walls, temples and palaces, storehouses, granaries, and harbour facilities. All these activities required a massive investment of resources and good management to see projects through to completion.

Early in his reign Darius I rebuilt the city of Susa and constructed a giant palace, 250 m on a side, containing hundreds of rooms. This palace became the principal residence of subsequent Persian kings. He also built a new residence some 400 km southeast of Susa at a place he called Parsa, but which is better known by its Greek name, Persepolis.[43] The main citadel was an enormous stone terrace, 450 m long by 300 m wide, which formed part of a vast complex that included many small palaces in the surrounding area. The building project was so expansive it was not completed in his lifetime, but continued during the reigns of his son and even his grandson. Until the creation of the Achaemenid Empire, the Persians had not been great builders, and skilled masons, woodworkers, and other specialized craftsmen had to be brought in from the four corners of the empire.[44] Darius undertook many building projects in other parts of the empire too.[45] Because they did not have their own monumental building tradition, Persian styles are eclectic, and the architectural motifs and decorations at Susa and Persepolis show influences from Mesopotamia, Egypt, and Greece.

Darius I in Egypt

Unlike his predecessor, Cambyses II, Greek classical sources depict Darius I as an intelligent, just, and generous ruler.[46] Early in his reign he convened the educated men of his kingdom to collect and record all the Egyptian writings on legislation down to the rule of the Egyptian pharaoh, Amasis II (570–526 BC). This project lasted for ten years. Darius I also resumed construction on the canal between the Nile River and the Red Sea begun by Necho II during the 26th Dynasty. The opening of the canal was a great event, probably as important as the opening of the Suez Canal by the French and the British 2500 years later. The first group of ships to pass through the canal were 24 vessels carrying goods to Persia.[47] To mark the opening, 24 large stone stelae praising Darius I's accomplishments were set up along the banks of the canal. Preserved fragments of these stelae show that they were inscribed in four languages, including Egyptian, Elamite, Akkadian, and, of course, Persian. They were decorated with the *sema-tawy*, the symbol that shows the two kingdoms being tied together, and represented Darius I as responsible for the continued union of Upper and Lower Egypt. Figures of the diverse subject peoples of the empire are shown pledging their loyalty to Darius I.

When the next Apis bull died, funds were collected throughout the kingdom to ensure that the sacred animal would have a proper burial, and to emphasize Persian respect for Egyptian religious practices. At the el-Kharga Oasis he built a great temple dedicated to the god Amun and other deities. In the temple Darius I is depicted as the pharaoh in the company of gods and goddesses. In one low-relief the goddess Mut is nursing him, and there is a rendering of Darius I seated on a throne over the *sema-tawy* unification symbol. Taken together, these artistic representations, building projects, and liberal use of Egyptian symbolism indicate that Darius I was wise enough to show respect for the religion, culture, and traditions of the Egyptians.

A remarkable discovery occurred in 1972, when French archaeologists excavating at Susa discovered a 3 m-high statue of Darius I.[48] The statue is inscribed in the four languages of the major groups of people under Persian rule – Elamite, Persian, Egyptian, and Akkadian – and praises the god Ahura-Mazda. Each depiction of the 24 peoples or ethnic groups shows unique facial features, native dress, and hairstyles. Unlike Egyptian depictions of subject peoples from earlier times, the people on the Darius statue are not shown as prisoners, but with their hands unfettered and extended upwards towards their new leader, the Persian pharaoh Darius I. This seems to indicate a spirit of acceptance and détente between the Persian ruler and his conquered subjects.

Egyptian rebellions against the Persians

Despite Persian attempts to appear benevolent and to create stronger bonds between themselves and their conquered subjects, there were still many Egyptians who wanted to rid the Two Lands of their Persian overlords. On at least three occasions between 486 and 343 BC, the Egyptians managed to overthrow their Persian rulers, with varying degrees of success.

The first attempt to oust the Persians occurred in 486 BC, but resulted in only a temporary re-establishment of native Egyptian power. The second occurred in 465 BC, when Inaros came to the throne for a short period. Finally, a third armed struggle saw the return of native Egyptians to the throne of the Two Lands in 404 BC.[49] This third period of independence lasted for 60 years until 343 BC.

The Egyptian rebellion of 486 BC

When Darius I died in 486 BC he was succeeded by the crown prince, Xerxes II, who reigned until 465 BC. The new king was the son of Atossa, one of Cyrus II's daughters, one of the women Darius I had married to prevent the creation of a rival dynasty. Atossa was a powerful woman who influenced at least three Persian kings: Cyrus II, Darius I, and Xerxes II. Despite temple-building programmes and other positive initiatives instituted by Persian leaders, the Egyptians wanted to rid the country of foreign conquerors and the year Darius I died, they rebelled against their Persian rulers. To counteract armed rebellions Xerxes II instituted a new policy towards nations that did not cooperate with their Persian overlords. Unlike Cambyses II and Darius I, who respected Egyptian customs and religion, Xerxes II vented his anger by ignoring Egyptian forms of rule and imposing his will on his rebellious subjects; he used the same policy in Babylonia a few years later. After a rebellion in Babylonia was put down in 482 BC, he ruled as a conqueror, not as the legitimate successor to previous kings of Mesopotamia.

Once revolts in both Babylonia and Egypt were put down, Xerxes II decided to revenge the Persian losses suffered by Darius I in Greece ten years earlier by making major territorial advances into southern Europe. After years of preparation for the occasion, Xerxes headed into Greek territory, marching his foot soldiers and their supplies over a floating pontoon bridge he had his engineers build across the Dardanelles straits. Compared to Greek forces, his army was huge, with perhaps as many as 350 000 soldiers,[50] but much smaller than the 1 700 000 claimed by Herodotus.[51] Despite his planning and preparations the Persians were defeated at a number of key battles, including the famous naval battle off the island of Salamis in 480 BC.[52] The Greek wars ended in failure resulting in significant losses for the Persians, and after a major defeat at the battle of Plataea in 479 BC the Persians were forced to withdraw from southern Europe and western Anatolia.

It is helpful to place the Egyptian quest for independence in the context of the whole Persian Empire. Egypt was not the only *satrapy* trying to reassert local rule. Similar struggles went on periodically in Greece, the eastern Mediterranean, and Mesopotamia, and created situations that were often quite unstable. The series of defeats suffered by the Persians at the hands of the Greeks had a profound effect on Egyptians who wanted to throw off the yoke of Persian rule.[53] Since Xerxes II was occupied at home dealing with internal problems, he appointed his son, Achaemenes, as the *satrap* (governor) of Egypt. Like his father, Achaemenes was also known for his cruelty, and he put down the Egyptian revolt with great brutality that was not forgotten by the defeated Egyptians.

The rebellion of Inaros

A few years later, in 465 BC, Inaros proclaimed himself pharaoh and took control of the Delta region of Lower Egypt. Unfortunately for him, the rest of the country, including Upper Egypt and the northern city of Memphis, did not join the revolt. However, the Athenian navy came to his aid and this time the Egyptian rebels killed Achaemenes, and emerged victorious, at least for a short period of time. The new Persian king, Artaxerxes I (465–424 BC) who was occupied over a thousand kilometres away with palace intrigues at home could not free himself and his troops to quell the Egyptian uprising. Instead, Artaxerxes sent his general, Megabyses, who defeated the Egyptian forces and had Inaros crucified. Despite initial success with the aid of their Greek allies, the Egyptians were once again defeated, and brought under the yoke of Persian rule for another half century.

The return of Egyptian independence

Some years later, and relying once again on their Greek allies in the city-state of Sparta, the Egyptian army under General Amyrtaios fought a nine-year struggle with Persian forces, and by 404 BC he took the throne at the head of an independent Egypt. But his short-lived 28th Egyptian Dynasty only lasted five years until 399 BC. The centre of Egyptian power then shifted to the city of Mendes, the capital during the 29th Dynasty. This dynasty included five kings and lasted until 378 BC. The 30th Dynasty (380–343 BC) lasted nearly twice as long and included three Egyptian kings.

The last native-born pharaoh of ancient Egypt was Nectanebo II, who ruled an independent Egypt for 16 years from 359 to 343 BC. Throughout the fourth century BC the Persians continued to lose their control over their western territories, and by the middle of century they could only maintain their presence in Egypt for little more than a decade. The last Persian Dynasty in Egyptian history, the 31st Dynasty, began with the reconquest of Egypt under Artaxerxes III in 343 BC. This final, short-lived period of Persian domination was made up of three Persian kings who could only hold on to power for a mere 11 years before they lost their control over the Two Lands in 332 BC. At that time a new conqueror and a new dynasty from southern Europe came to power in the Near East. A young and talented king from northern Greece dashed across the stage of history and quickly conquered Egypt, Mesopotamia, and the remnants of the Persian Empire in Iran. His name was Alexander III of Macedonia; he is also known as Alexander the Great.

The period of Persian rule of both Mesopotamia and Egypt was followed by a period of Greek or "Hellenistic" rule under Alexander the Great and his successors in Mesopotamia from 311 to 146 BC, and in Egypt until the death of Cleopatra in 30 BC. Greek rule in Egypt from the time of Alexander to the beginning of the Roman period in Egypt is known as the Ptolemaic period (332 to 30 BC) and ended when Egypt became a province of the Roman Empire.

In the east, after Alexander's death in 323 BC, the Greeks maintained control of Babylonia and even enjoyed popular support for a while.[54] A few years later, Seleucus I (305–281 BC), one of Alexander's successors, took control of Media, Persia, and Susa, and his short-lived empire stretched from Mesopotamia to Central Asia. The period of Greek rule in Mesopotamia from 311–146 BC is called the Seleucid period, and marks the time of greatest Greek cultural, political, and economic influence in the Tigris and Euphrates river valleys and Iran.

During the Seleucid period numerous Greek colonies were established throughout Mesopotamia, and Greek culture made a lasting impression on the region. Greek forms of architecture and art spread throughout many parts of the former Persian Empire. Greek law, theatre, philosophy, and literature were known from the Nile river valley all the way across the Iranian Plateau. With the Greek demise in the east and the shrinking of their power, first the Parni, or Parthians and then the Sassanians, both descendants of the Persians,[55] came to power. The Parthians[56] struggled against the Romans, who had replaced the Seleucids, and finally drove them out of Mesopotamia. Later the Sassanians[57] maintained control over Mesopotamia and Iran until the arrival of Islam, a new religious and cultural force that came out of the Arabian Peninsula and swept the eastern territories about AD 650. While the east was divided up between the Persians, Greeks, Parthians, and Sassanians, Egypt remained under the control of the Greeks and then the Romans. After centuries of occupation local leaders eventually regained control in Mesopotamia in the first millennium AD, but Egypt remained under foreign rule until AD 1952.

Epilogue
The twilight of the first civilizations

In less than two decades, first Mesopotamia (539 BC) and then Egypt (525 BC) fell victim to the Persians, and their collective conquests marked a turning point, the beginning of the end, of the two great river civilizations of the ancient Orient. Although they still experienced moments of greatness in art, architecture, literature, and religion, over the next few centuries both Egypt and Mesopotamia gradually lost many of their original and defining cultural characteristics. In the early years after the Persian conquest the two countries were managed reasonably well, and the average peasant or labourer probably perceived little difference in their lives or how things were run. However, in the final years of Persian rule temples were looted and burned, city defences razed, and precious manuscripts burned in an effort to suppress rebellion among native Egyptians and Babylonians. As in Egypt, when the Persians took over Mesopotamia it became one *satrapy* among many in a vast world empire that spanned thousands of kilometres, stretching from the southeastern tip of Europe all the way to India. Starting with the Persians the centre of power moved from the Nile and Tigris–Euphrates river valleys, to the Iranian Plateau, and then, under the control of the Greeks and later the Romans it moved to Europe.

From the fifth to the first century BC, outside influences pushed the traditional culture of Mesopotamia aside and its inhabitants, particularly the ruling elite, were forced to adopt new ways. The cuneiform script, which had been in use for more than 25 cen-turies, was progressively marginalized and replaced by alphabetic scripts, such as Aramaic and Greek, written on papyrus or parchment instead of clay tablets. Although the Persians and later Greeks did build new cities in the Tigris–Euphrates region, many major building projects were shifted to the Persian heartland, which had become the centre of political power in the ancient world, while in Mesopotamia palaces and temples fell into disuse and city walls crumbled. Under the Persians important trade routes by-passed cities like Nineveh[1] and Babylon,[2] forcing their inhabitants to move elsewhere to find their fortunes, and leaving these once great cities substantially diminished or, in some cases, abandoned.

Even though the Persians were generally tolerant of the religious beliefs and customs of the peoples they conquered, their greedy taxation schemes sapped the economic strength of Mesopotamia, Egypt, and surrounding countries. After their conquest, the residents of Babylonia and Assyria were forced to contribute immense sums of gold and food each year for the upkeep of the Persian court in Susa and Persepolis. Within a century prices doubled while wages stayed the same. Mesopotamia was no longer the land of opportunity it had once been, as bankers charged exorbitant annual interest rates of 40–50 per cent on loans to an increasingly impoverished population.[3] Despite deteriorating conditions, the city of Babylon remained a sacred site well into the third century BC, and kings like Antiochus I (281–260 BC) and Seleucus III (225–223 BC)[4] made offerings to the old gods and maintained at least some of their temples. But by the first century BC the city of Babylon had lost much of its population. Among the people remaining were a handful of astronomers and astrologers who lived among the city's ruins while clinging to the mostly discarded cuneiform writing system, and to the ancient city that symbolized the greatness of the once-vibrant Mesopotamian culture. Although other parts of Mesopotamia did eventually prosper once again, it was centuries before they recovered fully from earlier conflicts. Many of the ancient Sumerian cities languished, Nineveh was not the capital of a great empire, and Babylon was finally abandoned. When the Greek soldier Xenophon[5] marched his army past the broken-down walls of the city of Nineveh in 401 BC, it was deserted, and he failed to realize that the crumbled ruins (which he mistakenly called "Larissa") were once the capital of the mighty Assyrian Empire. Changes in the ethnic composition of the region also took their toll on Mesopotamian civilization as increasing numbers of Persians, and later Greeks, after Alexander the Great, moved into the Tigris–Euphrates river valley.

Egypt did prosper under the Greeks, despite foreign rule. Art flourished and some of the best examples of temple architecture were created in Egypt during the Late and Ptolemaic periods; the old religions and writing systems of Egypt survived intact for many centuries into Roman times. But with the spread of Greek and later Roman cultures – which included theatre, philosophy, mathematics, and new religions – the old pharaonic culture slowly died out. As the once-great temples and palaces were abandoned by their priests and worshippers the structures crumbled, were used as stone quarries for new building projects, or were burnt for lime fertilizer. In AD 356, Emperor Constantius II began closing Egyptian temples. The old religions suffered an additional blow in AD 391 when the priests of the Serapeum temple were all massacred, and by AD 395 Emperor Theodosius declared Christianity the official state religion of the Roman Empire, including Egypt. From that time on

Great pylons of the Temple of Horus at Edfu, built during the Hellenistic period (323–30 BC). The structure was begun by Ptolemy III Euergetes in 237 BC and finished in 57 BC by Ptolemy XIII. Niches held flagstaffs of the gods Horus and Hathor.

Columns from the Temple of Horus and Hathor at Edfu.

the religions of Egypt, which had existed for millennia, were forbidden by royal decree. By the fifth century AD, no one could read the hieroglyphic signs of ancient Egyptian, and the key to understanding their past was lost for more than 1400 years.

Mesopotamia and Egypt were the first regions on earth to adapt to changing population and climatic conditions in the millennia after the end of the last Ice Age, which brought about agriculture and the formation of the first civilizations. Elements of city life and social organization that can be traced back to the ancient Near East are still deeply rooted in modern societies and, to some extent, modern people share a common, albeit distant, bond with the civilizations of ancient Mesopotamia and ancient Egypt. Although the people of Mesopotamia and Egypt were the first to develop civilization, this does not mean that without them civilization would never have originated. The domestication of plants and animals, and the formation of complex societies, occurred independently in China and the New World and gave rise to the Olmecs, Incas, and Aztecs, without any contact with Egypt and Mesopotamia. Had civilization not developed first in the Tigris–Euphrates and Nile river valleys it most certainly would have developed elsewhere.

It would be inaccurate to say that either Egypt or Mesopotamia was superior to the other. Both were vital forces in the formation of early civilization. On the other hand, each possessed special talents and uniqueness that deserve to be mentioned. Ultimately, the character of any civilization is determined by its technology, institutions, and ideology. In the early periods of Mesopotamian history, a number of impressive inventions and innovations appeared that we in the modern world consider essential for the formation of civilization. In addition to being pioneers in the development of irrigation agriculture, cities, writing, and monumental architecture, the peoples of Mesopotamia produced the wheel and the plough, and then domesticated oxen, the tractors of the ancient world, to pull them. They built the first major road and postal systems, gathered together the first sizeable archives of written material, and took the first steps towards creating scientific astronomy. Along with these innovations are the characters and themes of Near Eastern literature and mythology, which have become the staples of our own Western traditions through the Bible and Greek and Roman literature.[6] Despite their important role in the past, there is no "mania",[7] no deep-felt attraction, in the modern world for things Mesopotamian.[8] Why this is so is unclear, but one reason may be that many Mesopotamian monumental structures and works of art are poorly preserved and unknown to the general public.

Egypt also made a number of important innovations, particularly in medicine, and calendar reckoning, but also in the visual arts, architecture, literature, and religion. Like Mesopotamia, Egyptian mythological stories and religious themes have made their way into the religions and literary traditions of the West. Egyptian masonry construction was unsurpassed anywhere in the ancient Near East, and when it comes to the beauty and grandeur of their mortuary structures and funerary preparations, no one in the ancient world could surpass the Egyptians.

Columns from the Temple of Horus and Hathor at Edfu.

Khafre and Khufu Pyramids, 4th Dynasty.

Stairway at Dur-Kurigalzu (Aqar Quf), Iraq, Kassite period.

Even though both Mesopotamia and Egypt left their imprints on the history and culture of the ancient world, it is Egypt that is most often remembered when modern people think of the world before the Greeks and Romans. The ancient Egyptians, their beautiful works of art, illuminated writing system, great temples, and majestic pyramids have succeeded in capturing the modern imagination. Egypt, probably more than any other ancient civilization, serves as a link to the past for modern people. In many ways it is the concept of Egypt as a land of beauty and mystery that is its greatest contribution to our collective memory. The fascination with ancient Egypt, "Egyptomania", can be seen today in films, books, visual arts, architecture, and even popular music. The uniqueness of Egypt is due in part to the art and architecture associated with death and the afterlife. The Egyptians buried their dead in subterranean chambers, often surrounded by paintings, jewellery, and sculpture: masterpieces of visual art. Perhaps it has something to do with the fear and mystery associated with death, but many people find skeletons and old cadavers wrapped with strips of cloth fascinating, and have a keen interest in mummies and the preparation of the dead for internment. In addition, the shape of the pyramids, as well as their size and grandeur, have a kind of mystical power that draws people to study and contemplate them.

But the first civilizations have not been lost forever. They live on today through the continued research of historians, archaeologists, and linguists. Egypt and Mesopotamia are archaeological time machines, open air museums for everyone to see and appreciate. Despite wars, both ancient and modern, and the ravages of time, portions of the broken mud-brick walls and palaces of Ashur and Babylon and the crumbled remains of the ziggurats of Ur and Nippur still remain today, and the grandeur of the temples of Karnak, Luxor, and Abu Simbel can easily be seen by visitors. The remains of pyramids still stand and, along the Nile, rock-cut tombs display their beautiful paintings. A few even contain mummies, sleeping away the centuries while visiting tourists gaze on. This combined legacy of art, architecture, and intellectual innovation creates a bridge between modern peoples and the cultural heritage of the first civilizations: ancient Mesopotamia and ancient Egypt.

Archaeological research at Nineveh, northern Iraq.

Notes

1: History and archaeology as tools for understanding the past

1. See Hans J. Nissen, "Mesopotamia: Prehistoric Mesopotamia" and "Mesopotamia: Ancient Mesopotamia", in *The Oxford Encyclopedia of Archaeology in the Near East*, E. Meyers (ed.), **3**, 476–84 (Oxford University Press, Oxford, 1997).
2. See A. Kirk Grayson, "Mesopotamia (Place)", in *The Anchor Bible Dictionary*, D. N. Freedman (ed.), **4**, 714 (Doubleday, Garden City, 1992).
3. Seton Lloyd, *The Archaeology of Mesopotamia* (Thames & Hudson, London, 1978), 12.
4. For an overview see Fredrick Cryer, "Chronology, Issues and Problems", in *Civilizations of the Ancient Near East*, J. Sasson (ed.), **1**, 651–64 (Charles Scribner's Sons, New York, 1995); Ian Shaw, "Introduction: Chronologies and Cultural Change in Egypt", in *The Oxford History of Ancient Egypt*, I. Shaw (ed.), 1–16 (Oxford University Press, Oxford, 2000); and Leo Dupydt, "On the Consistency of the Wandering Year as the Backbone of Egyptian Chronology", *Journal of the American Research Center in Egypt* **32** (1995), 43–58.
5. Anthony Spalinger, "Calendars", in *The Oxford Encyclopedia of Ancient Egypt*, D. Redford (ed.), **1**, 224–7 (Oxford University Press, Oxford, 2001).
6. The Sothic cycle is problematic and not everyone is in agreement about its exact length. The traditional length of 1460 years used in most publications is probably too high by at least four years, perhaps more. For a discussion see Rolf Kraus, *Sothis- und Monddaten: Studien zur astronomischen und technischen Chronologie Altägyptens* (Hildesheim, 1985), 86–127; Marshal Clagett, *Ancient Egyptian Science, Volume II, Calendars, Clocks and Astronomy* (American Philosophical Society, Philadelphia, 1995), 307–39; and Shaw (ed.), *The Oxford History of Ancient Egypt*, 11, 450.
7. See Asger Aaboe, "Babylonian Mathematics, Astrology, and Astronomy", in *The Cambridge Ancient History Volume 3, Part 2: The Assyrian and Babylonian Empires and Other States of the Near East, from the Eighth to the Sixth Centuries BC*, J. Boardman *et al.* (eds), 276–92 (Cambridge University Press, Cambridge, 1992), 280.
8. Simo Parpola, *Letters From Assyrian Scholars to the Kings Esarhaddon and Assurbanipal*, Alter Orient und Altes Testament 5, 2 vols (Butzon & Bercker, Kevelaer/Neukirchener, Neukirchen-Vluyn, 1970–1983).
9. Alan Gardiner, *Egypt of the Pharaohs* (Oxford University Press, Oxford, 1961), Ch. 15; and Cryer, "Chronology, Issues and Problems", 659.
10. Thorkild Jacobsen, *The Sumerian King List*, Assyriological Studies No. 11 (University of Chicago Press, Chicago, 1939); and Bernard Knapp, "Mesopotamia, History of (Chronology)", in Freedman (ed.), *The Anchor Bible Dictionary*, **4**, 714–20.
11. A. L. Oppenheim, "Babylonian and Assyrian Historical Texts", in *Ancient Near Eastern Texts Relating to the Old Testament*, 3rd edn, J. B. Pritchard (ed.), 305–12, 564–6 (Princeton University Press, Princeton, 1969); and Kirk Grayson, *Assyrian and Babylonian Chronicles* (J. J. Augustin, Locust Valley/Glückstadt Germany, 1989) and "Histories and Historians of the Ancient Near East", *Orientalia* **49** (1980), 1–51.
12. See C. C. Lamberg-Karlovsky and Jeremy Sabloff, *Ancient Civilizations: The Near East and Mesoamerica* (Waveland Press, Prospect Heights, 1995), Ch. 1.
13. E. H. Carr, *What is History?* (Pelican Books, Harmondsworth, 1961), 8.
14. Trevor Bryce, "The Trojan War: Is There Truth Behind the Legend?", *Near Eastern Archaeology* **65** (2002), 182–95; Hans Günter Jansen, "Troy: Legend and Reality", in Sasson (ed.), *Civilizations of the Ancient Near East*, 1121–34; and William H. Stiebing Jr, *Uncovering the Past: A History of Archaeology* (Prometheus Books, Buffalo, 1993), 123–34.
15. Heinrich Schliemann, *Ilios: The City and Country of the*

Trojans (John Murray Publishers, London, 1880).
16. Steibing, *Uncovering the Past*, 110–11.
17. Michel Fortin, "Rapport préliminaire sur la seconde campagne de fouilles (printemps 1987) a Tell 'Atij, sur le Moyen Khabour", *Syria* **67** (1990), 219–50, "Trois campagnes de fouilles à Tell 'Atij: Un comptoir commercial du IIIème millénaire en Syrie du Nord", *The Bulletin of the Canadian Society for Mesopotamian Studies* **18** (1989), 35–56, "Résultats de la 4ème Campagne de Fouilles à Tell 'Atij et à Tell Gudeda", *Echos du Monde Classique/Classical Views* **32**(12) (1993), 97–121 and *Syria, Land of Civilizations*, J. Macaulay (trans.) (Musée de la Civilization, Québec/Éditions de L'Homme, Montréal, 1999); and with Lisa Cooper, "Canadian Excavations at Tell 'Atij (Syria) 1992–1993", *The Bulletin of the Canadian Society for Mesopotamian Studies* **27** (May 1994), 33–50.
18. John Holladay, "Stratigraphy", in Meyers (ed.), *Oxford Encyclopedia of Archaeology*, **5**, 82–9; and Martha Joukowsky, *A Complete Manual of Field Archaeology: Tools and Techniques of Fieldwork for Archaeologists* (Prentice-Hall, Englewood Cliffs, NJ, 1980), Ch. 7.
19. H. J. Franken, "Pottery", in Freedman (ed.), *The Anchor Bible Dictionary*, **5**, 429–32; and James Armstrong, "Ceramics: Mesopotamian Ceramics", in Meyers (ed.), *Oxford Encyclopedia of Archaeology*, **1**, 453–9.
20. Daniel Snell, "Methods of Exchange and Coinage in Ancient Western Asia", in Sasson (ed.), *Civilizations of the Ancient Near East*, **3**, 1494; and John Betlyon, "Coinage", in Freedman (ed.), *The Anchor Bible Dictionary*, **2**, 1078–83.
21. See Chapter 2, note 21.
22. J.-C. Margueron, "Mari, l'Euphrat, et le Khabur au milieu du IIIème millénaire", *The Bulletin of the Canadian Society for Mesopotamian Studies* **21** (May 1991), 79–100 (esp. 95) and "Mari (Archaeology)", in Freedman (ed.), *The Anchor Bible Dictionary*, **4**, 525–9; and Jean-Marie Durand, "Mari (Texts)", in Freedman (ed.), *The Anchor Bible Dictionary*, **4**, 525–38.

2: Agriculture and the origins of civilization

1. See Charles Redman, *The Rise of Civilization: From Early Farmers to Urban Society in the Ancient Near East* (W. H. Freeman, San Francisco, 1978), 216–17; Ofer Bar-Yosef, "The Neolithic Period", in *The Archaeology of Ancient Israel*, A. Ben-Tor (ed.), 10–39 (Yale University Press, New Haven, 1992); and Lamberg-Karlovsky and Sabloff, *Ancient Civilizations*, Ch. 2.
2. David C. Hopkins, "Agriculture", in Meyers (ed.), *Oxford Encyclopedia of Archaeology*, **1**, 22–31.
3. Christopher Eyre, "The Agricultural Cycle, Farming, and Water Management in the Ancient Near East", in Sasson (ed.), *Civilizations of the Ancient Near East*, **1**, 175–89; Brian Hesse, "Animal Husbandry and Human Diet in the Ancient Near East", in Sasson (ed.), *Civilizations of the Ancient Near East*, **1**, 203–22; and Robert J. Wenke, *Patterns in Prehistory* (Oxford University Press, Oxford, 1990), 226–31.
4. Redman, *The Rise of Civilization*, Ch. 4; and Lamberg-Karlovsky and Sabloff, *Ancient Civilizations*, 41.
5. Wenke, *Patterns in Prehistory*, 338, estimates that Uruk had a population of 50 000 by 3000 BC. Elizabeth Stone, "The Development of Cities in Ancient Mesopotamia", in Sasson (ed.), *Civilizations of the Ancient Near East*, **1**, 235–48, estimates populations from 10 000 to 100 000. Hans J. Nissen, *The Early History of the Ancient Near East: 9000–2000 BC* (University of Chicago Press, Chicago, 1988), 10–11, defines city in terms of centre and space, or a central area and its relationship with surrounding territories. See also Henri Frankfort, *The Birth of Civilization in the Near East* (Anchor Press/Doubleday, New York, 1956), 49–89.
6. See the discussion in Wenke, *Patterns in Prehistory*, 287–8, 344; and Redman, *The Rise of Civilization*, 249–51.
7. Redman, *The Rise of Civilization*, 270–74; and notes 22 and 23 below.
8. Edwin Firmage, "Zoology", in Freedman (ed.), *The Anchor Bible Dictionary*, **6**, 1109–67.
9. Hesse, "Animal Husbandry and Human Diet", 206–13.
10. James Mellaart, *The Neolithic of the Near East* (Thames & Hudson, London, 1975), 28–38; Wenke, *Patterns in Prehistory*, 228; and Redman, *The Rise of Civilization*, 92.
11. V. Gordon Childe, *New Light on the Most Ancient East* (Praeger, New York, 1952), 25.
12. Childe, *New Light*, 25.
13. Redman, *The Rise of Civilization*, 98, 113, 115.
14. Robert Braidwood and B. Howe, *Prehistoric Investigations in Iraqi Kurdistan* (University of Chicago Press, Chicago, 1960); and Robert Braidwood, "Prehistoric Investigations in Southwestern Asia", *Proceedings of the American Philosophical Society* **116**(4) (1962), 310–20.
15. Redman, *The Rise of Civilization*, 78–81.
16. *Ibid.*, 97.
17. Richard Lee, "What Hunters do for a Living, or How to Make Out on Scarce Resources", in *Man the Hunter*, R. Lee (ed.), 30–48 (Aldine, Chicago, 1968); and Redman, *The Rise of Civilization*, 90.
18. Philip E. L. Smith and T. Cuyler Young Jr., "The Force of Numbers: Population Pressure in the Central W Zagros", in *The Hilly Flanks and Beyond, Volum* P. E. L. Smith *et al.* (eds), 141–62 (Oriental Institute lications, Chicago, 1983).
19. Mark N. Cohen, *The Food Crisis in Prehistory* (Yale University Press, New Haven, 1977), 279. But see Wenke, *Patterns in Prehistory*, 263.
20. Redman, *The Rise of Civilization*, 97; and Wenke, *Patterns in Prehistory*, 240–43.
21. Redman, *The Rise of Civilization*, 92. For an opposing view see Wenke, *Patterns in Prehistory*, 265–6.
22. Redman, *The Rise of Civilization*, 103–5.
23. *Ibid.*, 196, and plan.
24. Guillermo Algaze, *The Uruk World System* (University of Chicago Press, Chicago, 1993).
25. Denise Schmandt-Besserat, "The Earliest Precursor of Writing", *Scientific American* **238** (1978), 50–59, "An Ancient Token System: A Precursor to Numerals and Writing", *Archaeology* (Nov/Dec 1986), 32–9, *Before Writing, Volume I: From Counting to Cuneiform* (University of Texas Press, Austin, 1992), *Before Writing, Volume II, A Catalogue of Near Eastern Tokens* (University of Texas Press, Austin, 1992), and "Record Keeping Before Writing", in Sasson (ed.), *Civilizations of the Ancient Near East*, **4**, 2097–106; and Sabah Abboud Jasim and Joan Oates, "Early Tokens and Tablets in Mesopotamia", *World Archaeology* **17**(3) (1986), 348–62. See also the comments of H. Vanstiphout, "Memory and Literacy in Ancient Western Asia", in Sasson (ed.), *Civilizations of the Ancient Near East*, **4**, 2181–6. For opposing views see Paul Zimansky, "A Review of Schmandt-Besserat 1992", *Journal of Field Archaeology* **20** (1993), 513–17; Stephen Lieberman, "Of Clay Pebbles, Hollow Clay Balls, and Writing: A Sumerian View", *American Journal of Archaeology* **84** (1980), 339–58.
26. Schmandt-Besserat, "Record Keeping Before Writing", **4**, 2097–106, esp. 2102.
27. Christopher Walker, *Cuneiform* (University of California Press, Berkley, 1987), Preface; and Beatrice André-Leicknam and C. Ziegler, *Naissance de l'ecriture* (Éditions de la Réunion des Musées Nationaux, Paris, 1982). For the decipherment of the languages of the ancient Near East see Peter Daniels, "The Decipherment of Ancient Near Eastern Texts", in Sasson (ed.), *Civilizations of the Ancient Near East*, **1**, 81–93.
28. François Vallat, "The Most Ancient Scripts of Iran: The Current Situation", *World Archaeology* **17**(3) (1986), 335–47; André Lemaire, "Writing and Writing Materials", in Freedman (ed.), *The Anchor Bible Dictionary*, **6**, 999–1008; and Dietz Otto Edzard, "The Sumerian Lan-

guage", in Sasson (ed.), *Civilizations of the Ancient Near East*, **4**, 2107–116.

29. Burchard Brentjes, "The History of Elam and Achaemenid Persia: An Overview", in Sasson (ed.), *Civilizations of the Ancient Near East*, **2**, 1001–21; Vallat, "The Most Ancient Scripts of Iran", Ch. 4.

30. Shaw (ed.), *The Oxford History of Ancient Egypt*, 78.

31. Richard Wilkinson, *Reading Egyptian Art* (Thames & Hudson, London, 1992), 9–12; and Cyril Aldred, *Egyptian Art* (Thames & Hudson, New York/London, 1980), 17.

32. André Lemaire, "Writing and Writing Materials", **6**, 999–1008.

33. Antonio Loprieno, "Egyptian", in Meyers (ed.), *Oxford Encyclopedia of Archaeology*, **2**, 208–13.

34. Antonio Loprieno, "Ancient Egyptian and Other Afroasiatic Languages", in Sasson (ed.), *Civilizations of the Ancient Near East*, **4**, 2135–50, esp. 2139.

35. Donald Redford, *Egypt, Canaan, and Israel in Ancient Times* (Princeton University Press, Princeton, 1992), 18 and n. 65; H. W. F. Saggs, *Civilization Before Greece and Rome* (Yale University Press, New Haven, 1989), 72; and John D. Ray, "The Emergence of Writing in Egypt", *World Archaeology* **17**(3) (1986), 309.

36. However, new evidence from Abydos may force a reinterpretation of this long-held idea. See Eugene Cruz-Uribe, "Scripts", in Redford (ed.), *Oxford Encyclopedia of Ancient Egypt*, **3**, 192–8, esp. 192.

37. William D. Whitt, "The Story of the Semitic Alphabet", in Sasson (ed.), *Civilizations of the Ancient Near East*, **4**, 2380–82; and Ernst Doblehofer, *Voices in Stone* (Paladin, London, 1973), 203–5.

38. Whitt, "The Story of the Semitic Alphabet", 2384–5; and M. Carter and K. Schoville, *Sign, Symbol, Script* (University of Wisconsin, Madison, 1984), 32–47.

39. Lemaire, "Writing and Writing Materials", 1000.

40. Jonathan Tubb, *Canaanites* (University of Oklahoma Press, Norman, 1998), 14.

41. Redman, *The Rise of Civilization*, Ch. 7.

42. *Ibid.*, 18, 29, 237, 268.

43. John F. Robertson, "The Social and Economic Organization of Ancient Mesopotamian Temples", in Sasson (ed.), *Civilizations of the Ancient Near East*, **1**, 443–54, esp. 448; and Michael Roaf, *Cultural Atlas of Mesopotamia and the Ancient Near East* (Facts on File, New York, 1990), 58–78.

44. For a discussion of the word *edin* see Howard Wallace, "Eden, Garden of", in Freedman (ed.), *The Anchor Bible Dictionary*, **2**, 281–3.

45. See Genesis 2:14; and Mark Stratton Smith, "Myth and Mythmaking in Canaan and Ancient Israel", in Sasson (ed.), *Civilizations of the Ancient Near East*, **4**, 2038–9.

46. Algaze, *The Uruk World System*.

47. Robert McCormick Adams and Hans J. Nissen, *The Uruk Countryside: The Natural Setting of Urban Societies* (University of Chicago Press, Chicago, 1972), 9–33; and Redman, *The Rise of Civilization*, 265.

48. Robert McCormick Adams, *Heartland of Cities: Surveys of Ancient Settlement and Land Use on the Central Floodplain of the Euphrates* (University of Chicago Press, Chicago, 1981), 71.

49. Adams and Nissen, *The Uruk Countryside*, 17–18, 21; and Charles Maisels, *The Emergence of Civilization* (Routledge, London, 1990), Ch. 6.

50. Adams and Nissen, *The Uruk Countryside*.

3: The Early Dynastic period and the formation of the first city-states

1. W. T. Wright, "Mesopotamia, History of (Prehistory)", in Freedman (ed.), *The Anchor Bible Dictionary*, **4**, 720–24.

2. For brief overviews see Piotr Michalowski, "Sumerians", in Meyers (ed.), *Oxford Encyclopedia of the Archaeology*, **5**, 95–101; Amélie Kuhrt, *The Ancient Near East c.3000–330 BC*, 2 vols (Routledge, London, 1995), **1**, 19–73; Jerrold Cooper, "Sumerians", in Freedman (ed.), *The Anchor Bible Dictionary*, **6**, 231–4; and George Roux, *Ancient Iraq*, 2nd edn (Penguin Books, Harmondsworth, 1980), Chs 5–8. Book length treatments include S.N. Kramer, *History Begins at Sumer* (Doubleday, New York, 1959), *The Sumerians* (University of Chicago Press, Chicago, 1963); and Harriet Crawford, *Sumer and the Sumerians* (Cambridge University Press, Cambridge, 1991).

3. Joan Oates, *Babylon* (Thames & Hudson, London, 1986), 22; and Cooper, "Sumerians", 233.

4. Piotr Steinkeller, "Mesopotamia, History of, (Third Millennium BC)", in Freedman (ed.), *The Anchor Bible Dictionary*, **4**, 724–32.

5. Frank S. Frick, "Cities: An Overview", in Meyers (ed.), *Oxford Encyclopedia of Archaeology*, **2**, 14–17.

6. Redman, *The Rise of Civilization*, 319. Numbers range from 100 to 230 inhabitants per hectare. See Stone, "The Development of Cities", 244. See Nissen, *Early History of the Ancient Near East*, 71–3 for a comparison of the sizes of cities in the ancient world. In the 3rd millennium BC the city of Uruk was larger than Athens and Jerusalem and half the size of Rome in the 1st century AD.

7. Redman, *The Rise of Civilization*, 318.

8. Dominique Charpin, "The History of Ancient Mesopotamia: An Overview", in Sasson (ed.), *Civilizations of the Ancient Near East*, **2**, 807–29, esp. 809.

9. Both titles had a strong relationship to the gods. Nissen, *Early History of the Ancient Near East*, 140.

10. Steinkeller, "Mesopotamia, History of", **4**, 726, and Nissen, *Early History of the Ancient Near East*, 140–41.

11. Donald P. Hansen, "Kish", in Meyers (ed.), *Oxford Encyclopedia of Archaeology*, **3**, 298–9; and Charpin, "The History of Ancient Mesopotamia", **2**, 809.

12. *Ibid.*, 2, 809.

13. Steinkeller, "Mesopotamia, History of", **4**, 725. However, see Norman Yoffe, "The Economy of Ancient Western Asia", in Sasson (ed.), *Civilizations of the Ancient Near East*, **3**, 1387–99, esp. 1388.

14. J. N. Postgate, "Royal Ideology and State Administration in Sumer and Akkad", in Sasson (ed.), *Civilizations of the Ancient Near East*, **1**, 396.

15. Kuhrt, *The Ancient Near East*, **1**, 33.

16. Stone, "The Development of Cities", 236.

17. Yoffe, "Economy of Ancient Western Asia", 1394.

18. Redman, *The Rise of Civilization*, 304–5; Thorkild Jacobsen, "Primitive Democracy in Ancient Mesopotamia", *Journal of Near Eastern Studies* **2** (1943), 159–72; and Henri Frankfort, *Kingship and the Gods* (University of Chicago Press, Chicago, 1948), 229.

19. Lloyd R. Bailey, *Noah: The Person and the Story in History and Tradition* (University of South Carolina Press, Columbia, 1989) and Jack P. Lewis, "Flood", in Freedman (ed.), *The Anchor Bible Dictionary*, **2**, 798–803. Dated, but still interesting, is the discussion and translation in A. Heidel, *The Epic of Gilgamesh and Old Testament Parallels* (University of Chicago Press, Chicago, 1946). For other translations and discussions see Chapter 9.

20. Lewis, "Flood", 798.

21. G. S. Kirk, *Myth: Its Meaning and Functions in Ancient and Other Cultures* (Cambridge University Press, Cambridge, 1970).

22. U. Cassuto, *A Commentary on the Book of Genesis*, Part II (Magnes Press, Jerusalem, 1992), 3–140, esp. 24.

23. Genesis 8:4.

24. Lewis, "Flood", 798.

25. Bailey, *Noah*, 95–101 gives full details; and Lewis, "Flood", 798.

26. R. L. Raikes, "The Physical Evidence for Noah's Flood", *Iraq* **28** (1960), 52–63.

27. Leonard Woolley, *Ur of the Chaldees* (Norton, New York, 1956), 29, and *Excavations at Ur* (London, 1954), 34–6.

28. Max Mallowan, "Noah's Flood Reconsidered", *Iraq* **26**

(1964), 62–82, esp. 72; and Woolley, *Ur of the Chaldees* (1956), 29.

29. Mallowan, "Noah's Flood Reconsidered", 62–82.

30. Roux, *Ancient Iraq*, 113.

31. Mallowan, "Noah's Flood Reconsidered", n. 3, 62.

32. Michael Roaf, "Palaces and Temples in Ancient Mesopotamia", in Sasson (ed.), *Civilizations of the Ancient Near East*, 1, 432.

33. T. Jacobsen, "Sumer", in *The Encyclopedia of Ancient Civilizations*, A. Cotterell (ed.), 72–83 (Mayflower Books, New York, 1980), 76–7.

34. See Samuel N. Kramer, *The Sacred Marriage Rite* (Indiana University Press, Bloomington, Indiana, 1969); and Jean Bottéro, *Mesopotamia: Writing, Reasoning and The Gods* (University of Chicago Press, Chicago, 1992), 185.

35. Kuhrt, *The Ancient Near East*, 1, 39.

36. Mario Liverani, "The Deeds of Ancient Mesopotamian Kings", in Sasson (ed.), *Civilizations of the Ancient Near East*, 4, 2355–6.

37. Kuhrt, *The Ancient Near East*, 1, 42. There may have been a league of city-states. See Roaf, *Cultural Atlas of Mesopotamia*, 68. Jacobsen, "Sumer", 76, refers to it as the "Nippur League".

38. Eyre, "The Agricultural Cycle".

39. Karl W. Butzer, "Environmental Change in the Ancient Near East", in Sasson (ed.), *Civilizations of the Ancient Near East*, 1, 142–51.

40. Lucio Milano, "Ebla: A Third-Millennium City-State in Ancient Syria", in Sasson (ed.), *Civilizations of the Ancient Near East*, 2, 1219–30.

41. Paolo Matthiae, *Ebla: An Empire Rediscovered* (Doubleday, Garden City, 1981), 49.

42. Giovanni Pettinato, *The Archives of Ebla, An Empire Inscribed in Clay* (Doubleday, Garden City, 1981), Ch. 7.

43. Milano, "Ebla", 1224.

44. Matthiae, *Ebla*, 40.

45. Steinkeller, "Mesopotamia, History of", 726.

46. For an overview of Woolley's fascinating career see Brian Fagan, *Return to Babylon, Travelers, Archaeologists, and Monuments in Mesopotamia* (Little Brown, Boston, 1979), Chs 19, 20; and Seton Lloyd, *Foundations in the Dust* (Thames & Hudson, London, 1980), 187–9, and *The Archaeology of Mesopotamia*, Ch. 6.

47. Woolley, *Ur of the Chaldees*, rev. edn by P. R. S. Moorey (Cornell University Press, Ithaca, 1982).

48. Woolley, *Ur of the Chaldees* (1982), 75.

49. Henri Frankfort, *The Art and Architecture of the Ancient Orient* (Penguin Books, Harmondsworth, 1954), 34.

50. Amir Harrak, "The Royal Tombs of Nimrud and their Jewellery", *The Bulletin of the Canadian Society for Meso-*

potamian Studies 20, 5–14 gives some interesting parallels from the Neo-Assyrian period.

51. Frankfort, *Kingship and the Gods*, Ch. 19, n. 12, 400–401.

52. Woolley, *Ur of the Chaldees* (1956), 65.

53. Jo Ann Scurlock, "Death and the Afterlife in Mesopotamian Thought", in Sasson (ed.), *Civilizations of the Ancient Near East*, 3, 1883–93; Thorkild Jacobsen, "Death in Mesopotamia", in *Death in Mesopotamia*, B. Alster (ed.), 19–24 (Akademisk Forlag 8, Copenhagen, 1980), and *The Treasures of Darkness* (Yale University Press, New Haven, 1976), 215–19; and Bottéro, *Mesopotamia*, Ch. 15.

54. Thorkild Jacobsen, *The Harps that Once ... Sumerian Poetry in Translation* (Yale University Press, New Haven, 1987).

55. Redman, *The Rise of Civilization*, 298.

4: The Akkadians and the Ur III Dynasty

1. Benjamin Foster, "Akkadians", in Meyers (ed.), *Oxford Encyclopedia of Archaeology*, 1, 49–54; and Kuhrt, *The Ancient Near East*, 1, 44–55.

2. Gotthelf Bergsträsser, *Introduction to the Semitic Languages*, P. Daniels (trans.) (Eisenbrauns, Winona Lake, Indiana, 1983).

3. John Huehnergard, "Semitic Languages", in Sasson (ed.), *Civilizations of the Ancient Near East*, 4, 2117–28, and "Languages (Introductory)", in Freedman (ed.), *The Anchor Bible Dictionary*, 4, 155–70; and Gene B. Gragg, "Semitic Languages", in Meyers (ed.), *Oxford Encyclopedia of Archaeology*, 4, 516–27.

4. This chronology follows that of Roaf, *Cultural Atlas of Mesopotamia*, 96. See also C. J. Gadd, "The Dynasty of Agade", in *The Cambridge Ancient History, Volume 1, Part 2: Early History of the Middle East*, 3rd edn, I. E. S. Edwards *et al.* (eds) (Cambridge University Press, Cambridge, 1971), 417.

5. Gadd, "The Dynasty of Agade", 421.

6. *Ibid.*, 417.

7. Similar stories were attributed to religious leaders like John the Baptist, Siddartha Gautama (the Buddha), the Persian god Mithras, and Jesus of Nazareth. See David Leeming, *Mythology: The Voyage of the Hero*, 2nd edn (Harper and Row, New York, 1981), Ch. 1, 10–49; and Joseph Campbell, *The Hero With a Thousand Faces*, 2nd edn (Princeton University Press, Princeton, 1968), 341.

8. Exodus 2.

9. Sabina Franke, "Kings of Akkad: Sargon and Naram-Sin", in Sasson (ed.), *Civilizations of the Ancient Near East*, 2,

831–41, esp. 836–7; and E. A. Speiser, "Akkadian Myths and Epics", in Pritchard (ed.), *Ancient Near Eastern Texts*, 60–119 (supp. 501–18), esp. 119.

10. Harvey Weiss, "Akkade", in Meyers (ed.), *Oxford Encyclopedia of Archaeology*, 1, 41–4.

11. Foster, "Akkadians", 50.

12. Kuhrt, *The Ancient Near East*, 1, 44.

13. Franke, "Kings of Akkad", 832; and Saggs, *Civilization Before Greece and Rome*, 41.

14. Roux, *Ancient Iraq*, 146.

15. Franke, "Kings of Akkad", 832; Kuhrt, *The Ancient Near East*, 1, 49; and Roaf, *Cultural Atlas of Mesopotamia*, 96.

16. *Enkheduanna* was one of a number of female scribes in ancient Mesopotamia. See Laurie E. Pearce, "Scribes and Scholars of Ancient Mesopotamia", in Sasson (ed.), *Civilizations of the Ancient Near East*, 4, 2265–78, esp. 2266; and Franke, "Kings of Akkad", 835–36.

17. Roaf, *Cultural Atlas of Mesopotamia*, 97.

18. Saggs, *Civilization Before Greece and Rome*, Ch. 7.

19. It has also been suggested that it represents Sargon's grandson, Naram-Sin. See Roaf, *Cultural Atlas of Mesopotamia*, 99.

20. Irene J. Winter, "Aesthetics in Ancient Mesopotamian Art", in Sasson (ed.), *Civilizations of the Ancient Near East*, 4, 2569–82, esp. 2578.

21. Kuhrt, *The Ancient Near East*, 1, 51.

22. Postgate, "Royal Ideology and State Administration", 401.

23. Glen M. Schwartz, "Pastoral Nomadism in Ancient Western Asia", in Sasson (ed.), *Civilizations of the Ancient Near East*, 1, 249–58, esp. 254.

24. Franke, "Kings of Akkad", 832.

25. Gadd, "The Dynasty of Agade", 454–63.

26. Kuhrt, *The Ancient Near East*, 1, 57–8; and Jerrold S. Cooper, *The Curse of Agade* (Johns Hopkins University Press, Baltimore, 1983), 142.

27. Michalowski, "Sumerians".

28. Martha Roth, *Law Collections from Mesopotamia and Asia Minor, Volume 6* (Scholars Press, Atlanta, 1997), 13; and Samuel Greengus, "Legal and Social Institutions in Ancient Mesopotamia", in Sasson (ed.), *Civilizations of the Ancient Near East*, 1, 469–84.

29. Daniel Snell, *Life in the Ancient Near East, 3100–332 BCE* (Yale University Press, New Haven, 1997), 35.

30. For an overview see Saggs, *Civilization Before Greece and Rome*, 47–61; and Roaf, "Palaces and Temples", 429–31. In-depth studies are by André Parrot, *Ziggurats et Tour de Babel* (Éditions Albin Michel, Paris, 1949) and Th. A. Busink, "L'Origine et Evolution de la Ziggurat Babylonienne", *Jaarbericht Ex Oriente Lux* 21 (1970), 91–141.

31. Roux, *Ancient Iraq*, 157; and Roaf, *Cultural Atlas of Mesopotamia*, 104.
32. Donald Wiseman, *Nebuchadnezzar and Babylon* (Oxford University Press, Oxford, 1983), 72. The ziggurat of Dur Untash measured 105.2 m on a side and rose to a height of 52.6 m. See Pierre Amiet, *Art of the Ancient Near East* (Harry N. Abrams, New York, 1980), 547–9.
33. Wiseman, *Nebuchadnezzar and Babylon*, 68–73.
34. Saggs, *Civilization Before Greece and Rome*, 57.
35. Roux, *Ancient Iraq*, 156.
36. Busink, "L'Origine et Evolution", 93; and Parrot, *Ziggurats et Tour de Babel*, 200–217.
37. But see Busink, "L'Origine et Evolution", 120.
38. Saggs, *Civilization Before Greece and Rome*, 57.
39. Busink, "L'Origine et Evolution", 98–9.
40. Parrot, *Ziggurats et Tour de Babel*, 216.
41. A. Leo Oppenheim, "A New Prayer to the Gods of the Night", *Analecta Biblica* **12** (1959), 282–97.
42. Robert Chadwick, "Calendars, Ziggurats and the Stars", *The Bulletin of the Canadian Society for Mesopotamian Studies* **24** (1992), 7–24.
43. Genesis 1; and Oates, *Babylon*, 60.
44. Saggs, *Civilization Before Greece and Rome*, 60.
45. Oates, *Babylon*, 60.

5: Mesopotamia in the second millennium BC: the Babylonians and the Kassites (2000–1600 BC)

1. For an overview see Glenn Schwartz, "Pastoral Nomadism", in Sasson (ed.), *Civilizations of the Ancient Near East*, **1**, 249–58; George Mendenhall, "Amorites", in Freedman (ed.), *The Anchor Bible Dictionary*, **1**, 199–202; and Robert Whiting, "Amorite Tribes and Nations of Second Millennium Western Asia", in Sasson (ed.), *Civilizations of the Ancient Near East*, **2**, 1231–42.
2. Whiting, "Amorite Tribes and Nations", **2**, 1234.
3. Jack Sasson, "King Hammurabi of Babylon", in Sasson (ed.), *Civilizations of the Ancient Near East*, **2**, 901–15; and Samuel A. Meier, "Hammurapi", in Freedman (ed.), *The Anchor Bible Dictionary*, **3**, 39–42.
4. His name is usually spelled Hammurabi (meaning "the god Hammu is great"); G. R. Driver and John C. Miles, *The Babylonian Laws* (Oxford University Press, Oxford, 1955), 117–18. The name is sometimes spelled with a *-pi*, which changes the meaning, although the *-bi* spelling is more common and is used here. See André Finet, *Le Code de Hammurapi* (Éditions du Cerf, Paris, 1983), 7. The name Hammurapi means "the god Hammu is a healer". Hammu or 'Ammu was an ancient Amorite deity,

but in this case the name refers to a divinized "paternal uncle". See Sasson, "King Hammurabi of Babylon", 902; and Meier, "Hammurabi", 41–2.
5. Traditionally the reign of Hammurabi has been set at 1792–1750 BC, but these dates are open to question; see Peter J. Huber, A. J. Sachs, M. Stol *et al.* 1982, *Astronomical Dating of Babylon I and Ur III*, Occasional Papers on the Near East **1**(4) (Undena Publications, Malibu, 1982).
6. Roaf, *Cultural Atlas of Mesopotamia*, 120.
7. The modern name is *Tell Hariri*. Margueron, "Mari (Archaeology)"; and Kuhrt, *The Ancient Near East*, **1**, 95–108.
8. J.-C. Margueron, "Mari: A Portrait in Art", in Sasson (ed.), *Civilizations of the Ancient Near East*, **2**, 889.
9. Margueron, "Mari, Euphrat, et le Khabur".
10. J.-C. Margueron, "Mari", in Meyers (ed.), *Oxford Encyclopedia of Archaeology*, **3**, 413–17.
11. Margueron, "Mari (Archaeology)"; Stephanie Dalley, *Mari and Karana: Two Old Babylonian Cities* (Longman, London, 1984); and Durand, "Mari (Texts)".
12. Margueron, "Mari (Archaeology)", 528 and "Mari", 416.
13. Pierre Villard, "Shamshi-Adad and Sons: The Rise and Fall of an Upper Mesopotamian Empire", in Sasson (ed.), *Civilizations of the Ancient Near East*, **2**, 873–83.
14. The vast corpus of letters from Mari are published in an ongoing series of volumes under the general title *Archives Royales de Mari: Textes Transcrits et Traduits*, G. Dossin *et al.* (eds) (Librairie Orientaliste Paul Geuthner, Paris, 1950–). Translations can be found in Dalley, *Mari and Karana*.
15. Margueron, "Mari (Archaeology)", 529.
16. Oates, *Babylon*, 68.
17. In some instances it could also mean "women" or "minor" as well. See Roth, *Law Collections*, 72.
18. Oates, *Babylon*, 68; H. W. F. Saggs, *Everyday Life in Babylonia and Assyria* (Dorset Press, New York, 1965), 67–8; Roux, *Ancient Iraq*, 191–2; and Bottéro, *Mesopotamia*, 166.
19. See the discussion in Oates, *Babylon*, 69.
20. *Ibid.*, 69.
21. *Ibid.*, 69–70.
22. Saggs, *Everyday Life in Babylonia and Assyria*, 160–75; and Roth, *Law Collections*, 13–70.
23. For an overview see Saggs, *Everyday Life in Babylonia and Assyria*, 160–75; Bottéro, *Mesopotamia*, 156–84; and Samuel Greengus, "Law", in Freedman (ed.), *The Anchor Bible Dictionary*, **4**, 242–52. For translations see M. E. J. Richardson, *Hammurabi's Laws, Text, Translations and Glossary* (Sheffield Academic Press, Sheffield, 2000), and

Roth, *Law Collections*. For text in cuneiform characters see R. Borger, *Babylonisch-Assyrische Lesestücke*, 3 vols (Pontificum Institutum Biblicum, Rome, 1963).
24. Bottéro, *Mesopotamia*, 164; and Richardson, *Hammurabi's Laws*, 11.
25. The term used to refer to such decisions was *dīnāt mēsharim*, meaning "just verdicts". For a discussion see Bottéro, *Mesopotamia*, 164.
26. The rod and ring are symbols of royal power. Agnès Spycket, "Reliefs, Statuary, and Monumental Paintings in Ancient Mesopotamia", in Sasson (ed.), *Civilizations of the Ancient Near East*, **4**, 2583–600, esp. 2585.
27. Richardson, *Hammurabi's Laws*, 123.
28. Greengus, "Legal and Social Institutions", 473–5.
29. Richardson, *Hammurabi's Laws*, 60–61 and n. 36.
30. Greengus, "Legal and Social Institutions", 478–81.
31. Andrew George, *The Epic of Gilgamesh: A New Translation* (Barnes & Noble, New York, 1999), 194.
32. See, for example, Isaac Mendelson, "The Family in the Ancient Near East", in *The Biblical Archaeologist Reader 3*, E. F. Campbell and D. N. Freedman (eds), 147–54 (Anchor Press/Doubleday, Garden City, 1970).
33. Greengus, "Legal and Social Institutions", 475–8.
34. See Ch. 9, Pt II. Some popular books claim that Babylonian surgeons were capable of performing operations for cataracts, supposedly mentioned in the Hammurabi Laws. This seems unlikely. The eye surgery mentioned in the Hammurabi Laws was a form of scarification that offered relief from certain eye diseases. This practice was also known from later Alexandrian medicine. See A. L. Oppenheim, *Ancient Mesopotamia: Portrait of a Dead Civilization*, rev. and completed by E. Reiner (University of Chicago Press, Chicago, 1977), 293 and bibliographical references.
35. See Gernot Windfuhr, "Indo-European Languages", in Meyers (ed.), *Oxford Encyclopedia of Archaeology*, **3**, 149–58; and Garry Beckman, "Languages (Hittite)", in Freedman (ed.), *The Anchor Bible Dictionary*, **4**, 214–16.
36. Klaas Veenhof, "Kanesh: An Assyrian Colony in Anatolia", in Sasson (ed.), *Civilizations of the Ancient Near East*, **1**, 859–71.
37. J. G. Macqueen, "The History of Anatolia and the Hittite Empire: An Overview", in Sasson (ed.), *Civilizations of the Ancient Near East*, **2**, 1085–105. Macqueen's dates are higher than those used here, which follow more closely those of Trevor Bryce, *Life and Society in the Hittite World* (Oxford University Press, Oxford, 2002), xi.
38. Johan De Roos, "Hittite Prayers", in Sasson (ed.), *Civilizations of the Ancient Near East*, **3**, 1997–2005, esp. 2003.

39. Philo H. J. Houwink Ten Cate, "Hittite History", in Freedman (ed.), *The Anchor Bible Dictionary*, **3**, 219–25, esp. 222.

40. Diana Stein, "Kassites", in Meyers (ed.), *Oxford Encyclopedia of Archaeology*, **3**, 271–5. See also Huehnergard, "Languages (Introductory)", 165.

41. Walter Sommerfeld, "The Kassites of Ancient Mesopotamia: Origins, Politics, and Culture", in Sasson (ed.), *Civilizations of the Ancient Near East*, **2**, 917–30.

42. John Brinkman, *Materials and Studies for Kassite History, Volume I* (University of Chicago Press, Chicago, 1976), vii.

43. Edwin Firmage, "Zoology (Animal Profiles)", in Freedman (ed.), *The Anchor Bible Dictionary*, **6**, 1136–7.

44. Sommerfeld, "The Kassites of Ancient Mesopotamia", 925.

45. Stephanie Dalley, "Ancient Mesopotamian Military Organisation", in Sasson (ed.), *Civilizations of the Ancient Near East*, **1**, 413–22, esp. 414–17; and Saggs, *Civilization Before Greece and Rome*, 213–15. Also J. H. Crouwel and M. A. Littauer, "Chariots", in Meyers (ed.), *Oxford Encyclopedia of Archaeology*, **1**, 485–7, "Chariots", in Freedman (ed.), *The Anchor Bible Dictionary*, **1**, 888–92, and *Wheeled Vehicles and Ridden Animals in the Ancient Near East* (Brill Publishers, Leiden, 1979).

46. Stein, "Kassites", 272.

6: The Assyrians

1. For an overview see A. K. Grayson, "Mesopotamia, History of (Assyria)", in Freedman (ed.), *The Anchor Bible Dictionary*, **4**, 732–55, and "Assyrians", in Meyers (ed.), *Oxford Encyclopedia of Archaeology*, **1**, 228–33. See also Kuhrt, *The Ancient Near East*, **2**, 473–546.

2. Villard, "Shamshi-Adad and Son"; and Kuhrt, *The Ancient Near East*, 473–546.

3. Paul-Éugéne Dion, "Aramean Tribes and Nations of the First Millennium Western Asia", in Sasson (ed.), *Civilizations of the Ancient Near East*, **2**, 1281–94, and *Les Araméens, à l'âge du fer: histoire politique et structure socials* (Études Bibliques N.S. 34, Paris, Gabalda, 1997).

4. Kenneth Kitchen, *The Third Intermediate Period in Egypt (1100–650 BC)* (Aris & Phillips, Warminster, 1973); Anthony Spalinger, "Egypt, History of (Dyn 21–26)", in Freedman (ed.), *The Anchor Bible Dictionary*, **2**, 353–64; and John Taylor, "The Third Intermediate Period (1069–664 BC)", in Shaw (ed.), *The Oxford History of Ancient Egypt*, 330–68, esp. 334.

5. H. W. F. Saggs, *The Might that was Assyria* (Sidgwick & Jackson, London, 1984), 70–74.

6. Grayson, "Mesopotamia, History of (Assyria)", 741; and Roux, *Ancient Iraq*, 259–60.

7. Julian Read, *Assyrian Sculpture* (Harvard University Press, Cambridge, MS, 1983), 22–3.

8. Saggs, *Civilization Before Greece and Rome*, 187, emphasizes that the Assyrians were no more brutal than anyone else. While the Assyrians chopped off the heads of their adversaries and heaped them into piles, wall reliefs of the temple of Pharaoh Ramesses III at Medinet Habu depict the severed male sex organs of their enemies piled in heaps on the ground.

9. Kirk Grayson, "The Assyrian and Babylonian Empires and Other States in the Near East", in Boardman *et al.* (eds), *The Cambridge Ancient History*, 219.

10. Jeremy Black and Anthony Green, *Gods, Demons and Symbols of Ancient Mesopotamia* (University of Texas Press, Austin, 1992), 37–9.

11. Saggs, *The Might that was Assyria*, 247–8.

12. For an overview of the Assyrian military see Dalley, "Ancient Mesopotamian Military Organization"; and Grayson, "The Assyrian and Babylonian Empires", 217–21. See D. J. Wiseman, "The Assyrians", in *Warfare in the Ancient World*, J. Hackett (ed.) (Sidgwick & Jackson, New York, 1989), 36–53; and Roux, *Ancient Iraq*, 263–5. Saggs, *The Might that was Assyria*, Ch. 16 is devoted to the Assyrian army.

13. Wiseman, "The Assyrians", 42.

14. *Ibid.*, 38.

15. Dalley, "Ancient Mesopotamian Military Organization", 418.

16. Wiseman, "The Assyrians", 41–2.

17. *Ibid.*, 48.

18. *Ibid.*, 44–5, says they were effective up to 650 m, which seems exaggerated.

19. For illustrations see David Ussishkin, *The Conquest of Lachish by Sennacherib* (Institute of Archaeology, Tel Aviv University, Tel Aviv, 1982); and Mark Healy and Angus McBride, *The Ancient Assyrians* (Osprey Publishing, Oxford, 1991).

20. Grayson, "The Assyrian and Babylonian Empires", 218.

21. *Ibid.*, 219.

22. Saggs, *Civilization Before Greece and Rome*, 248–50.

23. See D. D. Luckenbill, *Ancient Records of Assyria and Babylonia*, 2 vols (University of Chicago Press, Chicago, 1926–27), nos 433, 445, 455 and 472.

24. Grayson, "Mesopotamia, History of (Assyria)", 742.

25. J. K. Anderson, "Hunting", in Meyers (ed.), *Oxford Encyclopedia of Archaeology*, **3**, 122–4.

26. Saggs, *The Might that was Assyria*, 64.

27. Grayson, "The Assyrian and Babylonian Empires", 222.

28. Paul Zimansky, *Ecology and Empire: The Structure of the Uartian State* (University of Chicago Press, Chicago, 1985), and "The Kingdom of Uartu in Eastern Anatolia", in Sasson (ed.), *Civilizations of the Ancient Near East*, **2**, 1135–46.

29. Grayson, "Mesopotamia, History of (Assyria)", 744; and Saggs, *The Might that was Assyria*, 85–9.

30. Gary Oller, "Messengers and Ambassadors in Ancient Western Asia", in Sasson (ed.), *Civilizations in the Ancient Near East*, **2**, 1465–72; and Barry Beitzel, "Travel and Communications, the Old Testament World", in Freedman (ed.), *The Anchor Bible Dictionary*, **6**, 644–8.

31. Bustenay Oded, *Mass Deportation and Deportees in the Neo-Assyrian Empire* (Dr. Ludwig Reichert, Wiesbaden, 1979).

32. *Ibid.*, 43.

33. *Ibid.*, 20.

34. *Ibid.*, 46–8.

35. Grant Frame, "Chaldeans", in Meyers (ed.), *Oxford Encyclopaedia of Archaeology*, **1**, 482–4; and Richard S. Hess, "Chaldea", in Freedman (ed.), *The Anchor Bible Dictionary*, **1**, 886–7.

36. Oates, *Babylon*, 116, and n. 3; and Kuhrt, *The Ancient Near East*, **2**, 497–9, 517–19.

37. Roux, *Ancient Iraq*, 287.

38. Saggs, *The Might that was Assyria*, 92–5.

39. David Stronach and Kim Codella, "Nineveh", in Meyers (ed.), *Oxford Encyclopedia of Archaeolog*, **4**, 144–8; and John Russell, "Nineveh" in *The Dictionary of Art, Volume 25*, J. Turner (ed.), 152–5 (Grove, London/New York, 1996).

40. Stone, "The Development of Cities", 244.

41. Thorkild Jacobsen and Seton Lloyd, *Sennacherib's Aqueduct at Jerwan* (University of Chicago Press, Chicago, 1935).

42. John Malcolm Russell, *Sennacherib's Palace Without Rival at Nineveh* (University of Chicago Press, Chicago, 1991).

43. Saggs, *The Might that was Assyria*, 100.

44. Oded, *Mass Deportation and Deportees*, 21.

45. See 2 Kings 18 and 19.

46. Ronald H. Sack, "Merodach-Baladan", in Freedman (ed.), *The Anchor Bible Dictionary*, **4**, 704–5; Oates, *Babylon*, 166; and Saggs, *The Might that was Assyria*, 101.

47. Simo Parpola, "The Murder of Sennacherib", in *Death in Mesopotamia*, B. Alster (ed.), 171–82 (Akademisk Forlag, Copenhagen, 1980), 174.

48. Erle Leichty, "Esarhaddon, King of Assyria", in Sasson (ed.), *Civilizations of the Ancient Near East*, **2**, 949–58.

49. Kuhrt, *The Ancient Near East*, **2**, 632–6; and Shaw, *The Oxford History of Ancient Egypt*, 352–9.
50. Ezra 4:9–10.
51. Saggs, *The Might that was Assyria*, 117–21.
52. Klaas Veenhof, "Libraries and Archives", in Meyers (ed.), *Oxford Encyclopedia of Archaeology*, **3**, 351–7; J. A. Black and W. J. Tait, "Archives and Libraries in the Ancient Near East", in Sasson (ed.), *Civilizations of the Ancient Near East*, **4**, 2197–209; Lionel Casson, *Libraries in the Ancient World* (Yale University Press, New Haven, 2001), 1–16, Oppenheim, *Ancient Mesopotamia*, 15–21; Oates, *Babylon*, 125.
53. Grayson, "Mesopotamia, History of (Assyria)", 747.
54. A. Kirk Grayson, "Assyrian Rule of Conquered Territory", in Sasson (ed.), *Civilizations of the Ancient Near East*, **2**, 959–68, esp. 967.
55. Grayson, "The Assyrian and Babylonian Empires", 216–17.

7: The Last Babylonian Dynasty

1. For an overview of this period see A. Kirk Grayson, "Mesopotamia, History of (Babylonia)", in Freedman (ed.), *The Anchor Bible Dictionary*, **4**, 755–77, esp. 764–77; Paul-Alain Beaulieu, "King Nabonidus and the Neo-Babylonian Empire", in Sasson (ed.), *Civilizations of the Ancient Near East*, **2**, 969–79; D. J. Wiseman, "Babylonia 605–539 BC", in Boardman *et al.* (eds), *The Cambridge Ancient History*, 229–51; Grant Frame, *Babylonia 689–627* (Nederlands Historisch-Archaeologisch Instituut, Istanbul, 1992), 210–13; and Kuhrt, *The Ancient Near East*, **2**, 573–622. For Babylon in general see H. W. F. Saggs, *The Greatness that was Babylon*, 2nd edn (Sidgwick & Jackson, London, 1988).
2. Kuhrt, *The Ancient Near East*, **2**, 590–97; Wiseman, *Nebuchadnezzar and Babylon*, 13–16, 29, 33, and *Chronicles of the Chaldean Kings (626–556 BC) in the British Museum* (British Museum, London, 1956). See also Saggs, *The Greatness that was Babylon*, 129–32.
3. Redford, *Egypt, Canaan, and Israel*, 449–55; and Oates, *Babylon*, 128–31.
4. Redford, *Egypt, Canaan, and Israel*, 454.
5. Grayson, "Mesopotamia, History of (Babylonia)", 765–6.
6. 2 Chronicles 36 and 2 Kings 24; and Wiseman, "Babylonia", 233–5, 392–409.
7. Philip King, "Jerusalem", in Freedman (ed.), *The Anchor Bible Dictionary*, **3**, 747–66; and Dan Bahat, "Jerusalem", in Meyers (ed.), *Oxford Encyclopedia of Archaeology*, **3**, 224–38.
8. Wiseman, *Nebuchadnezzar and Babylon*, 32.
9. There were 3 023 upper-class deportees according to Jeremiah 52:28–30, but 2 Kings 24:14–16 claims 10 000 were taken captive. See also, Moshe Beer, "Judaism (Babylonian)", in Freedman (ed.), *The Anchor Bible Dictionary*, **3**, 1076–83.
10. Wiseman, *Nebuchadnezzar and Babylon* , 36–9.
11. 2 Kings 25:7.
12. Evelyn Klengel-Brandt, "Babylon", in Meyers (ed.), *Oxford Encyclopedia of Archaeology*, **1**, 251–6; and Kuhrt, *The Ancient Near East*, **2**, 593–7, 610–21.
13. Oates, *Babylon*, 144–60; and Wiseman, "Babylonia", 236–9.
14. Roaf, *Cultural Atlas of Mesopotamia*, 199.
15. Roux, *Ancient Iraq*, 360.
16. Beaulieu, "King Nabonidus", 971; Stephanie Dalley, "Babylon and the Hanging Gardens: Cuneiform and Classical Sources Reconciled", *Iraq* **56** (1994), 45–76; D. W. W. Stevenson, "A Proposal for the Irrigation of the Hanging Gardens of Babylon", *Iraq* **54** (1992), 35–55; Irving Finkel, "The Hanging Gardens of Babylon", in *The Seven Wonders of the World*, P. A. Clayton and M. J. Price (eds), 38–58 (London, Routledge, 1988); and Wiseman, *Nebuchadnezzar and Babylon*, 56–60.
17. Grayson, "Mesopotamia, History of (Babylonia)", 771–7.
18. Daniels, "The Decipherment of Ancient Near Eastern Scripts".
19. Paul-Alain Beaulieu, *The Reign of Nabonidus, King of Babylon 556–539 BC* (Yale University Press, New Haven, 1989), 67–9, 88.
20. Beaulieu, *The Reign of Nabonidus*, 78, 90, 110–11.
21. *Ibid.*, 70.
22. *Ibid.*, 73.
23. *Ibid.*, 73, refers to this as a "*mythe fondateur*".
24. *Ibid.*, 108.
25. *Ibid.*, 184.
26. Roux, *Ancient Iraq*, 180; Oates, *Babylon*, 133; and Wiseman, "The Assyrian and Babylonian Empires", 246–7.
27. J. M. Cook, *The Persian Empire* (Schocken Books, New York, 1983), 28, suggests that Nabonidus may have used his Arabian sojourn to rebuild his military forces for eventual use against the Persians.
28. See Jacob Klein, "Akitu", in Freedman (ed.), *The Anchor Bible Dictionary*, **1**, 138–40; Jeremy Black, "The New Years Ceremonies in Ancient Babylon: 'Taking Bel by the Hand,' and a Cultic Picnic", *Religion* **11** (1981), 39–59; and Thorkild Jacobsen, "Religious Drama in Ancient Mesopotamia", in *Unity and Diversity*, H. Goedicke and J. J. Roberts (eds), 65–77 (Johns Hopkins, Baltimore, 1975). For an overview see Roux, *Ancient Iraq*, 365–9; and Roaf, *Cultural Atlas of Mesopotamia*, 201–2.
29. Jean Bottéro and Samuel Kramer, *Lorsque les dieux faisaient l'homme: Mythologie mésopotamienne* (Gallimard, Paris, 1989), 602–79; Stephanie Dalley, *Myths from Mesopotamia* (Oxford University Press, Oxford, 1989). English translations include Alexander Heidel, *The Babylonian Genesis* (University of Chicago Press, Chicago, 1951), and Speiser, "Akkadian Myths and Epics". For overviews see Jacobsen, *The Treasures of Darkness*, 166–91; and Bottéro and Kramer, *Lorsque les dieux faisaient l'homme*, Ch. 13.
30. Samuel Kramer, *Le Marriage Sacré* (Berg International, Paris, 1983).
31. A. T. Olmstead, *History of the Persian Empire* (University of Chicago Press, Chicago, 1948), 49. Roux, *Ancient Iraq*, 356, refers to a "pro-Persian party".
32. Pierre Briant, *From Cyrus to Alexander: A History of the Persian Empire*, P. Daniels (trans.) (Eisenbrauns, Winona Lake, Indiana, 2002), 40–43.
33. Beaulieu, *The Reign of Nabonidus*, 232.
34. Briant, *From Cyrus to Alexander*, 41; and Oppenheim, "Babylonian and Assyrian Historical Texts", 315–16.
35. Olmstead, *History of the Persian Empire*, 51.
36. Saggs, *The Greatness that was Babylon*, 138.
37. T. Cuyler Young, Jr., "Cyrus", in Freedman (ed.), *The Anchor Bible Dictionary*, **1**, 1231–2; and Kuhrt, *The Ancient Near East*, **2**, 659.
38. Isaiah 45:1.

8: Mythology and religion in Mesopotamia: the story of Gilgamesh and Enkidu

1. Useful editions with introductions include George, *The Epic of Gilgamesh*; Maureen Gallery-Kovacs, *The Epic of Gilgamesh* (Stanford University Press, Stanford, 1989); Benjamin Foster, *From Distant Days: Myths, Tales and Poetry of Ancient Mesopotamia* (CDL Press, Bethesda, 1995); and E. A. Speiser and A. K. Grayson, "The Epic of Gilgamesh", in Pritchard (ed.), *Ancient Near Eastern Texts*, 72–99 (supp. 503–7). For overviews and analyses see George, *The Epic of Gilgamesh*, xii–xxx; William Moran, "The Gilgamesh Epic: A Masterpiece from Ancient Mesopotamia", in Sasson (ed.), *Civilizations of the Ancient Near East*, **4**, 2327–36; and Jack Sasson, "Gilgamesh Epic", in Freedman (ed.), *The Anchor Bible Dictionary*, **2**, 1024–7.
2. Moran, "The Gilgamesh Epic", 2327.
3. Jacob Klein, "The Royal Hymns of Shulgi, King of Ur:

Man's Quest for Immortal Fame", *American Philosophical Society* **71**(7) (1981), 10.

4. In some versions from the first millennium BC a 12th tablet was added to the story. This tablet was not part of the original story and is not discussed here. Gallery-Kovacs, *The Epic of Gilgamesh*, xxi; and J. Tigay, *The Evolution of the Gilgamesh Epic* (University of Pennsylvania Press, Philadelphia, 1982), 104–7.

5. Jack Sasson, "On Musical Settings for Cuneiform Literature: A Discography", *Journal of the American Oriental Society* **103** (1983), 233–5; and Anne D. Kilmer, "Music and Dance in Ancient Western Asia", in Sasson (ed.), *Civilizations of the Ancient Near East*, **4**, 2601–13.

6. Moran, "The Gilgamesh Epic", 2328.

7. Tigay, *The Evolution of the Gilgamesh Epic*, 206–12.

8. *Ibid.*, 202–12, esp. 209.

9. Chadwick, "Celestial Episodes and Celestial Objects in Ancient Mesopotamia", *The Bulletin of the Canadian Society for Mesopotamian Studies* **22** (1991), 43–9, esp. 45–7.

10. The name Utnapishtim is formed from the Sumerian Zi-u4-sud-ra: "life of long days". Translated into Akkadian the signs give u4 = Ut, and Zi = *napishtim*: Tigay, *The Evolution of the Gilgamesh Epic*, 229.

11. Brian B. Schmidt, "Flood Narratives of Ancient Western Asia", in Sasson (ed.), *Civilizations of the Ancient Near East*, **4**, 2337–51.

12. Gallery-Kovacs, *The Epic of Gilgamesh*, 99, n. 3.

13. Lloyd R. Bailey, "Noah and the Ark", in Freedman (ed.), *The Anchor Bible Dictionary*, **4**, 1123–32; Schmidt, "Flood Narratives of Ancient Western Asia", 2343–8; and Heidel, *The Epic of Gilgamesh*, 224–69.

14. The name *Bilgamesh*, the original Sumerian spelling of Gilgamesh, may have meant "the old one is youthful": Tigay, *The Evolution of the Gilgamesh Epic*, 257.

9: Science and technology: astronomy and medicine in Mesopotamia and Egypt

1. Joseph Needham, *Science and Civilization in China, Volume III* (Cambridge University Press, Cambridge, 1959), 171–461; and N. Sivin, "Chinese Archaeoastronomy: Between Two Worlds", in *World Archaeoastronomy*, A. Aveni (ed.), 55–64 (Cambridge University Press, Cambridge, 1989).

2. Francesca Rochberg, "Astronomy and Calendars in Ancient Mesopotamia", in Sasson (ed.), *Civilizations of the Ancient Near East*, **3**, 1925–40.

3. Oppenheim, *Ancient Mesopotamia*, 206–27.

4. Ivan Starr, *Queries to the Sun God: Divination and Politics in Sargonid Assyria*, State Archives of Assyria IV (Helsinki University Press, Helsinki, 1990), xiii–lxxix.

5. Erica Reiner, "Babylonian Celestial Divination", in *Ancient Astronomy and Celestial Divination*, N. M. Swerdlow (ed.), 21–37 (MIT Press, Cambridge, 1999), 23.

6. David Pingree, "Astrology", in *Encyclopedia Britannica*, 28 vols, 15th edn (Encyclopedia Britannica, Chicago, 1974–84) **2**, 219.

7. Rochberg, "Astronomy and Calendars", 1925.

8. Bartel van der Waerden, *Science Awakening II: The Birth of Astronomy* (Noordhoff International Publishing, Leiden/New York, 1974), 48.

9. Hermann Hunger, *Astrological Reports to Assyrian Kings*, State Archives of Assyria VIII (Helsinki University Press, Helsinki, 1992): see numerous references listed in the subject index on 354, 362, 359.

10. A. L. Oppenheim, "Divination and Celestial Observation in the Last Assyrian Empire", *Centaurus* **14** (1969), 97–135.

11. *Ibid.*, 118–19.

12. *Ibid.*, 120.

13. Parpola, *Letters from Assyrian Scholars*, **1**, xxii–xxxii; and Bottéro, *Mesopotamia*, 138–55.

14. John Steele, "Eclipse Prediction in Mesopotamia", *Archive for the History of Exact Sciences* **54** (2000), 421–54.

15. See Francesca Rochberg-Halton, "Calendars", in Freedman (ed.), *The Anchor Bible Dictionary*, **1**, 810–14.

16. Otto Neugebauer, *The Exact Sciences in Antiquity*, 2nd edn (Brown University Press, Providence, 1969), 98.

17. Oppenheim, "Divination and Celestial Observation", 97–135, and Hunger, *Astrological Reports to Assyrian Kings*, *passim*.

18. Erica Reiner and David Pingree, *Babylonian Planetary Omens: Part Two* (Undena Publications, Malibu, California, 1981), 10–16.

19. Otto Neugebauer and Richard A. Parker, *Egyptian Astronomical Texts*, 3 vols (Brown University Press, Providence, 1969), **3**, 3; and Richard Parker, "Ancient Egyptian Astronomy", in *The Place of Astronomy in the Ancient World*, F. R. Hodson (ed.), 51–66 (Oxford University Press, Oxford, 1974), 60–61.

20. See the many examples and listings in Paul Gössmann, *Planetarium Babylonicum* (Des Papstlichen Bibelinstituts Verlag, Rome, 1959).

21. Rochberg, "Astronomy and Calendars", 1932.

22. Abraham Sachs, "Babylonian Horoscopes", *Journal of Cuneiform Studies* **6** (1952), 9–75.

23. Francesca Rochberg, "Babylonian Horoscopy: The Texts and their Relations", in *Ancient Astronomy and Celestial Divination*, N. Swerdlow (ed.), 39–59 (MIT Press, Cambridge, MS, 1999).

24. Francesca Rochberg-Halton, "New Evidence for the History of Astrology", *Journal of Near Eastern Studies* **43** (1984), 115–40, esp. 121.

25. Rochberg-Halton, "New Evidence for the History of Astrology", 117.

26. David Pingree, "Mesopotamian Astronomy and Astral Omens in Other Civilizations", *25e Rencontre Assyriologique Internationale à Berlin* **1**(2), 613–31 (Berliner Beiträge zum Vorderen Orient, 1978).

27. Asger Aaboe, "Babylonian Mathematics, Astrology, and Astronomy", in Boardman *et al.* (eds), *The Cambridge Ancient History*, 276–92, and "Scientific Astronomy in Antiquity", in Hodson (ed.), *The Place of Astronomy*, 21–42, John Britton and Christopher Walker, "Astronomy and Astrology in Mesopotamia", in *Astronomy Before the Telescope*, C. Walker (ed.), 42–67 (St. Martin's Press, New York, 1996), 67.

28. Neugebauer, *The Exact Sciences in Antiquity*, 71; and Parker, "Ancient Egyptian Astronomy", 51.

29. I. E. S. Edwards, *The Pyramids of Egypt*, rev. edn (Penguin Books, Harmondsworth, 1993), 247–51, figs 54–6. But see also a different approach to the problem by Otto Neugebauer, "On the Orientation of the Pyramids", *Centaurus* **24** (1980), 1–3.

30. Mark Lehner, "Some Observations on the Layout of the Khufu and Khafre Pyramids", *Journal of the American Research Centre in Egypt* **20** (1983), 7–25, esp. 19–25; and Edwards, *The Pyramids*, 247–51.

31. V. Trimble, "The Astronomical Investigations Concerning the So-called Air Shafts of the Cheops Pyramid", *Mitteilungen des Instituts für Orientforschung* **10** (1964), 183–7.

32. J. Hecht, "The Debunking of Egyptian Astronomers", *New Scientist* **17**(1439) (Jan 1985), 65.

33. O. R. Faulkner, "The King and the Star Religion in the Pyramid Texts", *Journal of Near Eastern Studies* **25** (1966), 153–61.

34. Gay Robins, "Mathematics, Astronomy and Calendars in Pharaonic Egypt", in Sasson (ed.), *Civilizations of the Ancient Near East*, **3**, 1799–814, esp. 1811–12.

35. R. A. Parker, *A Vienna Demotic Papyrus on Eclipse and Lunar Omina* (Brown University Press, Providence, 1959), 3.

36. Jean Leclant, "Éléments pour une étude de la divination dans l'Égypte pharaonique", in *La Divination*, A. Caqout and M. Leibovici (eds), 1–23 (Presses Universitaires de France, Paris, 1968), 22–3.

37. Neugebauer, *The Exact Sciences in Antiquity*, 168.
38. *Ibid.*, 81, 396.
39. Clagett, *Ancient Egyptian Science*, 280–81; and Olaf E. Kaper, "Myths: Lunar Cycle", in Redford (ed.), *The Oxford Encyclopedia of Ancient Egypt*, **2**, 480–82, esp. 481.
40. Parker, "Ancient Egyptian Astronomy", 54.
41. Clagett, *Ancient Egyptian Science*, 221–34.
42. Parker, "Ancient Egyptian Astronomy", 53.
43. Clagett, *Ancient Egyptian Science*, 53–65.
44. van der Waerden, *Science Awakening*, 64–7.
45. Pingree, "Mesopotamian Astronomy".
46. Aaboe, "Babylonian Mathematics", 292.
47. Hector Ignatio Avalos, "Medicine", Meyers (ed.), *Oxford Encyclopedia of Archaeology*, **3**, 450.
48. Avalos, "Medicine".
49. Mark Cohen, *Health and the Rise of Civilization* (Yale University Press, New Haven, 1989), 33–7.
50. *Ibid.*, 45.
51. Two examples are smallpox, related to cowpox, and bovine tuberculosis. Other animal-borne diseases include rabies, transmitted by domestic dogs, and tetanus, spread mainly by horses, but also by cattle and pigs. Well-known human diseases such as measles originated from cattle; distemper from dogs; influenza from pigs and chickens; the common cold from horses; and diphtheria from cattle. *Ibid.*, 47.
52. *Ibid.*, 40.
53. *Ibid.*, 136.
54. *Ibid.*, 139.
55. Guido Majno, *The Healing Hand: Man and Wound in the Ancient World* (Harvard University Press, Cambridge, 1975), Ch. 2.
56. Miranda Bayliss, "The Cult of Dead Kin in Assyria and Babylonia", *Iraq* **35–6** (1973–74), 115–25, esp. 116.
57. Erica Reiner, *Your Thwarts are in Pieces Your Mooring Rope Cut* (University of Michigan Press, Ann Arbour, 1985), 115, line 55.
58. See Walter Faber, "Witchcraft, Magic and Divination in Ancient Mesopotamia", in Sasson (ed.), *Civilizations of the Ancient Near East*, **3**, 1895–924, esp. 1897.
59. Robert Biggs, "Medicine, Surgery, and Public Health in Ancient Mesopotamia", in Sasson (ed.), *Civilizations of the Ancient Near East*, **3**, 1911–24, esp. 1912.
60. Biggs, "Medicine, Surgery, and Public Health", 1913.
61. G. Dossin and A. Finet, *Archives Royales de Mari, vol. X: Correspondance féminine* (Paul Geuthner, Paris, 1978), 129; and Biggs, "Medicine, Surgery, and Public Health", 1922.
62. Michel Civil, "Prescriptions Médicales Sumériennes",

Revue D'Assyriologie et Archéologie Orientale **54**(2) (1960), 59–72; and Avalos, "Medicine", 452.
63. Avalos, "Medicine", 452.
64. Oppenheim, *Ancient Mesopotamia*, 292.
65. Biggs, "Medicine, Surgery, and Public Health", 1923.
66. *Ibid.*, 1917–18.
67. J. Worth Estes, *The Medical Skills of Ancient Egypt* (Science History Publications, Canton, 1993), Ch. 5, n. 17, 152; and Majno, *The Healing Hand*, 109–11.
68. Oppenheim, *Ancient Mesopotamia*, 293; and Saggs, *Civilization Before Greece and Rome*, 265.
69. Biggs, "Medicine, Surgery, and Public Health", 1914.
70. Oppenheim, *Ancient Mesopotamia*, 295.
71. E. Ritter, "Magical Expert (=Âšipu) and Physician (=Asû): Notes on Two Complementary Professions in Babylonian Medicine", *Assyriological Studies* (Oriental Institute of the University of Chicago), H. G. Gütterbach and T. Jacobsen (eds), **16**, 299–321.
72. Reiner, refers to the *ashipu* as a "diagnostician": *Your Thwarts are in Pieces*, 111.
73. Hunger, *Astrological Reports to Assyrian Kings*, 178, line 18.
74. Cohen, *Health and the Rise of Civilization*, 194–8, gives infant mortality figures for a number of modern cities and countries from the 16th to the 20th centuries, where in some cases mortality rates among newborns were in the range 10–20% and rates for children under the age of 15 years in the range 30–50%. Similar rates were probably experienced in the ancient Near East.
75. Biggs, "Medicine, Surgery, and Public Health", 1917.
76. See Roth, *Law Collections*, Sumerian Laws 1 and 2, 43; rev. iii, 2–6, 26–7; Law 53, 174; Law 209, 122.
77. Roth, *Law Collections*, Middle Assyrian Laws, Law 53, 174; and Claudio Saporetti, *The Status of Women in the Middle Assyrian Period* (Undena Press, Malibu, 1979), 10.
78. Robert Ritner, "Medicine", in Redford (ed.), *The Oxford Encyclopedia of Ancient Egypt*, **2**, 353–6.
79. Kent Weeks, "Medicine, Surgery, and Public Health in Ancient Egypt", in Sasson (ed.), *Civilizations of the Ancient Near East*, **3**, 1787–98.
80. Ritner, "Medicine", 353.
81. Avalos, "Medicine", 452. For an overview see James E. Harris, "Dental Care", in Redford (ed.), *The Oxford Encyclopedia of Ancient Egypt*, **1**, 383–5.
82. Not everyone agrees that the hieroglyph of an elephant tusk really means "toother" or dentist. See Saggs, *Civilization Before Greece and Rome*, 243–4.
83. *Ibid.*, 243; and Harris, "Dental Care", 384.
84. Harris, "Dental Care".

85. Biggs, "Medicine, Surgery, and Public Health", 1916; and E. A. Speiser, "A Cosmological Incantation: The Worm and the Toothache", in Pritchard (ed.), *Ancient Near Eastern Texts*, 100–101.
86. Weeks, "Medicine, Surgery, and Public Health", 1791.
87. Ritner, "Medicine", 354, refers to this as the "first empirical, comprehensive disease theory in history". See also note 90 below.
88. Weeks, "Medicine, Surgery, and Public Health", 1788.
89. Guinea worms, *Filaria medinensis*, are parasitic threadworms that lodge beneath the skin, and cause abscesses and great pain. Tapeworms, *Tænia sainata* and others, are parasitic worms that attach themselves to the insides of the intestines of humans and other animals. They are flat, segmented, and can grow to over 6 m in length. Hookworms, *Necator Americanus*, are found in sandy soil, and enter the body through the foot, then lodge in the intestines and poison the intestinal system with their waste. Round worms, *Ascaris lumbricoides* are intestinal worms, 15–30 cm long.
90. Robert Ritner, "Innovations and Adaptations in Ancient Egyptian Medicine", *Journal of Near Eastern Studies* **59** (2000), 107–17, esp. 114–17.
91. Andrew Gordon, "Origins of Ancient Egyptian Medicine", *KMT: A Modern Journal of Ancient Egypt* **1**(2) (1990), 26–9, esp. 26.
92. Weeks, "Medicine, Surgery and Public Health", 1789.
93. Gordon, "Origins of Ancient Egyptian Medicine", 26–7.
94. Weeks, "Medicine, Surgery, and Public Health", 1789.
95. Bertrand Ebbell, *The Papyrus Ebers* (Levin & Munksgaard, Copenhagen, 1937).
96. James Breasted, *The Edwin Smith Surgical Papyrus* (University of Chicago Press, Chicago, 1930). It was named after an Englishman who purchased it on the antiquities market in 1862.
97. Alwin Burridge, "A Study of the Edwin Smith Surgical Papyrus", *The Journal of the Society for the Study of Egyptian Antiquities* **27** (1997), 9–26, esp. 10.
98. Weeks, "Medicine, Surgery, and Public Health", 1795.
99. Burridge, "Study of the Edwin Smith Surgical Papyrus", 16.
100. *Ibid.*, 24 n. 38, 25 n. 49.
101. Avalos, "Medicine", 452; and Joyce Filer, "Hygiene", in Redford (ed.), *The Oxford Encyclopedia of Ancient Egypt*, **1**, 133–6.
102. T. G. H. James, *Pharaoh's People* (University of Chicago Press, Chicago, 1984), 225–7, and n. 22.
103. James, *Pharaoh's People*, 228.
104. Gay Robins, "Women and Children in Peril: Pregnancy, Birth and Infant Mortality in Ancient Egypt", *KMT: A Modern Journal of Ancient Egypt* **5**(4) (1994–95), 24–35.

105. Ritner, "Innovations and Adaptations", 114–15.
106. Ritner, "Medicine", 354.

10: Egypt: the Black Land

1. Karl Butzer, "Environmental Change", 142.
2. Redman, *The Rise of Civilization*, 35–46.
3. Karl Butzer, "Nile", in Redford (ed.), *The Oxford Encyclopedia of Ancient Egypt*, **2**, 543–51.
4. *Ibid.*, 543.
5. *Ibid.* and *Early Hydraulic Civilization in Egypt* (University of Chicago Press, Chicago, 1976), 18–25.
6. Barry Kemp, *Ancient Egypt: Anatomy of a Civilization* (Routledge, New York, 1993), Ch. 1, 19–63; A. J. Spencer, *Early Egypt: The Rise of Civilization in the Nile Valley* (University of Oklahoma Press, Norman, 1995), Ch. 2; Fred Wendorf and Angela Close, "Prehistoric Egypt", in Meyers (ed.), *Oxford Encyclopedia of Archaeology*, **2**, 191–4; Peter Lacovara, "Predynastic Egypt", in Meyers (ed.), *Oxford Encyclopedia of Archaeology*, **2**, 194–5; and Stan Hendrickx and Pierre Vermeersch, "Prehistory from the Paleolithic to the Badarian Culture (c.700,000–4000 BC)", in Shaw (ed.), *The Oxford History of Ancient Egypt*, Ch. 2, and "The Naqada Period", in Shaw (ed.), *The Oxford History of Ancient Egypt*, Ch. 3.
7. Michael Hoffman, *Egypt Before the Pharaohs: The Prehistoric Foundations of Egyptian Civilization* (Alfred Knopf, New York, 1979), 161.
8. Bruce G. Trigger, "The Rise of Egyptian Civilization", in *Ancient Egypt: A Social History*, B. G. Trigger *et al.* (eds), 1–70 (Cambridge University Press, Cambridge, 1983), 20, 22, 25.
9. Wilma Wetterstrom and Mary Anne Murray, "Agriculture", in Redford (ed.), *The Oxford Encyclopedia of Ancient Egypt*, **1**, 37; and Redford, *Egypt, Canaan, and Israel*, 5.
10. Diana Craig Patch, "Merimde", in Meyers (ed.), *Oxford Encyclopedia of Archaeology*, 3, 471–2.
11. Fekri Hassan, "Cities", in Redford (ed.), *The Oxford Encyclopedia of Ancient Egypt*, **1**, 268–73, esp. 270–71.
12. Hassan, "Cities", 271.
13. Frankfort, *The Birth of Civilization*, and "The Origin of Monumental Architecture in Egypt", *American Journal of Semitic Languages and Literature* **58** (1941), 329–58; Marian Feldman, "Mesopotamia", in Redford (ed.), *The Oxford Encyclopedia of Ancient Egypt*, **2**, 384–90, esp. 384.
14. Kathryn Bard, "The Emergence of the Egyptian State (c. 3200–2686)", in Shaw (ed.), *The Oxford History of Ancient Egypt*, 61–88, esp. 66.

15. Redford, *Egypt, Canaan, and Israel*, 17.
16. Michael C. Astour, "Overland Traderoutes in Ancient Western Asia", in Sasson (ed.), *Civilizations of the Ancient Near East*, 3, 1405–20, esp. 1405–6.
17. Edwin Firmage, "Zoology (Animal Profiles)", in Freedman (ed.), *The Anchor Bible Dictionary*, 6, 1119–51, esp. 1137.
18. Trigger, "The Rise of Egyptian Civilization", 39; and Redford, *Egypt, Canaan, and Israel*, 19.
19. Barry Kemp, "Unification and Urbanization of Ancient Egypt", in Sasson (ed.), *Civilizations of the Ancient Near East*, **2**, 679–90, esp. 682–5.
20. Trigger, "The Rise of Egyptian Civilization", 39.
21. Redford, *Egypt, Canaan, and Israel*, 19–20.
22. Spencer, *Early Egypt*, 58; and Redford, *Egypt, Canaan, and Israel*, 22.
23. Cruz-Uribe, "Scripts", 192.
24. Spencer, *Early Egypt*, 62; Saggs, *Civilizations Before Greece and Rome*, 71.
25. Tomb U-j from the necropolis at Abydos. See Kemp, "Unification and Urbanization", 685.
26. Bard, "The Emergence of the Egyptian State", 78–82, and Spencer, *Early Egypt*, 63–71.
27. Bard, "The Emergence of the Egyptian State", 78.
28. Stiebing, *Uncovering the Past*, 55–60.
29. The word "Pharaoh" is often used for the Egyptian king. It first appeared in the 18th Dynasty and comes from the words for "great house or estate", which referred to the palace as an institution.
30. Daniels, "The Decipherment of Ancient Near Eastern Texts"; and Maurice Pope, *The Story of Archaeological Decipherment from Egyptian Hieroglyphs to Linear B*, 2nd edn (Thames & Hudson, London, 1999).
31. C. A. R. Andrews, "Decipherment", in Redford (ed.), *The Oxford Encyclopedia of Ancient Egypt*, **1**, 360–63.
32. J.-F. Champollion, *Lettre à M. Dacier, relative à l'alphabet des hiéroglyphes phonétiques* (Firmin Didor, Paris, 1822).
33. Kemp, "Unification and Urbanization"; and Spencer, *Early Egypt*, Ch. 3.
34. Kemp, "Unification and Urbanization", 686; and Spencer, *Early Egypt*, 63.
35. Anthony Spalinger, "Chronology and Periodization", in Redford (ed.), *The Oxford Encyclopedia of Ancient Egypt*, **1**, 264–76, esp. 264–8.
36. Bard, "The Emergence of the Egyptian State", 61–7.
37. William J. Murnane, "The History of Ancient Egypt: An Overview", in Sasson (ed.), *Civilizations of the Ancient Near East*, **2**, 691–717; Kemp, "Unification and Urbanization", 684–5; and Kuhrt, *The Ancient Near East*, **1**, 128–30.

38. Herman Te Velde, "Theology, Priests, and Worship in Ancient Egypt", in Sasson (ed.), *Civilizations of the Ancient Near East*, **3**, 1731.
39. Ma'at was also a goddess. See, for example, Manfred Lurker, *The Gods and Symbols of Ancient Egypt* (London: Thames & Hudson, 1980), 78.
40. Amihai Mazar, *Archaeology of the Land of the Bible: 10,000–586 BCE* (Doubleday, Garden City, 1992), 106–7; Bard, "The Emergence of the Egyptian State", 66; and Trigger, "The Rise of Egyptian Civilization", 49.

11: The Old Kingdom or the Pyramid Age (2575–2134 BC)

1. Miroslav Verner, "Old Kingdom: An Overview", in Redford (ed.), *The Oxford Encyclopedia of Ancient Egypt*, **2**, 585–91; Murnane, "The History of Ancient Egypt"; Gerald Kadish, "Egypt, History of (Dyn. 1–11)", in Freedman (ed.), *The Anchor Bible Dictionary*, **2**, 342–5; Jaromir Malek, "The Old Kingdom (c.2686–2125 BC)", in Shaw (ed.), *The Oxford History of Ancient Egypt*, 89–117; and Kuhrt, *The Ancient Near East*, **1**, 135–60.
2. David Lorton, "Legal and Social Institutions of Pharaonic Egypt", in Sasson (ed.), *Civilizations of the Ancient Near East*, **1**, 345–62.
3. Verner, "Old Kingdom: An Overview", 586.
4. *Ibid.*
5. A. G. McDowell, "Crime and Punishment", in Redford (ed.), *The Oxford Encyclopedia of Ancient Egypt*, **1**, 315–20.
6. Jean-Marie Kruchten, "Law", in Redford (ed.), *The Oxford Encyclopedia of Ancient Egypt*, **2**, 279.
7. Saggs, *Civilization Before Greece and Rome*, 170.
8. Lorton, "Legal and Social Institutions", 353.
9. Maya Müller, "Afterlife", in Redford (ed.), *The Oxford Encyclopedia of Ancient Egypt*, **1**, 32–7.
10. Siegfried Morenz, *Egyptian Religion* (Cornell University Press, Ithaca, 1973), Ch. 9; and Erik Hornung, *Conceptions of God in Ancient Egypt* (Cornell University Press, Ithaca, 1983).
11. Müller, "Afterlife", 32.
12. Henri Frankfort, *Ancient Egyptian Religion* (Harper & Row, New York, 1961), 91–2; Edwards, *The Pyramids*, 17–18; and A. J. Spencer, *Death in Ancient Egypt* (Penguin Books, Harmondsworth, 1982), 58–9.
13. R. O. Faulkner, *The Ancient Egyptian Pyramid Texts*, 2 vols (Oxford University Press, Oxford, 1969).
14. Edwards, *The Pyramids*, 18.
15. See the discussion of the *ba* in Frankfort, *Ancient Egyptian*

Religion, 96–9; and Morenz, *Egyptian Religion*, 157.

16. For a discussion see John Baines, "Society, Morality, and Religious Practice", in *Religion in Ancient Egypt: Gods, Myths, and Personal Practice*, Byron Shafer (ed.), 123–200 (Cornell University Press, Ithaca, 1992), 145 and n. 64; and Frankfort, *Ancient Egyptian Religion*, 100–102.

17. Leonard Lesko, "Death and the Afterlife in Ancient Egyptian Thought", in Sasson (ed.), *Civilizations of the Ancient Near East*, **3**, 1764.

18. Rolf Krauss has recently argued that the Egyptians meant the area north of the ecliptic and not the region of the circumpolar stars; see his "Astronomische Konzepte und Jenseitvorstellungen in den Pyramidentexten", *Ägyptologische Abhandlungen* **95** (Harrassowitz, 1997).

19. Faulkner, "The King and the Star Religion".

20. Kent Weeks, "Tombs: An Overview", in Redford (ed.), *The Oxford Encyclopedia of Ancient Egypt*, **3**, 418–25; Edwards, *The Pyramids*, 19–33; and Spencer, *Death in Ancient Egypt*, 29–33, 215–19.

21. Müller, "Afterlife", 32.

22. Müller, "Afterlife", 32.

23. Bard, "The Emergence of the Egyptian State", 71; Spencer, *Early Egypt*, 76–7.

24. Bard, "The Emergence of the Egyptian State", 72.

25. Mark Lehner, *The Complete Pyramids* (Thames & Hudson, London, 1997), 72–81.

26. Bard, "The Emergence of the Egyptian State", 61–88, see figure p. 63.

27. Spencer, *Death in Ancient Egypt*, 48.

28. *Ibid.*, 68, 139.

29. Lehner, *The Complete Pyramids*, 84–93.

30. Redford, *Egypt, Canaan, and Israel*, 49–55.

31. Spencer, *Death in Ancient Egypt*, 61.

32. Faulkner, *The Ancient Egyptian Pyramid Texts*, 267.

33. Lehner, *The Complete Pyramids*, 97–104; Edwards, *The Pyramids*, 90–97.

34. W. M. F. Petrie, E. Mackay and G. A. Wainwright, *Meydum and Memphis, Vol. III* (Murray, London, 1910).

35. George B. Johnson, "The Pyramid of Meidum: Part II", *KMT: A Modern Journal of Egyptology* **5** (1994), 74–5.

36. George B. Johnson, "The Pyramid of Meidum: Part I", *KMT: A Modern Journal of Egyptology* **4** (1993), 64–71, esp. 66–7; and Johnson, "The Pyramid of Meidum: Part II".

37. Kurt Mendelsshon, *The Riddle of the Pyramids* (Thames & Hudson, London, 1974), Ch. 4.

38. Ali el Khouli, *Meidum*, Australian Center for Egyptology: Report 3, G. Martin (ed.) (Sydney, 1991).

39. Edwards, *The Pyramids*, 282.

40. Breasted, *The Development of Religion and Thought*, 72.

41. Edwards, *The Pyramids*, 282–3; and Faulkner, *The Ancient Egyptian Pyramid Texts*, Spells 508 and 523.

42. Lehner, *The Complete Pyramids*, 97–100.

43. *Ibid.*, 18–19.

44. *Ibid.*, 97.

45. Miroslav Verner, "Pyramid", in Redford (ed.), *The Oxford Encyclopedia of Ancient Egypt*, **2**, 87–95, esp. 89.

46. Lehner, "The Complete Pyramids", 97, argues for Snefru as the builder, while Johnson, "The Pyramid of Meidum: Part 1", 66, argues for Huni. Edwards, *The Pyramids*, 114, suggests that it may have been built by both Huni and Snefru.

47. Rainer Stadelmann, "Giza", in Redford (ed.), *The Oxford Encyclopedia of Ancient Egypt*, **2**, 25–30; and Lehner, *The Complete Pyramids*, 106–19.

48. Stadelmann, "Giza", 25.

49. Dieter Arnold, *Building in Egypt: Pharaonic Stone Masonry* (Oxford University Press, New York, 1991), 7–27.

50. Stadelmann, "Giza", 29.

51. Stadelmann, "Giza", 29.

52. Herodotus, *The Histories*, rev. edn. Aubrey de Sélincourt (trans.) (Penguin Books, Harmondsworth, 1972), Book II, 122–4.

53. Rainer Stadelmann, "Builders of the Pyramids", in Sasson (ed.), *Civilizations of the Ancient Near East*, **2**, 719–34, esp. 731; and Verner, "Pyramid", 95.

54. Genesis 41:47–57.

55. See Lehner, "The Complete Pyramids", 38–45; and Saggs, *Civilization Before Greece and Rome*, 59.

56. Exodus 2:25–31, 2:35–40.

57. Mendelssohn, *The Riddle of the Pyramids*, 177–88; and William H. Steibing, *Ancient Astronauts, Cosmic Collisions and other Popular Theories about Man's Past* (Prometheus Books, Buffalo, 1984), 108–10.

58. However, see Stadelmann, "Giza", 28.

59. Herodotus, *The Histories*, Book II, 125.

60. Morris Bierbrier, *The Tomb Builders of the Pharaohs* (The American University in Cairo Press, Cairo, 1982), 12; and Saggs, *Civilization Before Greece and Rome*, 42–6.

61. Anthony Leahy, "Ethnic Diversity in Ancient Egypt", in Sasson (ed.), *Civilizations of the Ancient Near East*, **1**, 225–34, esp. 229; S. Allam, "Slaves", in Redford (ed.), *The Oxford Encyclopedia of Ancient Egypt*, **3**, 293–6.

62. Gardiner, *Egypt of the Pharaohs*, 78.

63. See discussion in Redford, *Egypt, Canaan, and Israel*, 144, 266, 289, 335.

64. Dieter Arnold, *Lexikon der Ägyptologie*, W. Helck, E. Otto and W. Westendorf (eds) (Otto Harrasowitz Verlag, Wiesbaden, 1984), **5**, 1–4.

65. Bierbrier, *The Tomb Builders of the Pharaohs*, 11.

66. Herodotus, *The Histories*, Book II, 126.

67. Edwards, *The Pyramids*, 92.

68. Saggs, *Civilization Before Greece and Rome*, 53.

69. Rolf Krauss, "The Length of Sneferu's Reign and How Long it Took to Build the 'Red Pyramid'", *Journal of Egyptian Archaeology* **82** (1996), 43–50.

70. Lehner, *The Complete Pyramids*, 212–15.

71. Edwards, *The Pyramids*, 246; and Lehner, "Some Observations on the Layout", 19–20, and diagrams on 24 and 25.

72. Stadelmann, "Builders of the Pyramids", 728–9; Arnold, *Building in Egypt*, 13–15 and notes 28 and 26.

73. Arnold, *Building in Egypt*, 13.

74. Lehner, "Some Observations on the Layout", 19–20.

75. Neugebauer, "On the Orientation of the Pyramids".

76. A. Badawy, "The Stellar Destiny and the So-called Air Shafts of the Cheops Pyramid", *Mitteilungen des Instituts für Orientforschung* **10** (1964), 189–206, and *Architecture in Ancient Egypt and the Near East* (MIT Press, Cambridge, 1966); and Trimble, "Astronomical Investigations".

77. Robert Chadwick, "Celestial Alignments and the Soul Shafts of the Khufu Pyramid", *The Journal of the Society for the Study of Egyptian Antiquities* **28** (2001), 15–25.

78. Faulkner, "The King and the Star Religion", 153–61; and Frankfort, *Ancient Egyptian Religion*, 100–101.

79. Lehner, *The Complete Pyramids*, 202–14.

80. *Ibid.*, 215–17; and William F. Petrie, *The Pyramids and Temples of Gizeh* (Field & Turner, London, 1883), 210.

81. However, see Verner, "Pyramid", 95.

82. Edwards, *The Pyramids*, 254–7.

83. Arnold, *Building in Egypt*, 57–72; Lehner, *The Complete Pyramids*, 202–11.

84. Lehner, *The Complete Pyramids*, 215–25.

85. Edwards, *The Pyramids*, 271–3.

86. Lehner, *The Complete Pyramids*, 240–43.

12: Funerary practices, rituals and mummification

1. See arguments against this interpretation in Redford, *Egypt, Canaan, and Israel*, 60.

2. Bierbrier, *The Tomb Builders of the Pharaohs*, 14.

3. John A. Wilson, *The Culture of Ancient Egypt* (University of Chicago Press, Chicago, 1951), 98–9.

4. Rosalie David, *The Pyramid Builders of Ancient Egypt: A Modern Investigation of Pharaoh's Workforce* (Routledge, London, 1996), 44. But see comments in Kuhrt, *The Ancient Near East*, **1**, 142.

5. Cyril Aldred, *Egypt to the End of the Old Kingdom* (Thames & Hudson, London, 1965), 130–31; and W. S. Smith, "The Old Kingdom in Egypt and the Beginning of the First Intermediate Period", in Edwards *et al.* (eds), *Cambridge Ancient History*, 195.

6. Lehner, *The Complete Pyramids*, 229.

7. Verner, "Old Kingdom: An Overview", 587.

8. Malek, "The Old Kingdom", 101–5.

9. Stephan Seidlmayer, "The First Intermediate Period (c.2160–2055)", in Shaw (ed.), *The Oxford History of Ancient Egypt*, 118–47, esp. 120.

10. Kuhrt, *The Ancient Near East*, **1**, 154–5; Seidlmayer, "The First Intermediate Period", 121.

11. Spalinger, "Chronology and Periodization".

12. Malek, "The Old Kingdom", 117; Butzer, *Early Hydraulic Civilization*, 28–9; Barry Kemp, "Old Kingdom, Middle Kingdom, and Second Intermediate Period c. 2686–1552 BC", in Trigger *et al.* (eds), *Ancient Egypt*, 71–182, esp. 178–82.

13. Seidlmayer, "The First Intermediate Period", 145; John A. Wilson, "The Admonitions of Ipu-Wer, Egyptian Oracles and Prophecies", in Pritchard (ed.), *Ancient Near Eastern Texts*, 441–4.

14. Seidlmayer, "The First Intermediate Period", Ch. 6, 118–47.

15. For overviews see Ronald Leprohon, "Egypt, History of (Dyn. 11–17)", in Freedman (ed.), *The Anchor Bible Dictionary*, **2**, 345–8; Detlef Franke, "Middle Kingdom", in Redford (ed.), *The Oxford Encyclopedia of Ancient Egypt*, **2**, 393–400; Kuhrt, *The Ancient Near East*, **1**, 161–82; and Gae Callender, "The Middle Kingdom Renaissance (c.2055–1650 BC)", in Shaw (ed.), *The Oxford History of Ancient Egypt*, 148–83.

16. Detlef Franke, "The Middle Kingdom in Egypt", in Sasson (ed.), *Civilizations of the Ancient Near East*, **2**, 735–48, esp. 735.

17. See Lehner, *The Complete Pyramids*, 168–9; and Edwards, *The Pyramids*, 197–205.

18. T. G. H. James (ed.), *Excavating in Egypt: The Egyptian Exploration Society: 1882–1982* (University of Chicago Press, Chicago, 1982), 63.

19. Edwards, *The Pyramids*, 205.

20. See Jadwiga Lipinska and George Johnson, "The Polish Archaeology Missions at Deir el Bahari", *KMT: A Modern Journal of Ancient Egypt* **3**(2) (1992), 46–51; and "The Way-Station of Thutmosis III at Deir El Bahari", *KMT: A Modern Journal of Ancient Egypt* **3**(3) (1992), 12–25.

21. Leprohon, "Egypt, History of", 345.

22. Franke, "Kings of Akkad", 736.

23. Kuhrt, *The Ancient Near East*, **1**, 164. However, see R. B. Parkinson, *The Tale of Sinuhe and other Ancient Egyptian Poems, 1940–1640 BC* (Oxford University Press, Oxford, 1998).

24. Miriam Lichtheim, *Ancient Egyptian Literature* (University of California Press, Berkeley, 1973), **1**, 139–45, and Antonio Loprieno (ed.), *Ancient Egyptian Literature: History and Forms*, Probleme der Ägyptologie 10 (E. J. Brill Publishers, Leiden, 1996).

25. Lichtheim, *Ancient Egyptian Literature*, **1**, 135–9.

26. Donald Redford, "Execration and Execration Texts", in Freedman (ed.), *The Anchor Bible Dictionary*, **2**, 681–2.

27. Robert Ritner, "Magic: Magic in Daily Life", in Redford (ed.), *Oxford Encyclopedia of Ancient Egypt*, **2**, 331–3.

28. Redford, *Egypt, Canaan, and Israel*, 87.

29. Kuhrt, *The Ancient Near East*, **1**, 164.

30. Lichtheim, *Ancient Egyptian Literature*, **1**, 135–9.

31. *Ibid.*, 118–20, and quoted in Kuhrt, *The Ancient Near East*, **1**, 168–71.

32. Betty Winkelman, "Buhen, Blueprints of an Egyptian Fortress", *KMT: A Modern Journal of Ancient Egypt* **6** (1995), 72–81.

33. Lehner, *The Complete Pyramids*, 179–83; Edwards, *The Pyramids*, 218–27.

34. Dieter Arnold, "Royal Cult Complexes of the Old and Middle Kingdoms", in *Temples of Ancient Egypt*, B. Shafer (ed.), 31–85 (Cornell University Press, Ithaca, 1997), 80; and with Adela Oppenheim, "Reexcavating the Senwosret III Pyramid Complex at Dashur", *KMT: A Modern Journal of Ancient Egypt*, **6** (1995), 44–56.

35. Arnold, *Building in Egypt*, 178. By the same author is the definitive work on this pyramid, *Der Pyramidenbezirk des Königs Amenemhet III. in Dahschur: Vol. 1* (Philipp von Zabern, Mainz, 1987).

36. Robert J. Wenke, "Faiyum", in Meyers (ed.), *Oxford Encyclopedia of Archaeology*, **2**, 299.

37. Franke, "Middle Kingdom", 399; and Callender, "The Middle Kingdom Renaissance", 164–5.

38. Alan B. Lloyd, "The Egyptian Labyrinth", *Journal of Egyptian Archaeology*, **56** (1970), 81–100.

39. Edwards, *The Pyramids*, 218–21.

40. J. Gwyn Griffiths, "Osiris", in Redford (ed.), *The Oxford Encyclopedia of Ancient Egypt*, **2**, 615–19; Jacobus Van Dijk, "Myth and Mythmaking in Ancient Egypt", in Sasson (ed.), *Civilizations of the Ancient Near East*, **3**, 1697–1709, esp. 1702–9.

41. See the somewhat out-of-date treatment by Frankfort, *Kingship and the Gods*, Ch. 15.

42. Lesko, "Death and the Afterlife", 1773.

43. Howard Carter, *The Tomb of Tutankhamen*, 3 vols (Sphere Books, London, 1972), 175 (originally published Cassell, London, 1923–33); Frankfort, *Kingship and the Gods*, 185–6; and Manfred Lurker, *The Gods and Symbols of Ancient Egypt* (Thames & Hudson, London, 1988), 41.

44. R. T. Rundle Clark, *Myth and Symbol in Ancient Egypt* (Thames & Hudson, 1959), 118–19.

45. Eberhard Otto, *Ancient Egyptian Art: The Cults of Osiris and Amon*, K. Bosse Griffiths (trans.) (Harry N. Abrams, New York, 1967), 61–4.

46. Another version of the story exists in which Seth chopped up the body of Osiris and scattered the pieces over Egypt. Isis retrieved the pieces, sewed them back together and revived Osiris. See Rundle Clark, *Myth and Symbol in Ancient Egypt*, 105 and 109.

47. Frankfort, *Kingship and the Gods*, 200–201.

48. Morenz, *Egyptian Religion*, 248–50.

49. Morenz, *Egyptian Religion*, 249; David, *The Ancient Egyptians* (Routledge & Kegan Paul, London, 1982), 174.

50. R. O. Faulkner, *The Egyptian Book of the Dead*, rev. edn C. Andrews (British Museum, London, 1985).

51. Erik Hornung, *The Ancient Egyptian Books of the Afterlife* (Cornell University Press, Ithaca, 1999), 13–22.

52. Lurker, *The Gods and Symbols*, 128–9.

53. David P. Silverman, "Divinity and Deities in Ancient Egypt", in Shafer (ed.), *Religion in Ancient Egypt*, 7–87, esp. 44.

54. Morenz, *Egyptian Religion*, 255–7; and David, *The Ancient Egyptians*, 175–7.

55. Ann Rosalie David, "Mummification", in Redford (ed.), *The Oxford Encyclopedia of Ancient Egypt*, **2**, 439–44; A. R. David and E. Tapp, *The Mummy's Tale: The Scientific and Medical Investigation of Natsef-Amun, Priest in the Temple at Karnak* (St. Martin's Press, New York, 1992); Leonard Lesko, "Death and the Afterlife"; Morenz, *Egyptian Religion*, 198–204; and Spencer, *Death in Ancient Egypt*, 112–38.

56. Spencer, *Death in Ancient Egypt*, 30, 33.

57. David, "Mummification", 439–40.

58. *Ibid.*, 440.

59. Spencer, *Death in Ancient Egypt*, 35.

60. *Ibid.*

61. David and Tapp, *The Mummy's Tale*, 43.

62. Spencer, *Death in Ancient Egypt*, 123.

63. David, "Mummification", 441.

64. Herodotus, *The Histories*, Book II, 86–8.

65. David, "Mummification", 439.

66. Ann Macy Roth, "Opening of the Mouth", in Redford (ed.), *Oxford Encyclopedia of Ancient Egypt*, **2**, 605–9.

67. David and Tapp, *The Mummy's Tale*.

68. Kent Weeks, "Valley of the Kings", in Redford (ed.), *The Oxford Encyclopedia of Ancient Egypt*, **3**, 471–4 and *The Lost Tomb* (William Morrow, New York, 1998); Richard Wilkinson and Nicholas Reeves, *The Complete Valley of the Kings, Tombs and Treasures of Egypt's Greatest Pharaohs* (Thames & Hudson, London, 1996).

69. Gerhard Haeny, "New Kingdom 'Mortuary Temples' and 'Mansions of Millions of Years'", in *Temples of Ancient Egypt*, B. Shafer (ed.), 86–126 (Cornell University Press, Ithaca, 1997), esp. 86–7.

70. Bierbrier, *The Tomb Builders of the Pharaohs*, 14.

71. Spencer, *Death in Ancient Egypt*, 63.

72. Bierbrier, *The Tomb Builders of the Pharaohs*, 111–17.

13: The Hyskos period and the New Kingdom

1. Franke, "Middle Kingdom", 393–9; Barry Kemp, "Old Kingdom, Middle Kingdom", 154.

2. Leprohon, "Egypt, History of", 347.

3. Manfred Bietak, "Hyksos", in Redford (ed.), *Oxford Encyclopedia of Ancient Egypt*, **2**, 136–43; James Weinstein, "Hyksos", in Meyers (ed.), *Oxford Encyclopedia of Archaeology*, **3**, 133–6; William A. Ward, "Egyptian Relations with Canaan", in Freedman (ed.), *The Anchor Bible Dictionary*, **2**, 402–3; Donald Redford and James Weinstein, "Hyksos", in Freedman (ed.), *The Anchor Bible Dictionary*, **3**, 341–8; Kuhrt, *The Ancient Near East*, **1**, 173–82; Janine Bourriau, "The Second Intermediate Period (c.1650–1550)", in Shaw (ed.), *The Oxford History of Ancient Egypt*, 185–217, Ch. 8; and John van Seters, *The Hyksos: A New Investigation* (Yale University Press, New Haven, CT, 1966).

4. Mazar, *Archaeology of the Land of the Bible*, 188–94.

5. See Kuhrt, *The Ancient Near East*, **1**, 175.

6. Redford, *Egypt, Canaan and Israel*, 119.

7. Niels Peter Lemche, "The History of Syria and Palestine", in Sasson (ed.), *Civilizations of the Ancient Near East*, **2**, 1195–218, esp. 1205.

8. Manfred Bietak, "Dab'a, Tell Ed", in Redford (ed.), *Oxford Encyclopedia of Ancient Egypt*, **1**, 351–4, esp. 351.

9. Redford, *Egypt, Canaan and Israel*, 116–17.

10. Redford and Weinstein, "Hyksos", "*aamu*"; Bourriau, "The Second Intermediate Period", 187; Whiting, "Amorite Tribes and Nations"; and Redford, *Egypt, Canaan and Israel*, 32, 100.

11. Borriau, "The Second Intermediate Period", 187–9; Lemche, "The History of Syria and Palestine", 1205.

12. Franke, "The Middle Kingdom in Egypt", 738. For a recent translation see Parkinson, *The Tale of Sinuhe* and an older translation of John A. Wilson, "The Prophecy of Neferti", in Pritchard (ed.), *Ancient Near Eastern Texts*, 444–6.

13. See the reference to *Papyrus Brooklyn Museum 35.1446* in Kemp, "Old Kingdom, Middle Kingdom", 155.

14. Mary Aiken Littauer and J. H. Crouwel, "Chariots", in Freedman (ed.), *The Anchor Bible Dictionary*, **1**, 888–92 and "Chariots", in Meyers (ed.), *Oxford Encyclopedia of Archaeology*, **1**, 485–7. Kathy Hansen, "The Chariotry in Egypt's Age of Chivalry", *KMT: A Modern Journal of Ancient Egypt* **5**(1) (1994), 51–61 contains useful illustrations.

15. Alan R. Schulman, "Chariots, Chariotry, and the Hyksos", *The Journal of the Society for the Study of Egyptian Antiquities* **10**(2) (1980), 105–53; Rupert Chapman, "Weapons and Warfare", in Meyers (ed.), *Oxford Encyclopedia of Archaeology*, **5**, 337; T. Säve-Söderbergh, "The Hyksos Rule in Egypt", *Journal of Egyptian Archaeolog* **37** (1951), 53–71.

16. Schulman, "Chariots, Chariotry, and the Hyksos", 105.

17. Säve-Söderbergh, "The Hyksos Rule in Egypt", 60.

18. Manfred Bietak, "Dab'a, Tell Ed", in Meyers (ed.), *Oxford Encyclopedia of Archaeology*, **2**, 99–101.

19. Bietak, "Dab'a, Tell Ed".

20. Bietak, "Hyksos", 141; Mazar, *Archaeology of the Land of the Bible*, 191–2.

21. John S. Holladay, "Maskhuta, Tell El", in Meyers (ed.), *Oxford Encyclopedia of Archaeology*, **3**, 432–7 and *Cities of the Delta III, Tell el-Maskhuta* (Undena Publishing, Malibu, CA, 1982).

22. Weinstein, "Hyksos", 134.

23. Bietak, "Dab'a, Tell Ed".

24. Redford, *Egypt, Canaan, and Israel*, 102–3.

25. Kemp, "Old Kingdom, Middle Kingdom", 158.

26. Timothy Kendall, "Kush", in Redford (ed.), *Oxford Encyclopedia of Ancient Egypt*, **2**, 250–52; and Redford, *Egypt, Canaan, and Israel*, 111–13.

27. Bietak, "Hyksos", 142.

28. Lana Troy, "New Kingdom: Eighteenth Dynasty to the Amarna Period", in Redford (ed.), *Oxford Encyclopedia of Ancient Egypt*, **2**, 525–31, esp. 527.

29. For overviews see the following articles by William J. Murnane. "New Kingdom: An Overview", in Redford (ed.), *Oxford Encyclopedia of Ancient Egypt*, **2**, 519–25; "The History of Ancient Egypt", in Sasson (ed.), *Civilizations of the Ancient Near East*, **1**, 702–9; and "Egypt, History of (Dyn. 18–20)", in Freedman (ed.), *The Anchor Bible Dictionary*, **2**, 348–53. See also Betsy M. Bryan, "The Eighteenth Dynasty Before the Amarna Period (c.1550–1352 BC)", in Shaw (ed.), *The Oxford History of Ancient Egypt*, 218–71.

30. Gardiner, *Egypt of the Pharaohs*, 52.

31. Murnane, "New Kingdom: An Overview", 519–20.

32. *Ibid.*, 521; Bryan, "The Eighteenth Dynasty", 226–30.

33. Jadwiga Lipinska, "Hatshepsut", in Redford (ed.), *Oxford Encyclopedia of Ancient Egypt*, **2**, 85–7; and G. Robins, *Women in Ancient Egypt* (Harvard University Press, Cambridge, 1993), 45–52.

34. Kuhrt, *The Ancient Near East*, **1**, 191–3.

35. Robins, *Women in Ancient Egypt*, 45.

36. *Ibid.*, 46.

37. Emily Teeter, "Hatshepsut", *KMT: A Modern Journal of Ancient Egypt* **1**(1) (1990), 8.

38. Teeter, "Hatshepsut", 4.

39. Robins, *Women in Ancient Egypt*, 51.

40. *Ibid.*

41. Teeter, "Hatshepsut", 4–5.

42. Murnane, "The History of Ancient Egypt", 703; Kuhrt, *The Ancient Near East*, **1**, 193; David O'Connor, "New Kingdom and Third Intermediate Period, 1552–664 BC", in Trigger *et al.*, *Ancient Egypt*, 219.

43. O'Connor, "New Kingdom and Third Intermediate Period", 219.

44. Robins, *Women in Ancient Egypt*, 47.

45. *Ibid.*, 50.

46. Franke, "The Middle Kingdom in Egypt", 746; and Robins, *Women in Ancient Egypt*, Ch. 2.

47. Spencer, *Early Egypt*, 64.

48. Bryan, "The Eighteenth Dynasty", 237–8.

49. Kuhrt, *The Ancient Near East*, **1**, 177.

50. Gay Robins, "Queens and Queenship in the 18th Dynasty Before the Amarna Period", *The Bulletin of the Canadian Society for Mesopotamian Studies* **26** (1993), 53.

51. Bryan, "The Eighteenth Dynasty", 238–42; and Haeny, "New Kingdom 'Mortuary Temples'", 93–5.

52. There is some confusion concerning the identity of her tomb in the Valley of the Kings. Bryan, "The Eighteenth Dynasty", 240, refers to it as KV 20.

53. Franciszek Pawlicki and George Johnson, "Behind the Third Portico", *KMT: A Modern Journal of Ancient Egypt* **5**(2) (1994), 40–49; Lipinska, "Hatshepsut", 87; Haeny, "New Kingdom 'Mortuary Temples'", 93–5.

54. Labib Habachi, *The Obelisks of Egypt* (Charles Scribner's Sons, New York, 1977), 59–73; Dieter Arnold, *Building in Egypt*, 67–70.

55. Habachi, *The Obelisks of Egypt*, Chs 6 and 7.

56. Robins, *Women in Ancient Egypt*, 47.

57. Denis Forbes, "Power Behind the Throne, Senenmut", *KMT: A Modern Journal of Ancient Egypt* **1**(1) (1990), 14–19.

58. Wilson, *The Culture of Ancient Egypt*, 176.

59. Donald Redford, *The History and Chronology of the Egyptian 18th Dynasty: Seven Studies* (University of Toronto Press, Toronto, 1967), 57–62.

60. Redford, *Egypt, Canaan, and Israel*, 151–2; and *History and Chronology*, 80.

61. Jadwiga Lipinska, "Thuthmosis III", in Redford (ed.), *Oxford Encyclopedia of Ancient Egypt*, 3, 401–3.

62. Murnane, "New Kingdom: An Overview", 521; Bryan, "The Eighteenth Dynasty", 243–8.

63. Andrea Gnirs, "Military: An Overview", in Redford (ed.), *Oxford Encyclopedia of Ancient Egypt*, 2, 400–406; Alan R. Schulman, "Military Organization in Pharaonic Egypt", in Sasson (ed.), *Civilizations of the Ancient Near East*, 1, 289–301.

64. Lipinska, "Thuthmosis III", 401.

65. Kuhrt, *The Ancient Near East*, 1, 289–300.

66. Troy, "New Kingdom", 525–31; Bryan, "The Eighteenth Dynasty", 260–71; and Betsy M. Bryan, Arielle Kozloff and Lawrence M. Berman, *Egypt's Dazzling Sun: Amenhotep III and His World* (Cleveland Museum of Art, Cleveland, and Indiana University Press, Bloomington, 1992).

14: Akhenaten and the Amarna period

1. H. R. Hall, "Egypt and the External World in the Time of Akhenaten", *Journal of Egyptian Archaeology* 14 (1928), 45–56, esp. 45.

2. Sigmund Freud, *Moses and Monotheism* (Vintage Books, New York, 1967), 21–3; and Jan Assmann, *Moses the Egyptian* (Harvard University Press, Cambridge, 1997), Ch. 5.

3. Edward F. Wente, "Monotheism", in Redford (ed.), *Oxford Encyclopedia of Ancient Egypt*, 2, 432–5, esp. 435.

4. Freud, *Moses and Monotheism*, 27.

5. James Henry Breasted, *A History of Ancient Egypt* (Bantam Books, New York, 1906), 297–8.

6. Donald B. Redford, *Akhenaten: The Heretic King* (Princeton University Press, Princeton, 1984), 235.

7. For an overview see, Erik Hornung, *Akhenaten and the Religion of Light* (Cornell University Press, Ithaca, 1995), 1–18; Juliette Bentley, "Akhenaten in the Eye of the Beholder", in *Amarna Letters 2*, 6–8 (KMT Publications, San Francisco, 1992); and Cyril Aldred, *Akhenaten: King of Egypt* (Thames & Hudson, London, 1988), 7 and Ch. 26.

8. Stephen Quirke, *The Cult of Ra: Sun-Worship in Ancient Egypt* (Thames & Hudson, London, 2001), Ch. 5; and Vincent A. Tobin, "Akhenaten as a Tragedy of History: A Critique of the Amarna Age", *The Journal of the Society for the Study of Egyptian Antiquities* 23 (1993), 5–28; this issue of the journal is devoted to Akhenaten.

9. Aldred, *Akhenaten: King of Egypt*, 237.

10. Redford, *Akhenaten: The Heretic King*, 176.

11. According to Redford, *ibid.*, 141, "He who is useful to the Sun-disc," or "Glorified of the Sun-disc"; Gardiner, *Egypt of the Pharaohs*, 222 translates "Serviceable to the Aten".

12. Gerald E. Kadish, "The New Kingdom: Amarna Period and the End of the Eighteenth Dynasty", in Redford (ed.), *Oxford Encyclopedia of Ancient Egypt*, 2, 531–4; Betsy Bryan, "Amarna, Tell El", in Redford (ed.), *Oxford Encyclopedia of Ancient Egypt*, 1, 60–65; Kemp, *Ancient Egypt: Anatomy of a Civilization*, 261–317; and Rolf Krauss, "Akhetaten: A Portrait in Art of an Ancient Egyptian Capital", in Sasson (ed.), *Civilizations of the Ancient Near East*, 2, 749–62; Donald Redford, "Akhenaten", in Freedman (ed.), *The Anchor Bible Dictionary*, 1, 135–7.

13. John L. Foster, "The Hymn to Aten: Akhenaten Worships the Sole God", in Sasson (ed.), *Civilizations of the Ancient Near East*, 3, 1751–61; and Aldred, *Akhenaten: King of Egypt*, 241.

14. W. L. Moran, *The Amarna Letters* (The Johns Hopkins University Press, Baltimore, 1992); Nadav Na'aman, "Amarna Letters", in Freedman (ed.), *The Anchor Bible Dictionary*, 1, 174–81.

15. Shlomo Izre'el, "The Amarna Letters from Canaan", in Sasson (ed.), *Civilizations of the Ancient Near East*, 4, 2411–19.

16. For example, Walter A. Fairservis Jr., *The Ancient Kingdoms of the Nile* (Mentor Books, New York, 1962), 139.

17. Wilson, *The Culture of Ancient Egypt* , 230–31.

18. Aldred, *Akhenaten: King of Egypt*, 120–21.

19. Wente, "Monotheism", 434–5; Marianne Eaton-Krauss, "Akhenaten", in Redford (ed.), *Oxford Encyclopedia of Ancient Egypt*, 1, 48–51; Hornung, *The Ancient Egyptian Books of the Afterlife*, 87–94.

20. See discussion in Assmann, *Moses the Egyptian*, 23–54; Morenz, *Egyptian Religion*, 146–50; Freud, *Moses and Monotheism*, 72–4.

21. William J. Murnane, "Egypt, History of"; Jacobus Van Dijk, "The Amarna Period and the Later New Kingdom (c.1352–1069)", in Shaw (ed.), *The Oxford History of Ancient Egypt*, 272–313.

22. Redford, *Akhenaten: The Heretic King*, 169–70; and Aldred, *Akhenaten: King of Egypt*, 239.

23. Aldred, *Akhenaten: King of Egypt*, 245.

24. Redford, "Akhenaten", 135; Lanny Bell, "Appendix I: Luxor Temple in the Reign of Akhenaten", in Shafer (ed.), *Temples of Ancient Egypt*, 127–84, esp. 180–82.

25. Hornung, *The Ancient Egyptian Books of the Afterlife*, 95–104.

26. Redford, *Akhenaten: The Heretic King*, 72, 152; Aldred, *Akhenaten: King of Egypt*, 265 suggests that the royal family was surrounded by a full-time "praetorian guard" like those used later to protect Roman emperors. See also Van Dijk, "The Amarna Period", 277–8.

27. Redford, *Akhenaten: The Heretic King*, 167–8, 194.

28. Robins, *Women in Ancient Egypt*, 53.

29. *Ibid.*, 54.

30. *Ibid.*

31. Aldred, *Akhenaten: King of Egypt*, 227, 230. A number of scholars believe that Nefertiti actually became the pharaoh and was co-regent with her husband. See Earl L. Ertman, "Is there Evidence for a 'King' Nefertiti?", in *Amarna Letters 2*, 50–55 (KMT Publications, San Francisco, 1992).

32. Redford, *Akhenaten: The Heretic King*, 191.

33. *Ibid.*, 192.

34. Kuhrt, *The Ancient Near East*, 1, 202 suggests a brother, while Quirke, *The Cult of Ra*, 164 argues that he was the son of one of Akhenaten's wives.

35. Nicholas Reeves, *The Complete Tutankhamun* (Thames & Hudson, London, 1990).

36. Some destruction began early in the reign of Tutankhamun; Eaton-Krauss, "Akhenaten", 50.

37. Aldred, *Akhenaten: King of Egypt*, 301–2.

38. *Ibid.*, 231.

39. *Ibid.*, 110; Redford, *Akhenaten: The Heretic King*, 58 says he was "hideous to behold".

40. Robert Steven Bianchi, "Ancient Egyptian Reliefs, Statuary, and Monumental Paintings", in Sasson (ed.), *Civilizations of the Ancient Near East*, 4, 2533–54.

41. Redford, *Akhenaten: The Heretic King*, 188, 193.

42. Cyril Aldred and A. T. Sandison, "The Pharaoh Akhenaten: A Problem in Egyptology and Pathology", *Bulletin of the History of Medicine* 36, 293–316. See also C. Aldred, *Akhenaten: Pharaoh of Egypt* (Thames & Hudson, London, 1968), 100–105; Aldred, *Akhenaten: King of Egypt*, 231–4; and Krauss, "Akhetaten: A Portrait in Art", 757.

43. A new medical hypothesis argues that Akhenaten's physical condition was caused by Marfan's Syndrome. See Alwyn Burridge, "Akhenaten: A New Perspective. Evidence of a Genetic Disorder in the Royal Family of 18th Dynasty Egypt", *The Journal of the Society for the Study of Egyptian Antiquities* 23 (1993), 63–74.

44. See John A. Larson, "Theodore M. Davis and the So-called Tomb of Queen Tiye, Part 1", *KMT: A Modern Journal of Ancient Egypt* 1 (1990), 48–53, 60–61 and

"Theodore M. Davis and the So-called Tomb of Queen Tiye, Part 2", *KMT: A Modern Journal of Ancient Egypt* **2** (1991), 43–51.

45. Aldred, *Akhenaten: King of Egypt*, 199; Eaton-Krauss, "Akhenaten", 50 accepts that the mummy in KV 55 was that of Akhenaten.

46. Gay Robins, *Proportion and Style in Ancient Egyptian Art* (University of Texas Press, Austin, 1994), 119–59; Krauss, "Akhetaten: A Portrait in Art".

47. Eaton-Krauss, "Akhenaten", 50.

48. Jean Yoyotte, "Das Neue Reich in Ägypten. I: Die XVIII Dynastie", in *Fischer Weltgeschichte, Vol. III: Die altorientalischen Reiche*, part 2, E. Cassin, J. Bottéro, J. Vercoutter (eds), 222–60 (Frankfort-am-Main, 1966), 250. Mentioned in O'Connor, "New Kingdom and Third Intermediate Period", 221.

49. Redford, *Akhenaten: The Heretic King*, 234.

50. Van Dijk, "The Amarna Period".

51. John Baines and Jaromir Málek, *Cultural Atlas of Ancient Egypt*, 2nd edn (Facts on File, New York, 2000), 46.

52. Van Dijk, "The Amarna Period", 292–4; Otto J. Schaden, "Courtier, Confidante, Councillor, King: The God's Father Ay", in *Amarna Letters 2*, D. C. Forbes (ed.), 92–115 (KMT Publications, San Francisco, 1992).

53. Kenneth A. Kitchen, *Pharaoh Triumphant: The Life and Times of Ramesses II* (Benben Publications, Mississauga, 1982), 15.

54. Ronald J. Leprohon, "A Vision Collapsed: Akhenaten's Reforms Viewed through Decrees of Later Reigns", in *Amarna Letters*, D. Forbes (ed.), 66–73 (KMT Publications, San Francisco, 1991).

55. Carter, *The Tomb of Tutankhamen*; Christiane Desroches-Noblecourt, *Tutankhamen* (George Rainbird, London, 1963).

56. James (ed.), *Excavating in Egypt*.

57. Weeks, *The Lost Tomb*.

58. Lyn Green, "A Lost Queen of Ancient Egypt, King's Daughter, King's Great Wife, Ankhesenamen", *KMT: A Modern Journal of Ancient Egypt* **1**(4) (1990), 22–9.

59. Kitchen, *Pharaoh Triumphant*, 15.

60. See Reeves, *The Complete Tutankhamun*, 23 and Quirke, *The Cult of Ra*, 146.

61. For the Hittite text see Albrecht Goetze, "Hittite Historical Texts", in Pritchard (ed.), *Ancient Near Eastern Texts*, 318–19.

62. Gardiner, *Egypt of the Pharaohs*, 241.

63. Aldred, *Akhenaten: King of Egypt*, 228–9; and Reeves, *The Complete Tutankhamun*, 23, 141.

64. Redford, *Egypt, Canaan, and Israel*, 179; and Redford, *Akhenaten: The Heretic King*, 217–21.

15: The 19th Dynasty and the Ramesside kings

1. Kenneth A. Kitchen, "New Kingdom: Nineteenth Dynasty", in Redford (ed.), *Oxford Encyclopedia of Ancient Egypt*, **2**, 534–8 and "Pharaoh Ramesses II and His Time", in Sasson (ed.), *Civilizations of the Ancient Near East*, **2**, 763–74; Murnane, "Egypt, History of", 351–3; and Van Dijk, "The Amarna Period", 297–302.

2. Gerhard Haeny, "Royal Cult Complexes of the Ramesside Period", in Shafer (ed.), *Temples in Ancient Egypt*, 107–23; and Otto, *Ancient Egyptian Art*, 50–58.

3. Kitchen, *Pharaoh Triumphant*, 51.

4. Kenneth A. Kitchen, "Ramesses II", in Redford (ed.), *Oxford Encyclopedia of Ancient Egypt*, **2**, 116–18.

5. Van Dijk, "The Amarna Period", 297.

6. For the dates of the reign of Ramesses II and related problems of Egyptian chronology, see Kitchen, *Pharaoh Triumphant* and "Egypt, History of (Chronology)", in Freedman (ed.), *The Anchor Bible Dictionary*, **2**, 321–31 and bibliography. Dates used here for Ramesses II follow Shaw (ed.), *The Oxford History of Ancient Egypt*, 481.

7. Alan R. Schulman, "Military Organization in Pharaonic Egypt" and *Military Rank, Title, and Organization in the Egyptian New Kingdom* (Münchner Ägyptologische Studien, Munich and Berlin, 1964). For an overview see Trevor Watkins, "The Beginnings of Warfare", in *Warfare in the Ancient World*, J. Hackett (ed.), 27–35 (Sidgwick & Jackson, London, 1989) and Kitchen, "Pharaoh Triumphant", 140–44.

8. James Hoffmeier, "Military: Materiel", in Redford (ed.), *Oxford Encyclopedia of Ancient Egypt*, **2**, 406–12, esp. 409.

9. Littauer and Crouwel, "Chariots". See additional references in Ch. 13.

10. A ratio of one chariot for every 500 infantry has been suggested, but this figure has never been confirmed and may be much lower. See note 29 below and Schulman, "Chariots, Chariotry, and the Hyksos", 132.

11. Van Dijk, "The Amarna Period", 297.

12. See Kitchen, *Pharaoh Triumphant*, 50–64 for battle details.

13. Kuhrt, *The Ancient Near East*, **1**, 258 calls it "a resounding defeat".

14. For Hittite military see Bryce, *Life and Society in the Hittite World*, 98–118 and J. G. Macqueen, *The Hittites and their Contemporaries in Asia Minor* (Thames & Hudson, London, 1986), 56–64. Ramesses II's own inscriptions claim they had 2500 chariots.

15. Kitchen, *Pharaoh Triumphant*, 61.

16. Macqueen, *The Hittites*, 49.

17. See Houwink Ten Cate, "Hittite History"; and Macqueen, "The History of Anatolia".

18. Kuhrt, *The Ancient Near East*, **1**, 258–62.

19. See photos in Kitchen, *Pharaoh Triumphant*, 76–7. Excerpts from the text follow on 78–9.

16: Egypt in the late second and first millenniums BC

1. Anthony Leahy, "Foreign Incursions", in Redford (ed.), *Oxford Encyclopedia of Ancient Egypt*, **1**, 548–52; Ian Shaw, "Egypt and the Outside World", in Shaw (ed.), *The Oxford History of Ancient Egypt*, 314–29.

2. Over the years some scholars have emphasized Egypt's geographical isolation while others have denied it. See, for example, Baines and Málek, *Cultural Atlas of Ancient Egypt*, 12; Wilson, *The Culture of Ancient Egypt*, 11; and Gardiner, *Egypt of the Pharaohs*, 31, 36–7. Aldred, *Egypt to the End of the Old Kingdom*, 48 did not agree.

3. See discussion in Kuhrt, *The Ancient Near East*, **2**, 385–6.

4. Chronology follows Shaw (ed.), *The Oxford History of Ancient Egypt*, 481.

5. Eliezer Oren, *The Sea Peoples and their World: A Reassessment* (University of Pennsylvania Press, Philadelphia, 2000); Trude Dothan and Moshe Dothan, *People of the Sea* (Macmillan, New York, 1992); Trude Dothan, "The 'Sea Peoples' and the Philistines of Ancient Palestine", in Sasson (ed.), *Civilizations of the Ancient Near East*, **2**, 1267–79; Anthony Leahy, "Sea Peoples", in Redford (ed.), *Oxford Encyclopedia of Ancient Egypt*, **3**, 257–60; and N. K. Sandars, *The Sea Peoples: Warriors of the Ancient Mediterranean*, rev. edn (Thames & Hudson, London, 1985), 32, 48–53.

6. Warren J. Heard, "Libya", in Freedman (ed.), *The Anchor Bible Dictionary*, **4**, 324; and Redford, *Egypt, Canaan, and Israel*, 247–50.

7. Kitchen, *Pharaoh Triumphant*, 24–6, 67, 71–2; and Kuhrt, *The Ancient Near East*, **2**, 385–93.

8. O'Connor, "New Kingdom and Third Intermediate Period", 273.

9. Kenneth Kitchen, "Nineteenth Dynasty", in Redford (ed.), *Oxford Encyclopedia of Ancient Egypt*, **2**, 534–8.

10. Pierre Grandet, "The New Kingdom: Twentieth Dynasty", in Redford (ed.), *Oxford Encyclopedia of Ancient Egypt*, **2**, 538–43; and Kuhrt, *The Ancient Near East*, **1**, 204–10.

11. Redford, *Egypt, Canaan, and Israel*, 248–50.

12. Kuhrt, *The Ancient Near East*, **2**, 386–7.

13. Shaw, "Egypt and the Outside World", 328; and

O'Connor, "New Kingdom and Third Intermediate Period", 276.

14. See Robert Drews, *The End of the Bronze Age* (Princeton University Press, Princeton, 1993), Ch. 6.

15. Kuhrt, *The Ancient Near East*, **2**, 388; and O'Connor, "New Kingdom and Third Intermediate Period", 276.

16. Bernard Knapp, "Island Cultures: Crete, Thera, Cyprus, Rhodes, and Sardinia", in Sasson (ed.), *Civilizations of the Ancient Near East*, **2**, 1433–49, esp. 1444. The Sherden had previously served as mercenaries in the armies of Ramesses II at the battle of Qadesh, and in the 18th Dynasty. See Kitchen, "Pharaoh Triumphant", 53.

17. Shaw, "Egypt and the Outside World", 328.

18. Oren, *The Sea Peoples and their World*. See note 3 above, and Mazar, *Archaeology of the Land of the Bible*, 300–313; O'Connor, "New Kingdom and Third Intermediate Period", 203–4, 253; and Redford, *Egypt, Canaan, and Israel*, 243, note 14.

19. Sandars, *The Sea Peoples*, 117–20.

20. Dothan, "The 'Sea Peoples' and the Philistines", 1267, 1273. See also Dothan and Dothan, *People of the Sea*, Ch. 14; Mazar, *Archaeology of the Land of the Bible*, 307–8; Redford, *Egypt, Canaan, and Israel*, 251 and sources quoted in note 48.

21. Redford, *Egypt, Canaan, and Israel*, 253–6. But Kuhrt, *The Ancient Near East*, **2**, 390–93 does not agree.

22. John Chadwick, *The Mycenaean World* (Cambridge University Press, Cambridge, 1976).

23. W. H. Van Soldt, "Ugarit: A Second Millennium Kingdom on the Mediterranean Coast", in Sasson (ed.), *Civilizations of the Ancient Near East*, **2**, 1255–66, esp. 1264–65.

24. O'Connor, "New Kingdom and Third Intermediate Period", 272.

25. Dothan and Dothan, *People of the Sea*, 211–12, and *passim*, Sandars, *The Sea Peoples*, 162 and 167.

26. Kuhrt, *The Ancient Near East*, **1**, 223–4.

27. O'Connor, "New Kingdom and Third Intermediate Period", 226.

28. Bierbrier, *The Tomb Builders of the Pharaohs*, 41–2.

29. Murnane, "Egypt, History of", 352.

30. Kuhrt, *The Ancient Near East*, **2**, 623–46; Kitchen, *The Third Intermediate Period*; Aidan Dodson, "Third Intermediate Period", in Redford (ed.), *Oxford Encyclopedia of Ancient Egypt*, **3**, 388–94; and Taylor, "The Third Intermediate Period".

31. Spalinger, "Egypt, History of".

32. *Ibid.*, 357–8.

33. Murnane, "The History of Ancient Egypt", 710.

34. Spalinger, "Egypt, History of", 356.

35. Leslie J. Hoppe, "Israel, History of (Monarchic Period)", in Freedman (ed.), *The Anchor Bible Dictionary*, **3**, 558–67, esp. 563.

36. Spalinger, "Egypt, History of", 357.

37. See the complexities of Egyptian chronology in Shaw, "Introduction: Chronologies and Cultural Change"; and Kitchen, "Egypt, History of (Chronology)", 327–30.

38. For discussions see Taylor, "The Third Intermediate Period", 338–46; Kuhrt, *The Ancient Near East*, **2**, 623–31; and O'Connor, "New Kingdom and Third Intermediate Period", 232–42.

39. Kendall, "Kush"; Derek Welsby, "Nubia", in Redford (ed.), *Oxford Encyclopedia of Ancient Egypt*, **2**, 551–7, esp. 555–7; Taylor, "The Third Intermediate Period", 352–9; and Robert Morkot, *The Black Pharaohs: Egypt's Nubian Rulers* (Rubicon, London, 2000) and "Special Report on Egypt and Nubia", *KMT: A Modern Journal of Ancient Egypt* **3** (1992), 27–69.

40. Kendall, "Kush", 251.

41. Kuhrt, *The Ancient Near East*, **2**, 633.

42. T. G. H. James, "Egypt in the Third Intermediate Period", in Boardman (ed.), *The Cambridge Ancient History*, 738ff.

43. Taylor, "The Third Intermediate Period", 356–8.

44. James, "Egypt in the Third Intermediate Period", 680.

45. *Ibid.*, 679–81.

46. O'Connor, "New Kingdom and Third Intermediate Period", 243.

47. Kuhrt, *The Ancient Near East*, **2**, 634–6.

48. Spalinger, "Egypt, History of", 359–60.

49. II Kings 18:21.

50. Taylor, "The Third Intermediate Period", 359.

51. Anthony Spalinger, "Twenty-sixth Dynasty", in Redford (ed.), *Oxford Encyclopedia of Ancient Egypt*, **2**, 272–4; A. B. Lloyd, "The Late Period (664–332 BC)", in Shaw (ed.), *The Oxford History of Ancient Egypt*, 369–94 and "The Late Period, 664–323 BC", in Trigger *et al.*, *Ancient Egypt*, 279–348.

52. John D. Ray, "Late Period: An Overview", in Redford (ed.), *Oxford Encyclopedia of Ancient Egypt*, **2**, 267–72, esp. 268.

53. Briant, *From Cyrus to Alexander*, 51; Nicolas Grimal, *A History of Ancient Egypt*, I. Shaw (trans.) (Blackwell, Oxford, 1994), 354.

54. Lloyd, "The Late Period (664–332 BC)", 371–7.

55. O'Connor, "New Kingdom and Third Intermediate Period", 251.

56. Ray, "Late Period: An Overview", 269; Lloyd, "The Late Period, 664–323 BC", 325–31.

57. Ray, "Late Period: An Overview", 268; Lloyd, "The Late Period (664–332 BC)", 374–6.

58. Rosalind M. H. Janssen, "Costume in New Kingdom Egypt", in Sasson (ed.), *Civilizations of the Ancient Near East*, **1**, 383–94, esp. 383.

59. Kuhrt, *The Ancient Near East*, **2**, 641; and James, "Egypt in the Third Intermediate Period", 720–26.

60. Herodotus, *The Histories*, Book II, 158.

61. Spalinger, "Egypt, History of", 361; and Georges Posener, "Le Canal à le Mer Rouge", *Chronique d'Egypte* **13** (1938), 259–73.

62. Herodotus, *The Histories*, Book II, 160.

63. See A. B. Lloyd, "Necho and the Red Sea: Some Considerations", *Journal of Egyptian Archaeology* **63** (1977), 142–55.

64. Herodotus, *The Histories*, Book IV, 42.

65. George F. Bass, "Sea and River Craft in the Ancient Near East", in Sasson (ed.), *Civilizations of the Ancient Near East*, **3**, 1421–31, esp. 1430. For another opinion see Edward Lipinski, "The Phoenicians", in Sasson (ed.), *Civilizations of the Ancient Near East*, **2**, 1321–33, esp. 1331.

66. Grayson, *Assyrian and Babylonian Chronicles*, 95.

67. Ray, "Late Period: An Overview", 268–9.

68. Lloyd, "The Late Period (664–323 BC)", 285.

69. James, "Egypt in the Third Intermediate Period", 735.

70. Briant, *From Cyrus to Alexander*, 53–5; and Cook, *The Persian Empire*, 46–9.

71. See discussion in Kuhrt, *The Ancient Near East*, **2**, 662–3; Cook, *The Persian Empire*, 48; and Grimal, *A History of Ancient Egypt*, 367–82.

72. Murnane, "The History of Ancient Egypt", 711.

17: The Persians

1. Sommerfeld, "The Kassites of Ancient Mesopotamia".

2. Leahy, "Foreign Incursions".

3. The name Iran (from *aryan*) comes from *aryanam khshathram*, meaning "the land of the Aryans", which later became *Iranshahr*, then shortened to Iran. The region east of the Zagros mountains was known as Persia until 1935, when the name was changed to Iran. See Brentjes, "The History of Elam", 1003.

4. *Ibid.*

5. Oscar White Muscarella, "Art and Archaeology of Western Iran in Prehistory", in Sasson (ed.), *Civilizations of the Ancient Near East*, **2**, 981–99, esp. 984; Robert H. Dyson Jr., "Iran, Prehistory of", in Freedman (ed.), *The Anchor Bible Dictionary*, **3**, 451–4.

6. Muscarella, "Art and Archaeology of Western Iran", 981–99.

7. Holly Pittman, "Susa", in Meyers (ed.), *Oxford Encyclopedia of Archaeology*, **5**, 106–11, esp. 108–9.

8. The major book-length treatment of the Persians is Briant, *From Cyrus to Alexander*; see also Pierre Briant, "Persian Empire", in Freedman (ed.), *The Anchor Bible Dictionary*, **5**, 237.

9. T. Cuyler Young Jr., "Persians", in Meyers (ed.), *Oxford Encyclopedia of Archaeology*, **4**, 295–300 and "Persia", in Cotterell (ed.), *The Encyclopedia of Ancient Civilizations*, 147.

10. B. A. Litvinsky, "Archaeology and Artifacts in Iron Age Central Asia", in Sasson (ed.), *Civilizations of the Ancient Near East*, **2**, 1067–83, esp. 1069.

11. Windfuhr, "Indo-European Languages"; Colin Renfrew, *Archaeology and Language: The Puzzle of Indo-European Origins* (Cambridge University Press, Cambridge, 1988), 178–210.

12. Herodotus, *The Histories*, Book I, 95–130.

13. Cuyler Young, "Persia", 147; and Briant, *From Cyrus to Alexander*, 18–21.

14. T. Cuyler Young Jr., "Medes", in Meyers (ed.), *Oxford Encyclopedia of Archaeology*, **3**, 448–50; and Briant, *From Cyrus to Alexander*, 24–8.

15. Cuyler Young, "Medes", 448–50; and Kuhrt, *The Ancient Near East*, **2**, 653–6.

16. See Luckenbill, *Ancient Records of Assyria and Babylonia*, §§739–40.

17. Briant, "Persian Empire", 236–44.

18. The names Cyrus, Darius, and others in the Persian language have traditionally been rendered in Hellenized forms in most scholarship on the subject. See discussion in Cook, *The Persian Empire*, 44–5; and Kuhrt, *The Ancient Near East*, **2**, 647–51.

19. David Stronach, "Pasargadae", in Meyers (ed.), *Oxford Encyclopedia of Archaeology*, **4**, 250–53.

20. Briant, *From Cyrus to Alexander*, 40–44.

21. *Ibid.*, 43.

22. Isaiah 45:1.

23. Sancisi-Weerdenburg, Heleen, "Darius I and the Persian Empire", in Sasson (ed.), *Civilizations of the Ancient Near East*, **3**, 1035–50, esp. 1040; and Lloyd, "The Late Period (664–323 BC)", 286.

24. Briant, *From Cyrus to Alexander*, 85–6.

25. T. Cuyler Young, Jr., "The Early History of the Medes and the Persians and the Achaemenid Empire to the Death of Cambyses", in *The Cambridge History of Iran, Volume 1*, J. Boardman (ed.), 1–52 (Cambridge University Press, Cambridge, 1988).

26. Lloyd, "The Late Period (664–332 BC)", 383–5.

27. Sancisi-Weerdenburg, "Darius I and the Persian Empire", 1041.

28. Dieter Kessler, "Bull Gods", in Redford (ed.), *The Oxford Encyclopedia of Ancient Egypt*, **1**, 209–13.

29. Nicolas Grimal, *A History of Ancient Egypt*, 356–7; Karol Myśliwiec, *The Twilight of Ancient Egypt* (Cornell University Press, Ithaca, 2000), 135.

30. Briant, *From Cyrus to Alexander*, 57.

31. Myśliwiec, *The Twilight of Ancient Egypt*, 136–7.

32. Sancisi-Weerdenburg, "Darius I and the Persian Empire".

33. David Stronach and Antogoni Zournatzi, "Bisitun", in Meyers (ed.), *Oxford Encyclopedia of Archaeology*, **1**, 330–31.

34. Gernot L. Windfuhr, "Persian", in Meyers (ed.), *Oxford Encyclopedia of Archaeology*, **4**, 292–5.

35. Mary Boyce, "Zoroaster, Zoroastrianism", in Freedman (ed.), *The Anchor Bible Dictionary*, **6**, 1168–74.

36. Briant, "Persian Empire", 238.

37. Kuhrt, *The Ancient Near East*, **2**, 665.

38. *Ibid.*, 689–92.

39. François Vallat, "Susa and Susiana in the Second-Millennium Iran", in Sasson (ed.), *Civilizations of the Ancient Near East*, **2**, 1023–33.

40. Herodotus, *The Histories*, Book I, 186.

41. Briant, *From Cyrus to Alexander*, 369–74.

42. Astour, "Overland Trade Routes", 1417–19.

43. D. Stronach and K. Codella, "Persepolis", in Meyers (ed.), *Oxford Encyclopedia of Archaeology*, **4**, 273–7.

44. Kuhrt, *The Ancient Near East*, **2**, 669–70.

45. Briant, *From Cyrus to Alexander*, 165–71.

46. Myśliwiec, *The Twilight of Ancient Egypt*, 136.

47. Sancisi-Weerdenberg, "Darius I and the Persian Empire", 1043; and Myśliwiec, *The Twilight of Ancient Egypt*, 136.

48. Jean Yoyotte, "Une statue de Darius découverte à Suse", *Journal Asiatique* **260** (1972), 250–60.

49. Lloyd, "The Late Period (664–323 BC)", 385–90.

50. Cook, *The Persian Empire*, 113–17.

51. Herodotus, *The Histories*, Book VII, 60.

52. For an overview of the Persian military see Nick Sekunda, "The Persians", in *Warfare in the Ancient World*, J. Hackett (ed.), 82–103 (Facts on File, New York, 1989).

53. See discussion in Briant, *From Cyrus to Alexander*, 535–42.

54. Alan B. Lloyd, "The Ptolemaic Period (332–30 BC)", in Shaw (ed.), *The Oxford History of Ancient Egypt*, 395–421.

55. Kuhrt, *The Ancient Near East*, **2**, 647.

56. E. J. Keal, "Parthians", in Meyers (ed.), *Oxford Encyclopedia of Archaeology*, **4**, 249–50.

57. E. J. Keal, "Sassanians", in Meyers (ed.), *Oxford Encyclopedia of Archaeology*, **4**, 491–5.

Epilogue: the twilight of the first civilizations

1. Astour, "Overland Trade Routes".

2. Roux, *Ancient Iraq*, 379.

3. Oates, *Babylon*, 138–9.

4. Roux, *Ancient Iraq*, 385.

5. Xenophon, *Anabasis* III, 4. C.L. Brownson, Loeb Classical Library, Harvard University Press, Cambridge, 1934. Afterwards, the site was redeveloped for a short time during the Seleucid period.

6. See H. W. F. Saggs, *Babylonians* (University of Oklahoma Press, Norman, 1995), 173–5.

7. Perhaps "Mesomania" would be a better term. For "Babyloniamania" see John M. Lundquist, "Babylon in European Thought", in Sasson (ed.), *Civilizations of the Ancient Near East*, **1**, 67.

8. John Maier, "The Ancient Near East in Modern Thought", in Sasson (ed.), *Civilizations of the Ancient Near East*, **1**, 107–20.

Bibliography

Aaboe, A. 1974, "Scientific Astronomy in Antiquity", in Hodson (ed.) (1974), 21–42.

Aaboe, A. 1992, "Babylonian Mathematics, Astrology, and Astronomy", in Boardman *et al.* (eds) (1992), 276–92.

Adams, R. McCormick 1981, *Heartland of Cities: Surveys of Ancient Settlement and Land Use on the Central Floodplain of the Euphrates*, University of Chicago Press, Chicago.

Adams, R. McCormick & H. J. Nissen 1972, *The Uruk Countryside: The Natural Setting of Urban Societies*, University of Chicago Press, Chicago.

Aldred, C. 1965, *Egypt to the End of the Old Kingdom,* Thames & Hudson, London.

Aldred, C. 1968, *Akhenaten: Pharaoh of Egypt*, Thames & Hudson, London. [Represents some of Aldred's early ideas on the subject.]

Aldred, C. 1980, *Egyptian Art*, Thames & Hudson, New York/London.

Aldred, C. 1984, *The Egyptians*, rev. edn, Thames & Hudson, London.

Aldred, C. 1988, *Akhenaten: King of Egypt*, Thames & Hudson, London.

Aldred, C. & A. T. Sandison 1962, "The Pharaoh Akhenaten: A Problem in Egyptology and Pathology", *Bulletin of the History of Medicine* 36, 293–316.

Algaze, G. 1993, *The Uruk World System*, University of Chicago Press, Chicago.

Ali el-Khouli, A. 1991, *Meidum*, Australian Center for Egyptology: Report 3, G. Martin (ed.), Sydney.

Allam, S. 2001, "Slaves", in Redford (ed.) (2001), 3, 293–6.

Alster, B. (ed.) 1980, *Death in Mesopotamia*, Copenhagen Studies in Assyriology 8, Akademisk Forlag, Copenhagen.

Amiet, P. 1980, *Art of the Ancient Near East*, Harry N. Abrams, New York.

Anderson, J. K. 1997, "Hunting", in Meyers (ed.) (1997), 3, 122–4.

André-Leicknam, B. & C. Ziegler 1982, *Naissance de l'ecriture*, Éditions de la Réunion des Musées Nationaux, Paris.

Andrews, C. A. R. 2001, "Decipherment", in Redford (ed.) (2001), 1, 360–63.

Armstrong, J. 1997, "Ceramics: Mesopotamian Ceramics", in Meyers (1997), 1, 453–59.

Arnold, D. 1984. *Lexikon der Ägyptologie*, vol. 5, W. Helck, E. Otto & W. Westendorf (eds), Otto Harrasowitz, Wiesbaden.

Arnold, D. 1987, *Der Pyramidenbezirk des Königs Amenemhet III. in Dahschur: Volume 1*, Philipp von Zabern, Mainz.

Arnold, D. 1991, *Building in Egypt: Pharaonic Stone Masonry*, Oxford University Press, New York.

Arnold, D. 1997, "Royal Cult Complexes of the Old and Middle Kingdoms", in *Temples of Ancient Egypt*, B. Shafer (ed.), 31–85, Cornell University Press, Ithaca.

Arnold, D. & A. Oppenheim 1995, "Reexcavating The Senwosret III Pyramid Complex at Dashur", *KMT: A Modern Journal of Ancient Egypt* 6, 44–56.

Asherman, N. 1982, *Digging for God and Country*, Alfred A. Knopf, New York.

Assmann, J. 1997, *Moses the Egyptian*, Harvard University Press, Cambridge.

Assmann, J. & A. Alcock 1995, *Egyptian Solar Religion in the New Kingdom: Re, Aman and the Crisis of Polytheism*, Kegan Paul International, London & New York.

Astour, M. 1995, "Overland Trade Routes in Ancient Western Asia", in Sasson (ed.) (1995), 3, 1405–20.

Avalos, H. 1995, *Illness and Health Care in the Ancient Near East: the Role of the Temple in Greece, Mesopotamia and Israel*, Scholars Press, Atlanta.

Avalos, H. 1997, "Medicine", in Meyers (ed.) (1997), 3, 450.

Badawy, A. 1964, "The Stellar Destiny and the So-called Air Shafts of the Cheops Pyramid", *Mitteilungen des Instituts für Orientforschung* 10, 189–206.

Badawy, A. 1966, *Architecture in Ancient Egypt and the Near East*, MIT Press, Cambridge.

Bahat, D. 1995, "Jerusalem", in Meyers (ed.) (1995), 3, 224–38.

Baikie, J. 1926, *The Story of the Pharaohs,* A. & C. Black, London.

Bailey, L. R. 1989, *Noah: The Person and the Story in History and Tradition*, University of South Carolina Press, Columbia.

Bailey, L. R. 1992, "Noah and the Ark", in Freedman (ed.) (1992), **4**, 1123–32.

Baines, J. & J. Málek 1991, "Society, Morality, and Religious Practice", in Shafer (ed.) (1991), 123–200.

Baines, J. & J. Málek 2000, *Cultural Atlas of Ancient Egypt*, 2nd edn, Facts on File, New York.

Bard, K. 2000, "The Emergence of the Egyptian State (c. 3200–2686)", in Shaw (ed.) (2000), 61–88.

Barnett, R. D. & A. Lorenzini 1975, *Assyrian Sculpture in the British Museum*, McClelland & Stewart, Toronto.

Bar-Yosef, O. 1992, "The Neolithic Period", in *The Archaeology of Ancient Israel*, A. Ben-Tor (ed.), 10–39, Yale University Press, New Haven.

Bass, G. F. 1995, "Sea and River Craft in the Ancient Near East", in Sasson (ed.) (1995), **3**, 1421–31.

Bayliss, M. 1973–74, "The Cult of Dead Kin in Assyria and Babylonia", *Iraq* **35–6**, 115–25.

Beaulieu, P.-A. 1989, *The Reign of Nabonidus, King of Babylon 556–539 BC*, Yale University Press, New Haven.

Beaulieu, P.-A. 1993, "An Episode in the Fall of Babylon", *Journal of Near Eastern Studies* **52**, 241–61.

Beaulieu, P.-A. 1995, "King Nabonidus and the Neo-Babylonian Empire", in Sasson (ed.) (1995), **2**, 969–79.

Beckman, G. M. 1983, *Hittite Birth Rituals*, Harrassowitz, Wiesbaden.

Beckman, G. 1992, "Languages (Hittite)", in Freedman (ed.) (1992), **4**, 214–16.

Beer, M. 1992, "Judaism (Babylonian)", in Freedman (ed.) (1992), **3**, 1076–83.

Beitzel, B. 1992, "Travel and Communications, The Old Testament World", in Freedman (ed.) (1992), **6**, 644–8.

Bell, L. 1997, "Appendix I: Luxor Temple in the Reign of Akhenaten", in Shafer (ed.) (1997), 127–84.

Bentley, J. 1992, "Akhenaten in the Eye of the Beholder", *Amarna Letters 2*, 6–8, KMT Publications, San Francisco.

Bergsträsser, G. 1983, *Introduction to the Semitic Languages*, P. Daniels (trans.), Eisenbrauns, Winona Lake.

Betlyon, J. 1992, "Coinage", in Freedman (1992), **1**, 1078–83.

Bianchi, R. S. 1995, "Ancient Egyptian Reliefs, Statuary and Monumental Paintings", in Sasson (ed.) (1995), **4**, 2533–54.

Bienkowski, P. & A. Millard 2000, *Dictionary of the Ancient Near East*, University of Pennsylvania Press, Philadelphia.

Bierbrier, M. 1982, *The Tomb Builders of the Pharaohs*, American University in Cairo Press, Cairo.

Bietak, M. 1997, "Dab'a, Tell Ed", in Meyers (ed.) (1997), **2**, 99–101.

Bietak, M. 2001, "Dab'a, Tell Ed", in Redford (ed.) (2001), **1**, 351–4.

Bietak, M. 2001, "Hyksos", in Redford (ed.) (2001), **2**, 136–143.

Biggs, R. 1987–1990, "Medizin. A.", *Reallexicon der Assyriologie und Vorderasiatischen Archäologie 7*, 623–9, Herausgegeben von Dietz Otto Edzard, Berlin [in English].

Biggs, R. 1995, "Medicine, Surgery, and Public Health in Ancient Mesopotamia", in Sasson (ed.) (1995), **3**, 1911–24.

Black, J. 1981, "The New Years Ceremonies in Ancient Babylon: 'Taking Bel by the Hand,' and a Cultic Picnic", *Religion* **11**, 39–59.

Black, J. & A. Green 1992, *Gods, Demons and Symbols of Ancient Mesopotamia*, University of Texas Press, Austin.

Black, J. A. & W. J. Tait 1995, "Archives and Libraries in the Ancient Near East", in Sasson (ed.) (1995), **4**, 2197–209.

Boardman, J., I. E. S. Edwards, N. G. L. Hammond & E. Sollberger (eds) 1992, *The Cambridge Ancient History, Volume 3, Part 2: The Assyrian and Babylonian Empires and Other States of the Near East, from the Eighth to the Sixth Centuries BC*, Cambridge University Press, Cambridge.

Borger, R. 1963, *Babylonisch–Assyrische Lesestücke*, 3 volumes, Pontificum Institutum Biblicum, Rome.

Bottéro, J. 1971, "The Dynasty of Agade and the Gutian Invasion", in Edwards *et al.* (eds) (1971), 417–63.

Bottéro, J. 1992, *Mesopotamia: Writing, Reasoning and the Gods*, University of Chicago Press, Chicago.

Bottéro, J. 2001, *Religion in Ancient Mesopotamia*, University of Chicago Press, Chicago.

Bottéro, J. & S. Kramer 1989, *Lorsque les dieux faisaient l'homme: Mythologie mesopotamienne*, Gallimard, Paris.

Bourriau, J. 2000, "The Second Intermediate Period (c.1650–1550)", in Shaw (ed.) (2000), 185–217.

Boyce, M. 1992, "Zoroaster, Zoroastrianism", in Freedman (ed.) (1992), **6**, 1168–74.

Braidwood, R. 1962, "Prehistoric Investigations in Southwestern Asia", *Proceedings of the American Philosophical Society* **116**(4), 310–20, American Philosophical Society, Philadelphia.

Braidwood, R. & B. Howe 1960, *Prehistoric Investigations in Iraqi Kurdistan*, University of Chicago Press, Chicago.

Breasted, J. H. 1906, *A History of Ancient Egypt*, Bantam Books, New York.

Breasted, J. H. 1906, *Ancient Records of Egypt*, University of Chicago Press, Chicago.

Breasted, J. H. 1912, *The Development of Religion and Thought in Ancient Egypt*, University of Pennsylvania Press, Philadelphia.

Breasted, J. H. 1912, *A History of Egypt*, 2nd edn, Charles Scribner's Sons, New York.

Breasted, J. H. 1916, *Ancient Times: A History of the Ancient World*, Ginn & Co., Boston.

Breasted, J. 1930, *The Edwin Smith Surgical Papyrus*, University of Chicago Press, Chicago.

Brentjes, B. 1995, "The History of Elam and Achaemenid Persia: An Overview", in Sasson (ed.) (1995), **2**, 1001–21.

Briant, P. 1992, "Persian Empire", in Freedman (ed.) (1992), 236–44.

Briant, P. 2002, *From Cyrus to Alexander: A History of the Persian Empire*, P. Daniels (trans.), Eisenbrauns, Winona Lake.

Brinkman, J. 1976, *Materials and Studies for Kassite History*, University of Chicago Press, Chicago.

Brinkman, J. 1991, "Babylonia in the Shadow of Assyria (747–626 BC)", in Boardman *et al.* (eds) (1991), 1–70.

Brinkman, J. 1991, "Assyria: Tiglath-pileser III to Sargon (744–705 BC)", in Boardman *et al.* (eds) (1991), 71–102.

Britton, J. & C. Walker 1996, "Astronomy and Astrology in Mesopotamia", in *Astronomy Before the Telescope*, C. Walker (ed.), 42–67, St. Martin's Press, New York.

Bryan, B. M. 2000, "The Eighteenth Dynasty Before the Amarna Period (c.1550–1352 BC)", in Shaw (ed.) (2000), 218–71.

Bryan, B. 2001, "Amarna, Tell El", in Redford (ed.) (2001), **1**, 60–65.

Bryan, B., A. Kozloff & L. M. Berman 1992, *Egypt's Dazzling Sun: Amenhotep III and His World*, Cleveland Museum of Art, Cleveland, and Indiana University Press, Bloomington.

Bryce, T. 2002, "The Trojan War: Is There Truth Behind the Legend?", *Near Eastern Archaeology* **65**, 182–95.

Bryce, T. 2002, *Life and Society in the Hittite World*, Oxford University Press, Oxford.

Burridge, A. 1993, "Akhenaten: A New Perspective. Evidence of a Genetic Disorder in the Royal Family of 18th Dynasty Egypt", *The Journal of the Society for the Study of Egyptian Antiquities* **23**, 63–74.

Burridge, A. 1997, "A Study of the Edwin Smith Surgical Papyrus", *The Journal of the Society for the Study of Egyptian Antiquities* **27**, 9–26.

Busink, Th. A. 1970, "L'Origine et Évolution de la Ziggurat Babylonienne", *Jaarbericht Ex Oriente Lux* **21**, 91–141.

Butzer, K. W. 1976, *Early Hydraulic Civilization in Egypt*, University of Chicago Press, Chicago.

Butzer, K. W. 1995, "Environmental Change in the Ancient Near East and Human Impact on the Land", in Sasson (ed.) (1995), **1**, 123–51.

Butzer, K. 1998, "Late Quaternary Problems of the Egyptian Nile: Stratigraphy, Environments, Prehistory", *Paléorient* **23**, 151–73.

Butzer, K. 2001, "Nile", in Redford (ed.) (2001), **2**, 543–51.

Callender, G. 2000, "The Middle Kingdom Renaissance (c.2055–1650 BC)", in Shaw (ed.) (2000), 148–83.

Campbell, J. 1968, *The Hero with a Thousand Faces*, 2nd edn, Princeton University Press, Princeton.

Carr, E. H. 1961, *What is History?*, Pelican, Harmondsworth.

Carter, E. & M. Stolper 1984, *Elam: Surveys of Political History and Archaeology*, University of California Press, Berkeley.

Carter, H. 1972, *The Tomb of Tutankhamen*, Sphere Books, London [originally published in 3 vols, Cassell, London, 1923–33].

Carter, M. & K. Schoville 1984, *Sign, Symbol, Script*, University of Wisconsin, Madison.

Carter, H. *et al.* 1917, *Beni Hasan*, vol. 4, London.

Casson, L. 2001, *Libraries in the Ancient World*, Yale University Press, New Haven.

Cassuto, U. 1992, *A Commentary on the Book of Genesis*, Part II, Magnes Press, Jerusalem.

Chadwick, J. 1976, *The Mycenaean World*, Cambridge University Press, Cambridge.

Chadwick, R. 1991, "Celestial Episodes and Celestial Objects in Ancient Mesopotamia", *Bulletin of the Canadian Society for Mesopotamian Studies* **22**, 43–9.

Chadwick, R. 1992, "Calendars, Ziggurats and the Stars", *The Bulletin of the Canadian Society for Mesopotamian Studies* **24**, 7–24.

Chadwick, R. 2001, "Celestial Alignments and the Soul Shafts of the Khufu Pyramid", *The Journal of the Society for the Study of Egyptian Antiquities* **28**, 15–25.

Champollion, J.-F. 1822, *Lettre à M. Dacier relative à l'alphabet des hieroglyphes phonétiques*, Firmin Didot, Paris.

Chapman, R. 1997, "Weapons and Warfare", in Meyers (ed.) (1997), **5**, 334–9.

Charles R. 1978, *The Rise of Civilization*, W. H. Freeman, San Francisco.

Charpin, D. 1995, "The History of Ancient Mesopotamia: An Overview", in Sasson (ed.) (1995), **2**, 807–29.

Childe, G. V. 1952, *New Light on the Most Ancient East*, Praeger, New York.

Chipiez, C. & G. Perrot 1882, *Histoire de l'art dans l'antiquité: Chaldée et Assyrie*, vol. II, Hachette, Paris.

Civil, M. 1960, "Prescriptions Médicales Sumériennes", *Revue D'Assyriologie et Archéologie Orientale* **54**(2), 59–72.

Civil, M. 1997, "Sumer", in Meyers (ed.) (1997), 95–101.

Clagett, M. 1995, *Ancient Egyptian Science, Volume II: Calendars, Clocks, and Astronomy*, American Philosophical Society, Philadelphia.

Clark, R. T. R. 1959, *Myth and Symbol in Ancient Egypt*, Thames & Hudson, London.

Clayton, P. A. 1994, *Chronicles of the Pharaohs*, Thames & Hudson, London.

Clive, J. 1987, *Not by Fact Alone: Essays on the Writing and Reading of History*, Alfred Knopf, New York.

Cohen, M. N. 1977, *The Food Crisis in Prehistory*, Yale University Press, New Haven.

Cohen, M. 1989, *Health and the Rise of Civilization*, Yale University Press, New Haven.

Cook, J. M. 1983, *The Persian Empire*, Schocken Books, New York.

Cooper, J. S. 1983, *The Curse of Agade*, Johns Hopkins University Press, Baltimore.

Cooper, J. 1992, "Sumerians", in Freedman (ed.) (1992), **6**, 231–4.

Cotterell, A. (ed.) 1980, *The Encyclopedia of Ancient Civilizations*, Mayflower Books, New York.

Crawford, H. 1991, *Sumer and the Sumerians*, Cambridge University Press, Cambridge.

Crouwel, J. H. & M. A. Littauer 1979, *Wheeled Vehicles and Ridden Animals in the Ancient Near East*, Brill Publishers, Leiden.

Crouwel, J. H. & M. A. Littauer 1992, "Chariots", in Freedman (ed.) (1992), **1**, 888–92.

Crouwel, J. H. & M. A. Littauer 1997, "Chariots", in Meyers (ed.) (1997), **1**, 485–7.

Cruz-Uribe, E. 2001, "Scripts", in Redford (ed.) (2001), **3**, 192–8.

Cryer, F. 1995, "Chronology, Issues and Problems", in Sasson (ed.) (1995), **1**, 651–64.

Curl, J. S. 1994, *Egyptomania: The Egyptian Revival, a Recurring Theme in the History of Taste*, Manchester University Press, Manchester.

Curtis, J. (ed.) 1982, *Fifty Years of Mesopotamian Discovery*, British School of Archaeology in Iraq, London.

Dalley, S. 1984, *Mari and Karana: Two Old Babylonian Cities*, Longman, London.

Dalley, S. 1989, *Myths from Mesopotamia*, Oxford University Press, Oxford.

Dalley, S. 1994, "Babylon and the Hanging Gardens: Cuneiform and Classical Sources Reconciled", *Iraq* **56**, 45–76.

Dalley, S. 1995, "Ancient Mesopotamian Military Organisation", in Sasson (ed.) (1995), **1**, 413–22.

Daniels, P. 1995, "The Decipherment of Ancient Near Eastern Texts", in Sasson (ed.) (1995), **1**, 81–93.

Daniels, P. 1997, "Writing and Writing Systems", in Meyers (ed.) (1997), **5**, 358–61.

David, A. R. 1982, *The Ancient Egyptians*, Routledge & Kegan Paul, London.

David, A. R. 1996, *The Pyramid Builders of Ancient Egypt: A Modern Investigation of Pharaoh's Workforce*, Routledge, London.

David, A. R. 2001, "Mummification", in Redford (ed.) (2001), **2**, 439–44.

David, A. R. & E. Tapp 1992, *The Mummy's Tale: The Scientific and Medical Investigation of Natsef-Amun, Priest in the Temple at Karnak*, St. Martin's Press, New York.

De Morgan, J. 1900, *Mémoires, Délegation en Perse*, vol. 1, Paris.

Denon, D. V. 1803, *Travels in Upper and Lower Egypt* [*Voyages dans la Haute et la Basse Égypte*], A. Aikin (trans.), Phillips, London.

Depuydt, L. 1995, "On the Consistency of the Wandering Year as the Backbone of Egyptian Chronology", *Journal of the American Research Center in Egypt* **32**, 43–58.

De Roos, J. 1995, "Hittite Prayers", in Sasson (ed.) (1995), **3**, 1997–2005.

De Sarzec, E. & M. Heuzey, 1912, *Découverts en Chaldée*, vol. 4, E. Leroux, Paris.

Desroches-Noblecourt, C. 1963, *Tutankhamen*, George Rainbird, London.

Dion, P.-É. 1995, "Aramean Tribes and Nations of the First Millennium Western Asia", in Sasson (ed.) (1995), **2**, 1281–94.

Dion, P.-É. 1997, *Les Araméens, à l'âge du fer: histoire politique et structure sociales*, Études Bibliques N.S. 34, Paris, Gabalda.

Doblehofer, E. 1973, *Voices in Stone*, Paladin, London.

Dodson, A. 2001, "Third Intermediate Period", in Redford (ed.) (2001), **3**, 388–94.

Dossin, G. & A. Finet 1978, *Archives royales de Mari, texts transcrits et traduits X: Correspondance féminine*, Librairie Orientaliste Paul Geuthner, Paris.

Dothan, T. 1995, "The 'Sea Peoples' and the Philistines of Ancient Palestine", in Sasson (ed.) (1995), **2**, 1267–79.

Dothan, T. & M. Dothan 1992, *People of the Sea*, Macmillan, New York.

Drews, R. 1993, *The End of the Bronze Age*, Princeton University Press, Princeton.

Driver, G. R. & J. C. Miles 1955, *The Babylonian Laws*, 2 vols, Oxford University Press, Oxford.

Durand, J.-M. 1988, "Maladies et medicines", *Archives royales de Mari, texts transcrits et traduits*, vol. 26, Paul Geuthner, Paris.

Durand, J.-M. 1992, "Mari (Texts)", in Freedman (ed.) (1992), **4**, 529–38.

Dyson Jr., R. H. 1992, "Iran, Prehistory of", in Freedman (ed.) (1992), **3**, 451–4.

Eaton-Krauss, M. 1990, "Akhenaten versus Akhenaten", *Bibliotheca Orientalia* **47**, 541–59.

Eaton-Krauss, M. 2001, "Akhenaten", in Redford (ed.) (2001), **1**, 48–51.

Eaton-Krauss, M, 2001, "Nefertiti", in Redford (ed.) (2001), **2**, 513–14.

Eaton-Krauss, M. 2001, "Tutankhamun", in Redford (ed.) (2001), **3**, 452–3.

Ebbell, B. 1937, *The Papyrus Ebers*, Levin & Munksgaard, Copenhagen.

Eberhard, O. & M. Hirmer 1960, *Ancient Egyptian Art: The Cults of Osiris and Amon*, Harry N. Abrams, New York.

Edwards, I. E. S. 1993, *The Pyramids of Egypt*, rev. edn, Penguin Books, Harmondsworth.

Edwards, I. E. S., C. J. Gadd & N. G. L. Hammond (eds) 1971, *The Cambridge Ancient History, Volume 1, Part 2: Early History of the Middle East*, 3rd edn, Cambridge University Press, Cambridge.

Edzard, D. O. 1995, "The Sumerian Language", in Sasson (ed.) (1995), **4**, 2107–16.

Erman, A. 1971 [1894], *Life in Ancient Egypt*, Dover Publications, New York.

Ertman, E. L. 1992, "Is There Evidence for a 'King' Nefertiti?", in *Amarna Letters 2*, 50–55, KMT Publications, San Francisco.

Estes, J. W. 1993, *The Medical Skills of Ancient Egypt*, Science History Publications, Canton.

Eyre, C. 1995, "The Agricultural Cycle, Farming, and Water Management in the Ancient Near East", in Sasson (ed.) (1995), **1**, 175–89.

Faber, W. 1995, "Witchcraft, Magic and Divination in Ancient Mesopotamia", in Sasson (ed.) (1995), **3**, 1895–924.

Fabrega Jr., H. 1997, *Evolution of Sickness and Healing*, University of California Press, Berkeley.

Fagan, B. 1979, *Return to Babylon, Travelers, Archaeologists, and Monuments in Mesopotamia*, Little Brown, Boston.

Fairservis Jr., W. A 1962, *The Ancient Kingdoms of the Nile*, Mentor Books, New York.

Faulkner, R. O. 1966, "The King and the Star Religion in the Pyramid Texts", *Journal of Near Eastern Studies* **25**, 153–61.

Faulkner, R. O. 1969, *The Ancient Egyptian Pyramid Texts*, 2 vols, Oxford University Press, Oxford.

Faulkner, R. O. 1973–78, *The Ancient Egyptian Coffin Texts*, 3 vols, Aris & Phillips, Warminster.

Faulkner, R. O. 1985, *The Egyptian Book of the Dead*, rev. edn C. Andrews, British Museum, London.

Fazzini, R. & M. E. McKercher, 2001, "Egyptomania", in Redford (ed.) (2001), **1**, 458–62.

Feldman, M. 2001, "Mesopotamia", in Redford (ed.) (2001), **2**, 384–90.

Filer, J. 2001, "Hygiene", in Redford (ed.) (2001), **1**, 133–6.

Finet, A. 1983, *Le Code de Hammurapi*, Éditions du Cerf, Paris.

Finkel, I. 1988, "The Hanging Gardens of Babylon", in *The Seven Wonders of the World*, P. A. Clayton and M. J. Price (eds), 38–58, Routledge, London.

Firmage, E. 1992, "Zoology", in Freedman (ed.) (1992), **6**, 1109–67; including "Zoology (Animal Profiles)", 1119–51.

Flandin, E. 1846, *Bas-reliefs assyriens découverts à Khorsabad*, E. Leroux, Paris.

Forbes, D. 1990, "Power Behind the Throne, Senenmut", *KMT: A Modern Journal of Ancient Egypt* **1**(1), 14–19.

Forbes, D. 1991, "Artists of the Aten: History's First Caricaturists", *KMT: A Modern Journal of Ancient Egypt* **2**, 38–43.

Fortin, M. 1988, "Rapport préliminaire sur la première campagne de fouilles (printemps 1986) à Tell 'Atij, sur le Moyen Khabour", *Syria* **65**, 139–71. [See also *Syria* **71** and **72**.]

Fortin, M. 1989, "Trois campagnes de fouilles à Tell 'Atij: Un comptoir commercial du IIIème millénaire en Syrie du Nord", *The Bulletin of the Canadian Society for Mesopotamian Studies* **18**, 35–56.

Fortin, M. 1990, "Rapport préliminaire sur la seconde campagne de fouilles (printemps 1987) à Tell 'Atij, sur le Moyen Khabour", *Syria* **67**, 219–50.

Fortin, M. 1993, "Résultats de la 4ème campagne de fouilles à Tell 'Atij et à Tell Gudeda", *Echos du Monde Classique/ Classical Views* **32**(12), 97–121.

Fortin, M. 1999, *Syria, Land of Civilizations*, J. Macaulay (trans.), Musée de la Civilisation, Québec/Éditions de L'Homme, Montréal.

Fortin, M. & L. Cooper 1994, "Canadian Excavations at Tell 'Atij (Syria) 1992–1993", *The Bulletin of the Canadian Society for Mesopotamian Studies* **27** (May), 33–50.

Foster, B. 1995, *From Distant Days: Myths, Tales and Poetry of Ancient Mesopotamia*, CDL Press, Bethesda.

Foster, B. 1997, "Akkadians", in Meyers (ed.) (1997), **1**, 49–54.

Foster, J. L. 1995, "The Hymn to Aten: Akhenaten Worships the Sole God", in Sasson (ed.) (1995), **3**, 1751–61.

Frame, G. 1992, *Babylonia 689–627*, Nederlands Historisch Archaeologisch Institut, Istanbul.

Frame, G. 1997, "Chaldeans", in Meyers (ed.) (1997), **1**, 482–4.

Franke, D. 1995, "The Middle Kingdom in Egypt", in Sasson (ed.) (1995), **2**, 735–48.

Franke, S. 1995, "Kings of Akkad: Sargon and Naram-Sin", in Sasson (ed.) (1995), **2**, 831–41.

Franke, D. 2001, "Middle Kingdom", in Redford (ed.) (2001), **2**, 393–400.

Franken, H. J. 1992, "Pottery", in Freedman (1992), **5**, 429–32.

Frankfort, H. 1941, "The Origin of Monumental Architecture in Egypt", *American Journal of Semitic Languages and Literature* **58**, 329–58.

Frankfort, H. 1961, *Ancient Egyptian Religion*, Harper & Row, New York.

Frankfort, H. 1948, *Kingship and the Gods*, University of Chicago Press, Chicago.

Frankfort, H. 1954, *The Art and Architecture of the Ancient Orient*, Penguin, Harmondsworth.

Frankfort, H. 1956, *The Birth of Civilization in the Near East*, Anchor Press/Doubleday, Garden City.

Freed, R. E., "Art", in Redford (ed.) (2001), **1**, 127–36.

Freedman, D. N. (ed.) 1992, *The Anchor Bible Dictionary*, Doubleday, Garden City.

Freud, S. 1967, *Moses and Monotheism*, Vintage Books, New York.

Frick, F. S. 1997, "Cities: An Overview", in Meyers (ed.) (1997), **2**, 14–17.

Gadd, C. J. 1971, "The Dynasty of Agade", in Edwards *et al.* (eds) (1971), 417–63.

Gallery-Kovacs, M. 1989, *The Epic of Gilgamesh*, Stanford University Press, Stanford.

Galter, H. D. 1993, *Die Rolle der Astronomie in den Kulturen Mesopotamiens*, Grazer Morgenländische Studien, 3, Graz [many articles in English].

Gardener, J. & J. Maier 1984, *Gilgamesh*, Alfred A. Knopf, New York.

Gardiner, A. 1961, *Egypt of the Pharaohs*, Oxford University Press, Oxford.

George, A. 1999, *The Epic of Gilgamesh: A New Translation*, Barnes & Noble, New York.

Ghalioungui, P. 1983, *The Physicians of Pharaonic Egypt*, Philipp von Zabern, Mainz Am Rhine.

Ghalioungui, P. & Z. el-Dawakhly 1965, *Health and Healing in Ancient Egypt*, Dar al-Maaref, Cairo.

Gnirs, A. 2001, "Military: An Overview", in Redford (ed.) (2001), **2**, 400–406.

Goetze, A. 1969, "Hittite Historical Texts", in Pritchard (ed.) (1969), 318–19.

Gordon, A. 1990, "Origins of Ancient Egyptian Medicine", *KMT: A Modern Journal of Ancient Egypt* **1**(2), 26–9.

Gössmann, P. 1959, *Planetarium Babylonicum*, Des Papstlichen Bibelinstituts Verlag, Rome.

Gragg, G. B. 1997, "Semitic Languages", in Meyers (ed.) (1997), **4**, 516–27.

Grandet, P. 2001, "The New Kingdom: Twentieth Dynasty", in Redford (ed.) (2001), **2**, 538–43.

Grayson, A. K. 1975, *Assyrian and Babylonian Chronicles*, J. J. Augustin, Locust Valley/Glückstadt, Germany.

Grayson, A. K. 1980, "Histories and Historians of the Ancient Near East", *Orientalia* **49**, 1–51.

Grayson, A. K. 1991, "Assyria 668–635 BC: The Reign of Ashurbanipal", in Boardman *et al.* (eds) (1991), 142–61.

Grayson, A. K. 1991, "Assyria: Sennacherib and Esarhaddon (704–669 BC)", in Boardman *et al.* (eds) (1991), 103–41.

Grayson, A. K. 1991, "Assyrian Civilization", in Boardman *et al.* (eds) (1991), 194–228.

Grayson, A. K. 1991, "The Assyrian and Babylonian Empires and Other States in the Near East", in Boardman *et al.* (eds) (1991), 217–21.

Grayson, K. 1992, "Mesopotamia, History of (Assyria)", in Freedman (ed.) (1992), **4**, 732–55.

Grayson, A. K. 1992, "Mesopotamia, History of (Babylonia)", in Freedman (ed.) (1992), **4**, 755–77.

Grayson, A. K. 1992, "Mesopotamia (Place)", in Freedman (1992), **4**, 714.

Grayson, K. 1995, "Assyrian Rule of Conquered Territory", in Sasson (ed.) (1995), **2**, 959–68.

Grayson, K. 1997, "Assyrians", in Meyers (ed.) (1997), **1**, 228–33.

Green, L. 1990, "A Lost Queen of Ancient Egypt, King's Daughter, King's Great Wife, Ankhesenamen", *KMT A Modern Journal of Ancient Egypt* **1**(4), 22–9, 67.

Greengus, S. 1992, "Law", in Freedman (ed.) (1992), **4**, 242–52.

Greengus, S. 1995, "Legal and Social Institutions of Ancient Mesopotamia", in Sasson (ed.) (1995), **1**, 469–84.

Griffiths, J. G. 2001, "Osiris", in Redford (ed.) (2001), **2**, 615–19.

Grimal, N. 1992, *A History of Ancient Egypt*, I. Shaw (trans.), Blackwell, Oxford.

Habachi, L. 1977, *The Obelisks of Egypt*, Charles Scribner's Sons, New York.

Haeny, G. 1997, "New Kingdom 'Mortuary Temples' and 'Mansions of Millions of Years'", in Shafer (ed.) (1997), 86–126.

Haeny, G. 1997, "Royal Cult Complexes of the Ramesside Period", in Shafer (ed.) (1997), 107–23.

Hall, H. R. 1928, "Egypt and the External World in the Time of Akhenaten", *Journal of Egyptian Archaeology* **14**, 45–56.

Handcock, P. 1912, *Mesopotamian Archaeology*, Macmillan, London.

Hansen, D. P. 1997, "Kish", in Meyers (ed.) (1997), **3**, 298–9.

Hansen, K. 1994, "The Chariotry in Egypt's Age of Chivalry", *KMT: A Modern Journal of Ancient Egypt*, **5**(1), 51–61.

Harrak, A. 1990, "The Royal Tombs of Nimrud and their Jewellery", *The Bulletin of the Canadian Society for Mesopotamian Studies* **20** (1990), 5–14.

Harris, J. E. 2001, "Dental Care", in Redford (ed.) (2001), **1**, 383–5.

Hassan, F. 2001, "Cities", in Redford (ed.) (2001), **1**, 268–73.

Healy, M. & A. McBride 1991, *The Ancient Assyrians*, Osprey Publishing, Oxford.

Heard, W. J. 1992, "Libya", in Freedman (ed.) (1992), **4**, 324.

Hecht, J. 1985, "The Debunking of Egyptian Astronomers", *New Scientist* **17**(1439) (Jan.), 65.

Heidel, A. 1946, *The Epic of Gilgamesh and Old Testament Parallels*, University of Chicago Press, Chicago.

Heidel, A. 1951, *The Babylonian Genesis*, University of Chicago Press, Chicago.

Helck, W., E. Otto & W. Westendorf (eds) 1972–, *Lexikon der Ägyptologie*, 7 vols, Otto Harrassowitz Verlag, Wiesbaden.

Hendrickx, S. & P. Vermeersch 2000, "Prehistory from the Paleolithic to the Badarian Culture (c.700,000–4000 BC)", in Shaw (ed.) (2000), 17–43.

Herodotus 1972, *The Histories,* rev. edn, Aubrey de Sélincourt (trans.), Penguin, Harmondsworth.

Hess, R. S. 1992, "Chaldea", in Freedman (ed.) (1992), **1**, 886–7.

Hesse, B. 1995, "Animal Husbandry and Human Diet in the Ancient Near East", in Sasson (ed.) (1995), **1**, 203–22.

Hinke, J. W. 1911, *A New Babylonian Boundary Stone*, E. J. Brill, Leiden.

Hodson, F. R. (ed.) 1974, *The Place of Astronomy in the Ancient World*, Oxford University Press, Oxford.

Hoffman, M. A. 1979, *Egypt Before the Pharaohs: The Prehistoric Foundations of Egyptian Civilization*, Alfred A. Knopf, New York [2nd edn, University of Texas Press, Austin, 1991].

Hoffmeier, J. 2001, " Military: Materiel", in Redford (ed.) (2001), **2**, 406–12.

Holladay, J. 1997, "Stratigraphy", in Meyers (ed.) (1997), **5**, 82–9.

Holladay, J. S. 1997, "Maskhuta, Tell El", in Meyers (ed.) (1997), **3**, 432–7.

Holladay, J. S. 1982, *Cities of the Delta III, Tell el-Maskhuta*, Undena Publishing, Malibu.

Hopkins, D. C. 1997, "Agriculture", in Meyers (ed.) (1997), **1**, 22–31.

Hoppe, L. J. 1992, "Israel, History of (Monarchic Period)", in Freedman (ed.) (1992), **3**, 558–67.

Hornung, E. 1983, *Conceptions of God in Ancient Egypt*, Cornell University Press, Ithaca.

Hornung, E. 1999, *Akhenaten and the Religion of Light*, D. Lorton (trans.), Cornell University Press, Ithaca.

Hornung, E. 1999, *The Ancient Egyptian Book of the Afterlife*, Cornell University Press, Ithaca.

Horowitz, W. 1998, *Mesopotamian Cosmic Geography*, Eisenbrauns, Winona Lake.

Houwink Ten Cate, P. H. J. 1992, "Hittite History", in Freedman (ed.) (1992), **3**, 219–25.

Huber, P. J., A. J. Sachs, M. Stol *et al.* 1982, *Astronomical Dating of Babylon I and Ur III*, Occasional Papers on the Near East **1**(4), Undena Publications, Malibu.

Huehnergard, J. 1992, "Languages (Introductory)", in Freedman (ed.) (1992), **4**, 155–70.

Huehnergard, J. 1995, "Semitic Languages", in Sasson (ed.) (1995), **4**, 2117–34.

Hunger, H. 1992, *Astrological Reports to Assyrian Kings*, State Archives of Assyria VIII, Helsinki University Press, Helsinki.

Hunger, H. & A. J. Sachs 1988, *Astronomical Diaries and Related Texts from Babylonia*, 2 vols, Verlag der Österreichischen Akademie der Wissenschaften, Vienna.

Hunger, H. & D. Pingree 1989, *MUL. APIN: An Astronomical Compendium in Cuneiform*, Archiv für Orient Forschung, 24, Horn, Austria.

Izre'el, S. 1995, "The Amarna Letters from Canaan", in Sasson (ed.) (1995), **4**, 2411–19.

Jackson, D. & R. Biggs 1992, *The Epic of Gilgamesh*, Bolchazy Carducci Publications, Wauconda.

Jacobsen, T. 1939, *The Sumerian King List*, Assyriological Studies No. 11, University of Chicago Press, Chicago.

Jacobsen, T. 1943, "Primitive Democracy in Ancient Mesopotamia", *Journal of Near Eastern Studies* **2**, 159–72.

Jacobsen, T. 1975, "Religious Drama in Ancient Mesopotamia", in *Unity and Diversity*, H. Goedicke & J. J. Roberts (eds), 65–77, Johns Hopkins, Baltimore.

Jacobsen, T. 1976, *The Treasures of Darkness*, Yale University Press, New Haven.

Jacobsen, T. 1980, "Akkad (Akkadê)", in Cotterell (ed.) (1980), 84–9.

Jacobsen, T. 1980, "Death in Mesopotamia", in *Death in Mesopotamia*, B. Alster (ed.), 19–24, Akademisk Forlag 8, Copenhagen.

Jacobsen, T. 1980, "Sumer", in Cotterell (ed.) (1980), 72–83.

Jacobsen, T. 1987, *The Harps that Once … Sumerian Poetry in Translation*, Yale University Press, New Haven.

Jacobsen, T. & S. Lloyd 1935, *Sennacherib's Aqueduct at Jerwan*, University of Chicago Press, Chicago.

James, T. G. H. (ed.) 1982, *Excavating in Egypt: The Egyptian Exploration Society 1882–1982*, British Museum Publications, London/University of Chicago Press, Chicago.

James, T. G. H. 1984, *Pharaoh's People*, University of Chicago Press, Chicago.

James, T. G. H. 1991, "Egypt in the Third Intermediate Period", in Boardman *et al.* (eds) (1991).

Jansen, H. G. 1995, "Troy: Legend and Reality", in Sasson (ed.) (1995), **2**, 121–1134.

Janssen, R. M. H. 1995, "Costume in New Kingdom Egypt", in Sasson (ed.) (1995), **1**, 383–94.

Jasim, S. A. & J. Oates 1986, "Early Tokens and Tablets in Mesopotamia", *World Archaeology* **17**(3), 348–62.

Jeffreys, D. (ed.) 2003, *Views of Ancient Egypt since Napoleon Bonaparte: Imperialism, Colonialism and Modern Appropriations, Encounters with Ancient Egypt*, UCL Press, London.

Johnson, G. B. 1993, "The Pyramid of Meidum: Part 1", *KMT: A Modern Journal of Ancient Egypt* **4**, 64–71.

Johnson, G. B. 1994, "The Pyramid of Meidum: Part 2", *KMT: A Modern Journal of Ancient Egypt*, **5**, 72–82.

Jomard, E.-F. (ed.) 1817, *Description de l'Égypte*, vol. 4.

Jones, A. 1997, "Babylonian Astronomy and Its Legacy", *Bulletin of the Canadian Society for Mesopotamian Studies* **32**, 11–16.

Joukowsky, M. 1980, *A Complete Manual of Field Archaeology: Tools and Techniques of Fieldwork for Archaeologists*, Prentice-Hall, Englewood Cliffs.

Kadish, G. 1992, "Egypt, History of (Dyn. 1–11)", in Freedman (ed.) (1992), **2**, 342–5.

Kadish, G. 2001, "Amarna Period and the End of the Eighteenth Dynasty", in Redford (ed.) (2001), **2**, 531–4.

Kadish, G. E. 2001, "The New Kingdom: Amarna Period and the End of the Eighteenth Dynasty", in Redford (ed.) (2001), **2**, 531–4.

Kaper, O. E. 2001, "Myths: Lunar Cycle", in Redford (ed.) (2001), **2**, 480–82.

Keal, E. J. 1997, "Parthians", in Meyers (ed.) (1997), **4**, 249–50.

Keal, E. J. 1997, "Sassanians", in Meyers (ed.) (1997), **4**, 491–5.

Kemp, B. 1983, "Old Kingdom, Middle Kingdom, and Second Intermediate Period c. 2686–1552 BC", in Trigger *et al.* (1983), 71–182.

Kemp, B. 1989, *Ancient Egypt: Anatomy of a Civilization*, Routledge, New York.

Kemp, B. 1995, "Unification and Urbanization of Ancient Egypt", in Sasson (ed.) (1995), **2**, 679–90.

Kendall, T. 2001, "Kush", in Redford (ed.) (2001), **2**, 250–52.

Kessler, D. 2001, "Bull Gods", in Redford (ed.) (2001), **1**, 209–13.

Kilmer, A. D. 1995, "Music and Dance in Ancient Western Asia", in Sasson (ed.) (1995), **4**, 2601–13.

King, P. 1992, "Jerusalem", in Freedman (ed.) (1992), **3**, 747–66.

Kirk, G. S. 1970, *Myth: Its Meaning and Functions in Ancient and Other Cultures*, Cambridge University Press, Cambridge.

Kitchen, K. 1973, *The Third Intermediate Period in Egypt (1100–650 BC)*, Aris and Phillips, Warminster.

Kitchen, K. 2001, "Nineteenth Dynasty", in Redford (ed.) (2001), **2**, 534–8.

Kitchen, K. A. 1982, *Pharaoh Triumphant: The Life and Times of Ramesses II*, Benben Publications, Mississauga.

Kitchen, K. A. 1992, "Egypt, History of (Chronology)", in Freedman (ed.) (1992), **2**, 321–31.

Kitchen, K. A. 1995, "Pharaoh Ramesses II and His Time", in Sasson (ed.) (1995), **2**, 763–74.

Kitchen, K. A. 2001, "New Kingdom: Nineteenth Dynasty", in Redford (ed.) (2001), **2**, 534–8.

Kitchen, K. A. 2001, "Ramesses II", in Redford (ed.) (2001), **2**, 116–18.

Klein, J. 1981, "The Royal Hymns of Shulgi, King of Ur: Man's Quest for Immortal Fame", *American Philosophical Society* **71**(7), Philadelphia.

Klein, J. 1992, "Akitu", in Freedman (ed.) (1992), **1**, 138–40.

Klengel-Brandt, E. 1995, "Babylon", in Meyers (ed.) (1995), **1**, 251–6.

Knapp, B. 1992, "Mesopotamia (Chronology)", in Freedman (1992), **4**, 714–20.

Knapp, B. 1995, "Island Cultures: Crete, Thera, Cyprus, Rhodes, and Sardinia", in Sasson (ed.) (1995), **2**, 1433–49.

Koldewey, R. 1911, *Die Tempel von Babylon und Borsippa*, Wissenschaftliche Veröffenlichungen der Deutschen Orient-Gesellschaft, Leipzig.

Koldewey, R. 1914, *Excavations at Babylon*, Macmillan, Toronto.

Kramer, S. N. 1959, *History Begins at Sumer*, Doubleday, Garden City.

Kramer, S. N. 1969, *The Sacred Marriage Rite*, Indiana University Press, Bloomington.

Kramer, S. N. 1963, *The Sumerians*, University of Chicago Press, Chicago.

Kramer, S. 1983, *Le Marriage Sacré*, Berg International, Paris.

Kraus, R. 1985, *Sothis- und Monddaten: Studien zur astronomischen und technischen Chronologie Altägyptens*, Hildesheim.

Krauss, R. 1995, "Akhetaten: A Portrait in Art of an Ancient Egyptian Capital", in Sasson (ed.) (1995), **2**, 749–62.

Krauss, R. 1996, "The Length of Sneferu's Reign and How Long it Took to Build the 'Red Pyramid'", *Journal of Egyptian Archaeology* **82**, 43–50.

Kruchten, J.-M. 2001, "Law", in Redford (ed.) (2001), **2**, 277–82.

Kuhrt, A. 1995, *The Ancient Near East, c.3000–330 BC*, 2 vols, Routledge, London.

Lacovara, P. 1997, "Predynastic Egypt", in Meyers (ed.) (1997), **2**, 194–5.

Lamberg-Karlovsky, C. C. 1997, "Persia: Ancient Persia", in Meyers (ed.) (1997), **4**, 279–86.

Lamberg-Karlovsky, C. C. & J. Sabloff 1995, *Ancient Civilizations: The Near East and Mesoamerica*, Waveland Press, Prospect Heights.

Larson, J. A. 1990, "Theodore M. Davis and the So-called Tomb of Queen Tiye, Part 1", *KMT: A Modern Journal of Ancient Egypt* **1**, 48–53, 60–61.

Larson, J. A. 1991, "Theodore M. Davis and the So-called Tomb of Queen Tiye, Part 2", *KMT: A Modern Journal of Ancient Egypt* **2**, 43–6.

Lauer, J.-P. 1974, *Le Mystère des Pyramides*, Presses de la Cité, Paris.

Layard, A. H. 1849, *The Monuments of Nineveh*, John Murray, London.

Layard, A. H. 1853, *A Second Series of Monuments of Nineveh*, John Murray, London.

Leahy, A. (ed.) 1990, *Libya and Egypt (c.1300–750 BC)*, London.

Leahy, A. 1995, "Ethnic Diversity in Ancient Egypt", in Sasson (ed.) (1995), **1**, 225–34.

Leahy, A. 2001, "Foreign Incursions", in Redford (ed.) (2001), **1**, 548–52.

Leahy, A. 2001, "Sea Peoples", in Redford (ed.) (2001), **3**, 257–60.

Leclant, J. 1968, "Éléments pour une étude de la divination dans l'Égypte pharaonique", in *La Divination*, A. Caqout & M. Leibovici (eds), 1–23, Presses Universitaires de France, Paris.

Lee, R. 1968, "What Hunters do for a Living, or How to Make Out on Scarce Resources", in *Man the Hunter*, R. Lee (ed.), 30–48, Aldine, Chicago.

Leeming, D. 1981, *Mythology: The Voyage of the Hero*, 2nd edn, Harper and Row, New York.

Lehner, M. 1983, "Some Observations on the Layout of the Khufu and Khafre Pyramids", *Journal of the American Research Centre in Egypt* **20**, 7–25.

Lehner, M. 1997, *The Complete Pyramids*, Thames & Hudson, London.

Leichty, E. 1995, "Esarhaddon, King of Assyria", in Sasson (ed.) (1995), **2**, 949–58.

Lemaire, A. 1992, "Writing and Writing Materials", in Freedman (ed.) (1992), **6**, 999–1008.

Lemche, N. P. 1995, "The History of Syria and Palestine", in Sasson (ed.) (1995), **2**, 1195–218.

Leprohon, R. J. 1991, "A Vision Collapsed: Akhenaten's

Reforms Viewed through Decrees of Later Reigns", *Amarna Letters*, D. Forbes (ed.), 66–73, KMT Publications, San Francisco.

Leprohon, R. 1992, "Egypt, History of (Dyn. 11–17)", in Freedman (ed.) (1992), **2**, 345–8.

Lepsius, R. 1849–59, *Denkmäler aus Ägypten und Äthiopien*, Berlin.

Lesko, L. 1995, "Death and the Afterlife in Ancient Egyptian Thought", in Sasson (ed.) (1995), **3**, 1763–74.

Lewis, J. P. "Flood", in Freedman (ed.) (1992), **2**, 798–803.

Lichtheim, M. 1973, *Ancient Egyptian Literature*, University of California Press, Berkeley, CA.

Lieberman, S. 1980, "Of Clay Pebbles, Hollow Clay Balls, and Writing: A Sumerian View, *American Journal of Archaeology* **84**, 339–58.

Lipinska, J. & G. Johnson 1992, "The Polish Archaeology Missions at Deir el Bahari", *KMT: A Modern Journal of Ancient Egypt* **3**(2), 46–51.

Lipinska, J. & G. Johnson 1992, "The Way-Station of Thutmosis III at Deir El Bahari", *KMT: A Modern Journal of Ancient Egypt* **3**(3), 12–25.

Lipinska, J. 2001, "Hatshepsut", in Redford (ed.) (2001), **2**, 85–7.

Lipinska, J. 2001, "Thuthmosis III", in Redford (ed.) (2001), **3**, 401–3.

Lipinski, E. 1995, "The Phoenicians", in Sasson (ed.) (1995), **2**, 1321–33.

Littauer, M. A. & J. H. Crouwel 1992, "Chariots", in Freedman (ed.) (1992), **1**, 888–92.

Littauer, M. A. & J. H. Crouwel 1997, "Chariots", in Meyers (ed.) (1997), **1**, 485–7.

Litvinsky, B. A. 1995, "Archaeology and Artifacts in Iron Age Central Asia", in Sasson (ed.) (1995), **2**, 1067–83.

Liverani, M. 1995, "The Deeds of Ancient Mesopotamian Kings", in Sasson (ed.) (1995), **4**, 2353–66.

Lloyd, A. B. 1970, "The Egyptian Labyrinth", *Journal of Egyptian Archaeology* **56**, 81–100.

Lloyd, A. B. 1983, "The Late Period (664–323 BC)", in B. Trigger *et al.* (1983), 279–348.

Lloyd, A. B. 2000, "The Ptolemaic Period (332–30 BC)", in Shaw (ed.) (2000), 395–421.

Lloyd, A. B. 2000, "The Late Period (664–332 BC)", in Shaw (ed.) (2000), 369–94.

Lloyd, A. B. 1977, "Necho and the Red Sea: Some Considerations", *Journal of Egyptian Archaeology* **63**, 142–55.

Lloyd, S. 1978, *The Archaeology of Mesopotamia*, Thames & Hudson, London.

Lloyd, S. 1980, *Foundations in the Dust*, Thames & Hudson, London [originally published 1947].

Loprieno, A. 1995, "Ancient Egyptian and Other Afroasiatic Languages", in Sasson (ed.) (1995), **4**, 2135–50.

Loprieno, A. 1995, "Egyptian", in Meyers (ed.) (1995), **2**, 208–13.

Loprieno, A. (ed.) 1996, *Ancient Egyptian Literature: History and Forms*, Probleme der Ägyptologie 10, E. J. Brill Publishers, Leiden.

Lorton, D. 1995, "Legal and Social Institutions of Pharaonic Egypt," in Sasson (ed.) (1995), **1**, 345–62.

Luckenbill, D. D. 1926–27, *Ancient Records of Assyria and Babylonia*, 2 vols, University of Chicago Press, Chicago.

Lundquist, J. M. 1995, "Babylon in European Thought", in Sasson (ed.) (1995), **1**, 67.

Lurker, M. 1980, *The Gods and Symbols of Ancient Egypt*, Thames & Hudson, London.

MacDonald, S. & M. Rice (eds), 2003, *Consuming Ancient Egypt: Encounters with Ancient Egypt*, UCL Press, London.

MacNish, R. S. 1990, *The Origins of Agriculture and Settled Life*, University of Oklahoma Press, Norman.

Macqueen, J. G. 1986, *The Hittites: And Their Contemporaries in Asia Minor*, Thames & Hudson, London.

Macqueen, J. G. 1995, "The History of Anatolia and the Hittite Empire: An Overview", in Sasson (ed.) (1995), **2**, 1085–105.

Maier, J. "The Ancient Near East in Modern Thought", in Sasson (ed.) (1995), **1**, 107–120.

Maisels, C. 1990, *The Emergence of Civilization*, Routledge, London.

Majno, G. 1975, *The Healing Hand: Man and Wound in the Ancient World*, Harvard University Press, Cambridge, MS.

Malek, J. 2000, "The Old Kingdom (c.2686–2125 BC)", in Shaw (ed.) (2000), 89–117.

Mallory, J. P. 1989, *In Search of the Indo-Europeans: Language, Archaeology and Myth*, Thames & Hudson, London.

Mallowan, M. 1964, "Noah's Flood Reconsidered", *Iraq* **26**, 62–82.

Margueron, J.-C. 1991, "Mari, l'Euphrat, et le Khabur au milieu du IIIème millénaire", *The Bulletin of the Canadian Society for Mesopotamian Studies* **21** (May), 79–100.

Margueron, J.-C. 1992, "Mari (Archaeology)", in Freedman (ed.) (1992), **4**, 525–9.

Margueron, J.-C. 1995, "Mari: A Portrait in Art", in Sasson (ed.) (1995), **2**, 889.

Margueron, J.-C. 1997, "Mari", in Meyers (ed.) (1997), **3**, 413–17.

Mariette, A. 1872, *Monuments divers recueillis en Egypte*, vol. 5, Hachette, Paris.

Matthiae, P. 1981, *Ebla: An Empire Rediscovered*, Doubleday, Garden City.

Mazar, A. 1990, *Archaeology of the Land of the Bible: 10,000–586 BCE*, Doubleday, Garden City.

McDowell, A. G. 2001, "Crime and Punishment", in Redford (ed.) (2001), **1**, 315–20.

Meier, S. A. 1992, "Hammurapi", in Freedman (ed.) (1992), **3**, 39–42.

Mellaart, J. 1975, *The Neolithic of the Near East*, Thames & Hudson, London.

Mendelson, I. 1970, "The Family in the Ancient Near East", *The Biblical Archaeologist Reader 3*, E. F. Campbell & D. N. Freedman (eds), 147–54, Anchor Press/Doubleday, New York.

Mendelsshon, K. 1974, *The Riddle of the Pyramids*, Thames & Hudson, London.

Mendenhall, G. 1992, "Amorites", in Freedman (ed.) (1992), **1**, 199–202.

Meyers, E. (ed.) 1997, *The Oxford Encyclopedia of Archaeology in the Near East*, Oxford University Press, Oxford.

Michalowski, P. 1997, "Sumerians", in Meyers (ed.) (1997), **5**, 95–101.

Midant-Reyens, B. 2000, "The Naqada Period (c.4000–3200 BC)", in Shaw (ed.) (2000), 44–60.

Milano, L. 1995, "Ebla: A Third-Millennium City-State in Ancient Syria", in Sasson (ed.) (1995), **2**, 1219–30.

Moorey, P. R. S. 1979, *The Origins of Civilization*, Clarendon Press, Oxford.

Moorey, P. R. S. 1982, *Ur "of the Chaldees": A Revised and Updated Edition of Sir Leonard Woolley's "Excavations at Ur"*, Cornell University Press, Ithaca.

Moran, W. L. 1992, *The Amarna Letters*, Johns Hopkins University Press, Baltimore.

Moran, W. 1995, "The Gilgamesh Epic: A Masterpiece from Ancient Mesopotamia", in Sasson (ed.) (1995), **4**, 2327–36.

Morenz, S. 1973, *Egyptian Religion*, Cornell University Press, Ithaca.

Morkot, R. 1992, "Special Report on Egypt and Nubia", *KMT: A Modern Journal of Ancient Egypt*, **3**, 27–69.

Morkot, R. 2000, *The Black Pharaohs: Egypt's Nubian Rulers*, Rubicon, London.

Müller, M. 2001, "Afterlife", in Redford (ed.) (2001), **1**, 32–6.

Murnane, W. J. 1985, *The Road to Kadesh*, University of Chicago Press, Chicago.

Murnane, W. J. 1992, "Egypt, History of (Dyn. 18–20)", in Freedman (ed.) (1992), **2**, 348–53.

Murnane, W. J. 1995, "The History of Ancient Egypt: An Overview", in Sasson (ed.) (1995), **1**, 691–717.

Murnane, W. J. 2001, "New Kingdom: An Overview", in Redford (ed.) (2001), **2**, 519–25.

Muscarella, O. W. 1995, "Art and Archaeology of Western Iran in Prehistory", in Sasson (ed.) (1995), **2**, 981–99.

Myśliwiec, K. 2000, *The Twilight of Ancient Egypt*, Cornell University Press, Ithaca.

Na'aman, N. 1992, "Amarna Letters", in Freedman (ed.) (1992), **1**, 174–81.

Needham, J. 1959, *Science and Civilization in China, Volume III*, Cambridge University Press, Cambridge.

Nelson, H. H. 1930, *The Earliest Historical Records of Ramesses III, Medinet Habu*, vol. 1, University of Chicago Press, Chicago.

Neugebauer, O. 1942, "The Origins of the Egyptian Calendar", *Journal of Near Eastern Studies* **1**, 396–403.

Neugebauer, O. 1953, *Astronomical Cuneiform Texts*, 3 vols, Brown University Press, Providence.

Neugebauer, O. 1969, *The Exact Sciences in Antiquity*, 2nd edn, Brown University Press, Providence.

Neugebauer, O. 1980, "On the Orientation of the Pyramids", *Centaurus* **24**, 1–3.

Neugebauer, O. & R. A. Parker 1969, *Egyptian Astronomical Texts*, 3 vols, Brown University Press, Providence.

Nielsen, H. 1987, *Medicaments used in the Treatment of Eye Diseases in Egypt, the Countries of the Near East, India and China in Antiquity*, Odense University Press, Odense.

Nissen, H. J. 1988, *The Early History of the Ancient Near East, 9000–2000 BC*, University of Chicago Press, Chicago.

Nissen, H. J. 1997, "Mesopotamia: Prehistoric Mesopotamia" and "Mesopotamia: Ancient Mesopotamia", in Meyers (1997), **3**, 476–84.

Nunn, J. F. 1996, *Ancient Egyptian Medicine*, University of Oklahoma Press, Norman.

Nunn, J. F. 2001, "Disease", in Redford (ed.) (2001), **1**, 396–401.

O'Connor, D. 1983, "New Kingdom and Third Intermediate Period, 1552–664 BC", in Trigger *et al.* (1983), 183–278.

O'Connor, D. 2000, *Ancient Nubia: Egypt's Rival in Africa*, University of Pennsylvania Press, Philadelphia.

O'Connor, D. & D. Silverman (eds) 1995, *Ancient Egyptian Kingship*, E. J. Brill, Leiden.

Oates, J. 1979, *Babylon*, Thames & Hudson, London.

Oates, J. 1991, "The Fall of Assyria (635–609 BC)", in Boardman *et al.* (eds) (1991), 163–93.

Oates, D. & J. Oates 1976, *The Rise of Civilization*, Elsevier-Phaidon, Oxford.

Oded, B. 1979, *Mass Deportation and Deportees in the Neo-Assyrian Empire*, Dr. Ludwig Reichert, Wiesbaden.

Oller, G. 1995, "Messengers and Ambassadors in Ancient Western Asia", in Sasson (ed.) (1995), **3**, 1465–72.

Olmstead, A. T. 1948, *History of the Persian Empire*, University of Chicago Press, Chicago.

Oppenheim, A. L. 1959, "A New Prayer to the Gods of the Night", *Analecta Biblica* **12**, 282–97.

Oppenheim, A. L. 1969, "Assyrian King Lists", in Pritchard (ed.) (1969), 564–6.

Oppenheim, A. L. 1969, "Babylonian and Assyrian Historical Texts", in Pritchard (ed.) (1969), 265–317; including "Texts from the Accession Year of Nabonidus to the Fall of Babylon", 305–12.

Oppenheim, A. L. 1969, "Divination and Celestial Observation in the Last Assyrian Empire", *Centaurus* **14**, 97–135.

Oppenheim, A. L. 1977, *Ancient Mesopotamia: Portrait of a Dead Civilization*, revised and completed by E. Reiner, University of Chicago Press, Chicago.

Oppenheim, A. L. 1978, "Man and Nature in Mesopotamian Civilization", in *Dictionary of Scientific Biography: Volume 15*, C. Gillespie (ed.), 634–66, Charles Scribner's Sons, New York.

Oren, E. 1997, *The Hyksos: New Historical and Archaeological Perspectives*, University of Pennsylvania Press, Philadelphia.

Oren, E. 2000, *The Sea Peoples and their World: A Reassessment*, University of Pennsylvania Press, Philadelphia.

Otto, E. 1967, *Ancient Egyptian Art: The Cults of Osiris and Aman*, K. Bosse Griffiths (trans.), Harry N. Abrams, New York.

Pardee, D. 1997, "Alphabet", in Meyers (ed.) (1997), vol. **1**, 75–9.

Parker, R. A. 1950, *The Calendars of Ancient Egypt*, University of Chicago Press, Chicago.

Parker, R. A. 1959, *A Vienna Demotic Papyrus on Eclipse and Lunar Omina*, Brown University Press, Providence.

Parker, R. A. 1974, "Ancient Egyptian Astronomy", in Hodson (ed.) (1974), 51–66.

Parkinson, R. B. 1998, *The Tale of Sinuhe and other Ancient Egyptian Poems, 1940–1640 BC*, Oxford University Press, Oxford.

Parkinson, R. B. 2002, *Poetry and Culture in Middle Kingdom Egypt: A Dark Side to Perfection*, Continuum, London.

Parpola, S. 1970–1983, *Letters From Assyrian Scholars to the Kings Esarhaddon and Assurbanipal*, Alter Orient und Altes Testament 5, 2 vols, Butzon & Bercker, Kevelaer/Neukirchener, Neukirchen-Vluyn.

Parpola, S. 1980, "The Murder of Sennacherib", in *Death in Mesopotamia*, B. Alster (ed.), 171–82, Akademisk Forlag, Copenhagen.

Parrot, A. 1937, *Studia Mariana*, vol. 18, Leiden.

Parrot, A. 1949, *Ziggurats et Tour de Babel*, Éditions Albin Michel, Paris.

Patch, D. C. 1997, "Merimde", in Meyers (ed.) (1997), **3**, 471–2.

Pawlicki, F. & G. Johnson 1994, "Behind the Third Portico", *KMT: A Modern Journal of Ancient Egypt*, **5**(2), 40–49.

Pearce, L. E. 1995, "Scribes and Scholars of Ancient Mesopotamia", in Sasson (ed.) (1995), **4**, 2265–78.

Petrie, W. M. F. 1883, *The Pyramids and Temples of Gizeh*, Field & Turner, London.

Petrie, W. M. F., E. Mackay & G. A. Wainwright 1910, *Meydum and Memphis: Vol. III*, Murray, London.

Pettinato, G. 1981, *The Archives of Ebla, An Empire Inscribed in Clay*, Doubleday, Garden City.

Pinches, T. G. 1898, *Cuneiform Texts from Babylonian Tablets in the British Museum*, pt. IV, London.

Pingree, D. 1974–84, "Astrology", in *Encyclopedia Britannica*, 28 vols, 15th edn, **2**, 219, Encyclopedia Britannica, Chicago.

Pingree, D. 1978, "Mesopotamian Astronomy and Astral Omens in Other Civilizations", *25e Rencontre Assyriologique Internationale à Berlin* **1**(2), 613–31. Berliner Beiträger zum Vorder Orient.

Pingree, D. 1996, "Astronomy in India", in *Astronomy Before the Telescope*, C. Walker (ed.), 123–42, British Museum Press, London.

Pittman, H. 1997, "Susa", in Meyers (ed.) (1997), **5**, 106–111.

Pope, M. 1999, *The Story of Archaeological Decipherment from Egyptian Hieroglyphs to Linear B*, 2nd edn, Thames & Hudson, London.

Posener, G. 1938, "Le Canal à le Mer Rouge", *Chronique d'Egypte* **13**, 259–73.

Postgate, J. N. 1995, "Royal Ideology and State Administration in Sumer and Akkad", in Sasson (ed.) (1995), **1**, 395–411.

Pritchard, J. B. (ed.) 1969, *Ancient Near Eastern Texts Relating to the Old Testament*, 3rd edn, Princeton University Press, Princeton.

Quirke, S. 2001, *The Cult of Ra: Sun-Worship in Ancient Egypt*, Thames & Hudson, London.

Raikes, R. L. 1960, "The Physical Evidence for Noah's Flood", *Iraq* **28**, 52–63.

Ray, J. D. 1986, "The Emergence of Writing in Egypt", *World Archaeology* **17**(3), 307–16.

Ray, J. D. 2001, "Late Period: An Overview", in Redford (ed.) (2001), **2**, 267–72.

Read, J. 1983, *Assyrian Sculpture*, Harvard University Press, Cambridge.

Redford, D. 1967, *History and Chronology of the Egyptian 18th Dynasty. Seven Studies*, University of Toronto Press, Toronto.

Redford, D. 1970, "The Hyksos Invasion in History and Tradition", *Orientalia* **39**, 1–51.

Redford, D. 1984, *Akhenaten: The Heretic King*, Princeton University Press, Princeton.

Redford, D. 1992, *Egypt, Canaan, and Israel in Ancient Times*, Princeton University Press, Princeton.

Redford, D. 1992, "Akhenaten", in Freedman (ed.) (1992), **1**, 135–7.

Redford, D. 1992, "Execration and Execration Texts", in Freedman (ed.) (1992), **2**, 681–2.

Redford, D. (ed.) 2001, *The Oxford Encyclopedia of Ancient Egypt*, Oxford University Press, Oxford.

Redford, D. & J. Weinstein 1992, "Hyksos", in Freedman (ed.) (1992), **2**, 341–8.

Redman, C. 1978, *The Rise of Civilization: From Early Farmers to Urban Society in the Ancient Near East*, W. H. Freeman, San Francisco.

Reeves, N. 1990, *The Complete Tutankhamun*, Thames & Hudson, London.

Reiner, E. 1985, *Your Thwarts are in Pieces Your Mooring Rope Cut*, University of Michigan Press, Ann Arbour, MI.

Reiner, E. 1999, "Babylonian Celestial Divination", in *Ancient Astronomy and Celestial Divination*, N. M. Swerdlow (ed.), 21–37, MIT Press, Cambridge.

Reiner, E. & D. Pingree 1975, *The Venus Tablets of Ammizaduga*, Undena Publications, Malibu, CA.

Reiner, E. & D. Pingree 1981, *Enuma Anu Enlil, Tablets 50 51*, Undena Publications, Malibu, CA.

Reiner, E. & D. Pingree 1981, *Babylonian Planetary Omens: Part Two*, Undena Publications, Malibu, CA.

Renfrew, C. 1976, *Before Civilization*, Penguin Books, Harmondsworth/Cambridge University Press, Cambridge [1979].

Renfrew, C. 1988, *Archaeology & Language: The Puzzle of Indo-European Origins*, Cambridge University Press, Cambridge.

Richardson, M. E. J. 2000, *Hammurabi's Laws, Text, Translations and Glossary*, Sheffield Academic Press, Sheffield.

Ritner, R. 2000, "Innovations and Adaptations in Ancient Egyptian Medicine", *Journal of Near Eastern Studies* **59**, 107–17.

Ritner, R. 2001, "Medicine", in Redford (ed.) (2001), **2**, 353–6.

Ritner, R. 2001, "Magic: Magic in Daily Life", in Redford (ed.) (2001), **2**, 331–3.

Ritter, E. 1965, "Magical Expert (=Âšipu) and Physician (=Asû): Notes on Two Complementary Professions in Babylonian Medicine", *Assyriological Studies* (Oriental Institute of the University of Chicago), H. G. Gütterbach & T. Jacobsen (eds), **16**, 299–321.

Roaf, M. 1990, *Cultural Atlas of Mesopotamia and the Ancient Near East*, Facts on File, New York.

Roaf, M. 1995, "Palaces and Temples in Ancient Mesopotamia", in Sasson (ed.) (1995), **1**, 423–41.

Robertson, J. F., "The Social and Economic Organization of Ancient Mesopotamian Temples", in Sasson (ed.) (1995), **1**, 443–54.

Robins, G. 1994–95, "Women and Children in Peril: Pregnancy, Birth and Infant Mortality in Ancient Egypt", *KMT: A Modern Journal of Ancient Egypt*, **5**(4), 24–35.

Robins, G. 1995, "Mathematics, Astronomy and Calendars in Pharaonic Egypt", in Sasson (ed.) (1995), **3**, 1799–1814.

Robins, G. 1990, "While the Woman Looks On: Gender Inequality in the New Kingdom", *KMT: A Modern Journal of Ancient Egypt* **1**(3), 18–21, 64–5.

Robins, G. 1993, *Women in Ancient Egypt*, Harvard University Press, Cambridge.

Robins, G. 1993, "Queens and Queenship in the 18th Dynasty Before the Amarna Period", *The Bulletin of the Canadian Society for Mesopotamian Studies* **26**, 53–8.

Robins, G. 1994, *Proportion and Style in Ancient Egyptian Art*, University of Texas Press, Austin.

Rochberg, F. 1995, "Astronomy and Calendars in Ancient Mesopotamia", in Sasson (ed.) (1995), **3**, 1925–40.

Rochberg, F. 1999, "Babylonian Horoscopy: The Texts and Their Relations", in *Ancient Astronomy and Celestial Divination*, N. M. Swerdlow (ed.), 39–59, MIT Press, Cambridge, MS.

Rochberg-Halton, F. 1984, "New Evidence for the History of Astrology", *Journal of Near Eastern Studies* **43**, 115–40.

Rochberg-Halton, F. 1992, "Calendars", in Freedman (ed.) (1992), **1**, 810–14.

Roehring, C. 1990, "Hatshepsut and the Metropolitan", *KMT: A Modern Journal of Ancient Egypt* **1**(1), 28–33.

Roth, A. M. 2001, "Opening of the Mouth", in Redford (ed.) (2001), **2**, 605–9.

Roth, M. 1997, *Law Collections from Mesopotamia and Asia Minor, Volume 6*, 2nd edn, Scholars Press, Atlanta.

Roux, G. 1980, *Ancient Iraq*, 2nd edition, Penguin, Harmondsworth.

Rundle Clark, R. T. 1959, *Myth and Symbol in Ancient Egypt*, Thames & Hudson, London.

Russell, J. M. 1991, *Sennacherib's Palace Without Rival at Nineveh*, University of Chicago Press, Chicago.

Russell, J. 1996, "Nineveh", in *The Dictionary of Art, Volume 25*, J. Turner (ed.), 152–5, Grove, London/New York.

Sachs, A. 1952, "Babylonian Horoscopes", *Journal of Cuneiform Studies* **6**, 49–75.

Sachs, A. 1974, "Babylonian Observational Astronomy", in Hodson (ed.) (1974), 43–50.

Sack, R. H. 1992, "Merodach-Baladan", in Freedman (ed.) (1992), **4**, 704–5.

Saggs, H. W. F. 1965, *Everyday Life in Babylonia and Assyria*, Dorset Press, New York.

Saggs, H. W. F. 1984, *The Might that was Assyria*, Sidgwick & Jackson, London.

Saggs, H. W. F. 1988, *The Greatness that was Babylon*, 2nd edn, Sidgwick & Jackson, London.

Saggs, H. W. F. 1989, *Civilization Before Greece and Rome*, Yale University Press, New Haven.

Saggs, H. W. F. 1995, *Babylonians*, University of Oklahoma Press, Norman.

Sancisi-Weerdenburg, H. 1995, "Darius I and the Persian Empire", in Sasson (ed.) (1995), **3**, 1035–50.

Sancisi-Weerdenburg, H., *et al.* (eds), 1987–1994, *Achaemenid History*, Proceedings of the Achaemenid History Workshops, 8 vols, Nederlands Instituut voor het Nabije Oosten, Leiden.

Sandars, N. 1985, *The Sea Peoples: Warriors of the Ancient Mediterranean*, rev. edn, Thames & Hudson, London.

Saporetti, C. 1979, *The Status of Women in the Middle Assyrian Period*, Undena Press, Malibu.

Sasson, J. 1983, "On Musical Settings for Cuneiform Literature: A Discography", *Journal of the American Oriental Society* **103**, 233–5.

Sasson, J. 1992, "Gilgamesh Epic", in Freedman (ed.) (1992), **2**, 1024–7.

Sasson, J. (ed.) 1995. *Civilizations of the Ancient Near East*, Charles Scribner's Sons, New York.

Sasson, J. 1995, "King Hammurabi of Babylon", in Sasson (ed.) (1995), **2**, 901–15.

Säve-Söderbergh, T. 1951, "The Hyksos Rule in Egypt", *Journal of Egyptian Archaeology* **37**, 53–71.

Schaden, O. 1992, "Courtier, Confidante, Councillor, King: The God's Father Ay", in *Amarna Letters 2*, D. C. Forbes (ed.), 92–115, KMT Publications, San Francisco.

Schäffer, H. & W. Andrae 1925, *Die Kunst des Alten Orient*, Propyläen Verlag, Berlin.

Schliemann, H. 1880, *Ilios: The City and Country of the Trojans*, John Murray Publishers, London.

Schlögl, H. A. 2001, "Aten", in Redford (ed.) (2001), **1**, 156–8.

Schmandt-Besserat, D. 1978, "The Earliest Precursor of Writing", *Scientific American* **238**, 50–59.

Schmandt-Besserat, D. 1986, "An Ancient Token System: A Precursor to Numerals and Writing", *Archaeology* (Nov/Dec), 32–9.

Schmandt-Besserat, D. 1992, *Before Writing, Volume I, From Counting to Cuneiform*, University of Texas Press, Austin.

Schmandt-Besserat, D. 1992, *Before Writing, Volume II, A Catalog of Near Eastern Tokens*, University of Texas Press, Austin.

Schmandt-Besserat, D. 1995, "Record Keeping Before Writing", in Sasson (ed.) (1995), **4**, 2097–106.

Schmidt, B. B. 1995, "Flood Narratives of Ancient Western Asia", in Sasson (ed.) (1995), **4**, 2337–51.

Schulman, A. R. 1964, *Military Rank, Title, and Organization in the Egyptian New Kingdom*, Münchner Ägyptologische Studien, Munich and Berlin.

Schulman, A. R. 1980, "Chariots, Chariotry, and the Hyksos", *The Journal of Society for the Study of Egyptian Antiquities* **10**(2), 105–53.

Schulman, A. R. 1995, "Military Organization in Pharaonic Egypt", in Sasson (ed.) (1995), **1**, 289–301.

Schwartz, G. M. 1995, "Pastoral Nomadism in Ancient Western Asia", in Sasson (ed.) (1995), **1**, 249–58.

Scurlock, J. A., "Death and the Afterlife in Mesopotamian Thought", in Sasson (ed.) (1995), **3**, 1883–93.

Seidlmayer, S. 2000, "The First Intermediate Period (c.2160–2055)", in Shaw (ed.) (2000), 118–47.

Sekunda, N. 1989, "The Persians", in *Warfare in the Ancient World*, J. Hackett (ed.), 82–103, Facts on File, New York.

Shafer, B. E. (ed.) 1991, *Religion in Ancient Egypt: Gods, Myths, and Personal Practice*, Cornell University Press, Ithaca.

Shafer, B. (ed.) 1997, *Temples of Ancient Egypt*, Cornell University Press, Ithaca.

Shaw, I. 2000, "Egypt and the Outside World", in Shaw (ed.) (2000), 314–29.

Shaw, I. 2000, "Chronologies and Cultural Changes in Egypt", in Shaw (ed.) (2000), 1–16.

Shaw, I. (ed.) 2000, *The Oxford History of Ancient Egypt*, Oxford University Press, Oxford.

Silverman, D. P. 1991, "Divinity and Deities in Ancient Egypt", in Shafer (ed.) (1991), 7–87.

Sivin, N. 1989, "Chinese Archaeoastronomy: Between Two Worlds", in *World Archaeoastronomy*, A. Aveni (ed.), 55–64, Cambridge University Press, Cambridge.

Smith, M. S. 1995, "Myth and Mythmaking in Canaan and Ancient Israel", in Sasson (ed.) (1995), **4**, 2038–9.

Smith, P. E. L. 1976, *Food Production and Its Consequences*, Cummings Press, Menlo Park.

Smith, P. E. L. & T. Cuyler Young Jr. 1983, "The Force of Numbers: Population Pressure in the Central Western Zagros", in *The Hilly Flanks and Beyond, Volume 36*, P. E. L. Smith *et al.* (eds), 141–62, Oriental Institute Publications, Chicago.

Smith, W. S. 1971, "The Old Kingdom in Egypt and the Beginning of the First Intermediate Period", in Edwards *et al.* (eds) (1971), 145–207.

Snell, D. 1995, "Methods of Exchange and Coinage in Ancient Western Asia", in Sasson (ed.) (1995), **3**, 1487–97.

Snell, D. 1997, *Life in the Ancient Near East, 3100–332 BCE*, Yale University Press, New Haven.

Sollberger, E. 1962, *The Babylonian Legend of The Flood*, British Museum Publications, London.

Sommerfeld, W. 1995, "The Kassites of Ancient Mesopotamia: Origins, Politics, and Culture", in Sasson (ed.) (1995), **2**, 917–30.

Spalinger, A. 1992, "Egypt, History of (Dyn 21–26)", in Freedman (ed.) (1992), **2**, 353–64.

Spalinger, A. (ed.) 1994, *Revolutions in Time, Studies in Ancient Egyptian Calendars*, Van Siclen Books, San Antonio.

Spalinger, A. 2001, "Calendars", in Redford (ed.) (2001), **1**, 224–7.

Spalinger, A. 2001, "Chronology and Periodization", in Redford (ed.) (2001), **1**, 264–76.

Spalinger, A. 2001, "Twenty-sixth Dynasty", in Redford (ed.) (2001), **2**, 272–4.

Speiser, E. A. 1969, "Akkadian Myths and Epics", in Pritchard (ed.) (1969), 60–119 (supp. 510–18).

Speiser, E. A. 1969, "A Cosmological Incantation: The Worm and the Toothache", in Pritchard (ed.) (1969), 100–101.

Speiser, E. A.& A. K. Grayson 1969, "The Epic of Gilgamesh", in Pritchard (ed.) (1969), 72–99 (supp. 503–7).

Spencer, A. J. 1982, *Death in Ancient Egypt*, Penguin Books, Harmondsworth.

Spencer, A. J. 1995, *Early Egypt: The Rise of Civilization in the Nile Valley*, University of Oklahoma Press, Norman.

Spycket, A. 1995, "Reliefs, Statuary, and Monumental Paintings in Ancient Mesopotamia", in Sasson (ed.) (1995), **4**, 2583–600.

Stadelmann, R. 1995, "Builders of the Pyramids", in Sasson (ed.) (1995), **2**, 719–34.

Stadelmann, R. 2001, "Old Kingdom: Fourth Dynasty", in Redford (ed.) (2001), **2**, 593–7.

Stadelmann, R. 2001, "Giza", in Redford (ed.) (2001), **2**, 25–30.

Starr, I. 1990, *Queries to the Sun God: Divination and Politics in Sargonid Assyria*, State Archives of Assyria IV, Helsinki University Press, Helsinki.

Steele, J. 2000, "Eclipse Prediction in Mesopotamia", *Archive for the History of Exact Sciences* **54**, 421–54.

Stein, D. 1997, "Kassites", in Meyers (ed.) (1997), **3**, 271–5.

Steinkeller, P. 1992, "Mesopotamia, History of (Third Millennium BC)", in Freedman (ed.) (1992), **4**, 724–32.

Stevenson, D. W. W. 1992, "A Proposal for the Irrigation of the Hanging Gardens of Babylon", *Iraq* **54**, 35–55.

Stiebing Jr, W. H. 1984, *Ancient Astronauts, Cosmic Collisions and other Popular Theories about Man's Past*, Prometheus Books, Buffalo.

Stiebing Jr, W. H. 1993, *Uncovering the Past: A History of Archaeology*, Prometheus Books, Buffalo.

Stol, M. 1993, *Epilepsy in Babylonia*, Groningen: STYX Publications.

Stol, M. 2000, *Birth in Babylonia*, Brill, Leiden.

Stone, E. C. 1995, "The Development of Cities in Ancient Mesopotamia", in Sasson (ed.) (1995), **1**, 235–48.

Stronach, D. 1997, "Pasargadae", in Meyers (ed.) (1997), **4**, 250–53.

Stronach, D. & K. Codella 1997, "Persepolis", in Meyers (ed.) (1997), **4**, 273–7.

Stronach, D. & A. Zournatzi 1997, "Bisitun", in Meyers (ed.) (1997), **1**, 330–31.

Stronach, D. & K. Cordella 1997, "Nineveh", in Meyers (ed.) (1997), **4**, 144–8.

Tadmor, H. & M. Weinfeld 1983, *History, Historiography and Interpretation*, Magnes Press, Israel.

Taylor, J. 1859, *The Great Pyramid: Why Was It Built and Who Built It?*, Longman, London.

Taylor, J. 2000, "The Third Intermediate Period (1069–664 BC)", in Shaw (ed.) (2000), 330–68.

Teeter, E. 1990, "Hatshepsut", *KMT: A Modern Journal of Ancient Egypt* **1**(1), 4–13, 56–7.

Te Velde, H. 1995, "Theology, Priests, and Worship in Ancient Egypt", in Sasson (ed.) (1995), **3**, 1731.

Thorwald, J. 1962, *Science and Secrets of Early Medicine: Egypt, Mesopotamia, India, China, Mexico, Peru*, Thames & Hudson, London.

Thureau-Dangin, F. & M. Dunand 1936, *Til Barsip*, Paul Geuthner, Paris.

Tigay, J. 1982, *The Evolution of the Gilgamesh Epic*, University of Pennsylvania Press, Philadelphia.

Tobin, V. A. 1993, "Akhenaten as a Tragedy of History: A Critique of the Amarna Age", *The Journal of the Society for the Study of Egyptian Antiquities* **23**, 5–28.

Trigger, B. 1978, *Time and Traditions: Essays in Archaeological Interpretation*, Columbia University Press, New York.

Trigger, B. G. 1983, "The Rise of Egyptian Civilization", in Trigger *et al.* (1983), 1–70.

Trigger, B. G., B. J. Kemp, D. O'Connor & A. B. Lloyd (eds) 1983, *Ancient Egypt: A Social History*, Cambridge University Press, Cambridge.

Trimble, V. 1964, "The Astronomical Investigation Concerning the So-called Air Shafts of the Cheops' Pyramid", *Mitteilungen des Instituts für Orientforschung* **10**, 183–7.

Troy, L. 2001, "New Kingdom: Eighteenth Dynasty to the Amarna Period", in Redford (ed.) (2001), **2**, 525–31.

Tubb, J. 1998, *Canaanites*, University of Oklahoma Press, Norman.

Ussishkin, D. 1982, *The Conquest of Lachish by Sennacherib*, Institute of Archaeology, Tel Aviv University.

Vallat, F. 1986, "The Most Ancient Scripts of Iran: The Current Situation, *World Archaeology* **17**(3) (1986), 335–47.

Vallat, F. 1995, "Susa and Susiana in the Second-Millennium Iran", in Sasson (ed.) (1995), **2**, 1023–33.

van der Waerden, B. 1974, *Science Awakening II: The Birth of Astronomy,* Noordhoff International Publishing, Leiden New York.

Van Dijk, J. 1995, "Myth and Mythmaking in Ancient Egypt", in Sasson (ed.) (1995), **3**, 1697–1709.

Van Dijk, J. 2000, "The Amarna Period and the Later New Kingdom (c.1352–1069)", in Shaw (ed.) (2000), 272–313.

Van Seters, J. 1966, *The Hyksos: A New Investigation,* Yale University Press, New Haven.

Van Seters, J. 1983, *In Search of History: Historiography in the Ancient World and the Origins of Biblical History*, Yale University Press, New Haven.

Van Soldt, W. H. 1995, "Ugarit: A Second Millennium Kingdom on the Mediterranean Coast", in Sasson (ed.) (1995), **2**, 1255–66.

Vanstiphout, H. 1995, "Memory and Literacy in Ancient Western Asia", in Sasson (ed.) (1995), **4**, 2181–6.

Veenhof, K. 1995, "Kanesh: An Assyrian Colony in Anatolia", in Sasson (ed.) (1995), **1**, 859–71.

Veenhof, K. 1997, "Libraries and Archives", in Meyers (ed.) (1997), **3**, 351–7.

Verner, M. 2001, "Old Kingdom: An Overview", in Redford (ed.) (2001), **2**, 585–91.

Verner, M. 2001, "Pyramid", in Redford (ed.) (2001), **2**, 87–95.

Villard, P. 1995, "Shamshi-Adad and Sons: The Rise and Fall of an Upper Mesopotamian Empire", in Sasson (ed.) (1995), **2**, 873–83.

Walker, C. 1987, *Cuneiform,* University of California Press, Berkeley.

Walker, C. & J. Britton 1983, "Episodes in the History of Babylonian Astronomy", *The Bulletin of the Canadian Society for Mesopotamian Studies* **5**, 18–26.

Wallace Budge, E. A. 1895, *The Book of the Dead (The Papyrus of Ani), Egyptian Text, Transliteration, Translation,* Trustees of the British Museum, London.

Wallace Budge, E. A. 1895, *The Mummy: Chapters on Egyptian Funerary Archaeology,* Cambridge University Press, Cambridge.

Wallace Budge, E. A. 1904, *The Gods of the Egyptians,* vol. 2, Methuen, London.

Wallace Budge, E. A. 1925, *The Mummy: A Handbook of Egyptian Funerary Archaeology,* Cambridge University Press, Cambridge.

Wallace Budge, E. A. 1930, *Amulets and Superstitions,* Oxford University Press, Oxford.

Wallace, H. 1992, "Eden, Garden of", in Freedman (ed.) (1992), **2**, 281–3.

Ward, W. A. 1992, "Egyptian Relations with Canaan", in Freedman (ed.) (1992), **2**, 399–408.

Watkins, T. 1989, "The Beginnings of Warfare", in *Warfare in the Ancient World,* J. Hackett (ed.), 27–35, Sidgwick & Jackson, London.

Weeks, K. R. 1995, "Medicine, Surgery and Public Health in Ancient Egypt", in Sasson (ed.) (1995), **3**, 1787–98.

Weeks, K. R. 1998, *The Lost Tomb,* William Morrow, New York.

Weeks, K. 2001, "Tombs: An Overview", in Redford (ed.) (2001), **3**, 418–25.

Weeks, K. 2001, "Valley of the Kings", in Redford (ed.) (2001), **3**, 471–4.

Weidner, E. F. 1967, *Gestirn-Darstelleungen auf Babylonischen Tontafelen,* Kommissionsverlag Österreichische Akademie der Wissenschaften, Vienna.

Weinstein, J. 1997, "Hyksos", in Meyers (ed.) (1997), **3**, 133–6.

Weiss, H. 1997, "Akkade", in Meyers (ed.) (1997), **1**, 41–4.

Weissbach, F. H. 1903, *Babylonische Miscellen,* Hinrichs'sche Buchhandlung, Leipzig.

Welsby, D. 2001, "Nubia", in Redford (ed.) (2001), **2**, 551–7.

Wendorf, F. & A. Close 1997, "Prehistoric Egypt", in Meyers (ed.) (1997), **2**, 191–4.

Wenke, R. J. 1990, *Patterns in Prehistory,* Oxford University Press, Oxford.

Wenke, R. J. 1997, "Faiyum", in Meyers (ed.) (1997), **2**, 299.

Wente, E. F. 2001, "Monotheism", in Redford (ed.) (2001), **2**, 432–5.

Wettersrom, W. & M. A. Murray 2001, "Agriculture", in Redford (ed.) (2001), **1**, 37.

Whitehouse, H. 1995, "Egypt in European Thought", in Sasson (ed.) (1995), **1**, 15–31.

Whiting, R. 1995, "Amorite Tribes and Nations of Second Millennium Western Asia", in Sasson (ed.) (1995), **2**, 1231–42.

Whitt, W. D. 1995, "The Story of the Semitic Alphabet", in Sasson (ed.) (1995), **4**, 2379–97.

Wilkinson, J. G. 1853, *A Popular Account of the Ancient Egyptians,* John Murray, London.

Wilkinson, R. 1992, *Reading Egyptian Art,* Thames & Hudson, London.

Wilkinson, R. & N. Reeves 1996, *The Complete Valley of the Kings, Tombs and Treasures of Egypt's Greatest Pharaohs,* Thames & Hudson, London.

Wilson, J. A. 1951, *The Culture of Ancient Egypt,* University of Chicago Press, Chicago.

Wilson, J. A. 1969, "Egyptian Historical Texts", in Pritchard (ed.) (1969), 227–64.

Wilson, J. A. 1969, "The Admonitions of Ipu-Wer, Egyptian Oracles and Prophecies", in Pritchard (ed.) (1969), 441–4.

Wilson, J. A. 1969, "The Prophecy of Neferti", in Pritchard (ed.) (1969), 444–6.

Windfuhr, G. L. 1997, "Indo-European Languages", in Meyers (ed.) (1997), **3**, 149–58.

Windfuhr, G. L. 1997, "Persian", in Meyers (ed.) (1997), **4**, 292–5.

Winkelman, B. 1995, "Buhen, Blueprints of an Egyptian Fortress", *KMT: A Modern Journal of Ancient Egypt* **6**, 72–81.

Winter, I. J. 1995, "Aesthetics in Ancient Mesopotamian Art", in Sasson (ed.) (1995), **4**, 2569–82.

Wiseman, D. J. 1956, *Chronicles of the Chaldean Kings (626 556 BC) in the British Museum,* British Museum, London.

Wiseman, D. J. 1985, *Nebuchadnezzar and Babylon,* Oxford University Press, Oxford.

Wiseman, D. J. 1989, "The Assyrians", in *Warfare in the Ancient World,* J. Hackett (ed.), 36–53, Sidgwick & Jackson, New York.

Wiseman, D. J. 1992, "Babylonia 605–539 BC", in Boardman *et al.* (eds), (1992), 229–51.

Woolley, L. 1954, *Excavations at Ur,* London.

Woolley, L. 1982, *Ur of the Chaldees,* rev. edn by P. R. S. Moorey, Cornell University Press, Ithaca [originally published by Norton, London, 1956].

Wright, W. T. 1992, "Mesopotamia, History of (Prehistory)", in Freedman (ed.) (1992), **4**, 720–24.

Xenophon 1934, *Anabasis,* Book III, 4, C. L. Brownson (trans.), Harvard University Press, Cambridge.

Yoffe, N. 1988, "Context and Authority in Early Mesopotamian Law", in *State Formation and Political Legitimacy,* R. Cohen & J. Toland (eds), 95–113, Transaction Books, New Brunswick NJ and Oxford.

Yoffe, N. 1995, "The Economy of Ancient Western Asia", in Sasson (ed.) (1995), **3**, 1387–99.

Young, Jr., T. C. 1980, "Persia", in Cotterell (ed.) (1980), 147–54.

Young, Jr., T. C. 1988, "The Early History of the Medes and the Persians and the Achaemenid Empire to the Death of Cambyses", in *The Cambridge History of Iran, Volume 1,* J. Boardman (ed.), 1–52, Cambridge University Press, Cambridge.

Young, Jr., T. C. 1992, "Cyrus", in Freedman (ed.) (1992), **1**, 1231–2.

Young, Jr., T. C. 1997, "Medes", in Meyers (ed.) (1997), **3**, 448–50.

Young, Jr., T. C. 1997, "Persians", in Meyers (ed.) (1997), **4**, 295–300.

Yoyotte, J. 1966, "Das Neue Reich in Ägypten. I: Die XVIII Dynastie", in *Fischer Weltgeschichte, vol. III: Die altorientalischen Reiche*, part 2, E. Cassin, J. Bottéro & J. Vercoutter (eds), 222–60, Frankfort-am-Main.

Yoyotte, J. 1972, "Une statue de Darius découverte à Suse", *Journal Asiatique* **260**, 250–60.

Zimansky, P. 1985, *Ecology and Empire: The Structure of the Uartian State*, University of Chicago Press, Chicago.

Zimansky, P. 1993, "A Review of Schmandt-Besserat 1992", *Journal of Field Archaeology* **20**, 513–17.

Zimansky, P. 1995, "The Kingdom of Uartu in Eastern Anatolia", in Sasson (ed.) (1995), **2**, 1135–46.

Index

Page numbers for maps and illustrations are italicized.